CRIMINAL INVESTIGATION

second edition

Michael D. Lyman

Columbia College of Missouri

PEARSON

Boston Columbus Indianapolis New York San Francisco Upper Saddle River
Amsterdam Cape Town Dubai London Madrid Milan Munich Paris Montréal Toronto
Delhi Mexico City São Paulo Sydney Hong Kong Seoul Singapore Taipei Tokyo

Editorial Director: Andrew Gilfillan
Product Manager: Gary Bauer
Program Manager: Tara Horton
Editorial Assistant: Lynda Cramer
Director of Marketing: David Gesell
Senior Marketing Manager: Mary Salzman
Senior Marketing Coordinator: Alicia Wozniak
Senior Marketing Assistant: Les Roberts
Project Management Team Lead: JoEllen Gohr
Project Manager: Jessica H. Sykes

Procurement Specialist: Deidra Skahill
Senior Art Director: Diane Ernsberger
Cover Designer: Cenveo
Full-Service Project Management: Bev Kraus, S4Carlisle
    Publishing Services
Composition: S4Carlisle Publishing Services
Printer/Binder: R.R. Donnelley/Roanoke
Cover Printer: Lehigh-Phoenix Color/Hagerstown
Text Font: MinionPro-Regular 10/12

10 9 8 7 6 5 4 3 2 1

ISBN 10:   0-13-358794-0
ISBN 13: 978-0-13-358794-4

Dedication

*This book is dedicated
to the most important
people in my life, my wife
Julie and my daughter
Kelsey, who have offered
their continual support
of me in the painstaking
preparation of this book.
Their understanding of this
huge undertaking played
no small role in this book's
successful completion.
Thanks, guys.*

Brief Contents

Contents

PART 2   Follow-Up Investigative Processes

PART 6   Terrorism

Preface

This Book's Theme

This book is now in its second edition. It is intended to meet the needs of students and others interested in criminal justice by presenting information in an easy-to-read, logical flow, paralleling the steps and considerations observed in an actual criminal investigation. Additionally, it is designed to fulfill an ongoing need for an abbreviated book that explains clearly and thoughtfully the fundamentals of criminal investigation as practiced by police investigators on the job in communities across the nation.

The book is written with several observations in mind. First, it is designed to blend scientific theories of crime detection with a practical approach to criminal investigation. Its underlying assumption is that sound criminal investigations depend on an understanding of the science of crime-detection procedures and the art of anticipating human behavior. There is yet another critical observation made in the book: It recognizes that both the uniformed officer and the criminal investigator play important roles in the field of criminal investigation. The duties of each are outlined throughout the book, recognizing that there is a fundamental need for both to work in tandem throughout many aspects of the criminal investigation process.

Another underlying theme of the book is that, as with all police endeavors, criminal investigation is a law enforcement responsibility that must be conducted within the framework of the U.S. Constitution and the practices of a democratic society. Consequently, court decisions and case studies have been quoted extensively for clarification of issues and general reader information.

Additional Highlights to the Author's Approach

- A 16-chapter format specifically designed to enable the instructor to cover the entire book in a standard semester and to enable the student to read without being pressured to cover numerous chapters in a short period of time

- An enhanced graphical interface affording the student an additional venue for learning

- Recent and meaningful case studies that begin and end each chapter

- Boxed features specifically designed to allow the student to consider how chapter material applies to the real world of criminal investigation

- A dedicated chapter on terrorism and the investigation of such crimes

- Coverage of the latest investigative methods for dealing with eyewitness testimony, missing and abducted persons, computer/Internet crime, and other "hot-button" issues in criminal investigation

New to This Edition

- Updated case studies throughout

- Statistics are now updated for this edition

- More detail about crime scene searches and evidence

- Learning outcomes identified throughout each chapter

- New graphics throughout the book

- New "Think About It" sections in each chapter

- Refreshed photos and informational boxes throughout the book

- Revised "Learning Outcomes" at the end of each chapter

▶ *Instructor Supplements*

- *Instructor's Manual with Test Bank.* Includes content outlines for classroom discussion, teaching suggestions, and answers to selected end-of-chapter questions from the text. This also contains a Word document version of the test bank.

- *TestGen.* This computerized test generation system gives you maximum flexibility in creating and administering tests on paper, electronically, or online. It provides state-of-the-art features for viewing and editing test bank questions, dragging a selected question into a test you are creating, and printing sleek, formatted tests in a variety of layouts.

Select test items from test banks included with TestGen for quick test creation, or write your own questions from scratch. TestGen's random generator provides the option to display different text or calculated number values each time questions are used.

- *PowerPoint Presentations.* Our presentations offer clear, straightforward outlines and notes to use for class lectures or study materials. Photos, illustrations, charts, and tables from the book are included in the presentations when applicable.

To access supplementary materials online, instructors need to request an instructor access code. Go to **www.pearsonhighered.com/irc**, where you can register for an instructor access code. Within 48 hours after registering, you will receive a confirming email, including an instructor access code. Once you have received your code, go to the site and log on for full instructions on downloading the materials you wish to use.

Pearson Online Course Solutions

Criminal Investigation is supported by a variety of online course and media solutions. Go to **www.pearsonhighered.com** or contact your local representative for the latest information.

Alternate Versions

- *eBooks*. This text is also available in multiple eBook formats including Adobe Reader and CourseSmart. *CourseSmart* is an exciting new choice for students looking to save money. As an alternative to purchasing the printed textbook, students can purchase an electronic version of the same content. With a *CourseSmart* eTextbook, students can search the text, make notes online, print out reading assignments that incorporate lecture notes, and bookmark important passages for later review. For more information, or to purchase access to the *CourseSmart* eTextbook, visit **www.coursesmart.com**.

▶ Acknowledgments

No book can be written entirely as a solo effort, and this project was no exception. The preparation of the second edition represents hundreds of painstaking hours maintaining continuous contact with criminal justice agencies, federal information clearinghouses, police practitioners, and colleagues in the field of criminal justice. In addition, to offer the reader the most up-to-date and relevant information, it was important to consult libraries, police journals, periodicals, newspapers, government publications, and other sources of literature germane to the field of crime detection on an ongoing basis.

Many persons were helpful in the preparation of this book, including practitioners in the field as well as experts in academe. Among these, the contributions of certain persons deserve special recognition. Included are the men and women of the Columbia, Missouri, Police Department, the Missouri State Highway Patrol, agents from the Federal Bureau of Investigation and Drug Enforcement Administration, contributors from the Department of Homeland Security, and the International Association of Chiefs of Police.

A special debt of gratitude goes to Detective Michael Himmel of the Columbia Police Department (ret.) and Brian Hoey of the Missouri State Highway Patrol Crime Laboratory, who both provided a number of crime-scene and laboratory photos for this new edition. Without the cooperation and guidance of these persons and organizations, this book would not have been possible.

A special thank you is also well deserved for Program Manager Megan Moffo and Product Manager Gary Bauer, along with the many other dedicated publishing professionals at Pearson for their hard work and support of this text. Finally, I would like to extend special thanks to those criminal justice academics and practitioners who painstakingly reviewed the manuscript of this book. Without the support and assistance of all these people and many more, this book would not have become a reality. Thank you all.

—Michael D. Lyman

▶ About the Author

Michael D. Lyman is a Professor of Criminal Justice at Columbia College, located in Columbia, Missouri. In addition to being a teaching faculty member, he serves as the program coordinator for the Master of Science of Criminal Justice Program and the founder of the college's Forensic Science Program. Before entering the field of college teaching, he was employed as a certified police trainer and also served as a sworn criminal investigator for state police organizations in Kansas and Oklahoma. He has taught literally thousands of law enforcement officers in the proper police techniques and methods of professional criminal investigation. Dr. Lyman has authored numerous textbooks in criminal justice dealing with the areas of criminal investigation, policing, organized crime, drug enforcement, and drug trafficking. He received both his bachelor's and master's degrees from Wichita State University and his Ph.D. from the University of Missouri–Columbia. He has been called upon on an estimated 275 occasions by the law enforcement and legal communities to review criminal investigations and render the results of his evaluations and his opinions in federal court proceedings nationwide.

Textbooks such as this are an ongoing work in progress, and the author welcomes communication and correspondence about his work. Dr. Lyman can be contacted at Columbia College, 1001 Rogers Street, Columbia, MO 65216 or at mlyman@cougars.ccis.edu. Thank you for using this textbook.

"Our current system of criminal investigation is a direct result of what we have learned and what we have inherited from the past."

Foundations of Criminal Investigation

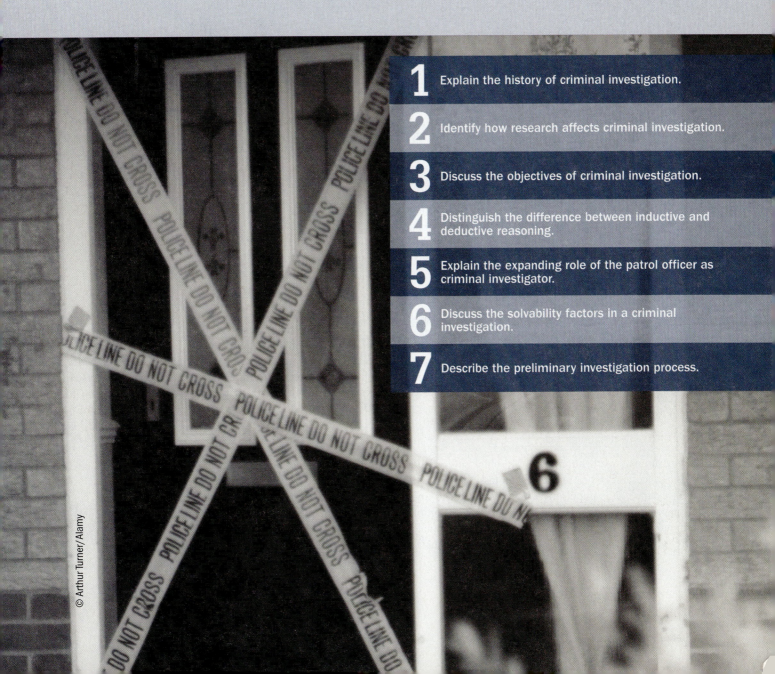

1 Explain the history of criminal investigation.

2 Identify how research affects criminal investigation.

3 Discuss the objectives of criminal investigation.

4 Distinguish the difference between inductive and deductive reasoning.

5 Explain the expanding role of the patrol officer as criminal investigator.

6 Discuss the solvability factors in a criminal investigation.

7 Describe the preliminary investigation process.

© Arthur Turner/Alamy

INTRO · WHEN HATE BECOMES MURDER

In April 2014, on the eve of Passover, a Jewish holiday, a shotgun-wielding man opened fire at the Jewish Community Center of Greater Kansas City, which is in Overland Park, and at Village Shalom, a retirement home. The shooter was later identified as 73-year-old Frazier Glenn Cross (also known as Frazier Glenn Miller). The investigation into the incident showed that Cross first went to the community center and opened fire on two people in the parking lot in front of the Lewis and Shirley White Theatre. Then, in the back area of the center, gunfire erupted at the community center as hundreds of high school singers from across the metro area were readying to audition for the KC SuperStar singing scholarship contest and actors were rehearsing for a production of *To Kill a Mockingbird*.

After the shootings, police blanketed the area and found Cross in the parking lot of a nearby elementary school, where he was arrested. Investigators looked at several things found in Cross's car that could be used as evidence. According to investigators, before being driven off to jail, Cross began ranting while in police custody. A TV news video showed Cross yelling what appeared to be "Heil Hitler!" from the backseat of a police car.

The investigation into the incident revealed that Cross was a former "Grand Dragon" of the Ku Klux Klan and had a lengthy history of running an illegal paramilitary organization and intimidating minorities. Furthermore, Cross had a violent criminal record dating back to a 1987 nationwide manhunt after violating a court order prohibiting him from operating a paramilitary organization. Cross and three associates were eventually arrested in 1987 in Ozark, Missouri, during a federal raid of a trailer where authorities found enough weapons "for a small army" after Cross declared war on the U.S. government. Authorities found guns, thousands of rounds of ammunition, grenades, crossbows, police scanning radios, and $14,800 in cash. In September 1987, he pleaded guilty to a federal charge of mailing threatening communications and possessing automatic weapons.

The Kansas City Jewish Community Center shootings illustrate the complexity of active shooters. The event also shows what challenges face law enforcement with regard to proactive investigations and predicting the likelihood of such crimes before they occur.

Photo of Frazier Glenn Cross Following His Arrest in May 2014.

David Eulitt/MCT/Newscom

DISCUSS Whether motivated by anger or hate, the presence of an active shooter in a public location is one of the greatest public concerns. Is it possible for police investigators to proactively predict if and where an active shooter might be next? What are some methods or techniques that could make this a reality?

The study of criminal investigation involves probing several different fields at once, and is therefore a difficult task about which to write. For example, it is important for an investigator to understand the basic techniques of collection and preservation of evidence, but to do so, a fundamental understanding of criminalistics or forensic science is often required. In addition to technical competence, modern-day investigators must be well versed in the law. Legal skills include a working knowledge of criminal law, constitutional law, and rules of evidence, all of which are essential for successful prosecution of a criminal case. This chapter is designed to give the reader the underlying essentials of this field of policing, which is both rewarding and challenging.

Criminal investigation is one of the most charismatic, engaging, and rewarding endeavors in the field of criminal justice. The theme of this book is its underlying "true north." That is, the premise of the book is that the function of criminal investigation is both an art and a science. It calls on the abilities of the most competent, professional, and hard-working personnel in the criminal justice field. In order for this to take place, investigations must be conducted with the understanding that the end does not justify the means, that integrity and constitutional principles of searching for the truth must be tempered by reasonableness and knowledge of the best practices of contemporary crime detection. In addition to constitutional considerations, investigations must be conducted with regard to requirements of agency policy and a proper sense of what is the right thing to do under the circumstances. That said, investigations must be fueled by the understanding that the goal of criminal investigation is as much to identify the guilty as to eliminate those who are not, and that investigations are never complete until each and every credible investigative lead has been properly considered.

▶ The History of Criminal Investigation

The roots of America's system of criminal investigation go back to the towns and cities of England during the eighteenth and nineteenth centuries. The ensuing crime wave forced law enforcement officials to take drastic measures. As a result, **thief catchers** were recruited from the riffraff of the streets to aid law enforcement officials in locating criminals. Two classes of thief catchers were identified: (1) hirelings, whose motivations were mercenary in nature; and (2) social climbers, who would implicate their accomplices in order to move up the social ladder.

LEARNING OUTCOMES 1 Explain the history of criminal investigation.

Criminal Investigation in England

During the 1750s, crimes such as burglary and street robbery were rampant in England. Henry Fielding, an author and magistrate, took on the challenge of reducing the profits realized by criminals. Working relationships were established with local business owners, in particular pawnbrokers, who were provided with lists of stolen property. Fielding encouraged them to contact him if any stolen property came to their attention. Fielding took seriously his new duty as crime fighter and promptly employed new crime-fighting methods. One such method was the appointment of a handful of parish constables acclimated to night watchman duties. These trackers soon began performing criminal investigation functions and became well known as successful thief takers by using their ties with London's criminal underworld. Originally called "Mr. Fielding's People," they soon became known as the

Bow Street Runners, the first well-known investigative body in England. Fielding's runners were not paid as police officers but rather in terms of thief-taker rewards, a percentage of all fines resulting from successful prosecution of thieves.

The Bow Street Runners were forerunners of a trend in policing for specialization within the police force. In fact, by 1800, the Bow Street Police Office was considered by many to be the leading law enforcement organization in the area.

The great watershed in British police development occurred in 1829 with the establishment of the London Metropolitan Police Department. Officers of the department were dubbed **bobbies**. after the department's founder, Home Secretary Sir Robert Peel. The "new" police were England's first paid, full-time police force, consisting of about 1,000 uniformed officers. In addition, they replaced the old constables, such as the Bow Street Runners, who had ultimately gained a reputation of incompetency and inefficiency.

The Creation of Scotland Yard

For many people, much misunderstanding has existed about the function and role of **Scotland Yard**. Some believe that it represents a single police authority in Great Britain. In fact, it is the headquarters of London's Metropolitan Police and has never exerted any authority over other police organizations in Great Britain. Although London's Metropolitan Police was founded in 1829, it took more than 10 years to organize a detective branch. Even then, however, "the Yard" was only a small division within the department. The strength of the force was increased in 1867 after an incident in which an explosion occurred when a small

Alison Wright/Corbis

Modern-Day English "Bobby" Police Officer.

group of Irishmen were trying to free a prisoner from the Clerkenwell House of Detention. Several citizens were killed. A decade later, another reorganization occurred when several senior detectives of Scotland Yard were convicted of corruption charges.

Criminal Investigation in the United States

As the American frontier moved westward during the nineteenth century, outlaws posed serious problems in newly settled areas. Mining camps and cattle towns seemed to experience more violence than other areas. The westward migration had moved men and women far from the institutions that had served them previously. Law enforcement agencies and criminal courts, if present at all, made only minor strides in protecting the vast areas under their jurisdictions. Indeed, it was in these areas that criminals could easily hide and witnesses would often move away, making detection and apprehension of criminals a discouraging task.

Following the lead of London's police force, the first professional police forces were established in the United States at Boston in 1837, New York in 1844, and Philadelphia in 1854.

By the 1870s, almost all major U.S. cities had municipal police departments. As in England, criminal investigation by public law enforcement was viewed as politically hazardous because it favored only those who could pay. But the rapid growth of cities produced violence, crime, and vice activities that demonstrated a breakdown of social order in small communities. Growing incidents of mob violence between Protestants and Catholics, immigrants and Native Americans, and abolitionists and pro-slavery groups were probably the most crucial catalysts for expanded police functions.

Medford Historical Society Collection/Corbis

Allen Pinkerton with Secret Service Agents.

The Pinkerton National Detective Agency

Pinkerton's National Detective Agency, founded in 1850 by Scottish immigrant Allan Pinkerton, was the first organization of its type in the United States. In fact, its organizational structure was later adopted by the Federal Bureau of Investigation (FBI). The Pinkerton Agency was called on by communities to handle cases that local law enforcement officers were unable to investigate due to incompetency or limited resources. Pinkerton offered the field of criminal investigation several innovations in crime detection. For example, he was the first to devise a **rogues' gallery**, which was a compilation of descriptions, methods of operation, hiding places, and names of associates of known criminals.

Pinkerton agents were hired to track western outlaws Jesse James, the Reno Gang, and the Wild Bunch (including Butch Cassidy and the Sundance Kid). On March 17, 1874, two Pinkerton detectives and Deputy Sheriff Edwin P. Daniels met the Younger brothers (associates of the James-Younger Gang); John Younger and one Pinkerton agent were killed. In Union, Missouri, a bank was robbed by George Collins, aka Fred Lewis, and Bill Randolph; Pinkerton Detective Chas Schumacher trailed them and was killed. Collins was subsequently hanged on March 26, 1904, and Randolph was hanged on May 8, 1905, in Union, Missouri. Pinkerton agents were also hired for the purposes of transporting money and other high-quality merchandise between cities and towns. This made them extremely vulnerable to the outlaws. As such, Pinkerton agents were usually well paid and well armed.

Due to Pinkerton agents' conflicts with labor unions, labor organizers and union members still associate the term *Pinkerton* with strikebreaking. Accordingly, Pinkerton agents moved away from labor spying following disclosures by the La Follette Committee hearings in 1937. Pinkerton agents' criminal detection work also underwent problems resulting from the police modernization movement, which saw the rise of the FBI and the bolstering of detective branches and resources of the public police. Without the labor and criminal investigation work on which Pinkerton agents flourished for decades, the company became increasingly involved in protection services, and in the 1960s, the word "Detective" disappeared from the agency's letterhead. In July 2003, the Pinkerton agency was acquired along with longtime rival the William J. Burns Detective Agency (founded in 1910), one of the largest security companies in the world.

The Introduction of Metropolitan Detectives

As far back as 1845, New York City had 800 plainclothes officers. But not until 1857 were the police authorized to designate 20 patrol officers as detectives. In 1857 the New York City Police Department established a rogues' gallery of photographs of known offenders arranged by criminal specialty and height—and by the following year, it had over 700 photographs for detectives to study so that they might recognize criminals on the street.[1]

Pinkerton National Detective Agents Badge (1860).

Geoff Brightling/Dorling Kindersley, Ltd.

Photographs from rogues' galleries of that era reveal that some offenders grimaced, puffed their cheeks, rolled their eyes, and otherwise tried to distort their appearance to lessen the chance of later recognition.

In 1884, Chicago established this country's first municipal Criminal Identification Bureau. The Atlanta Police Department's Detective Bureau was organized in 1885 with a staff of one captain, one sergeant, and eight detectives.[2] In 1886 Thomas Byrnes, the dynamic chief detective of New York City, published *Professional Criminals in America*, which included pictures, descriptions, and the methods of all criminals known to him. Byrnes thereby contributed to information sharing among police departments. To supplement the rogues' gallery, Byrnes instituted the **Mulberry Street Morning Parade**. At 9 o'clock every morning, all criminals arrested in the past 24 hours were marched before his detectives, who were expected to make notes and to recognize the criminals later.[3]

State and Federal Initiatives

From the very beginning, the federal government utilized criminal investigators to detect revenue violations. In 1865, Congress created the United States Secret Service for the purposes of detecting counterfeiting. Following the assassination of President McKinley, in 1903 the Secret Service was also assigned responsibilities regarding the president.

Following the passing of Prohibition in 1920, the Bureau of Internal Revenue assumed responsibility for enforcement of Prohibition. In time, the number of bureau agents swelled to an enormous 4,000. The Bureau of Internal Revenue, however, was housed within the Department of the Treasury, so its agents were nicknamed "T-men."

The Creation of the FBI

Probably the single most significant development in criminal investigation in the United States was the establishment of the FBI in 1924. The FBI originated from a force of special agents created in 1908 by Attorney General Charles Bonaparte during the presidency of Theodore Roosevelt. The two men first met when they both spoke at a meeting of the Baltimore Civil Service Reform Association. Roosevelt, then Civil Service commissioner, boasted of his reforms in federal law enforcement. It was 1892, a time when law enforcement was often political rather than professional. Roosevelt spoke with pride of his insistence that Border Patrol applicants pass marksmanship tests, with the most accurate getting the jobs. Following Roosevelt on the program, Bonaparte countered, tongue in cheek, that target shooting was not the way to get the best men: "Roosevelt should have had the men shoot at each other and given the jobs to the survivors."

Roosevelt and Bonaparte both were "Progressives." They shared the conviction that efficiency and expertise, not political connections, should determine who could best serve in government. Theodore Roosevelt became the president of the United States in 1901; four years later, he appointed Bonaparte to be attorney general. In 1908, Bonaparte applied that Progressive philosophy to the Department of Justice by creating a corps of special agents. It had neither a name nor an officially designated leader other than the attorney general. Yet, these

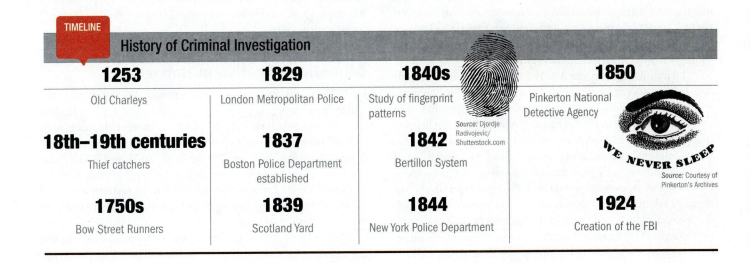

TIMELINE	History of Criminal Investigation			
1253	**1829**	**1840s**		**1850**
Old Charleys	London Metropolitan Police	Study of fingerprint patterns		Pinkerton National Detective Agency
18th–19th centuries	**1837**	**1842**		
Thief catchers	Boston Police Department established	Bertillon System	*Source:* Djordje Radivojevic/ Shutterstock.com	
1750s	**1839**	**1844**		**1924**
Bow Street Runners	Scotland Yard	New York Police Department		Creation of the FBI

WE NEVER SLEEP

Source: Courtesy of Pinkerton's Archives

J. Edgar Hoover.

no investigators of its own except for a few special agents who carried out specific assignments for the attorney general, and a force of examiners (trained as accountants) who reviewed the financial transactions of the federal courts. Since its beginning in 1870, the Department of Justice used funds appropriated to investigate federal crimes to hire private detectives first and later investigators from other federal agencies. (Federal crimes are those that were considered interstate or occurred on federal government reservations.)

By 1907, the Department of Justice most frequently called upon Secret Service "operatives" to conduct investigations. These men were well trained, dedicated—and expensive. Moreover, they reported not to the attorney general, but to the chief of the Secret Service. This situation frustrated Bonaparte, who wanted complete control of investigations under his jurisdiction. Congress provided the impetus for Bonaparte to acquire his own force. On May 27, 1908, it enacted a law preventing the Department of Justice from engaging Secret Service operatives.

The following month, Attorney General Bonaparte appointed a force of special agents within the Department of Justice. Accordingly, 10 former Secret Service employees and a number of Department of Justice peonage (i.e., compulsory servitude) investigators became special agents of the Department of Justice. On July 26, 1908, Bonaparte ordered them to report to Chief Examiner Stanley W. Finch. This action is celebrated as the beginning of the FBI.

Both Attorney General Bonaparte and President Theodore Roosevelt, who completed their terms in March 1909, recommended that the force of 34 agents become a permanent part of the Department of Justice. Attorney General George Wickersham, Bonaparte's successor, named the force the Bureau of Investigation on March 16, 1909. At that time, the title of chief examiner was changed to chief of the Bureau of Investigation.

When new federal laws governing interstate transportation of stolen automobiles were passed, the bureau gained considerable notoriety. John Edgar (J. Edgar) Hoover, the bureau's newly named director, announced in 1924 that he would strive to eliminate corruption and get the agency out of politics. In doing so, he raised the qualifications of agent personnel, reduced the number of agents nationwide, and closed some field offices. Today, the FBI is one of many federal investigative agencies that has made great strides in professionalizing the field of criminal investigation.

Other Investigative Initiatives

In 1933, when Prohibition was repealed by the Eighteenth Amendment to the U.S. Constitution, many former bootleggers and other criminals turned to other forms of criminality such as bank robbery and kidnapping. During the Depression, some people saw John Dillinger, "Pretty Boy" Floyd, and Bonnie and Clyde "as plain folks" and did not grieve over a bank robbery or the kidnapping of a millionaire. Given the restricted roles of other federal investigative agencies, it became the FBI's role to deal with these criminals.

Under Hoover, who understood the importance and uses of information, records, and publicity as well as Allan Pinkerton had, the FBI became known for investigative efficiency. In 1932,

former detectives and Secret Service men were the forerunners of the FBI.

Today, most Americans take for granted that our country needs a federal investigative service, but in 1908, the establishment of this kind of agency at a national level was highly controversial. The U.S. Constitution is based on "federalism": a national government with jurisdiction over matters that crossed boundaries, like interstate commerce and foreign affairs, with all other powers reserved to the states. Throughout the 1800s, Americans usually looked to cities, counties, and states to fulfill most government responsibilities. However, by the twentieth century, easier transportation and communications had created a climate of opinion favorable to the federal government establishing a strong investigative tradition.

The impulse among the American people toward a responsive federal government, coupled with an idealistic, reformist spirit, characterized what is known as the Progressive Era, from approximately 1900 to 1918. The Progressive generation believed that government intervention was necessary to produce justice in an industrial society. Moreover, it looked to "experts" in all phases of industry and government to produce that just society.

President Roosevelt personified Progressivism at the national level. A federal investigative force consisting of well-disciplined experts and designed to fight corruption and crime fit Roosevelt's Progressive scheme of government. Attorney General Bonaparte shared his president's Progressive philosophy. However, the Department of Justice under Bonaparte had the FBI established a crime laboratory and made its services available free to state and local police. In 1935 it started the **National Academy**, a training course for state and local police. In 1967 the **National Crime Information Center (NCIC)** was made operational by the FBI, providing data on wanted persons and property stolen from all 50 states. Altogether, these developments gave the FBI considerable influence over law enforcement throughout the country. Although some people argue that such federal influence is undesirable, others point out that Hoover and the FBI strengthened police practices in this country, from keeping crime statistics to improving investigation.

The Harrison Act (1914) made the distribution of non-medical drugs a federal crime. Enforcement responsibility was initially given to the Internal Revenue Service, although by 1930 a separate Federal Bureau of Narcotics (FBN) was established in the Treasury Department. In 1949 a federal commission noted that federal narcotics enforcement was fragmented among several agencies, including the Border Patrol and Customs, resulting in duplication of effort and other ills. In 1968 some consolidation of effort was achieved with the creation of the Bureau of Narcotics and Dangerous Drugs (BNDD) in the Department of Justice, and in 1973, with the creation of its successor, the **Drug Enforcement Administration (DEA)**.

Today the DEA devotes many of its resources to fighting international drug traffic. Like the FBI, the DEA trains state and local police in investigative work. The training focuses on recognition of illegal drugs, control of drug purchases, surveillance methods, and handling of informants. In 2002 several federal agencies were consolidated to form Immigration and Customs Enforcement (ICE) in the Department of Homeland Security (DHS).

Contributions of August Vollmer

A discussion of the history of policing would not be complete without addressing the vast contributions of August Vollmer. August Vollmer is one of the most important figures in the historic evolution of professional policing.

When he was alive he was one of the most famous people in the nation. He was Marshal in Berkley, California from 1905 to 1909 and advanced his career by becoming Berkeley's chief of police. He remained in that position from 1909 to 1931. During that time, Vollmer introduced numerous concepts that transformed policing into what it is today.

When Vollmer first came into office, police officers were known more for their brutality and corruption than their skills in crime control and order maintenance. Gambling dens and opium parlors operated openly in Berkeley because the owners paid off city officials. Vollmer, who only had a sixth-grade education, banned graft and gratuities, and instituted a series of reforms that are credited with transforming policing into a modern profession.[4] Vollmer's many contributions included:

- In 1910, he was the first chief to put officers on bicycles, then on motorcycles a year later, and then in patrol cars in 1913. He then put radio communications in the cars in 1928.
- In 1906 he created a centralized police records system, one of the first in the United States.

- He was the first chief in the United States, in 1907, to insist his department use blood, fiber, and soil analysis to solve crimes. Vollmer's emphasis on scientific investigation prompted the creation of numerous crime laboratories around the state.
- In 1907, he started the world's first police school where officers could learn about the laws of evidence.
- In 1914, he was the first to use radio communications between officers. Also that year he formed the first juvenile division in the country.
- Vollmer was the first police chief to require officers get college degrees.
- In 1916, he pioneered the teaching of criminal justice classes by starting a program at UC Berkeley.
- Vollmer outlawed the use of "third-degree" tactics, meaning police officers could no longer brutalize detainees to extract information.
- In 1921, Vollmer was the first chief to use the lie detector in investigations and was one of the first to use fingerprints to identify suspects.
- In 1919, Vollmer hired one of the nation's first African-American officers and the first female officer in 1925.
- He suggested that the role of police is to prevent crime rather than just to solve it. To better understand the criminal mind, Vollmer visited the jail each morning to talk to prisoners and corresponded extensively with men he had put in prison.
- Vollmer was also opposed to capital punishment.

Vollmer became so associated with police reform that he took extended leaves of absence from Berkeley to help out other departments.[5] He helped reorganize police departments in Los Angeles, Chicago, San Diego, and Dallas, as well as in Cuba. On November 4, 1955, at the age of 79 and suffering from cancer, Vollmer committed suicide at his Berkeley home.

Historical Highlights in Forensic Science

The origins of criminalistics or forensic science are largely European. Forensic science draws from diverse disciplines, such as geology, physics, chemistry, biology, and mathematics, to study physical evidence related to crime. The first major book describing the application of scientific disciplines to criminal investigation was written in 1893 by **Hans Gross**, a public prosecutor and later a judge from Graz, Austria. Translated into English in 1906 under the title *Criminal Investigation*, it remains highly respected today as the seminal work in the field.

The Frenchman **Edmond Locard** established the first forensic laboratory in Lyon in 1910. All crime scenes are searched on the basis of **Locard's exchange principle**, which asserts that when perpetrators come into contact with the scene, they will leave something of themselves and take away something from the scene, for example, hairs and fibers. Expressed somewhat differently, Locard's exchange principle states that there is something to be found. He is also recognized as the father of poreoscopy, the study of pores, and for advocating that if there were 12 points of agreement between two compared fingerprints the identity was certain.

Although the field of forensic science has seen periods of stability, on the whole it is dynamic and a work in progress. Examples of this principle of dynamic change can be seen in the histories of two commonly used services—biometric-based identification and firearms identification.

Biometric-Based Identification

Technology in crime detection began to flourish during the nineteenth century with the creation of a personal identification system by Alphonse Bertillon, the director of the criminal identification section of the Paris Police Department. The **Bertillon system**, also known as **anthropometry**, was based on the idea that certain aspects of the human body, such as skeletal size, ear shaping, and eye color, remained the same after a person had reached full physical maturity. It used a combination of photographs with standardized physical measurements. **Dactylography** is the study of fingerprints. Fingerprints were used on contracts during China's T'ang Dynasty in the eighth century as well as on official papers in fourteenth-century Persia and seventeenth-century England. In the first century, the Roman lawyer Quintilianus introduced a bloody fingerprint in a murder trial, successfully defending a child against the charge of murdering his father.

In 1684 in England, Dr. Nehemiah Grew first called attention to the system of pores and ridges in the hands and feet. Just two years later, Marcello Malpighi made similar observations. In 1823, John Perkinje, a professor at the University of Breslau, named nine standard types of fingerprint patterns and outlined a broad method of classification. Despite these early stirrings, it was not until 1900 in England that dactylography was used as a country-wide system of criminal identification.

In the mid-1840s, the study of fingerprint patterns became a popular means to identify suspects in crime. Although the use of fingerprints is commonplace today, it wasn't until the late nineteenth century that it was learned that a person's fingerprints could act as a unique, unchangeable method of personal identification. Such discoveries have been credited to the Englishmen William J. Herschel and Henry Fields, who were working in Asia at the time.

Firearms Identification

In the United States, the historic frequency of shootings has made firearms identification extremely important. As a specialty within forensic science, firearms identification extends far beyond the comparison of two fired bullets. It includes identification of types of ammunition, knowledge of the design and functioning of firearms, restoration of obliterated serial numbers on weapons, and estimation of the distance between a gun's muzzle and a victim when the weapon was fired.

In 1835, one of the last of the Bow Street Runners, Henry Goddard, made the first successful attempt to identify a murderer from a bullet recovered from the body of a victim. Goddard noticed that the bullet had a distinctive blemish or gouge on it. At the home of one suspect, Goddard seized a bullet mold with a defect whose location corresponded exactly to the gouge on the bullet. When confronted with this evidence, the owner of the mold confessed to the crime.

Professor Lacassagne removed a bullet in 1889 from a corpse in France. On examining it closely, he found seven grooves made as the bullet passed through the barrel of a gun. Shown the guns of a number of suspects, Lacassagne identified the one that could have left seven grooves. On the basis of this evidence, a man was convicted of the murder. However, any number of guns manufactured at that time could have produced seven grooves. There is no way of knowing whether the right person was found guilty.

A CLOSER LOOK

Current Applications of Firearms and Toolmark Analysis

Today, physical scientists/forensic examiners, physical science technicians, firearms specialists, and ammunition specialists all utilize forensic techniques to examine not just firearms but other devices used in criminality. These are examples:

Firearms Identification
- Comparing bullets to barrels
- Comparing cartridge cases to firearms
- Firearms function testing
- Silencer testing
- Gunshot distance determination
- Serial number restoration
- Accidental discharge determination
- Trigger pull measurements
- Ejection pattern testing
- Shot pattern examinations

Toolmark Identification
- Comparing tools with toolmarks found at the crime scene
- Comparing stamps with stamped impressions for identification
- Fracture matching
- Lock and key examinations

Source: Federal Bureau of Investigation. (2014). Retrieved from http://www.fbi.gov.

In 1898 a German chemist named Paul Jeserich was given a bullet taken from the body of a man murdered near Berlin. After firing a test bullet from the defendant's revolver, Jeserich took microphotographs of the fatal and test bullets and, on the basis of the agreement between both their respective normalities and abnormalities, testified that the defendant's revolver fired the fatal bullet, contributing materially to the conviction obtained. Unknowingly at the doorstep of scientific greatness, Jeserich did not pursue this discovery any further, choosing instead to return to his other interests.

Gradually, attention began to shift from just bullets to other aspects of firearms. In 1913 Professor Balthazard published perhaps the single most important article on firearms identification. In it, he noted that the firing pin, breechblock, extractor, and ejector all leave marks on cartridges and that these vary among different types of weapons.

► The Evolution in Research and Science in Forensic Science

As discussed, the seeds of modern forensic science were sown in the last quarter of the nineteenth century. Progress from that time has been slow but steady. The American Academy of Forensic Sciences (AAFS), a professional organization of forensic scientists in America, was established in 1948. Specific areas of expertise of AAFS members include pathology and biology, toxicology, criminalistics, questioned documents, and forensic odontology and anthropology.

LEARNING OUTCOMES 2 Identify how research affects criminal investigation.

In addition to the development of fingerprinting as an aid to criminal detection, several other forensic advances were either being developed or had already been placed into service by the late nineteenth century. Historic strides in criminal investigation included study in serology, forensic dentistry, and ballistics. For example, research into human blood was vastly expanded during the early twentieth century by Paul Uhlenhuth, a German physician. Uhlenhuth's work created serums that enabled one to distinguish one species of animal blood from another. Consequently, **serology** was a procedure that was established to study human bloodstains and distinguish them from the blood of most other animals.

Forensic pathology is a branch of pathology concerned with determining the cause of death by examination of a corpse. The pathologist, at the request of a coroner or medical examiner, performs the autopsy, usually during the investigation of criminal cases and civil suit cases in some jurisdictions. Forensic pathologists are also frequently asked to confirm the identity of a corpse.

The *forensic pathologist* is a medical doctor who has completed training in anatomical pathology and who has subsequently subspecialized in forensic pathology. Forensic pathologists perform autopsies/postmortem examinations to determine the cause of death. The autopsy report contains an opinion about the following:

- The pathologic process, injury, or disease that directly resulted in or initiated a series of events that led to a person's death (also called mechanism of death), such as a bullet wound to the head, exsanguinations due to a stab wound, manual or ligature strangulation, myocardial infarction due to coronary artery disease, and so on

- The "manner of death"—the circumstances surrounding the cause of death—which in most jurisdictions includes the following:
  - Homicide
  - Accidental
  - Natural
  - Suicide
  - Undetermined

The autopsy is also an opportunity for other issues raised by the death to be addressed, such as the collection of trace evidence or determining the identity of the deceased. Pathologists also have the following responsibilities:

- Examine and document wounds and injuries, both at autopsy and occasionally in a clinical setting.

- Collect and examine tissue specimens under the microscope in order to identify the presence or absence of natural disease and other microscopic findings, such as asbestos bodies in the lungs or gunpowder particles around a gunshot wound.

- Collect and interpret toxicological analyses on bodily tissues and fluids to determine the chemical cause of accidental overdoses or deliberate poisonings.

- Serve as expert witnesses in civil or criminal cases.

Think About It...

Pathology as a Forensic Career Although not a law enforcement officer, the forensic pathologist is one of criminal investigation's most valuable assets. Could you perform the duties of a pathologist? Why or why not?

Darren Baker/Shutterstock.com

Researcher in Lab.

Modern Fields of Forensic Science

The area of forensic science has grown considerably over the last 150 years and more so since the mid-1980s. Here are examples of fields of forensic science that may be of interest to future criminal investigators:

- Forensic accounting is the study and interpretation of accounting evidence.

- Forensic anthropology is the application of physical anthropology in a legal setting, usually for the recovery and identification of skeletonized human remains.

- Forensic archaeology is the application of a combination of archaeological techniques and forensic science, typically in law enforcement.

- Forensic astronomy uses methods from astronomy to determine past celestial constellations for forensic purposes.

- Forensic botany is the study of plant life in order to gain information regarding possible crimes.

- Forensic chemistry is the study of detection and identification of illicit drugs, accelerants used in arson cases, and explosive and gunshot residue (GSR).

- Computational forensics concerns the development of algorithms and software to assist forensic examination.

- Criminalistics is the application of various sciences to answer questions relating to examination and comparison of biological evidence, trace evidence, impression evidence (such as fingerprints, footwear impressions, and tire tracks), controlled substances, ballistics, firearm and toolmark examination, and other evidence in criminal investigations. In typical circumstances, evidence is processed in a crime laboratory.

- Forensic dactyloscopy is the study of fingerprints.

- Digital forensics is the application of proven scientific methods and techniques in order to recover data from electronic/digital media. Digital forensic specialists work in the field as well as in the lab.

- Forensic document examination or questioned document examination answers questions about a disputed documents using a variety of scientific processes and methods. Many examinations involve a comparison of the questioned document, or components of the document, to a set of known standards. The most common type of examination involves handwriting analysis, wherein the examiner tries to address concerns about potential authorship.

- Forensic DNA analysis takes advantage of the uniqueness of an individual's DNA to answer forensic questions such as paternity/maternity testing or placing a suspect at a crime scene (for example, in a rape investigation).

- Forensic engineering is the scientific examination and analysis of structures and products relating to their failure or cause of damage.

- Forensic entomology deals with the examination of insects in, on, and around human remains to assist in the determination of time or location of death. It is also possible to determine if the body was moved after death.

- Forensic geology deals with trace evidence in the form of soils, minerals, and petroleum.

- Forensic limnology is the analysis of evidence collected from crime scenes in or around freshwater sources. Examination of biological organisms, in particular, diatoms, can be useful in connecting suspects with victims.

- Forensic linguistics deals with issues in the legal system that require linguistic expertise.

- Forensic meteorology is a site-specific analysis of past weather conditions for a point of loss.

- Forensic odontology is the study of the uniqueness of dentition, better known as the study of teeth.

- Forensic optometry is the study of glasses and other eyewear in relation to crime scenes and criminal investigations.

- Forensic pathology is a field in which the principles of medicine and pathology are applied to determine a cause of death or injury in the context of a legal inquiry.

- Forensic psychology is the study of the mind of an individual, using forensic methods. Usually it determines the circumstances behind a criminal's behavior.

- Forensic seismology is the study of techniques to distinguish the seismic signals generated by underground nuclear explosions from those generated by earthquakes.

- Forensic serology is the study of body fluids.

- Forensic toxicology is the study of the effect of drugs and poisons on/in the human body.

- Forensic video analysis is the scientific examination, comparison, and evaluation of video in legal matters.

- Mobile device forensics is the scientific examination and evaluation of evidences found on a mobile phone (for example, call history, deleted SMS, and SIM card forensics).

- Trace evidence analysis is the analysis and comparison of trace evidence, including glass, paint, fibers, hair, and so on.

- Forensic podiatry is an application of the study of a foot, footprint, or footwear and their traces to analyze the scene of a crime and to establish personal identity in forensic examinations.

▶ Criminal Investigation Research

As with other aspects of criminal justice, research plays an important role in helping us to understand how criminal investigations can be more effective. Early studies by both the RAND Corporation and the Police Executive Research Forum challenged long-held opinions about criminal investigation and made some practical recommendations.

The RAND Corporation Study

In the late 1970s, the National Institute of Law Enforcement and Criminal Justice awarded a grant to the RAND Corporation to undertake a nationwide study of criminal investigations by police agencies in major U.S. cities. The goals of the study were to determine how police investigations were organized and managed, as well as to assess various activities as they relate to the effectiveness of overall police functioning. Until this study, police investigators had not been placed under as much scrutiny as those in patrol functions or other areas of policing.

Design of the Study

The focus of the RAND study was the investigation of "index" offenses: serious crimes such as murder, robbery, and rape. Other less serious crimes, such as drug violations, gambling, and prostitution, were not considered in the study. A national survey was conducted that assessed the investigative practices of all municipal and county police agencies employing more than 150 sworn personnel or serving a jurisdiction with a population over 100,000. Observations and interviews were conducted in more than 25 departments, which were chosen to represent various investigative methods.

The *Uniform Crime Reports* (UCRs), administered by the FBI, were used to determine the outcome of investigations. Data on the allocation of investigative endeavors were obtained from a computerized network operated by the Kansas City Police Department. In addition, information from the National Crime Victimization Survey and the UCRs were linked to identify the effectiveness of arrest and the overall relationships between departments. Finally, the study analyzed case samples to determine how specific cases were solved.

Recommendations of the Study

The RAND study resulted in the following recommendations:

1. Postarrest activities should be coordinated more closely with the prosecutor's office. This could be accomplished by assigning an investigator to the prosecutor's office or by permitting prosecutors discretionary guidance over the practices of investigators, thus increasing the number of prosecutable cases.

2. Patrol officers should be afforded greater responsibilities in conducting preliminary investigations, which will provide greater case-screening capabilities for investigators while eliminating redundancy. The study suggests that many cases can be closed at the preliminary investigation stage. Therefore, patrol officers should be trained to perform such duties.

3. Forensic resources should be increased for processing latent prints and developing a system to organize and search fingerprint files more effectively.

4. With regard to investigations of cases that the agency chose to pursue, a distinction should be made between cases that require routine clerical skills and those that require special investigative abilities. Investigations falling into the second category should be handled through a specialized investigation section.

In addition to the RAND Corporation's study, several others have offered support for its findings. Block and Weidman's study of the New York Police Department and Greenberg et al.'s decision-making model for felony investigations both support the idea that patrol officers make the majority of arrests during preliminary investigations and can provide excellent case-screening benefits for investigations.[6]

The PERF Study

In one important study, the Police Executive Research Forum (PERF) considered the roles played by detectives and patrol officers in the course of burglary and robbery investigations. The study examined three areas: DeKalb County, Georgia; St. Petersburg, Florida; and Wichita, Kansas. Of the major findings of the study, several observations were made.[7] For example, PERF concluded that detectives and patrol officers contributed equally to the resolution of burglary and robbery cases. However, it was determined that in most cases, a period of four hours (stretched over several days) was sufficient to close cases and that 75 percent of burglary and robbery cases were suspended in less than two days due to a lack of leads. In the remainder of cases, detectives played a major role in follow-up work conducted to identify and arrest suspects. It was determined, however, that both detectives and patrol personnel are too reliant on victim information for identification purposes, as opposed to checking leads from sources such as informants, witnesses, and other information sources in the police department.

Results of the PERF study suggest the following:

1. There is not as much waste or mismanagement in investigations as earlier thought as a result of similar studies. The value of follow-up investigations by detectives in identifying and arresting suspects is also thought to be much greater than indicated by earlier studies.

2. Greater emphasis should be placed on the collection and use of physical evidence when applicable. Although physical evidence is seldom used in identifying suspects, it can be effective in corroborating other evidence of suspect identification, indicating that although not all police departments use extensive training of evidence technicians, many have established policies regulating situations in which they should be used.

3. Police departments should develop policies and guidelines regulating the use of evidence technicians in routine cases such as burglary and robbery when there has been no physical injury to victims. This policy should be based on the assumption that if the suspects can be found through other means of identification, physical evidence is not likely to be useful.

4. Officers should dedicate greater effort to locating witnesses through the use of a neighborhood canvass. This was not found to be common practice by patrol officers in the cities studied because initial information was commonly learned via interviews with witnesses and victims. It was suggested that to expand the scope of their investigations, patrol officers seek additional witnesses and victims through a neighborhood canvass.

5. Patrol officers should make more extensive use of department records and informants to develop and identify suspects. Although checking department records would be a relatively easy task, the skills needed to develop and interview informants are not common among patrol officers. Supervisors in the patrol area could make a greater effort to provide such training to street officers to help them develop informants.

▶ The Objectives of Criminal Investigation

 Discuss the objectives of criminal investigation.

Because of the changing nature of criminal activity and the role of the investigator, the objectives of the criminal investigation may be more complex than people imagine. The objectives of criminal investigations are to

- Detect crime
- Locate and identify suspects in crimes
- Locate, document, and preserve evidence in crimes
- Arrest suspects in crimes
- Recover stolen property
- Prepare sound criminal cases for prosecution

The premise behind the criminal investigation field is that people make mistakes while committing crimes. For example, a burglar may leave behind broken glass or clothing fibers, or a rapist may leave fingerprints, skin tissue, semen, or blood. As a result of these oversights, evidence of who committed the crime is also left behind. It is the job of the criminal investigator to know how, when, and where to look for such evidence. In doing so, he or she must be able to draw on various resources:

- Witnesses and informants, for firsthand information about the crime
- Technological advances in evidence collection and preservation
- Their own training and experience in investigative techniques

In summary, almost all crimes require some degree of investigation. The extent to which any particular violation is investigated depends largely on resources available to the department and how the department prioritizes the violation.

Inductive and Deductive Reasoning

After an initial evaluation of evidence in a case, the criminal investigator draws conclusions through a process of reasoning. This process is typically achieved through inductive or deductive reasoning. The distinctions between the two are described next.

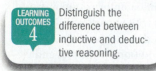 Distinguish the difference between inductive and deductive reasoning.

Inductive Reasoning

Induction or **inductive reasoning**, sometimes called inductive logic, is reasoning that takes us beyond what we know (our current evidence or information) to conclusions about what we don't know. Induction is used, for example, in drawing general conclusions from "specific" propositions, as in the following examples:

"All of John Wayne Gacy's victims found to date were male [specific]; thus, Gacy did not kill females [general]."

Or:

"This ice is cold, and all ice I have ever touched was cold [specific.] . . . to infer general; thus, all ice is cold [general]."

The calculus of inductive reasoning can also be broken down into conclusions that are strong versus those that are not so strong or even weak. For example, the following are examples of strong and weak induction.

Strong Induction

"All observed crows are black; therefore, all crows are black."

This exemplifies the nature of induction: inducing the universal from the particular. However, the conclusion is not certain. Unless one can systematically falsify the possibility of crows being another color, the conclusion that all crows are all black may actually be false.

Technically speaking, one could examine a crow's genome and learn whether it's capable of producing a differently colored bird. In doing so, we could discover that, in fact, colored crows are genetically possible. Consequently, a strong induction is an argument in which the truth of the premises would make the truth of the conclusion probable but not necessary.

Weak Induction

"I always hang pictures on nails; therefore, all pictures hang from nails."

Assuming the first statement to be true, this example is built on the certainty that "I always hang pictures on nails" leading to the generalization that "All pictures hang from nails." However, the link between the premise and the inductive conclusion is weak. In other words, there is no reason to believe that just because one person hangs pictures on nails that there are no other ways for pictures to be hung or that other people cannot do other things with pictures.

Of course, not all pictures are hung from nails, and for that matter; many pictures aren't hung at all. So the conclusion cannot be strongly inductively made from the premise. Using other knowledge, we can easily see that this example of induction would lead us to a clearly false conclusion. Conclusions drawn in this manner are usually overgeneralizations that are in need of further investigation. Consider another example of weak induction:

"Many speeding tickets are given to teenagers; therefore, all teenagers drive fast."

In this example, although the premise is built upon a certainty, it is not one that leads to a reasonable conclusion. Not every teenager observed has been given a speeding ticket. In other words, unlike "The sun rises every morning," there are already plenty of examples of teenagers who have not received speeding tickets. Therefore, the conclusion drawn can easily be true or false, and the inductive logic does not give us a strong conclusion. In both of these examples of weak induction, the logical means of connecting the premise and conclusion (with the word "therefore") are faulty and do not give us a strong inductively reasoned statement.

Deductive Reasoning

Sometimes called deductive logic, **deductive reasoning** is reasoning based on specific pieces of evidence to establish proof that a suspect is guilty of an offense—for example, identifying muddy footprints outside a window where a burglary has occurred. An issue would be whether the footprints belonged to an occupant of the house, to the burglar, or to someone else.

Deductive reasoning is often contrasted with inductive reasoning. For example, by thinking about phenomena such as how apples fall and how the planets move, Isaac Newton induced his theory of gravity. In the nineteenth century, Adams and LeVerrier applied Newton's theory (general principle) to deduce the existence, mass, position, and orbit of Neptune (specific conclusions) from perturbations in the observed orbit of Uranus (specific data).

In the context of criminal investigation, investigators must anticipate all possible scenarios and know what evidence is needed to support prosecution of the case because each issue in dispute must be supported by evidence. The more evidence an investigator collects, the stronger the case and the stronger the proof of guilt. Conversely, the criminal investigator must also consider what evidence is available to exonerate innocent parties.

Challenging Inductive and Deductive Reasoning

In 2002, Jon J. Nordby questioned the processes of inductive and deductive reasoning in his book *Dead Reckoning: The Art of Forensic Detection*. Nordby suggested that it's not enough to just collect and analyze evidence; investigators also need a guiding theory that's flexible enough to accommodate new information and sufficiently logical to show a clear pattern of cause and effect.[8]

For example, Nordby states that a homicide investigation could show that the killer did not need to break in to a residence because he or she had a key. This theory would significantly narrow the possibilities. It is important for investigators to have a theory that guides the investigation, but also important is that any theory that is contradicted must be discarded. In other words, it is important for investigators to understand how logic and science work together.

Abduction is the process, in line with this reasoning, of proposing a likely explanation for an event that must then be tested. For example, the likely explanation that the killer had a key to the victim's home must then be followed up with testing. Nordby suggests,

> Induction is the wrong way of looking at science . . . because the classic problem of induction is the contrary instance [something that contradicts the claim].

Let us consider the notion that once a crime scene investigator observes a hair or piece of fiber, he or she now has their evidence. The reality is that many if not most crime scenes exist in dirty, debris-filled rooms. Such places are abundant with hair and fibers. So what is the investigator actually looking for? Which of all of those hairs and fibers is actually evidence? Unless the criminal

Inductive Reasoning

Sometimes called inductive logic, inductive reasoning is reasoning that takes us beyond what we know (our current evidence or information) to conclusions about what we don't know. Induction is used, for example, in using "specific" propositions. There are two types of inductive reasoning, strong and weak inductive reasoning.

Strong Induction

"All observed crows are black; therefore, all crows are black."

This exemplifies the nature of induction: inducing the universal from the particular. However, the conclusion is not certain. Unless one can systematically falsify the possibility of crows being another color, the conclusion that all crows are all black may actually be false.

Weak Induction

"I always hang pictures on nails; therefore, all pictures hang from nails."

Assuming the first statement to be true, this example is built on the certainty that "I always hang pictures on nails" leading to the generalization that "All pictures hang from nails." However, the link between the premise and the inductive conclusion is weak. In other words, there is no reason to believe that just because one person hangs pictures on nails that there are no other ways for pictures to be hung or that other people cannot do other things with pictures.

Conclusions drawn in this manner are usually overgeneralizations that are in need of further investigation.

Deductive Reasoning

Deductive reasoning is based on specific pieces of evidence to establish proof that a suspect is guilty of an offense—for example, identifying muddy footprints outside a window where a burglary has occurred. An issue would be whether the footprints belonged to an occupant of the house, to the burglar, or to someone else.

Deductive reasoning is often contrasted with inductive reasoning. For example, by thinking about phenomena such as how apples fall and how the planets move, Isaac Newton induced his theory of gravity. In the nineteenth century, Adams and LeVerrier applied Newton's theory (general principle) to deduce the existence, mass, position, and orbit of Neptune (specific conclusions) from perturbations in the observed orbit of Uranus (specific data).

Inductive and Deductive Reasoning.

COMPARISON TABLE OF CRITICAL THINKING AND SCIENTIFIC METHODOLOGY

In addition to the use of deductive and inductive logic in interpreting evidence, criminal investigators must incorporate skills of critical thinking with known scientific methods in their investigations. Let's look at how these two approaches to criminal investigation compare.

Scientific Methodology

In contrast with critical thinking, the scientific method refers to techniques for investigating phenomena, acquiring new knowledge, or correcting and integrating previous knowledge. To be termed scientific, a method of inquiry must be based on gathering empirical and measurable evidence.[i]

A scientific method consists of the collection of data through observation and experimentation and the formulation and testing of hypotheses. Each element of a scientific method is subject to peer review for possible mistakes.

The processes of critical thinking and scientific method need not be mutually exclusive. Rather, reasonable and informed investigators consider both as tools in their investigative arsenal, allowing for critical thinking in determining the direction of the investigation and scientific methods in evaluating the value of and usefulness of evidence.

Critical thinking

Critical thinking is the use of rational skills, worldviews, and values to get as close as possible to the truth. It is judgment about what to believe or what to do in response to observations or experiences. Critical thinking can also involve determining the meaning and significance of what is observed to determine whether there is adequate justification to accept whether a conclusion is true.

In contemporary usage, "critical" has the connotation of expressing disapproval, which is not always true of critical thinking. A critical evaluation of an argument, for example, might conclude that it is good.

Whereas thinking is often *casual* or routine, critical thinking deliberately evaluates the *quality* of thinking. In an early study on critical thinking in 1941, Edward Glaser wrote that the ability to think critically involves the following three things[ii]:

1. An attitude of being disposed to consider in a thoughtful way the problems and subjects that come within the range of one's experiences
2. Knowledge of the methods of logical inquiry and reasoning
3. Some skill in applying those methods

Critical thinking calls for a persistent effort to examine any belief or supposed form of knowledge in the light of the evidence that supports it and the further conclusions to which it tends. It also generally requires ability to recognize problems and to find workable means for meeting those problems. Critical thinking may occur whenever one judges, decides, or solves a problem—essentially, critical thinking may be used whenever one must figure out what to believe or what to do and do so in a reasonable and reflective way.

Critical thinking is important because it enables one to analyze, evaluate, explain, and restructure one's thinking, thereby decreasing the risk of adopting, acting on, or thinking with a false belief.

[i] Newton. (1999). Rules for the study of natural philosophy. From the General Scholium, which follows Book 3, *The system of the world* 794–796.

[ii] Glaser, E. M. (1941). *An experiment in the development of critical thinking.* Teacher's College, Columbia University.

---

investigator has an idea or theory that will make one object relevant and another irrelevant, the evidence-collection process will be overwhelming. In order to have purpose in what is being done, the investigator must have something in mind. That comes from abduction.

Developing an explanation that can be tested moves the investigation forward and guides the accumulation of knowledge, giving way only when contradicted. Abduction helps to make links among events, and the development of the overall theory of a crime depends on adding new links. Nordby suggests that abduction keeps guessing to a minimum.

Critical Thinking and Scientific Methodology

In addition to the use of deductive and inductive logic in interpreting evidence, criminal investigators must incorporate skills of critical thinking with known scientific methods in their investigations. Let's look at how these two approaches to criminal investigation compare.

The processes of critical thinking and the scientific method need not be mutually exclusive. Rather, reasonable and informed investigators consider both as tools in their investigative arsenal, allowing for critical thinking in determining the direction of the investigation and scientific methods in evaluating the value and usefulness of evidence.

▶ The Emergence of the Police Specialist

Within law enforcement agencies in the United States, a division typically exists between officers whose responsibility it is to maintain order and those who investigate crimes. In larger departments, specialized squads typically perform the investigative function in law enforcement agencies. In fact, many such departments have several internal detective divisions, each dealing with different categories of crime, such as crimes against persons (for example, rape, assault, and robbery), crimes against property (for example, burglary, larceny, and auto theft), and vice crimes (for example, drug violations, gambling, and prostitution). Smaller rural departments often lack the financial resources to specialize, so patrol officers often conduct criminal investigations in addition to their patrol duties.

In some types of crime, such as homicide, investigators must develop leads through interviews with friends, family, and associates of the victim as well as witnesses to the crime. In other cases, investigative leads are developed by sifting through files and prior police records and establishing the suspect's mode of operation (MO). In all cases, the investigative process uses traditional and historical methods of detection through the use of official records, photographs, fingerprints, and so on, as opposed to daily face-to-face contacts with the citizenry, such as with the patrol division. The investigative specialist is generally an older person who has had considerable experience in police work. Most detectives are former patrol personnel who have worked up through the ranks due to the common practice of promoting from within.

Types of Investigations

The mission of law enforcement is complex and demanding but contains some fundamental components, including the maintenance of peace in our communities and the protection of lives and property. When people choose to violate laws that provide for these essentials, the perpetrators must be identified and brought before a court. It is the task of identifying such offenders that is the quintessence of criminal investigation. Criminal investigators confront investigations in several areas in the regular course of their duties:

- Personal background, to determine a person's suitability for appointment to sensitive public trust positions
- Suspected violations of criminal law
- Infractions of civil law
- Vice (drug and organized crime activity)

Crime-Scene Investigators

The popular television show *CSI: Crime Scene Investigation* has brought the role of the crime-scene investigator to the public, creating considerable interest in forensic science. Of course, crime-scene investigators require very specific training with regard to crime-scene protection and the identification and preservation of evidence, and not every law enforcement agency is able to support a dedicated crime-scene investigation (CSI) unit. A description of the crime-scene unit (CSU) is provided by Michael Weisberg (2001):[9]

> The crime-scene unit (CSU) can be described as a specialized investigative unit that supports the crime scene investigation by identifying, documenting and preserving evidence. Services include fingerprinting, sketching and photographing physical evidence. Members of the CSU respond to the scene of the crime and in addition to locating physical evidence, specialists assist in identifying witnesses, victims and suspects. Depending on the structure of the law enforcement organization, members of the CSU may be sworn or non-sworn.[10]

Modes of Investigation

Criminal investigations are conducted through the use of three different responses: reactive, proactive, and preventive.

The **reactive response** addresses crimes that have already occurred, such as murder, robbery, and burglary. In this case, investigators typically respond to a crime, collect evidence, locate and interview witnesses, and identify and arrest a suspected perpetrator. Investigations are also conducted as a **proactive response** to anticipated criminal activity, as with many vice and organized crime investigations. Proactive investigations differ from reactive investigations in two major regards: (1) The investigation is conducted before the crime is committed (rather than after), and (2) the suspect is identified before he or she commits the crime. Finally, investigations are sometimes conducted as a **preventive response**. Prevention through deterrence is sometimes achieved by arresting the criminal and by aggressive prosecution.

The Role of the Criminal Investigator

As indicated earlier, many myths exist regarding the role of criminal investigators. Perhaps these are best summarized by Herman Goldstein, who wrote[11]

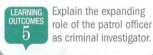

LEARNING OUTCOMES 5 — Explain the expanding role of the patrol officer as criminal investigator.

> Part of the mystique of detective operations is the impression that a detective has difficult-to-come-by qualifications and skills; that investigating crime is a real science; that a detective does much more important work than other police officers; that all detective work is exciting; and that a good detective can solve any crime. It borders on heresy to point out that, in fact, much of what detectives do consists of very routine and very elementary chores, including much paper processing; that a good deal of their work is not only not exciting but downright boring; that the situations they confront are often less demanding and challenging than those handled by patrol officers; that it is arguable whether special skills and knowledge are required for detective work; that a considerable amount of detective work is usually undertaken on a hit-or-miss basis; and that the capacity of detectives to solve crimes is greatly exaggerated.

Indeed, some studies have suggested that the role played by investigators is overrated and that their time could probably be spent more productively by focusing on crimes with the best likelihood of clearance.[12] Other researchers suggest that the investigative process is a valid utility in crime detection but should be augmented by the use of proactive patrol programs.

Characteristics of the Investigator

What characteristics best define a professional criminal investigator? Certainly, standards vary from one law enforcement agency to the next, but certain commonalities can be identified. To recognize these qualities, many police agencies implement a supervisory performance appraisal system to evaluate suitability for appointment to investigator. Once taken, the police manager can choose from candidates who possess the most sought-after qualities. The qualities involved in investigative performance are listed in Figure 1–1.

Investigators are specialists. They undertake activities related primarily to law enforcement; patrol officers, on the other hand, routinely spend their time in order maintenance (for example, maintaining peace) and the provision of general services (for example, emergency aid, finding lost children, traffic control). Despite the diversity of tasks performed by patrol officers, investigators also assume many substantial duties. For example, detectives gather crime information, effect arrests, and prepare cases for prosecution and trial.

The Patrol Officer as an Investigator

Traditionally, the responsibility of patrol officers in criminal investigations has been limited. Patrol officers have been required only to collect and record the most basic information by asking simple questions of the victims and witnesses and recording their answers on a report form. Although in the past patrol officers have studied crime scenes for physical evidence, usually the time spent on any one incident has been minimal. As a rule, reports have been reviewed by a supervisor and then sent to the detective division or an investigative unit for follow-up. In many cases, this process has resulted in the duplication of efforts by investigators.

Over the past decade, many police departments have expanded the role of the patrol officer to responsibilities that are traditionally assigned to investigators. These new responsibilities include the following:

- The patrol officer provides immediate assistance to victims, locates witnesses, interviews both victims and witnesses, and records information about the crime scene. Depending on the seriousness of the crime or the presence of physical evidence, the patrol officer may call for a more specialized search by evidence technicians. To a great extent, this procedure initiates the case.

- The patrol officer has the authority to initiate and complete investigation of certain classifications of crime, such as all misdemeanors, cases that involve property value up to $1,500, and auto larceny cases. Investigations of more serious crimes continue to be referred to specialized investigative units. The practical effect of this "sorting out" of responsibilities for different types of investigations is that patrol officers investigate high-volume crimes that can be investigated as effectively by patrol as by criminal investigators. Conversely, investigations that require more time, specialized skill, and effort are handled by trained criminal investigators.

According to a study by the National Institute of Justice (NIJ), investigative traits most commonly desired include[i]:

Motivation

Intuition

Stability

Judgment

Street knowledge

Teamwork

Persistence

Reliability

Intelligence

Dedication

Integrity

[i]National Institute of Justice. (1987, September). *Investigators who perform well*. Washington, DC: U.S. Department of Justice, September.

Investigative Traits Most Desired.

Qualities Involved in Investigative Performance

Gathering Information	Intelligence	Prosecutions
Crime-scene management	Perseverance	Quantity
Communication skills	Initiative	Presentation of testimony
Field Operations	Judgment	Percent of convictions
Stakeouts	Teamwork	**Personnel Performance**
Patrol	Involvement	Absenteeism
Crime-pattern analysis	Dedication	Complaints
Developing informants	**Arrests**	Awards
Street knowledge	Quantity	Dedication
Personal Traits	Quality	**Qualifications**
Motivation	**Public Victim Satisfaction**	Education
Stability	Crime reduction	Training
Persistence	Diminution of fear	Previous assignments in department

FIGURE 1–1 Qualities Involved in Investigative Performance.

- In rare cases, the police officer may be given responsibility for the entire investigative process. In these situations, the patrol officer carries out all investigative functions. Investigators, if there are any, perform as consultants to the patrol officers.

For the most part, police administrators agree that these changes in the patrol officers' roles have produced a number of benefits, including the following:

- The cases are handled completely and expeditiously.

- Relationships and communications between patrol officers and investigators have improved.

- The frequency of morale problems among patrol officers has decreased, and the decrease is attributable to the officers' belief that their skills are being better used in the investigative process.

- An increase in investigator productivity has resulted from a light caseload, which produced more time to focus investigative resources on specific high-profile cases.

- There is better management of the entire investigative effort by the police administrator.

Solvability Factors

A police department's reporting system and the investigative role of the patrol officer are inextricably bound. The redefining of the role of patrol officer is intended to ensure that evidence supporting the continual investigation or case closure is collected at the earliest possible point in the investigative process. This reporting system serves as the foundation for the criminal investigation.

LEARNING OUTCOMES 6 Discuss the solvability factors in a criminal investigation.

The reporting system is defined by two basic components, which in combination form the basis for an initial investigation. The first is a format that logically guides the identification leads, or **solvability factors**, that experience and research have demonstrated are most likely to result in case solution. The second provides an opportunity for details of the investigation thus far expended so the follow-up plans do not unnecessarily duplicate tasks already completed.

A police department's reporting system should indicate not only that solvability factors are present but it should also identify the investigative effort expended in searching for leads. For example, if witnesses have been sought in a number of locations, the report should indicate where the search was conducted, who was contacted, and what was found. Without this description, the follow-up investigator will not have a clear idea of where the patrol officer has located the existing solvability factors and will end up duplicating his or her efforts.

Unless the patrol officer is able to make an immediate, on-scene arrest, 12 essential questions need direct answers. These solvability factors are logically based on existing police practices. All agencies may have different capabilities and procedures that result in slightly different solvability factors.

From an investigative standpoint, these 12 structured questions serve to define what the patrol officer should accomplish.

Primary Solvability Factors

1. Immediate availability of witnesses
2. Name(s) of the suspect
3. Information about the suspect's location
4. Information about the suspect's description
5. Information about the suspect's identification
6. Information about the suspect's vehicle and vehicle movement
7. Information about traceable property
8. Information about significant MO
9. Information about significant physical evidence
10. Discovery of useful physical evidence
11. Judgment by the patrol officer that there is sufficient information available to conclude that anyone other than the suspect could not have committed the crime
12. Judgment by the patrol officer on case disposition. If the officer believes there is enough information available and with a reasonable investment of investigative effort that the probability of the case solution is high, then the investigation should be continued.

Patrol officers directing their activities to areas that were the most promising for a successful case solution not only broadened their roles but also established effective limitations as to where patrol officers should terminate their investigation. Furthermore, utilization of the solvability factors emphasizes the importance of a thorough initial investigation even when it is being turned over for a continuing investigation. The patrol officer has provided the direction of the investigation, up to this point.

Think About It...

Signature Murders One of the first things investigators consider in evaluating a homicide case is whether the method of operation, or "MO," was used in other crimes. In some extreme cases, not only is the same MO used, but also a "signature" of sorts is left at the scene that specifically identifies that scene with a particular killer. A signature crime is a crime that exhibits characteristics idiosyncratic to specific criminals, known as signature aspects, behaviors, or characteristics. Can you think of any "signature" crimes you have heard about? On one hand, the discovery of a signature crime provides the investigator with investigative leads, but can investigators wrongfully target a suspect just because a crime has similar aspects?

Courtesy of Mark C. Ide

Police Investigating a Crime Scene.

In summary, the expanded role of patrol officers in recent years has meant increased efficiency and effectiveness in policing in general and in criminal investigation specifically. It has also helped to enlighten those who serve the community in the capacity as patrol officers and to make them more aware of their important role as first responders to crime scenes and as the police department's eyes and ears on the street. In their role as first responders to crime scenes, patrol officers have many specific duties. These duties are encompassed in a process known as the preliminary investigation.

► *The Preliminary Investigation*

Although the primary purpose of a patrol force is to prevent crime, patrol officers have assumed many other responsibilities,

LEARNING OUTCOMES 7 Describe the preliminary investigation process.

including the investigation of crimes (discussed earlier). In modern police departments, the patrol force participates fully in the preliminary investigation of crimes.

The preliminary investigation is the responsibility of the first officer at the crime scene. His or her actions at the scene can greatly influence the ultimate success or failure of the investigation. In other words, a job well done during a preliminary investigation should provide the information or evidence needed to build a solid case. Conversely, errors made during the preliminary investigation, especially those that involve a failure to properly safeguard or identify physical evidence, cannot be rectified at a later time.

From the time the officer receives information to proceed to a crime scene, his or her preliminary investigation objectives are the following:

- Determine what has happened.
- Locate witnesses and sources of evidence that aid in determining what has occurred.
- Locate and preserve physical evidence.
- Determine what further investigative steps should be taken.
- Obtain and evaluate the accuracy of witnesses' statements.
- Determine whether to act on the statements and evidence found at the scene.
- Record what has been done, what has been learned, and what is left to be done.
- Complete the investigation and make an apprehension if appropriate.

One of the primary objectives of the preliminary investigation is to establish whether the necessary elements of a crime exist. All information obtainable at the scene of a crime should be gathered and reported at the time of the initial police response. The follow-up investigation by specialists is a second step—provided this second step won't unnecessarily postpone the successful completion of the investigation.

The preliminary investigation should begin when an officer is assigned to proceed to a crime scene and only terminate when he or she has completed the task to the point at which a delay in further action does not substantially affect the successful outcome of the investigation. For the most part, the nature of the crime and the relationship between the time of occurrence and the time of arresting the perpetrator determine whether or not the offense is investigated to conclusion by the patrol officer. When a suspect is arrested at or near the scene of a crime or during or shortly after the crime, the limits of a preliminary investigation need to be extended. If an extensive search of the crime scene for physical evidence is necessary, the preliminary and follow-up investigations overlap into a single operation. An example of this is homicide investigations.

Typically, patrol officers proceed to crime scenes with bits and pieces of information that must first be verified and then expanded to be of investigative use. However, as far as only crime-scene response is concerned, the patrol officer usually has two facts that shape his or her preliminary plans: the type of crime and the location of the crime. These facts usually indicate the urgency of a call and thus the degree to which a patrol officer can conduct the preliminary investigation.

The Crime-Scene Response

While approaching the crime scene, the responding officer must remain observant for potential suspects fleeing the area. The officer should note descriptions of people and vehicles leaving the crime area. A critical decision needs to be made by the responding officer when he or she observes a suspect. The officer must decide whether to stop his or her approach to the crime scene and investigate a suspicious person who may be fleeing or to proceed directly to the crime scene. The decision to stop must be based on the likelihood that the suspicious person is the offender fleeing the crime scene.

If it is necessary to stop a suspicious person, the officer should notify the dispatcher immediately so that other units are aware of the situation. The dispatcher should assign a backup

The Crime-Scene Response

Aid to the injured → Evaluate the situation → Obtain basic information → Interview witnesses

unit to assist the officer and then send another officer to the crime scene.

Aid to the Injured

The first duties of police officers at the scene of the crime are to administer first aid and obtain medical assistance for injured parties when required. All considerations are secondary to the well-being of injured parties. Even the capture of suspects and the integrity of valuable clues or evidence may need to be sacrificed to aid a victim. Obviously, if other apparently qualified persons are at the crime scene to provide first aid, an officer can then pursue fleeing suspects.

While rendering aid, officers should disturb the scene as little as possible. They should not unnecessarily move furniture, use facilities, or litter the area. For example, first aid supplies should be collected after use. Ambulance personnel should be directed how to enter and work within the crime scene so as not to needlessly disturb it.

Evaluate the Situation

After caring for any injured people, the officer should make an evaluation of the crime scene before proceeding with the preliminary investigation. Evaluation of the scene at this time often prevents false moves and mistakes. By observing the overall crime scene, a police officer can gain a reasonably accurate mental image of how the crime occurred and where it was committed. Of course, if additional assistance is needed at the crime scene, the officer should request it immediately.

After arriving at the scene, the officer must exercise extreme caution. He or she should concentrate on identifying potential evidence and avoid disturbing the likely locations of fingerprints and other evidence. For example, the swinging double doors common to many commercial establishments should be pushed open at a point lower than normally touched by a person. After the doors are identified as possible sources of fingerprints, they can be protected from contamination by locking them or tying them open.

The officer should observe and record the details of the scene. This is done by beginning to take notes as soon as possible. The longer the officer waits, the greater the danger becomes of omitting small but often important facts. The type of small details include whether a door was closed or locked, the lights were all on or off, or the blinds were open or closed.

Obtain Basic Information

For the most part, the preliminary sources of immediate information at a crime scene are victims and witnesses. From them, the officer can obtain the essential facts of the case. Although a lengthy inquiry cannot be conducted when the officer first arrives, he or she should establish the following points:

- The identities of victims, witnesses, and others present at the scene when the officer arrived
- A brief account from each witness or victim of what occurred, including descriptions of any suspects

After basic information has been obtained, the officer should broadcast a lookout alert or BOLO ("be on the lookout"). Alerting other field units about the nature of the offense and the details about the suspect, mode and direction of travel, description of the vehicle, proceeds of the crime, and type of weapon used may lead to an immediate arrest of a fleeing suspect.

Interview Witnesses

The first officer at the scene must detain witnesses. The officer should quickly remove all persons from the crime scene and should not allow them to return until all of the necessary crime-scene work is completed. The witnesses should be separated so they cannot discuss the case with each other. Such discussions among witnesses about the crime can adversely influence the witnesses' memories and statements.

The officer must obtain adequate information to identify and locate witnesses. Some witnesses may volunteer and offer to provide information to the officer. However, witnesses are not always easy to find. Many persons are reluctant to accept the role of witness, and they avoid becoming involved with the investigation in any manner.

One technique for identifying witnesses is watching the crowd for persons who are describing what they observed. Also, the officer should ask each witness to point out anyone else who was present at the time of the crime. In major crimes, the license numbers of vehicles parked near the crime scene and in the immediate neighborhood should be documented.

The officer should determine which witnesses have the most helpful information and obtain full details from them. Other witnesses who have not observed a significant part of the crime should be permitted to give a brief statement.

When a crime is committed within a residential building, the number of possible witnesses may be few. On the other hand, when a crime is committed in a store or on the street, a large number of persons may typically have witnessed the offense. The officer may need to visit adjoining places of business, apartments, or homes to determine if other persons might have knowledge of the crime.

The officer's inquiries must go beyond simply taking statements. He or she cannot accept without question anything stated by a witness. The officer must be observant and quick to recognize discrepancies or unusual behavior on the part of witnesses. Furthermore, the officer must examine the interrelationships between the accounts of witnesses and other evidence

When possible, witnesses and others should be interviewed in the following order:

1. Victim

2. Eyewitnesses

3. Persons observing the suspect entering or leaving the crime scene

4. Persons having knowledge of events leading up to the crime

5. Persons in the neighborhood

The Proper Order of Interviews.

in the case. This involves more than establishing that the witness has personal knowledge of the circumstances of the crime; it also involves an examination of the statements of witnesses in relation to their physical ability, the geographic layout of the crime scene, weather, and degree of visibility. Other factors include reasons for the witness being present at the scene.

In conclusion, criminal investigation is a dynamic and challenging police endeavor. Its roots are deeply embedded in our English heritage, and the slow evolution of techniques and research has resulted in our current system of investigative crime detection. Methods of approaching the crime scene are numerous but include time-honored techniques such as inductive and deductive reasoning coupled with critical thinking skills and scientific methodology.

Not everyone is well suited to be a criminal investigator, as research has shown that the preferable candidate should possess certain personality traits. Once the right individual is ready for the job, he or she must work closely with patrol first responders to properly access the crime scene and identify, collect, and properly preserve evidence.

Anatomy of a Home Invasion

In the late afternoon of July 22, 2007, Jennifer Hawke-Petit and her daughter Michaela went to a local grocery store in Cheshire, Connecticut. They had been targeted by Steven Hayes and his accomplice Joshua Komisarjevsky, who followed them home, and planned to later rob the family by home invasion. Anticipating their deeds, Hayes and Komisarjevsky exchanged text messages that were later introduced in court. According to Hayes's confession, the two men planned to rob the house and flee the scene with the family bound and un-harmed, but there was a change in their plan. They beat the husband William Petit with a bat Komisarjevsky had found in the yard, then tied him up in the basement at gunpoint. The children and their mother were each bound and locked in their respective rooms. Hayes convinced Jennifer to withdraw $15,000 from her line of credit. Video surveillance at a gas station showed Hayes purchasing $10 worth of gasoline in two cans he had taken from the Petit home.

Hayes and Komisarjevsky escalated their crime when Komisarjevsky sexually assaulted the 11-year-old daughter, Michaela, and photographed his assault on his cell phone. He then provoked Hayes to rape Jennifer. Hayes strangled Jennifer, and doused her body and parts of the house, includ-ing the daughter's room, with gasoline. A fire was then ignited, and Hayes and Komisarjevsky fled the scene, leaving the family members to die from smoke inhalation. The invasion lasted

© Arthur Turner/Alamy

seven hours, and Hayes and Komisarjevsky were found guilty of their role in the home invasion and murders. Although this was a horrific crime, we learn from this case that many crimes of violence leave a considerable amount of evidence behind.

Sources: Neighbors, schools mourn Petit family—Family's charitable work honored." (2007). *Channel 3 Eyewitness News.* Retrieved from www .thebostonchannel.com/r/13744337/detail.html; Goodall, J., & Hawks, C. (2005). *Crime scene documentation.* San Clemente, CA: LawTech Custom Publishing.

Criminal investigators must learn to look beyond the horror of the crime and evaluate what occurred from a scientific and analytical point of view:

1. Using the chapter material and the information about this home invasion, what do you think about the role of the investigators and the solvability of this crime?
2. Please explain what you have learned in this chapter about the history of criminal investigation that might be relevant to this case.

LEARNING OUTCOMES 1

Explain the history of criminal investigation.

Our current system of criminal investigation is a product of our English heritage and occurrences and events taking place here in the United States. Not only is it significant that our English ancestors paved the way for our current system of criminal investigation, but the many scientific advances have slowly but surely led us to a system whereby the identification of perpetrators is more accurate, thus providing justice for the victims and their families and decreasing the chance that an innocent person might go to prison.

1. Why were criminal investigations and apprehension difficult in the American frontier?

2. Where was the first professional police force established in the United States?

3. Why is the creation of the FBI considered one of the most significant developments in the history of law enforcement in America?

4. What is the role of a forensic pathologist in criminal investigations?

thief catchers People recruited from the riffraff of the streets to aid law enforcement officials in locating criminals during the European Industrial Revolution.

Bow Street Runners A group of English crime fighters formed by Henry Fielding during the eighteenth century.

bobbies The name of London Metropolitan Police Department officers; They were named this after Home Secretary Sir Robert Peel.

Scotland Yard One of the first criminal investigative bodies originally formed in England in the mid-nineteenth century.

rogues' gallery A compilation of descriptions, methods of operation, hiding places, and the names of associates of known criminals in the 1850s.

Mulberry Street Morning Parade An event in 1966 by Thomas Byrnes who showcased all criminals arrested in the previous 24 hours.

National Academy An extensive management training course sponsored by the FBI.

National Crime Information Center (NCIC) Criminal data maintained by the FBI on wanted persons and property stolen from all 50 states.

Drug Enforcement Administration (DEA) A United States federal law enforcement agency tasked with drug offenses such as trafficking, manufacture and abuse of illicit drugs.

Hans Gross A public prosecutor and later a judge from Graz, Austria who in 1893 wrote the first major book describing the application of scientific disciplines to criminal investigation.

Edmond Locard A Frenchman who in 1910 established the first forensic laboratory.

Locard's exchange principle A scientific principle which holds that the perpetrator of a crime will bring something into the crime scene and leave with something from it, and that both can be used as scientific evidence in a criminal investigation.

Bertillon system An early criminal identification or classification system based on the idea that certain aspects of the human body, such as skeletal size, ear shape, and eye color, remained the same after a person had reached full physical maturity. This system used a combination of photographs and standardized physical measurements.

anthropometry Another name for the Bertillon system which was based on the idea that certain aspects of the human body, such as skeletal size, ear shaping, and eye color, remained the same after a person had reached full physical maturity.

dactylography The study of fingerprints.

 LEARNING OUTCOMES 2

Identify how research affects criminal investigation.

In many law enforcement organizations, the crime-scene technician is the person trained to respond to the scene of a crime and identify, collect, and preserve evidence. The investigation is then taken over by the criminal investigator, who responds in a reactive or preventive manner. Investigations can also be of a proactive nature.

1. As it relates to criminal investigations, what were the most significant recommendations following the RAND study?

2. As it relates to criminal investigations, what were the most significant recommendations following the PERF study?

3. In terms of findings/recommendations, what is the primary similarity among the three studies noted in the chapter?

serology The scientific analysis of blood.

forensic pathology A subspecialty of pathology that focuses on determining the cause of death by examining a corpse.

Discuss the objectives of criminal investigation.

LEARNING OUTCOMES 3

Because of the changing nature of criminal activity and the role of the investigator, the objectives of the criminal investigation may be more complex than people imagine. These include detecting crime, locating and identifying suspects, and documenting and preserving evidence. The premise behind the criminal investigation field is that people make mistakes while committing crimes. For example, a burglar may leave behind broken glass or clothing fibers, or a rapist may leave fingerprints, skin tissue, semen, or blood. As a result of these oversights, evidence of who they are is also left behind.

1. What are the primary objectives of the criminal investigation?
2. What is the basic premise of the criminal investigation?
3. What are the three primary resources used by a criminal investigator?
4. What are some mistakes criminals often make when committing crimes?

Distinguish the difference between inductive and deductive reasoning.

LEARNING OUTCOMES 4

After an initial evaluation of evidence in a case, the criminal investigator draws conclusions through a process of reasoning. This process is typically achieved through inductive or deductive reasoning. Inductive reasoning is sometimes called inductive logic; it is reasoning that takes us beyond what we know (our current evidence or information) to conclusions about what we don't know. Deductive reasoning is reasoning based on specific pieces of evidence to establish proof that a suspect is guilty of an offense.

1. Why is critical thinking an important skill for criminal investigators?
2. How can critical thinking and the scientific method be used simultaneously in problem solving?
3. In criminal investigations, what is the danger in using inductive reasoning over deductive reasoning?
4. How does the concept of abduction apply to criminal investigations?

inductive reasoning Reasoning in which the premises seek to supply strong evidence for (not absolute proof of) the truth of the conclusion.

deductive reasoning The process of reasoning from one or more general statements or premises to reach a logical conclusion.

abduction The process of proposing a likely explanation for an event that must then be tested.

Explain the expanding role of the patrol officer as criminal investigator.

LEARNING OUTCOMES 5

The traditionally limited responsibility of the patrol officer has expanded to include locating witnesses, conducting interviews, recording information about the crime scene, and initiating and completing investigations. Most police administrators agree that these changes have been beneficial to the department.

1. What are the fundamental components of law enforcement?
2. What are the three modes of investigation?
3. What is the difference between reactive and proactive responses?
4. How has the role of the patrol officer changed over the years, and what benefits to law enforcement in general and in criminal investigations specifically has this change produced?
5. What qualities do professional investigators have in common?

reactive response An approach to crime solving that addresses crimes that have already occurred, such as murder, robbery, and burglary.

proactive response An investigative approach to crime solving in which criminal activity is investigated before it occurs.

preventive response Prevention through deterrence that is sometimes achieved by arresting the criminal and by aggressive prosecution.

Discuss the solvability factors in a criminal investigation.

LEARNING OUTCOMES 6

Solvability factors are identification leads that have proven to be valuable and are most likely to result in case solution. Examples include availability of witnesses, information about the suspect, significant physical evidence, and judgment by the patrol officer that there is enough information to continue an investigation.

1. What are three primary solvability factors in criminal investigations?
2. How does the patrol officer guide the direction of an investigation?
3. A police department's reporting system is defined by what two basic components?

solvability factors Factors that logically guide the investigation and are likely to result in case solution.

Describe the preliminary investigation process.

For many criminal investigations, the investigative process begins with the preliminary investigation. It is during this phase that patrol officers typically arrive at the scene before the investigator and conduct some extremely important duties. These duties include securing the scene, arresting any perpetrators, providing first aid to the injured, and identifying and separating witnesses. Typically, the officer conducting the preliminary investigation will take some notes and turn over all information to the criminal investigator upon his or her arrival.

1. What are the objectives of the preliminary investigation?

2. Why are preliminary investigations important in the investigative process?

3. What are the steps in the crime-scene response?

4. Who are the most important witnesses to be interviewed by a first responder?

Additional Links

http://content.met.police.uk/Home
This is the official website of the Scotland Yard/Metropolitan Police in London. This site contains links to the history of Scotland Yard and the history of policing. Other links include archives, famous cases, news links, crimes, recruitment, and how to report a crime.

www.fbi.gov
This is the official website of the Federal Bureau of Investigation. This site contains links to the history of the FBI, including famous cases. In addition, visitors will find *Uniform Crime Report* statistics, reports and publications, videos, photos, news, most wanted lists, crime alerts, jobs and internship programs, as well as fun and games links for teens and children.

www.aafs.org
The site of the American Academy of Forensic Sciences (AAFS) contains links and information on membership, news and current events, archives, resources for students including choosing a career, and colleges and universities that have forensic science programs.

www.nij.gov
The National Institute of Justice (NIJ) is the research, development, and evaluation agency of the Department of Justice. This organization's site includes links for publications, training, and courses for criminal justice professionals. The site also includes multimedia presentations.

"A fundamental premise of criminal investigation is that investigators have the ability to reconstruct the facts and circumstances surrounding each case."

The Crime Scene: Field Notes, Documenting, and Reporting

1 Explain what specific field notes should be taken during a criminal investigation.

2 Identify the qualities of a good investigative report.

3 Identify the main components of a fact sheet or initial complaint.

4 Explain the correct methods for photographing the crime scene.

5 Summarize the legal precedents for the admissibility of photographs as evidence in court.

6 Determine what types of information should be included in a photographic log.

7 Explain the types of photography commonly used in criminal investigations.

8 Describe how crime-scene sketches are made.

INTRO A KILLER AMONG US

On January 8, 2011, shortly after 10 A.M., U.S. representative from Arizona Gabrielle Giffords was holding a public meeting outside a Safeway grocery store in Casas Adobes, a northwest suburb of Tucson, Arizona. The meeting was Giffords's first "Congress on Your Corner" gathering of the year. Giffords had set up a table outside the store and about 20 to 30 people were gathered around her when a gunman arrived, ran up to the crowd, and began firing an estimated 20 to 30 shots. The gunman was 22-year-old Jared Lee Loughner. The weapon he used was a 9mm Glock model 19 pistol with a 33-round magazine.

A total of six people were killed, including federal judge John Roll and Giffords's congressional aide and community outreach director Gabe Zimmerman. A nine-year-old girl, Christina Taylor Green, was also pronounced dead at the hospital. Fourteen others were wounded. Other victims with gunshot wounds were transported to the Northwest Medical Center; four people were listed in critical condition. Twenty people were shot, of whom six died. Giffords was shot in the side of the head but miraculously survived.

Actors from *CSI* TV Show.

The investigation into Loughner's background revealed some "red flags" from fall 2010. Specifically, from the time Loughner showed up for his first algebra class at Pima County Community College in the summer 2010, he began to experience conflict with students and teachers alike.[1]

The 2011 Arizona shooting represents a high-profile incident that consumed the popular media for days. Because of intense emotion stemming from the killings and the persons wounded, it is clear that a proper and thorough investigation of the incident would be essential. Even though the shooter in this case was captured, a number of important questions still remained unanswered. To what extent could the actions of Jared Loughner have been prevented through timely intervention? Moreover, considering the confusion and turmoil following the shooting, how can the scene of the shooting best be preserved and how can important evidence such as witness statements and physical evidence best be identified and preserved?

DISCUSS **To what extent could the actions of Jared Loughner have been prevented through timely intervention? Moreover, considering the confusion and turmoil following the shooting, how can the scene of the shooting best be preserved and how can important evidence such as witness statements and physical evidence best be identified and preserved?**

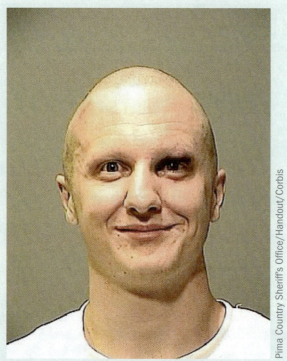
Photo of Jared Lee Loughner following his arrest in January 2011.

A fundamental premise of criminal investigation is that investigators have the ability to reconstruct the facts and circumstances surrounding each case. This is generally accomplished through well-written reports, photographs, and crime-scene sketches. Accompanying such evidence are the ever-important laboratory testing of objects seized from the scene and supportive testimony by investigators and laboratory technicians. With the exception of unusual circumstances, such as the removal of injured parties or inclement weather at a crime scene, all evidence at the scene is properly recorded before any objects are collected or removed.

▶ The Role of Field Notes in a Criminal Investigation

When one thinks of a police officer taking field notes, the Hollywood portrayal of an officer writing down bits and pieces of information on the inside of a matchbook cover may come to mind. Unfortunately, in some cases, this is a reality, but it is not the prescribed method of note taking. **Field notes** have many benefits for both the officer and the department. Most notes result from interviews, but there are other uses as well. For example, notes may be the most important step in the initial documentation of a crime scene. An investigator's field notes are his or her most personal and readily available record of the crime-scene search. It is difficult, if not impossible, to recommend a particular form of field note taking because most officers usually adopt their own style. However, one objective of this process remains clear: The notes taken at a crime scene must adequately reflect the condition and state of the location at the time of the crime-scene search.

LEARNING OUTCOMES 1 — Explain what specific field notes should be taken during a criminal investigation.

68/George Doyle/Ocean/Corbis

Police Officer Taking Notes.

When to Take Notes

The investigative process begins as soon as an officer gets a call to the scene of a crime. Accordingly, the note-taking process also begins at this time. Officers should remember that note taking is a continual process that occurs throughout the duration of an officer's involvement in an investigation. Some victims or witnesses may be intimidated by an officer taking down what is said during an interview. If it appears that this is the case, the investigator should take the time to explain the importance of brief notes and how they will benefit the overall investigation. If a subject simply refuses to talk while comments are being recorded, the officer can wait and make the required notes immediately after the interview.

What to Write Down

It would be ideal if investigative notes could begin with the assignment of the officer to the case and follow through in a logical flow of events to the culmination of the investigation. In reality, however, notes most likely are written in the order in which information is learned, resulting in fragmented bits of information being logged. This is not unusual and should not pose a problem for the investigator provided that notes are complete and well organized. Remember to get the specifics.

When first encountering a witness or victim, it is important for the investigator to allow the person to state in his or her own words what occurred. This is best accomplished by asking the simple question, "What happened?" It is likely that much of the desired information will be communicated to the investigator at that point. After the subject provides his or her

initial explanation, then more specific questions should be asked to pinpoint exactly what occurred. Most information can be learned with answers to who, what, when, where, why, and how. For example, certain specifics should be included in the note-taking process. Figure 2–1 identifies examples of essential topics of information.

Developing a Note-Taking System

It is advisable for a system of note taking to be developed to allow an officer greater swiftness in his or her interviews. For example, initials can be used in place of complete names. This can be illustrated by using "S" for suspect, "V" for victim, "W-1" for witness number 1, "C" for complainant, and so on. When adopting this system, officers should be careful not to move into "shorthand," making it difficult for others to interpret what the notes are trying to say. Remember that field notes may be required later as evidence in court. Figure 2–1 shows sample crime-scene field notes, and Figure 2–2 notes essential information to include.

Field Interview Cards

One unique and successful method of documenting information on the street is through the use of **field interview cards** (FI cards). These are used when patrol officers happen on people or circumstances that appear suspicious but there is not sufficient cause for arrest. The FI card is used to document names, addresses, and other pertinent information. At the end of the officer's watch, he or she turns in the FI cards, and they are filed for future reference.

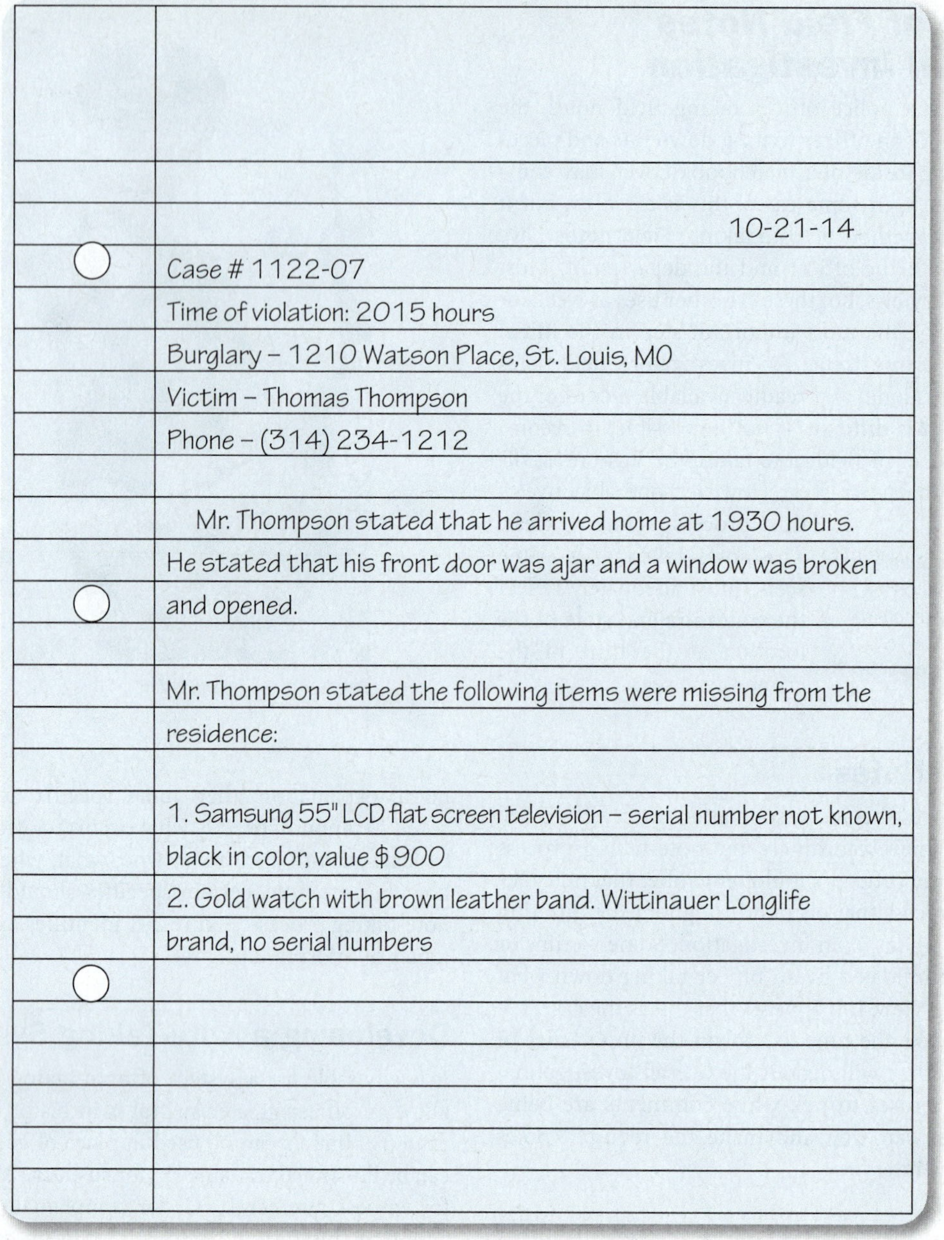

FIGURE 2–1 Sample Crime-Scene Field Notes.

The field notes read:

10-21-14

Case # 1122-07

Time of violation: 2015 hours

Burglary – 1210 Watson Place, St. Louis, MO

Victim – Thomas Thompson

Phone – (314) 234-1212

Mr. Thompson stated that he arrived home at 1930 hours. He stated that his front door was ajar and a window was broken and opened.

Mr. Thompson stated the following items were missing from the residence:

1. Samsung 55" LCD flat screen television – serial number not known, black in color, value $900

2. Gold watch with brown leather band. Wittinauer Longlife brand, no serial numbers

▶ Writing the Official Investigative Report

A criminal investigator's written report represents the final product of his or her investigative efforts. The report informs others of what events have occurred and provides a permanent record useful in numerous ways as evidentiary matter at trial, intelligence information, and crime-analysis data. To many readers, the report represents their only opportunity to learn about the background of the investigation. Consequently, it is essential that the report be written so it can be understood and, more important, so it is not misunderstood.

Many police officers write mediocre reports. A poorly prepared report can easily become evident when one officer tries to read another officer's reports and tries to interpret what is being said. If an official report is difficult to understand, the complaint-issuing process will be bogged down, and it will be difficult for the prosecutor to decipher the facts and circumstances of the case. In addition, a poorly written report gives the defense attorney a tool to use during trial to confuse the officer's testimony and to muddle the issue.

Investigators should remember that the official police report is the backbone of the criminal prosecution process. It is a permanent record of the complaint and of the facts and events leading up to the arrest of the suspect. An important three-pronged rule to remember is that official reports should be factual, thorough, and to the point because they will be under close scrutiny when the case goes to court. Box 2–1 outlines the steps in report writing.

LEARNING OUTCOMES 2 Identify the qualities of a good investigative report.

1. **Dates, times, and locations.** Record these in the notes. Officers should also include from whom they received the assignment. Supplementary information should include the exact time of arrival at the crime scene, the location of the scene, lighting and weather conditions, and the names of other officers contacted and other persons present at the scene.

2. **Description of victim.** This information should include all identifiers of the victim, including name, age, Social Security number, height, weight, color of hair and eyes, and so on. In addition, clothing should be noted as to style (if possible) and color of garment. Special attention should be given to extemporaneous identifiers such as complexion, tattoos, and scars.

3. **Wounds on the victim.** Notes regarding the type and location of wounds should be documented carefully. It is important to emphasize descriptions of the wound, and if it is a bruise, its color should be noted.

4. **Overall description of the crime scene.** Investigators must note anything unusual at the crime scene. This includes items damaged or in disarray, items that seem misplaced or that don't seem to belong in the scene, open (or closed) doors or windows, and so on.

5. **Notes on photographs taken of the scene.** For every photograph taken of the scene, the F-stop, shutter speed, distance, and direction of the photo should be logged in an officer's notes. Also included should be the time and location of each photograph. In the event that a video camera is used to document the scene, an officer's notes should include the type of camera and any special attachments that may have been used.

6. **Type and location of each piece of evidence.** Document adequately the location of each piece of evidence found at the crime scene. This includes its description, location, the time it was discovered and by whom, the type of container in which it was placed, how the container was sealed and marked, and the disposition of the item after it was collected.

7. **Absence of items.** Document items not at the crime scene that probably should be such as certain articles of clothing missing from the deceased or certain home furnishings absent from the scene.

---

1. Mar. 23, 2014 - etc.

2. Jane doe, ~20 years old, SSN, 5'2", brown hair, brown eyes, etc.

3. Gunshot wound ~1/4" in diameter to the left temple and ~1 1/2" from the left eye. A dark gray circle ~1/4" in diameter surrounds the entire wound.

4. Broken window, open door, etc.

5. Photo of window: F18, 1/6" sec., 6', facing outside.

6. 9mm cal. S & W model 669 semiautomatic handgun, nickel plated with wooden grips, Serial #36348. 71 inches from the S.W. corner of the master bedroom, 16 inches E. of S. edge of W. door. Marked "WT" on evidence tag placed on trigger guard. Placed in manila evidence envelope, sealed with tape, and marked #11 WT 7-21-01 at 03:25 hrs. Released to Officer Mary Schultz, laboratory firearms examiner, 09:35 hrs. 7-21-14 WT.

7. Missing TV, stereo system, etc.

FIGURE 2–2 Information Needed in Properly Written Field Notes.

Factuality

The police report must be prepared carefully so that it accurately reflects all pertinent facts learned by investigators. Special attention should be given to dates, times, and other details of the investigation. In addition, these facts must be written in such a manner that the reader of the report can easily understand them. It is important that the police report be factual and not contain hearsay information, speculation, or opinions of the investigator. Facts are generally defined as information learned personally by the investigator and not conclusions presumed by him or her. For example, if an informant tells the investigator that a suspect is a heroin addict, this information should be verified before stating it as fact in the official report.

After the information has been verified, the investigator should include in the report how the information was validated.

BOX 2–1 STEPS IN REPORT WRITING

1. Collect information about the crime scene, informants, and witnesses.
2. Take complete notes.
3. Organize the information.
4. Prepare the report.
5. Proofread and evaluate the report.

Think About It…

Many investigations, especially those that are high profile with considerable media attention, require a speedy response. This is because perpetrators can still be on the scene, witnesses may still be present, evidence may be contaminated or otherwise destroyed if not promptly collected, and so on. For those investigations where many investigative steps are taken in a short period of time, what are some consequences of either not responding on a timely basis or not properly or thoroughly processing the scene?

Detective Collecting Evidence.

corepics/Shutterstock.com

For example, were undercover officers used to converse with the suspect, or were court orders obtained for disclosure of medical records? In the event that verification is not possible, the investigator should mention that the information was "alleged" to be true by the source (for example, confidential informant, witness, newspaper article).

Thoroughness

All facts learned pertaining to the investigation should be included in the official report. This practice is necessary for completeness of the report and for the credibility of the investigation. For example, if an undercover officer was offered illegal drugs and declined to purchase them, the offer should be documented in the event that the dealer later claims to have sold the drugs to the officer. In addition to the narrative aspect of the report, copies of related documentation should be attached with every report. For example, if investigators are looking at a check-kiting ring, copies of the suspect's checks should be attached to the report. Additionally, if surveillance photos are taken, they become part of the official report.

The report should also reflect the **chain of custody** of all evidence in the case. For example, in a drug case, the report should reflect how the drugs were collected, who handled them after seizure, where and how they were stored, and who now has possession of them (for example, the crime laboratory).

Getting to the Point

The best investigative report is one that is not only thorough but is concise as well. In preparing such a report, the investigator must be aware that although details and completeness are important, excess information can bog down the report and possibly confuse the reader.

Accuracy and Objectivity

An investigator's ability to report accurately is highly dependent on both the ability to conduct an objective and thorough investigation and to express the results of this inquiry in writing. In order to report objectively, the investigator must distinguish between facts and **hearsay evidence** and be able to relay exactly a factual accounting of the incident.

It is essential that all relevant facts and details should be presented in an unbiased manner without any indication of the officer's feelings or opinions about the case. Writing the report should be considered as an extension of the investigation in which the officer is basically an inquirer whose purpose is to gather information. Even when conclusions or opinions are called for in the report summary, the officer must make sure that such judgments reflect his or her thinking and not his or her feelings. The officer must be sure to clearly indicate when a statement is his or her opinion.

Word Choice

The narrative portion of the report, in which the reporting officer brings the facts together in a story form, requires the effective use of language. In writing the narrative section of the report, the officer should be concerned with two basic items: presentation and diction (choice and use of words). As a rule, the most effective report presentation is a chronological narrative, in which events are described as they occurred from the officer's perspective. Accordingly, the narrative should unfold from the point when the officer received a service call or otherwise became involved in the case.

One of the most difficult aspects of writing well is the proper choice and use of words. This is especially true with police reports because accuracy and brevity are all-important characteristics. The following are suggestions for writing effective police reports:

1. Avoid the use of unnecessary words; for example, in "the aforementioned suspect," the word "aforementioned" is not needed. If more than one suspect is involved, they should be identified in some other way.

2. Avoid the use of elaborate or unfamiliar words when a small or commonly used term will do; for example, "the victim is cognizant of" should be written as "the victim knows."

3. Use specific words rather than vague terms; for example, "the victim said she proceeded to the living room" should be written as, "the victim said she (walked, ran, limped, hurried, etc.) to the living room."

4. Try to use the active voice; for example, "The message was received from the dispatcher at 10:40 A.M." can be improved by stating, "I received a message from the dispatcher at 10:40 A.M."

5. Use standard abbreviations; other persons will not necessarily understand individual abbreviations.

6. Write short, simple sentences whose meanings are clear and direct. Do not try to crowd many ideas into one sentence.

7. Avoid the use of double negatives such as, "No evidence could not be found at the crime scene." At the least, such expressions are confusing and, in some cases, the double negative can be misunderstood as a positive statement.

8. Be sure modifiers, adjectives, and adverbs are used sparingly because these words usually do not contribute much to a fact-finding report.

9. Use standard English rather than jargon or slang except when quoting witnesses, victims, and suspects.

▶ The Main Components of a Fact Sheet or Initial Complaint

The report should be structured so that the reader is able to learn pertinent information quickly and succinctly. To best accomplish this, the effective organization of information on the report is critical.

LEARNING OUTCOMES 3 — Identify the main components of a fact sheet or initial complaint.

Documenting Interviews

In forming questions for taking reports, the criminal investigator is much like a newspaper reporter. The investigator needs to know the answers to questions who, what, when, where, and how. More specifically, the following items are considered essential information:

- *Preliminary information.* This category of data includes the time and manner in which the complaint was received; identification of the location, time, and nature of the crime; and full identification of the victim.

- *Witnesses.* This grouping refers to information provided by victims, witnesses, or other persons at the crime scene.

- *Physical evidence.* The search for a discovery of evidentiary items must be included in the officer's records.

- *Modus operandi.* This is an extremely important category because, in many cases, the method of operation is a clue to determining the suspect.

Obtaining information from victims, witnesses, or bystanders is more demanding than recording conversations at a crime scene. Interviews involve a variety of skills, both communicative and investigative, that require the investigator's full attention.

The use of basic interviewing techniques opens up communication between the investigator and the person being interviewed. However, the investigator must be skilled at forming questions and "digging" for information either temporarily forgotten or considered unimportant by the person being interviewed. At the same time, the investigator should guide the interview so that information flows sequentially and logically. This makes the investigator's job as recorder a much simpler task.

Conclusions that are unsubstantiated by fact should be presented as opinion. For example, "The witness heard gunfire in the vicinity of his home" should be stated as "The witness heard a loud noise that he believes was gunfire in the vicinity of his home."

As a rule, investigations are documented by the initial complaint (the face sheet) and supplemental reports (describing new findings). Formats for these reports are considered next.

The Initial Complaint

Also called the *face sheet* or *initial page*, the complaint depicts an "at-a-glance" summary of the investigation. This information includes the suspect's name and related identifiers as well as a brief summary of the facts and circumstances surrounding the case (for example, times, dates, locations, who did what, who saw what, and what evidence was collected). The initial complaint is the first report seen by anyone examining the file of the investigation, so it is important to keep it direct and to the point. Although individual departmental policies dictate the precise manner in which the reports are organized, the items listed in Figure 2–3 are usually included.

Supplemental Reports

As the case progresses, investigators will undoubtedly develop new sources of information, such as new witnesses, physical evidence, and documents. As this information is gathered, a supplemental report is generated to update the case. The supplemental report is considerably longer than the initial complaint because it goes into much greater detail on pertinent aspects of the case. In fact, it is the supplemental report that incorporates the who, what, when, where, how, and (sometimes) why of the case.

The report begins with a brief synopsis of the subject of the report, which gives the reader an overall view of the body of the report. The main portion is the details section. As the investigator formulates this section, events are prepared in paragraphs and in chronological order. For example, a report of a drug purchase by an undercover agent should contain the following information in the details section of the report:

Type of offense (for example, possession, distribution)

Date and time of offense

Location of violation (for example, suspect's residence, parking lot)

Description of suspect's vehicle

Description of weapons possessed by suspect

Description of how the violation was discovered (for example, through informant information, undercover agents, search warrants)

Who (undercover agent or informant) was wearing concealed transmitters and names of officers monitoring the conversation, if relevant

Description of evidence in the case (for example, drugs, weapons, videotape of transaction, statement of informant)

Field test results of drugs seized

Each report must also reflect additional details of the case, such as the following:

Chain of custody of evidence

Statements made by suspects (before and after arrest)

Elements of the Report

- Who the officer was met by at the crime scene

- What the officer found at the scene

- What the officer did at the scene (e.g., administered first aid, notified immediate supervisor)

- Description of injuries to victim or suspect

- Type of weapon used

- Description of all evidence

- Names and identifiers of all suspects arrested

- Names of all witnesses

- Copies of written statements given by witnesses

1. **Type of crime.** Depending on the department, crimes are generally designated as crimes against property, crimes against persons, or vice crimes. In addition, they are indexed according to the specific act that is being alleged, such as robbery, burglary, or drug distribution.

2. **Date.** This is the date of the offense.

3. **Case number.** Before any paperwork is filed at the department, it must have a case number assigned by the records division. This number will be used on all subsequent reports in the investigation.

4. **Officer's name.** This is the investigator's full legal name (no nicknames), rank, and badge number.

5. **Suspect's name and address.** This includes the suspect's full legal name, monikers, addresses, date of birth, Social Security number, and any other pertinent information known about the suspect.

6. **Victim.** The name of the victim(s) and address(es). No additional identifiers are required. For vice cases, the victim part of the report will either remain blank or reflect the jurisdiction in which the offense occurred (e.g., the state of Washington).

7. **Witnesses.** This includes the names and addresses of witnesses of the crime.

8. **Synopsis of crime and investigation.** This section should be no longer than one paragraph and should contain all general details of the case.

9. **Details of crime and investigation.** This section is much longer than the synopsis because it encompasses all pertinent details of the investigation in a logical progression.

10. **Attachments.** This section includes a list of all evidence relating to the case. Included are drugs, weapons, statements by victims and witnesses, references to videotapes used by investigators, photos, and so on.

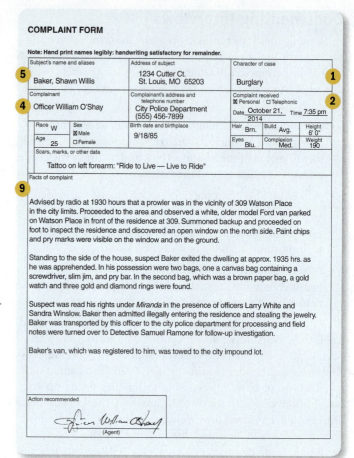

FIGURE 2–3 Information Included on a Complaint Form.

How the suspect was identified

Names of all witnesses in the case (for example, officers, informant [identify by number, not name])

List of property seized (for example, cars, guns)

Copies of legal documents (for example, search warrants, search warrant returns, vehicle seizure forms, informant statements) should be attached to the report.

▶ Methods for Photographing the Crime Scene

As with the use of crime-scene sketches (discussed later), the use of photographs in crime-scene investigations has been fundamental for decades. It is important to note that both photos and sketches are necessary in criminal investigations because photos may distort distance, color, and so on. Today, the practice of crime-scene photography has been extended to digital recorders to depict crime scenes. In this section, the term *photograph* (or *photo*) will refer to either or both forms of audiovisual reproduction.

Although the adage "a picture is worth a thousand words" might seem unrealistic, a visual portrayal of the crime scene clearly adds a dimension to both the investigation and prosecution of the case that no other medium can emulate. In fact, without the benefit of pictures, a witness or juror may be influenced by past experiences, preconceptions, stereotypes, and biases in making decisions about a crime scene. Indeed, photos and videotapes may convey information to the court more accurately than verbal descriptions of the crime.

Photographs as Evidence

The principal requirements to admit a photograph into evidence are relevance and **authentication**. In general, a photograph is admitted into evidence at the discretion of the trial judge. In rare cases, a chain of custody is required, or the best evidence rule may be invoked if the photograph is offered for its truth and is the basis of a controlling issue in the case.

The most important requirement is authentication. Specifically, the party seeking to introduce the photograph into evidence must be prepared to present testimony that the photograph is accurate and correct. In most cases, the testimony need not be from the photographer; a qualified witness who has knowledge of the scene and can testify that the photograph accurately portrays the scene will suffice. Some courts will rule that a photograph is self-authenticating or presumptively

LEARNING OUTCOMES 4 Explain the correct methods for photographing the crime scene.

authentic. If the authenticity of the photograph is challenged, it is usually a question for the trier of fact (for example, the jury).[2]

Preserving Digital Images

From an evidentiary standpoint, digital images must be handled with special care and consideration to preserve their integrity as evidence. As a rule, digital images are stored on removable media such as Secure Digital (SD) cards and Memory Sticks™. Images saved to these storage media must be stored immediately, or as soon as reasonable, on a compact disc (CD) or other protected medium to create the "master disc." Digital images contained on this master disc must not be altered or manipulated in any way. Of course, the master disc must then be properly stored and protected so images can be viewed in the future. After the master disc is successfully made, the original medium contained in the camera may be erased and reused for subsequent investigations.

A "working copy" of the master disc can then be made for investigative purposes while protecting the original images contained on the master disc. Images contained on the working copy can be manipulated for investigative purposes. However, any changes or adjustments must be properly documented. Finally, the master disc must be safely maintained until such time as there is an official determination that there will be no future need for the images.[3]

What to Photograph

Extensive expertise in photography and audio electronics is always a clear benefit to a crime-scene investigator, but such training is not always required for good pictures of the scene. Any camera is better than no camera at all, and many relatively low-cost cameras come equipped with auto focus and rewind features. In any case, one important point to remember is that when photographing a crime scene, there can never be too many pictures. Depending on the crime scene, 100 to 200 photos may be typical for proper documentation. When using digital technology, it is vital for the investigator to back up crime scene photos and digital video (as discussed previously).

Because digital media are relatively inexpensive, most departments can afford to take numerous photographs. In doing so, mistakes or problems encountered with one photo can usually be circumvented through the choice of others depicting the same scene or item. Photographs of the crime scene are usually taken in three stages: from the general view to the medium-range view to the close-up view. This approach enables a picture of all circumstances to be painted for jurors while leading up to the most critical part of the crime scene.

General Views

The general photograph is a sweeping view of the crime-scene area (that is, an overall scene, such as the neighborhood, including angles from all streets leading up to the crime scene). It demonstrates what the scene looks like in its own environment. Examples are as follows:

- Photo of a bank that was robbed
- Photo of a house that was burglarized
- Abandoned "getaway" car in a wooded area

Photos depicting such scenes should be taken at a distance to reveal the natural surroundings of the location. In the case of a bank robbery, the bank should be photographed from across the street and from both sides of the building. This will give jurors a perspective of where the structure was situated and the location of possible escape routes.

Medium-Range Views

As we move in closer to the subject of the crime scene, additional photos should be taken. These photos should be taken at a distance no greater than 20 feet away from the subject or item being photographed. The intent of the medium-range photo is to depict specific items or objects in the crime scene. Some examples are blood splatters on the walls or an open window that served as the entry point for an intruder. Different lenses can be used to accomplish this phase of photography. For example, a wide-angle digital lens should be considered for a broad panoramic view of the scene. The purpose of the medium-range photography process is to allow jurors to link each print with the general crime-scene photos.

Close-Up Views

Moving from the broad to the specific, the last phase in photographing the crime scene is the close-up. These photos are taken at a distance of less than 5 feet using the zoom feature on the digital camera, and they should focus on small segments of a larger surface or on specific objects in the scene. Examples are bullet holes in the walls, weapons, blood-splatter stains, latent fingerprints, and so on. As with medium-range photos, these photographs should include some identifiable item from the medium-range photos to link the object(s) being photographed with the general crime scene. It is also important to note that close-up photos should be taken with and without a small ruler or other item, such as a coin, to provide perspective.

Other Hints

Because many types of evidence undergo significant changes at the crime scene, it is important for investigators to photograph the crime scene in a timely fashion. This should typically precede most other tasks of the crime-scene processing because objects cannot be examined adequately until after they are photographed from every angle. Accordingly, it is important that all camera angles and settings be recorded on the crime-scene sketch.

Photos of the interior scenes should be conducted to depict the entire area. This is accomplished by overlapping photos from one scene to the next and working in one direction around the room. In the use of video, a slow panorama of the crime scene is necessary. It is usually advisable to either use a tripod or to attempt to keep the camera at eye level for all the photos. Fox and Cunningham offer several other considerations that crime-scene photographers should consider:[4]

- Approaches to and from the scene
- Surrounding areas (for example, the yard of a house in which the homicide occurred, the general area surrounding an outdoor crime scene)

Benefits

- Provide easy storage and retrieval of data on the crime scene

- Remove many inferences by practically placing the judge and jury at the crime scene

- Give the investigator a source of reference as to the location of evidence at the scene

Disadvantages

- Do not show true or actual distances

- Can distort color and perceptions

- Can be ruined by mechanical errors in processing

Advantages and Disadvantages of Photographs.

- Close-up photographs of the entrance and exit to the scene, or if these are not obvious, those most likely to have been used

- A general scenario shot showing the location of the body and its position in relation to the room or area in which it was found

- At least two photographs of the dead body at 90-degree angles to each other, with the camera placed as high as possible, pointing downward toward the body

As many close-ups of the dead body should be taken as needed to show wounds or injuries, weapons lying near the body, and the immediate surroundings. After the body is removed and after the removal of each item of evidence, the area underneath should be photographed if there is a mark, stain, or other apparent change. All fingerprints that do not need further development or that cannot be lifted should be photographed. Areas in which fingerprints were discovered are photographed to show the locations if these areas were not included in other photographs. Bloodstains should always be photographed, including their locations. Today, color digital images are considered the norm and, almost without exception, are accepted by courts as the best photographic evidence.

Perspective

It is important that the crime-scene photographer show the relationship between one item of evidence and another. This is accomplished by showing the location of the articles in accordance with recognizable backgrounds. In the event that an item to be photographed is smaller than 6 inches, two photos should be taken. The first should be taken at close range, and the second should be taken from at least 6 feet away. This portrays the object in proper perspective.

Suitable Lighting

As a rule, the crime-scene photographer will find that natural light at the scene is inadequate for good-quality photos and that artificial lighting is required. Investigators must therefore select the proper equipment for this task. Whether a flash or a more elaborate lighting system is used, it is of utmost importance to avoid unnecessary shadows. Shadows tend to hide details, some of which might be of grave significance to the investigation. In addition, the part of the photo that is closest to the flash may become washed out, and details might be lost. A good solution to this problem is the strategic use of floodlights to ensure consistent illumination.

Use of Markers

A generally accepted practice in crime-scene photography is the use of measuring or other identifying devices in photos (see Figure 2–4 of a bloody shoeprint). These include rulers, tapes, coins, and so on. **Markers** such as these are included in the finished photograph and call attention to specific objects or enable the viewer of the photo to get a sense of the size of the object or the distance between objects. Some markings can be made with chalk to show specific locations of objects such as dead bodies, footprints, or weapons. Other markers include ink markings made on the surface of photographs after they have been printed.

Because the use of a marker introduces something foreign into the crime scene, investigators should take a photo of the area before placement of the marker and then take a second photo of the same setting after the marker is in place. Another marking technique is to place over the photo a transparent overlay containing all necessary arrows, circles, and so on to depict relevant information. This technique preserves the original photo and allows for comparison between the two.

FIGURE 2–4 A Bloody Shoeprint.

Courtesy of Michael D. Lyman, Ph.D.

▶ Legal Considerations for the Admissibility of Photographs

LEARNING OUTCOMES 5 Summarize the legal precedents for the admissibility of photographs as evidence in court.

Trial courts bear the responsibility of determining the admissibility of photographs as evidence in court. Such determinations have been based on several legal precedents:

Materiality. The object portrayed in the photo must be material and relevant to the case at hand. All photographs, provided that they serve to prove a particular point in the issue, should be admitted into evidence.

a. A *material photograph* is one that relates to and makes a substantive contribution to the specific case in question.

b. A *relevant photograph* also applies to the matter in question and is used to support testimony. It is representative of the evidence that relates it to the matter in question to determine the truth of the circumstances (*Barnett* v. *State*, 1922).

Prejudicial images. Any photograph or image admitted must not prejudice, or appeal unfairly, to the emotions of the jury. Some judges have suppressed photos depicting unusually gruesome crime scenes. In one recent case, photos were taken of a defendant immediately after his arrest, showing him as dirty and unkempt. The photos were offered as evidence to contrast the defendant's clean and polished image in the courtroom. The judge refused to admit the image into evidence on the basis that it was prejudicial.

Distorted photos. Photographs must be kept free of distortion. Three types of distortion have generally been common in crime-scene photographs: incorrect point of view, perspective, and misrepresentation of tone or color. These problems commonly occur through improper use of angles of the photo. For example, a handgun lying next to a dead body may be photographed to appear much larger in size than it actually is, thus distorting the perception of the scene. Another example is bruises on a body, which might indicate the extent of the wound or even the time it was inflicted. Therefore, if the tone of a bruise is shown in a photo as greenish in color rather than bluish, a different conclusion may be made as to the extent of the injuries. Because of this, the photographer or laboratory technician may be subjected to rigorous cross-examination regarding his or her expertise in the processing of digital images. Such distortions must be avoided because they will taint the case and will probably cause the images to be excluded as evidence.

Think About It…

To what extent should the criminal investigator be concerned about the legality of crime-scene photos? We know that many crime scenes, especially those where violent crimes have occurred, require numerous photographs—sometimes hundreds depending on the nature of the scene. Investigators have their hands full in trying to properly document and properly photograph the scene. But will concerns about admissibility merely bog down the crime-scene photographer, or should he or she be aware of the law as it relates to the admissibility of photos? In other words, should the investigator simply let the prosecutor consider the legality of the photos?

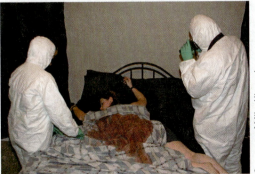

Investigators in Biohazard Suits Photographing Crime Scene.

Courtesy of Mike Himmel

Items at a Crime Scene.

Monalyn Gracia/Corbis

Additionally, photos and physical evidence have different requirements regarding the chain of custody. For example, it is not necessary for the person taking the photograph to be the one to testify about it in court. In *State v. Fournier* (1963), however, the court held that evidence must be offered to show that the photograph is an accurate representation of the object(s) portrayed (as mentioned previously). Such evidence is usually given by an officer who was present at the crime scene and who can vouch for the validity of the photo.

Information Included in the Photographic Log

It is of critical importance for investigators to log their photos carefully as to date, time, and sequence number, as seen in Figure 2–5. The photographic log is the best way to organize photos of the scene and evidence associated with the scene.

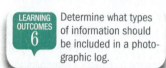

This is because crime-scene photos in many crime scenes can amount to several hundred photos. Included should be the following:

- Type of case
- Description of subject of photo
- Location

- Names of persons handling evidence
- Assigned case number
- Any other relevant information

Using this technique will reduce hours of sorting out finished photos and trying to determine what picture goes where.

Surveillance Photographs

Surveillance photography is used covertly in establishing identities or in documenting criminal behavior. Photography of this nature is selective and may have many benefits. For example, it may aid officers in identifying the physical locations of criminal activity or in formulating a raid plan for serving a search warrant. Covert **surveillance** is now used commonly in banks and convenience stores as a deterrent for would-be robbers and as an aid in prosecution. Some systems use single-reflex cameras with telephoto lenses, and others use infrared film.

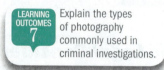

Most investigations using surveillance photography are vice and organized crime operations, and a specially outfitted van or truck is usually used by investigators. In these operations, illegal transactions are made discreetly among criminals, and thorough documentation is necessary to establish proof beyond

---

PHOTOGRAPHIC LOG

PAGE __1__ of __1__

LOCATION Living Room

DATE 10-21-14

CASE # 0211-10

OFFICERS Lt. Johnson, Officer Watson, Officer Smith

CAMERA #31

CAMERA TYPE Nikon Coolpix P-1 digital

COMMENTS SD Disk #14

Photo #	Description of Subject Photographed	Scale	Misc. Comments	Sketch (if required)
1	Long-range shot — living room		Photos from top	
2	Close-up — defense wound			
3	Medium-range shot — knife			
4	Close-up — powder burns			
5	Long-range shot — hallway		From left side	
6	Medium-range shot — handgun		From right side	
7	Close-up — handgun			
8	Close-up — knife			

FIGURE 2–5 Photographic Log.

a reasonable doubt. Such photography can be problematic, however, in that proper lighting is sometimes difficult to come by. In response, many police agencies have purchased night-vision devices that affix to surveillance cameras. These devices use natural light emitted by stars or the moon and usually produce identifiable images.

Sketching a Crime Scene.

▶ *The Crime-Scene Sketch*

The crime-scene sketch complements photographs and videos taken of the scene. With increased use of video and digital cameras at crime scenes, one might argue that preparation of the sketch is no longer needed. In actuality, because videos and photos may tend to distort the dimensions of the crime scene, a properly prepared crime-scene sketch is all the more important to a properly documented crime scene. In other words, whereas a photograph represents the scene as it is perceived by the viewer, the diagram represents the scene as it actually is.

In many ways, the crime-scene sketch can show certain details better than a photograph. For example, photographs are two-dimensional and may fail to show the distance between objects. Also, a photograph cannot show the entire crime scene, whereas a sketch can.

A crime-scene sketch is a scale drawing that locates evidence in relation to other factors. As a rule, the sketch will not identify such items as the color of a wall, the type of floor, the general condition of the area, and non-evidential matter.

A properly prepared sketch is an important tool for the prosecutor as well. The sketch can become the focus point of courtroom testimony. Witnesses can show on the diagram their relationship to observations of the crime, and each item of evidence can be pinpointed.

Putting It Together

Several methods have been developed over the years to best conduct a detailed sketch of the scene. One should remember that the objective of the crime-scene sketch is to portray the scene accurately, not artistically. Too much detail in a crime-scene sketch will remove the advantage of a sketch over a photograph. Thus, most officers can be expected to produce a sketch successfully.

In each crime-scene sketch, some items are considered essential. As with note taking, however, such items should not be considered the only items needed for complete documentation of the scene. The crime-scene sketch should include the following information:

- The investigator's complete name and rank
- The date, time, type of crime, and assigned case number
- The complete names of other officers assisting in the making of the sketch
- The address of the crime scene, its position in a building, landmarks, and so on

- The scale of the drawing (if no scale, indicate by printing "not to scale")
- The primary items of physical evidence and other critical features of the crime scene, located by detailed measurements from at least two fixed points of reference
- A key or legend identifying the symbols or points of reference used in the sketch

Measurement

One general rule of sketching is that the sketch should reflect as accurately as possible the important details of the scene. Such information must be recorded uniformly. For example, if the dimensions of a dead body in a field are recorded accurately but the location of a handgun found near the body is estimated only roughly, the sketch is virtually useless. Accordingly, all measures of distance must be conducted by using the same method. Specifically, one part of the scene should not be paced off and another area of the scene measured with a tape measure.

After the case goes to court and a measurement error is discovered, the explanation of such an error may prove embarrassing and difficult. Use of a tape measure is therefore considered the most effective method of measuring the scene.

Rough and Finished Sketches

There are generally two sketches for every crime scene: a rough sketch and a finished sketch. The **rough sketch** is the one drawn by officers at the crime scene. Generally, it is not drawn to scale but should reflect accurate dimensions and distances between objects of importance. At times, it might be necessary to draw more than one rough crime-scene sketch. For example, one sketch might portray the overall scene, and a second sketch could show only the body and its immediate surroundings. Alterations to the rough sketch should not be made after the investigator leaves the scene.

The **finished sketch** is simply a completed sketch drawn to scale. This is drawn from information contained on the rough sketch and should accurately reflect all measurements indicated on the rough sketch. With the finished sketch being drawn

Ferrerilavarialiotti/Fotolia

Tools for Crime-Scene Sketching

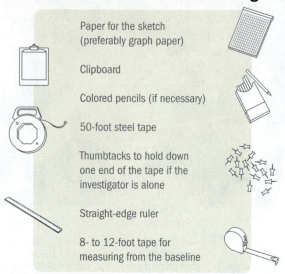

Paper for the sketch
(preferably graph paper)

Clipboard

Colored pencils (if necessary)

50-foot steel tape

Thumbtacks to hold down
one end of the tape if the
investigator is alone

Straight-edge ruler

8- to 12-foot tape for
measuring from the baseline

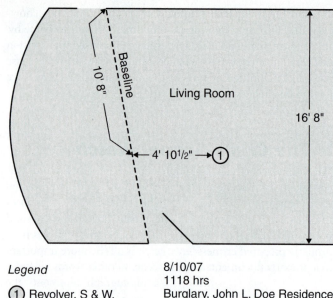

Legend

① Revolver, S & W,
.38 cal.
Ser. #984210

8/10/07
1118 hrs
Burglary, John L. Doe Residence
1st Floor Living Room
18 Birch Avenue
Kansas City, Mo.
Measured and sketched by
Sgt. John Smith, KCPD

FIGURE 2–6 Baseline or Coordinate Method.

to scale, however, it is not necessary to include the specific measurements on the sketch itself. If the finished sketch is not drawn to scale, measurements are required. Finished sketches need not be prepared by the crime-scene investigator, although in court, the investigator will be required to affirm that the finished sketch is an accurate portrayal of the scene. In many cases, the finished sketch is prepared by a professional draftsperson or is made with the use of specially designed computerized programs.

Choosing the Best Method

Different crime scenes present different sketching problems. Let's now consider three of the most widely used sketching methods:

1. *Coordinate method.* The **coordinate method** uses the practice of measuring an object from two fixed points of reference. One such procedure, as shown in Figure 2–6, is the **baseline technique**, in which a line is drawn between two known points. The baseline could also be a wall or a mathematically derived point along a designated area where exact measurements can be determined. The measurements of a particular item are then taken from left to right along the baseline to a point at right angles to the object that is to be plotted. This distance is noted in the legend with a circled number after the name of the object.

2. *Triangulation method.* The **triangulation method**, shown in Figure 2–7, is a bird's-eye view of the scene that uses fixed objects from which to measure. This is particularly useful for sketching outdoor crime scenes where there are no easily identifiable points of reference. In this procedure, two or more widely separated points of reference are required. The item of interest is then located by measuring along a straight line from the reference points.

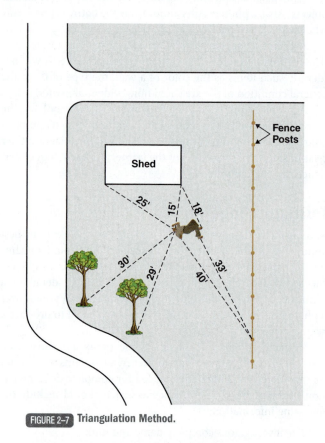

FIGURE 2–7 Triangulation Method.

3. *Cross-projection method.* The **cross-projection method**, shown in Figure 2–8, is used in indoor crime scenes. It is basically a top-down view of the crime scene, with the walls of the room "folded" down to reveal locations of bullet holes,

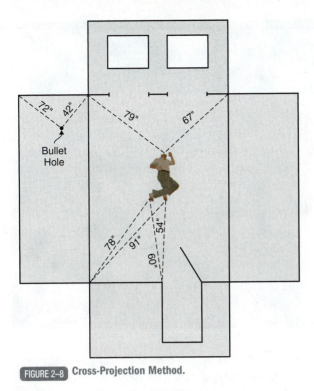

FIGURE 2–8 Cross-Projection Method.

blood-spatter evidence, and so on, which would not be apparent otherwise. Measurements are then made from a designated point on the floor to the area on the wall in question.

On completion of the sketch, the investigator should be prepared to do two things: (1) photocopy the sketch and attach the copy to the officer's report and (2) file the original sketch in a secure location so it is ready for presentation in court at a later date. The officer should remember that both the rough and finished sketches are admissible in court if they are prepared or witnessed by the investigator, provided that they both portray the crime scene accurately.

Think About It...

Considering that crime scenes can be outdoors, indoors, in a vehicle, and under an array of weather and other conditions, it is sometimes difficult to document such scenes. Under what circumstances, if any, would the criminal investigator create more than one type of crime-scene sketch (for example, a baseline and a cross-projection method sketch)? Give examples of various types of crime scenes that might require more than one type of sketch.

Drawing a Sketch.

Courtesy of Michael D. Lyman, Ph.D.

Investigative "Tunnel Vision"—The Duke Lacrosse Rape Case

In May 2007, North Carolina Attorney General Roy A. Cooper dismissed rape charges that were brought against three former members of the Duke University lacrosse team, saying that the players were innocent of all charges. Those charges were brought by Durham County Prosecutor Michael B. Nifong after an exotic dancer, Crystal Gail Mangum, who had performed at a house party in 2006, told police she had been raped, sodomized, strangled, and beaten by the partygoers. Contradictions in the accuser's statements, however, along with a lack of DNA and other evidence, convinced Cooper that the attack never occurred. Public accusations against investigators with the Durham Police Department also resulted from the Duke rape case, alleging methods of the photo identification process were placed into question, and that police had been allegedly known to use intimidation tactics on witnesses.

James A. Boardman/Shutterstock

Lawyers and media reports alike suggested that the photo identification process was severely flawed. For example, during the photo identifications, Mangum was told that she would be viewing Duke University lacrosse players who attended the party, and she was asked if she remembered seeing them at the party and in what capacity. At least two photo lineups were reported by the media. Ross (the only player she identified as attending the party with 100 percent certainty during both procedures) provided to police investigators indisputable evidence through cell phone records and a sworn affidavit from a witness that he was with his girlfriend at North Carolina State University before, during, and after the party. Another person Mangum identified in April also provided police with evidence that he did not attend the party at all. These examples of how investigators conducted their investigation show how police can be blinded and mistakenly led by a prosecutor whose "tunnel vision" blinds them to all available evidence. One day later, Cooper dismissed the criminal charges and Nifong apologized to the students, and was disbarred in 2007 after an ethics hearing by the North Carolina Bar Association. He was later found guilty of criminal contempt of court and spent only one day in jail.

Sources: Benjamin, N., & Blythe, A. (2006, December 24). As Duke rape case unravels, D.A.'s judgment questioned: Defense describes him as willing to skirt law for conviction. *San Francisco Chronicle*; Biesecker, M., Niolet, B., & Neff, J. (2007, June 16). Easley awaiting Nifong resignation. *News and Observer.* Retrieved from http://www.newsobserver.com/2007/06/18/84082/easley-awaiting-nifong-resignation.html.

Proper documentation is the key to a successful investigation:

1. Given what the chapter tells us, in what ways should criminal investigators have changed their tactics to ensure a fair and partial investigation?

2. What do you consider the importance of the photographic documentation in this case?

LEARNING OUTCOMES 1

Explain what specific field notes should be taken during a criminal investigation.

An investigator's field notes are his or her most personal and readily available record of the crime-scene search. Allow victims and witnesses to state in their own words what occurred. Be sure they answer the who, what, when, where, why, and how of what occurred. An investigator's notes might be required later on for court purposes.

1. What is the purpose of properly written notes taken at a crime scene?

2. How can an officer alleviate fears and concerns of witnesses during the interview process?

3. Why is it important to note the absence of items at a crime scene?

4. What are the six most important questions to ask in criminal investigation interviews?

5. In what order should field notes be taken?

6. Why, when first encountering a witness or victim, is it important for the investigator to allow the person to state in his or her own words what occurred?

field notes An investigator's most personal and readily available record of the crime-scene search.

field interview cards A method for documenting information on the street through the use of cards.

LEARNING OUTCOMES 2

Identify the qualities of a good investigative report.

The police report is the formal record of the offense and a record of investigative steps taken to solve the crime. As with field notes, the rule to remember is to seek answers to the questions of who, what, when, why, how, and where. The police report should also be prepared chronologically and should be factual (that is, contain no personal observations). The police report must also be thorough and to the point.

1. In what ways is the official investigative report used?

2. What are the ramifications of a poorly written police report?

3. What is the rule for remembering what information to include in a properly written police report?

4. What are the two basic components of effective report writing?

5. Why is the official report considered the backbone of the criminal prosecution process?

6. What are the key steps in report writing?

7. Why is the effective use of language important in the report-writing process?

chain of custody Documentation of all who handle evidence in a criminal case.

hearsay evidence Second-party statements offered to the court by a person who did not originate the statement.

LEARNING OUTCOMES 3

Identify the main components of a fact sheet or initial complaint.

This information includes the suspect's name and related identifiers as well as a brief summary of the facts and circumstances surrounding the case (for example, times, dates, locations, who did what, who saw what, what evidence was collected).

1. What is the best way to organize the fact sheet in a criminal investigation?

2. Why is the information contained in the fact sheet important to the integrity of the investigation?

3. How are supplemental reports used by criminal investigators?

4. What are the most important elements of a fact sheet?

5. What similarities do journalists and criminal investigators share?

LEARNING OUTCOMES 4

Explain the correct methods for photographing the crime scene.

Photos of the scene should include general, medium-range, and close-up views. Photos must be taken and preserved so as to be admissible in court. The principal requirements to admit a photograph into evidence are relevance and authentication. From the investigator's standpoint, the most important requirement is authentication (that is, the photo must be accurate and correct). In addition to being material and relevant, crime-scene photos must not be prejudicial or distorted in any fashion. Doing so will risk the possibility that the photo might not be admitted into evidence.

1. What are the benefits of surveillance photos?

2. What are the most common mistakes in crime-scene photography?

3. What are the disadvantages of crime-scene photographs?

4. What are the three stages of crime-scene photography?

5. What is the purpose of the medium-range photograph?

6. Why is it important to take as many photographs of the crime scene as possible?

7. What is the most important requirement when photographs are being considered as evidence in a case?

8. How can photographs combat mistakes made by witnesses?

authentication A principal requirement to admit a photograph into evidence.

markers Items placed in crime-scene photos that call attention to specific objects or enable the viewer of the photo to get a sense of the size of the object or the distance between objects.

Summarize the legal precedents for the admissibility of photographs as evidence in court.

Trial courts bear the responsibility of admissibility of photographs as evidence in court. Such determinations have been based on several legal precedents. These include determinations regarding whether photos accurately reflect the crime scene.

1. What are the legal requirements for the admissibility of crime-scene photos?

2. Why is it important to observe legal precedents when photographing the crime scene?

3. What are the three types of distortion common in crime-scene photographs?

4. What is the difference between a material photograph and a relevant photograph?

5. When are photographs not allowed into evidence?

6. Who decides the admissibility of photographs as evidence in a trial?

Determine what types of information should be included in a photographic log.

It is of critical importance for investigators to log their photos carefully as to date, time, and sequence number. Doing so will ensure the integrity of the investigation and the subsequent prosecution of the suspect.

1. What is the purpose for maintaining a photographic log?

2. What are the benefits of having a properly prepared photographic log?

3. How can a photographic log help investigators in terms of efficiency and time management?

4. Why is it important to note the names of people handling evidence?

5. What is the best way to organize photos of a crime scene and evidence?

6. What information is pertinent in a photographic log?

Explain the types of photography commonly used in criminal investigations.

Photography is commonly used in covert criminal investigations as well as crime-scene investigations. The limits of what can be done are subject only to the investigator's imagination. One good example is surveillance photos. Surveillance photography is used covertly in establishing identities or in documenting criminal behavior. Photography of this nature is selective and may have many benefits.

1. What are some of the ways covert surveillance photos further a criminal investigation?

2. From a practical standpoint, what limitations does the criminal investigator face regarding surveillance photographs?

3. What is the purpose of surveillance photography?

4. How do non-police entities such as banks and convenience stores use surveillance photography?

5. What are the benefits of surveillance photography in criminal investigations?

surveillance Surreptitious observation.

LEARNING OUTCOMES 8

Describe how crime-scene sketches are made.

The crime-scene sketch can show certain details better than a photograph. It is a scale drawing that locates evidence in relation to other factors. Items such as the color of a wall, the type of floor, the general condition of the area, and non-evidential matter are normally not depicted. A sketch that is properly prepared can virtually always be used in court, but photographs that inflame the jury might be excluded in court.

1. What are the differences between the rough sketch and the finished sketch?

2. What are the benefits of the coordinate method of crime-scene sketching?

3. How can crime-scene sketches be more accurate than photographs?

4. How are crime-scene sketches used by prosecutors?

5. What is the objective of the crime-scene sketch?

6. Why is it important to record information uniformly when preparing a crime-scene sketch?

7. Which method is most effective for sketching indoor crime scenes?

rough sketch The initial crime-scene sketch drawn by officers on the crime scene.

finished sketches A completed crime-scene sketch drawn to scale.

coordinate method Measuring an object from two fixed points of reference.

baseline technique Crime-scene measuring technique in which a line is drawn between two known points.

triangulation method A bird's-eye view of the crime scene using fixed objects from which to measure.

cross-projection method Used in indoor crime scenes, it is basically a top-down view of the crime scene where the walls of the room have been "folded" down to reveal locations of bullet holes, blood-spatter evidence, and so on.

Additional Links

www.findlaw.com
This site calls itself the leading Internet source for all things law. Visitors may browse a myriad of different topics related to law. It includes a criminal law center link, which lists common crimes, their definitions, and criminal cases, as well as information on the process of a criminal class. There are links to other important topics such as juvenile crime and civil rights issues found on the website.

www.today.duke.edu/showcase/lacrosseincident
This site provides in-depth coverage of the Duke Lacrosse Team case. Links include media coverage and opinion pieces. There is also a link to a previous site in its final version, which was provided up-to-the-minute news, analysis, and information regarding the case until it was dismissed in May 2007.

www.science.howstuffworks.com/crime-scene-photography.htm
This site provides those interested in crime-scene photography with an overview of this special part of forensic science. It includes information on basic terminology as well as the types of photographs taken during criminal investigations.

3

"The initial steps of crime scene processing, such as protecting the scene and identifying and fingerprinting witnesses, are some of the most crucial steps in crime-scene investigation. Following proper investigative protocols will help ensure the timely capture of perpetrators and their successful prosecution."

Processing the Crime Scene

1 Describe the preliminary investigation.

2 Identify types of crime-scene evidence.

3 Summarize the responsibilities of the first responding officer.

4 Explain how to secure and protect the crime scene.

5 Explain how to collect and search for evidence at the scene.

6 Explain how to properly perform a follow-up investigation.

On the morning of September 8, 2011, Yale University doctoral student Annie Le left her apartment and took Yale transit to the Sterling Hall of Medicine on the Yale campus. Around 10:00 A.M., she walked from Sterling Hall to another campus building at 10 Amistad Street, where her research laboratory was located. Le had left her purse, cell phone, credit cards, and cash in her office at Sterling Hall. According to footage from the building's security cameras, Le entered the Amistad Street building just after 10:00 A.M. She was never seen leaving the building. On the evening of September 8 at about 9:00 P.M., one of her five housemates called police to report her missing.

Five days later, on September 13, her strangled body was found stuffed inside a wall of a campus lab building. Le had planned to marry Columbia graduate student Jonathan Widawsky on the day her body was found. The investigation into Le's death revealed that she had been placed into the wall upside down, with her bra pushed upward toward her head and her panties pulled down around her ankles. It was also determined that among other injuries, her jaw and one collarbone had been broken at some point before her death.

Four days later, on September 17, investigators arrested Raymond J. Clark III, a Yale lab technician who worked in the building. Clark subsequently pleaded guilty to Le's murder and was sentenced to 44 years in prison. In the fall of 2011, both Yale University and the Yale School of Medicine were named as defendants in a civil lawsuit brought by Le's family.

DISCUSS **Is it possible for criminal investigators to identify indicators as to whether a person is a possible target for murder? If so, how?**

The case of Annie Le helps us realize the complexities of a crime scene and just how important it is to preserve any and all evidence. The actions taken by patrol and investigative personnel at a crime scene often determine the success or failure of a criminal investigation. The survival of victims, the apprehension of the perpetrator, and the ultimate outcome of any resulting criminal prosecution may depend entirely upon prompt and proper responses by the officers at the scene. All personnel must understand, and be prepared to carry out correctly, the operational procedures established by the department for the management of crime scenes. Police officers responding to a crime scene have several very important responsibilities. They must:

- Be prepared to inform superiors of their findings,
- Assist victims,
- Secure and protect the crime scene,
- Apprehend the perpetrator,
- Collect and preserve evidence,
- Interview witnesses, and
- Perform other necessary operational functions.

Even though some of these tasks may be the responsibility of departmental specialists, every officer in the department should be able to conduct all of these functions properly if called upon to do so. Above all, the patrol officers initially responding to the scene must understand that they have a heavy responsibility to ensure that the appropriate actions are taken to protect life and property, preserve evidence, and make it possible for subsequent investigative work to be successful.

Technicians Processing Crime Scene.

Ashley Cooper/Corbis

▶ Understanding the Preliminary Investigation

A logical procedure for identifying, collecting, and preserving evidence is essential. The practice of following prescribed steps in the identification and collection of evidence is critical in making an arrest and in subsequent prosecution of the offender. The evidence-collection process begins immediately after the discovery of a crime. In most situations, this precursory investigative phase is known as the **preliminary investigation**. Generally, the term *preliminary investigation* is defined as an initial inquiry by

LEARNING OUTCOMES 1 — Describe the preliminary investigation.

officers to establish the facts and circumstances of a suspected crime and to preserve any evidence related to that crime. The preliminary investigation includes the following:

- Securing the crime scene
- Considering the possible arrest of a suspect
- Locating and questioning witnesses and victims
- Documenting the crime scene
- Identifying and collecting evidence

The function of the preliminary investigation is closely linked with the duties of the first officer to arrive at the crime scene (discussed later), who, in most cases, is a respondent from the patrol division. In any crime scene, the first officer and investigators should consider the scene itself as evidence. This is because much valuable information can be learned from items left on the scene, provided that it has not been tampered with or altered in any way.

Mock Murder Crime Scene.

Dave King/Dorling Kindersley, Ltd.

▶ Types of Crime-Scene Evidence

Crime-scene evidence is dynamic. Protection and preservation of the scene are therefore crucial because both avert the possibility of **contamination of evidence**, loss of evidence, or unnecessary movement of physical evidence. In the evidence-collection process, contamination of evidence occurs most commonly when evidence is not properly secured, is wrongfully mixed with other types of evidence, or is altered significantly from its original condition at the **crime scene**. When this occurs, the evidence is usually rendered inadmissible or "incompetent" by the court.

LEARNING OUTCOMES 2 — Identify types of crime-scene evidence.

The preliminary investigation involves the identification and preservation of evidence, much of which is minute or "trace" evidence. Trace evidence is any type of material left at—or taken from—a crime scene or the result of contact between two surfaces, such as shoes and the floor covering or soil or fibers from where someone sat on an upholstered chair.

The **Locard exchange principle**, also known as Locard's theory or the transfer of evidence theory, was first put forward by twentieth-century forensic scientist Edmond Locard. Locard was the director of the first-known crime laboratory, located in Lyon, France.[1]

For the most part, Locard's principle is applied to crime scenes where the perpetrator of a crime comes into contact with the scene, so he or she will both bring something into the scene and leave with something from the scene. Every contact leaves a trace. For example, Locard stated the following:

Wherever he steps, whatever he touches, whatever he leaves, even unconsciously, will serve as a silent witness against him. Not only his fingerprints or his footprints, but his hair, the fibers from his clothes, the glass he breaks, the tool mark he leaves, the paint he scratches, the blood or semen he deposits or collects. All of these and more, bear mute witness against him. This is evidence that does not forget. It is not confused by the excitement of the moment. It is not absent because human witnesses are. It is factual evidence. Physical evidence cannot be wrong, it cannot perjure itself, it cannot be wholly absent. Only human failure to find it, study and understand it, can diminish its value. (Edmond Locard)

An easier way to remember this is, "Every contact leaves a trace."

What Can Physical Evidence Do?

- **Prove the elements of a crime or reveal that a crime has been committed.** *Case example:* A search warrant served on the residence of a suspected drug dealer revealed a quantity of cocaine, scales, paraphernalia, business records showing drug dealing, and large amounts of cash concealed in shoeboxes.

- **Place the suspect at the scene.** *Case example:* Shoe impressions found in the mud outside a burglary victim's residence were found to match those of a known burglar in the community.

- **Eliminate innocent persons.** *Case example:* A murderer was careful not to leave fingerprints at the crime scene. However, blood samples taken from the scene later revealed, through DNA typing, the true identity of the perpetrator.

- **Lead to a suspect's confession.** *Case example:* Although a convenience store robbery suspect was wearing a ski mask at the time of the robbery, he admitted his role in the crime when a hidden-camera shot of him during the crime revealed a recognizable torn edge on the corner of his jacket.

- **Support witness testimony.** *Case example:* A neighbor told the police that she heard glass breaking at about 1:30 A.M. Investigators later located a broken pane of glass in a nearby house and, through use of the witness's statement, were able to determine the time of the offense.

- **Positively impact juries in criminal cases.** *Case example:* As the nickel-plated .38-caliber handgun was handed to the first jury member for inspection, fellow jurists leaned forward and watched while anticipating their chance to touch and hold the weapon that the prosecutor claimed was used in the crime.

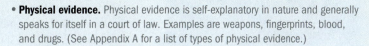

Types of Evidence

- **Physical evidence.** Physical evidence is self-explanatory in nature and generally speaks for itself in a court of law. Examples are weapons, fingerprints, blood, and drugs. (See Appendix A for a list of types of physical evidence.)

- **Direct or *prima facie* evidence.** *Prima facie* evidence is evidence established by law that at face value proves a fact in dispute. For example, states establish the minimum blood alcohol content to show that a person is under the influence.

- **Indirect or circumstantial evidence.** Circumstantial evidence merely tends to incriminate a person without offering conclusive proof. For example, although a person's footprint located outside a burglary victim's residence doesn't show that the person who left the print was the burglar, it does suggest that he or she could be.

- **Testimonial evidence.** Testimonial evidence consists of a verbal statement offered by a witness while under oath or affirmation. It may also be evidence offered by way of a sworn pretrial deposition. Although many people define testimony in the same way as evidence, they are clearly distinct. Simply, testimony is evidence offered in an oral manner and is used most commonly to explain some form of physical evidence (e.g., gunpowder residue, fingerprints).

- **Trace evidence.** Trace evidence consists of extremely small items of evidence, such as hair or clothing fibers. With the aid of modern forensic analysis, trace evidence plays a greater role today than ever before in solving capital cases.

- **Demonstrative evidence.** Demonstrative evidence is evidence used to demonstrate or clarify an issue rather than to prove something. An example is the use of anatomical dolls to aid in the testimony of children in a sexual molestation case.

Material transferred in this fashion is usually referred to as **trace evidence**, which generally refers to minute or even microscopic bits of matter that are not immediately apparent to the naked eye. Consequently, such evidence is extremely difficult to locate at the crime scene. Because of its microscopic nature, the criminal may be far less likely to eliminate it purposely than with more telltale evidence such as blood splattering or fingerprints.

In criminal investigations, the utility of physical evidence should be clearly understood. Some types of physical evidence are more obvious in nature than others.

Forms of Evidence

Evidence can also be classified in several distinct ways. Classifications can be considered either individually or in combination with other classes of evidence. In general, there are two commonly used classifications: *corpus delicti* and associative evidence. The term ***corpus delicti*** simply refers to evidence that establishes that a crime has been committed, such as pry marks on a doorjamb. Conversely, **associative evidence** (such as fingerprints, footprints, bloodstains, and fibers) links a suspect with a crime.

▶ Responsibilities of the First Officer

The initial response to a call by the responding officer is a critical phase of any criminal investigation. This response is usually made by patrol officers who must be prepared to initiate a preliminary investigation and carry out the functions discussed next until they are relieved by superior officers or specialists (for example, detectives or crime-scene specialists) who then assume responsibility for their specific functions at the scene.

LEARNING OUTCOMES 3 — Summarize the responsibilities of the first responding officer.

Unfortunately, improper actions by responding patrol officers can cause a loss of evidence or otherwise conduct so prejudice to an investigation that a subsequent successful criminal prosecution becomes impossible. Furthermore, in some instances, improper initial actions may result in aggravation of injuries to victims, endangerment of other officers, and even loss of life. Therefore, the responding officers must be prepared to carry out the following initial actions promptly and correctly.

In certain situations, it may not be possible to perform the actions described next in the order in which they are listed.

Police Officer and Investigator.

However, all of the actions, when appropriate, should be taken as soon as circumstances permit.

1. *Actions while en route to the crime scene.* While en route to the location, officers must be alert to the possible presence of perpetrators or perpetrators' vehicles fleeing from the scene. Although actions taken to detain suspicious vehicles or persons must comply with legal requirements for investigative detention and arrest, the information furnished to the responding units by the dispatcher or by other officers normally provides sufficient "reasonable suspicion" to justify detention of persons or vehicles found in or leaving the crime-scene area. In addition, the suspects' own conduct (for example, suspicious appearance or behavior, traffic violations, and so on) may provide grounds for an investigatory stop. Although the opportunity to apprehend a perpetrator while en route to the crime scene may not arise in a large percentage of cases, officers while en route to the location of a crime should always be alert for such possibilities.

2. *Initial actions upon arrival.* Upon arrival at the location, officers should, if possible, first verify that a crime has been committed. In many instances, it will be obvious that a crime has been committed or that, at the very least, there is sufficient evidence to justify further investigation. However, officers should be aware that unless the circumstances are sufficient to justify a reasonable belief that a major crime has occurred or is occurring within a dwelling or that some other exigent situation exists, they may not enter that dwelling without a warrant. To do so risks subsequent suppression of evidence and possible civil liability. Even when circumstances do not justify an immediate entry, officers may remain outside to protect the premises while additional information or a warrant is obtained. Reasonable belief that a crime has been or is being committed may be based on such various factors as information from dispatchers, statements provided by neighbors upon arrival, physical aspects of the scene (for example, broken windows or doors), or sounds from within the premises indicating that a crime is in progress (for example, screams or gunshots).

Deciding whether or not to enter premises where a crime may have been committed is often difficult. Such entries are considered "searches," and often the police on the scene must make an on-the-spot decision under circumstances that are adverse and confusing. Although each case is different and state or local law may vary, in general it may be said that under "exigent" (that is, emergency) circumstances, officers are permitted to enter any premises, even using force if necessary, without a warrant and conduct a "protective" search of the premises when the officers have reasonable grounds to believe that a person within the premises is in immediate need of assistance or a perpetrator is present.[2]

Officers entering premises under these circumstances are not permitted to search the premises for evidence. The **protective search** is limited by law to a "sweep" of the premises to discover victims or perpetrators. A protective search is for officer safety and includes a quick search of the premises for additional suspects/persons or any weapons that could be acquired by such persons. Any search beyond the scope of a protective sweep requires a search warrant. However, if in the course of the protective sweep, evidence is discovered in plain view, it may be seized without a warrant or noted for later removal after a warrant has been obtained.

Whenever possible, verification of a crime at the location, or the responding officers' reasonable suspicion thereof, should be communicated immediately to the dispatcher or superiors so that decisions can be made regarding backup, entry into the structure, dispatch of medical assistance or crime-scene specialists to the location, and so on. Failing to communicate promptly may endanger victims, the responding officers, and all subsequent aspects of the investigation.[3]

In many instances, circumstances do not permit transmission of complete information at the time of the initial arrival at the scene. In that event, follow-up communications should be made to provide the necessary additional information. (See "Follow-up communications.")

3. *Assistance to victims and protection of witnesses and bystanders.* Administering first aid to and summoning medical assistance for any victims present must be a top priority of responding officers. If the victim is still in danger, either because of the perpetrator or because of other circumstances (for example, fire), immediate steps must be taken to ensure the victim's safety. Similar protection must be rendered to witnesses and other bystanders. However, unless the bystanders are in danger or circumstances otherwise make it necessary, the officers should avoid ordering bystanders from the scene until it has been determined which, if any, of the bystanders is also a witness or potential witness to some aspect of the crime.

4. *Arrest of the perpetrator.* If the perpetrator is at the scene and probable cause for arrest exists or an arrest warrant has been issued, the perpetrator should be arrested in accordance with departmental policy and local law.

If officers need to leave the scene to effect the arrest (for example, the perpetrator is fleeing from the scene and must be pursued by officers), the officers must determine whether it is appropriate to leave the crime scene at that time. Conflicting considerations are often present in such circumstances. For example, the officers must balance the need to remain on the scene to render assistance to victims or to protect others from harm against the risk to the public if the perpetrator escapes. Ideally, sufficient personnel will be available to perform both functions simultaneously; if not, the officers present must decide where the priorities lie. Circumstances will dictate the decision, but in general, protecting the crime scene, any victims present, and the witnesses and bystanders will be the first consideration. Other units may then be alerted to pursue the fleeing perpetrator.

5. *Follow-up communications.* As noted previously, initial communication at the time of the officers' arrival at the crime scene is essential. However, circumstances may not permit the responding officers to furnish complete information to their headquarters at that point. Further communications should be made to provide, at a minimum, the following information.

Superiors must be informed of the apparent nature of the offense discovered by the officers. When possible, reports should be factual in nature. When it is necessary to state opinions or conclusions in such transmissions, these opinions or conclusions should be supported by the known facts. Approved departmental codes may be used when appropriate.[4] If the exact nature or seriousness of the crime cannot yet be determined, the possibility of the more serious offense should be made clear in the transmission.

If the perpetrator has fled the scene, a full description of the perpetrator, together with any information regarding the perpetrator's mode and direction of flight, should be communicated as soon as possible. If there were accomplices, similar information about them should be included. Likewise, if a vehicle was involved either in the commission of the crime or in the flight of the perpetrator(s) from the scene, this information should also be communicated.

If the perpetrator is known or believed to be armed, it is especially important that this information be transmitted as soon as possible. Any information available regarding the number and nature of the weapons possessed by the perpetrator should be provided. This permits other officers who may encounter the perpetrator to assess the threat level and proceed appropriately.

If not already requested during the initial transmission, support units may be requested during follow-up communications.

6. *Identification of witnesses and vehicles.* The identification and preliminary interviewing of witnesses are extremely important considerations for officers arriving at a crime scene. These functions are discussed in detail next.

License numbers and descriptions of vehicles parked in the area should be noted. In addition, the license number and description of any vehicle moving through the area in a slow, repeated, or otherwise suspicious manner should be recorded.

Officers should also be alert for suspicious persons who, although not present in the immediate vicinity of the crime scene, are observed in the general area. Such persons should be approached; identified; and, if circumstances justify it, detained for further investigation.

7. *Briefing investigators and superiors.* Officers should be prepared to brief investigators and other authorized personnel when they arrive on the scene. All information gathered, together with a summary of the actions taken by the responding officers up to that time, should be provided. Unfortunately, experience shows that in many instances, valuable information known to the officers making the initial response is not communicated to detectives, superiors, or other personnel. Responding officers should therefore make it a point to communicate all known facts accurately and completely to investigators or other authorized persons arriving on the scene.

Broadcasting a Flash Description

Additional preliminary duties may include the broadcasting of a **flash description** of the suspect and the suspect's vehicle (also called a BOLO—"be on the lookout"). If able to determine certain facts about possible suspects, weapons, and vehicles, the responding officer should put out a flash description to other officers in case the suspects are still in the vicinity. Flash descriptions vary in nature, depending on the specific law enforcement agency. Generally, they should be precise and to the point. The flash description consists of the following information:

1. The type of crime, location of crime, and time of occurrence

2. The number of suspects involved in the crime

3. A physical description of those involved:
   - Gender
   - Race
   - Age
   - Height
   - Weight
   - Eye color
   - Hair color
   - Style or type of hair
   - Length of hair
   - Facial hair, if any
   - Clothing description
   - Other outstanding physical characteristics (for example, tattoos, scars)

Actions of the First Officer

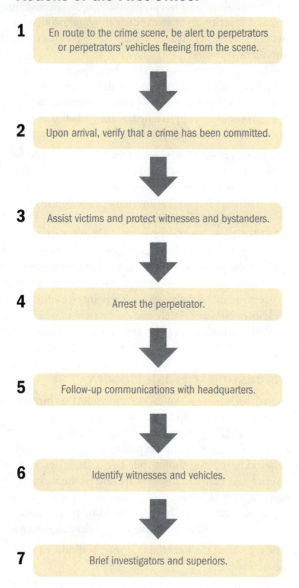

1 En route to the crime scene, be alert to perpetrators or perpetrators' vehicles fleeing from the scene.

2 Upon arrival, verify that a crime has been committed.

3 Assist victims and protect witnesses and bystanders.

4 Arrest the perpetrator.

5 Follow-up communications with headquarters.

6 Identify witnesses and vehicles.

7 Brief investigators and superiors.

4. Weapons used

5. Direction in which the suspect was last observed proceeding and how long ago

6. Means of escape (mention any possible route that suspects may take)

7. If anyone was wounded

8. Any vehicle used

When broadcasting flash descriptions of vehicles, remember the **CYMBL** rule, which helps officers remember to include the necessary information for a suspect vehicle description:

C: color

Y: year

M: make, model

B: body style

L: license number

Responsibilities of the First Responder The reality is that when an officer is the first responder on the scene, he or she has a tremendous responsibility to ensure that the process starts and proceeds without flaws in order to protect the integrity of the case. He or she has no idea whether or not the case will be closely or loosely scrutinized by the public, so all effort must be made to do this work properly every time. How should the first officer on the scene deal with media cameras present upon arrival and reporters attempting to walk within the crime-scene area?

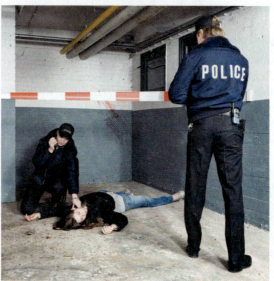

corepics/Shutterstock.com

Responding Officers Making Initial Determinations at Crime Scene.

▶ Securing and Protecting the Scene

One of the more important functions of responding officers is to ensure that neither their actions nor the actions of others will disturb the crime scene unnecessarily. Protecting the crime scene has always been essential to good police work, and this is doubly true today because scientific evidence analysis techniques are becoming an increasingly important part of criminal investigations. Unnecessary or improper entry into the crime scene may

LEARNING OUTCOMES **4** Explain how to secure and protect the crime scene.

- Destroy or contaminate important evidence,

- Introduce items or substances into the crime scene that may mislead investigators, and

- Provide defense attorneys with a basis for discrediting the investigators or the findings of a crime laboratory.

Unless circumstances or departmental policies dictate otherwise, after these initial functions have been performed, the responding officers should thereafter avoid entering the crime scene and prevent others from doing so until superiors, detectives, or crime-scene specialists relieve the responding officers of that responsibility.

Although, as mentioned previously, responding officers must often enter the crime scene to perform their essential preliminary functions, every entry into a crime-scene area has the potential to destroy evidence and introduce irrelevant substances into the scene. Therefore, even when entering the crime scene to perform necessary actions as described previously, responding officers should, to the greatest extent possible, avoid touching or moving objects at the scene or entering areas where entry is unnecessary to accomplish the previously stated purposes. In addition, whenever possible, the crime scene should be entered only by one narrowly defined route to avoid the destruction of evidence, the contamination of possible scent trails, and so on.

In addition to keeping their encroachment upon the crime scene to a minimum, officers should also carefully note the portions of the scene through which they have passed, the routes taken, the objects they have touched, and any other actions they have taken that may have altered or tainted the scene. This information will assist investigators in determining the original state of the crime scene and will enable them to disregard matters that are not relevant to the crime itself.

After the responding officers have completed their preliminary examination of the scene, the scene should be secured to protect it from encroachment by unauthorized persons. This is not always a simple task, and circumstances may dictate what can and cannot be done. However, in general, the following actions should be taken:

1. *The area to be declared a crime scene must be defined.* This includes any portion of the premises that may reasonably be anticipated to contain useful evidence. Although it is often impossible to cordon off all of the surrounding areas that might conceivably hold such evidence, the area designated as a crime scene should be as large as the circumstances require or permit. Remember that it is always a better practice to secure a larger area and narrow it down than to identify a small scene and attempt to expand it at a later time.

   The seriousness of the crime, the location of the crime, the nature of the surrounding environment, the amount of manpower available to maintain a perimeter, and similar factors determine the definition and extent of the crime scene in a given case. The specific nature of the suspected crime may also dictate the definition of the crime scene. For example, in a homicide case, the place where the body is found is obviously considered the crime scene, even though the actual death may later be determined to have occurred elsewhere; in the case of a suspected kidnapping, the place where the victim was last seen should be regarded as a crime scene and treated accordingly. If the perpetrator has fled or a victim or other significant person is believed to be missing from the scene, the widest possible area should be protected to preserve any evidence present, including any possible scent trails leading away from the immediate scene.

2. *Backup should be requested to help restrict access to the defined crime scene and to control onlookers.* Only rarely will one or two responding officers be able to maintain complete control of a crime scene by themselves. Assistance should be obtained quickly before others encroach upon the scene and evidence is lost.

3. *The interior of the crime scene area should be cleared.* Persons other than law enforcement officers or other officials actively engaged in crime-scene duties should be removed from the premises.[5] The crime scene should be secured by the use of tape, rope, barricades, locks, or other appropriate measures (see Box 3–1). After the crime scene has been secured, access to the scene should be restricted to authorized personnel.

BOX 3–1 INVESTIGATOR'S CHECKLIST: CRIME-SCENE EQUIPMENT

- *Surveillance equipment.* Night vision equipment, listening devices.

- *Cameras.* The digital camera has surpassed the 35-mm camera as the photographic tool of choice for crime-scene documentation. Both cameras and editing software have now become affordable for even the smallest departments. Digital video cameras are another recent innovation in crime-scene documentation, offering the best evidence of crimes in progress and fresh crime-scene evidence. Camera accessories such as lenses, tripods, and lighting attachments may be required for unusual crime scenes.

- *Lights.* Handheld flashlight (for example, Streamlight), emergency flashing strobes instead of vehicle fog lights, handheld floodlights for crime scenes.

- *Notebook.* Sketching material for producing rough sketches while on the scene. Writing utensils such as pencils, pens, and markers must be available.

- *Other materials.* Tape measures (both cloth and metal), evidence tape, a carpenter-type ruler, eraser, chalk, tweezers, scissors, labels, tongue depressors, a clipboard, and outdoor and indoor templates.

- *Containers.* Envelopes, boxes, plastic and paper bags, and glass bottles of all sizes and shapes.

- *First aid kit.* To treat injured parties at the scene.

- *Casting material.* Plaster or dental stone to make casts (for example, pry marks, footprints).

Securing a Crime Scene

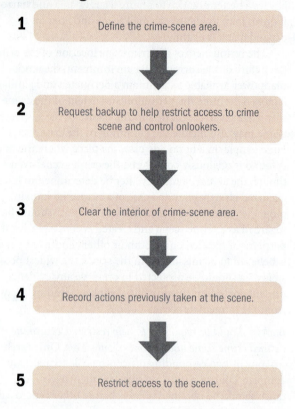

1 Define the crime-scene area.

2 Request backup to help restrict access to crime scene and control onlookers.

3 Clear the interior of crime-scene area.

4 Record actions previously taken at the scene.

5 Restrict access to the scene.

4. *Record actions previously taken at the scene.* Responding officers should note and record any alterations that may have occurred to the crime scene due to their own activities or the activities of personnel rendering emergency assistance to victims. In addition, officers should determine if any actions of the persons reporting the crime or of other persons present on the scene before the arrival of the officers may have altered or tainted the crime scene in any way. In particular, actions involving moving or otherwise disturbing the victim's body should be noted. All of this information should be communicated to investigators, superiors, or both at the earliest possible opportunity.

5. *Restrict access to the scene.* After the crime scene has been defined, cleared, and secured, access to the scene should be limited to authorized personnel directly involved in the investigation. In the case of major crimes, the identities of all persons entering the perimeter should be recorded, and, if possible, the times at which they entered and left the scene should be noted. Attempts by news media personnel, nonessential city or county officials, and others to gain access to the scene should be referred to the supervisor in charge of the scene or other officer designated to handle requests for entry.[6] When a decision is made to allow any such persons to have access to the scene, they should be escorted by an officer during the period of their entry to prevent their taking any action that might result in the loss of evidence or otherwise endanger the investigation. In this regard, a **contamination log** should also be kept to document all persons entering the scene.[7] The

contamination log documents any evidence that has been compromised or for which the chain of custody has not been observed.

▶ The "Walk-Through"

Conducting a scene "walk-through" provides the investigator with an overview of the entire scene. The walk-through provides the investigator with the first opportunity to locate and view the body, identify valuable and/or fragile evidence, and determine initial investigative procedures providing for a systematic examination and documentation of the scene and body. The initial scene walk-through is essential to minimize scene disturbance and to prevent the loss and/or contamination of physical and fragile evidence.

▶ Establishing "Chain of Custody"

Ensuring the integrity of the evidence by establishing and maintaining a chain of custody is crucial to a successful investigation. Doing so will protect against subsequent allegations of tampering, theft, planting of evidence, and contamination of evidence. So before any evidence is removed, the custodian(s) of evidence shall be identified and designated and should maintain a chain of custody for all evidence collected. Such persons must perform the following tasks:

- Document location of the scene and time of arrival of the death investigator at the scene.
- Determine custodian(s) of evidence, determine which agency or agencies are responsible for collection of specific types of evidence, and determine evidence-collection priority for fragile/fleeting evidence.
- Identify, secure, and preserve evidence with proper containers, labels, and preservatives.
- Document the collection of evidence by recording its location at the scene, time of collection, and time and location of disposition.
- Develop personnel lists, witness lists, and documentation of times of arrival and departure of personnel.

▶ Using Legal "Tools"

The investigator, prior to or upon arrival at the death scene, should work with other agencies to:

- Determine the need for a search warrant (discuss with appropriate agencies).
- Identify local, state, federal, and international laws (discuss with appropriate agencies)
- Identify medical examiner/coroner statutes and/or office standard operating procedures (discuss with appropriate agencies).

Following and utilizing laws related to the collection of evidence will ensure a complete and proper investigation in compliance with state and local laws, admissibility in court, and adherence to departmental policies and procedures.

▶ Collecting and Searching for Evidence at the Scene

After an investigator has documented a crime scene, the actual search must begin. Generally speaking, evidence discovered at the crime scene will serve four objectives: (1) to determine the facts of the crime, (2) to identify the lawbreaker, (3) to aid in the arrest of the perpetrator, and (4) to aid in the criminal prosecution of the perpetrator. History has shown that there are many different ways to search a crime scene for evidence. Indeed, methods for crime-scene searching vary according to the types of crime scenes and evidence at hand. Varieties of crime-scene evidence include firearm evidence, trace material collection, toolmark evidence, collection of bodily fluids, standards of evidence, fire and explosion evidence, outdoor crime scenes, vehicle searches, and interior and victim searches. The search of the crime scene consists of several distinct phases:

LEARNING OUTCOMES 5 Explain how to collect and search for evidence at the scene.

- Surveying the crime scene
- Documenting the crime scene through sketches and photographs
- Recording all physical evidence
- Searching for fingerprints

Search Patterns

Of the methods of searching used most often, several have been most commonly used over time. The most common search patterns include the spiral search method, grid search method, strip or line search method, and quadrant or zone search method (see Figure 3–1). Some methods of searching are best suited for indoor scenes, others are more applicable to outdoor crime scenes, and other scenes present unique problems; each of these is discussed next. Whichever method is adopted, the rule to remember is that the search must be thorough.

Indoor Crime-Scene Searches

It is generally recommended that at least two officers search an indoor crime scene. This may best be accomplished by dividing the room in half and having each investigator search half of the room (also known as the quadrant or **zone search method**). At the conclusion of the search, the investigators switch halves. In this fashion, each half of the room is searched twice.

Think About It…

Collecting and Searching for Crime-Scene Evidence There are numerous variables related to properly searching for and collecting crime-scene evidence. As noted, evidence can possibly be fragile and easily damaged or contaminated, therefore requiring care in the search as well as preservation once evidence is found. How would you deal with any coworkers you might observe using improper techniques to collect evidence (especially infected evidence), such as not wearing appropriate hand or eye protection?

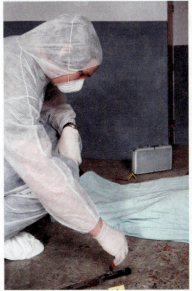

corepics/Shutterstock.com

What Can Physical Evidence Do?

Spiral Search Method

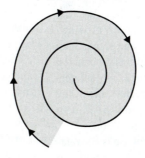

Grid Method

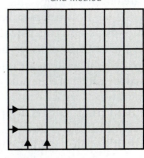

Strip or Line Search

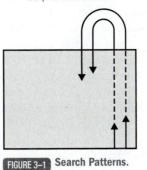

Quadrant or Zone Search

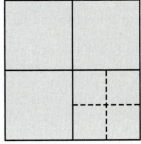

FIGURE 3–1 Search Patterns.

Outdoor Crime-Scene Searches

In most cases, the outdoor crime scene covers a broader area than those that are indoors. If this is the case, more investigators are required. Accordingly, with the increased size of the scene, a more systematic searching method must be used. One way is to rope off the scene into a grid, referred to as the **grid search method**. Each square, averaging about 6 square feet, represents a specific search area that is a manageable size for each investigator.

Nighttime Crime-Scene Searches

If possible, investigators should wait until daylight to search a crime scene. Obviously, circumstances may require investigators to proceed with the search at night. These may include inclement weather or other emergency circumstances. In the event that such a search is to be conducted, lighting generators should be used to provide sufficient illumination for the search.

Vehicle Searches

The search of a vehicle requires the same degree of attention as indoor and outdoor searches. Obviously, the nature of the crime dictates the area of the vehicle to be searched. For example, whereas a drug smuggling or murder case requires closer examination of the interior of the vehicle, a hit-and-run investigation necessitates examination of the exterior of the vehicle. Similar to an interior search, a vehicle should also be searched for fingerprints. This should be done after other trace evidence has been sought.

The Crime-Scene Search

Evidence of crimes is dynamic. That is, it is unique, often fragile, and may constantly be undergoing change. Experience indicates that there is usually only one chance to search a crime scene properly, so for this reason, it is a good idea to survey the scene carefully before embarking on the search process itself.

There are two approaches to crime-scene searches. As a first step, the investigator should consider all information provided to him or her by officers who arrived earlier on the scene. Such information includes the officers' perceptions of what occurred and the nature of the evidence. Next, investigators should determine which evidence items seem to play the greatest role in the alleged crime. In brief, the principal concern at this point is to observe and document the scene rather than take action.

Of specific importance in the observation phase is the relative distance of any object to the victim. The distance between an object and a victim may play a greater role in the evidence-collection phase than the item itself. For example, if the crime scene consists of a dead person who has apparently been shot and a 9mm handgun, the locations of spent shell casings could indicate the angle of the weapon or the position of the victim at the time the gun was discharged. Such a determination could point to either suicide or homicide and may subsequently alter the character of the investigation. As indicated, while observations are being carried out, notes should be taken to organize the sequence of events. Witnesses' statements should be taken as well, regarding the victim(s) or related information. Additionally, video recordings and digital photographs should be made during this phase to document the scene adequately for future reference. Both of these considerations are discussed in greater detail later in the book.

Collecting Evidence

There is a tendency on the part of many investigators to rush the evidence-collection process and focus attention on the obvious. Understandably, the task of observing firsthand the scene of another's misfortune is a difficult one for many, and one might appreciate the desire for expeditiousness on the part of the investigator. It is a fact, however, that much critical evidence, often seemingly unimportant, can be located in and around the scene of almost every crime. As discussed in the earlier section on crime-scene searches, investigators must choose which method of searching is best suited for the crime in question.

Regardless of the method used, evidence must be collected in a comprehensive, nondestructive manner; within a reasonable period; and with unnecessary movement about the scene kept to a minimum. Although every criminal case is unique and should be evaluated on an individual basis, experience has shown that the following general recommendations are beneficial in organizing the search and preventing errors.

Gathering and Preserving Evidence

After the initial crime-scene search has been completed and the sketching and photographing of the scene have been done, evidence should be collected. The manner in which evidence is collected must be consistent with each law enforcement agency's policies and procedures and should be in keeping with accepted rules of evidence. The evidence collected first is usually that which is most fragile. Therefore, fingerprints should be lifted as a priority. Next, other fragile evidence, such as blood and other trace evidence, should be collected. It is important for officers to search the crime scene a second time after the evidence has been collected. This should uncover any evidence overlooked accidentally. When possible, one investigator should serve as the evidence collector. This designation ensures that all evidence gets recorded and processed at the scene in a uniform and correct manner. It also ensures that evidence will be moved only when the collector decides that it can be moved.

When the case goes to court, both the investigator who discovered the evidence and the collector are usually required to testify. The greatest advantage to using this system is that all evidence is collected in a uniform manner, where one officer is responsible for packaging and marking the evidence and filling out the necessary paperwork. This reduces the need to tie up additional officers back at the office for such a task. See Figure 3–2 for instructions on proper sealing of evidence.

Chain of Custody

Evidence that has been collected must be safeguarded until the case goes to court. During the trial, if it is determined that labels are missing and evidence is not properly initialed or is otherwise missing or altered, the evidence may be considered inadmissible and the case thrown out. The total accounting of evidence is known as the **chain of custody**. This is made up of all persons

Proper Sealing of Evidence

The method shown below permits access to the invoice letter without breaking the inner seal. This allows the person entitled to receive the evidence to receive it in a sealed condition just as it was packed by the sender.

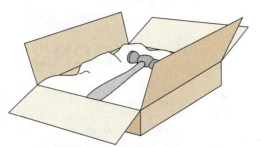

1 Pack bulk evidence securely in box.

2 Seal box and mark as evidence.

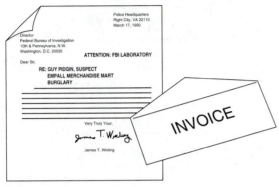

3 Place copy of transmittal letter in envelope and mark "INVOICE."

4 Stick envelope to outside of sealed box.

5 Wrap sealed box in outside wrapper and seal with gummed paper.

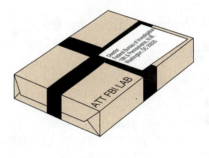

6 and mark: Attention FBI Laboratory
(or your local crime lab)

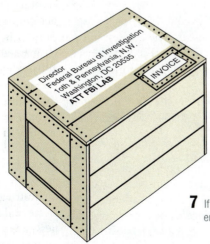

7 If packing box is wooden—tack invoice envelope to top under a clear plastic cover.

FIGURE 3–2 **Proper Method for Sealing Evidence.**

(usually, law enforcement personnel) who have taken custody of the evidence since its collection and who are therefore responsible for its protection and storage. The chain of custody is established by adhering to certain guidelines:

- The number of persons handling evidence from the time that it is safely stored should be limited. If the evidence leaves the possession of an officer, he or she should record to whom the evidence was given, the date and time, and the reason it was turned over.

- Anyone who handles evidence should affix his or her name and badge number to the package containing evidence.

- A signed receipt should be obtained from the person accepting the evidence. In turn, the investigator should sign a receipt or log when the item is returned.

- When a piece of evidence is turned in, the investigator should check his or her identification mark on it to ensure that it is the same item.

- After an item is returned to the investigator, he or she should determine if the item is in the same condition as when it was discovered. Any change in the physical appearance of the evidence should be called to the attention of the court.

Evidence can be stored in vehicle trunks, strongboxes, property rooms, locked file cabinets, evidence lockers, or

Details to Include on an Evidence Label

EVIDENCE

Case Number _____

Exhibit Number (when numerous items are seized) _____

Date and time of seizure _____

Name and description of articles _____

_____

_____

Location at time of discovery _____

_____

_____

Signature or initials of officer making the discovery _____

Name or initials of others witnessing the discovery _____

Recommendations for Dealing with Infected Evidence

- **Human bites.** Viral transmission through saliva is unlikely; however, if bitten, after milking the wound, rinse well and seek medical attention.

- **Saliva, urine, and feces.** Viral transmission through saliva is unlikely. In urine, the virus is isolated in very low concentrations and nonexistent in feces. No AIDS cases have been associated with urine or feces.

- **Cuts and puncture wounds.** When searching areas hidden from view, use extreme caution to avoid sharp objects. Cases involving needle sticks are very rare.

- **Cardiopulmonary resuscitation (CPR) and first aid.** Minimal risk is associated with CPR, but it is a good idea to use masks or airways and gloves when in contact with bleeding wounds.

- **Body removal.** As with all crime scenes, when in contact with a dead body, always wear protective gloves.

- **Casual contact.** No AIDS cases or HIV infections have been associated with casual contact.

- **Any contact with bodily fluids or blood.** Wear protective gloves if contact with blood or bodily fluids is likely. If contact is made, wash the area thoroughly with soap and water. Clean up spills with 1 part water and 10 parts household bleach.

- **Contact with dried blood.** No cases of infection have been traced to exposure to dried blood. The drying process itself seems to deactivate any viruses in blood. However, it is still a good idea to wear protective clothing such as gloves.

vaults. The only stipulation is that it be marked properly and protected from tampering and destruction. Most evidence is turned over to an evidence custodian, who is usually an employee of the crime lab. This person signs off on an evidence form as the recipient of the evidence. The seizing officer then indicates in his or her investigative report the person to whom the evidence was given.

Marking the Evidence

Another important rule to remember during the evidence-collection process is that all evidence must be marked immediately upon seizure to ensure proper identification later because it is common for the officer who seizes evidence to identify it at trial. Such testimony ensures the integrity of the chain of custody. Proper marking of each piece of evidence also ensures organization of all items of evidence for restructuring the events of the crime and the questioning of witnesses. Generally, it does not matter how the officer marks evidence as long as the initials of the seizing officer and the date of the seizure are clearly indicated on the seized item and on any container used to enclose the object, such as an envelope or cardboard box.

In many cases, the officer's department will require additional information. Such information includes the assigned case number, the type of crime, and the victim's name as well as the defendant's name, address, and date of birth. After physical evidence has been marked, sealed, counted, weighed (if necessary), and placed within a sealed container, a label is affixed containing identifying information.

▶ Performing the Follow-Up Investigation

The investigator's duties don't end at the crime scene. Indeed, they may very well extend into the community to virtually any source of information that may be of value in the investigation. Accordingly, officers should not construe the follow-up investigation as a negative reflection on their investigative abilities. Conversely, it demonstrates that officers are conscientious enough to follow up on leads even after the preliminary investigation has long been concluded. Double checking addresses, possible escape routes, and other leads may provide the investigator with priceless new information. Tasks required of the follow-up investigator include the following:

LEARNING OUTCOMES 6 — Explain how to properly perform a follow-up investigation.

- Contacting the medical examiner
- Conducting a neighborhood canvass
- Preparing crime-scene reports

In addition, officers should analyze reports of officers conducting the preliminary phases of the investigation; review official reports; gather information on friends and associates of suspects; examine the victim's background; check police intelligence files to develop potential suspects; and organize police actions, such as neighborhood canvassing, raids, and search warrants. Let's now consider a few of the most important follow-up duties.

Contacting the Medical Examiner

The official determination regarding the death of the victim and circumstances surrounding the death is typically made by the **medical examiner** (or, in small jurisdictions, county coroner). The responding law enforcement agency's standard operating procedure (SOP) should set forth the circumstances regarding when these persons are contacted.

For example, some police organizations wait to call the medical examiner until after the crime-scene technicians have conducted preliminary investigations on the crime scene. Investigators must realize that in almost all jurisdictions, the medical examiner will have jurisdiction over the body, so police without proper authorization may not move it.

In the event that the responding officer must move the body, its position should be documented through the use of both

photographs and sketching. Additionally, tape or chalk should be placed on the floor to indicate to crime-scene investigators how the head, arms, and legs of the body were positioned. If possible, officers must take care to see that the body remains in exactly the same position in which it was found. Specifically, limbs that are bent should not be straightened; if the body was discovered lying face down, it should be left in or returned to the same position to avoid any shifting of the blood and subsequent altering of lividity.

Conducting a Neighborhood Canvass

A **neighborhood canvass** may also be in order during the early phases of an investigation. Although investigators may perform this function, the first officer on the scene might be directed to conduct a neighborhood or door-to-door canvass of the area to identify witnesses. This could focus not only on residents but also on employees of stores, delivery personnel, utility personnel, bus and taxi drivers, and so on—those who have specific knowledge of the crime or parts of the crime and general witnesses who can provide important background information about the victim and possible suspects.

Preparing Crime-Scene Reports

Both responding officers and those conducting follow-up investigations should prepare reports in accordance with departmental policy. At a minimum, crime-scene reports should include the following information:

- The date and time at which the officers arrived on the scene

- Relevant conditions at the time of arrival at the crime scene, including the weather and other observations

- The manner in which the crime was discovered and reported and the identity of the reporting individuals, if known, including their relationships to the victim or other persons involved

- Identity of any police officers or emergency personnel who were present at the time of arrival of the reporting officer or who arrived thereafter

- Physical evidence collected and the identities of those who collected it (special note should be made of any valuables discovered or collected, such as currency or jewelry)

- Full identification information, including name, address, telephone number, and other identifying data regarding witnesses to the crime

- The results of interviews with victims and witnesses, including the identities and descriptions of suspects, the methods of operation and other actions of the suspects, the means and route of escape used by the suspects, and so on

- Diagrams, sketches, photographs, videotapes, and other information prepared at the scene or afterward, including the identity of the persons, whether officers or civilians, who recorded or prepared these items

- Recommendations that may be helpful to the follow-up investigation (for example, the names of witnesses or other persons who may be able to provide additional information)

Performing the Follow-Up Investigation

The investigator's duties don't end at the crime scene. Indeed, they may very well extend into the community to virtually any source of information that may be of value in the investigation. Accordingly, officers should not construe the follow-up investigation as a negative reflection on their investigative abilities. Conversely, it demonstrates that officers are conscientious enough to follow up on leads even after the preliminary investigation has long been concluded. The investigator should remember that the follow-up investigation should build on what has been learned in the preliminary investigation. Double checking addresses, possible escape routes, and other leads may provide the investigator with priceless new information. Tasks required of the follow-up investigator include:

- Analyzing reports of officers conducting the preliminary phases of the investigation

- Reviewing official departmental records and mode of operation (MO) files

- Gathering information on friends and associates of suspects

- Examining the victim's background

- Checking police intelligence files to develop potential suspects

- Organizing police actions, such as neighborhood canvassing, raids, and search warrants

In summary, investigators must possess organizational skills that enable them to sift through detailed and fragmented pieces of information. As with organizational skills, personality traits can aid in communicating with people in the community who may possess valuable information.

Pressure, and More Pressure—The Impact of TV on Crime-Scene Processing

An Augusta, Georgia, television station recently joined in on what has been called by many the "CSI effect." Simply put, for many fans of the now numerous TV shows about crime-scene investigation and how it allegedly works, there is an "expectation" some viewers have about what is realistic and what is not when it comes to processing real crime-scene evidence. From older cases like the O. J. Simpson trial, which hinged on evidence the defense argued was contaminated at the crime scene, to the more recent JonBenét Ramsey case citing the quality of crime-scene evidence, this reality of expectations the public has is a growing concern to criminal justice professionals.

The CSI effect appears to be most visible in the courtroom, particularly among jurors. Prosecutors are concerned about the CSI effect among juries because they may question why everything isn't subject to forensic analysis when in fact not everything has to be. Equally, defense attorneys are concerned about the CSI effect because jurors may perceive the science of forensics as completely objective and totally accurate, thus ignoring the possibility of human or technical error.

Examples of the CSI effect include the following:

- A murder trial where jurors alerted the judge that a bloody coat introduced as evidence had not been tested for DNA. In fact, the tests were not needed because the defendant acknowledged being at the murder scene. The judge stated that TV had taught jurors about DNA tests, but not enough about when to use them.

corepics/Shutterstock.com

- A murder trial where jurors asked the judge if a cigarette butt found during the crime-scene investigation could be tested to see if it could be linked to the defendant. The defense team had ordered the tests but hadn't introduced them into evidence. Upon doing so, the tests exonerated the defendant, and he was acquitted.

- The fact that prosecutors are now being allowed to question potential jurors about their TV-watching habits.

Sources: Muniz, S. (2011). "Special assignment: CSI syndrome." WRDW-TV News 12, May 27; Roane, Kit R. [Dan Morrison]. (2005). "The CSI effect." *U.S. News & World Report*, April 17; Willing, R. (2004). "CSI effect has juries wanting more evidence." *USA Today*, August 5. Retrieved from www.usatoday.com/news/nation/2004-08-05-csi-effect_x.htm.

It has been said that because of movies and television shows portraying crime-scene investigations, jurors are becoming more and more insistent on forensic evidence. If this is true, then investigators must ensure that all proper investigative steps have been taken during each investigation—whether forensic evidence is discovered or not:

1. Using the chapter material and this information about the CSI effect, what do you think police departments and courts might do in order to address this phenomenon?

2. What responsibility (if any) do you think the entertainment industry might have in portraying crime-scene processing as accurately as possible? Provide detail in your response.

CHAPTER 3 — Processing the Crime Scene

Describe the preliminary investigation.

Generally, the term *preliminary investigation* is defined as an initial inquiry by officers to establish facts and circumstances of a suspected crime and to preserve any evidence related to that crime. Preliminary investigation includes securing the crime scene, considering the possible arrest of a suspect, locating and questioning witnesses and victims, documenting the crime scene, and identifying and collecting evidence.

1. How is the term *preliminary investigation* defined?

2. How does it apply to a crime scene?

3. What is the primary goal of the first officer responding to a crime scene?

4. What are the elements of the preliminary investigation?

preliminary investigation A term referring to the early stages of crime-scene processing, usually conducted by the first officer on the crime scene.

Identify types of crime-scene evidence.

Crime-scene evidence is dynamic. Protection and preservation of the scene are therefore crucial because both avert the possibility of contamination, loss, or unnecessary movement of physical evidence. In the evidence-collection process, contamination of evidence occurs most commonly when evidence is not properly secured, is wrongfully mixed with other types of evidence, or is altered significantly from its original condition at the crime scene.

1. What can investigators learn from physical evidence?

2. What are the two commonly used classifications of evidence, and how do they differ?

3. What role does trace evidence play in solving criminal cases?

4. Given the Locard exchange principle, why are all crimes ultimately solvable?

contamination of evidence The act of adversely affecting evidence by allowing it to be tampered with or by not protecting the chain of custody.

crime scene The location where the crime took place.

Locard exchange principle A criminological theory asserting that when perpetrators come into contact with the scene, they will leave something of themselves and take away something from the scene, for example, hairs and fibers.

trace evidence A minute or even a microscopic fragment of matter such as a hair or fiber that is not immediately detectable by the naked eye.

***corpus delicti* evidence** Evidence that establishes that a crime has been committed.

associative evidence Evidence that links a suspect with a crime.

Summarize the responsibilities of the first responding officer.

Remember that the initial response to a call by the responding officer is a critical phase of any criminal investigation. This response is typically made by patrol officers who must be prepared to initiate a preliminary investigation and carry out important and timely functions until they are relieved by supervisors or investigators.

1. What is the most important role of the responding officer to a crime scene?

2. What are the preliminary duties of the responding officer at a crime scene?

3. What measures must be taken to ensure that a crime scene is secured?

4. What information is included in a flash description?

5. In the description of suspects, why is it important to go beyond simple markers such as race and gender?

6. What are the dangers of improper initial actions of responding officers?

7. Why is it essential for responding officers to have excellent communication and organizational skills?

protective search A search conducted for officer safety that includes a quick search of the premises for additional suspects/persons or any weapons that could be acquired by such persons.

flash description An emergency radio broadcast, generally made by the first officer to reach a crime scene to other officers in the area, in which descriptions of the suspect and his or her vehicle are communicated.

CYMBL A rule that helps officers remember to include the necessary information for a suspect vehicle description: Color, Year, Make and model, Body style, License number.

LEARNING OUTCOMES 4

Explain how to secure and protect the crime scene.

One of the more important functions of responding officers is to ensure that neither their actions nor the actions of others will disturb the crime scene unnecessarily. Much too often, criminal evidence and many criminal cases have been lost because the crime scene was not adequately secured and protected.

1. What is the potential harm when a crime scene is not adequately secured and protected?

2. How is a contamination log used?

3. In securing a crime scene, what are the most important steps taken by responding officers?

4. What factors determine the definition and extent of a crime scene in a given case?

5. Name some equipment required at a crime scene.

contamination log Documents any evidence that has been compromised or for which the chain of custody has not been observed.

LEARNING OUTCOMES 5

Explain how to collect and search for evidence at the scene.

It is important to remember that after an investigator has properly documented a crime scene, the actual search must begin. Generally speaking, evidence discovered at the crime scene serves four objectives: (1) to determine the facts of the crime, (2) to identify the lawbreaker, (3) to aid in the perpetrator's arrest, and (4) to aid in the criminal prosecution of the perpetrator.

1. With the exception of any unusual circumstances, why is evidence at a crime scene recorded before any objects are collected or removed?

2. What is meant by the term *contamination of evidence*?

3. How is evidence discovered at the crime scene used in the investigative process?

4. What are examples of crime-scene evidence?

5. What are the phases of the crime-scene search?

6. How do the four common search patterns differ?

7. Which search-pattern method is best for outdoor crime scenes?

8. What is meant by the statement "evidence of crimes is dynamic"?

9. Why is the chain of custody an important aspect of the investigative procedures?

zone search method A searching technique; also known as the quadrant method.

grid search method A crime-scene search method whereby an area is sectioned off in square areas. Each square, averaging about 6 square feet, represents a specific search area that is a manageable size for each investigator.

chain of custody Documentation of all who handle evidence in a criminal case.

LEARNING OUTCOMES 6

Explain how to properly perform a follow-up investigation.

The investigator's duties don't end at the crime scene. Indeed, they may very well extend into the community to virtually any source of information that may be of value in the investigation. Accordingly, officers should not construe the follow-up investigation as a negative reflection on their investigative abilities. Conversely, it demonstrates that officers are conscientious enough to follow up on leads even after the preliminary investigation has long been concluded.

1. Why are follow-up investigations important?

2. How does the preliminary investigation relate to the follow-up investigation?

3. What are the responsibilities of the follow-up investigator?

4. What role does the medical examiner play in the investigation process?

5. Why is the neighborhood canvass important in the investigative process?

6. What are the most vital facts found in a crime-scene report?

medical examiner A public official who makes official determinations of the cause and time of death in wrongful death cases.

neighborhood canvass A door-to-door search of the area of a crime to identify witnesses.

Additional Links

www.science.howstuffworks.com

For those interested in learning more about Locard's exchange principle, this site provides an overview of the theory as well as background on Edmond Locard—the theory's creator. Additional articles include overviews on conducting autopsies, DNA analysis, and blood-pattern analysis, as well as other forensic science topics.

http://criminology.fsu.edu/faculty/nute/FScareers.html

For those who are interested in careers as medical examiners, this site provides information on medical examiner education, including a list of medical schools and colleges that offer programs, courses and classes overviews, and education requirements. **Degreedirectory.com** also includes job duties and career outlook information.

"The crime laboratory plays a pivotal role in successful criminal investigations."

4

Identifying Criminal Suspects: Field and Laboratory Processes

1 Summarize the role of the crime laboratory in a criminal investigation.

2 Identify the types and patterns of fingerprints, as well as how to search for fingerprints.

3 Explain the development and preservation of latent fingerprints.

4 Discuss the Integrated Automated Fingerprint Identification System.

5 Explain the role of DNA in criminal investigations.

6 Describe handwriting analysis.

7 Describe criminal composites.

8 Discuss the role of investigative analysis to solve crimes.

9 Explain the proper methods for conducting lineups.

TRACKING A SERIAL RAPIST

Aaron Thomas was considered by his New Haven, Connecticut, neighbors as no more than an odd nuisance—a man who lifted weights in the front yard, parked his tractor-trailer in his residential neighborhood, and rode his bicycle extraordinary distances. His girlfriend's son even described him as a laid-back person. But in February 2011, police collected DNA off of a discarded cigarette that subsequently matched the DNA database in the state police forensic lab confirming that Thomas was the "East Coast Rapist." The East Coast Rapist was wanted for 17 rapes and other attacks in Connecticut, Maryland, Rhode Island, and Virginia that began in 1997.

During the course of their 14-year-long investigation, police put up electronic billboards in the states where the attacks occurred and in neighboring states as well. A tip originated from Prince William County, Virginia, that directed investigators to Thomas. Although the origination of the tip, as well as Thomas's arrest, occurred during a short period of time, police worked for years pursuing the case. To the frustration of investigators, Thomas was able to elude the police even though the crimes he committed were typically committed outdoors. In some cases, the attacker was reported as wearing a mask or hooded sweatshirt to conceal his face. He would typically approach women outdoors on foot and threaten them with a knife, screwdriver, or handgun.

One can see by the Thomas case that of paramount importance to any criminal investigation is establishment of the identity of the perpetrator or victim. In the case of Thomas, it was DNA that revealed the perpetrator's identity, but determining the identity of a suspect can be accomplished through numerous investigative techniques.

DISCUSS Other than electronic billboards, what other techniques would you suggest that would encourage tips by the public to identify the rapist?

Although many investigative techniques used in suspect identification involve forensic procedures, forensics is not the primary focus of this text. Rather, the intent is to provide the reader with a basic understanding of some of the technological advances in suspect identification through brief offerings of some of the most innovative and effective techniques in this area.

▶ The Role of the Crime Laboratory in Criminal Investigation

The crime laboratory plays a pivotal role in criminal investigation. Thus, criminalists are major contributors to the investigative process. The duties and qualifications of criminalists vary

LEARNING OUTCOMES 1 Summarize the role of the crime laboratory in a criminal investigation.

greatly from one position to the next. For example, positions in crime labs include specialists in DNA (blood), trace evidence, handwriting analysis, toxicology, and ballistics, to name only a few. Students interested in becoming criminalists must be mindful of the very different job requirements and specific college coursework required to successfully compete.

Trace Evidence

The trace evidence unit identifies and compares specific types of trace materials that could be transferred during the commission of a violent crime. These trace materials include human hair, animal hair, textile fibers and fabric, ropes, and wood. Physical contact between a suspect and a victim may result in the transfer of trace materials such as hairs and fibers. The identification and comparison of these materials may often link a suspect to a crime scene or to physical contact with another individual. Torn pieces of fabric may be positively associated with a damaged garment, and broken pieces of wood can be fit together. Odontology (forensic dentistry) and physical anthropology (skeletal remains) examinations assist in the identification of human remains.

Questioned Documents

The questioned documents unit examines and compares data appearing on paper and other evidentiary materials. These surface data include handwriting, hand printing, typewriting, printing, erasures, alterations, and obliterations. Impressions in the surface of paper, such as those from indented writing or use of a check writer or dry seal, are also routinely evaluated by unit examiners, as are shoeprints and tire-tread impressions.

DNA Analysis

A crime laboratory's DNA analysis unit analyzes bodily fluids and bodily fluid stains recovered as evidence in violent crimes. Examinations include the identification and characterization of blood, semen, saliva, and other bodily fluids using traditional serological techniques and related biochemical analysis. After the stain has been identified, it is characterized by DNA analysis using the restriction fragment length polymorphism (RFLP) or polymerase chain reaction (PCR) technique. The results of the analyses are compared with results obtained from known blood or saliva samples submitted from the victims or suspects.

In 1996, a number of DNA crime laboratory analysis units began using mitochondrial DNA (mtDNA) analysis, which is applied to evidence containing small or degraded quantities of

DNA from hair, bones, teeth, and bodily fluids. The results of mtDNA analysis are compared with blood, saliva, or both submitted from victims or suspects. The unit examines evidence that may not have been suitable for significant comparison purposes before the development of this technique.

The **Mitochondrial DNA Population Database** is composed of complete nucleotide sequences of the first and second hypervariable segments of the control region of the human mitochondrial genome and consists of two main data sets. The first data set contains individuals from populations of forensic relevance and is contributed mostly by the Scientific Working Group on DNA Analysis Methods and forensic laboratories. The second data set, based on mtDNA concordance, contains nucleotide sequences from ethnic groups around the world.

Mitochondrial DNA Analysis

Both data sets are bundled in MitoSearch, a software package specifically designed for the compilation and analysis of mtDNA databases. MitoSearch estimates the relative frequency of specific sequences for the various populations represented within the database and assesses the relative relatedness of each population with reference to the size of each database.

Ballistics

The forensic ballistics unit receives and examines evidence related to firearms, firearm components, ammunition, ammunition components, tools, and toolmarks. Evidence in a typical case may include a number of recovered rifles, pistols, shotguns, silencers and other muzzle attachments, magazines, holsters, and a variety of fired and unfired cartridges. Lead and other metal fragments, shot wads, shot cups, and bullets removed from bodies during an autopsy are also frequently received items in firearms-related casework. Evidence submitted in toolmark cases may include screwdrivers, scissors, knives, pliers, wrenches, crowbars, hammers, saws, wire, sections of sheet metal, chains, safety deposit boxes, human bone or cartilage, plates, locks, doorknobs, bolts, and screens.

Latent Prints

The latent print unit conducts all work pertaining to the examination of latent prints on evidence submitted to the Federal Bureau of Investigation (FBI) laboratory. Latent prints are impressions produced by the ridged skin on human fingers, palms, and the soles of the feet. Unit examiners analyze and compare latent prints with known prints of individuals in an effort to make identifications or exclusions. The uniqueness, permanence, and arrangement of the friction ridges allow unit examiners to positively match two prints and determine whether an area of a friction ridge impression originated from one source to the exclusion of all others.

Various techniques, including use of chemicals, powders, lasers, alternate light sources, and other physical means, are used

The forensic photography unit is typically responsible for the following:

- Crime-scene and evidentiary photography
- Forensic photography
- Surveillance photography
- Aerial photography
- Venue photography
- Tactical imaging
- Photographic scanners
- Field photographic equipment
- Regional color photographic processing minilaboratories
- Silver-based and digital darkrooms
- Digital imaging technologies
- Courtroom presentations and exhibits

in the detection and development of latent prints. In instances in which a latent print has limited quality and quantity of detail, unit personnel utilize **Amido black protein**. This is an amino-acid-staining diazo dye used in biochemical research to stain for total protein on transferred membrane blots in microscopic examinations to affect conclusive comparisons.

Forensic Photography

A crime lab's forensic photography unit is responsible for imaging operations. This unit captures, processes, produces, analyzes, archives, and disseminates images using traditional silver-based photographic processes and digital imaging technologies.

Forensic photography is part of the process of evidence collection. It provides the investigator with photos of victims, places, and items involved in the crime. Photos of accidents show broken machinery, damaged vehicles, and so on. Photography of this kind involves choosing correct lighting, accurate angling of lenses, and a collection of different vantage points. Scales, items of length measurement or objects of known size, are often used in the picture so that dimensions of items are recorded on the image.

▶ Types and Patterns of Fingerprints

Identifying criminal suspects through the use of fingerprinting has proven to be one of the most effective methods for apprehending persons who might otherwise go undetected and continue their criminal activities. In addition to identifying criminal suspects, the use of fingerprinting also makes it possible to learn accurately the suspect's number (and type) of previous arrests and convictions. This, of course, often results in more appropriate sentences being handed down to repeat or career criminals. Early on, fingerprinting, because

LEARNING OUTCOMES 2

Identify the types and patterns of fingerprints, as well as how to search for fingerprints.

of its peculiar adaptability to the field, had been associated in the layperson's mind almost exclusively with criminal identification. Interestingly, the civil fingerprint file of the FBI contains three times as many fingerprints as the criminal file. Such files also provide a humanitarian benefit to society in general by identifying missing persons, amnesia victims, and unknown deceased people.

Few developments in crime solving have played a more exciting role than that dramatized by the fascinating loops, whorls, and arches etched on the fingers and palms of a human being. Although faults have been found with earlier identification systems, to date no two fingerprints have been found to be identical (see Figure 4–1).

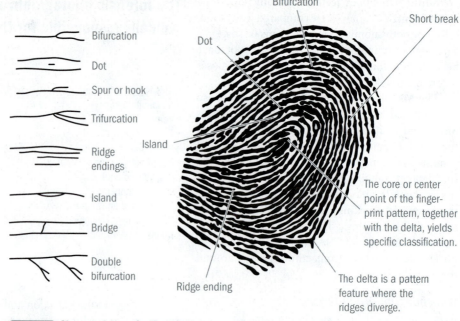

FIGURE 4–1 Characteristics of a Fingerprint.

Types of Prints

Among the most valuable clues for the investigator at the crime scene are fingerprints and palm prints. After such prints have been collected by investigators and evaluated by classification experts, a definitive determination can be made as to the exact identity of the suspect(s). Generally, fingerprints can be divided into three main groups: latent, plastic, and visible (see Box 4–1 and Figure 4–2).

Types of Patterns

The use of fingerprints for identification purposes is based on distinctive ridge outlines that appear on the bulbs on the inside

BOX 4–1 Types of Fingerprints

A **latent fingerprint** (also called a *patent fingerprint*) is one that occurs when the entire pattern of whorls on the finger, which contain small amounts of grease, oil, perspiration, or dirt, for example, is transferred to an object when it is touched. The grease and oil are usually natural and are transferred to the fingers when the person touches other areas of his or her body containing various bodily excretions. Latent prints include those not only visible to the naked eye but also those that can be examined properly only after development. Those are usually found on paper and smooth surfaces.

A **plastic fingerprint** results when a finger presses against plastic material and leaves a negative impression of friction ridges. Typically, these are found on recently painted surfaces; in wax, grease, tar, and putty; in the gum on stamps or envelopes; and on adhesive tape.

A **visible fingerprint** (also called a *dust print*) is a print that has been adulterated with foreign matter. If a finger is placed in a thin layer of dust, for example, the dust may cover the friction ridges. If the finger subsequently touches a clean surface, a visible fingerprint may result. A visible fingerprint may also develop as a result of touching other substances such as blood, flour, ink, or oil.

of the end joints of the fingers and thumbs. These ridges have definite contours and appear in several general pattern types. Each type has general and specific variations of the pattern, depending on the shape and relationship of the ridges (see Figure 4–1 for examples of fingerprint characteristics.) The ridge outlines appear most clearly when inked impressions are taken on paper, so that the ridges are black against a white background. This results from the ink adhering to the friction ridges. Impressions can be made by a variety of substances, including blood, dirt, grease, or any other foreign matter present on the ridges or the saline substance emitted by the glands through the ducts or pores that constitute their outlets. The background or medium may be paper, glass, porcelain, wood, cloth, wax, putty, silverware, or any smooth, nonporous material.

Fingerprints may be resolved into three large general groups of patterns: the arch, the loop, and the whorl. Each group bears the same general characteristics. Patterns can be further subdivided by means of the smaller differences existing between patterns in the same general group. Patterns are divided as follows:

- Arch loop
- Whorl
- Plain radial
- Plain tented
- Ulnar
- Accidental double
- Central pocket

Figure 4–2 shows examples of basic fingerprint patterns.

Before pattern definition can be understood, it is necessary to understand the meaning of a few technical terms used in fingerprint work. As far as classification is concerned, the

Plain Arch Tented Arch Plain Loop

Plain Loop Whorl Central Pocket Loop

Lateral Pocket Loop Twinned Loop Accidental

FIGURE 4-2 **Basic Fingerprint Patterns.**

Broken pieces of glass don't always fall inside a residence. Indeed, they may or may not be in the structure at all, or the burglar might pick up the pieces and throw them outside, out of the way. When attempting to climb through the window, the burglar may leave fingerprints on a window jamb, frame, or sill. The search for fingerprints should begin at the place of entry by the criminal.

Some burglars have been known to eat food or drink something while in a residence. The investigator must anticipate this and take care to preserve any fingerprints left on glassware (including liquor bottles) and even on some types of food (detectable by superglue fuming, discussed later). Electric light switches, circuit breakers, and light bulbs should also be examined closely for prints. If it has been determined that the burglar was wearing gloves, places where gloves would be awkward to wear

pattern area is the only part of the finger impression worth focusing on. It is present in all patterns, of course, but in many arches and tented arches, it is impossible to define. This is not important, however, because the only patterns in which one needs to define pattern areas for classification purposes are loops and whorls. The U.S. Department of Justice defines the pattern area as follows: the part of a loop or whorl in which appear the cores, deltas, and ridges with which we are concerned when classifying.[1] Type lines enclose the pattern areas of loops and whorls. *Type lines* may be defined as the two innermost ridges, which start parallel, diverge, and then surround or tend to surround the pattern area. Fingerprint impressions can be made from blood, dirt, grease, or the saline substance emitted by the glands through ducts or pores in the skin.

Searching for Prints

Investigators must be judicious in their search for fingerprints, as such evidence may be located in not-so-obvious places at the crime scene. In a burglary case, for example, the search for prints should begin at the place of entry by the criminal. Investigators should be able, at that point, to determine whether or not the burglar's hands were protected. If a door has been forced open, prints may be located on the lock or its immediate surroundings or in the general area of entry. When entry is gained through windows, broken glass should be searched for and documented. Generally, this method of entry involves the criminal breaking a piece of glass just large enough for a hand to reach through and open the latch.

Peter Kim Shutterstock.com

Investigator Using a Fiber Duster Fingerprint Brush to Dust for Fingerprints at the Crime Lab.

should be examined because the burglar may have removed the gloves to accomplish a particular task. Experience shows that this is common and that it typically occurs early in the commission of a crime. Many police officers have grown accustomed to wearing gloves during their crime-scene search. Today, this has become a recommended practice for the investigator's safety as well as to safeguard against contaminating the evidence.

► Development and Preservation of Latent Fingerprints

The sole purpose of developing, or lifting, a latent fingerprint impression is to make it visible so that it can be preserved and compared. Several powders and chemicals are used for this purpose in addition to several techniques designed to develop such evidence.

LEARNING OUTCOMES 3 — Explain the development and preservation of latent fingerprints.

The "Tools" of the Trade

Powders

When a latent print is clearly visible, it should be photographed before attempts are made to develop it. Accordingly, wet fingerprints should be allowed to dry before any attempt is made to develop them. Failure to do so will probably result in the print being destroyed. The powder method is used to develop fingerprints by making them show up on a surface where they would otherwise go unnoticed. To develop a latent fingerprint with powder, the powder used should contrast with the color of the surface of the print. The powder is lightly brushed over the print so it will adhere to the oils on the surface of the print pattern. Generally, gray and black powders are best for latent fingerprint development: gray for dark backgrounds and black for light backgrounds.

When brushing, the investigator should try to identify the contour of the ridges of the print so that brush strokes can go in the same direction. Powder particles will then affix themselves to the oily ridges of the fingerprint, and the print will become visible. Typically, beginners tend to use too much powder and too little brushing, thus making the print unidentifiable.

Iodine

Iodine is used on the premise that it attacks the object and changes its color. The grease and oils naturally produced by the skin discolor very easily and naturally become good candidates for development with iodine. Iodine prints, generally used on paper and wood, are temporary and begin to fade after the fuming has stopped. It is therefore necessary for the investigator to be prepared to photograph the prints immediately.

Ninhydrin

Another process, involving the development of prints using amino acids present as a result of perspiration, is generally the most common method of fingerprint development for latent prints. Solutions of ninhydrin in powder or aerosol form can be acquired from fingerprint supply companies. Similar to chlorides, amino acids permeate the friction ridges of the fingerprint and remain unchanged for an extremely long time. In some cases, prints have been developed on paper 30 or 40 years after they were deposited. One fundamental requirement is that the paper must have been stored under dry conditions from the time deposited to the time developed.

Silver Nitrate

Latent impressions developed by the use of silver nitrate are caused by the reaction of sodium chloride present in perspiration. When a person touches a surface with a sweaty finger, sodium chloride remains (almost indefinitely) while the other chemical compounds decompose. If a solution of silver nitrate is used on the impression, a chemical reaction occurs between the sodium chloride and the silver nitrate, resulting in the appearance of two new chemicals: sodium nitrate and silver chloride. Through the use of ultraviolet radiation or sunlight, the silver chloride is reduced to metallic silver, bringing out a brownish print.

Superglue Fuming

Cyanoacrylate resin, or superglue, was developed in the late 1950s as a bonding adhesive for metals and plastics. The substance was first used in fingerprinting, however, by the Japanese national police in 1978. Since then, the process has been refined and accepted as valuable for developing latent fingerprints on various types of surfaces. The use of superglue fuming is a relatively simple procedure and is particularly valuable in developing prints on plastic bags, metal foil, waxed paper, lacquered wood, leather, and almost all hard surfaces. Even fruits, vegetables, and dinner rolls have been processed successfully with this procedure. The process occurs as the fumes adhere to the friction ridges and then harden as ridge detail is built up on the print.

Lasers

The detection and development of latent fingerprints left at crime scenes have taken a quantum leap forward with the use of laser technology. Since its development in 1976, this technique has been used to develop prints that could not have been developed through the use of powders, iodine, ninhydrin, silver nitrate, or superglue fuming. The laser procedure is a clean, relatively easy method to develop prints, and pretreatment of the specimen is not required.

Preserving Fingerprints

Because of the importance of latent fingerprints in any criminal investigation, great care must be taken to preserve them for later examination and use in court. Fingerprints remain on affected areas for varying amounts of time, depending on whether they are plastic, visible, or latent. Generally, plastic and latent prints may remain for years, depending on the type of surface on which they are located. Methods of fingerprint preservation include photography of the print and lifting techniques.

Often, fingerprints are left on a surface that can be transported to the crime laboratory for examination. Undoubtedly,

The FBI's National DNA Database: CODIS

When scientists James Watson and Francis Crick first mapped the structure of the DNA double helix a half century ago, little did they know that they were also unleashing a powerful weapon in the fight against crime and terrorism. DNA can uniquely identify an individual in ways that even fingerprints can't. DNA is found in virtually every human cell. It can be extracted from hair, teeth, bones, and body fluids (blood, saliva, semen, even sweat!). It leaves traces on everything from cigarette butts to postage stamps, from shirt collars to napkins. And it lasts for years—even in harsh conditions, and even when there's little left of human remains. For example, after the September 11, 2001, attacks, investigators were able to find traces of DNA in the rubble of the World Trade Center that identified victims and brought some measure of closure and relief to their devastated families.

In 1990, the FBI began a pilot project called the **Combined DNA Index System**, or **CODIS**—which became fully operational in 1998. CODIS is a three hitter:

1. Computer technology (a database program and software)

2. Forensic science (DNA profiles rigorously measured and maintained)

3. Telecommunications (the ability of local, state, and federal labs to share information and communicate electronically)

Simply put, CODIS stores DNA profiles from across the country in a series of local, state, and national databases—all linked via computers—that enable crime labs at every level to share and compare DNA profiles electronically. Lightning-fast searches using CODIS can link DNA found at one crime to other crime scenes and to convicted criminals whose DNA is already on file.

The overwhelming majority—more than 1.5 million DNA profiles—come from convicted felons. Depending on the state, the felons include those serving time for rape, murder, crimes against children, robbery, burglary, kidnapping, and assault and battery.

The National DNA Index System (NDIS) also includes more than 78,000 DNA samples collected from crime scenes, more than 100 from missing persons and another 300 from relatives of missing persons, and some 150 from unidentified human remains. DNA samples from suspected terrorists are also collected today, but they are not uploaded to NDIS. When you add it all up, there are more than 1.6 million DNA profiles in the national system.

CODIS is used by a total of 175 crime labs in all 50 states and Puerto Rico, as well as the FBI lab and the U.S. Army Crime Lab. And, in a sign of how effective the system is, 31 labs in 18 nations worldwide also use CODIS, but they are not connected to any DNA databases here in the United States. They simply borrow the FBI's technology to help investigations in their own countries.

The success of CODIS is measured primarily by keeping tabs on the number of investigations helped by CODIS through a hit or match that wouldn't have otherwise been developed. According to the FBI, the National DNA Index (NDIS) contains over 10,867,894 offender profiles, 1,830,544 arrestee profiles, and 547,682 forensic profiles as of March 2014.[2] Ultimately, the success of the CODIS program is measured by the crimes it helps to solve. As of March 2014, CODIS had produced over 239,158 hits assisting in more than 229,704 investigations.[3]

Source: Federal Bureau of Investigation. (2014). Biometric analysis. Retrieved from http://www.fbi.gov/about-us/lab/biometric-analysis/codis/ndis-statistics.

---

this is the preferred way to facilitate classification of the print. Unfortunately, however, many prints must be processed at the crime scene because they are found on surfaces too large to transport. In general, plastic and latent prints can remain for years, depending on the type of surface on which they are located.

Fingerprint lifters are used to remove the print from surfaces that are curved or otherwise difficult to photograph. For surfaces such as these, rubber lifters are recommended. Rubber lifters are available at fingerprint supply houses and consist of a thin black or white flexible material coated with an adhesive. The adhesive side is guarded by a thin cover that is removed just before it is placed on the print and then replaced just after use. As a general rule, the latent fingerprint is dusted with print powder. The adhesive side of the lifter is then placed against the print and slowly pulled away. The print is preserved by the fingerprint powder being pressed against the lifter. After the print is lifted, the lifter cover is replaced.

Prints from Gloves

The notoriety of the success of fingerprinting has resulted in the use of gloves by many criminals as a protective measure.

Investigators may discover "smearing" from gloves at a crime scene but may give the matter little consideration. Indeed, such gloves—if located—may produce valuable evidence in locating the perpetrator. The glove itself may have a unique, identifiable pattern, as with a fingerprint.

▶ The Integrated Automated Fingerprint Identification System

The **Integrated Automated Fingerprint Identification System**, more commonly known as **IAFIS**, is a national fingerprint and criminal history database maintained by the FBI's Criminal Justice Information System (CJIS) Division. The IAFIS provides automated fingerprint search capabilities, latent searching capability, electronic image storage, and electronic exchange of fingerprints and responses 24 hours a day, 365 days a year. It combines with criminal histories, mugshots, scar and tattoo photos, height, weight, hair and eye color, and aliases to help match

LEARNING OUTCOMES 4 — Discuss the Integrated Automated Fingerprint Identification System.

evidence with identities. As a result of submitting fingerprints electronically, agencies receive electronic responses to fingerprint submissions within two hours for criminal cases and within 24 hours for civil fingerprint submissions.

The IAFIS maintains the largest biometric database in the world, containing the fingerprints and corresponding criminal history information for more than 47 million subjects in the Criminal Master File. The fingerprints and corresponding criminal history information are submitted voluntarily by state, local, and federal law enforcement agencies.

Just a few years ago, substantial delays were a normal part of the fingerprint identification process because fingerprint cards had to be physically transported and processed. A fingerprint check could often take three months to complete. The FBI formed a partnership with the law enforcement community to revitalize the fingerprint identification process, leading to the development of the IAFIS. The IAFIS became operational in July 1999, and some of its success stories are noted in Box 4–2.

▶ DNA and Criminal Investigations

Because of its success in identifying suspects, fingerprinting has proven to be one of the most effective methods in law enforcement. However, a dramatic advance in forensic science may now overshadow the technique of fingerprinting: **DNA technology**. DNA has given scientists the means with which to detect the remarkable variability existing between individuals. The re-

LEARNING OUTCOMES 5 Explain the role of DNA in criminal investigations.

sults of this technology hold great promise in aiding the criminal justice system in making positive determinations of criminal identity.

BOX 4–2 SUCCESSFUL STORIES OF THE IAFIS

Since its implementation, the IAFIS has been responsible for the successful identification of suspects in hundreds of cases. Examples are as follows:

1. *The case of the cocaine murderer.* In April 2004, a man was arrested in Connecticut by a drug task force for possession of cocaine. He was fingerprinted, and his electronic prints were sent to IAFIS. Ten minutes later, there was a match. It turns out he'd been wanted in Miami since September 2002 for fleeing the state to avoid being prosecuted for homicide, and he'd been wanted in Fort Lauderdale since October 2003 on homicide charges. In no time, he was picked up and extradited to Florida for prosecution.

2. *The case of the vicious rapist.* In June 2004, a man was arrested by police in New Jersey for simple assault and endangering the welfare of children. That turned out to be the tip of the iceberg. When officers fingerprinted the man and sent his prints to IAFIS, 13 minutes later there was a match! It turns out he'd been wanted in Norfolk, Virginia, since October 2000 for charges of rape and sexual abduction, and he'd been wanted in Yorktown, Virginia, since May 2001 for charges of kidnapping and sexual assault. In no time, he was facing charges in New Jersey before being shipped off to Virginia to face charges there.

3. *The case of the Christmas murderer.* In September 2004, a 57-year-old man was arrested in Massachusetts for slashing another man with a pocket knife. They'd been on a public bus, words were exchanged, and out came the knife. Fingerprints were taken at the booking station and sent to IAFIS. Turns out he was the man accused of a horrific crime in Baltimore in 1974. It was Christmas Eve, 30 years earlier, when police department employee McKinley Johnson was helping to put together food baskets for the poor. Suddenly, a young man approached and stole a can of lunch meat from one of the baskets. Johnson ran after him—and the thief shot him point blank. Before dying, Johnson identified his alleged assailant from photographs, and the hunt had been on ever since. Since that time, the suspect had lived in different places, assumed 10 different identities, and was arrested five times in Boston in the 1980s for charges from shoplifting to weapon possession. In the meantime, though, IAFIS was created, allowing matches of fingerprints nationwide. And so, with the slash of a pocket knife, 30 years on the run came to an end.

Source: Federal Bureau of Investigation. (2014). Retrieved from http://www.fbi.gov/about-us/cjis/fingerprints_biometrics/iafis/iafis.

Analyzing DNA

Genetic patterns found in blood or semen can be just as distinctive as fingerprints. Traditional serology tests on bodily fluids often do not discriminate enough to either exclude or include a suspect in a crime. DNA analysis provides much more conclusive analysis. The unique genetic patterns found in each person's DNA make it possible, with a high degree of accuracy, to associate a suspect with (or exclude a suspect from) a crime. Except in the case of identical twins, every person's DNA and resulting DNA pattern are different. (Figure 4–3 shows the steps of DNA analysis.) The process of analyzing, or "typing," DNA begins with DNA source material such as blood or semen. After the DNA is removed from the sample chemically, restriction enzymes known as endonucleases are added that cut the DNA into particles or fragments. The particles are then mixed with a sieving gel and sorted out according to size by a process called electrophoresis. In this process, the DNA moves along the gel-coated plate, some faster than others. At the completion of the process, the double-stranded fragments of DNA are treated so that the strands separate from each other.

Next, a transfer method developed by Edward Southern, called Southern blotting, is used. In this process, the DNA is transferred to a nylon membrane in much the same way that ink is transferred to a blotter. The nylon sheet is then treated with radioactively labeled DNA probes, single-stranded pieces of DNA that can bind through complementary base pairing with target DNA. Whereas a single-locus probe "looks" for only one field, a multilocus probe looks for numerous fields simultaneously.

The radioactive probe then merges with the specific DNA sequences found on the membrane fragments. The images that result from X-ray film placed in contact with the membrane to detect the probe configuration look like the price bar codes used on supermarket products.

These images are analyzed visually or by computer. Although not yet considered a routine procedure for all police agencies, it is clear that DNA will prove to be one of the most exciting and valuable investigative tools developed in recent decades, possibly even more significant than fingerprinting technology. As time goes on, there will undoubtedly be significant legal and scientific challenges to the application of DNA technology in crime solving. Certainly, however, as the "bugs" are worked out, society as a whole will be the beneficiary of this captivating science, which enables virtually positive identification of both criminal suspects and their victims.

Elimination Samples

As with fingerprints, the effective use of DNA may require the collection and analysis of elimination samples.[4] Elimination samples can be used to determine whether the evidence comes from the suspect or from someone else. It is important for the investigator, while still at the crime scene, to think ahead to the time of trial and possible defenses. For example, in the case of a residential burglary in which the suspect may have drunk a glass of water at the crime scene, an officer should identify appropriate people, such as household members, for future elimination sample testing.

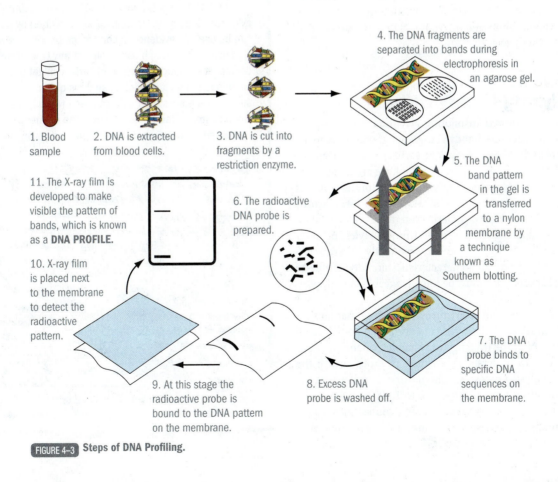

1. Blood sample
2. DNA is extracted from blood cells.
3. DNA is cut into fragments by a restriction enzyme.
4. The DNA fragments are separated into bands during electrophoresis in an agarose gel.
5. The DNA band pattern in the gel is transferred to a nylon membrane by a technique known as Southern blotting.
6. The radioactive DNA probe is prepared.
7. The DNA probe binds to specific DNA sequences on the membrane.
8. Excess DNA probe is washed off.
9. At this stage the radioactive probe is bound to the DNA pattern on the membrane.
10. X-ray film is placed next to the membrane to detect the radioactive pattern.
11. The X-ray film is developed to make visible the pattern of bands, which is known as a **DNA PROFILE.**

FIGURE 4–3 Steps of DNA Profiling.

What Is DNA?

In all life forms, from viruses to human beings, the basis for difference lies in the genetic material known as deoxyribonucleic acid (DNA). In every living organism, with the exception of certain viruses that possess ribonucleic acid (RNA), DNA represents a genetic facsimile, or "blueprint," of that organism. Additionally, in every cell within each human body, the DNA is identical. This applies whether the cell is a white or a red blood cell, a piece of skin, spermatozoa, or even a follicle of hair.

Although DNA is extremely complex chemically, it consists of only five basic elements: carbon, hydrogen, oxygen, nitrogen, and phosphorus. These five elements combine to form certain molecules known as nucleotides. The four bases that code genetic information in the polynucleotide chain of DNA are thymine, cytosine, adenine, and guanine (T, C, A, and G, respectively). Although just four letters exist in this short alphabet, a variety of different sequences of nucleotides exist. A single strand of DNA can be millions of nucleotides long. For example, 6 billion nucleotides constitute the DNA in one human being.

In human beings, 23 pairs of chromosomes originate from each parent: one of each pair from the mother and one from the father at the time of conception. Therefore, when a person is born, his or her genes are made up of a combination of maternal and paternal genes. Because of this, no two persons are exactly alike except identical twins.

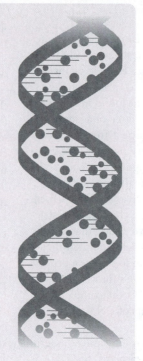

object containing handwritten or type-written markings and whose source or authenticity is in doubt may be referred to as a questioned document.[5]

Collection of Exemplars

Cases involving questioned documents require a comparison between the suspect document and a sample or exemplar (also known as a *standard*). Two types of **exemplars** exist: the requested and the collected. In both cases, its origin must be well documented before analysis to ensure genuineness.

Requested Exemplars

A requested handwriting standard is obtained from a suspect at the formal request of a law enforcement officer and is performed solely as a means to acquire a comparison document. It is logical to assume that no two samples of a suspect's handwriting are identical.

These samples may be needed for comparison with the saliva found on the glass to determine whether the saliva is valuable evidence. In homicide cases, be sure to collect the victim's DNA from the medical examiner at the autopsy, even if the body is badly decomposed. This may serve to identify an unknown victim or distinguish between the victim's DNA and other DNA found at the crime scene.

▶ Analyzing Handwriting

Similar to skills acquired in piloting an aircraft or interpreting a polygraph, accurate handwriting analysis requires many years of study and practice. From our earliest years in elementary school, we are taught how to sculpt letters of the alphabet meticulously to form words and sentences. People often adopt unique styles of their own, frequently characteristic only of that person. Such characteristics are identifiable to handwriting experts, who must be knowledgeable in both photography and microscopy.

LEARNING OUTCOMES 6 — Describe handwriting analysis.

Writings may occur in many forms, including that on personal correspondence, desks, walls, and even dead bodies. In all cases, they may offer the investigator valuable evidence in identifying suspects. To understand how best to proceed with the handwriting analysis process, we should first consider that the average handwriting specimen has 500 to 1,000 characters, including elements such as form, movement, connections, alignment, punctuation, slant, spacings, and embellishments. Any

Think About It . . . .

"That's Not My Writing Your Honor!" Unlike using video evidence, documents containing words written by a suspect can be used as evidence in connection to crimes given the circumstances. In such cases, almost any type of written document on almost any type of surface might shed light on someone's guilt. As noted, analysis of handwriting is an arduous process, sometimes even involving obtaining samples from dead bodies. What is the difference between "collected" and "requested" exemplars, and why are they important?

Photo of a Handwritten Note Found at a Crime Scene. The Analysis of Such Evidence can produce viable suspects.

Bruce Amos/Shutterstock.com

Therefore, a sufficient number of exemplars must be collected to demonstrate to the examiner the range of natural variations in a suspect's writing peculiarities. In the event that investigators might not be successful in obtaining exemplars of a suspect's handwriting, an exemplar may be obtained directly from the suspect.

Collected Exemplars

A collected handwriting exemplar is a sample of the suspect's handwriting that was not written for the purpose of examination and is not evidence in the crime under investigation. The obvious reason for this is that the sample document must be one that the suspect has not prepared or altered deliberately to match a suspect document.

The most valuable collected document is one that has been acquired close to the time the suspect document was produced. For example, if the document questioned was produced on a typewriter, an exemplar of the suspected typewriter would be collected. Accordingly, if the suspect's signature is in question, a standard of his or her handwriting must be collected. Typically, collected exemplars can be acquired from such documents as insurance policies, credit card receipts, canceled checks, and personal letters.

The Writing Medium

The process of collecting handwriting exemplars includes being sure that the writing instruments (for example, paper, pencils) used in the sample are the same as those used in the suspect document. Things to look for in selection of paper include its size, thickness, color, and condition. In short, the sample paper should match, as closely as possible, that used by the suspect.

If more than one sample document is being acquired from the suspect, they should not be stacked on top of each other. This is because writing impressions might press through one page to another and hinder their examination. Additionally, each handwriting sample should be taken from the suspect's sight as soon as it is obtained. This prevents the suspect from attempting to compare his writing from one exemplar to another.

The same type of instrument used for the document questioned should be furnished to the suspect for the control exemplar. This includes pencils, pens, felt-tip markers, and so on. Special attention should also be given to matching the lead number of a pencil, the color of an ink pen, and the width of a felt-tip marker to that used on the questioned document.

▶ *Criminal Suspect Composites*

One method of developing an idea of the suspect's general description is to have the witness provide information to a police artist so that a *facial composite* can be generated. In previous years, construction of the **composite** was done by a trained artist through drawing, sketching, or painting in consultation with a witness or crime victim. In the 1960s, techniques were devised for use by those who are less artistic, using interchangeable templates of separate facial features, such as

Smith & Wesson's **Identi-Kit**. More recently, computer-generated imaging systems have been developed, such as Smith & Wesson's Identi-Kit 2000®. Today the FBI maintains that hand drawing is still the correct method for constructing a facial composite. Many police agencies, however, use software because developed artistic talent is often not available. Technologically, the most popular software in the United States is FACES®, although other popular products are CompuSketch®, Mac-a-Mug®, and SuspectID®.[6]

LEARNING OUTCOMES 7 — Describe criminal composites.

Although the classic use of the facial composite is in a citizen recognizing the face as an acquaintance, there are other ways that a facial composite can prove useful. The facial composite can assist law enforcement in a number of ways:

- Identifying the suspect in a wanted poster
- Gathering additional evidence against a suspect
- Assisting investigation in checking leads
- Warning the public against serial offenders[7]

Facial composites have been used successfully to identify suspects in numerous cases. Included are the Oklahoma "Murrah Building" bomber Timothy McVeigh and the Baton Rouge serial killer Derrick Todd Lee.[8] They have also been used extensively in television programs, such as *America's Most Wanted*,[9] that aim to reconstruct major unsolved crimes with the intent of gaining information from the members of the public.

PHANTOMBILD LKA NRW 251 / 07

Police Composite Sketch of Subject.

Ho Police/Afp/Getty Images

WANTED

SAN FRANCISCO POLICE DEPARTMENT

NO. 90-69   WANTED FOR MURDER   OCTOBER 18, 1969

ORIGINAL DRAWING   AMENDED DRAWING

Supplementing our Bulletin 87-69 of October 13, 1969. Additional information has developed the above amended drawing of murder suspect known as "ZODIAC".

WMA, 35-45 Years, approximately 5'8", Heavy Build, Short Brown Hair, possibly with Red Tint, Wears Glasses. Armed with 9 MM Automatic.

Available for comparison: Slugs, Casings, Latents, Handwriting.

ANY INFORMATION:
Inspectors Armstrong & Toschi
Homicide Detail   THOMAS J. CAHILL
CASE NO. 696314   CHIEF OF POLICE

Sketch of the "Zodiac Killer."

▶ Investigative Analysis to Solve Crimes

For years, the means of identifying the type of person responsible for a particular crime was known as personality profiling. Today, the process, known as **criminal investigative analysis**, is accomplished by identifying psychological and social characteristics surrounding the crime as well as the manner in which it was committed. An example is the Unabomber case, in which mail bombs killed

LEARNING OUTCOMES 8 — Discuss the role of investigative analysis to solve crimes.

four people in a period spanning 15 years. Forensic investigators subsequently determined that the bomber chose his postage carefully, using Frederick Douglass stamps when he wanted to injure his targets and stamps of playwright Eugene O'Neill when he intended to kill. O'Neill's plays were known for their dark themes.

One of O'Neill's plays, *Dynamo*, was highly critical of America's growing reliance on machinery and industrialization,

a theme echoed in the Unabomber's manifesto. The profiling technique can be advantageous in illuminating certain clues at the crime scene that may not be apparent upon first examination. For example, hate, passion, fear, and confusion may all have certain indicators somewhere at the scene, such as postmortem slashing or cutting, rapes, lust and mutilation murders, and so on.

The practice of profiling was developed during World War II by government psychologist William Langer to predict Adolph Hitler's future actions. As it relates to criminal investigation, profiling is based on the notion that crime is, directly or indirectly, based on the personality of the person committing it. Profilers typically scrutinize evidence found at the crime scene and attempt to re-create the circumstances surrounding the crime and to predict the offender's frame of mind. The profile is then used to narrow down the list of suspects as it develops. From a practical standpoint, profiling can be helpful in investigating any crime in which the evidence suggests that the suspect is irrational or mentally or emotionally unstable.

Profiling gained popularity during the 1980s, when the FBI became heavily involved in the profiling of violent sex offenders and arsonists. More recently, caregivers with a disorder called Munchausen syndrome by proxy (MSBP) have become the subject of profilers. The disorder involves offenders who injure or cause illnesses in their children to gain attention and sympathy for themselves. Past cases have revealed that most suspects are women who victimize their children so as to become the center of attention by police, doctors, family members, and others. MSBP is thought to be a serial offense usually affecting families with more than one child. Characteristics of offenders include a history of self-inflicted wounds, past psychiatric treatment, past attempted suicides,

The profiling technique requires the collection of certain types of information:

- **Photographs** focused on the extent and depth of wounds

- **Neighborhood information**, including racial, ethnic, and social data

- **Medical examiner's report**, including photos of damage to the body—such as stabs, gunshots, bruises, and lividity—and information regarding toxicology, postmortem wounds, and personal observations of the medical examiner

- **Map of the victim's travel before death**, including residence and employment information, where last seen, and crime-scene location

- **Complete investigation report of the incident**, such as date, time, location, type of weapon used, and detailed interviews of witnesses

- **Background of victim**, including age, race, gender, physical description, marital status, lifestyle, sexual preference, medical history (physical and mental), personal habits, use of alcohol or drugs, and friends or enemies

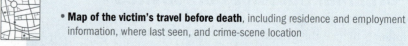

a middle- to upper-class background, a better-than-average education, and knowledge of the medical field and related procedures.

The field of psychological profiling continues to grow as new areas are developed. Two of the newest areas include hostage negotiation and terrorism.[10] The psychological profiling technique was used successfully by the FBI in the investigation of Theodore (Ted) Bundy, the serial murderer responsible for the murders of 30 young women in the northwestern United States between 1973 and 1978.

According to John Douglas and Robert Ressler of the FBI, most (normal) persons have personality traits that are more or less identifiable. However, an abnormal person tends to become more ritualized and tends to display a "pattern" to his or her behavior. Often, the suspect's personality is reflected in both the crime scene and in the furnishings of his or her home. Because of the nature of such evidence, the profiling procedure has limitations and should be used in conjunction with other investigative techniques.

As noted, the psychological profiling technique recognizes that emotions such as hate, passion, fear, and confusion may all have certain indicators somewhere at the scene. After the information has been collected, the investigator analyzes the information and attempts to reconstruct the event. Techniques used are brainstorming to critique the case, use of intuition to follow hunches, and educated guessing. Profiling factors do not consist of clinical observations solely, but rather a collection of investigative data from which to draw inferences about the suspect, victim, and motive of the crime.

▶ Conducting Lineups

One recurring problem in criminal investigation is the overreliance by criminal investigators on eyewitness accounts of crimes. This is especially a concern when the identification of a criminal suspect relies heavily on the word of eyewitnesses or victims. The problem is pervasive. For example, in 2009 the Innocence Project reported: "Eyewitness misidentification is the single greatest cause of wrongful convictions nationwide, playing a role in more than 75% of convictions overturned through DNA testing."[11] For more than 30 years, research has proven the unreliability of eyewitnesses testimony.[12] For example, (1) criminal suspects have been identified by eyewitnesses seated in the back of a patrol vehicle, a long distance away on a dimly lit street; (2) witnesses have been shown photo arrays in which only one photo is clearly marked with an "R"; (3) witnesses have changed their physical description of a criminal suspect after speaking with police and learning additional information about the suspect; (4) eyewitnesses and victims have been reluctant in identifying a suspect, but at trial prosecutors inform the jury that witnesses did not waiver in their identification.[13] Many such cases have resulted in innocent persons being wrongfully accused and convicted of crimes they did not commit.

LEARNING OUTCOMES 9 — Explain the proper methods for conducting lineups.

It is common in criminal investigations for investigators to place an overreliance on eyewitness identifications. Experience and research have shown that civilian eyewitnesses frequently prove to be unreliable observers, and erroneous identifications are often the result. Numerous factors contribute to misidentifications by eyewitnesses. For example, human perception tends to be inaccurate, especially under stress. The average citizen, untrained in observation and subjected to the stress of being a victim of or witness to a crime, is seldom able to describe a perpetrator accurately even, in some cases, after coming face to face with the individual. Also, a witness, especially one who is unsure what the perpetrator actually looked like, may be easily influenced by suggestions conveyed to him or her during the identification process. This fact was recognized in *United States v. Wade*, in which the Supreme Court of the United States stated,

> The influence of improper suggestions upon identifying witnesses probably accounts for more miscarriages of justice than any other single factor. Perhaps it is responsible for more such errors than all other factors combined.[14]

Law enforcement officers can also cause misidentifications by suggestive words or conduct. The average witness, anxious to make an identification and influenced by the police officer's image as an authority figure, tends to be very sensitive to any suggestion made by the police regarding the identity of the perpetrator. Officers may, intentionally or unintentionally, convey to the witness by words or conduct that a particular person being viewed is the perpetrator.

As a result, great care must be taken by officers conducting identification sessions of any type to avoid any action that might lead to an erroneous identification. Carefully adhering to the proper identification procedures will help avoid misidentifications that may lead to unjust accusations or even erroneous convictions of innocent persons and divert the investigation away from the actual offender. In addition, even if the actual offender is caught and brought to trial, using improper identification procedures during the investigation often causes the

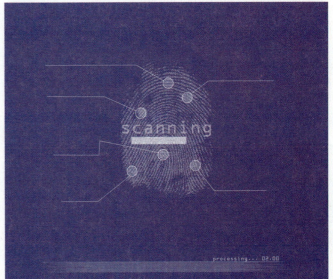

Fingerprint Recognition Interface.

wavebreakpremium/Fotolia

Factors Determining Reliability of Suspect Identification.

suppression of identification evidence at trial, resulting in dismissal of the charges or otherwise making it difficult or even impossible to convict the guilty party.

If a court determines that an identification procedure was excessively suggestive, the court may prohibit introduction of the evidence in question. It may rule that any in-court identification of the accused by the victim is inadmissible, suppress other evidence that was obtained as a result of an improper pre-trial identification procedure, or both. Of course, any of these actions may result in prosecution being thwarted.

Today, in evaluating proper identification procedure, the courts are generally concerned with whether it was suggestive. If the court finds that the procedure was suggestive, the court will then proceed to determine whether, despite the suggestiveness, the identification was reliable when considering the "totality of the circumstances."[15]

If, in view of these various factors, it appears that the identification was reliable despite the suggestiveness of the procedure, evidence of the identification will be admissible to bolster a subsequent in-court identification.

Identification Procedures

For purposes of this chapter, identification procedures may be categorized as photo identifications, lineups, or show-ups. Photo identification procedures may involve the showing of one or several photographs to a witness for the purpose of obtaining an identification. In a **lineup**, eyewitnesses are presented simultaneously with a number of individuals.

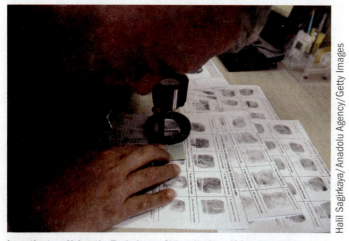

Investigators Using the Technique of Visually Classifying Fingerprints Located on Fingerprint Cards.

Halil Sagirkaya/Anadolu Agency/Getty Images

Types of Lineups

For the most part, the function of a police lineup is to identify a suspect. Lineups are typically shown to victims of crimes or eyewitnesses to crimes. From a procedural standpoint, a police lineup involves placing a suspect among people not suspected of committing the crime (fillers) and asking the victim or eyewitness if he or she can identify the perpetrator. This can be done using a live lineup of people or, as more commonly done in the nation's police departments, a lineup of photographs. Live lineups typically use five or six people (a suspect plus four or five fillers) and photo lineups include six or more photographs.[16] Most police departments in the United States use photo lineups. There are two common types of lineups: simultaneous and sequential.

The type of lineup used by most police departments across the nation is the **simultaneous lineup**.[17] In this lineup, the eyewitness views all the people or photos at the same time. In comparison, a **sequential lineup** involves people or photographs that are presented to the witness one at a time.

In either model, the lineup administrator can be blind—meaning he or she does not know the identity of the suspect—or non-blind—meaning the administrator knows the identity of the suspect.

Historically, the investigator knows who the suspect is.[18] Critics suggest that in these cases, lineup administrators might either knowingly or unintentionally give the witness verbal or nonverbal cues as to the identity of the suspect. For example, if the eyewitness identifies a filler, the investigator might say to the witness, "Take your time. . . . Make sure you look at all the photos."

Such a statement may effectively lead the witness away from the filler.[19] However, in a "double-blind" lineup, neither the officer administering the lineup nor the witness knows the identity of the suspect, so there is no way the officer administering the lineup can influence the witness in any way.[20] In 2008, the National Institute of Justice reported that other variables can affect the outcome of police lineups, including the following:[21]

- *Pre-lineup instructions given to the witness.* This includes explaining that the suspect may or may not be present in the lineup. Research on pre-lineup instructions by Nancy Steblay, Ph.D., professor of psychology at Augsburg College in Minneapolis, Minnesota, revealed that a "might or might not be present" instruction reduced mistaken identification rates in lineups where the suspect was absent.[22]

- *The physical characteristics of fillers.* Fillers who do not resemble the witness's description of the perpetrator may cause a suspect to stand out.[23]

- *Similarities and differences between witness and suspect's age, race, or ethnicity.* Research suggests that when the offender is present in a lineup, young children and elderly people perform nearly as well as young adults in identifying the perpetrator. When the lineup does not contain the offender, however, young children and elderly people commit mistaken identifications at a rate higher than young adults. Research has also indicated that people are better able to recognize faces of their own race or ethnic group than faces of another race or ethnic group.[24]

Live Police Lineups: How Do They Work?*

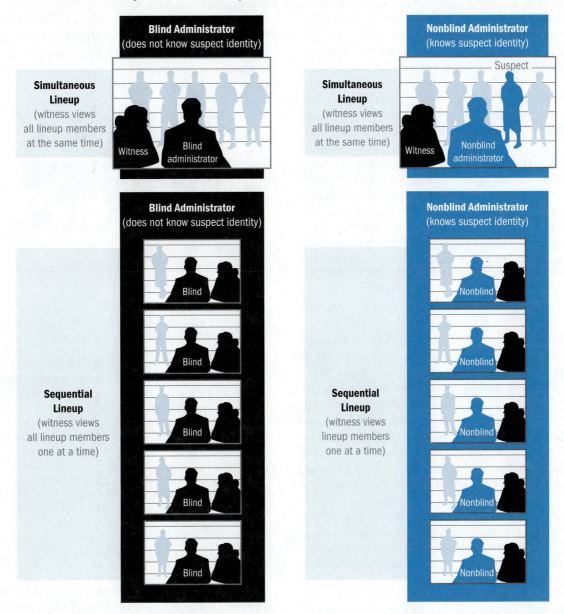

* Most U.S. police departments use photo lineups. The same concepts depicted in this graphic—simultaneous and sequential, blind and nonblind—apply in photo lineups.

- *Incident characteristics, such as the use of force or weapons.* The presence of a weapon during an incident can draw visual attention away from other things, such as the perpetrator's face, and thus affect an eyewitness's ability to identify the holder of the weapon.[25]

In summary, the most common lineup procedure in use by law enforcement is the simultaneous lineup.[26] Researcher Gary Wells argues, however, that during simultaneous lineups, witnesses use **relative judgment**. This means that they compare lineup photographs or members with each other rather than to their memory of the offender. This is a problem when the

perpetrator is not present in the lineup because the witness will often choose the lineup member who most closely resembles their recollection of the perpetrator.[27]

On the other hand, during sequential lineups, witnesses must make a decision about each photograph or member before moving on to the next, prompting them to use **absolute judgment**. In other words, witnesses compare each photograph or person only with their memory of what the offender looked like.[28]

Research shows that the double-blind sequential method, in which the officer conducting the lineup does not know the identity of the suspect, produces fewer false identifications than the traditional simultaneous method.[29]

Photo Lineups The photo lineup is a commonly used investigative technique to identify suspects. When used improperly, however, innocent persons can be singled out for prosecution. This very thing occurred in the case of Calvin Willis.

Late one night in 1982, three young girls were sleeping in their Shreveport, Louisiana, home when a man wearing cowboy boots entered their house and raped the oldest girl, who was only 10 years old. The police responded, and during their investigation learned that all three girls remembered the attack differently. One investigator reported that the victim did not see her attacker's face. In a different report that was never produced at trial, a suspect who resided in the neighborhood, Calvin Willis, was named as the attacker. During the trial, the victim's mother testified that the neighbors had mentioned Willis's name when speculating who might have committed the crime. The 10-year-old victim testified at trial that she was shown photos and instructed to pick the man without a full beard. She also stated that she didn't pick anyone but investigators said she picked Willis. The jury convicted Willis and sentenced him to life in prison. In 2003, DNA testing proved that Willis did not commit the crime and he was released from prison after serving 22 years.[30]

Photo identifications may take a number of forms. If a single photo is shown to the witness, the photo identification has all of the shortcomings of the show-up (discussed on pages 79–80) and is generally regarded by the courts as improper and suggestive. Consequently, multiple-photo procedures are preferable. In such procedures, the photos may be shown individually, one at a time, or displayed simultaneously in a book or array. This procedure is similar to a physical lineup (discussed next), and virtually all of the cautions set forth for lineups in the preceding discussion apply to multiple-photo identification procedures as well.

The courts have approved the proper use of photographs to obtain identification of a perpetrator.[31] However, the courts appear to prefer that photo identification procedures be used only to develop investigative leads. Some courts have criticized the practice of using photo identifications after the suspect has been arrested, preferring that after the suspect is in custody and therefore readily available, a lineup be used for eyewitness identification.[32]

Physical Lineups The lineup, if properly conducted, is significantly less suggestive than the show-up and hence is generally far preferable. Nevertheless, police officers conducting a lineup must use caution to avoid suggestive influences. Studies of witness psychology reveal that lineup witnesses tend to believe that the guilty party must be one of the individuals in the lineup. Consequently, witnesses tend to pick out the person in the lineup who most closely resembles their perception of the perpetrator, even though the perpetrator is not in fact present.

In addition, it is possible that witnesses, in an effort to please the police officers conducting the lineup, feel obligated to pick out someone from the lineup rather than "disappoint" the officers.[33] Such witnesses are often sensitive to, and strongly influenced by, clever clues conveyed by the officers that may indicate to the witness that the officer believes a particular individual in the lineup is the perpetrator. This makes it even more important that officers conduct the lineup—and their own behavior—in a nonsuggestive manner.

Preparing for a lineup may be as important to the validity of the procedure as actually conducting it. Selecting individuals for the lineup is a particularly important issue. In determining which individuals are to be presented to the witnesses in a lineup, the following principles should be observed:

1. *The lineup should consist of individuals of similar physical characteristics.* Witnesses tend to pick out anyone who stands out from the rest of the group in any significant way. Therefore, the individuals who appear in the lineup should be reasonably similar with respect to age; height; weight; hair color, length, and style; facial hair; clothing; and other characteristics, such as glasses. Of course, the individuals must be of the same race and gender. Absolute uniformity of the lineup participants is obviously unattainable and is not procedurally necessary.[i]
2. *The lineup should consist of at least five or six persons.* The smaller the lineup, the less objective it is. A lineup with only two or three persons is little better than a show-up, and suggestive factors become excessively influential. As a result, most authorities recommend that at least five, preferably six, persons be in the lineup. In addition, some authorities caution against the use of plainclothes police officers in lineups because they do not naturally look or act like suspects, a factor that causes witnesses to reject them as possibilities.

[i] *U.S.* v. *Lewis*, 547 F. 2d 1030, 1035 (8th Cir. 1976)

Preparing a witness for viewing the lineup is another important consideration. Preparation should be limited to nonsuggestive statements, such as explaining the procedure that will be used and making it clear that the individuals in the lineup will be unable to see him or her. Officers should avoid taking any action or making any statement that will adversely affect the validity of the lineup. In particular, before a lineup, officers should avoid the following:

1. Showing the witness any photos of the suspect[34]

2. Conducting a show-up with the suspect or allowing the witness—accidentally or otherwise—to see the suspect, such as in an office or holding cell, before the lineup

3. Making suggestive statements to the witness, such as telling the witness that the person whom the police suspect will be in the lineup. Professional standards in criminal investigation now require investigators to tell the witness that the perpetrator may not be among those in the lineup.

Other common errors that should be avoided include telling the witness that another witness has identified someone in the same

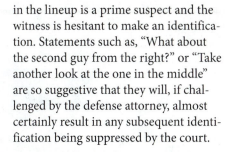
lineup, advising the witness to take special notice of some particular individual in the lineup, or making any other statement or action that may cause the witness to focus on a particular individual or to think that he or she must pick out somebody. Finally, if more than one witness is to view a lineup, the witnesses should be kept separated before the lineup and should not be permitted to discuss the case with each other, compare descriptions, and so forth.

As a safeguard, officers who are not associated with the case should handle the procedure if possible. This helps to minimize the possibility that the officers who are conducting the investigation will, in their zeal to solve the case, convey (inadvertently or otherwise) clues to the witness as to which person to pick out or put pressure on the witness to pick out somebody.

The following should also be observed in conducting lineups:

1. *Statements that put pressure on the witness to make an identification should be avoided.* Witnesses are anxious to please the officers conducting the lineup, so they should not be made to feel that they are expected to pick out someone. For example, telling a witness that the person the police suspect is in the lineup or urging a hesitant witness to make an identification or to "try harder" would be improper.

2. *Statements that may cause the witness to focus on a particular individual should be avoided.* The same sort of statements discussed in regard to witness preparation should be avoided during the actual conduct of the lineup. Officers are often tempted to prompt a witness when someone

in the lineup is a prime suspect and the witness is hesitant to make an identification. Statements such as, "What about the second guy from the right?" or "Take another look at the one in the middle" are so suggestive that they will, if challenged by the defense attorney, almost certainly result in any subsequent identification being suppressed by the court.

3. *The lineup should be presented to one witness at a time.* The common practice of having a group of witnesses view a lineup simultaneously should not be permitted. Courts, including the U.S. Supreme Court,[35] have disapproved of multiple-witness lineups. If, for some reason, more than one witness must be present simultaneously, witnesses should be required to make their identifications silently in writing and should not be permitted to discuss the identification aloud with each other or with the officers present.

4. *If possible, conduct a "blank" lineup.* Conducting two or more lineups, where one lineup includes the suspect and the others do not, assists the prosecution in later refuting any claim by the defense that the lineup was too small or was suggestive.

5. *If multiple lineups are to be conducted for the same witnesses, do not put the suspect in more than one.* Seeing the same face in a second lineup may cause the witness to erroneously "recognize" the person as the perpetrator, merely because the face is familiar from the first lineup. Because of this, the courts have disapproved of this practice.[36]

After the lineup, certain precautions should be taken. For example, as mentioned, when more than one witness has viewed a lineup, witnesses should be kept separate after the lineup procedure has been completed. Although discussions between witnesses following a lineup will presumably not render any previously made identification invalid, they may affect the admissibility of a subsequent in-court identification of the defendant by these witnesses during the trial itself.

Additionally, witnesses should not be praised or congratulated for picking out the suspect. This may serve to reinforce a shaky identification, convincing the witness that he or she has picked out the actual perpetrator when the witness is in some doubt. In addition to increasing the chances of a miscarriage of justice, this may lead to suppression of a later in-court identification of the perpetrator by the same witness.

Show-Ups

In a "show-up," the witness is confronted with one suspect only (as opposed to an array). The show-up has been widely

When used, station house show-ups should, at a minimum, be subject to the following guidelines:

1. Show-ups should not be conducted when the suspect is in a cell, manacled, or dressed in jail clothing.
2. Show-ups should not be conducted at a late hour.
3. Show-ups should not be conducted with more than one witness present at a time. If show-ups are conducted separately for multiple witnesses, the witnesses should not be permitted to communicate before or after the show-up regarding the identification of the suspect.
4. The same suspect should not be presented to the same witness more than once.
5. Show-up suspects should not be required to put on clothing worn by the perpetrator, to speak words uttered by the perpetrator, or to perform other actions mimicking those performed by the actual perpetrator.[i]
6. Words or conduct by the police that may suggest to the witness that the individual is or may be the perpetrator should be scrupulously avoided. For example, one should never tell the witness that the individual was apprehended near the crime scene, that the evidence points to the individual as the perpetrator, or that other witnesses have identified the individual as the perpetrator. Unfortunately, the mere fact that the individual has been presented to the witness for identification strongly suggests that the officers believe him or her to be the guilty party.

[i] Although such requirements may sometimes be properly imposed during a lineup, the show-up is so inherently suggestive that the same court that would approve its use in a lineup may find it excessively suggestive when used during a show-up.

condemned by the courts and by experts in law, law enforcement, and law enforcement identification procedures.[37] Whereas the courts have not held show-ups to be categorically improper, they have ruled that the determination of whether a specific show-up was excessively suggestive will be made based on the "totality of the circumstances" attending that particular show-up. In practice, evidence deriving from show-ups is frequently suppressed because the show-up is so inherently suggestive that it is virtually impossible to eliminate suggestion from the procedure.

Consequently, the use of show-ups should be avoided whenever possible. Only when exigent circumstances make it absolutely necessary should this technique be used. When it must be used, certain guidelines should be followed to minimize the **suggestiveness** of the procedure and the risk of suppression of any resultant identification evidence. A suggestive identification technique is one that unduly narrows down the victim's/witnesses' options so that a particular suspect is chosen.

Even when these guidelines are followed, it is entirely possible that a court may suppress the resulting evidence on the grounds that no amount of care can eliminate suggestion, and hence unreliability, from the procedure.

Yet exigent circumstances may justify the use of show-ups in certain instances. For example, in certain instances, a station house show-up may be tolerated by the courts if it can be demonstrated that time or other factors prevented the police from arranging a proper lineup. However, the reasons for not taking the time to prepare and conduct a lineup must be substantial

and reasonably explained. Even then, they may not be accepted by the courts.

Exigent circumstances may also justify a show-up in the field. A show-up conducted shortly after the commission of the offense and in reasonable proximity to the crime scene may be tolerated by courts. The court may recognize that the realities of the situation often make it vital that a witness view a suspect immediately at or near the scene. Courts have noted that this procedure has potential advantages both for the suspect and the police. If the identification is negative, it will result in the freeing of the suspect and permit the officers to devote their time and attention to other leads. If the identification is positive, the police can focus their attention on the identified suspect. Consequently, some courts are more willing to tolerate this type of show-up.

The Right to Counsel at Eyewitness Identifications

In 1967, the Supreme Court of the United States held that a suspect has a right to counsel at a postindictment lineup (see Box 4–3).[38] Subsequently, the Court expanded this ruling to provide for a right to counsel at any lineup conducted after formal adversary proceedings have been initiated against the suspect, whether by way of formal charge, preliminary hearing, indictment, information, or arraignment.[39] There is, however, no right to have counsel present at a lineup conducted before such adversary proceedings have been initiated. These same rules apply to show-ups. However, there is no right to counsel at photo identification sessions.[39] The purpose of having counsel present at the identification is to enable counsel to detect any suggestiveness or other irregularities in the procedure. It should be recognized, however, that the presence-of-counsel requirement may actually help the police in certain instances. First, the department's goal should be to avoid any possibility of an erroneous identification and a resultant miscarriage of justice.

Therefore, the presence of counsel may be regarded as a positive step in preventing any such occurrence. In addition, if counsel is present and acquiesces in the procedure being used, this may preclude any subsequent defense contention that suggestiveness or other impropriety occurred. This will strengthen the prosecution's case. Therefore, to the extent that defense counsel is responsible and objective, cooperation with counsel in constructing and conducting a nonsuggestive and otherwise proper identification procedure may benefit all concerned.

DNA's First Case: The Narborough Murders

The November 1983 discovery of a murdered 15-year-old girl in the English village of Narborough ultimately had an enormous impact on international criminal investigation.

Before the four-year murder investigation was completed, a scientific discovery was applied that not only solved a double criminal homicide but also completely revolutionized forensic identification: the mapping of DNA fragments. At first, the murder of Lynda Mann was barely noticed outside the area known as Leicestershire, but it soon launched one of the biggest homicide investigations in English history. A squad of more than 150 detectives was formed and exhausted every lead in the case. So thorough was the investigation that every male between the ages of 13 and 34 living in the area of the murder was noted and in many cases questioned. Nonetheless, no murder suspect was apprehended.

lightpoet/Shutterstock.com

Then, in July 1986, 15-year-old Dawn Ashworth, also of Leicestershire, was found brutally raped and strangled. The MO indicated the same killer and alerted authorities to the possibility of a serial killer. This time, more than 200 investigators from all across the country were placed on the case. Word of the killings began to be cause for concern in almost all of England, but investigators were still unable to develop significant indicators as to whom the killer might be. At last, a case against one suspect was developed. A 17-year-old hospital kitchen porter linked to the murder through circumstantial evidence was arrested. After interrogation, the suspect admitted to the second killing but denied the first, despite the belief by the police that both victims were murdered by the same person.

The ultimate solution to the problem was found only a short distance away, at Leicester University. Alec J. Jeffreys, a university scientist working in the field of genetic research since the early 1980s, had recently discovered a process of human identification based on the DNA molecule. Whether the suspect's father or the British police first initiated contact with Jeffreys is still under dispute, but the scientist was well known for his work in a paternity lawsuit in which DNA technology established the identity of the father. In the Narborough murders, Jeffreys analyzed a semen sample from the body of Lynda Mann and then analyzed a sample from the Dawn Ashworth crime scene. The technique yielded a DNA image that was identical for both

murders. Then, from the suspect's blood sample, Jeffreys obtained a comparison DNA fingerprint. Alarmingly, the suspect's DNA failed to match up with either murder, including the murder to which the suspect had already confessed. The suspect was then released from custody.

Certain of one fact—that the same person had killed both teenagers—investigators decided to single out the perpetrator through genetic fingerprinting. Accordingly, in January 1987, all males 17 to 40 years of age living in the village were asked to submit blood samples. More than 4,500 samples were examined before the police, in September 1987, arrested a local baker, Colin Pitchfork, and charged him with the murders. Pitchfork had a long history of sexual assault and indecent exposure, and an informant had alerted police that he had cheated on his blood examination by persuading a coworker to submit a blood sample for him. When a legitimate test of the suspect's blood was conducted, an identical match was made with fingerprints found at both murder scenes. Based solely on DNA fingerprinting and the resulting confession, Pitchfork was convicted of both murders.

Sources: Batt, E. (1999, April). DNA fingerprinting: The capture of a murderer. Retrieved from http://www.suite101.com/article.cfm/leicestershire/ 17877; Leicestersound. Retrieved from http://www.leicestersound.co.uk/ Article.asp?id=1283518; Wambaugh, J. (1990). *The blooding: True story of the Narborough murders.* New York: Bantam Books.

The investigation of the Narborough murders introduced criminal investigation to a new era of scientific detection:

1. Blood and DNA evidence were used to solve the Narborough murders. Identify how other investigative methods could have possibly been used to solve this crime.
2. Can you identify recent cases in your community that have been solved using DNA technology?
3. During the investigation of more than one murder, should investigators focus on one murder at a time or compare and contrast investigative leads and evidence between murders?

CHAPTER 4 — Identifying Criminal Suspects: Field and Laboratory Processes

 LEARNING OUTCOMES 1

Summarize the role of the crime laboratory in a criminal investigation.

Crime labs play a pivotal role in the investigation process. They have specialists in DNA (blood) analysis, trace evidence, handwriting analysis, toxicology, and ballistics.

1. What are the various functions of the crime laboratory?
2. How is DNA analysis used in criminal investigations?
3. What are examples of trace material?

Mitochondrial DNA Population Database One of several DNA databases in the world.

Amido black protein An amino acid-staining diazo dye used in biochemical research to stain for total protein on transferred membrane blots.

 LEARNING OUTCOMES 2

Identify the types and patterns of fingerprints.

The use of fingerprints for identification purposes is based on distinctive ridge outlines that appear on the bulbs on the inside of the end joints of the fingers and thumbs. These ridges have definite contours and appear in several general pattern types. Each type has general and specific variations of the pattern, depending on the shape and relationship of the ridges.

1. What are the three main groups of fingerprints?
2. How does a latent fingerprint differ from a plastic print?
3. What are the different types of patterns of fingerprints?

latent fingerprints Fingerprints that are not visible unless developed through a fingerprint-lifting process.

plastic fingerprints A fingerprint impression left when a person presses against a plastic material, such as putty, wax, or tar.

visible fingerprints A type of fingerprint left at a crime scene that results from being adulterated with some foreign matter, such as blood, flour, or oil.

 LEARNING OUTCOMES 3

Explain the development and preservation of latent fingerprints.

The sole purpose of developing, or lifting, a latent fingerprint impression is to make it visible so that it can be preserved and compared. Several powders and chemicals are used for this purpose in addition to several techniques designed to develop such evidence.

1. What are the various ways investigators locate and identify fingerprints at a crime scene?

2. What is the significance of the new role that IAFIS fingerprinting technology offers the field of criminal investigation and identification?

Combined DNA Index System (CODIS) The generic term used to describe the FBI's program of support for criminal justice DNA databases as well as the software used to run these databases.

 LEARNING OUTCOMES 4

Discuss the Integrated Automated Fingerprint Identification System.

The Integrated Automated Fingerprint Identification System, more commonly known as IAFIS, is a national fingerprint and criminal history database maintained by the FBI's CJIS Division. The IAFIS provides automated fingerprint search capabilities, latent searching capability, electronic image storage, and electronic exchange of fingerprints and responses 24 hours a day, 365 days a year.

1. What are the different variables searched for by IAFIS to make a match?

2. How quickly do criminal investigators receive results back from IAFIS for criminal and civil cases?

3. How is IAFIS used in criminal investigations?

Integrated Automated Fingerprint Identification System (IAFIS) A national fingerprint and criminal history database maintained by the FBI's CJIS Division.

Explain the role of DNA in criminal investigations.

DNA has given scientists the means with which to detect the remarkable variability existing between individuals. The results of this technology hold great promise in aiding the criminal justice system in making positive determinations of criminal identity.

1. To what extent has DNA technology improved methods of criminal identification?

2. Why are recent court rulings addressing the admissibility of DNA evidence in the courtroom significant?

3. What is the Southern blotting method of DNA analysis? Who developed it?

4. What is meant by elimination samples?

DNA technology The science of identifying the genetic facsimile, or "blueprint," of any particular organism in every cell within each human body.

Describe handwriting analysis.

People often adopt unique writing styles of their own, frequently characteristic only of that person. Such characteristics are identifiable to the handwriting expert. Writings may occur in many forms, including that on personal correspondence, desks, walls, and even dead bodies.

1. Why it is important to verify the origin of a requested exemplar?

2. Why is it important to be sure that the writing instruments (for example, paper, pencils) used in the sample are the same as those used in the suspect document?

3. What are two skills needed by handwriting experts?

4. How are requested and collected exemplars used in handwriting?

exemplars Samples, as of a suspect's handwriting.

Describe criminal composites.

One method of developing an idea of the suspect's general description is to have the witness provide information to a police artist so that a facial composite can be generated. In previous years, construction of the composite was done by a trained artist through drawing, sketching, or painting in consultation with a witness or crime victim. Today, most composites are computer generated.

1. What are some of the well-known cases in which criminal composites have been used to identify suspects?

2. What are some disadvantages of using a criminal composite?

3. According to the FBI, what is the correct method for constructing a facial composite?

4. In what ways does a facial composite assist law enforcement?

composite A freehand drawing of a suspected criminal.

Identi-Kit A computer-generated composite of a suspected criminal.

Discuss the role of investigative analysis to solve crimes.

Criminal investigative analysis, formerly known as personality profiling, is the means of identifying the type of person responsible for a particular crime. This is accomplished by identifying psychological and social characteristics surrounding the crime as well as the manner in which it was committed.

1. How has investigative analysis been used in the past to capture criminals?

2. What is the process of criminal profiling and how does it assist criminal investigations?

3. What is Munchausen syndrome by proxy?

4. What psychological and social characteristics are used by investigators to identify perpetrators and solve crimes?

criminal investigative analysis Identifying psychological and social characteristics surrounding the crime as well as the manner in which it was committed.

LEARNING OUTCOMES 9

Explain the proper methods for conducting lineups.

The function of a police lineup is to identify a suspect. Lineups are typically shown to victims of crime or eyewitnesses to a crime. Great care must be taken by officers conducting identification sessions of any type to avoid any action that might lead to an erroneous identification. Carefully adhering to the proper identification procedures will help avoid misidentifications that may lead to unjust accusations or even erroneous convictions of innocent persons and divert the investigation away from the actual offender.

1. What is the proper method of conducting a photo lineup?

2. What is the value of the composite sketch in identifying a criminal suspect?

3. In what ways do criminal composites assist the criminal investigator?

lineup The police practice of allowing witnesses or victims to view several suspects for identification purposes.

simultaneous lineup A lineup procedure whereby the eyewitness views all the people or photos at the same time.

sequential lineup A police lineup method whereby people or photographs are presented to a witness one at a time.

relative judgment When eyewitnesses compare lineup photographs or members with each other rather than with their memories of the offender.

absolute judgment When eyewitnesses compare each photograph or person in a lineup only with their memories of what the offender looked like.

suggestiveness An identification technique that unduly narrows down the victim's/witnesses' options so a particular suspect is chosen.

Additional Links

www.dna.gov
This site provides information related to research and statistics on DNA technology. This information is pertinent to investigators, scientists, officers of the court, lawmakers, victim advocates, or the casual observer interested in DNA technology. Links include statutes and case law, DNA databases, and tools for forensic scientists.

www.exploreforensics.co.uk
This site offers articles on various aspects of forensic science, including evidence collection and analysis as well as types of forensics.

www.forensicscience.net
This site is a forensic science education site. It includes career links and fun stuff such as criminology resources, criminology blogs, and "ridiculous scenes from shows such as CSI."

www.criminaljusticeprofiles.org; www.criminaljusticeusa.com
These sites offer information on the work of criminalists, including training required, salary, and skills needed. They also contain links to colleges and universities offering criminal justice programs that include forensic science.

5

Legal Issues in Criminal Investigation

"Criminal and constitutional law provide law enforcement officers with the critical framework within which they must operate."

1 Identify the legal guidelines for conducting searches.

2 Explain the exceptions to the exclusionary rule.

3 Summarize what information must be contained on a search warrant.

4 Explain when warrantless searches are authorized under law.

5 Define an arrest.

6 Explain what is required for an arrest to be legal.

7 Explain when police officers can use force.

8 Explain when police officers can use deadly force.

INTRO — THE MAKING OF AN ARREST

On May 15, 2014, former New England Patriots tight end Aaron Hernandez was indicted on murder charges for the killings of 29 year-old Daniel Jorge Correia de Abreu and 28 year-old Safiro Teixeira Furtado. The charges stemmed from a June 2013 investigation of a double murder that took place on July 16, 2012, in Boston's South End. According to the police, Abreu and Furtado, who both resided in Dorchester, were killed by gunshots fired into their vehicle.

Two days later, Hernandez's house was searched by police in connection with an investigation into the shooting death of another victim, Hernandez's friend, Odin Lloyd. Lloyd's body was found in an industrial park about a mile away from Hernandez's house with multiple gunshot wounds to the back and chest. The Massachusetts State

Police obtained a search warrant after evidence surfaced that Hernandez had intentionally destroyed his home security system. A cell phone belonging to Hernandez was turned over to police "in pieces" and Hernandez allegedly hired a "team of house cleaners" the same day Lloyd's body was discovered, raising additional suspicion.

On June 26, 2013, Hernandez was taken from his home in handcuffs and into police custody. The Patriots released Hernandez from the team about 90 minutes later, even before officially knowing the charges against him. Later that day, Hernandez was charged with first-degree murder, in addition to five gun-related charges. On August 22, 2013, he was indicted by a grand jury for the murder of Odin Lloyd. Since then he has maintained his innocence.

While the Aaron Hernandez case is ongoing at the time of the preparation of this text, the case against him illustrates the importance of evidence and observing legal requirements to support an arrest.

Aaron Hernandez is escorted into the courtroom of the Attleboro District Court for his hearing on August 22, 2013, in North Attleboro, Massachusetts. Former New England Patriot Aaron Hernandez has been indicted on a first-degree murder charge for the death of Odin Lloyd.

Photo by Jared Wickerham/Getty Images

Epitavi/Fotolia

DISCUSS This case illustrates the many uses of legal instruments such as the search warrant and arrest warrant. Investigators are duty-bound to follow legal requirements for searching and seizing evidence and persons in the course of their investigations.

▶ Legal Guidelines for Conducting Searches

LEARNING OUTCOMES 1 Identify the legal guidelines for conducting searches.

Investigators must remember that they not only should have legal grounds to begin a search but that while conducting the search, they must not contaminate any evidence. Doing so will result in the dismissal of such evidence in the courtroom. Additionally, searches must first be justified under law. In the past, officers have not always followed the rules, as the case histories discussed in this chapter show.

The Probable Cause Requirement

For decades courts have scrutinized virtually every aspect of the Fourth Amendment. The probable cause requirement is one of the most important components of the Fourth Amendment because it lies at the heart of police officers' authority to search, seize, and make arrests. Simply put, **probable cause** is the minimum amount of information necessary to warrant a reasonable person to believe that a crime has been or is being committed by a person who is about to be arrested. Officers generally establish probable cause through their own observations. For example,

- Did the suspect attempt to run away when approached by the officer?
- Did the suspect admit to any part of the alleged crime?
- Did the suspect behave furtively, as if he or she were trying to hide something?

It is unlikely that a single fact or circumstance will establish probable cause, but several such facts put together might.

The Exclusionary Rule

The **exclusionary rule** relates primarily to cases involving issues of search and seizure, arrests, interrogations, and stop-and-frisk violations. In addition, it pertains to any evidence obtained illegally even though it may be both relevant and material. The exclusionary rule states that courts will exclude any evidence that was illegally obtained even though it may be relevant and material.

The exclusionary rule originated with the 1914 case of *Weeks* v. *United States*, 232 U.S. 383 (1914). In the *Weeks* case, the U.S. Supreme Court unanimously held that the warrantless seizure of items from a private residence constitutes a violation of the Fourth Amendment. It also established the exclusionary rule that prohibits admission of illegally obtained evidence but was geared to apply to federal, not state, governments.

In 1920, *Silverthorne Lumber Co.* v. *United States*, 251 U.S. 385 (1920), also addressed the exclusionary rule. It was a U.S. Supreme Court Case in which Silverthorne attempted to avoid paying taxes. Federal agents illegally seized tax books from Silverthorne and made copies of the records. The issue in this case is whether or not evidence derived from illegal evidence is permissible in court. The ruling was that to permit illegally seized evidence would encourage police to circumvent the Fourth Amendment. Consequently, the illegally copied evidence was held tainted and inadmissible. This precedent is known as "fruit of the poisonous tree" and is an extension of the exclusionary rule.

Although the *Weeks* and *Silverthorne* cases were virtually ignored by state courts, the subsequent *Mapp* decision (*Mapp* v. *Ohio*, 1961) expanded the scope of the exclusionary rule by applying it to both federal and state courts. In 1957, Cleveland police officers went to the residence of Dolree Mapp while acting on information that a fugitive was in hiding there. Mapp refused to admit officers to the residence without a search warrant. The officers left but maintained surveillance on the residence. Three hours later, more officers arrived and forced their way into the Mapp residence. By this time, Mapp's attorney had arrived, but officers ignored him. Mapp then demanded to see a search warrant, at which time one of the officers held up a piece of paper, claiming that it was a search warrant. Mapp grabbed the piece of paper and stashed it in her blouse. A struggle ensued, and the officers retrieved the paper and arrested Mapp for being "belligerent." The officers then began to search the entire home. Although they never located the fugitive they were looking for, they ran across some obscene material for which Mapp was subsequently arrested and convicted. The U.S. Supreme Court overturned the conviction, stating that the methods used by officers to obtain the evidence were a violation of her constitutional rights.

Although the state supreme court in Ohio upheld the conviction, the U.S. Supreme Court overturned it. In addition to imposing federal constitutional standards on state law enforcement personnel, the Court pointed out that there is a relationship between the Fourth and Fifth Amendments that makes up the legal basis for the exclusionary rule.

Search Incident to Lawful Arrest

Chimel v. *California* (1969) was a watershed case that dealt with areas that are not in plain view that are searched without a warrant. It established that a search made incidental to a lawful arrest must be confined to the area around the suspect's immediate control.

In this case, Ted Chimel was approached in his home by officers who possessed an arrest warrant for him. The officers then advised him that they wanted to "look around" and proceeded to search the premises without his permission. After a one-hour search, some coins were located and seized as evidence. Although initially convicted, Chimel appealed the case, which was reversed by the U.S. Supreme Court because the coins were not lawfully seized.

TIMELINE

1914	1920	1961
Weeks v. *United States*—The birth of the exclusionary rule but attached only to federal officers	*Silverthorne Lumber Co.* v. *United States*—The fruit of the poisonous tree doctrine	*Mapp* v. *Ohio*—The exclusionary rule is expanded to include both state and federal courts

The *Chimel* case held that the officers who searched Chimel's house went far beyond any area where he might have either hidden a weapon or been able to destroy any evidence. Therefore, there was no constitutional basis for an extended search of the house. The *Chimel* case is important, as it relates to criminal investigation; it changed the policy with regard to the **scope of the search**, as it relates to an officer's authority to search incident to an arrest. Before the *Chimel* case, officers had more leeway to search the area around an arrested suspect.

▶ Exceptions to the Exclusionary Rule

Since the *Mapp* and *Chimel* cases, the U.S. Supreme Court has developed several exceptions to the exclusionary rule. These play a considerable role in shaping the manner in which police officers are allowed to behave before, during, and after a search and seizure of evidence.

LEARNING OUTCOMES 2 — Explain the exceptions to the exclusionary rule.

The Good-Faith Exception

In the years since the *Weeks* and *Silverthorne* cases, some people have criticized the U.S. Supreme Court for a "chipping away" of the exclusionary rule. One such case emerged in the summer of 1984 when the laws dealing with search and seizure changed dramatically in *United States* v. *Leon*, when the first good-faith exception to the exclusionary rule was decided. During the course of a drug trafficking investigation by the Burbank, California, Police Department, officers secured a search warrant for the residence of Alberto Leon. Three prosecutors reviewed the warrant before its being issued by a state court judge. The subsequent search netted large quantities of drugs, and Leon was arrested and charged with drug trafficking. The defense challenged the validity of the warrant based on the unreliability of the informant and moved to suppress the evidence. The district court and the U.S. Court of Appeals both held that the affidavit was insufficient, but the U.S. Supreme Court supported the prosecution, holding that the exclusionary rule was designed only as a deterrent for the abuse of police authority. The Court specified that evidence might be excluded if (1) police officers were dishonest in preparing the affidavit, (2) the warrant was deficient on its face (for example, a wrong or missing description of the place to be searched) such that no officer could reasonably serve it, or (3) if the magistrate was not found to be neutral.

The practical effect of the *Leon* case is that any evidence seized through a search warrant is immune from suppression even if the judge signing the warrant was wrong and there was not probable cause to believe that contraband or other evidence would be discovered under the warrant. The *Leon* case allows the use of evidence obtained by officers acting in reasonable reliance on a search warrant issued by a neutral magistrate but that is ultimately found invalid.

The Inevitable Discovery Doctrine

The inevitable discovery exception to the exclusionary rule was developed in the 1984 *Nix* v. *Williams* case. This exception states that evidence that has been seized illegally or evidence stemming from illegally seized evidence (for example, fruit of the poisonous tree; *Wong Sun* v. *United States*, 1963) is admissible if the police can prove that they would have inevitably discovered it anyway by lawful means.

The Computer Errors Exception

In the 1995 *Arizona* v. *Evans* case, the Court created a computer errors exception to the exclusionary rule. The exception held that a traffic stop, which led to the seizure of marijuana, was legal even though officers conducted the stop based on an arrest warrant stored improperly in their computer. In *Arizona* v. *Evans* the court reasoned that officers should not be held responsible for a clerical error made by a court worker and held that the arresting officers acted in good faith based on the information available to them at the time of the arrest.

▶ Searches with a Warrant

Over the years, the **search warrant** has proven to be one of the most valuable tools in criminal investigation. It authorizes the search of homes, businesses, and vehicles of suspects; typically results in the arrest of multiple suspects; and expedites investigation and subsequent case closure.

LEARNING OUTCOMES 3 — Summarize what information must be contained on a search warrant.

When Are Search Warrants Necessary?

If the warrant specifies a certain person to be searched, the police can search only that person unless they have independent probable cause to search other persons who happen to be present at the scene of a search. However, if an officer has a reasonable suspicion that an onlooker is engaged in criminal activity, the officer can question the onlooker and, if necessary for the officer's safety, can frisk for weapons.

Technically, a person may require the police to produce a warrant before admitting them into his or her home for a search.

However, people sometimes run into trouble when they "stand on their rights" in this way. A warrant is not always legally necessary, and a police officer may have information of which a person is unaware that allows the officer to make a warrantless entry. If an officer announces an intention to enter without a warrant, a person should not risk injury or a separate charge of "interfering with a police officer." Rather, the person should stand aside, let the officer proceed, and allow a court to decide later whether the officer's actions were proper. At the same time, the person should make it clear that he or she does not consent to the search.

**IN THE DISTRICT COURT OF THE FIFTH JUDICIAL DISTRICT
IN AND FOR:
JACKSON COUNTY, MISSOURI**

BEFORE _____ JUDGE, DISTRICT COURT OF
JACKSON COUNTY, MISSOURI

State of Missouri } ss.
Jackson County }

Affidavit for Search Warrant

On this _21_ day of _October_, 14, _Agent Brian Johnson_ being first sworn, upon oath deposes and says:

That a certain _Residence_ within said County and State, located and described as follows, to wit:

2304 N.W. 38th Place, Kansas City, Missouri located in Jackson County being a single family wood frame dwelling facing South, and under the control of Lance T. Anderson, and wife Chelsea. The garage area of the house is to the West end of the South side. The house is on the North side of the street with tan colored brick along the lower third of the front, while being fenced in, with a chain link fence, around the back yard area.

the same being the _residence_ of _Lance and Chelsea Anderson_ whose more full, true and correct name is unknown to the affiant, there is located certain property particularly described as follows, to-wit:

Controlled substances to include marijuana, Schedule I, LSD, Schedule I, Cocaine, Schedule II, and one fifty dollar bill ($50.00) U.S. currency bearing serial number JO3744496B, and any other records or documents showing illicit business dealings in controlled drugs.

which said property is subject to search and seizure as set out by the laws of Missouri for the following grounds, to-wit:

Violation of the state criminal code controlled substances section RsMo 195.233.

and that the probable cause of the affiant believing such facts exist as follows, to-wit:

1) Your affiant is a sworn police officer with the Kansas City Police Department, who has been a full time narcotics investigator for three years and seven months. 2) On October 21, 2014 at approximately 1630 hours, Officer Johnson purchased one (1) kilo of marijuana for $2500 from Chelsea Anderson which was contained in a black trunk located in the hallway of the residence. 3) On October 21, 2014 at approx. 1945 hours Officer Johnson purchased 100 units of LSD for $4350 from Lance Anderson which he acquired from the freezer area of the kitchen. 4) On October 21, 2014 Lance Anderson also displayed approx. one (1) ounce of white powder claiming it to be cocaine which was also kept in the refrigerator area of the kitchen.

_____
Affiant

Subscribed and sworn before me this _21_ *day of* _October_, *2014*

_____
Judge, District Court of
Jackson County, Missouri

FIGURE 5–1 Sample Search Warrant Affidavit.

Advantages of Searching with a Search Warrant

Among the many tools afforded the criminal investigator, the search warrant has proven to be of substantial worth. It represents an authorization by the court for officers to enter a designated location or structure and search for specific items. It can be useful to a criminal investigator in many situations. The search warrant can be used to do the following:

- Recover stolen property
- Seize drugs or other contraband
- Seize any other type of property used in the commission of a crime

The search warrant must contain specifics about the location to be searched, the objects being sought, the probable cause that indicates that there is property to seize, and a signature of the judge authorizing the search. Evidence obtained through the use of a search warrant may also be more readily accepted by courts than evidence that was seized without a warrant or incident to arrest. In addition, the officer is protected from civil liability when a warrant is obtained. A search warrant also benefits the prosecutor by shifting the legal burden to the defendant. Instead of the prosecutor having to justify a presumably unreasonable search, it becomes the burden of the defendant to show that the evidence was seized illegally. This factor alone has encouraged officers to obtain search warrants when possible.

The Search Warrant

Basically, the search warrant sets forth the same facts as outlined in the affidavit. Prior to signing the affidavit, the affiant (the officer) must be certain that he or she is first sworn in by a judge. The judge must then sign and date all pages of the affidavit and warrant. See Figures 5–1 and 5–2 for examples of an affidavit and a search warrant.

IN THE DISTRICT COURT OF THE FIFTH JUDICIAL DISTRICT IN AND FOR:
JACKSON COUNTY, MISSOURI

BEFORE _____ JUDGE, DISTRICT COURT OF
JACKSON COUNTY, MISSOURI

State of Missouri } ss. **SEARCH WARRANT**
Jackson County

In the name of the State of Missouri, to any sheriff, constable, marshal, policeman, or peace officer in the County of Jackson, State of Missouri.

Proof by affidavit having been this day made before me, by _Agent Brian Johnson_ that there is probable cause for believing that in the herein described _residence_ is located the following property particularly described as follows, to-wit:

Controlled substances to include marijuana, Schedule I, LSD, Schedule I, and Cocaine, Schedule II, and one fifty dollar bill U.S. currency bearing serial number: JO3744496B

and that the herein described _residence_ should be searched by reason of the following grounds to-wit:

Possession of the above described controlled dangerous substances and currency is evidence of violation of the state criminal code controlled substances section RsMo 195.233.

YOU ARE THEREFORE COMMANDED at any time of day or night to make immediate search of the _residence_ of _2304 N.W. 38th Place, Kansas City, Missouri_ whose more full, true and correct name is unknown, located and described as follows, to-wit:

a single family wood frame dwelling facing South, and under the control of Lance Thomas Anderson, and wife Chelsea. The garage area of the house is to the West end of the south side. The house is on the north side of the street with tan colored brick along the lower third front, while being fenced in, with a chain link fence, around the back yard area.

for the said property above described, and, if you find the same or any part thereof to bring it forthwith before me at my office in Kansas City, Jackson County, Missouri.

Dated this _21_ day of _October_, 2014.

_____
Judge, District Court of
Jackson County, Missouri

FIGURE 5–2 Sample Search Warrant.

United States v. Grubbs

Respondent Jeffrey Grubbs purchased a videotape containing child pornography from a website operated by an undercover postal inspector. Officers from the postal inspection service arranged a controlled delivery of a package containing a videotape to Grubbs's residence. A postal inspector submitted a search warrant application (an affidavit) describing the proposed operation in detail. The affidavit stated the following:

> Execution of the search warrant will not occur unless and until the parcel has been received by a person(s) and has been physically taken into the residence . . . at that time, and not before, the search warrant will be executed by me and other United States Postal Service inspectors, with appropriate assistance from other law enforcement officers in accordance with this warrant's command.

In addition to describing this triggering condition, the affidavit referred to two attachments, which described Grubbs's residence and the items officers would seize. These attachments, but not the body of the affidavit, were incorporated into the requested warrant.

The magistrate judge issued the warrant as requested. Two days later, an undercover postal inspector delivered the package. Grubbs's wife signed for it and took the unopened package inside. The inspectors detained Grubbs as he left his home a few minutes later and then entered the house and commenced the search. Approximately 30 minutes into the search, Grubbs was provided with a copy of the warrant, which included both attachments but not the supporting affidavit that explained when the warrant would be executed. Grubbs consented to interrogation by the postal inspectors and admitted ordering the videotape. He was placed under arrest, and various items were seized, including the videotape. Grubbs subsequently pleaded guilty but reserved his right to appeal the denial of his earlier motion to suppress the evidence.

Anticipatory Search Warrants

An anticipatory search warrant is a warrant based on an affidavit showing probable cause to believe that at some future time, particular evidence of a crime will be located at a particular place. Anticipatory warrants may not be executed until some specific event (other than the passage of time) has occurred. The specified events are called **triggering conditions**, and even though the warrant has been issued and is in the hands of the police, until the triggering condition has arisen, the search may not be carried out.

Anticipatory search warrants have been the subject of a great deal of litigation, much of which is based on the argument that all anticipatory warrants are unconstitutional because they violate the Fourth Amendment requirement of probable cause. The contention of many defendants has been because, by definition, anticipatory search warrant affidavits show only that there will be probable cause to search the premises at some later time—not that there is at present probable cause to search—the Fourth Amendment requirement is not satisfied. Although this argument has been repeatedly rejected by various federal courts of appeals, the issue came before the Supreme Court of the United States in the case of *United States* v. *Grubbs*, 377 F.3d 1072 (2004). Even though the case involved a warrant obtained by federal officers for a federal crime, the Supreme Court's opinion in that case, described in "A Closer Look," is of value to all law enforcement officers and agencies in understanding anticipatory search warrants and their use.

▶ *Warrantless Searches*

Officers must remember that the rules applying to searches differ from those applying to arrests. An arrest and a search are two completely separate and distinct law enforcement procedures. For example, depending on certain statutory restraints, an officer might be empowered to make an arrest without an arrest warrant, provided that probable cause exists. In addition, arrests are permissible even when there is time for the officer to get a warrant. For searches, the rules are different. The Fourth Amendment says that all searches must be preceded by the officer obtaining a search warrant. Regardless of how much probable cause an officer may have, if he or she searches without a search warrant, there is a legal presumption that the search is unconstitutional. Several exceptions have been developed in which a warrantless search is authorized under law:

LEARNING OUTCOMES 4 — Explain when warrantless searches are authorized under law.

- Consent searches
- Searches under exigent circumstances
- Searches incident to lawful arrest
- Stop-and-frisk searches
- Plain-view searches
- Automobile searches
- Open-field searches

Search by Consent

Police can search without a warrant when a suspect gives them permission to do so. Searches in this instance must, of course, be subsequent to an initial detention that was lawful. As a case in point, *Florida* v. *Royer* (1983) held that evidence obtained as a result of a **consent search** when the detention was made without probable cause is a violation of the defendant's Fourth Amendment rights and will be excluded.

The consent search can be especially useful in cases in which officers have no legal basis for obtaining a search warrant. It is important to remember, however, that a consent search must be authorized voluntarily, with no coercion from officers. This was affirmed in *Bumper* v. *North Carolina* (1968) in a decision in which the U.S. Supreme Court held that a search is not justified on the basis of consent when consent

The following factors, among others, may be considered by a court in determining whether the contact was a consensual encounter or a field interview.

Interference with the suspect's freedom of movement

Case example: If officers position themselves or their vehicles in such a manner as to block the suspect's path, this indicates that the suspect is not free to leave and may render the encounter an investigative stop.

Number of officers and their behavior

Case example: Confrontation of the suspect by more than one officer may create an atmosphere of intimidation that will cause the courts to consider the contact an investigative stop. Excessive display of weapons, such as drawn or pointed firearms, will have the same effect. Even the prolonged or repeated display of badges or other police identification may be considered intimidating.[i] A threatening or bullying manner may lead to the same result.

Physical contact with the suspect

Case example: Any physical contact with the suspect for purposes of stopping or holding the individual or to search for weapons or evidence will almost certainly cause the contact to be considered a nonconsensual (that is, an investigative) stop or even a full-fledged arrest.

Retaining personal property of the suspect

Case example: If the officer wishes the contact to be regarded as consensual, any personal property taken from the suspect, such as a driver's license or other identification, should be returned promptly to the suspect. Prolonged retention by the officer of such items may lead a court to conclude that the suspect was not free to leave.

---

[i]Officers must, for reasons of both legality and personal safety, adequately identify themselves as police officers. Proper identification as a police officer does not render an encounter nonconsensual. It is only the excessive, unnecessary, or deliberately intimidating display of authority that affects the consensual nature of the encounter.

---

was given only after the officer conducting the search asserted possession of a warrant. Although it is legal for officers to search on the word of the suspect, it is a better idea to have the person sign a consent-to-search waiver authorizing the search in writing. For the consent to be valid, officers must first establish that the person giving consent has legal authority to do so. Just because a suspect is present in a particular residence, he or she may not have legal authority to grant a search. Dominion and control can be verified through the seizing of utility bills, for example, that bear the name of the suspect and the associated address. See Figure 5–3 for an example of a consent-to-search form.

Emergency Searches

In the case of an emergency or **exigent circumstances**, a search may also be conducted without a warrant provided that probable cause exists. As a general rule, the police are authorized to

CITY POLICE DEPARTMENT
CONSENT TO SEARCH

DATE _____

LOCATION _____

I, _____, having been informed of my constitutional right
not to have a search made of the premises hereinafter described without a search warrant and of my
right to refuse to consent to such a search, hereby authorize _____
_____, officers of the City Police Department, to conduct a complete
search of my:

Premises ___

Curtilage ___

Vehicles ___

These officers are authorized by me to take from my premises any letters, papers, materials, or other
property which they may desire, after receipting me for same. I further state that I am the proper
person to give the consent and authorization referred to herein.

This written permission is being given by me to the above named officers(s) voluntarily and without
threats or promises of any kind.

_____
Signature

WITNESSES:

_____

_____

_____

FIGURE 5–3 Sample Consent to Search Form.

make an emergency warrantless search when the time it would take to get a warrant would jeopardize public safety or lead to the loss of important evidence.

Any one of the circumstances noted in Box 5–1 may create an exception to the Fourth Amendment's warrant requirement. It is incumbent on investigating officers to demonstrate that a dire situation existed that justified their actions. Failure to do so will result in the evidence seized being deemed illegal. However, if a judge decides that an officer had time to obtain a search warrant without risking injury to people or the loss of evidence, the judge should refuse to allow into evidence whatever was seized in the course of the warrantless search.

Stop-and-Frisk Searches

In 1968, the Supreme Court of the United States declared in the case of *Terry* v. *Ohio* (1968)[1] that a police officer may stop a person for questioning if the officer reasonably suspects that the person has committed, is committing, or is about to commit a crime. It is not necessary that the officer have probable cause to arrest the individual at the time that the stop is made. All that is required is that the officer has a reasonable suspicion that the individual is involved in criminal activity. However, to be reasonable, this suspicion must be based on articulable facts that would lead a reasonable person to suspect that the individual is involved in criminal activity.

BOX 5-1

Here are some situations in which judges would most likely uphold a warrantless search:

- *A threat of the removal or destruction of evidence. Case example:* After a street drug arrest, an officer enters the house after the suspect shouts into the house, "Eddie, quick, flush our stash down the toilet." The officer arrests Eddie and seizes the stash.

- *A danger to life. Case example:* A police officer on routine patrol hears shouts and screams coming from a residence, rushes in, and arrests a suspect for spousal abuse.

- *The threat of a suspect escaping:* Knowledge of a suspect who is known to be in a location and who has already escaped or is aware that he is being sought by police.

The Supreme Court further declared in *Terry* v. *Ohio* that an officer who has stopped a suspect may ". . . search for weapons for the protection of the police officer, where he has reason to believe that he is dealing with an armed and dangerous individual."[2] This case is the landmark legal decision that grants officers the authority to conduct field interviews (also called "investigative detentions" or *Terry* stops) and pat-down searches (an investigative detention is commonly referred to as a **stop and frisk**). Numerous federal and state court decisions have interpreted and applied the principles of *Terry*. In addition, many states have enacted statutes dealing with field interviews and pat-down searches.[3]

Factors Defining a Field Interview

The U.S. Supreme Court has held that a police–citizen encounter is consensual (that is, does not amount to a seizure of the person) as long as the circumstances of the encounter are such that a reasonable person would feel that he or she was "free to leave," to terminate the encounter and depart at any time.[4]

An officer may ask the suspect to move to another area during the encounter without altering the consensual nature of the contact if it is made clear to the suspect that the request to move to another location is just that—a request only—and that the suspect is free to refuse the request.

The Consensual Encounter versus Investigative Detention

Police contacts with citizens that do not involve an interrogation or arrest are referred to as consensual encounters. An officer may conduct a consensual encounter in any location where the officer has a legal right to be present and, if conducted properly, the encounter may result in citizen cooperation and often produces information helpful in a criminal investigation.

Stopping to talk to a citizen is not improper but investigating officers must remember that the citizen may refuse to speak with the officer and may be allowed to simply walk away. The citizen's ability to walk away hinges on the whether the encounter is a consensual encounter or whether the officer has reasonable suspicion to detain the citizen where he or she is not free to leave. In order for the officer to stop the citizen from walking away, thus beginning an investigative detention, reasonable suspicion is required.

A Citizen's Right to Refuse the Contact or to Answer Questions

The citizen has the right to refuse to answer questions asked by an officer. When this happens, this is not a basis for any further action by the officer. This means that after such a refusal to cooperate, the citizen must be allowed to walk away.

Freedom to Leave

Based on the preceding, one of the primary distinctions between the *Terry* stop and the consensual encounter is the degree of freedom of action enjoyed by the citizen during the encounter. If there are no grounds for reasonable suspicion that the individual being interviewed is engaged in criminal behavior, he or she is free at all times to discontinue the interview and, as the courts have said, "go about his (or her) business," that is, walk away from the officer.

When a Consensual Encounter Escalates into an Investigative Detention

In some cases, what begins as a consensual contact may evolve into something more based on information developed by the officer during the contact. This can occur when statements are made or other circumstances create reasonable suspicion to believe that the citizen has committed, is committing, or is about to commit a crime. The contact may then become an investigative detention, with all of the aspects of such a detention, including a possible right to frisk the suspect.

The officer, however, must be able to point to specific facts, when taken together with rational inferences, reasonably warrant the stop. Such facts include but are not necessarily limited to the following:

1. The appearance or demeanor of a subject suggests that he or she is engaged in a criminal act.

2. The actions of the subject indicate that he or she is engaged in a criminal activity.

3. The hour of day or night is inappropriate for the subject's presence in the area.

4. The subject's presence in a neighborhood or location is inappropriate.

5. The subject is carrying a suspicious object.

6. The subject's clothing bulges in a manner consistent with carrying a weapon.

7. The subject is located in proximity (time and place) to an alleged crime.

8. The officer has knowledge of the subject's prior involvement in criminal activity.

Therefore, if the officer feels that a consensual encounter has become an investigative detention, the officer should be prepared to clearly articulate the factors that, in the officer's mind, created this transition.

That said, two additional points should be made. First, the refusal of a citizen to cooperate in a police–citizen contact does not form the basis for reasonable suspicion. Some officers believe that a citizen who does not cooperate with the police has "something to hide" or simply has no respect for police authority. Second, refusal to cooperate, especially when accompanied by hostile statements or behavior, may be construed by an officer as disrespectful to him or her personally and his or her authority (e.g., "contempt of cop"). Although it is certainly true that such conduct may reflect a dislike for police and a desire to avoid contact with them, it is equally true that such attitudes and behaviors do not constitute a basis for reasonable suspicion of criminal activity for purposes of a *Terry* stop.

When a Subject Runs

Sometimes, police will observe a subject who runs after seeing the officers. The United Supreme Court has addressed this and concludes that flight from contact with police officers provides an additional basis for conducting an investigative detention. In some instances when a police officer attempts to make a citizen contact, the citizen in question may make efforts to avoid the contact by fleeing or making a quick exit from the immediate location.

In the U.S. Supreme Court case *Illinois* v. *Wardlow* (2000), it was determined that fleeing constitutes an additional factor for determining reasonable suspicion to conduct an investigative detention.[5] The Supreme Court further noted in *Wardlow*, as it has in previous cases, that nervous, evasive behavior, although not alone sufficient to constitute reasonable suspicion, is a pertinent factor in determining whether or not reasonable suspicion exists.[6]

Pat-Down Searches

As noted earlier, *Terry* v. *Ohio*, other court decisions, and various state statutes give officers the authority to conduct a pat-down search[7] or "frisk" of a suspect who has been the subject of a valid investigative stop if the officer reasonably believes that the suspect may possess a weapon.

Plain-View Searches

Police officers have the opportunity to begin investigations or confiscate evidence without a warrant based on what they find in plain view and open to public inspection. This has become known as the **plain-view doctrine**, a doctrine first stated in the Supreme Court ruling in *Harris* v. *United States* (1968). A police officer found evidence of a robbery while inventorying an impounded vehicle. The court ruled, "objects falling in the plain view of an officer who has a right to be in the position to have that view are subject to seizure and may be used as evidence." This doctrine has been widely used by investigators in such cases as crimes in progress, accidents, and fires. An officer might enter an apartment, for example, while responding to a domestic disturbance and find drugs on a living room table. He or she would be within his or her rights to seize the drugs as evidence without having a search warrant. The criteria for a valid plain-view search were identified in *Coolidge* v. *New Hampshire* (1971). In that decision, the court identified three criteria that must be present:

1. The officer must be present lawfully at the location to be searched.

2. The item seized must have been found inadvertently.

3. The item is contraband or would be useful as evidence of a crime.

The plain-view doctrine has been restricted by subsequent court decisions, such as the case of *United States* v. *Irizarry* (1982), in which the court held that officers cannot move objects to gain a better view of evidence otherwise hidden from view. This view was affirmed in the case of *Arizona* v. *Hicks* (1987), which stated that evidence seized must be in plain view without the need for officers to move or dislodge it.

Automobile Searches

The precedent established for warrantless searches of automobiles is the automobile exception, or the *Carroll* doctrine (*Carroll* v. *United States*, 1925). This decision established that the right to search a vehicle does not depend on the right to arrest the driver but on the premise that the contents of the vehicle contain evidence of a crime. In this case, George Carroll, a bootlegger, was convicted for transporting intoxicating liquor in a vehicle, a violation of the National Prohibition Act. At the trial, Carroll's attorneys contended that the liquor need not be admitted into evidence because the search and seizure of the vehicle were unlawful and violated the Fourth Amendment. Because of the mobility of the automobile, the warrantless search under *Carroll* is justified. After the *Carroll* decision, there existed some uncertainty about the moving vehicle doctrine. Much of this doubt was laid to rest in 1970, however, when the U.S. Supreme Court reaffirmed the right of officers to search a vehicle that is moving or about to be moved out of their jurisdiction, provided that probable cause exists that the vehicle contains items that officers are entitled to seize.

Since the ruling of the *Carroll* doctrine, related cases have raised the question of whether officers searching under *Carroll* also have the right to search closed containers in a car. In a 1981 decision, the U.S. Supreme Court held that warrantless seizures of evidence in the passenger compartments of a car, after a lawful arrest, are valid (*New York* v. *Belton*, 1981).

In a high-impact case, *California* v. *Acevedo* (1991), much of the confusion about vehicle searches was eliminated. Stated simply, the *Acevedo* case holds that if an officer has probable cause to believe that a container in an automobile holds contraband, the officer may open the container and seize the evidence, provided that the evidence is in fact contraband. Two subsequent cases further clarified the authority with which police officers may search vehicles.

The law on vehicle searches has changed dramatically over the past 20 years, enabling police officers more latitude in their search and seizure authority. For example, in *Pennsylvania* v. *Labron* (1993), the Supreme Court ruled that there is no need for a search warrant in vehicle searches if the vehicle is readily mobile, even if there is time to obtain a warrant. In a related case, the Court held that police officers with probable cause to search a car may inspect passengers' belongings found in the car that are capable of concealing the object of the search (*Wyoming* v. *Houghton*, 1999).[8]

Vehicle Inventory Search

In 1970, the U.S. Supreme Court reaffirmed the right of officers to search a vehicle that is moving or is about to be moved,

The Distinction between Arrest and Investigative Detention

There is a practical and legal distinction between a person's arrest and investigative detention. Simply put, the standard for placing a person under arrest is probable cause, whereas the standard for investigative detention is reasonable suspicion—a lower standard of proof than probable cause. Longstanding and nationally recognized police procedures permit an investigative detention based upon the officer's reasonable suspicion that the person detained has committed, is committing, or is about to commit a crime.

The practice of identifying and detaining persons in a residence is recognized as an appropriate control method during the service of a search warrant. Officers should take precautionary measures for their own safety during an investigative detention. These typically include the display of firearms or handcuffing the detainee.

provided that there is probable cause to believe that the vehicle contains items that are legally seizeable. In the *Chambers* v. *Maroney* (1970) case, the Court referred to the earlier case of *Carroll* v. *United States* and determined that a search warrant is unnecessary provided that probable cause exists that contraband is contained in the vehicle, that the vehicle is movable, and that a search warrant is not readily obtainable. This doctrine applies even if the vehicle has been driven to the police station by a police officer and there was time to secure a search warrant.

When a vehicle is seized, its contents are routinely inventoried to prevent subsequent claims by the defendant that items were taken. The search and the inventory are, however, two separate processes under law but can be conducted simultaneously. Evidence located as a result of the inventory search is admissible in court.

Open-Field Searches

In *Oliver* v. *United States* (1984), the U.S. Supreme Court reaffirmed its position that open fields are not protected by the Fourth Amendment. This differs from constitutional protection over buildings, houses, and the area surrounding them, known as *curtilage*. The curtilage is considered one's yard; thus, both the house and yard are protected and cannot be searched without a warrant or one of the exceptions mentioned. Open fields and pastures outside the curtilage are not protected by the Constitution; thus, searches made by the government of those areas are not considered "unreasonable."

This case is significant because the Court essentially stated that a person's "reasonable expectation of privacy" under the Fourth Amendment does not apply when the property involved is an open field.

Defining Curtilage

In a 1987 decision, *United States* v. *Dunn*, the Supreme Court ruled that the warrantless search of a barn that is not part of the curtilage is valid. From this decision came four factors that laid out whether an area is considered a part of the curtilage.

The *Dunn* decision, although still subject to imprecise application, is helpful because it narrows the definition of what buildings should be considered curtilage of the main residence.

Four Factors of Curtilage

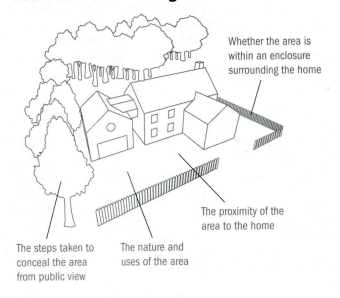

Whether the area is within an enclosure surrounding the home

The proximity of the area to the home

The nature and uses of the area

The steps taken to conceal the area from public view

▶ Making an Arrest

Criminal investigations often result in the arrest of a suspect or suspects. An improper or illegal arrest can negate all investigative efforts and result in the suspect going free. Legally speaking, an arrest is a seizure of a person. The Fourth Amendment reads, "The right of the people to be secure in their persons, houses, papers, and effects, against unreasonable searches and seizures, shall not be violated, and no warrants shall issue, but upon probable cause, supported by Oath or affirmation, and particularly describing the place to be searched, and the persons or things to be seized." It has been said that an estimated 80 percent of a criminal investigator's duties are uneventful, routine, and unglamorous. But the successful completion of an investigation will end in the arrest of a suspect, who will then be prosecuted. This process is far from routine. It is the arrest that is one of the most critical aspects of an investigator's responsibilities. Arrests are always dangerous and often result in injury or even death of the arresting officer. Therefore, certain considerations must be kept in mind by professional investigators before exercising this important police function.

LEARNING OUTCOMES 5 — Define an arrest.

What Is an Arrest?

One of the fundamental charges of criminal investigation is to identify a suspect in a crime and take him or her into custody. Indeed, when a suspect has been arrested pursuant to the filing of criminal charges or when an officer invokes the criminal process pursuant to the filing of charges, the officer must be familiar with certain critical legal guidelines.

The term **arrest** may take on many different interpretations. For example, it is the official interaction between a peace officer (law enforcement officer) and a suspected lawbreaker when the suspect is captured and delivered before the court. It may also be construed as the simple restriction of one's freedom by an agent of the government. There might not be an announcement of "You're under arrest" by the arresting officer, and *Miranda* warnings might not be given. In some cases, the suspect may not even consider himself or herself to be under arrest. When a person is arrested, he or she forfeits many constitutional rights. Consequently, because of the severe legal implications, the arresting officer must ensure fair and lawful treatment of the arrestee and the legal process of criminal apprehension.

The Lawful Arrest

Probable cause is required for a lawful arrest. The general test the courts consider to determine whether probable cause exists for an arrest is whether facts and circumstances within the officer's knowledge are sufficient to warrant a prudent person to believe a suspect has committed, is committing, or is about to commit a crime (see Box 5–2).[9]

LEARNING OUTCOMES 6 — Explain what is required for an arrest to be legal.

Fourth Amendment Requirements for a Constitutional Arrest

There are two types of arrests: formal (that is, intentional) arrests and detentions that last too long or are too invasive to constitute a *Terry* stop.

☑ The Fourth Amendment requires probable cause for an arrest.

☑ An arrest warrant is mandatory under the Fourth Amendment only when the police make a nonconsensual entry into a private residence to arrest someone inside (*Payton* v. *New York*, 1980).

An arrest warrant has two advantages over an arrest without a warrant:

☑ It ensures that evidence seized during an arrest will be admissible.

☑ It immunizes the officer from a civil suit.

However, both of the advantages above will be lost if the officer

• deliberately or recklessly includes false information in his or her affidavit, or

• fails to include enough factual information to enable a magistrate to make an independent determination as to whether probable cause exists for the arrest.

A defendant who is arrested without a warrant and not released on bail is entitled to a judicial determination of probable cause without undue delay after the arrest. Absent extraordinary circumstances, this detention must take place within 48 hours after a warrantless arrest.

Laws of arrest vary from one jurisdiction to another, but peace officers are generally authorized to make an arrest on the authority of an arrest warrant for either a misdemeanor or a felony offense. In many cases, the only restriction placed on the officer in these circumstances is the time of day that the arrest is authorized. As a general rule, whereas misdemeanor arrest warrants are authorized only during the daytime hours, felony warrants are typically authorized for daytime or nighttime service. Under the strictest interpretation of the U.S. Constitution, a warrant should be required for all arrests. However, the courts have loosely interpreted this requirement in allowing officers to arrest without a warrant if they personally observe any violation of the law.

Realistically speaking, arrests result after a situation between the officer and suspect develops, whereupon the officer requests information from the suspect. Only when the suspect attempts to leave and tests the limits of the officer's response may the suspect realize that he or she is really under arrest. The "free-to-leave" test was created in 1994 in *Stansbury* v. *California* in an effort to create a test to determine the point at which an arrest had been made.

The most common type of arrest is that which follows the questioning of a suspect. After a decision to arrest is reached, the officer must come to the conclusion that a crime has been committed and that the suspect is probably the one who committed it. The presence of these elements constitutes the probable cause needed for a legal arrest. Under any circumstance, probable cause is the minimum requirement for arrest, and when a suspect is caught in the process of committing a crime, the officer has the immediate probable cause required for arrest. Most jurisdictions permit a felony arrest without a warrant when a crime is not in progress, provided that probable cause has been established. In the case of *Payton* v. *New York* (1980), the U.S. Supreme Court ruled that unless the suspect gives permission or an emergency exists, an arrest warrant is necessary if an arrest requires entry into a suspect's private residence.

In a related Supreme Court ruling, *County of Riverside* v. *McLaughlin* (1991), a person arrested without a warrant must generally be provided with a judicial determination of probable cause within 48 hours after arrest. Arrests are authorized under the following conditions:

• When the officer has probable cause to believe that the person to be arrested has committed a violation of the law "in his or her presence"

• When the officer has probable cause to believe that the person to be arrested has committed a felony but "not in his or her presence"

• When the officer has probable cause to believe that the person to be arrested has committed a felony whether or not a crime has been committed

The in-presence requirement generally refers to the context of sight, but court rulings have supported prudent use of all five senses to support probable cause for a warrantless arrest. Other cases also have addressed the significance of the probable cause requirement. For example, *Draper* v. *United States* (1959) found that specific information as to the location of a suspect, when provided by a reliable informant, can also constitute probable cause for

BOX 5–2 🛡 Probable Cause

- An officer has probable cause to make an arrest whenever the totality of facts and circumstances known to the officer creates a fair probability that a particular person is guilty of a crime.

- Probable cause is analogous to reasonable suspicion in all ways but one: Probable cause requires evidence that establishes a higher probability of guilt.

- The Fourth Amendment requires probable cause for four different purposes: (1) a warrantless arrest, (2) issuance of an arrest warrant, (3) issuance of a search warrant, and (4) warrantless search and seizure.

an arrest. In *Brinegar* v. *United States* (1949), the courts underscored the importance of the probable cause requirement as it relates to arrests by stating that a relaxation of the requirement would leave law-abiding citizens at the mercy of the personal whims of police officers.

Detention versus Arrest

What constitutes an arrest? How does an arrest differ from an investigative **detention**? There are many different types of situations in which it might appear that an officer has arrested someone but has not. In his well-known book on police operations, Thomas Adams states that police intervention may be classified as a contact, a consensual encounter, an investigative detention, or an arrest:[10]

- *Contact.* In this situation, the subject is free to walk away if he or she so desires. It is the sole decision of the subject whether or not to cooperate with an officer.

- *Consensual encounter.* In this situation, the officer may not exert any authority over the subject. Officers can continue to seek the subject's cooperation but cannot demand it.

- *Investigative detention.* This is defined as something less than an arrest but more than a consensual encounter. Generally, this is when a person thinks that he or she cannot just walk away (*Terry* v. *Ohio*).

- *Arrest.* This is the act of placing a person in custody for a suspected violation of criminal law.

Investigatory Stops

Terry v. *Ohio* (1968) is the seminal case that recognized investigative stops (the investigative detention) as a separate category of seizures allowed on a lower degree of suspicion. Three constitutional requirements exist for an investigative detention, or a **Terry stop**, to be lawful:

1. The officer must be able to point to objective facts and circumstances that would warrant a reasonable police officer to link the detainee's conduct with possible criminal activity.

2. The officer must proceed with the investigation as expeditiously as possible to avoid unnecessarily prolonging the period of involuntary detention.

3. The officer must stay within the narrow investigative boundaries allowed for reasonable suspicion in *Terry* stop situations.

To satisfy the reasonable suspicion standard, the officer must possess objective grounds for suspecting that the person detained has committed, is committing, or is about to commit a crime. To satisfy this standard, the officer must be able to point to specific facts that, taken together with rational inferences that arise from them, provide a rational basis for suspecting the detainee of criminal activity.

Examples of how reasonable suspicion may affect criminal investigators

- **Criminal profiles.** Criminal profiles are groupings of behavioral characteristics commonly seen in a particular class of offenders. Although police are allowed to consider criminal profiles in evaluating the evidentiary significance of things they observe, the fact that a suspect exhibits characteristics included in the criminal profile is not a guarantee that a court will find that the officer possessed sufficient reasonable suspicion.

- **Tips from the public.** Police officers may not act on information received from members of the public without independent corroboration unless they have a rational basis for believing this information to be reliable.

- **Officer-to-officer information.** An officer who makes an investigatory stop (or an arrest) at the direction of another police department or officer need not be informed of the evidence that supports the action. However, if the officer making the stop lacks grounds to support the action, the stop will be constitutional only if the department or officer requesting the action had grounds to support it.

BOX 5-3 🛡

BOX 5-4 🛡 **A *Terry* stop must be . . .**

Police should also avoid doing the following during a *Terry* stop:
• Giving *Miranda* warnings before police have developed grounds for an arrest, unless highly intrusive safety measures become necessary during the stop
• Performing a weapons frisk without a reasonable suspicion that the detainees may be armed or dangerous
• Transporting detainees to a second location, unless this action is necessary for officer safety or to further the investigation
• Displaying weapons, using handcuffs, placing detainees in a patrol car, or performing other acts traditionally associated with an arrest, unless these precautions appear reasonably necessary for officer safety or to further the investigation

1. Brief (90 minutes maximum)
2. Conducted efficiently so as to avoid unnecessarily prolonging the period of involuntary detention
3. Confined to investigating the suspicion that prompted the stop unless clear grounds for reasonable suspicion of unrelated criminal activity developed during the stop

Whether the facts known to the officer provide an objective basis for reasonable suspicion is determined from the vantage point of a trained police officer. Courts consider "rational inferences that arise from the facts," as well as the facts themselves, in deciding whether the officer's information was sufficient to satisfy the reasonable suspicion standard.

Investigatory stops are allowed on a lower degree of suspicion than arrests because they are designed to be less intrusive than arrests. When the police overstep the lawful boundaries of an investigatory stop (see Box 5–3), the stop automatically escalates into an arrest, resulting in a violation of the detainee's Fourth Amendment rights unless probable cause for an arrest has already been established. Box 5–4 summarizes the element of a *Terry* stop.

When Is a Person under Arrest?

In most cases, it is easy to determine when a person is under arrest: A suspect is taken into custody based on a warrant or probable cause. Handcuffs are applied, and the suspect is read his or her *Miranda* warning and transported off to jail. However, is a person under arrest simply when an officer displays his or her "authority" to arrest (for example, turning on the red lights on a police car, ordering a person to stop, and so on)? The answer is that such actions may, indeed, not constitute a legal arrest.

The courts have held that a suspect is seized within the meaning of the Fourth Amendment whenever a law enforcement officer restricts his or her freedom to leave. This occurs when the suspect's liberty is restrained and brought under an officer's control, either through submission to a show of legal authority or physical restraint:

• *Seizure by submission to a show of legal authority.* The test for whether there has been a show of authority is objective— whether a reasonable person in the suspect's place would feel that he or she was not free to ignore an officer's request and walk away.

• *Seizure by physical restraint.* If the suspect does not submit to an officer's show of legal authority, no seizure occurs until the suspect is actually brought under the officer's control. The free-to-leave test has been repeatedly adopted by the court as the test for a seizure.[11]

This issue was considered in the *California* v. *Hodari* (1991) case, where the court ruled that a Fourth Amendment seizure does not occur when law enforcement officers are chasing a fleeing suspect unless the officers apply physical force or the suspect submits to the officer's show of authority. A juvenile named Hodari was standing with three other youths on a street corner in downtown Oakland, California. When an unmarked police car was observed approaching, the youths ran in different directions. An officer exited the police car, pursued, and finally caught up with Hodari. Just before being tackled, Hodari tossed away a bag containing crack cocaine that was later used as evidence to convict Hodari of possession of cocaine.

On appeal, the California Court of Appeal held that Hodari had been constructively seized as soon as the chase began; therefore, an arrest had taken place. The officer's display of authority was sufficient to place him under arrest. Consequently, because there was no probable cause for the arrest before the cocaine was discovered, it was inadmissible as evidence. The conviction was overturned.

Upon review by the U.S. Supreme Court, the justices considered the issue of whether or not an arrest had been made. There was no doubt that the officer had displayed his authority, that he wanted Hodari to stop, and that the suspect recognized all of this. However, even though the suspect had not submitted to arrest, was an arrest made? In a majority decision, Justice Antonin Scalia said, "An arrest requires either physical force . . . or, where that is absent, submission to the assertion of authority." He later added, "Neither usage nor common-law tradition makes an attempted seizure a seizure." The conviction was reaffirmed.

When there is no physical contact between an officer and a suspect, the totality of the circumstances must be considered when deciding if an arrest has been made. It must be shown that the officer's words or actions would have led a reasonable person to believe that he or she was not free to leave before the officer attempts seizure of the person. Also, the person must somehow show his or her submission to the officer's authority before the seizure actually occurs. Other factors affecting the legality of an arrest include the following:

• The officer must have the appropriate legal authority to do so (for example, jurisdiction).

• Arresting officers must be sure that persons arrested fall under the authority of the law (for example, being physically placed into custody by the officer or submitting to the assertion of authority).

Related U.S. Supreme Court decisions include the following:

- *County of Riverside* v. *McLaughlin* (1991). Detention of a suspect for 48 hours is presumptively reasonable. If the time to hearing is longer, the burden of proof shifts to the police to prove reasonableness. If the time to hearing is shorter, the burden of proof of unreasonable delay shifts to the suspect.

- *Florida* v. *Bostick* (1991). The test to determine whether a police–citizen encounter on a bus is a seizure is whether, taking into account all of the circumstances, a reasonable passenger would feel free to decline the officer's requests or otherwise terminate the encounter.

▶ Use of Force

Police are granted specific legal authority to use force under certain conditions (see Box 5–5). But the authority of officers to use force is limited. Penalties for abuse of authority can be severe, so police officers must be clear as to what they can and cannot do. The management of force by police officers is a constant challenge facing law enforcement managers. Balancing issues of a violent society with the safety concerns of police personnel creates many obstacles and concerns in developing departmental policies and procedures. The prevailing police perspective is based on a serious concern for the welfare of officers who must cope with the constant threat of a violent society. In contrast, citizens are fearful that police officers may exceed their legal bounds and use force as a means of punishment rather than control.

LEARNING OUTCOMES 7 — Explain when police officers can use force.

Police officers deal every day with persons who are violent, under the influence of drugs or alcohol, mentally deranged, or just desperate to avoid arrest. To cope, officers are granted specific legal authority to use force under constitutional law and the laws of most states. However, as noted, the authority of officers to use force is limited. Those limitations may be enforced through the use of criminal prosecution, civil lawsuits, and disciplinary actions. Our society recognizes three legitimate and responsive forms of force:[12]

BOX 5-5 🛡 Use of Force in Making an Arrest or Other Seizure

Use of excessive force is regulated by three provisions of the Constitution: the Fourth, Eighth, and Fourteenth Amendments.

- The Fourth Amendment standard used to evaluate whether unconstitutional force has been used in making a seizure is whether a reasonable police officer on the scene would have considered this amount of force necessary. This is called the *objective reasonableness standard.*

- Physical force may be used for the following three purposes only:

  1. To protect the officer or others from danger
  2. To overcome resistance
  3. To prevent escape

1. The right of self-defense, including the valid taking of another person's life to protect oneself

2. The power to control those for whom some responsibility for care and custody has been granted an authority figure, such as a prison guard

3. The institution of a police group that has relatively unrestricted authority to use force as required

Police officers are taught that the penalties for abusing their authority to use force can be severe. To avoid harsh penalties, police officers must be aware of the rules that govern the use of force. Such rules are included in state law, federal law, and department policy. The federal standard for police use of force was established by the U.S. Supreme Court in *Graham* v. *Connor* (1989). In that case, the Court recognized that the police officer's duty to make arrests and to conduct searches and investigatory stops carries with it the authority to use force reasonably or to threaten the use of force. The *Graham* decision allows officers to use force for two reasons only: defense and control, not punishment. One must remember that the Fourth Amendment protects the "right of the people to be secure in their persons . . . against unreasonable searches and seizures and shall not be violated." Because a police officer's use of force constitutes a seizure, using excessive force is a violation of a citizen's rights under the Fourth Amendment.

When police are compelled to use force, a court will use the following standard to determine whether such force was reasonable. First, the officer's conduct will be compared with that of a "reasonable officer" confronted by similar circumstances. Second, when the judge and jury evaluate the officer's actions, they must do so from the "standing in your shoes" standard. This means they can only make use of information the officer had at the time that he or she exerted force; 20/20 hindsight cannot be considered in this analysis.

The Commission set forth guidelines that identify levels of force and the permissible use-of-force techniques within each level:

1. Social control (uniformed presence)
2. Verbal control
3. Weaponless control techniques (including pressure or pain holds), starting at "hands-on" with no pain, stunning (diffused impact with soft striking surfaces), and mechanical (skeletal)
4. Electronic control weapons
5. Chemical agents
6. Control instruments (equivalent to weaponless pressure or pain holds)
7. Impact weapons (equivalent to weaponless mechanical modes)
8. Firearms (and other means of force that could cause death or serious bodily damage when used)

Remember, modern-day police officers must not only know how to use force techniques, such as the swinging of a baton, but must also know when to apply those techniques. The use of force by police officers stems from the premise that in a modern democratic society, citizens are discouraged by law from using force to solve personal disputes. Instead, they are expected to rely on the justice system to arbitrate and resolve conflicts. With few exceptions, such as cases involving self-defense, this restriction applies to most situations.

Understanding Reasonableness

Under the *Graham* decision, the Court identified three key factors based on the totality of the circumstances to use in evaluating an officer's use of **reasonable force**:

1. The severity of the crime committed
2. Whether the suspect posed an immediate threat to the safety of officers or others
3. Whether the suspect actively resisted arrest or attempted to evade arrest by flight

According to the *Graham* decision, active resistance to arrest includes any physical actions by the suspect that make the arrest physically more difficult to accomplish. Active resistance to arrest includes pushes and shoves as well as more obscure actions, such as holding on to the steering wheel while being removed from a car. An interesting finding of the *Graham* decision was an explanation of the standards under which officers' conduct should be judged by a jury and trial judge. First, the actions of the officer(s) will be compared to actions of a "reasonable officer" involved in a similar situation. Second, the Court said that when the judge and jury evaluate the officer from within the "shoes" of the officer under review, they must make their decision based on the information the officer had at the time that he or she took action. Thus, hindsight cannot be used to consider the behavior of the officers in question.

Levels of Force

In 1991, the Christopher Commission, which investigated the Los Angeles Police Department in the Rodney King beating

incident, found that there was a significant number of officers who regularly used force against the public and who often ignored department guidelines for the use of force. Under department guidelines, officers were required to exercise the minimum amount of force necessary to control a suspect.

Although it is important to consider this continuum in determining the various levels of force, it is also important to consider operational basics that apply to all police officers regarding the use of force. For example, experience tells us that although modern aerosol sprays can cause considerable discomfort, they seldom (if ever) result in bodily injury. In comparison, use of a baton may result in serious tissue damage, depending on the area targeted by the officer. So because using aerosol spray has a lower propensity for causing pain or injury, it has a low level of force.

Another example is the use of impact weapons, such as a baton or a flashlight. The flashlight has a greater propensity to create damage than the baton, and although the flashlight is commonly used as an impact weapon, it is not designed for this use. In comparing the two, it is easy to see that a flashlight would be on a higher level of force than a baton. Officers should constantly consider their options when approaching what they perceive to be a dangerous situation. In doing so, if the need to use force becomes a reality, proper application of force will be available quickly. Figure 5–4 shows a continuum used by many law enforcement agencies in the United States to determine appropriate use of force.

▶ Use of Deadly Force

In 1967, the President's Commission on Law Enforcement and the Administration of Justice noted that most police departments had no policy to guide them on the use of **deadly force**. At the time, most state laws were extremely broad in defining the circumstances under which officers could use deadly force. In its most commonly used parlance, the term *deadly force* refers to actions of police officers that result in the killing of a person. As mentioned previously, police officers are legally authorized to use deadly force under certain circumstances.

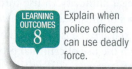

LEARNING OUTCOMES 8 — Explain when police officers can use deadly force.

As a rule, such actions result from situations in which persons are fleeing the police, assaulting someone, or attempting to use lethal force against another person (including a police officer). If deadly force is used improperly or illegally, the officers responsible may be criminally liable, and both the officers and the police department may be sued in a civil action. Most rules regarding the use of deadly force come from federal statutes and case law and, as a rule, are concerned with police use of deadly force to arrest fleeing felons engaged in nonviolent felonies. These cases are different from those pertaining to suspects committing violent felonies, such as murder, assault, rape, robbery, or other types of behavior that represent a substantial risk of bodily harm or death. Figure 5–5 shows the three factors that must be present to justify deadly force.

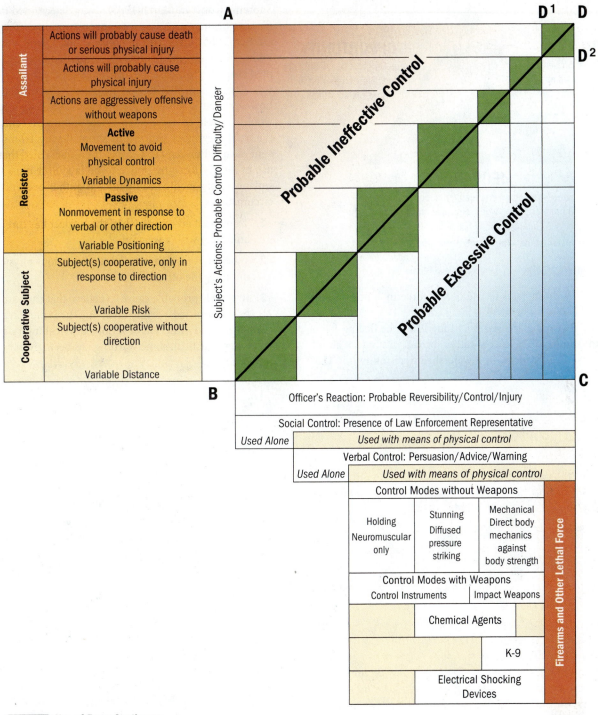

							D¹	D

A

Assailant
- Actions will probably cause death or serious physical injury
- Actions will probably cause physical injury
- Actions are aggressively offensive without weapons

Resister
- **Active** Movement to avoid physical control
- Variable Dynamics
- **Passive** Nonmovement in response to verbal or other direction
- Variable Positioning

Cooperative Subject
- Subject(s) cooperative, only in response to direction
- Variable Risk
- Subject(s) cooperative without direction
- Variable Distance

Subject's Actions: Probable Control Difficulty/Danger

Probable Ineffective Control

Probable Excessive Control

D¹ **D** **D²**

B **C**

Officer's Reaction: Probable Reversibility/Control/Injury

Social Control: Presence of Law Enforcement Representative

Used Alone | *Used with means of physical control*

Verbal Control: Persuasion/Advice/Warning

Used Alone | *Used with means of physical control*

Control Modes without Weapons

Holding Neuromuscular only	Stunning Diffused pressure striking	Mechanical Direct body mechanics against body strength

Control Modes with Weapons

Control Instruments	Impact Weapons

Chemical Agents

K-9

Electrical Shocking Devices

Firearms and Other Lethal Force

FIGURE 5–4 Use-of-Force Continuum.

The Fleeing-Felon Rule

Until the mid-1980s, the shooting of a suspect by police was tolerated by many police agencies. Although this is currently not the case, it was prevalent in the early development of policing, when most felonies were punishable by death and there was an assumption that all felons would avoid arrest at any cost. Therefore, the **fleeing-felon rule** was developed during a time when apprehension of felons was considered more dangerous than it is today. Police officers in those early days often worked alone and lacked sophisticated communications technology with which to track suspects who were wanted by police.

The concern was that felons would escape arrest and retreat to another community, where they could begin a new life of crime. As time went by and more efficient means were developed for apprehension, arrests became easier for law enforcement officials. For a period of time, police still relied on the ability to use deadly force even though some felons were not considered dangerous and posed no particular threat to the officer or the community. Before 1985, police officers were legally

ABILITY
Attacker must possess
the power to kill or
inflict crippling injury

OPPORTUNITY
Attacker must be capable of
immediately employing that
power in an attack

JEOPARDY
Attacker must act in a manner that a reasonable
and prudent person would conclude that the attacker
has intent to kill or inflict crippling injury

FIGURE 5–5 **Decision Model: The Deadly Force Triangle.**
Source: From Olson, D. T. (1998). Improving deadly force decision
making. *FBI Law Enforcement Bulletin* February: 1–8.

authorized by most states to use deadly force in apprehending fleeing felons.

Over the years, many states had modified the fleeing-felon rule, but some still allowed rather broad discretion about when to use deadly force. In a watershed decision by the U.S.

Supreme Court in March 1985, it was determined that Tennessee's fleeing-felon law was unconstitutional. *Tennessee* v. *Garner* (1985) involved the police shooting and subsequent killing of an unarmed boy as the youth fled from an unoccupied house. In this case, the officer could see that the suspect was a youth and that he was unarmed. The officer argued, however, that if the youngster were able to leap a fence, he would be able to escape. The state statute in Tennessee at the time permitted officers to shoot fleeing felons to prevent escape. Pursuant to *Garner*, the Court ruled that for the use of deadly force by police to be lawful, it must be "reasonable." Reasonable deadly force is authorized under three circumstances:

1. To prevent an escape when the suspect has threatened an officer with a weapon

2. When there is a threat of death or serious physical injury to the officer or others

3. If there is probable cause to believe that the suspect has committed a crime involving the infliction or threatened infliction of serious physical injury and, when practical, some warning has been given by the officer

The Search for the Craigslist Ripper

First appearing in 2007, the Long Island Serial Killer (also referred to by media sources as the "Gilgo Killer" and the "Craigslist Ripper") is an unknown serial killer who is thought to have murdered at least four prostitutes and dumped their bodies along the Ocean Parkway, near the remote beach towns of Gilgo Beach and Oak Beach in Suffolk County and the area of Jones Beach State Park in Nassau County. As of April 10, 2011, eight bodies had been dumped just feet from Ocean Parkway, a highway leading to the popular Jones Beach State Park. In December 2010, investigators, while following the disappearance of a New Jersey woman who was seen working as a Craigslist escort, happened upon the corpses of four women. The women were identified as missing prostitutes who had booked clients over the Internet. Four additional bodies were found when officers returned to the area in late March 2011. All eight bodies were located within an eight-mile radius on the north side of the parkway. Investigators determined that some of the victims had been dead for a long time and that the four women found in December 2010 were probably killed somewhere else and dumped by the beach highway. Investigators approached the investigation slowly and methodically, looking at the evidence to see what might be similar or dissimilar about the victims. In May 2011, the investigation continued as the search for more bodies moved to Nassau County, where police cadaver dogs and additional

Frances A. Miller/Shutterstock.com

mounted police units joined the search. As of the preparation of this text, a suspect has not yet been identified in the killings. The disturbing nature of this case demonstrates the importance of a thorough investigation and one whereby evidence must be gathered properly and legally.

Sources: Police widen search for more victims of Craigslist Ripper as they believe his killing spree could have spanned over four years. *Associated Newspapers Ltd* part of *The Daily Mail, The Mail on Sunday & Metro Media Group.* Retrieved from http://www.dailymail.co.uk/news/article-1373774/Craigslist-killer-Rippers-killing-spree-4-years-long-body-count-rises-9.html.

The investigation of serial homicide cases represents one of the greatest challenges to criminal investigation:

1. Using the chapter material and the preceding case, how do you think information for a search warrant could be relevant or important to the case?

2. Given this case, what are your thoughts on the use of warrantless searches, based on the chapter material?

Identify the legal guidelines for conducting searches.

Of paramount importance in criminal investigations is the officer's ability to be aware of and work within constitutional (and departmental) guidelines. Investigators must remember that they not only must have legal grounds to begin a search but that while conducting the search, they must not contaminate any evidence.

1. Explain the roles played by the Fourth, Fifth, and Sixth Amendments in searches and seizures and how they relate to the investigative process.

2. Define "scope of the search" and how it relates to criminal investigation.

3. What is probable cause?

4. What facts help establish probable cause?

5. What are some of the important cases involving police searches?

probable cause The minimum amount of information necessary to cause a reasonable person to believe that a crime has been or is being committed by a particular person.

exclusionary rule The legal rule that excludes evidence that has been determined to have been obtained illegally.

scope of the search An officer's authority to search incident to an arrest.

Explain the exceptions to the exclusionary rule.

The exclusionary rule states that courts will exclude any evidence that was illegally obtained even though it may be relevant and material. The U.S. Supreme Court has developed several exceptions to the exclusionary rule, including the good-faith exception, the inevitable discovery doctrine, and the computer errors exception.

1. Explain the practical benefits of the exclusionary rule and how the rule impacts criminal investigations—negatively and positively.

2. What are the historic legal origins of the exclusionary rule?

3. Explain the three major exceptions to the exclusionary rule.

4. What is the impact of these exceptions on police work and behavior?

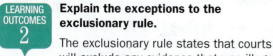

Summarize what information must be contained on a search warrant.

The search warrant is one of the most valuable tools in criminal investigation. It authorizes the search of homes, businesses, and vehicles of suspects; typically results in the arrest of multiple suspects; and expedites investigation and subsequent case closure.

1. What are the advantages of searching with a search warrant?

2. What are ways in which obtaining a search warrant benefits the criminal investigator?

3. What specific information must be included in a search warrant?

4. How can a search warrant be used?

5. In what ways does the search warrant aid the prosecutor?

search warrant A legal document enabling a police officer to search.

triggering condition An anticipated future event giving rise to a probable cause to search.

Explain when warrantless searches are considered lawful.

Depending on certain statutory restraints, an officer can make an arrest without an arrest warrant, provided that probable cause exists. A number of exceptions to the search warrant requirement have been identified by the courts.

1. Under what conditions can a search be conducted without a search warrant?

2. What are the legal justifications for searching without a warrant?

3. Which constitutional amendment deals with warrant requirements?

4. What are some situations in which a judge may uphold a warrantless search?

consent search When police gain permission to search without a warrant.

exigent circumstances Circumstances whereby a search may be legally conducted without a warrant.

stop and frisk When an officer stops and searches a person for weapons.

plain-view doctrine A legal doctrine whereby police officers have the opportunity to confiscate evidence, without a warrant, based on what they find in plain view and open to public inspection.

Define an arrest.

The successful completion of an investigation will end in the arrest of a suspect. An officer has probable cause to make an arrest whenever the totality of facts and circumstances known to the officer creates a fair probability that a particular person is guilty of a crime. In most cases, it is easy to determine when a person is under arrest: A suspect is taken into custody based on a warrant or probable cause, handcuffs are applied, and the suspect is read his or her *Miranda* warning and transported off to jail.

1. Identify the legal and practical effects of making an arrest that is illegal and how doing so affects criminal investigations.

2. Explain the legal requirement for making a lawful arrest.

3. What is the most common type of arrest?

4. What is the difference between detention and arrest?

5. What is meant by reasonable suspicion?

arrest The act of a police officer taking a person into custody after making a determination that he or she has violated a law.

detention Something less than an arrest but more than a consensual encounter.

***Terry* stop** An investigative detention.

Explain what is required for an arrest to be legal.

Probable cause is required for a lawful arrest. The general test the courts consider to determine whether probable cause exists for an arrest is whether facts and circumstances within the officer's knowledge are sufficient to warrant a prudent person to believe a suspect has committed, is committing, or is about to commit a crime. Officers generally establish probable cause through their own observations. Examples include,

1. Did the suspect attempt to run away when approached by the officer?

2. Did the suspect admit to any part of the alleged crime?

3. Did the suspect behave furtively, as if he or she were trying to hide something?

Explain when police officers can use force.

Police are granted specific legal authority to use force under certain conditions. But the authority of officers to use force is limited. Physical force may be used for the following three purposes only: to protect the officer or others from danger, to overcome resistance, and to prevent escape.

1. Explain the use-of-force continuum and under what circumstances an officer's escalation of force is justified.

2. Identify the constitutional standard for use of force by police as identified under *Graham* v. *Conner*.

3. What is the fleeing-felon rule?

4. What Supreme Court case established the rules for use of force by law enforcement officers?

reasonable force The amount of force that is considered reasonable to capture or subdue a criminal suspect.

Explain when police officers can use deadly force.

It is critical to remember that an officer's force response to a suspect pivots on that suspect's level of threat of resistance.

deadly force Actions of police officers that result in the killing of a person.

fleeing-felon rule A legal doctrine, no longer in effect, allowing police officers to shoot suspected felons.

Additional Links

www.Star-Telegram.com
For in-depth stories on the Michael A. Gilbert case mentioned earlier in the chapter, visit the site of the Fort Worth Star-Telegram.

www.Supremecourt.gov
This is the official site of the U.S. Supreme Court. The site gives visitors access to various court documents, including oral arguments and opinions. The site has video resources, press releases, and media advisories. It includes links for jobs and internship programs as well as related organizations such as the Federal Judicial Center and the United States Sentencing Commission. Visitors can also search for documents and docket files.

www.hrw.org
This is the website of the Human Rights Watch, which conducts investigations of human rights abuses in 70 countries. The site has a report on the Christopher Commission, which investigated the Los Angeles Police Department following the Rodney King beating in 1991. It also includes a police brutality report for 14 major metropolitan areas in the United States. New Orleans; Atlanta; Washington, D.C.; and New York are among the cities profiled.

www.americanbar.org
This is the site of the American Bar Association, which calls itself the national representative of the legal profession. The site contains information on basic criminal law, the police and your rights (*Miranda* rights), rules on search and seizure, and victims' rights.

"The information-gathering process through interviews and interrogations is one of the most important in the criminal justice process."

Interviews and Interrogations

1 Differentiate between interviews and interrogations.

2 Describe effective interviewing and interrogation techniques.

3 Describe the procedures for conducting the cognitive interview technique.

4 Explain the procedures for proper interrogations.

5 Summarize the legal requirements of interviewing and interrogation, including *Miranda* rights.

6 Identify how lying and deception are detected.

7 Explain why people confess.

8 Summarize how to take written and recorded statements.

INTRO WHEN POLICE IGNORE THE RULES

On April 9, 1993, Morris and Ruth Gauger, both in their 70s, were found murdered on their property in McHenry County, Illinois. Morris Gauger was discovered by his son, Gary Gauger; Ruth Gauger was later found by McHenry County deputies.

After the grisly discovery, Gary Gauger was subjected to a nearly day-long interrogation by police, during which they claimed to have found evidence of the murders both on Gauger's person and in his bedroom. Investigators had found no such evidence—and thus there was no physical evidence to use against Gauger in court—but they insisted on its existence. Although Gauger initially claimed that he had been asleep at the time of his parents' murders, after the interrogation he confessed, believing that perhaps he had committed the murders even though he had no memory of them.

At his trial, Gauger was found guilty of both murders and was sentenced to death early the next year. Gauger spent nearly two years in prison before, on March 8, 1996, the Second District Illinois Appellate Court ordered a new trial. Gauger's incriminating statements and alleged confession, the court said, should not have been admitted at the trial because his arrest had been made without probable cause, and those statements were the product of that arrest.

As the confession had been the strongest bit of evidence against Gauger, without it the charges against him had to be dropped, and he was released. Although the McHenry County state's attorney continued to claim that Gauger was guilty of the murders, two members of a Wisconsin motorcycle gang were eventually indicted for the murder of the Gaugers.

DISCUSS **In what ways can society ensure that police play by the rules?**

The Gauger case illustrates the influence of an interrogation and confession in a criminal investigation. It also demonstrates the importance of a properly conducted interrogation that is free of coercion, influence, and suggestibility.

In their authoritative book *Criminal Interrogation and Confessions*, Inbau and his associates illustrate the importance of gleaning information through interviews and interrogations. They state, ". . . the art and science of criminal investigation have not developed to a point where the search for and the examination of physical evidence will always . . . reveal a clue to the identity of the perpetrator. . . ."[1] In fact, experience has shown that in many cases, physical evidence is completely absent, and the only remaining approach is the *interview* of witnesses or the *interrogation* of the suspect.

In cases in which physical evidence is identified and implicates a suspect, the investigator's job is still not finished. The matter of proof and prosecution remains. It is the duty of each investigator to attempt to secure a confession from suspects they have arrested. Again, legal considerations must always be kept in mind to ensure that all statements are admissible in court.

▶ *Interview versus Interrogation*

During the course of an investigation, an investigator will probably conduct many interviews and several interrogations. The

LEARNING OUTCOMES 1 Differentiate between interviews and interrogations.

distinction between an interview and an interrogation is often blurred, but it can be expressed in terms of the purpose of the contact.

An **interview** is a question-and-answer session with a suspect, victim, or witness that is non-accusatory in nature. The objective of an interview is to learn information and evaluate the subject's credibility. Examples of investigative questions include, "Where were you at 11:30 last night?" or "Do you own or have access to a pistol?" or "Do you know who Laurie Stevenson is?" Other interview questions are specifically designed to produce behavioral responses from the subject. For example, "Do you think this woman really was raped?" or, "Tell me why you wouldn't force a woman to have sex with you."

During this process, it is crucial that the investigator maintain a non-accusatory demeanor during the interview. This even applies when the investigator is convinced that the subject has lied or is clearly being deceptive to a question designed to cause a behavioral response. In this case, if the investigator challenges the subject, he will become cautious and less willing to offer information. On the other hand, a subject will offer considerably more important information if he does not feel threatened. So, an investigator should allow, and even encourage, subjects to lie during an interview. As long as the subject continues to respond to the investigator's questions, the investigator is learning something.

According to John Reed & Associates, during an interview the investigator should talk about 20% of the time and the person being interviewed 80%.[2] To achieve this balance the investigator should keep his or her questions concise and, whenever possible, prompt a narrative response from the subject (opposed to a one-word response such as "yes" or "no"). One investigative pitfall is when the investigator reveals more information to the subject through their questions than the subject has revealed about their possible role in the crime. The role of the interrogation is to elicit the truth from a person who, according to the investigator, has lied during an interview. The interrogation is therefore an effort to persuade the subject to tell the truth. In some cases, an innocent person will be the subject of an interrogation. When this happens, interrogation tactics used must not be so aggressive as to result in a false confession. One way to avoid this is to warn the subject about possible consequences followed up with an assurance of leniency if the subject confesses to the crime.

The **interrogation** should not consist of questions that are accusatory because this will result in continued denials from the subject. Instead, it should consist of a monologue during which the investigator makes statements crafted to convince the subject to tell the truth. The monologue typically addresses the circumstances that led up to the subject's commission of the crime. Furthermore, logic and rational arguments (based on evidence known by the investigator) can be used to convince the subject to tell the truth.

During an interrogation, the investigator's demeanor should be understanding toward the subject's criminal behavior. It is psychologically much easier for a subject to tell the truth to someone who appears to understand why he or she committed the crime. At no time should the investigator remind the subject of the seriousness of the offense or the possible punishment for it. Such reminders merely reinforce the subject's effort to avoid consequences through continued denials.

If the investigator's persuasive statements have an impact on the subject, the guilty subject often exhibits signs indicating that he or she is considering telling the truth. At this point the investigator asks a question that offers the subject two choices concerning some aspect of the crime. For example, "Did you plan this out for months and months in advance or did it pretty much happen on the spur of the moment?" If the subject now acknowledges that the crime happened on the spur of the moment, this represents his or her initial admission of guilt.

Once the subject makes an initial admission of guilt, active persuasion stops and the investigator returns to the interviewing mode, where a full confession is elicited by asking non-accusatory questions. If the subject is truly guilty of the offense, he or she will be able to provide the investigator with details of the crime that only the guilty person would know.

On the other hand, if the investigator makes no clear distinction between interviewing and interrogation, less information will be learned when questions are asked during the interaction that resembles "interviewing" and the persuasive impact of the "interrogation" stage will be minimized. Of most concern, however, is that the guilty subject may never truly be persuaded to reach a stage where he or she is willing to openly talk about the crime (the first admission of guilt). Under this circumstance, often active persuasion is used to extract details of the confession piece by piece. The voluntariness of that confession, and even its trustworthiness, may later be challenged in court.

▶ The Interview Process

The interview is a form of communication used extensively by law enforcement. It is used in many ways to glean information from the subject being interviewed. Investigators should take the time to prepare properly for the interview. Occasionally, this preparation must be done quickly and may consist of no more than a mental review of the details of the case, but some type of preparation should precede actual contact with the subject being interviewed. Generally,

the most common interviews that investigators will conduct are with witnesses, cooperating citizens, victims, informants, and suspects. Let's look at the fundamentals of each of these (see Box 6–1).

Interviewing Witnesses, Citizens, and Victims

Investigators must remember that although the interview process is geared toward those believed simply to have information about a crime, witnesses often turn out to be suspects. Sources for interviews include the victim, witnesses, and the complainant. These subjects should be separated before questioning begins.

▶ The Cognitive Interview

Another widely accepted interviewing technique is the cognitive interview. As a rule, the cognitive interview technique is used for eliciting information from victims and witnesses, as opposed to obtaining confessions from suspects. The primary focus of the cognitive interview is to make witnesses and victims of a situation aware of all the events that transpired.[3]

Describe the procedures for conducting the cognitive interview technique.

Two main forces were behind the development of the cognitive interview. The first was the need to improve the effectiveness of police interviews when questioning witnesses. The second was to apply the results of psychological research in this area, particularly the work of Elizabeth Loftus, whose research had already dispelled the myth that an eyewitness's memory operates like a video camera.[4] As a result, Ronald P. Fisher of Florida International University and Edward Geiselman of UCLA developed the technique of cognitive interviewing.[5]

A number of differences can be identified between traditional interviewing techniques and the cognitive approach. For example, traditional interviewers attempt to bring out information by asking specific questions; they target a question for each content area that they need to address. For instance, if an investigator needs to find out how tall the perpetrator was, then he or she asks the question, "How tall was the perpetrator?" And if the investigator wants to determine the angle of the plane that was approaching the airport, he or she would ask a direct question such as, "What was the angle of the plane as it approached the airport?"

The traditional interviewer asks many questions, each of which elicits a very brief response. The cognitive interview, on the other hand, is less directive and is in some ways a questionless interview. The goal is to ask as few questions as possible so that witnesses give you long narrative responses that each contains that much more information than a traditional interview.[6] The objective is to try to elicit information, not extract information. The good interviewer tries to create a social environment so the witness generates information without having to wait for questions to be asked.

The cognitive interview is carried out in a series of several steps.[7] First, an introduction is made that establishes a

BOX 6-1 🛡 The Following Considerations Should Be Observed during the Interview Process:

- *Develop a plan of action.* The investigator should be familiar with pertinent data about the incident in question before initiating the interview. He or she should take care to develop questions designed to elicit the particular task at hand. For example, questions directed to a witness should be tailored to obtain specific facts for the police report. Questions that are prepared in advance will tend to add to the flow of conversation and give direction to the interview.

- *Conduct the interview in private.* It is sometimes easier to fulfill this requirement than others, depending on the circumstances. In all cases, it is important to provide interviewees with the greatest amount of privacy possible, both to encourage clarity of thought and to protect the confidentiality of the interview.

- *Place the interviewee at ease.* Most interviews involve a great amount of stress and emotional discord for the interviewee. This is usually created by a sense of uncertainty about the expectations of the investigator and the uniqueness of the situation. If a degree of fear develops in the person being interviewed, he or she may withhold information. Indeed, it is during the preliminary phase of the interview that the investigator's personality will be tested rigorously. The investigator should therefore take great care to make the person being interviewed as comfortable as possible and to build rapport. In addition, the investigator should attempt to uncover any reasons for the interviewee's reluctance to cooperate. It is also important to relax the person being interviewed because comments made by a calm person are easier to evaluate than those made by someone who is nervous. This can be accomplished by beginning the interview casually with friendly conversation. Certainly, a strained or awkward initial contact with the subject might convey the message that the investigator doesn't like something about the interviewee. A friendly approach will help defuse any negative feelings in the subject and reinforce positive ones.

- *Be a good listener.* After the communication barrier is lifted, the investigator must learn to let the interviewee speak freely. Indeed, this is a great shortcoming of many investigators because many feel the need to interrupt or share their personal opinions with interview subjects. It is the job of the interviewer to listen closely and evaluate not just *what* is being said but *how* it is being said. In short, it is the responsibility of the investigator to control the interview but not to dominate it.

- *Ask the right questions.* Not only is it important to know what questions to ask the subject but also how those questions should be asked. During the conversation, the investigator's emotions should be in check at all times, along with an attempt to make the questions easy to comprehend. In addition, the phrasing of questions is critical to the success of the interview. For example, close-ended questions, requiring a simple yes or no response, should be used sparingly. This type of question doesn't elicit personal information from the subject; it simply permits the person to confirm or deny information being offered. A preferable technique is to ask open-ended questions, which force the interviewee to relate in his or her own words what was observed. Hypothetical questions should also be avoided because they tend to make the interviewee guess at a certain response or to tell the interviewer what he or she wants to hear. Finally, the interviewer should avoid asking loaded, or leading, questions that contain the answer and require the person being interviewed to choose between the lesser of two evils.

- *Don't dispute the subject's answers.* The emotional reactions of the investigator must be kept under control at all times. After the subject gives his or her interpretation of what happened, the investigator can later go back and document any discrepancies.

- *Maintain control of the interview.* Frequently during an interview, the subject might try to steer the conversation away from the subject at hand. Again, proper preparation is the key to having a good plan and to staying on track.

- *Take brief notes.* After the interviewee begins to talk freely, the investigator should avoid interruptions. An attempt to take complete notes while a citizen is narrating a story will probably disrupt the flow of information. This generally occurs because the witness sees the investigator writing profusely and will slow down just to accommodate him or her. In doing so, the witness may become distracted and forget important details. Furthermore, some people are just naturally nervous speaking in the presence of someone recording everything they say. Brief notes are therefore the prescribed method of recording the conversation. These generally consist of names, addresses, and certain phrases that will outline the narrative for review. Most important, however, the investigator should listen carefully and not lose eye contact with the witness.

- *Adjourn the interview properly.* Just as the interview process begins with a proper introduction, it should also end appropriately. Generally, a concluding remark is appropriate, such as, "OK, you may leave—thank you for your time." It might also be advisable to summarize the interview briefly with the witness before dismissal. Such expressions of courtesy during and after the interview create a favorable impression and encourage further cooperation.

relationship between the witness and the interviewer. At this point the interviewer introduces the four retrieval rules to the witness and asks him or her to use these techniques. The interviewer then gives the witness an opportunity to provide an uninterrupted narration of what he or she saw. During this time, the interviewer is able to construct a strategy for carrying out the remainder of the interview. The interviewer will then guide the witness through several fact-based scenarios, after which the interviewer will evaluate the witness's recollections. The completion of this last step is followed by the completion of the interview. Although a two-hour interview is possible, the optimal length for a cognitive interview is about an hour.[8]

The two major subtypes of cognitive interviewing methods are think-aloud interviewing and verbal-probing techniques.[9]

"Think-Aloud" Interviewing

The think-aloud interview derives from psychological procedures described by Ericsson and Simon (1980).[10] The term *think-aloud* is used to describe a very specific type of activity in which subjects are explicitly instructed to "think aloud" as they answer the survey questions. The interviewer reads each question to the subject and then records or otherwise notes the processes that the subject uses in arriving at an answer to the question. The interviewer interjects little else, except to say, "Tell me what you're thinking" when the subject pauses.[11]

The advantages of the "think-aloud" interview technique is that it elicits responses from the subject that are free from interviewer bias and that little formal training is required to prepare the interviewer for the use of the technique. The disadvantages are that it is easy for the subject to lose focus and stray from the task.[12]

Verbal-Probing Techniques

As an alternative to the think-aloud technique, the use of verbal probing is the basic technique that has increasingly come into favor with cognitive researchers.[13] After the interviewer asks the survey question and the subject answers, the interviewer then asks for other, specific information relevant to the question or to the specific answer given. In general, the interviewer "probes" further into the basis for the response. Examples of the probing technique include the following:

> "You stated that you saw the man entering her apartment. What means did he use to gain entry?"

> "When you say you saw the men drive away, describe the manner in which they were operating the car."

The advantages of the probing technique are that the investigator can control the interview with relative ease, and the subject of the interview can easily adjust to the method used by the investigator.[14]

▶ The Suspect Interrogation Process

During any case, it is important for information to be obtained by means of a direct interview with a suspect. As indicated earlier, it is not at all uncommon during the progress of a case for a person who was interviewed as a witness or victim to become a

primary suspect at a later date. In that event, as the case progresses, the investigator can use information learned in the earlier interview.

Goals of the Interrogation

The interrogation is designed to match new information with a particular suspect to secure a confession; the goals of the process are shown in Box 6–2.

Safeguarding against Police Misconduct

Several types of behavior have been identified as improper (even illegal) for police investigators and will result in any confession obtained from the suspect being deemed inadmissible

by the courts. These behaviors include coercion or duress, physical constraint, unreasonable delay in arraignment, and refusing legal counsel during interrogation.

BOX 6–2 🛡 The Goals of the Interrogation Process Are as Follows:[15]

- To learn the truth of the crime and how it happened
- To obtain an admission of guilt from the suspect
- To obtain all facts to determine the method of operation and the circumstances of the crime
- To gather information that enables investigators to arrive at logical conclusions
- To provide information for use by prosecutors in possible court action

Coercion and Duress

Coercion and duress are similar in that they both create an environment of intimidation during the interrogation process.

Coercion is defined as the use, or threat of use, of illegal physical methods to induce a suspect to make an admission or confession. **Duress** is the imposition of restrictions on physical behavior, such as prolonged interrogation and deprivation of water, food, or sleep. In *Brown* v. *Mississippi* (1936), the U.S. Supreme Court ruled that physical coercion used to obtain a confession was a violation of the Fourteenth Amendment. Following this ruling, the Court focused its attention on cases in which "psychological" rather than physical coercion was used to prompt a confession.

The Suspect's Right to Legal Counsel

The legal guidelines to protect the rights of the accused were defined further by the U.S. Supreme Court in such cases as *Escobedo* v. *Illinois* (1964) and *Miranda* v. *Arizona* (1966). Surprisingly, before 1964, there were no legal rules requiring the presence of an attorney during the interrogation of a criminal suspect. In a ruling in May 1964, the U.S. Supreme Court reversed the conviction of a lower court because prosecutors had used incriminating statements made by the defendant to a friend that were overheard by a federal agent. The remarks were made after the defendant was indicted and while he was out on bail. The Court held that the statement was made by the defendant without the advice of his attorney, whom he had already retained. So, according to the Court, the defendant was deprived of his Sixth Amendment right to an attorney.

The Miranda Warning

In the *Miranda* v. *Arizona* (1966) case, a 23-year-old, Miranda, was arrested and transported from his home to the police station for questioning in connection with a kidnapping and rape. He was poor and uneducated. After two hours of questioning, officers obtained a written confession that was used against him in court. He was found guilty of the kidnapping and rape.

The legal question in this case is "Do the police have a responsibility to inform a subject of an interrogation of his or her constitutional rights involving self-incrimination and a right to counsel before questioning?" Again, the answer is yes.

In addition to being informed of these rights, the suspect must also agree, freely and voluntarily, to waive them before police can

STATEMENT OF RIGHTS AND WAIVER	CITY POLICE DEPARTMENT	DATE
PLACE		
NAME	CASE NO. *(If applicable)*	

Before we ask you any questions, you must understand your rights. You have the right to remain silent. Anything you say can be used against you in court or other proceedings. You have the right to talk to a lawyer for advice before we ask you questions, and to have him with you during questioning. You have this right to the advice and presence of a lawyer even if you cannot afford to hire one. In such a case you have a right to have a court-appointed attorney present at the interrogation. If you wish to answer questions now without a lawyer present, you have the right to stop answering questions at any time. You also have the right to stop answering at any time until you talk to a lawyer.

You may waive the right to advice of counsel and your right to remain silent and answer questions or make a statement without consulting a lawyer if you so desire.

WAIVER

I ☐ have read ☐ had read to me the statement of my rights shown above. I understand what my rights are and I elect to waive them. I am willing to answer questions and make a statement. I do not want a lawyer. I understand and know what I am doing. No promises or threats have been made to me and no pressure of any kind has been used against me. I was taken into custody at *(time)* _____ ☐ A.M. ☐ P.M., on *(date)* _____, and have signed this document at *(time)* _____ ☐ A.M. ☐ P.M., on *(date)* _____.

WITNESS	SIGNATURE OF PERSON WAIVING RIGHTS
WITNESS	

FIGURE 6–1 Sample Waiver of Rights Form.

begin questioning (see Figure 6–1). Accordingly, the suspect may invoke his or her right to stop answering questions at any time during the interrogation. Several court cases have arisen over the years that relate to *Miranda* and custodial interrogations. For example, *Rhode Island* v. *Innis* (1980) interpreted the meaning of interrogation by stating that in addition to direct questioning, interrogation also refers to any actions or remarks made by police that are designed to elicit an incriminating response.

The Public Safety Exception to Miranda

The public safety exception to *Miranda* was ruled on in *New York* v. *Quarles* (1984). This decision found that police officers who are reasonably concerned for public safety may question persons who are in custody and who have not been read the *Miranda* warning (see Figure 6–2). The U.S. Supreme Court also found that subsequent statements are admissible

MIRANDA WARNING

1. You have the right to remain silent.
2. Anything you say can and will be used against you in a court of law.
3. You have the right to talk to a lawyer and have him present with you while you are being questioned.
4. If you cannot afford to hire a lawyer, one will be appointed to represent you before any questioning, if you wish.
5. You can decide at any time to exercise these rights and not answer any questions or make any statements.

FIGURE 6–2 Sample *Miranda* Warning Card Carried by Officer.

in court. In this case, a woman complained to two officers that an armed man had just raped her. After giving the officers a description of the man, they proceeded to a nearby supermarket, where Benjamin Quarles was located. After a brief chase, the officers frisked Quarles and discovered an empty shoulder holster. After the suspect was in handcuffs, the officer asked Quarles where the gun was, and he nodded in the direction of some empty cartons and said, "It's over there." The gun was retrieved, and Quarles was arrested and read the *Miranda* warning.

When the case went to trial, the court ruled that under the requirements of *Miranda*, the statement "It's over there" and subsequent seizing of the weapon were inadmissible at the defendant's trial. On review, the U.S. Supreme Court acknowledged that Quarles should have been given the *Miranda* warnings. However, the Court recognized that the need to have the suspect talk was more important than the reading of the *Miranda* warning. The Court also ruled that if *Miranda* warnings had deterred the suspect from giving such information, the cost to society would have been much greater than the simple loss of evidence: As long as the gun remained in the pile of cartons, it posed a public safety hazard.

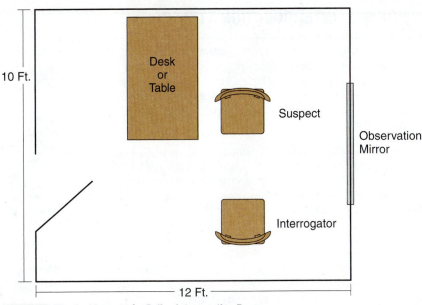

FIGURE 6–3 Physical Layout of a Police Interrogation Room.

Defining Custody

Miranda applies only when testimonial evidence is being sought. In addition, it applies only to **custodial interrogations**, not to circumstances in which the suspect is free to leave. The custodial interrogation rule applies not only when the suspect has been arrested before questioning but also when his or her liberty has been restricted to a degree that is associated with arrest. Therefore, an interview itself can also be considered custodial even though no arrest has been made. It depends on the circumstances. For example, if the suspect is being questioned in a relaxed atmosphere at his or her own residence, the *Miranda* warning need not be given. Conversely, if the suspect is approached in his or her own home by officers possessing an arrest warrant, the *Miranda* warning must be given before questioning. In brief, the test is whether the interview is custodial, not whether the investigation has focused on a particular person being interviewed.

The Interrogation Setting

In addition to the manner in which the interrogator treats the suspect, it is also important to consider the physical surroundings where the questioning occurs. Because of pressure from peers and family members who might be present at the scene, it is important to remove the suspect from familiar surroundings and take him or her to a location with a more sterile and less threatening atmosphere. A key psychological factor contributing to successful interrogations is privacy. This encourages the suspect to feel comfortable in unloading the burden of guilt. The structure of the interrogation setting should also be conducive to

the obtaining of confessions. Its surroundings should reduce fear and therefore encourage the suspect to discuss his or her role in the crime. Consequently, the interrogation room should reflect a more business-like atmosphere than a police-like environment.

The interrogation should be conducted in a room specifically designed for that purpose only (see Figure 6–3). It should be isolated from the bustling activity of the rest of the office, the sound of police radios, overhead intercoms, and other interruptions. Ideally, a soundproof room best serves this purpose. The interrogation room should be well lit but not to the extent that its lights are glaring. In addition, it should be protected from interruptions and equipped with some means of communicating with the outside, such as a buzzer or office intercom. Furnishings should be minimal, consisting of chairs, preferably without a desk, and containing pencil and paper but otherwise nondescript, with no distracting decorations.

Ideally, no obstacles such as tables or desks should block the interviewer's full view of the subject's body. A large portion of nonverbal behavior emanates from the lower body, not just from the hands and face. Feet that fidget or point to the door communicate discomfort. If subjects sit behind a desk or table, the investigator should instruct them to relocate. Deceivers often use soda cans, computer screens, and other objects (both large and small) to form barriers between themselves and the interviewer—behaviors consistent with dishonesty.[16]

▶ The Interrogation Procedure

As a rule, two investigators handle the interrogation: One actually conducts the questioning, and the second acts as a witness to statements made by the suspect. Obviously, the two investigators should meet before the interrogation to discuss their "roles." Frequently, one investigator will assume one approach to the suspect, and the other will assume a different and sometimes contrasting style (see Box 6–3). The suspect may be more receptive to one approach than the other.

BOX 6–3 INTERROGATION STYLES

Investigators have developed a variety of interrogation styles and techniques over the years. The decision to choose one style over the other may depend on many factors, including the personality of the suspect, the personality of the interrogator, and the nature of the case. Some of the most common styles of interrogation are described here.

- *Logical style.* In a case in which the evidence seems to be overwhelming, such as a drug trafficking case involving a drug purchase from an undercover agent, the investigator may try to appeal to the suspect's sense of logic. In doing so, the investigator, it is hoped, will persuade the suspect that cooperation is the only way the charges against him or her can be lessened. It is important to note here that promises of leniency to the suspect should not be made without direct authorization from the prosecuting attorney. The only promise that can be made is that his or her cooperation will be brought to the attention of the prosecutor for consideration of some kind of leniency.

- *Sympathetic style.* If the investigator thinks that the suspect is easily affected by an emotional appeal, the sympathetic approach might be a good technique. The interrogation is approached by speaking in low tones and will include expressions of concern and understanding for the suspect and his or her spouse, children, business, and so on. The investigator stimulates feelings of self-pity in the suspect when he or she blames others for his or her plight. Ideally, further relief of guilt

is achieved by the suspect's agreeing to cooperate with the investigator.

- *Indifferent style.* In this technique, the investigator acts as though he or she does not really care if the suspect cooperates or not but thinks that he or she must go through the motions of making the opportunity available to the suspect. This style suggests that the investigator would rather see the suspect punished severely by the court rather than give him or her the opportunity to gain leniency through cooperation.

- *Face-saving style.* In this approach, the investigator attempts to give the suspect a "way out" that will justify his or her participation in the crime. By systematically rationalizing the suspect's actions up to the point of the violation, describing them as natural consequences of some other problem, the investigator tries to get the suspect to start talking about his or her actions. Periodically, the investigator interjects comments that tend to diminish the importance of the suspect's own involvement in the crime.

- *Egotistical style.* Here the investigator plays on the suspect's sense of pride and precision in the commission of the crime. It is pointed out how daring and difficult the crime was to implement and that it took a great degree of planning and intelligence to pull it off. This approach encourages the suspect to brag about his or her involvement in the crime and to provide additional details to impress the investigator.

▶ Detecting Deception

Verbal Symptoms of Deception

Because of certain psychological and cultural differences, a perceptive investigator can sometimes readily identify the manner in which people lie. For example, a trained listener can observe a pattern of evasiveness in the suspect and after a period is able to identify these statements as lies or efforts to deceive.

LEARNING OUTCOMES 6 · Identify how lying and deception are detected.

Liars and Lying

Lying requires the deceiver to keep the facts straight, make the story believable, and withstand scrutiny. When individuals tell the truth, they often make every effort to ensure that other people understand. In contrast, liars attempt to manage others' perceptions. Consequently, people unwittingly signal deception via nonverbal and verbal cues. Unfortunately, no particular nonverbal or verbal cue demonstrates deception.[17] The ability of an investigator to detect deceptive behavior depends largely on his or her ability to observe, catalogue, and differentiate human behavior. The more observations investigators make, the greater the probability of detecting deception. Here are some indicators of deceptive behavior:

Research has shown that vocal changes occur 95 percent of the time when a person lies. A liar's speech rate and voice pitch will also increase 95 percent of the time.[18] In

addition, liars will usually stall before giving an answer, to give them time to decide if they should lie or tell the truth, or to decide just how big a lie to tell. Liars will always attempt to con the investigator. They may choose to tell a big lie, a misleading statement, or the complete truth. In most cases, they will attempt to dodge the truth. For example, they may restate the question or ask to have it repeated. They might say "I can't remember" or that they don't understand the question. If the subject stammers, stutters, or has a mental block before answering the question, most of the time he or she is lying.[19]

Lying Techniques

Liars often lie by using *specifics*. For example, the suspect may say, "I don't even own a gun!" Although this could be a true statement at face value, he or she might have borrowed a gun to commit the crime but is relying on the fact that the statement is a true one, and the investigator will, it is hoped, infer that the suspect didn't commit the crime. Liars tend to admit only what the investigator can prove and deny what can't be proved. In addition, they sometimes make an issue out of trivial things. For example, if a suspect complains about the manner in which the government has treated him in the past, he is probably attempting to sway away from the real issue.

Other lying techniques commonly used include the following:

- The suspect tries to confuse the interviewer by arguing about trivial points rather than addressing the real issues.

Think About It...

"Aren't They Just Questions?" There are a lot of folks who interchangeably use the terms "interview" and "interrogation" to refer to police discussions as part of their official duties; however, interviews are non-accusatory whereas interrogations are accusatory. What most people do not consider is that interviews and interrogations require mastery of various techniques in order to do them effectively. So, simply having the authority to conduct either an interview or interrogation does not correlate to successful police work. What are some of the interview and interrogation techniques offered in the chapter, and why might some of them be particularly important?

© Marmaduke St. John/Alamy

Suspect Being Interrogated by Detective.

- A debating tactic is used in which the suspect tries to discount the investigator's argument in advance. For example, if the investigator makes a statement regarding a piece of evidence, the suspect replies, "You don't really expect anyone to believe that, do you?" The big lie or repeated assertion is based on the assumption that if you say something over and over, people will start to believe it. Repeated denial of the violation only reinforces the suspect's ability to lie.

- The "you don't understand" tactic is used by experienced liars to block an in-depth interrogation. This is attempted by saying, "You wouldn't understand," "You don't know how these things work," or "How would someone like you be expected to know?"

- The "loophole" liar is a dodger who is unsure just how much the investigator knows about the crime. Loophole liars typically respond by saying, "I can't remember" or "to the best of my recollection." This technique gives the person a way out in case he or she is later confronted with contradictory evidence.[20]

Use of the Polygraph

Of the mechanical devices that have been designed to aid investigators in obtaining information, the **polygraph**, or "lie

Physical Characteristics of Lying

Head Position

- *Tilted:* cooperative, interested, probably truthful
- *Jutting forward, no tilt, jaw up:* angry, aggressive, stubborn
- *Chin on chest, no tilt:* depressed, bored, probably lying

Eyes

- *Breaks eye contact* (1 to 2 seconds is common): suddenly tensed, probably lying; may not resume eye contact until a new subject is discussed
- *Looks at ceiling and blinks:* just decided to confess
- *Pupils fully dilated:* high degree of emotional arousal, probably lying
- *Closes eyes:* trying to mentally escape, probably lying
- *Narrowed eyes:* looking for trouble, anticipating the worst
- *Rapid blinking:* nervous, probably lying

Legs

- *Men with crossed legs:* probably lying

Eyebrows

- *Both raised with mouth partly open:* surprised, probably truthful
- *One raised:* confused, skeptical, probably truthful
- *Squeezed together and lowered:* angry, worried, confused

Hands

- *Covers both eyes:* probably lying
- *Hands over mouth:* probably lying
- *Hand on chin:* probably truthful
- *Touches or rubs nose while talking:* probably lying
- *Hands clasped together, holding back of head:* probably truthful

Feet

- *Moves feet beneath chair:* probably lying
- *One foot tucked beneath the other:* probably truthful

detector," has proven to be of extreme value. Proper use of this tool can help an investigator determine a suspect's guilt or innocence. However, because of recent court rulings restricting the use of the polygraph in certain settings, the investigator should view this device as an aid only, not as a last resort or panacea.

The polygraph is designed simply to measure whether or not the person being tested is being deceptive. As the subject is asked different questions, the graphs observed by the operator will, it is hoped, indicate a truthful or a deceptive response. Indeed, the device does not actually do what its moniker indicates—it does not detect lies. What it does do is measure the physiological responses from the subject, including fear, anxiety, excitation, and other emotions. So the critical consideration in the use of a polygraph is not the machine itself but the operator's ability to interpret its results accurately.

Accuracy of the Polygraph

The criminal justice field is divided as to its acceptance of polygraph results. In fact, most courts do not accept the findings of a polygraph exam as absolute evidence except when stipulated to by all parties. Problems with the use of the polygraph have been in its application. Specifically, the machine should be used to identify statements as being false, not for the purpose of actually detecting lies.

Think About It…

Deceptions Abound . . . There are many who believe that certain techniques for detecting physical characteristics of lying apply to all cases. This can often be dangerous if the circumstances of the situation are not taken into account. Such belief can also be dangerous if someone exhibits one characteristic, but not a combination (for example, some people are in the habit of crossing their legs). What are some of the physical characteristics of lying, and how are they supposed to be considered by investigators?

Stephen Orsillo/Shutterstock.com

A CLOSER LOOK

Is the Polygraph Junk Science?

Although the courts still call it "junk science," the lie detector or polygraph has never been so widely used by criminal justice agencies as a tool for determining the truth. In 1998, the U.S. Supreme Court ruled against the use of polygraph evidence in criminal court, but police agencies still rely on the polygraph exam to make critical personnel decisions from hiring to firing. Over the years, the percentage of police agencies using polygraphs to screen new employees increased from 16 percent in 1962, for example, to 62 percent in 1999, according to a study conducted by Michigan State's School of Criminal Justice. The same survey shows that police are confident of exam results—more than three-fourths believe that polygraphs are 86 to 100 percent reliable.

At the Federal Bureau of Investigation (FBI), which employs over 11,000 agents, senior officials have requested permission to administer up to 225 polygraphs per year in investigations of suspected employee misconduct. That figure is in addition to the 3,000 tests given each year to new agents and witnesses and informants in major criminal investigations. The Central Intelligence Agency (CIA), National Security Agency, Defense Department, Treasury Department, and many large police departments across the nation also depend on the polygraph. Failing a polygraph, as in the case of scientist Wen Ho Lee at Los Alamos National Laboratory in New Mexico, can end a career just as quickly as a guilty verdict. Lee was fired after he failed an FBI-administered polygraph in March 1999 and refused to co-operate with the government's investigation of Chinese espionage at the facility, which is the nation's premier weapons facility.

Fearing unwarranted invasions of individual privacy, Congress passed the *Employee Polygraph Protection Act* of 1988 to curb what had

Polygraph.

pefostudio5/Shutterstock.com

been a growing use of polygraph tests in private businesses. In 1998, the U.S. Supreme Court expressed concerns about the reliability of polygraphs when it upheld the military's ban on use of them in criminal trials. Yet government agencies still consider polygraphs a valuable personnel tool.

Given concerns about the accuracy of the polygraph and its admissibility in court, how can this investigative tool be used in the course of an investigation? Is it more prudent for a law enforcement organization to rely on cognitive interviewing techniques than the use of the polygraph to elicit admissions and confessions? Explain your response.

Sources: Johnson, K. (1999, April 6. Government agencies see truth in polygraphs. *USA Today*, 11A; McCarthy, S. (2000). The truth about the polygraph. Health & Body website. Retrieved from http://archive.salon.com/health/feature/2000/03/02/polygraph/index.html.

The value of an examination can be looked at in two regards: reliability and validity. *Reliability* refers to the consistency of the examination's results. This can be shown through reproducing the examination repeatedly and obtaining the same results. Indeed, when properly administered, the polygraph can produce very reliable results. *Validity* refers to the accuracy of the examination. Validity can be affected by two considerations. First is the ability of the polygraph examiner to interpret the results of the examination accurately. Second, if the measurements that are recorded by the instrument fail to indicate lying directly, the examination lacks validity.

Admissibility of Polygraph Results

Over the years, the courts have addressed various aspects of the issue of polygraph results and their admissibility in court. Clearly, the machine can only detect certain changes in the human body, and estimates are that such changes can be detected up to 95 percent of the time. Despite arguments in favor of the use of the polygraph, its results are not currently admissible as absolute evidence in court. One early court case upheld a ruling of a trial court that refused acceptance of the results of the polygraph (*Frye* v. *United States*, 1923). Later that same year, the court in *People* v. *Forts* considered the results of the polygraph inadmissible based on doubts about the instrument's reliability. The *State* v. *Bohner* (1933) case also failed to accept the results of the polygraph but acknowledged its usefulness. Exceptions occur, however, when all parties stipulate to the acceptance of the results before administration of the exam.

The Voice Stress Analyzer

An investigative tool gaining considerable popularity with law enforcement agencies is the voice stress analyzer (VSA; see Figure 6–4). Unlike the computer polygraph, the VSA requires no wires to be attached to the subject being tested. The VSA uses only a microphone plugged into the computer to analyze the subject's responses. As the subject speaks, the computer displays each voice pattern, numbers it, then saves each chart to file. Unlike the polygraph, drugs do not affect the results of the exam, and there are no known countermeasures that will cause the ubiquitous "inconclusive" results associated with the polygraph.

Rapidly supplanting the polygraph, the VSA has been used in many investigative situations such as homicide, sex crimes, robbery, white-collar crimes, and internal affairs investigations, as well as preemployment examinations for background investigators. The system has been used as an investigative tool for verifying statements of witnesses and denials of suspects and for determining the validity of allegations made against police officers.

Microtremors are tiny frequency modulations in the human voice. When a test subject is lying, the autonomic, or involuntary, nervous system causes an inaudible increase in the microtremors' frequency. The VSA detects, measures, and displays changes in the voice print frequency. A laptop computer processes these voice frequencies and graphically displays a picture of the voice patterns. Furthermore, the VSA is not restricted to "yes" and "no" answers and is able to accurately analyze tape recordings of unstructured conversations.

▶ Why Suspects Cooperate and Confess

When we consider that self-destruction and self-condemnation are not normal human behavioral characteristics, it is perplexing why someone would openly confess to a crime. In addition, one could conclude that when a person is arrested and taken to a police station for questioning, he or she will not readily admit (and will even choose to lie about) his or her part in a crime. Many criminals, particularly career criminals, have developed a keen sense of observation over the years. It is likely that this sense has aided them in the past in avoiding detection by police. Such criminals can easily see the direction in which an interrogation is going. Logically, then, one would think that the dialogue between the suspect and investigator would be brief. Strangely, because of complex psychological factors, this is not always the case.

LEARNING OUTCOMES 7 — Explain why people confess.

Searching for Information

Depending on the crime in question and the particular suspect, it is logical to assume that many criminals follow the progress

FIGURE 6–4 Modern-Day Lie Detector.

Courtesy of Mike Himmels

of the police through media accounts of the investigation. Still, they really don't have a good sense of exactly what the investigator knows and doesn't know about the suspect. It is the desire of the criminal to want to know exactly what the investigator knows about the crime. This "paranoia" frequently drives the suspect to accompany the investigator willingly to the police station for an interview. Once at the station, however, the suspect not only tries to learn what the investigator knows about the investigation but also attempts to lead him or her away from the focus of the investigation.

Closing the Communication Gap

Research indicates that most guilty persons who confess are, from the outset, looking for the proper opening during the interrogation to communicate their guilt to investigators.[21] Suspects also make confessions when they believe that cooperation is the best course of action. Before they talk, they need to be convinced that investigators are willing to listen to all the circumstances surrounding the crimes. Finally, suspects confess when interrogators are able to speculate correctly on why the crimes were committed. They want to know ahead of time that interrogators will believe what they have to say and will understand what motivated them to commit the crime.

Admission versus Confession

Although seemingly alike, there is a notable difference between the admission of a criminal act and the confession of one's complicity in a crime. An **admission** is a self-incriminating statement made by the suspect that falls short of an acknowledgment of guilt. It is, however, an acknowledgment of a certain fact or circumstance from which his or her guilt can be inferred. Conversely, a **confession** is direct acknowledgment by the suspect of his or her guilt in the commission of a specific crime or as being an integral part of a specific crime. For the confession to be lawful, the investigator must be mindful of the constitutional checks governing its admissibility.

False Confessions

For a number of reasons, innocent people sometimes confess to crimes they did not commit. These reasons include mental health issues and law enforcement tactics that place undue pressure on suspects to "cooperate."

Although it can be hard to understand why someone would falsely confess to a crime, psychological research has provided some answers. Moreover, in 2009, the Innocence Project reported that through DNA exonerations, the problem has been revealed as more widespread than many people think. For example, in approximately 25 percent of the wrongful convictions overturned with DNA evidence, defendants made false confessions, admissions, or statements to law enforcement officials.[22]

▶ *Written Statements*

A confession from the suspect should substantiate the elements of the charge or at least contain information related to the investigation. In addition, the statement of the confession should contain any details of extenuating circumstances or explanations offered by the suspect that might be grounds for additional inquiry. Several variables determine what methods are used to take the statement.

LEARNING OUTCOMES 8 — Summarize how to take written and recorded statements.

These include the intelligence level of the suspect, the amount and nature of information to be recorded, and the availability of stenographic services. In many cases, the suspect will be willing to give a verbal statement about his or her involvement in a crime but might be unwilling to have it written down at the time. If this occurs, the investigator should not interrupt the remarks being made by the suspect just to ask for a signed statement. Instead, after the suspect is finished giving his or her account of what happened, the investigator should ask if the suspect would be willing to sign (or write) a statement to that effect. The suspect should be assured that only the information given to the investigator will be included in the statement and that he or she will have the prerogative of not signing it if it is not accurate.

If these techniques are adopted, the investigator must use the same phrases that were used by the suspect. The completed statement should then be shown to the suspect so that any changes can be made. Once corrections are in order, the statement is signed. The investigator should be careful to make the written statement reflect only one crime because in a criminal trial, the court will ordinarily not permit the introduction of evidence of additional crimes. Exceptions to this are when additional crimes tend to show intent, the identity of the defendant, or the scheme used in the commission of the crime in question. Therefore, the best policy is to obtain a separate written statement for each crime committed.

Structuring the Written Statement

The statement should begin with the place, date, identification of the maker, and the name of the person who is giving the statement. It is acceptable for the body of the statement to be in narrative or expository form. In addition, it should include all the elements of the crime as well as any facts that connect the suspect with the crime. If the investigator or stenographer prepares the statement, the suspect should be asked to read and sign each page at the bottom. To ensure that the suspect actually reads the statement, he or she should be asked to correct any typographical errors and to initial any corrections in ink. Finally, each page should be labeled "page _____ of _____ pages." The concluding paragraph should state that the suspect has read the statement consisting of so many pages and that the statement is "true and correct." After the suspect signs the statement in the space provided, two witnesses should sign it under the suspect's signature. Normally, the witnesses are the interrogators. Any more than two witnesses could leave the impression with the court that the suspect was intimidated by a large number of police at the time of the statement. See Figure 6–5 for an example of a voluntary statement form.

▶ Recorded Statements

Frequently, the investigator will choose to record a statement made by a suspect. This can be especially advantageous when the suspect cannot read or write or when he or she is only fluent in a foreign language. One important point to remember is that when the investigator chooses to record the statement, the interrogation should still be conducted first. When it is time to record the statement, the investigator uses his or her notes from the first interrogation to develop the recorded statement. When the recording is complete, the recorded statement is then played back for the suspect to hear so he or she can verify that it is a true and accurate representation of what was said during the interrogation.

Confessions on Video

On the basis of a national survey, it is estimated that one-third of all large police and sheriff's departments in the United States record at least some interrogations on video, a practice that is most common in cases of homicide, rape, and aggravated assault.[23] Proponents claim that documenting the interrogation through video has a number of benefits, such as deterring coercive behavior on the part of investigators and providing a more complete and accurate record of the confession for the judge and jury to evaluate the voluntariness and veracity of the defendant's statement.[24]

For evidentiary purposes, an interrogation that is captured on video should provide a complete and objective record of police–suspect interaction. But the question is still raised: What is a complete and accurate record? For example, in an actual police confession in New York, police were convinced that they recorded a confession from a "neutral" camera angle. The camera was positioned behind the investigator and focused directly on the suspect. Although this may seem innocent enough, research suggests that it is not. On the basis of studies showing that people make causal attributions to factors that are visually salient, Lassiter and his colleagues recorded mock interrogations from three different camera angles so that the suspect, the interrogator, or both were visible to mock jurors. The result was that those who saw only the suspect judged the situation as less coercive than those focused on the investigator. By directing visual attention on the suspect, the camera can lead jurors to underestimate the amount of pressure actually exerted by the "hidden" investigator.[25]

CITY POLICE DEPARTMENT
VOLUNTARY STATEMENT

_____
Case #

_____
Date

I _____ am _____ years of age and
currently reside at _____ which is located in the city
of _____.

Statement:

_____

_____

_____

_____

_____

_____

_____

_____

_____

_____

I have read this statement which consists of _____ page(s) and I affirm that it was given
voluntarily and that all the facts are truthful and accurate.

This statement was given at _____ (location) on the
_____ day of _____, 20___, at _____ (am) (pm).

_____
Signed

_____
Witness

_____
Witness

FIGURE 6–5 Sample Voluntary Statement Form.

The Stephanie Crowe Murder Investigation

The case of 12-year-old Stephanie Crowe illustrates how interviews and interrogations can result in the incorrect implication of a suspect. In 1998, noise from Stephanie's alarm clock radio caused her grandmother, Judith Kennedy, to go her room; she was soaked in blood from having been stabbed. Police learned that six hours before Stephanie's body was discovered, witnesses saw Richard Raymond Tuite, a 28-year-old transient, standing in the Crowes' driveway looking up at their house. The police questioned him about the murder then turned their focus toward the family.

After Stephanie's body was discovered, the police separately interviewed each member of the entire Crowe family. They specifically focused their attention on Stephanie's 14-year-old brother Michael, who was questioned for 27 hours over a three-day period. They also extensively interviewed two of his closest friends. By the time the interrogations ended, the police had obtained a confession from Michael and one of his friends and enough incriminating evidence from the third boy to file murder charges against them all. Although the boys allegedly confessed, there was a great deal of doubt concerning the accuracy of their statements and the method used to get them. The police allegedly used lies, false promises, isolation from parents and attorneys, and even threats of adult prison and predatory older inmates as persuasive techniques to get a confession. False confession expert Richard Leo analyzed the recorded interrogations and came to a shocking conclusion. He determined that the interrogations were textbook examples of how not to question suspects, finding that it amounted to a form of psychological torture so coercive that the boys would have said almost anything to make it stop. Charges against Michael Crowe

© AF archive / Alamy

were subsequently dropped and Richard Tuite was charged with the murder six years later when three drops of blood were found on his shirt.

Not only does this case illustrate the importance of conducting a proper and professional interrogation, but it also shows how when a suspect is incorrectly identified, the real perpetrator goes free. It is no small miracle that Tuite did not claim another victim after being released from his initial detention with police.

Sources: Chacon, D. J. (2004, May 26). Verdict brings mixed reaction in Escondido. *Union-Tribunes SignonSan-Diego.com*; Sauer, M., & Wilkens, J. (1999, May 11). Haunting questions: The Stephanie Crowe murder case. *Union-Tribunes SignonSanDiego.com*; Witt, A., & Schwartzman, P. (2001, June 7). Prince Georges prosecutor targets questioning; police must provide interrogation notes. *Washington Post*.

The investigation of serial homicide cases represents one of the greatest challenges to criminal investigation:

1. From a proactive investigative standpoint, in what ways can crimes such as this be prevented? Consider investigative efforts by patrol officers and investigators.
2. Discuss the ways in which interrogators can formulate questions that are improper, leading, and likely to elicit incriminating answers from the suspect.

CHAPTER 6 · Interviews and Interrogations

LEARNING OUTCOMES 1

Differentiate between interviews and interrogations.

Investigators must make a clear distinction between the two processes of interviewing and interrogating suspects. An interview should precede every interrogation. An interview is a relatively formal conversation conducted for the purpose of obtaining information. An interrogation is the systematic questioning of a suspect for the purpose of obtaining a confession.

1. What are the practical differences between the terms *interview* and *interrogation*?

2. What are the legal implications of the term *in custody*?

3. Who are some of the people most likely to be interviewed by investigators?

4. What is the ultimate goal of an interrogation?

interview A relatively formal conversation conducted for the purpose of obtaining information.

interrogation The systematic questioning of a person suspected of involvement in a crime for the purpose of obtaining a confession.

LEARNING OUTCOMES 2

Describe effective interviewing and interrogation techniques.

The investigator will have a more productive interview if it can be conducted at a location where the subject is mentally relaxed, the subjects are separated before questioning begins, and the investigator asks the right open-ended questions. It is the job of the interviewer to listen closely and evaluate not just *what* is being said but also *how* it is being said.

1. What are the circumstances and/or environment under which an investigator can conduct an investigative interview?

2. How should investigators prepare for an interview?

3. Why shouldn't all witnesses be asked the same questions?

4. What are the most effective questions to use during an interview?

5. What are the five goals of the interrogation process?

6. What types of questions should be avoided during the course of an interview?

7. Why should questions be prepared in advance of the interview?

LEARNING OUTCOMES 3

Describe the procedures for conducting the cognitive interview technique

The cognitive interview technique is used for eliciting information from victims and witnesses, as opposed to obtaining confessions from suspects. A number of differences can be identified between traditional interviewing techniques and the cognitive approach. For example, traditional interviewers attempt to bring out information by asking specific questions; they target a question for each content area that they need to

address. The objective is to try to elicit information, not extract information.

1. What type of person/witness/victim is the best candidate for a cognitive interview?

2. How is a cognitive interview best utilized in a criminal investigation?

3. Describe the process of conducting a cognitive interview.

LEARNING OUTCOMES 4

Explain the procedures for proper interrogations.

The interrogation is designed to match new information with a particular suspect to secure a confession. As a rule, two investigators handle the interrogation: One actually conducts the questioning, and the second acts as a witness to statements made by the suspect. Obviously, the two investigators should meet before the interrogation to discuss their "roles." Frequently, one

investigator will assume one approach to the suspect, and the other will assume a different and sometimes contrasting style.

1. Explain the differences between a properly conducted interrogation and one that is not.

2. Describe the physical environment of a properly conducted interrogation.

LEARNING OUTCOMES 5

Summarize the legal requirements of interviewing and interrogation, including *Miranda* rights.

Several types of behavior are improper (even illegal) for police investigators and will result in any confession obtained from the suspect being deemed inadmissible by the courts. These behaviors include coercion or duress, physical constraint, unreasonable delay in arraignment, and refusing legal counsel during interrogation. The suspect must be informed of his or her *Miranda* rights, and must also agree, freely and voluntarily, to waive them before police can begin questioning.

1. How does coercion differ from duress?

2. What amendment to the U.S. Constitution guarantees a defendant the right to an attorney?

3. Before police begin an interrogation, what activities are paramount?

4. What are key factors that contribute to successful interrogations?

5. What factors impact the type of interrogation style employed by investigators?

coercion The use or threat of illegal physical means to induce a suspect to make an admission or confession.

duress The imposition of restrictions on physical behavior such as prolonged interrogation and deprivation of water, food, or sleep.

custodial interrogation A process of questioning a suspect when his or her liberty has been restricted to a degree that is associated with arrest.

LEARNING OUTCOMES 6

Identify how lying and deception are detected.

An investigator can detect deceptive behavior by observing, cataloguing, and differentiating human behavior. Some indicators of deceptive behavior include changes in speech rate and voice pitch, stalling, restating the question, requesting that the question be repeated, stammering, stuttering, and/or mental blocks. Mechanical devices used to detect deception are the polygraph, or "lie detector," and the voice stress analyzer (VSA).

1. From an investigator's point of view, what are the most obvious indicators of deceptive behavior?

2. From an investigator's point of view, what are more subtle indicators of deceptive behavior?

3. How does body language indicate lying?

4. What affects validity when it comes to polygraph tests?

5. What are some of the physical characteristics of lying?

polygraph A mechanical device designed to aid investigators in obtaining information.

LEARNING OUTCOMES 7

Explain why people confess.

Suspects may make confessions when they believe that cooperation is the best course of action or when interrogators are able to speculate correctly on why the crimes were committed. False confessions may be the result of duress, coercion, intoxication, diminished capacity, mental impairment, ignorance of the law, fear of violence, infliction of harm, threat of a harsh sentence, and misunderstanding of the situation.

1. What factors contribute to a false confession?

2. What is the difference between an admission and a confession?

3. How does the cognitive interview differ from the traditional interview?

4. What are the objectives of a cognitive interview?

5. Why might the verbal-probing technique be more effective than the think-aloud technique of interviewing?

admission A self-incriminating statement made by a suspect that falls short of an acknowledgment of guilt.

confession Direct acknowledgment by the suspect of his or her guilt in the commission of a specific crime or as an integral part of a specific crime.

LEARNING OUTCOMES 8

Summarize how to take written and recorded statements.

The intelligence level of the suspect, the amount and nature of information to be recorded, and the availability of stenographic services determine what methods are used to take a statement. If a suspect is willing to give a verbal statement, the investigator should ask for a signed statement. The investigator may record a statement when the suspect cannot read or write or when he or she is only fluent in a foreign language.

1. What variables help determine the methods used to take written statements?

2. What are the benefits of recording an interrogation on video?

3. How can camera angles affect juror perceptions?

4. What are key techniques that can be used when a suspect decides to sign a written statement?

5. The use of recorded interrogations is most common in what types of criminal cases?

Additional Links

www.innocenceproject.org
This is the website of the Innocence Project, a national litigation and public policy organization, which has as its mission the exoneration of wrongfully convicted people through the use of DNA. The site includes news and resources links, legal information, fact sheets, e-newsletters, reports, and publications. The Fix the System menu has material on federal legislation.

www.lanl.gov
This is the website of Los Alamos National Laboratory, a science and technology institution that conducts research in national security, space, renewable energy, and nanotechnology. The site includes a news center, publications, education outreach links, and a career center with a job search engine.

www.crimeandclues.com; www.ifpo.org
For more information regarding investigative interviewing and interrogations, see either of these sites. Crime and Clues contains information covering criminal investigation and forensic science; www.ifpo.org is the site of the International Foundation for Protection Officers.

"The intelligence and surveillance functions of criminal investigation are two integral functions that often result in invaluable suspect information."

Criminal Intelligence and Surveillance Operations

1 Summarize the types of criminal intelligence.

2 Distinguish between the criminal intelligence and criminal investigation functions.

3 Explain the procedures for the intelligence-gathering process.

4 Explain the procedures for flowcharting used in intelligence-gathering operations.

5 Explain the types of surveillance in criminal investigation.

6 Describe how a stakeout is conducted.

7 Summarize the legal requirements of electronic surveillance.

Bjarne Henning Kvaale/Shutterstock.com

THE HIGH PRICE OF INFORMATION

FILES/AFP/Newcom

Robert Hanssen.

Federal Bureau of Investigation Special Agent Robert Hanssen was 56 years old at the time of his arrest at a park in Vienna, Virginia, in February 2001. At the time, he was secretly placing a package containing classified information at a prearranged, or "dead drop," site for pick-up by his Russian han-dlers. On an estimated 20 occasions, Hanssen had received substantial sums of money from the Russians after clandestinely leaving packages for the KGB and its successor agency, the SVR, at dead-drop sites in the Washington, D.C., area. He also provided more than two dozen computer diskettes containing additional disclo-sures of information. Overall, Hanssen gave the KGB and SVR more than 6,000 pages of valuable documentary material. During the time of his illegal activities, Hanssen was assigned to New York and Washington, D.C., where he held key counterintelligence positions. As a result of his assignments, Hanssen had direct and legitimate access to voluminous information about sensitive programs and operations. Hanssen used his training, expertise, and experience as a counterintelligence agent to avoid detection, including keeping his identity and place of employment from his Russian handlers and avoiding all the customary "tradecraft" and travel usually associated

RJ Lerich/Shutterstock

Plainclothes Investigator Taking Surveillance Photos.

with espionage. The turning point in this investigation came when the FBI was able to secure original Russian documentation of an American spy who appeared to the FBI to be Hanssen, which the investigation into his activi-ties later confirmed.[1]

DISCUSS What are some consequences of intelligence falling into the wrong hands? How does intelligence play a role in criminal investigation?

Information gathering, whether done consciously or uncon-sciously, is a regular part of a police officer's daily responsibili-ties.[2] The collection of criminal intelligence is another important function of the criminal investigative process and is one that has resulted in significant identification and arrest of major crime figures. Illustrating the importance of the intelligence func-tion, arguments can be made regarding the need for developing criminal intelligence. For example, some experts believe that physical measures don't actually reduce terrorism but rather just temporarily displace the threat. The cost of physical secu-rity to society is enormous, and such measures cannot protect everything, everywhere, all the time. If sufficiently motivated, a terrorist wanting to detonate a bomb in New York City to kill countless people can do it. Thus, reducing the threat of terror-ism has little to do with controlling access or taking measures to make sure the concrete wall is appropriately thick. Rather, the answer is to pursue the terrorists themselves and dismantling their organizations.[3]

Unfortunately, at the national level, the United States appar-ently lacks the intelligence capabilities necessary to adequately combat terrorism, according to a major interagency study of federal capabilities and defenses. The 73-page report, commis-sioned by the U.S. Justice Department, pinpoints a lack of intel-ligence sharing on domestic terrorists as a significant problem, and notes that "the single most significant deficiency in the nation's ability to combat terrorism is a lack of information, particularly regarding domestic terrorism."[4]

Although the preceding deals specifically with domestic and international terrorism, the same observations hold true with regard to the prevention and interdiction of many other seri-ous crimes. Information collection and analysis in respect to all criminal activity must be performed in a systematic and respon-sible manner to ensure both its accuracy and its effectiveness. This "collection, collation, evaluation, analysis, and dissemina-tion for use of information relating to criminal or suspected criminal activities of a wide variety"[5] makes up the tactical and strategic intelligence that law enforcement uses in the protec-tion of citizens and society.

▶ *The Usefulness of Intelligence*

As with all tactics used by law enforcement agencies to pre-vent crime, criminal intelligence operations certainly can be misused, but when regulated and carried out properly they can prove to be an indispensable tool for law enforcement. Informa-tion that is gathered can then be evaluated and disseminated for use in investigation of a variety of criminal activities. A report by the Justice Department notes that U.S. intelligence resources can be greatly improved in regards to new types of terrorism (for example, biological and nuclear), but we should also appre-ciate the successes that intelligence operations have achieved.

Although the terrorist attacks of September 11, 2001, on the World Trade Center and the Pentagon were shocking, they not only showed us what law enforcement is lacking in regard to the intelligence gathering needed to prevent such attacks, but also what law enforcement is doing correctly. Both before and since those attacks, evolving criminal intelligence tactics have prevented numerous similar attacks on domestic soil. This has been achieved through the combined efforts of local, state, and federal agencies.

While terrorist attacks against the United States continue, most of them occur on foreign soil. Attacks within U.S. borders have been kept to a minimum, with the majority being bombings carried out by activist groups, such as the Animal Liberation Front and Up the IRS. These groups generally focus on urban areas and are motivated by extremist ideologies regarding race, the environment, the government, or any number of other issues.

Although many of these groups continue to be quite active, others have been quieted through information gathering and the application of intelligence collected from those operations. When group leaders are tracked and arrested, their groups often are forced to either disband or at the very least halt their activities. Similar to some of these activist groups, organized crime in the United States has also suffered at the hands of effective intelligence operations. It still poses a threat, but being the long-time focus of aggressive intelligence operations has caused it to lose some ground to law enforcement. State and local law enforcement work together to combat these threats. Local and state contributions to national intelligence have proven invaluable.

| CITY POLICE DEPARTMENT | File: |
| **INTELLIGENCE REPORT** | Date: 10-21-14 |

SUBJECT: (Name and any identifying numbers)

SOURCE IDENTIFICATION:
Private Citizen ☐ (Name or Number) _____
Criminal Source ☐
Govt. Agency ☐ Personal Knowledge ☐ Documents ☐ Hearsay/Rumor ☐ Hypothesis ☐
Law Officer ☐ Other _____

EVALUATION OF SOURCE:
Highly Reliable ☐ Usually Reliable ☐ Reliability Questionable ☐ Unevaluated ☐

BY:

INFORMATION CONTENT:
Partially Verified ☐
Unverified ☐
Verified ☐

INFORMATION FILES CHECKED:
State Criminal Record ☐ Similar Info.
State Driver's License ☐ In File No. _____
NCIC ☐
Other _____

RECOMMENDED FOLLOW-UP:
Investigator to Verify ☐ Source to Verify ☐ Analyst to Research ☐ File Only ☐

DISSEMINATION:

FIGURE 7–1 Intelligence Report.

Overt and Covert Intelligence Collection

Overt information collection includes personal interaction with people, many of whom are witnesses to crimes, victims of crimes, or the suspects themselves. To best facilitate the overt collection process, agency administrators should require officers from all divisions to document any information on suspected criminal activity and to pass on such information to intelligence officers. The patrol division can be especially instrumental in the overt intelligence collection process by noting any activity around residences or businesses operated by major criminals in the area. Findings should be reported on a special intelligence report form (see Figure 7–1) and forwarded to the proper investigators.

Covert information collection is the most common and includes a process known as **intelligence gathering**. This is a process of data collection on criminal acts that have not yet occurred but for which the investigator must prepare. Covert intelligence collection methods use physical surveillance, electronic surveillance, informants, and undercover officers. In this

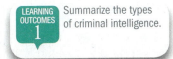
LEARNING OUTCOMES 1 Summarize the types of criminal intelligence.

chapter, we discuss both the intelligence-collection functions of criminal investigation and techniques for obtaining information through interviews and interrogation.

Criminal Intelligence and Criminal Investigation

The process of intelligence gathering originated as a function of the military but has now expanded to include "criminal" intel-

ligence as it applies to domestic law enforcement. Despite its technological and scientific advancements, criminal intelligence gathering is one of the least understood aspects of criminal investigation. Additionally, it is probably one of the most valuable (yet underused) resources of the police function.

Defining Criminal Intelligence

To set the pace for this chapter, we should first attempt to define the term *criminal intelligence.* According to the federally funded Regional Information Sharing Systems (RISS) projects, criminal intelligence is defined as knowledge of past, present, or future criminal activity that results from the collection of information that, when evaluated, provides the user with a basis for rational decision making.[6] Many law enforcement agencies assign sworn personnel to the criminal intelligence division. However, many departments have difficulty adequately defining the mission of the intelligence unit or the tasks of officers working within it, so officers often conduct multiple duties within the unit. Some of these duties are not relevant to the intelligence collection objective. In a practical sense, because it serves the department by delivering information to line personnel, the role of intelligence personnel is more of a staff than

a line function. Officers may therefore experience difficulty adjusting to their staff-related duties.

Types of Intelligence

The distinction between the different types of intelligence is often unclear because various methods are commonly used by different departments. To best understand the most common types of intelligence—strategic and tactical—the following definitions will be considered:

1. **Strategic intelligence** plays a role in the investigation of crimes by providing the investigator with a tool for long-range planning. Simply stated, it provides the investigator with information as to the capabilities and intentions of

Think About It...

Intelligence vs. Enforcement. . . Intelligence within a law enforcement agency can serve many useful purposes, and it is imperative that agencies are diligent to keep investigative files separate from criminal intelligence files. The thought of how potentially misunderstood police work might be if all types of files were either accessible or made public without discretion could be harmful merely even based on implication of potential wrongdoing, even when none really exists. Again, successful intelligence operations are determined by their ability to catalog or create actual intelligence, which might be used either now or in the future. What is the difference between strategic intelligence and tactical intelligence?

Confidential File.

Technically, the role of intelligence personnel is to deliver information to line personnel. To resolve any confusion about the differences between the criminal intelligence function and the criminal investigation function, the four fundamental differences between the two are listed below.

1. Criminal investigations are usually reactive in nature. Intelligence gathering, conversely, is a proactive function.
2. Criminal investigators generally work with deductive logic. This works by a logical progression through a sequence of events—the general to the specific. An example is collecting evidence from the crime scene, interviewing any witnesses, checking a suspect's criminal records, and so on. Intelligence unit personnel, conversely, exercise inductive logic. This affords them the luxury of beginning with the specific and expanding to the general.
3. Investigation case files are generally considered **open files**. They contain information developed for the purpose of eventually making an arrest and gaining a conviction in a court of law. In comparison, intelligence files are **closed files**. They contain information regarding ongoing criminal activity, but much of this information has not been verified as factual.
4. Intelligence files must therefore be maintained apart from criminal investigation files to prevent unauthorized inspection of data. The successful culmination of a criminal investigation is the arrest or conviction of a suspect in a crime. Successful intelligence operations are gauged by the cataloging of an intelligence product.

Intelligence-Gathering Process.

target subjects. Strategic intelligence has proved most useful in organizing long-range plans for interdiction in areas of criminal activity over extended periods.

2. **Tactical intelligence** targets criminal activity considered to be of immediate importance to the investigator. Specifically, tactical intelligence furnishes the police agency with specifics about individuals, organizations, and different types of criminal activity.

It is important to note that many police organizations have established criminal intelligence units that work with criminal investigators. These units are excellent resources of information for investigators who are following leads such as the identification of suspects or suspect associates, where suspects bank or hang out, what vehicles they drive, and other relevant information. On the national level, for example, the FBI is the lead agency for preventing and investigating intelligence activities on U.S. soil. In fact, it is the second highest priority for the FBI because foreign espionage poses a threat to the nation's national security.[7]

▶ Procedures for Intelligence Gathering

Intelligence collection should be thought of as a process of connecting a series of interrelated components of information. Failure on the part of the investigator to adequately connect any of these components could jeopardize the success of the investigation. Therefore, everyone associated with the collection process must have a keen understanding of the entire intelligence function and its various components. The intelligence function includes target selection, data collection, data **collation** and **analysis**, and **dissemination** (see Figure 7–2).

Careers: DEA Intelligence Research Specialist Job Description

As a Drug Enforcement Administration (DEA) intelligence research specialist, you will have the opportunity to be a part of the nation's leading drug law enforcement agency. You will be recognized worldwide for your skills, commitment, and achievements in working closely with DEA special agents to conduct the most significant drug investigations and counter-drug operations within the United States and abroad. Need an exciting place to live? DEA intelligence research specialist positions are located in most major U.S. cities, other domestic areas, and foreign countries that need the DEA's support in combating drug trafficking, violent crime, and terrorism. Use your intelligence skills at the DEA to contribute to our nation's war on drugs and terrorism.

Qualifications are as follows:

The DEA's Intelligence Division seeks candidates who have experience that demonstrates the ability to do the following:

- Analyze information, identify significant factors, gather pertinent data, and develop solutions

- Plan and organize work

- Communicate effectively orally and in writing

Such experience may have been gained in administrative, professional, or technical positions.

Employment requirements are as follows:

—Intelligence research specialists are subject to reassignment to any location in the United States depending on the needs of the DEA. All applicants must be available for relocation throughout their career with DEA and will be required to sign a statement to this effect when accepting an offer of employment.

Newly hired intelligence research specialists must complete the Basic Intelligence Research Specialist Training. All applicants interested in applying for jobs at the DEA must also be able to meet all DEA employment requirements and comply with the DEA's drug policy.

All applicants must meet the certain conditions of employment to be eligible for employment at DEA. These conditions include the following:

- U.S. citizenship

- Successfully pass a DEA-administered drug test for illegal drugs

- Complete a DEA drug questionnaire to show compliance with the DEA drug policy (see DEA drug policy for more information)

- Successfully pass a background investigation

- Register with the Selective Service System, if male and born after December 31, 1959

You will not be eligible for employment at the DEA if you do not meet these requirements. All of these requirements are thoroughly reviewed during the entire employment process. Please make sure you can meet all of these requirements before applying for a position with the DEA.

Background Investigations

The DEA—in its unique capacity as the world's eminent drug law enforcement agency—identifies, investigates, and targets for prosecution organizations and individuals responsible for the production and distribution of illegal drugs. In many cases, DEA work is sensitive in nature. Therefore, all employees are required to go through an extensive background investigation. Once you have received and accepted a conditional offer of employment, the DEA will initiate a background investigation. This investigation includes a credit and criminal records check; interviews of you, coworkers, employers, personal friends, educators, and neighbors; and for some occupations a polygraph examination. Additionally, there are certain employment requirements employees must meet to be eligible for employment at the DEA.

DEA Drug Policy

Drug testing is required and continues throughout a career at the DEA. Applicants who are found, through investigation or personal admission, to have experimented with or used narcotics or dangerous drugs, except those medically prescribed, will not be considered for employment with the DEA. Exceptions to this policy may be made for applicants who admit to limited youthful and experimental use of marijuana. Such applicants may be considered for employment if there is no evidence of regular, confirmed usage and the full background investigation and results of the other steps in the process are otherwise favorable. Compliance with this policy is an essential requirement of all DEA positions.

Source: Drug Enforcement Administration 2009. Retrieved from http://www .justice.gov/dea/resources/careers/opportunity/intel-research-spec.html.

Utility. This is the worth of the successful result. If the desired information is collected, how valuable is the result? Consider type, amount and frequency, and impact of criminal activity.

Probability of success. What are the chances of success with this target? Consider the following.
• Amount of effort to be expended
• Experience and expertise of the intelligence unit personnel
• Past success rate in similar operations
• Availability of sources of information

PHASE 1: TARGET SELECTION

Intelligence targets must be selected in a systematic manner. They may be based entirely on the utility, or size, of the target or available resources of the department.

FACTORS IN SELECTING A SUITABLE TARGET

Required resources. What resources are required to collect the desired information?
• Personnel hours—the primary required resource
• Equipment
• Confidential funds
• Travel expenses

Objective. Guarantee that intelligence efforts are focused toward targets that are an acceptable balance to merit or value, probability of a successful result, and resources used.

PHASE 2: DATA COLLECTION

Collection of criminal information may be done overtly, covertly, or as a combination of both. Written policy should dictate exactly what types of information may or may not be gathered. Because the collection of both personal and sensitive information on individuals could be a high-liability issue for some communities, great care is warranted by the police agency. Generally, intelligence information regarding any suspected criminal activity can be gathered.

Information can be gathered from organizations that

advocate the use of violence or other unlawful means to affect any unit of government.

possess or attempt to control shipments of arms, explosives, or controlled chemicals or biological weapons for unlawful purposes.

finance violent or unlawful activity.

Sources of Information

take actions that constitute unlawful activity targeted toward other organizations or individuals.

Investigators assigned to the intelligence unit

NOTE: Information should not be gathered merely because of a person's membership in organizations unless such organizations meet the criteria set forth previously and are found to present a clear and present danger to society. Under no circumstances should information be gathered solely on the basis of race, creed, color, national origin, sexual preference, or political or religious beliefs.

Nonintelligence departments of the agency: offense reports, arrest records, field interrogation reports, identification photos, fingerprint files, warrant files, traffic records

DATA STORAGE AND RETRIEVAL: This is generally done on computer, but some departments prefer index cards as a simplified and more secure system.

Other federal, state, and local jurisdictions

Non–law enforcement: newspapers, credit agencies, trial records, utility companies, banks, professional associations, insurance companies

FIGURE 7–2 Intelligence-Gathering Process.

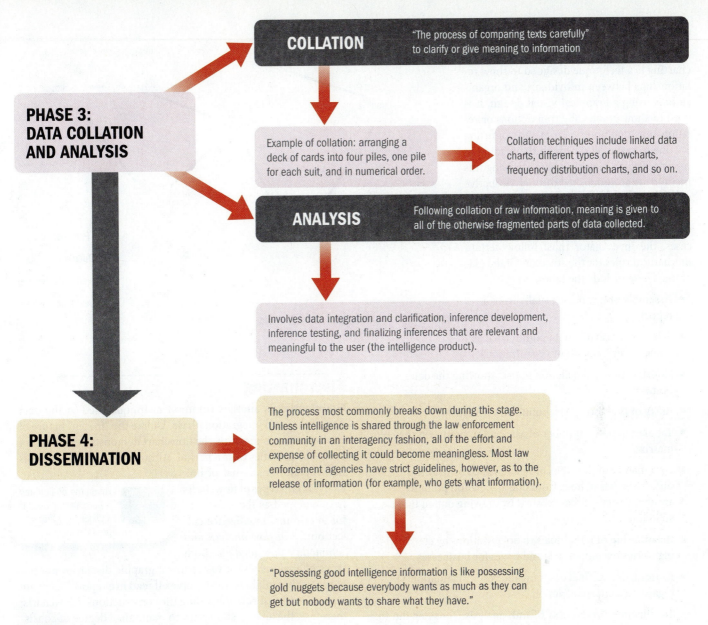

COLLATION — "The process of comparing texts carefully" to clarify or give meaning to information

PHASE 3: DATA COLLATION AND ANALYSIS

Example of collation: arranging a deck of cards into four piles, one pile for each suit, and in numerical order.

Collation techniques include linked data charts, different types of flowcharts, frequency distribution charts, and so on.

ANALYSIS — Following collation of raw information, meaning is given to all of the otherwise fragmented parts of data collected.

Involves data integration and clarification, inference development, inference testing, and finalizing inferences that are relevant and meaningful to the user (the intelligence product).

PHASE 4: DISSEMINATION

The process most commonly breaks down during this stage. Unless intelligence is shared through the law enforcement community in an interagency fashion, all of the effort and expense of collecting it could become meaningless. Most law enforcement agencies have strict guidelines, however, as to the release of information (for example, who gets what information).

"Possessing good intelligence information is like possessing gold nuggets because everybody wants as much as they can get but nobody wants to share what they have."

FIGURE 7–2 *Continued*

► Analyzing the Information

The purpose of analysis is to make fragmented information flow in a logical sequence to make it purposeful to the user, such as taking a group of surveillance reports and arranging them in the order in which they occurred to determine primary suspects, locations most frequently, vehicles driven, and so on. Intelligence gathering can be problematic in and of itself. For example, when officers are working with large amounts of information regarding individuals and organizations, the sources of that information may be varied and unorganized and may include confidential informants, surveillance reports, police reports, investigative reports, and so on.

> **LEARNING OUTCOMES 3** Explain the procedures for the intelligence-gathering process.

Link Analysis

To make sense out of the multitudes of information, a process known as *data description and integration* is used. One of the most common methods of data description and integration is link analysis. **Link analysis** charting is a technique designed to show relationships between individuals and organizations using a graphical visual design. It is used to show graphically transactions or relationships that are too large and confusing for one to assimilate through the reading of reports. Typically, decisions made using this method are accomplished through deductive reasoning.

There are several ways to illustrate this type of collation technique suitably. In all cases, the investigator must follow certain mechanical rules for the structure of the diagram. These include the following:

- Assembly of raw data (usually from a report)

- Selection of certain data points, such as names of individuals or organizations

- Construction of a collation matrix showing the data points

- Entry of the association points on the matrix

- Tabulation of the number of association points on the matrix

- Designation of the types of relationships by drawing different types of lines from one association point to another (usually accomplished by drawing dotted lines, solid lines, and so on)

- Relationship of individuals to organizations by constructing circles for individuals and boxes for businesses

- Examination of final diagram and recommendation(s) regarding a course of action

To illustrate the process of link analysis, consider the following scenario as if it were information from a surveillance report. The objective should be to determine the most appropriate target. Intelligence information, supported by criminal history records, shows that suspect Johnson has financial interest in both the Cloud Nine Tavern and the After Five Bar. Johnson is a known associate of convicted drug trafficker Weaver. Johnson also has financial interest in another business, On-line Productions, that is co-owned by suspect Willis. Willis is an associate of two other known street-level drug dealers who own a private investigation company, Independent Investigators Co. It is suspected that drugs are being financed by money made from Johnson's businesses and that Willis is the middle man/distributor who is using Hansen and Smith as retail street dealers. Suspect Baker is a known associate of Willis and is suspected of also associating with Independent Investigators Co.

Understanding the criminal relationships between these suspects and the businesses they own or associate with can form the basis for understanding a drug distribution network in which multiple suspects may be arrested and a number of businesses may be seized because they are supporting the drug enterprise (see Figure 7–3).

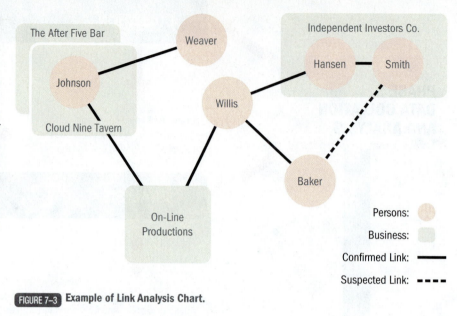

FIGURE 7–3 Example of Link Analysis Chart.

Persons: ⬤
Business: ▢
Confirmed Link: ——
Suspected Link: - - - -

Flowcharting

Flowcharting is another common technique used in the data description and integration phase. Unlike the "frozen" nature of the link analysis diagram, the flowchart demonstrates a chain of events or activities over a period. Although use of flowcharts is not as common as that of link analysis, two types of flowcharts have emerged as the most useful in criminal intelligence collection: *event flow analysis* and *commodity flow analysis*. Both types of analysis give investigators a graphic display of a series of events that might be too complex if read in a report. There are no hard-and-fast rules regarding the construction of flowcharts; therefore, the analyst should try to maintain a degree of consistency throughout the chart regarding the symbols used.

LEARNING OUTCOMES 4 — Explain the procedures for flowcharting used in intelligence-gathering operations.

Event Flow Analysis

Event flow analysis is usually conducted early in an investigation. Examples of flow analysis include charting a brief description of an event enclosed in a symbolic area such as a circle or rectangle. As different events are documented, they are connected by arrows to indicate the direction of the sequence. Consider the following scenario and think about how smuggled cocaine and its transition to street cocaine can best be portrayed by using the event flowchart.

The Role of the Intelligence Analyst

- To guide data collection
- To suggest operational recommendations
- To provide information to decision makers
- To assume a position of noninvolvement in policy formation

Typically, when cocaine is smuggled in from outside the country it is of considerably higher purity than when it hits the street. This is because once arriving in the country it is diluted or "cut," thus doubling, tripling, or even quadrupling the initial amount of the drug. For example, an initial kilo (2.2 lbs.) may be 90 percent pure, but after being "cut" there may be 4 kilos (8.8. lbs.) but at 22 percent purity. This is then re-packaged and delivered to a retail outlet (e.g., a crack house) and then distributed by street dealers. It can also be converted to crack cocaine and repackaged for retail distribution. Criminal investigators need to know the process of what happens to the cocaine from the time it arrives in the United States to when it is distributed on the streets. This will assist them in identifying suspects for arrest and their assets for criminal forfeiture (see Figure 7–4).

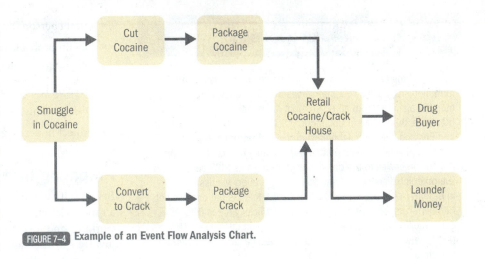

FIGURE 7–4 Example of an Event Flow Analysis Chart.

Commodity Flow Analysis

Commodity flow analysis may greatly simplify the investigative process by charting the logical flow of such commodities as drugs, money, and illegal arms shipments. For example, in a drug distribution network, if money can be traced from its origin to certain key individuals, an investigation will probably result in an arrest and conviction. This is particularly useful when the main drug kingpins don't typically possess the drugs themselves.

The structure of a commodity flowchart is generally the same as that of the event flowchart, except that rather than descriptions of events being placed in circles or rectangles, persons or businesses are used. A scenario follows in which commodity flowcharting might best be used. Study this case information and observe how the resulting flowchart illustrates and clarifies the facts and circumstances of the case.

One of your informants has informed you that a known methamphetamine cook named Earl Thomas is preparing to cook a new batch and that he has ordered chemicals, solvents, glassware, and hardware from different companies. Your investigation shows that in fact Thomas has ordered supplies from three different companies: Tri-state Chemical Supply, ABC Industrial Solvents, and Acme Laboratory Distributors. These companies have received orders from what appears to be two "front" (fake) companies: K.C. Industrial Supply and Professional Industries. Thomas has been connected with both of these "front" companies. Surveillance and phone records also indicate that Thomas has been making numerous phone calls to two known meth distributors: Brandon Phillips and Steve Russell. In order to initiate a conspiracy investigation, a commodity flowchart is constructed to clarify the various relationships (see Figure 7–5).

Auditing and Purging Files

Intelligence files that are no longer accurate, are not relevant to the mission of the unit, do not pertain to investigative interests and activities, or contain insufficient supporting documentation are among those that should be purged. When files are deficient in one or more of these areas, consideration may be given to updating or improving them through validation and other means.

However, when the basic information contained in these files is of such an age or of such poor quality as to make these efforts either too costly or unproductive, a decision should be made to purge the file. A record of any purged files should be maintained by the department.

Use of a qualified outside auditor is typically the best approach to purging intelligence files. This is because independent third parties remove much of the bias or the appearance of bias that may be evident when using in-house intelligence personnel. Although a yearly review of the files for purposes of purging useless materials is recommended, this does not preclude the

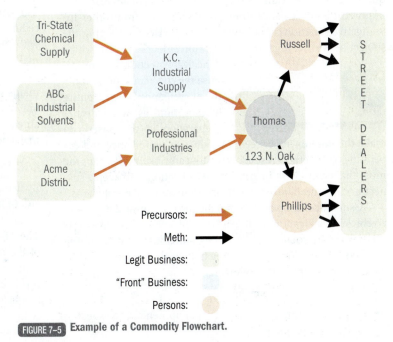

FIGURE 7–5 Example of a Commodity Flowchart.

destruction of files on an ad hoc basis when appropriate and with the approval of the intelligence or investigative unit.

▶ Surveillance Operations

Similar to undercover operations, conducting surveillance requires using the team concept. The considerable resources required for surveillance draw personnel away from other investigative functions. The potential also exists for alerting the subject of the investigation to law enforcement's interest, which conceivably could compromise the covertness of not only the surveillance but the entire investigation as well. Proper preparation at the onset can make the difference between a productive surveillance and expending considerable resources without any results.[8] Perhaps the most challenging task in criminal investigation is to keep a suspect under surveillance without arousing his or her suspicions.

LEARNING OUTCOMES 5 — Explain the types of surveillance in criminal investigation.

A surveillance operation may be directed toward a person, a vehicle, or a location for the purpose of bringing an investigation into sharp focus. By identifying individuals and obtaining detailed information about their activities, the criminal investigator can accomplish the following:

- Obtain evidence of a crime
- Prevent the commission of an act or apprehend a suspect in the commission of an act

- Locate persons or watch their hangouts and associates
- Obtain probable cause for obtaining search warrants
- Obtain information for later use in an interrogation
- Develop leads and information received from other sources
- Obtain admissible legal evidence for use in court
- Protect undercover officers or corroborate their testimony

Preparing for the Surveillance

Before initiation of the surveillance, a study should be made of all files relating to the suspects, their activities in crimes, their working and neighborhood environments, and the vehicles involved in the case. In studying information relating to the suspects, the officer should focus on names and aliases used by suspects and detailed physical descriptions, including photographs when available. When possible, the suspect should be pointed out to the surveillance officers.

Foot Surveillance

Generally, the foot surveillance technique is used only during relatively short distances or to maintain contact with a suspect after he or she has left a vehicle. There are four principal methods for conducting a moving surveillance on foot: one-officer surveillance; two-officer surveillance; the ABC method; and the progressive, or leapfrog, method.

One-Officer Surveillance

The single-officer technique is extremely difficult to conduct because the suspect must be kept in view at all times and close contact is required to enable the officer to immediately observe the suspect if he or she enters a building, turns a corner, or makes other sudden moves.

Two-Officer Surveillance

This method affords greater security against detection and reduces the risk of losing the suspect. On streets that are crowded with pedestrian or vehicular traffic, both officers should normally remain on the same side of the street as the suspect. The first officer trails the suspect fairly closely. The second officer remains some distance behind the first. On a less crowded street, one officer should walk on the opposite side of the street nearly abreast of the suspect. To avoid detection, the two officers should make periodic changes in their positions relative to the suspect.

ABC Method

By using a three-officer surveillance team in this technique, the risk of losing the suspect is further reduced. Under most conditions, this method provides greater security against detection. The ABC method also permits a greater variation in the position of the officers and allows an officer who suspects he has been spotted by the suspect to drop out of close contact. Under normal traffic conditions, officer A keeps a reasonable distance behind the suspect. Officer B follows A and concentrates on keeping A in view. Officer B also checks if an associate of the subject is being used to detect the surveillance (countersurveillance).

Preparing for Surveillance

Mannerisms: Identifying characteristics and mannerisms of the suspect should also be studied by the officers. The habits and normal routines of the suspects should be examined, as well as their probable suspicion of, and ability to elude, the surveillance operation. The identities and descriptions of known or suspected contacts or associates should be known, and the officer should be knowledgeable about the scope and extent of crimes and activities in which the suspects are involved.

Area: The officers must also familiarize themselves with the type of neighborhood in which the operation will take place, concentrating on such aspects as the type of inhabitants, their dress, and their use of language. This information will assist the officers in blending in with the neighborhood.

Equipment: The types of equipment used by surveillance officers are limited only by the improvisational ability of the officers themselves. For example, on a short-term surveillance of a building, the surveillance officers may use utility belts with tools and hard hats to adopt the appearance of public utility employees or may use some other type of "cover" equipment.

Recon: A physical reconnaissance should study the areas where the surveillance will take place and identify vantage points suitable for the officers. Similarly, traffic conditions should be observed, and the officers should become familiar with the names and locations of streets in the area, including locations of dead-end streets that may be used by the suspect to spot surveillance officers. The reconnaissance will also yield information on the neighborhood and its inhabitants that would not be in the police files.

Endurance: The officer must mentally and physically prepare him- or herself for surveillance operations. The officer needs to realize that he or she must be patient and possess endurance. Perseverance is needed while waiting for the suspect to appear or to doggedly follow a suspect through the same routine day after day.

Resourcefulness: The officer must be alert and resourceful because regardless of careful planning, there are always many unanticipated occurrences in surveillance work. The officer must develop keen powers of observation and memory because often he or she is unable to write down all events, descriptions of contacts, or times as they occur. Furthermore, the officer must prepare a logical explanation for being in a particular place at a particular time in the eventuality that he or she is approached by the subject and accused of following him or her.

Blend in: The officer must address and adopt the demeanor of local inhabitants to blend into the setting. The type of clothing to be worn will determine whether concealment of weapons or use of personal radios jeopardizes the operation. Ideally, the officer should have an ordinary appearance to avoid attracting the suspect's attention. Doing so will better ensure that the officer is able to blend in to the target's environment. The officer must have the ability to act naturally under all circumstances as if he or she belongs at that scene.

Clothing: Officers should also have such items as caps, jackets, and glasses available to quickly change appearance if needed. Flexibility and versatility are the keys to any surveillance. A change of clothing may suffice for one individual, but another may use clothing to suggest a trade or service. The clothing and behavior should be coordinated to communicate some cover or excuse for being in a neighborhood.

Officer C walks on the opposite side of the street slightly behind the suspect. On streets with little or no traffic, officers B and C may be on the opposite side of the street, or officer C may be in front of the suspect. On crowded streets, however, all three officers should generally be on the same side of the street.

Progressive or Leapfrog Method

In the progressive or leapfrog method of surveillance, the suspect is observed intermittently as he or she moves along a certain habitual route. The surveillance officer stations him- or herself at a fixed point until the suspect disappears from view. If a suspect follows the same route each day, the destination may be determined without constant surveillance. The officer should station him- or herself each day where the suspect disappeared from view the previous day. More than one officer can be used to extend the period of observation. This method may be of value in locating hideouts or meeting places when the risk of trailing a suspect is too great.

Vehicle Surveillance

As is the case with foot surveillance, there are four types of vehicular surveillance, or **mobile surveillance** (see Figure 7–6): the one-, two-, and three-car surveillance and the leapfrog method. If only one car is available for surveillance, its position should be behind the suspect car, the distance varying with the amount of traffic in the area. In city traffic, no more than two vehicles should be permitted between the suspect's car and the

Surveillance Kit Checklist

- Department two-way radio

- Handheld portable radio with spare battery

- Cellular phone

- Digital camera with telephoto lens (if available) with extra storage media and spare battery

- Digital video camera

- Stabilizing device such as a tripod

- Binoculars or thermal-imaging device

- Detailed road maps, compass, or GPS navigation device

- Flashlight with extra batteries

- Change of clothing, including hat and toiletries

- Food and water

- Cash, including coins for toll lanes

- Extra set of car keys

- Towels and glass cleaner

- Equipment bag to contain above items

When possible, there should be another car between the surveillance vehicle and the suspect car.

Whenever possible, the surveillant's car should be occupied by two officers—one driver and one observer to take notes. The second officer can also take over surveillance on foot if necessary. The seating arrangements and appearance of these two officers should be changed periodically to avoid recognition by suspects.

When conducting two-car surveillance in city areas during daylight hours, both cars should be behind the suspect's car. In three-car surveillance, parallel routes can be more readily used, and the positions of the cars can be changed frequently enough to prevent discovery of the surveillance. One car may be used to lead the suspect vehicle while observing it through the rearview mirror.

▶ Stakeouts, or "Stationary Surveillance"

In a **stakeout**, officers watch from a fixed or **stationary surveillance** vantage point such as a room, house, or camouflaged outdoor fixture located near the premises being observed (as illustrated in Figure 7–7). A stakeout is the tactical deployment

 LEARNING OUTCOMES 6 Describe how a stakeout is conducted.

surveillance vehicle. In rural areas, it is advisable to give the suspect a good lead. If intersections and road forks are far between, the lead can be extended to a point where the suspect car may be even temporarily lost from view over hills or around curves.

Courtesy of Mike Himmel

FIGURE 7–6 Detective Conducting a "Moving" or Vehicle Surveillance.

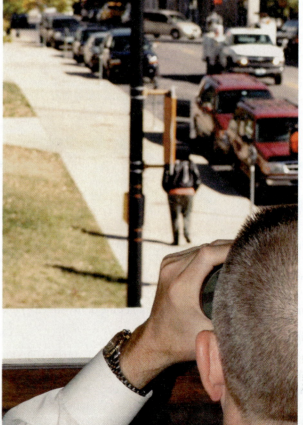

Courtesy of Mike Himmel

FIGURE 7–7 Detective Conducting a "Stakeout" or Fixed Surveillance.

of police officers in anticipation of the commission of a crime at a specific location. The anticipated perpetrators may be known individuals or may be suspects known only by their mode of operation (MO). The purpose of the stakeout is to arrest the suspect(s) during the attempted or actual commission of a crime.

However, the murder conviction in the *Jackson* case was upheld because Spokane County investigators took the precaution of getting a court order, even as they argued that it wasn't needed. It is possible that federal courts could reach a different conclusion because the U.S. Supreme Court, for more than 20 years, has authorized law enforcement to plant electronic transmitters on vehicles without a warrant and to track them, as long as the vehicles do not enter private property.

In addition to tracking criminal suspects, some law enforcement agencies also use GPS devices to check on the activities of their own employees. For example, between 1999 and 2003, law enforcement agencies in Des Moines, Iowa; Omaha, Nebraska; Orlando, Florida; and other cities have used GPS devices on police cars to track the cars' whereabouts during duty hours. In one case, in Clinton Township, New Jersey, in 2001, five officers were let go after their handwritten activity logs conflicted with information collected by GPS devices. In this case, one night shift officer reported that he had spent about two hours checking the security of a residence and several local businesses. The global positioning data indicated that his cruiser had been parked at a McDonald's restaurant the entire time.

Investigative Procedures

Generally, a stakeout consists of an inside team and an outside team of two officers each. The **outside team** is normally designated as the arrest team. Enforcement action should not be taken by the inside team unless a life-threatening situation develops. After the subjects have exited the stakeout location, the inside team is also responsible for securing the location to ensure that the suspects do not reenter and possibly create a barricade or hostage situation.

The **inside team** is responsible for briefing officers concerning their actions if a crime occurs. They should ensure that employees do not initiate any independent action and should remove any privately owned weapons. All employees must understand that they should not inform anyone that police are present, nor should they seek assistance from the stakeout team for crimes such as shoplifting. If necessary, uniformed officers may respond as usual to handle these offenses. Such incidents should be handled as quickly as possible, and uniformed officers should exit the area after the call for service has been handled.

Poststakeout Procedures

The potential for the use of deadly force is a part of nearly all stakeouts. However, this potentiality does not constitute grounds for an exception to existing policies and procedures that govern the use of deadly force in individual agencies. The safety of officers and citizens alike and overall reverence for

human life remain important issues. As in other circumstances, officers should use deadly force only as a last resort after all other reasonable alternatives are exhausted.

► Electronic Surveillance and Wiretaps

Surveillance is a term referring to the monitoring of the behavior or activities of persons in a covert manner. It most typically refers to observation of individuals or groups by government organizations. With the growing use of high technology to investigate crime and uncover violations of criminal law, courts throughout the nation are evaluating the applicability of constitutional guarantees with regard to high-tech surveillance. Recent technology makes possible increasingly complex forms of communication. One of the first Supreme Court decisions involving electronic communications was the 1928 case of *Olmstead* v. *United States*. In the *Olmstead* case, bootleggers used their home telephones to discuss and transact business.[9] Agents tapped the lines and based their investigation and ensuing arrests on conversations they overheard. The defendants were convicted and eventually appealed to the High Court, arguing that the agents had, in effect, seized information illegally without a search warrant in violation of the defendant's Fourth Amendment right to be secure in their homes.

LEARNING OUTCOMES 7 — Summarize the legal requirements of electronic surveillance.

The Court ruled, however, that telephone lines are not an extension of the defendant's home and therefore are not protected by the constitutional guarantee of security. However, subsequent federal statutes have substantially modified the significance of the *Olmstead* decision.

Recording devices carried on the body of an undercover agent or informant were ruled to produce admissible evidence in *On Lee* v. *U.S.* (1952) and *Lopez* v. *U.S.* (1963).[10] The 1967 case of *Berger* v. *New York* permitted wiretaps and "bugs" in instances in which state law provided for the use of such devices and officers had obtained a warrant based on probable cause.[11]

The Court appeared to undertake a significant change of direction in the area of electronic eavesdropping when it decided the case of *Katz* v. *U.S.* (1967). Federal agents had monitored a number of Katz's telephone calls from a public phone using a device separate from the phone lines and attached to the glass of a phone booth. The Court, in this case, stated that a warrant is required to unveil what a person makes an effort to keep private, even in a public place. In the words of the Court, "the government's activities in electronically listening to and recording the petitioner's words violated the privacy upon which he justifiably relied while using a telephone booth and thus constituted a search and seizure within the meaning of the Fourth Amendment."

In *Lee* v. *Florida* (1968), the Court applied the Federal Communications Act to telephone conversations that might be the object of police investigation and held that evidence obtained without a warrant could not be used in state proceedings if it resulted from a wiretap.[12] The only person who has the authority to permit eavesdropping, according to that act, is the sender of the message.

The Federal Communications Act, originally passed in 1934, does not specifically mention the potential interest of law enforcement agencies in monitoring communications. Title III of the Omnibus Crime Control and Safe Streets Act of 1968, however, mostly prohibits wiretaps but does allow officers to listen to electronic communications when (1) an officer is one of the parties involved in the communication, (2) one of the parties is not the officer but willingly decides to share the communication with the officer, or (3) officers obtain a warrant based on probable cause. In the 1971 case of *U.S.* v. *White*, the Court held that law enforcement officers may intercept electronic information when one of the parties involved in the communication gives his or her consent, even without a warrant.[13]

In 1984, the Supreme Court decided the case of *U.S.* v. *Karo*, in which Drug Enforcement Administration (DEA) agents had arrested James Karo for cocaine importation.[14] Officers placed a radio transmitter inside a 50-gallon drum of ether purchased by Karo for use in processing the cocaine. The device was placed inside the drum with the consent of the seller of the ether but without a search warrant. The shipment of ether was followed to the Karo house, and Karo was arrested and convicted of cocaine trafficking charges. Karo appealed to the U.S. Supreme Court, claiming that the radio beeper had violated his reasonable expectation of privacy inside his premises and that, without a warrant, the evidence it produced was tainted. The Court agreed and overturned his conviction.

Satellite-Assisted Surveillance

Global positioning system (GPS) technology is being used more and more to aid law enforcement in gathering information and performing surveillance. Where once individual investigators had to physically track suspects or survey people and places of interest, GPS tracking devices can now do much of the work. Global positioning systems use satellites and cell phone towers to track movements and pinpoint locations, often in real time and often with the ability to transmit information to a remote location, such as a computer in a police station. GPS devices receive signals from four or more GPS satellites, which are maintained by the U.S. government, and are then able to calculate their own position (see Figure 7–8). This can be done anywhere on Earth, so long as at least four unobstructed satellites are available.

One case in which GPS technology played an integral role in aiding police was the December 2002 disappearance of Laci Peterson in Modesto, California. Her husband, Scott Peterson, claimed no involvement in his pregnant wife's disappearance, but police did not entirely believe his story. GPS devices attached by the police to his cars showed that in the month following his wife's death Peterson twice drove to the San Francisco Bay area near where her body and that of her unborn son later washed ashore. This information was used by the prosecution against Peterson at his murder trial. He was convicted of first-degree murder for killing his wife and second-degree murder for killing her unborn child.

Computer Surveillance

Computer surveillance is another common investigative target for criminal investigators. To a great extent, it involves the monitoring of data and traffic on the Internet. In the United

Think About It…

Surveillance and Privacy The Communications Assistance for Law Enforcement Act enhances law enforcement agencies' ability to conduct electronic surveillance. This includes monitoring of phone calls, e-mail, Web traffic, and instant messaging. Does it make you uneasy to know that every conversation you have could be monitored, or do you feel safer knowing that law enforcement can access the communication of possible criminals or terrorists?

Maxim Tupikov/Shutterstock.com

Photo of the Numerous Ways in Which Digital Information Can Be Retrieved from Laptop Computers.

Tracking Vehicles with Satellites

To track a vehicle using a global positioning system (GPS), a device about the size of a paperback book is attached to the vehicle. The device reads signals from a network of 24 satellites and calculates its location based on its distance from each satellite.

The device can be attached under a car with a magnet.

GPS device

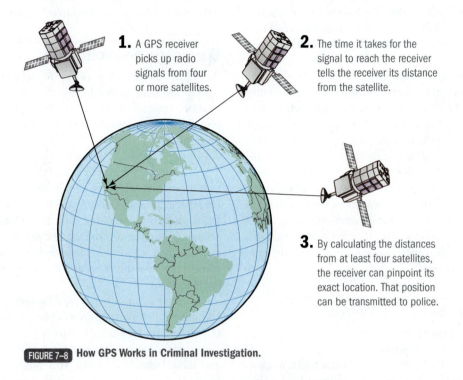

1. A GPS receiver picks up radio signals from four or more satellites.

2. The time it takes for the signal to reach the receiver tells the receiver its distance from the satellite.

3. By calculating the distances from at least four satellites, the receiver can pinpoint its exact location. That position can be transmitted to police.

FIGURE 7–8 How GPS Works in Criminal Investigation.

States, for example, under the Communications Assistance for Law Enforcement Act, all phone calls and broadband Internet traffic (e-mail, Web traffic, instant messaging, and so on) are required to be available for unrestricted real-time monitoring by law enforcement agencies on the federal level.

Due to the vast amount of data on the Internet, it is impossible for human investigators to manually search through all of it. So, automated Internet surveillance computers go through the vast amount of Internet traffic and report to human investigators traffic considered interesting due to (1) the use of certain "trigger" words or phrases, (2) visits to certain types of websites, or (3) communication via e-mail or chat with suspicious individuals or groups.

Billions of dollars per year are spent—by agencies such as the Information Awareness Office, National Security Agency (NSA), and the FBI—to develop, purchase, implement, and operate systems such as Carnivore, NarusInsight, and ECHELON to intercept and analyze this data and extract only information that is useful to law enforcement and intelligence agencies.

Personal computers are also a common police surveillance target because of the personal data stored on them. Through the use of computer forensics software such as the FBI's "Magic Lantern" and CIPAV, investigators can readily gain access to and

seize this data. Another form of computer surveillance, known as TEMPEST, involves reading electromagnetic discharges from computing devices in order to extract data from them at great distances. The NSA also runs a database known as "Pinwale," which stores and indexes large numbers of e-mails of both American citizens and foreigners.

Telephones and Mobile Telephones

The tapping of telephone lines is a long-time investigative tool for law enforcement. In the United States the Communications Assistance for Law Enforcement Act (CALEA) requires that all telephone and "VoIP" communications be available for real-time wiretapping by federal law enforcement and intelligence agencies. Two major telecommunications companies in the United States—AT&T and Verizon—are known to have contracts with the FBI, requiring them to keep their phone call records easily searchable and accessible for federal agencies, in return for $1.8 million dollars per year.[15]

Between 2003 and 2005, the FBI sent out more than 140,000 "National Security Letters" ordering phone companies to hand over information about their customers' calling and Internet histories. About half of these letters requested information on

U.S. citizens.[16] Investigators are not required to monitor most calls. Instead, speech-to-text software generates machine-readable text from intercepted audio, which is then processed by automated call-analysis programs. Such programs are currently being used by agencies such as the Information Awareness Office and companies such as Verint, and Narus, which search for certain words or phrases to decide whether to dedicate a human agent to the call.

Law enforcement in the United States currently possesses technology to remotely activate the microphones in cell phones, by accessing the phone's diagnostic/maintenance features, in order to listen to conversations that take place nearby the person who holds the phone.[17]

Mobile phones are also commonly used to retrieve data on location. The geographical location of a mobile phone (and thus the person carrying it) can be determined easily (whether or not it is in use), using a technique known as multilateration. Multilateration calculates the differences in time for a signal to travel from the cell phone to each of several cell towers near the owner of the phone.[18] The technique has been criticized by individual rights advocates who are concerned about the lawfulness of such techniques, and particularly whether a warrant or court order is required. But the technique is commonly used, as records for one cell phone carrier alone (Sprint) showed that in a given year federal law enforcement agencies requested customer location data 8 million times.[19]

Surveillance of Social Networks

One common form of surveillance is to create maps of social networks based on data from social networking sites such as Facebook, MySpace, and Twitter as well as from traffic analysis information from phone call records such as those in the NSA call database and others. These social network "maps" are then data mined to extract useful information such as personal interests, friendships and affiliations, wants, beliefs, thoughts, and activities.

As of the preparation of this text, U.S. government agencies such as the Defense Advanced Research Projects Agency (DARPA), the National Security Agency (NSA), and the Department of Homeland Security (DHS) are currently investing heavily in research involving social network analysis. The intelligence community believes that the biggest threat to U.S. power comes from decentralized, leaderless, geographically dispersed groups of terrorists, subversives, extremists, and dissidents. These types of threats are most easily countered by finding important nodes in the network and removing them. Doing so requires a detailed map of the network.

AT&T developed a programming language called "Hancock" that is able to sift through enormous databases of phone call and Internet traffic records, such as the NSA call database, and extract "communities of interest"—groups of people who call each other regularly, or groups that regularly visit certain sites on the Internet.

AT&T originally built the system to develop "marketing leads," but the FBI has regularly requested such information from phone companies such as AT&T without a warrant, and

after using the data, stores all information received in its own databases, regardless of whether or not the information was ever useful in an investigation.

Some people believe that the use of social networking sites is a form of "participatory surveillance," where users of these sites are essentially performing surveillance on themselves, putting detailed personal information on public websites where it can be viewed by corporations and governments. About 20 percent of employers have reported using social networking sites to collect personal data on prospective or current employees.[20]

Biometric Surveillance

Biometric surveillance refers to technologies that analyze human physical and/or behavioral characteristics for authentication, identification, or screening purposes. Examples of physical characteristics include DNA, facial patterns, and fingerprints.

Facial recognition is the use of the unique configuration of a person's facial features to accurately identify that person, typically from surveillance video. Both the Department of Homeland Security and DARPA are heavily funding research into facial recognition systems. The Information Processing Technology Office ran a program known as Human Identification at a Distance, which developed technologies that are capable of identifying a person at up to 500 feet by analyzing that person's facial features.

Another form of behavioral biometrics, based on affective computing, involves computers recognizing people's emotional state based on an analysis of their facial expressions, how fast they are talking, the tone and pitch of their voice, their posture, and other behavioral traits. This might be used, for instance, to see if a person is acting "suspicious" (looking around furtively, "tense" or "angry" facial expressions, waving arms, and so on).[21]

A more recent development is DNA fingerprinting, which looks at some of the major markers in the body's DNA to produce a match. The FBI is currently spending $1 billion to build a new biometric database, which will store DNA data, facial recognition data, iris/retina (eye) data, fingerprints, palm prints,

Biometric Surveillance.

and other biometric data of people living in the United States. The computers running the database will be contained in an underground facility that is about the size of a football field.[22] In 2008, the Los Angeles Police Department installed automated facial recognition and license plate recognition devices in its police cars, and provided handheld face scanners, which officers can use to identify subjects while on patrol.

Thermal Imaging

In 1996, the California appellate court decision in *People* v. *Deutsch* identified the kinds of issues that are likely to be encountered as the United States and law enforcement expand their use of high technology.[23] In this case, judges faced the question of whether a warrantless scan of a private dwelling using a thermal imaging device constitutes an unreasonable search within the meaning of the Fourth Amendment. These devices, also known as **forward-looking infrared (FLIR)** systems, measure radiant heat energy and display their readings as thermographs. Images that a thermal imager produces can be used (as in the case of Dorian Deutsch) to reveal unusually warm areas or rooms that might be associated with the cultivation of drug-bearing plants, such as marijuana. Two hundred cannabis plants, which were being grown hydroponically under high-wattage lights in walled-off portions of Deutsch's home, were seized after an exterior thermal scan of the home was conducted by a police officer who drove by the residence at 1:30 A.M.

Because the officer had not anticipated entering the house, he proceeded without a search warrant. A California court ruled that the scan was an illegal search because "society accepts reasonable expectation of privacy" surrounding "non-disclosed activities within the home."

In a similar case, *Kyllo* v. *U.S.* (2001), the U.S. Supreme Court reached much the same conclusion. Based on the results of a warrantless search conducted by the officers using a forward imaging device, investigators applied for a search warrant of Kyllo's home.[24] The subsequent search uncovered more than 100 marijuana plants that were being grown under bright lights. The Court held "where, as here, the government uses a device that is not in general public use, to explore details of a private home that would previously have been unknowable without physical intrusion, the surveillance is a Fourth Amendment search, and is presumptively unreasonable without a warrant."

A typical GPS tracking device is about the size of a paperback book and can be affixed to a car's undercarriage with a magnet. The cost for such a device is minimal, at about $1,000. As of the writing of this text, questions over whether police need a court's permission (a court order) to use GPS devices in investigations have become the subject of concern in state and federal courts across the nation.

Wiretaps and property searches ordinarily must be authorized by a state or federal judge, who determines whether such tactics are needed to investigate a crime. The surveillance on public roads ordinarily does not require such court orders. Because GPS devices are a substitute for ordinary visual surveillance, many police departments believe they can be used without a court order. Civil rights advocates are concerned that the technology has advanced to where police can track thousands of people anywhere, anytime, and police don't have to give a reason.

Courts are just beginning to address issues raised by GPS use in criminal investigations. In the *Jackson* case in Washington State, police argued that the devices do not require a court order because they provide the same information as a visual search. The state's court of appeals agreed, finding that the GPS devices used to track Jackson were "merely sense augmenting" and revealed information open to "public view" as Jackson traveled county roads. However, the state Supreme Court disagreed, stating that under Washington's state constitution, GPS surveillance requires a court order because it amounts to a search. In September 2003, Justice Barbara Madsen wrote in an opinion supported by all nine of the Court's justices, "the intrusion into private affairs made possible with the GPS devices is quite extensive . . . vehicles are used to take people to a vast number of places; they can reveal preferences, associations, personal habits and foibles." She continued to say that "GPS can provide a detailed picture of one's life."

Thermal Imaging of a House using a Forward Looking Infrared Device.

The Mechanics of Thermal Imaging

In its simplest terms, thermal imagers operate like the human eye, but are much more powerful. Energy from the environment passes through a lens and is registered on a detector. In the case of the thermal imager, that energy is in the form of heat. By measuring very small relative temperature differences, invisible heat patterns are converted by the thermal imager into clear, visible images that can be viewed by the operator through a viewfinder or monitor. Thermal imagers are usually very sensitive and can detect temperature variations smaller than 0.1°C.

Thermal imagers "see" nothing more than the heat emitted by all objects in the camera's field of view. They do not see visible light, nor do they see rays or beams of energy. Thermal imagers are completely passive and nonintrusive. Because these devices see heat and not light, they can be used for both daytime and nighttime operations.

Thermal imagers can be compared with image intensifiers, which are another type of night vision technology and one that has been used by law enforcement and the military for years. In contrast to image intensifiers, thermal imagers are unaffected by the amount of light in a scene and will "bloom" or shut down indirect light. Unlike image intensifiers, thermal imagers can see through dust, smoke, light fog, clouds, haze, and light rain because infrared wavelengths are longer than visible wavelengths of light.

Surveillance and the Killing of Osama Bin Laden

The utility of surveillance cannot be overstated. In both military and civilian law enforcement it has proven to be one of the government's greatest investigative tools. For example, on April 29, 2011, a team of U.S. Navy SEALs from the Naval Special Warfare Development Group (SEAL Team Six), working with the Central Intelligence Agency (CIA), raided a fortified compound in Northwest Pakistan. The operation, dubbed Operation Geronimo, was authorized and monitored by President Barack Obama. Intelligence information was that international terrorist Osama bin Laden was hiding out there. The SEALs entered the compound in two helicopters. Once inside, bin Laden, three other men, and a woman were located and killed in a firefight that did not result in any U.S. casualties. The entire raid, including intelligence sweeps of the compound, was completed in less than 40 minutes.

Osama bin Laden was the founder of the al-Qaeda organization, responsible for the September 11, 2001, attacks on the United States and numerous other attacks resulting in mass American casualties. Bin Laden was on the FBI's list of Ten Most Wanted Fugitives and Most Wanted Terrorists for his involvement in the 1998 U.S. Embassy bombing. From 2001 to 2011, bin Laden and his organization were major targets of the "War on Terror," which had resulted in an estimated 80,000 to 1.2 million civilian deaths in Iraq, Afghanistan, and Somalia between 2001 and 2007. The September 11 attacks resulted in the deaths of over 3,000 men, women, and children in the United States.

The covert surveillance of bin Laden's couriers provided the necessary information for the operation to move forward. It was initially thought that bin Laden was hiding near the border between Afghanistan and Pakistan's Federally Administered Tribal

Bjarne Henning Kvaale/Shutterstock.com

Areas, but he was actually found 100 miles (160 km) away in a million-dollar three-story mansion. Among those killed in the raid were one of bin Laden's sons, a man described as a courier, and the courier's brother. Four years of surveillance of the courier led to the intelligence that made the raid possible. It was reported that the courier was the owner of the compound where the assault took place. Although the bin Laden killing was a military operation, the principles and usefulness of surveillance operations are similar to those used in law enforcement.

Sources: Schabner, D., & Travers, K. (2011, May 1). Osama bin Laden killed: "Justice is done," president says. *ABC News Tonight with Diane Sawyer.* Retrieved from http://abcnews.go.com/Blotter/osama-bin-laden-killed/story?id=13505703; Marx, Gary T. (1989). *Undercover: Police surveillance in America.* University of California Press.

The intelligence collection process is a highly specialized criminal investigation endeavor:

1. Using the chapter material and the preceding case, how important is the ability of intelligence officials to work in secrecy?
2. Given this case, what are your thoughts on the use of the various surveillance techniques covered in the chapter (be specific)?

Summarize the types of criminal intelligence.

The collection of criminal intelligence is an important function of the criminal investigative process. A systematic approach is essential to put information and data to use in a constructive manner. Sufficient safeguards must be built into screening, reviewing, and managing intelligence files.

1. What is the goal of the intelligence function as it pertains to the collection of criminal information?

2. What information does the criminal intelligence unit provide criminal investigators?

3. What federal agency is responsible for preventing and investigating intelligence activities on U.S. soil?

4. What are the major types of intelligence?

overt information collection A method of collecting information involving personal interaction with individuals, many of whom are witnesses to crimes, victims of crimes, or the suspects themselves.

covert information collection A clandestine process of data collection on criminal acts that have not yet occurred but for which the investigator must prepare.

intelligence gathering The covert process of gathering information on criminal activity.

Distinguish between the criminal intelligence and criminal investigation functions.

Criminal intelligence is defined as knowledge of past, present, or future criminal activity resulting from the collection of information that is used for rational decision making. Criminal investigations are reactive in nature. Intelligence gathering is a proactive function. Investigation case files contain information developed for the purpose of eventually making an arrest and gaining a conviction in a court of law.

1. What are the four fundamental differences between criminal investigation and criminal intelligence gathering?

2. What is the difference between open and closed files?

3. How is criminal intelligence defined by the federal RISS project?

open files Criminal information developed for the purpose of eventually making an arrest and gaining a conviction in a court of law.

closed files Intelligence files that are maintained apart from criminal investigation files to prevent unauthorized inspection of data.

strategic intelligence Information that provides the investigator with intelligence as to the capabilities and intentions of target subjects.

tactical intelligence Information that supports police operations on a tactical level—such as raid planning—and that furnishes the police agency with specifics about weapons, dangerous individuals, and different types of criminal activity.

Explain the procedures for the intelligence-gathering process.

Intelligence collection should be thought of as a process of connecting a series of interrelated components of information. Failure on the part of the investigator to adequately connect any of these components could jeopardize the success of the investigation. Therefore, everyone associated with the collection process must have a keen understanding of the entire intelligence function and its various components. The intelligence function includes target selection, data collection, data collation and analysis, and dissemination. To make sense out of the multitudes of information, a process known as *data description and integration* is used. One of the most common methods of data description and integration is link analysis.

1. What are the four phases of the intelligence process?

2. Why is the dissemination phase critical in the intelligence-gathering process?

3. What sources other than law enforcement organizations are useful in data collection?

4. What factors must be considered when examining target utility in intelligence gathering?

5. How is link analysis conducted, and how does it benefit the intelligence process?

collation The process of comparing texts carefully to clarify or give meaning to information.

analysis A scientific examination.

dissemination The phase of the intelligence process whereby information is shared with other law enforcement agencies.

link analysis A charting technique designed to show relationships between individuals and organizations using a graphic visual design.

LEARNING OUTCOMES 4

Explain the procedures for flowcharting used in intelligence-gathering operations.

Flowcharting is used in the data description and integration phase of the intelligence-gathering operation. The flowchart demonstrates a chain of events or activities over a period. Two types of flowcharts have emerged as the most useful in criminal intelligence collection: *event flow analysis* and *commodity flow analysis*. Both types of analysis give investigators a graphic display of a series of events that might be too complex if read in a report. There are no hard-and-fast rules regarding the construction of flowcharts; therefore, the analyst should try to maintain a degree of consistency throughout the chart regarding the symbols used.

1. Describe the types of investigations in which an event flowchart is useful.
2. What is the method of structuring a commodity flowchart?
3. What are the basic differences between event Aand commodity flowcharting?
4. What are the advantages of flowcharting versus link analysis?

Flowcharting An intelligence organization technique that demonstrates a chain of events or activities over a period of time.

Commodity flow analysis An investigative process whereby the logical flow of commodities as drugs, money, and illegal arms shipments is charted.

LEARNING OUTCOMES 5

Explain the types of surveillance in criminal investigation.

The four principal methods for conducting a moving surveillance on foot are one-officer surveillance; two-officer surveillance; the ABC method; and the progressive, or leapfrog, method. As is the case with foot surveillance, there are four types of vehicular surveillance (or mobile surveillance): the one-, two-, and three-car surveillance and the leapfrog method.

1. What role and function do surveillance operations play in criminal investigations?

2. What are the similarities and differences in the types of surveillance methods?
3. What are the principal methods in conducting foot surveillance?
4. What can an investigator accomplish in a surveillance operation (that is, what information can an investigator gather during the process)?
5. What is the most effective method of surveillance?

mobile surveillance Observing a criminal suspect from a moving vehicle.

LEARNING OUTCOMES 6

Describe how a stakeout is conducted.

A stakeout is the tactical deployment of police officers in anticipation of the commission of a crime at a specific location. During a stakeout, officers watch from a stationary surveillance point such as a room, house, or camouflaged outdoor fixture near the premises being observed. The purpose of the stakeout is to arrest the suspect(s) during the attempted or actual commission of a crime.

1. What are the two types of briefings preceding deployment of a stakeout?

2. What is the primary objective of the stakeout?
3. How are the functions of the inside and outside teams different?
4. What is the purpose of poststakeout operations?

stakeout Another term for stationary or fixed surveillance.

stationary surveillance Another term for fixed surveillance or stakeout.

outside team The arrest team in a surveillance.

inside team A surveillance team responsible for briefing officers concerning their actions if a crime occurs.

LEARNING OUTCOMES 7

Summarize the legal requirements of electronic surveillance.

Courts throughout the nation are evaluating the applicability of constitutional guarantees with regard to high-tech surveillance. In 1986, Congress passed the Electronic Communications Privacy Act (ECPA), which brought major changes in the requirements law enforcement officers must meet to intercept wire communications. Investigators must be aware of other applicable laws that regulate their actions in the use of electronic surveillance techniques.

1. How are law enforcement agencies using new technology for surveillance purposes?

2. According to the Omnibus Crime Control and Safe Streets Act, under what circumstances can officers listen to electronic communications?
3. How does the Federal Communications Act affect electronic surveillance?
4. What types of surveillance methods were used to find and kill Osama bin Laden?

global positioning system (GPS) A space-based global navigation satellite system (GNSS) that provides location and time information in all types of weather, anywhere on or near the earth where there is an unobstructed line of sight to four or more GPS satellites.

forward-looking infrared (FLID) A surveillance technology that measures radiant energy in the radiant heat portion and displays readings as thermographs.

Additional Links

www.cia.gov
The official site of the Central Intelligence Agency (CIA) provides news and information, publications, and contact information. It includes links to the World Factbook, CIA history, student opportunities including internships and co-ops, and CIA Interactive (games and puzzles, kids' page, headquarters tour, CIA museum).

www.justice.gov/dea/
The site of the Drug Enforcement Administration (DEA) includes DEA publications, a press room that houses press releases and a multimedia library, drug information resources, legislative resources, and a careers link.

www.dhs.gov/index.shtm
The Department of Homeland Security site includes news on the latest threats, advisories, planning tips, and job opportunities. Also, links on the site include counterterrorism, border security, cybersecurity, news, career opportunities, and a job finder.

www.cdt.org
Students can read more on the Electronic Communications Privacy Act at the site of the Center for Democracy and Technology. Blog posts and resources related to issues such as free expression, security and surveillance, and digital copyright are included on the site.

American Civil Liberties Union: **http://www.reformthepatriotact.org/**
The American Civil Liberties Union site includes news, information, and opinions regarding criminal law reform, technology and liberty, national security, and the Patriot Act.

"Informants, while potentially problematic, are one of the most important tools of the criminal investigator."

8

Informant Management and Undercover Operations

1 Identify informants and their various uses.

2 Explain how to properly document and process an informant.

3 Explain how to maintain control of an informant during an investigation.

4 Summarize the legal framework for informant management.

5 Summarize the usefulness of undercover investigations.

6 Describe types of undercover operations.

7 Describe the undercover working environment.

8 Explain how to protect the undercover officer's "cover."

9 Explain methods of infiltration and the risks involved in undercover operations.

WHEN CRIMINALS ARE CAUGHT BY CITIZENS

INTRO

Over a 10-month period beginning in 2003, motorists in Ohio were terrorized by a sniper firing random shots at vehicles along Interstate 270 that killed at least two persons. The two dozen shootings had struck a variety of targets such as cars, trucks, buses, schools, and homes in the Columbus area. Initially, investigators had little to go on in their investigation and publicly expressed their frustration in not having developed a suspect in the shootings. But finally, in early 2004, ballistic tests on a 9mm handgun connected Charles McCoy, Jr., to the Ohio interstate shootings as well as at least eight other shootings.

In March 2004, McCoy checked into the Budget Suites Hotel in Las Vegas, Nevada, at 3:00 A.M. under his own name. That evening, Conrad Malsom, a 60-year-old unemployed car salesman who lived in Las Vegas, spotted McCoy reading a *USA Today* article about himself in the sports betting parlor of the Stardust Casino. The two even shared a pizza as Malsom got a closer look. As they talked, Malsom learned where McCoy was staying and even took a sheet of paper containing some notes that McCoy was writing down. Malsom called the Las Vegas police, who arrested McCoy outside his hotel at 2:45 A.M. the following day.

Security Cameras Monitoring Public Places are Becoming More and More Common as Concern about Street Violence Grows.

sframe/Fotolia

DISCUSS **Do you think it is always a good idea to report a suspected criminal to the police?**

Discuss what would have occurred in this case had Malsom been wrong and the wrong person was arrested.

The concept of informants in society is nothing new. In fact, both police and civilians attempt from time to time to encourage public participation in solving crimes. One well-known program is Crimestoppers, which encourages citizens to engage in "anonymous" informing to assist police in developing suspects in crimes or to catch criminals in the act of committing them. Although some people complain that Crimestoppers makes "snitches" out of law-abiding citizens, others argue that it is simply a system of public responsibility similar to the old days of the "hue and cry," when all citizens assumed responsibility for public order.

In addition to allowing tipsters to call the police anonymously, many informants receive cash rewards for their cooperation. The amount of the reward depends on the "quality of information" provided by the citizen—that is, information that results in an arrest. All communication between the police and the citizen is accomplished by the assignment of a number to the caller. That number is used in lieu of a name for the remainder of the citizen–police relationship, negating the need for the police ever to know the true name of the tipster.

Along lines similar to Crimestoppers are efforts by victims of crimes to convince the community to become more involved with identifying known criminals and reporting violators to police. One example of this is the well-known television show *America's Most Wanted*. The show has helped track down more than 800 fugitives.[1] Other shows, including *Unsolved Mysteries* and *U.S. Customs*, have had similar success.

Another public forum for locating criminals that has been around longer than the television shows discussed previously is the Top Ten Most Wanted list of the Federal Bureau of Investigation (FBI). The FBI has maintained its Most Wanted list since 1950, and although it was once a mainstay in crime fighting, it has all but lost its appeal in today's high-tech age of television, computers, and the Internet. Still, it is designed to encourage citizen participation in sharing information with the police about crime and criminals who are wanted. The Most Wanted list was invented by a wire service reporter and later adopted by the publicity-driven director of the FBI, J. Edgar Hoover. As of 1997, 422 of the 449 fugitives who appeared on the list have been captured, a 94 percent success rate.[2]

In its earliest stages, when few Americans owned televisions, the Most Wanted list contained bank robbers, burglars, and car thieves—criminals who dominated the crime scene. Today's Most Wanted list includes cop killers, drug dealers, and international terrorists who aren't even in the country.[3] Skeptics argue that the list has outlived its use-fulness because of the age of modern technology (the Internet, electronic billboards, and television). In 1992, the U.S. Post Office discontinued putting Top 10 posters on its walls. Perhaps it could be argued that the FBI's "list" has become ineffective, especially with the advent of so many different high-tech media showcasing the nation's fugitives. Of late, some victims have taken the ini-tiative to seek help from the public by using their own money and resources.

During August 1997, the parents of murder victim JonBenét Ramsey ran their fourth advertisement in a local newspaper appealing for help from the public. The ad included samples of handwriting from the ransom note and commented, "the killer appears to be obsessed with tech-nocrime movies and phrases from them."[4] In addition, the ad included quotes from the movies *Dirty Harry* and *Speed* that the family claimed were similar to the ones used in the ransom note.

In any case, whether it is a paid police informant or an anon-ymous tip, police rely heavily on information from the public to solve crimes. Experience has shown that a primary component of crime control is proactive law enforcement. Proactive investiga-tions include vice cases such as drug trafficking, prostitution, and gambling, in which investigators actually seek out potential crimes and intervene "before" the crimes occur. Accordingly, the use of *informants* as a source of criminal information in such crimes has proved to be invaluable. Consequently, law enforcement officers are insistent in protecting the identities of their sources so that the well-being of the informants will not be jeopardized and so they will continue to be of use to the officer in future criminal investigations.

Generally, people who become informants can be classified into four general groups:

1. *Average citizens.* Although not necessarily a criminal source, people falling into this group may still be an excellent source of information. Most good investigators have several informants of this type who are contacted periodically for leads. Examples of these informants are waitresses, bartenders, dancers, and private investigators.
2. *Fellow law enforcement officers.* On an average day, investigators exchange valuable information with other investigators many times. Although much of this information is between "friends" who are investigators, a considerable amount is also exchanged by officers working in other units within the department. In addition, investigators who befriend officers with other local, state, or federal agencies can also benefit from useful information about criminals and criminal activity.
3. *Mentally ill persons.* It is unfortunate, but a percentage of informants fall into the category of mentally ill or deranged. An experienced investigator can detect when such persons are simply fabricating information or passing on news stories or gossip. One should also consider, however, that although an informant is mentally ill, his or her information might still have some validity.
4. *Criminals or their associates.* Without question, criminal informants have proven to be most valued in many police investigations. These are people who are currently, or have been, associated with a particular criminal element and are therefore in an excellent position to supply firsthand information about criminal activity.

Informants are a dynamic group of people who come from diverse backgrounds and frequently view their role in different ways. For example, one informant may give information with no reservations about his or her identity becoming known. Conversely, others may have valuable information to render but may do so only with the understanding that their identities remain concealed. Those falling into the latter category typically want their identities to be kept secret for their own protection and because if their true identities become known, their func-tion as informants would be ended.

▶ Using Informants

Although a frequent source of valuable information, the use of an informant in a criminal investigation can be problematic. There-fore, the use of an informant should not be considered if similar results could be achieved through other means. Problems that stem from the use of informants are due to three variables. First, informants are often difficult to control. Many of them have been criminals for long periods and are very independent by nature. This independence sometimes results in the informant attempt-ing to manipulate the investigator and manage the investigation.

Second, an informant can become a source of public em-barrassment for the law enforcement agency. For example, an informant might be arrested for a high-visibility crime during the time that he or she is working with the police. The local me-dia could then make headlines that could jeopardize the inves-tigation in which the informant was involved. Such situations are sometimes unavoidable but can usually be minimized with proper management techniques.

A third area of concern is the informant's questionable **credibility** in court. Depending on the role of the informant in the investigation, he or she might have to testify in court pro-ceedings. A good defense council can expose the criminal back-ground of such people and show that their testimony is not to be believed. If this is accomplished, juries will have difficulty finding the defendant guilty "beyond a reasonable doubt."

▶ Who Becomes an Informant?

Although the word **informant** has many negative synonyms, such as "snitch" and "stoolie," the term could best be defined as "any-one who provides information of an investigative nature to law enforcement."[5] Exclusions to this definition, of course, are victims of crime who have re-ported specific criminal activity to law enforcement. This makes their role more that of a complainant.

LEARNING OUTCOMES 1 — Identify informants and their various uses.

Indeed, the informant is most typically used in cases in which there is no complainant. These typically include vice and victimless crimes such as drug violations, gambling, and prosti-tution. Because informants can be virtually anyone in a commu-nity, a good investigator should consider anybody with whom he or she comes in contact as a potential source of criminal information. That is, the premise of locating a knowledgeable informant is to realize that someone somewhere is aware of var-ious crimes committed. It is therefore the investigator's respon-sibility to locate and develop relationships with such people.

After the decision has been made to use the services of an informant, he or she can be used in a number of ways:

- Make observations in areas where strangers would be suspect
- Furnish information from a source not readily available to the investigator
- Conduct "controlled" undercover transactions or introduce undercover agents to criminal suspects
- Collect intelligence information (for example, determine street prices of drugs and identify suspects, their associates, and their residences)

The criminal investigator has the responsibility to evaluate every informant used. This saves time and effort if it is determined that the informant's information is unreliable or that the informant harbors a hidden agenda. Thus, the motive is extremely important to identify with each informant candidate because it may directly affect the credibility of the case.

Informant Motivations

Successful recruitment and management of informants pivot on the investigator's ability to recognize the **motivation** of the informant. Because the negative stigma of being an informant is so great in the United States, it is sometimes difficult to develop

Think About It…

"So, Tell Us What You Expect to Get Out of This Deal." People new to policing operations can sometimes be surprised as to what might motivate an informant. The reality is that informants are human beings with needs and desires, just like anyone else, but there is often some additional reality associated with a potential informant that might make that individual even more motivated (for example, financial need, anger/revenge). What are some of the most compelling motivations for people to become informants?

Copyright © Bonnie Kamin/ PhotoEdit

An Investigator Talking to an Informant Posing as a Mechanic.

Motivations for a criminal informant fall into a number of categories:

- *The fearful informant.* Many persons agree to cooperate with law enforcement when fear is the chief motivator. Fear comes in many forms, such as fear of detection by law enforcement or retribution from criminal associates. Typically, this incentive arises when a person is arrested for an offense and fears being convicted and imprisoned. Given the opportunity, the arrestee may choose to provide information to investigators in exchange for leniency. Investigators must be careful not to make any promises to persons arrested without the consent of the prosecutor, who is generally vested with such authority. The investigator may, however, advise the informant that such a recommendation may be made pending any cooperation.

- *The financially motivated informant.* "Mercenary" informants give information in exchange for a fee. Often, the financially motivated informant will prove to be a valuable contributor to the investigation. Such persons may, however, attempt to manipulate the investigation to prolong payments to them. This is typically done by extending the investigation by providing misleading information or by "setting up" suspects in criminal violations that they are not predisposed to commit (that is, entrapment).

- *The revengeful informant.* Revenge is not uncommon to the criminal underworld, and wrongs committed by one criminal against another are often settled outside the law. Frequently, however, informants motivated by revenge can produce favorable investigative results. Although those motivated by revenge are seldom concerned about revealing their identity in court, investigators must be careful to recognize an exaggerated or embellished story. In addition, such persons frequently have drifting allegiances and may reconcile with their former adversaries midway through the investigation, thus ruining credibility and jeopardizing the well-being of investigators.

- *The egotistical informant.* Many people take great delight in passing on information to others. Informants falling into this category may also be of great value to an investigator. This motivation is sometimes dubbed the *police complex* because of a person's desire to associate with law enforcement. It is typically characterized by a small-time criminal alleging to have inside information on high-level crime figures.

- *The perversely motivated informant.* People who display a perverse motivation are those who inform with a hidden benefit or advantage to themselves. Sometimes informants with this motivation are trying to eliminate their competition, learning investigative techniques, determining if any of their criminal associates are under investigation by police, or learning the identity of undercover officers. In all cases, the investigator must be aware of such motivations to avoid "setups" and compromising situations.

- *The reformed informant.* Informants characterized by this motivation act out of a sense of guilt from wrongdoing. Such informants are rare but when encountered may provide reliable information to the investigator.

such people successfully. Police occasionally consider average citizens as informants provided that they are willing to offer relevant information in an investigation. The motivation of such people is a sense of civic duty.

As one might guess, mentally ill informants (depending on their illness) are motivated by very different reasons. These reasons are usually very complicated and difficult to determine, and frequently, information furnished by these persons is worthless to the investigator. When a mentally ill informant gives valuable information, however, the person may be motivated by the same reasons as those that motivate criminal informants. Indeed, the criminal informant is the most valuable of all informant categories.

Documenting Your "Source"

LEARNING OUTCOMES 2 Explain how to properly document and process an informant.

Proper management of informants is essential in avoiding allegations of unethical, immoral, or unprofessional conduct later in an investigation. The investigator must remember that informants belong to the agency and are not the "personal" resource of the investigator. This understanding will ensure that a system of checks and balances through records and verification of information can be officially maintained (see Figure 8–1).

All candidates for informants should be well documented. They should, therefore, be fingerprinted, photographed, and carefully interviewed by investigators before being used as an informant. Interviews should reflect the informant's true name and any aliases, address, employment history, and so on. In addition, criminal records, if any, should be verified through the National Crime Information Center as well as through local and state law enforcement agencies. All such procedures should be contained in an official informant file established specifically

During the informant interview, the interviewer must be careful to solicit certain information. Some typical questions asked of potential informants include the following:

- What is his or her motivation?
- Has the informer been reliable in the past?
- What is the intelligence of the informant?
- How does he or she know about the violation?
- Does he or she have a personal interest, and if so, what?
- Does he or she have direct knowledge?
- Does he or she have access to additional knowledge?
- Does he or she harbor any vengeance toward the suspect?
- Is he or she withholding some kind of information?
- Has he or she lied about information in the past?
- Is he or she willing to testify in court?

for that person. The file should then be indexed by number, not by name, and that number should be used in all subsequent reports referring to the informant.

After the informant responds to the preceding questions, the investigator should have adequate information to proceed with a final evaluation of the person's potential worth. If the informant poses more of a liability than a benefit, he or she should be eliminated from further consideration.

Maintaining Control

Customarily, the investigator who develops an informer is the one who is assigned to him or her. A cardinal rule in working with informants is for the investigator to command control of the investigation, not the informant. This is sometimes difficult to accomplish because many informants possess strong, manipulative personalities. Although informants should be asked frequently for their opinions, each suggestion should be considered carefully. Additionally, investigators must be careful not to promise anything they cannot deliver (for example, money, a reduced charge, relocation of the informant's family, police protection).

LEARNING OUTCOMES 3 Explain how to maintain control of an informant during an investigation.

Control of informants is best achieved through frequent personal contacts with them. These interactions are the best method for debriefing informers and maintaining rapport with them. The officer assigned should make most, if not all, contacts with informants. Doing so reduces additional demands of the informant and ensures the person's allegiance to the control officer. Another critical area of instruction for the informant is **entrapment**. Criminal suspects must be given an "opportunity" for the commission of a crime and not the "motivation" for doing so. If the entrapment issue is not remembered during the course of an investigation, the case may result in the dismissal of charges against the suspect and a soiled reputation for the department.

Legal Considerations

Information gathering is a complex process that raises many ethical and legal questions regarding the techniques used by investigators. For example, when police pay informants for information, critics argue that the informant might be tempted to entrap persons into committing crimes so that the informant can realize some income. Another common use of informants is *flipping*. This is a procedure in which an arrested person is given the choice of providing information to police in exchange for dropping the charges against the individual. Flipping is a widely used procedure requiring approval of the local prosecutor, but it still raises questions about the ethical appropriateness of the procedure.

LEARNING OUTCOMES 4 Summarize the legal framework for informant management.

CITY POLICE DEPARTMENT
COOPERATING INDIVIDUAL AGREEMENT

I, _____, the undersigned, state that it is my intent to associate myself, of my own free will and without any coercion or duress, with the City Police Department as a cooperating individual.

As a cooperating individual, I understand and agree that I have no police powers under the laws of the state of (____) and have no authority to carry a weapon while performing my activity as a cooperating individual. Further, I understand and agree that my only association with the city of (____) is as a cooperating individual on a case-by-case or time-to-time basis as an independent contractor, and not as an employee of the police department. Any payment I receive from the City Police Department will not be subject to federal or state income tax withholding or social security. I understand that it is my responsibility to report any income and also that I am not entitled to either workmen's compensation or unemployment insurance payments for anything I do as a cooperating individual.

In consideration for being allowed to associate with the City Police Department as a cooperating individual, and in consideration for any payment I may receive, I agree to be bound by the following terms and conditions and procedures while so associated.

1. I agree that under no circumstances will I purchase or possess any controlled substances or suspected controlled substances without the direction and control of a police officer and then will make a purchase only with monies supplied by him.

2. I agree not to use or sell, dispense, or transfer any controlled substance except that I may use any controlled substance prescribed to me by a licensed physician.

3. I agree to maintain a strict accounting of all funds provided to me by the City Police Department and I understand that misuse of city funds could be grounds for criminal prosecution against me.

4. I agree not to divulge to any person, except the officer with whom I am associated, my status as a cooperating individual for the City Police Department unless required to do so in court, and shall not represent myself to others as an employee or representative of the City Police Department nor use the department or any of its officers as personal references or as credit or employment references.

5. I understand that any violation of the above listed provisions may be grounds for my immediate removal as a cooperating individual and that any violation of law may result in my arrest and prosecution.

I understand that association with the City Police Department as a cooperating individual may involve strenuous physical activity and may become hazardous to my physical well-being and safety. Nevertheless, it is my desire to associate myself with the department, on an independent contractor basis, as a cooperating individual. I am associating myself with the department in this status freely and without any coercion or duress. In consideration for being accepted as a cooperating individual, I release and discharge the City of (____), the City Police Department and its elected officials, officers, employees, and agents from all claims, demands, actions, judgments, and executions which I may have or acquire and subsequently claim to have against the City for personal injuries and property damage I may sustain which arises out of or in connection with my association with the city. I make this release for myself, my heirs, executors, and administrators. Also, I agree not to maintain any action against the City of (____), the City Police Department, or its elected officials, officers, employees, or agents for personal injuries and property damage I sustain which arise out of or in connection with my association with the City Police Department.

_____
Cooperating Individual

_____
Date

WITNESSES:

_____
Officer

_____
Officer

FIGURE 8–1 Sample Informant Agreement.

Simply put, the informer's primary role is to provide probable cause to police for arrests and search warrants. The case of *Aguilar* v. *Texas* (1964) established a two-pronged test to the effect that an informant's information could provide probable cause if both of the following criteria are met:

- The source of the information is made clear
- The police officer has a reasonable belief that the information is reliable

The two-pronged *Aguilar* test was intended to prevent the issuance of warrants on the basis of false or fabricated information. But two subsequent cases have provided exceptions to the two-pronged test. *Harris* v. *United States* (1968) acknowledged the assumption that when an informant provided information that was damaging to him or her, that information was probably true. In the *Harris* case, an informant told police that he had purchased nontax-paid whiskey from another person.

Because the information actually implicated the informant in a crime, it was taken at face value as being true even though it failed the second prong of the two-pronged test. In 1969, the case of *Spinelli* v. *United States* created an exception to the requirements of the first prong. In that case, the U.S. Supreme

Other Problems with Informants

- *Investigators becoming too friendly with informants.* Because investigators and their informers work together closely, it is possible that an officer can become caught up in an informant's personal problems. Certainly, the investigator should lend a sympathetic ear when possible, but investigators should be cautioned that becoming too close to an informant could jeopardize the investigator's level of control over the person.
- *Informants of the opposite sex.* Over the years, many investigators have fallen victim to allegations of sexual misconduct with informants of the opposite sex. Although some have proved truthful, many have had no basis but resulted in disciplinary action against the officer and a termination of the investigation. To avoid such allegations, a second officer should always accompany the investigator. The location of meeting spots with informants should also be considered very carefully, particularly if a second officer is not present.
- *Crimes committed by the informant.* During initial meetings between the investigator and potential informants, officers should stress that any criminal activity on the part of the informant will not be tolerated. History has shown that after being arrested for a crime, informants will sometimes mention the name of their control officer in hopes of being released or of receiving special treatment.
- *Officers who "own" their informants.* Over the years, some corrupt officers have claimed that meetings between themselves and criminals were in fact meetings with informants. Informants should be considered the "property" of the entire department and should be sufficiently documented. This avoids any allegations of misconduct on the part of investigators if seen with known criminals.

Court ruled that some information can be so highly specific that it must be accurate even if its source is not revealed. Then, in 1983, in *Illinois* v. *Gates*, the Court adopted a totality of circumstances approach, which held that sufficient probable cause for issuing a warrant exists where an informant can reasonably be believed on the basis of everything that is known by the police.

Under the *Gates* decision, however, the Court held that although it is still important to consider the two-pronged test, each part of the test should be viewed separately and independently. The totality of the circumstances approach, therefore, permits any deficiencies of one part of the test to be overcome by the other with available evidence. In its decision, the Court stated the following:

> For all these reasons we conclude that it is wiser to abandon the two-pronged test established by our decisions under *Aguilar* and *Spinelli*. In its place we reaffirm totality of the circumstances analysis that traditionally has informed probable cause determinations. The task of using the magistrate is simply to make a practical, common-sense decision whether, given all the circumstances set forth in the affidavit before him, including the "veracity and basis of knowledge" of persons supplying hearsay information, there is a fair probability that contraband or evidence of a crime will be found in a particular place. And the duty of a reviewing court is simply to ensure that the magistrate had a "substantial basis for conclud[ing]" that probable cause existed.

In 1990, the case of *Alabama* v. *White* was reviewed by the Supreme Court, which held that an anonymous tip, even in the absence of other corroborating information about a suspect, could form the basis for an investigatory stop when the informant accurately predicts the "future" behavior of the suspect. The Court reasoned that the ability to predict a suspect's behavior demonstrates a significant degree of familiarity with the suspect's affairs.

At times, information provided by informants is of such value that informants are paid for the information they supply. The investigator should be careful not to pay for information that has not been verified or that is not considered useful in the investigation. Accordingly, informant payments should be sufficiently modest as to avoid defense accusations of entrapment. When this occurs, the defense will maintain that the investigator's payment to the informant was so high that the informant was enticed into "setting up" the suspect solely for the monetary reward.

▶ Undercover Operations

Undercover operations are an important part of the criminal investigation function but one that is highly specialized and not practiced by all law enforcement agencies. Investigators require specialized training to successfully perform this function. Stories abound regarding both investigative successes and failures in this area. From a practical standpoint, undercover work and surveillance are viable options for police investigators because they provide considerable information that is not otherwise available through traditional investigative methods.

LEARNING OUTCOMES 5 — Summarize the usefulness of undercover investigations.

For example, in February 2009, the U.S. Drug Enforcement Administration (DEA) arrested 52 persons in California, Minnesota, and Maryland as part of *Operation Xcellerator*. This investigation targeted the Sinaloa Cartel, a major Mexican drug trafficking organization.

In recent years, the Sinaloa Cartel has been responsible for bringing multi-ton quantities of narcotics, including cocaine

Think About It...

"Like Herding Cats . . ." Not every law enforcement official is able to properly handle informants. As noted, there are often ethical and legal challenges involved, among other problems, that can make management of informants difficult. What are some of the problems associated with managing informants?

© Michael Matthews/Police Images/Alamy

Police Conducting a Field Interview of a Man.

ELEMENTS OF AN UNDERCOVER OPERATION

1 THE INTRODUCTION

2 THE ACCEPTANCE

3 THE BUY

4 THE ARREST/COVERING THE INFORMANT

5 AFTER ACTION

The informant typically makes the "introduction" of the undercover operative to the suspect. This is the initiation of the case. From this point on, the "acceptance" phase takes over when the undercover agent is either accepted or not. In the event the suspect does not accept the officer, it might be necessary for the informant to meet the suspect at a later time without the undercover officer to determine why the suspect was suspicious. In the event the officer is not accepted, the informant can bring in a second officer with a different cover story. This time, both the officer and informant will try to overcome the difficulties experienced during the first contact.

After the introduction, there is a short period of "bobbing, weaving, and circling": The suspect gets to know or feel if he or she can trust the undercover officer. If a feeling of trust is established, the conversation will quickly turn to the criminal activities in which the suspect is involved.

In the case of an undercover drug operation, for example, this conversation generally results in the undercover agent asking for or obtaining samples, and the suspect will quote the purchase price. After the samples have been delivered and the undercover agent has had an opportunity to examine them, the purchase price is discussed.

This purchase, or the "buy," may or may not go through. In other words, a decision must be made whether or not to arrest a suspect when he or she delivers the contraband (also known as a **buy-bust**) or to take that action after subsequent deliveries (known as a **buy-walk**). If it is determined that the investigation should continue, no arrests should be made and nothing should be done to arouse the suspect's suspicion or to identify accidentally the true role of the undercover operative. This is known as *covering the informant.*

In drug investigations, the first buy is usually a small one whereby the agency doesn't mind losing its **seed money** so that the undercover officer can make a bigger purchase at a later time. Subsequent purchases of contraband are known as the "after action." As a rule, the second purchase or, if necessary, several subsequent purchases. are large enough to warrant not only the appearance of a suspect but also some of the people connected with him or her. These individuals could be present in several capacities, including countersurveillance, protection, main participants, or equal partners, and perhaps even higher-ups. Sometimes it is necessary because of the development of circumstances surrounding the case to arrest a suspect when an initial delivery is made.

and marijuana, from Mexico into the United States through distribution cells in the United States and Canada. The cartel is also believed to be responsible for laundering millions of dollars in drug money. Suspects in this investigation were charged with engaging in a continuing criminal enterprise by violating various felony provisions of the Controlled Substances Act, conspiracy to import controlled substances, money laundering, and possession of unregistered firearms.[6]

The subjects of undercover operations and surveillance are discussed in this chapter because of their close relationship with each other and because of their importance to the investigative function. Typically, undercover work has been associated with drug enforcement, but it is a tool that can be useful in the investigation of a number of criminal activities.

Undercover operations have been used by police agencies for decades. However, they present many problems and concerns for the department because of the delicate nature of undercover work and the officer's role in determining whether someone is committing criminal violations.[7] Undercover work forces the officer to assume a different identity and, sometimes, a lifestyle that thrusts him or her into the criminal subculture, where he or she can be tempted to do things that would otherwise be immoral or even illegal (for example, using illegal drugs). This has the potential to exact a heavy price on individual officers because, depending on the nature of the assignment, they may be separated from family, friends, and other department members for extended periods of time.

Undercover work is street-level work at its best (or worst, however you wish to view it). Officers are required to participate in undesirable activities, and those who remain in undercover positions for too long of a period may begin to adopt the very behaviors of the criminals they are investigating, including undesirable mannerisms and foul language at the least. Even worse, the department can become involved in illegal activities during the course of an investigation. For example, New York City undercover officers ran a pornographic bookstore as part of an undercover sting operation. Officers, as part of their undercover investigation, purchased 1,200 pornographic films and resold them for considerable profit. After eight months, the officers finally arrested several film distributors.

Langworthy observes that some undercover operations result in additional criminal activities.[8] As a result of his analysis of a Birmingham undercover antifencing operation, he concluded that the operation caused a substantial amount of crime by creating a market for stolen goods. If the police operation had not existed, no market would have existed, and criminals would have stolen less often.

Any undercover operation is subject to claims of entrapment. Officers are permitted to do things that provide the opportunity for a suspect to commit a crime, but they may not induce someone to commit a crime. Because undercover operations generally may be initiated without prior judicial authorization, the results are subject to strict scrutiny by the courts. Allowing police to make the decision to initiate an undercover operation based on mere suspicion has been the subject of much criticism.[9] Recognizing the magnitude of the problem, the FBI now requires that large-scale undercover operations first be reviewed by the FBI's Criminal Undercover Operations Review Committee.

Informants are particularly useful and often necessary in the investigation of vice crimes. They can be problematic, however, because police sometimes overlook illegal acts committed by informers to pursue their investigations. For example, narcotics users or lower-level dealers may be allowed to continue violating the law to make cases against their suppliers. Consequently, to move up the distribution network, undercover officers may find it necessary to cooperate with dealers who are selling a significant amount of drugs.

Undercover operations require a number of decisions. Administrative discretion is exercised in determining what activities will be pursued, and operational discretion is exercised in determining who will be targeted for investigation. Because police do not have the resources to investigate every crime, they engage in selective enforcement, enforcing only particular types of violations or targeting specific types of offenders. The decision-making process for vice crimes is subject to the factors previously discussed. The most important criterion for officers is the seriousness of the offense.[10] Most forms of vice, when considered alone, could be viewed as relatively minor crimes.

▶ Types of Undercover Operations

The use of undercover agents is not recommended for every police organization because of the resources required for a suc-

cessful undercover operation. These resources include manpower, training, funding, specialized equipment, and other unique resources.

Police administrators must be careful in the selection of the proper candidate(s) for undercover work. Not every police officer can function properly and professionally in an undercover capacity. Typically, an undercover officer works with minimal direct supervision.[11] As such, officers can be exposed to a number of enticements, which could result in the compromising of the officer's integrity or the investigation. Because of this, the undercover officer must have considerable personal integrity.

One of the greatest challenges to undercover officers is the development of skills that maximize their efforts to match wits with some of the most intelligent and artful criminals on the street. Undercover assignments are either performed in the short term or long term (or "deep cover"). Short-term undercover operations are normally considerably safer for the officer than those that are **deep cover**. Short-term operations permit the help of surveillance officers and protection that undercover agents working in a deep-cover capacity do not have. However, the benefits of working a deep-cover undercover operation allow an undercover agent time to gain the total trust of the criminal suspect to the point of openly discussing criminal operations. This is a great advantage to an undercover agent because, as a rule, criminals are very suspicious about meeting new "clients" who could be (and sometimes are) police informers or undercover officers.

Although no two cases are exactly the same, Motto and June point out that there are certain elements common to each undercover operation: the introduction, the acceptance, the buy, the arrest, covering the informant, and the "after action."[12]

▶ The Undercover Working Environment

Although undercover operations have unique benefits, they also have a serious downside. On one hand, undercover is an investigative method by which officers can see firsthand the inner workings of criminal organizations. Officers can converse and strategize with their criminal targets and learn the ways criminal minds work. Conversely, this close interaction may place officers in jeopardy because they might inadvertently reveal something inconsistent with their cover story. Furthermore, exposure to criminal elements in a close, undercover capacity for extended periods of time might result in the undercover officer acting and speaking in a manner other than he or she is accustomed to, even when off duty, reflecting poorly on the officer's credibility.

To minimize problems associated with undercover operations, a certain degree of preparation is imperative. This includes establishing a sound cover story and understanding specialized infiltration techniques.

The Cover Story

A prerequisite for assuming an undercover role is to establish a **cover story**. Simply defined, the cover story is a fictitious story that the agent will convey to suspects concerning his or her background, including his or her name, address, hometown (or area), and employment, if applicable. Other details may be included, but it is a good idea to keep the cover story simple in case an agent must deal with inquisitive criminal suspects.

The cover story should fit with the area and people involved with the investigation. When an officer chooses to associate him- or herself with a particular town or area, it should be one with which the officer is already familiar, in case he or she later meets someone from that area. Officers should remember that mixing a partial truth with the cover story makes an officer more believable to the suspect.

When claiming a place of employment, the officer should choose one that cannot be easily checked out by suspects. This is more of a problem in rural areas because people are more likely to know each other. It may be desirable to choose an out-of-town place of employment that requires a lot of travel or to present a fictitious job in which the officer is self-employed, thus making it harder for criminal suspects to verify. Whatever story is chosen, the officer should be provided with business cards, customized stationery, credit cards, checking and savings account books, and other supporting credentials to corroborate the cover story. Moreover, the officer should be familiar with the profession chosen for the cover story for the same reasons he or she should be familiar with the purported hometown.

Think About It...

A Life Wrapped in a Lie . . . Media often glamorize the life of undercover work. The reality is that people involved in this work assume not only dangers of a serious nature, but additional stressors that many people probably could not handle. Undercover operatives must work so hard to protect their cover that it can be difficult not to become paranoid. The cost of not being careful though, can include anything from a ceased investigation, to torture, to even death. How might it be difficult for an undercover operative to balance a real life and a "cover" life?

Undercover Officer Searching a Suspect.

The officer's appearance and mannerisms should also fit the cover story. If the officer claims to be an oil field worker, for example, it might be out of character for the officer to be seen by the suspect in an expensive business suit. On the other hand, if the officer's cover story is that of financier for a big money deal, then expensive clothing might be more appropriate. It might also be necessary for an undercover officer to wear expensive jewelry to help convince sellers of his or her cover story. Depending on the nature of the investigation, expensive jewelry can sometimes be borrowed from local stores for short periods; however, the safety and security of the jewelry are the responsibility of the undercover officer.

An investigator should also be aware that criminals can be quite tricky and cunning when trying to expose possible police infiltration. For example, they may

- attempt to intoxicate the officer in the hope that he or she will say something inconsistent with the cover story while under the influence of alcohol.
- use prostitutes, girlfriends or boyfriends, or associates to attempt to seduce the officer; in doing so, the upper torso will be felt for body mikes, the waist area for weapons, and pockets for police credentials or anything else indicating an association with police work.
- ask the officer questions about his or her cover story when the suspects already know the answer; the suspects hope to observe nervousness on the part of the officer.
- ask the officer to furnish drugs to a friend or an associate, knowing that it is against regulations for a law enforcement officer to do so.
- ask the officer to consume drugs furnished by the suspect.
- attempt to learn information about the officer's family (spouse, children, other relatives, or friends) so that an officer's story can be more easily verified.
- ask the officer to perform various illegal acts.
- attempt to rummage through the officer's car or personal belongings to locate police-related material or information showing that the officer was lying about his or her cover story.
- ask the undercover officer excessive questions to see how many he or she is willing to answer before becoming suspicious or angry.

▶ Protecting the Undercover Officer's "Cover"

After the cover story has been established, the undercover officer is committed to it. Certainly the basics—name, hometown, and location—cannot easily be changed without jeopardizing the officer's safety and the integrity of the investigation. Even if changes are not necessary, however, the undercover officer must be able to detect and withstand attempts by suspects and their associates to test and invalidate the officer's cover story.

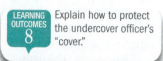

LEARNING OUTCOMES 8 · Explain how to protect the undercover officer's "cover."

Typically, suspects will barrage the officer with questions in an attempt to catch any inconsistency in the cover story. If they are successful, or believe they are, suspects usually attempt to frighten or intimidate the officer into admitting he or she is a law enforcement agent or into abandoning the investigation out of fear for their personal safety.

Panic is the undercover officer's worst enemy. Officers must realize two important things: paranoia is common among drug dealers, and no matter what suspects say they know about the agent, many times they're just attempting to lock the officer into an admission for which they have no proof. If the officer keeps the cover story general, most questioning and suspicion should be easily overcome. Moreover, if the officer has been properly trained and responds to the suspects according to his or her training, a bond of trust may develop between the officer and suspects that can pave the way to a successful investigation.

Different criminals use different methods to expose undercover police agents. Even though good field training should prepare undercover personnel for most of these obstacles, not every confrontation can be anticipated. Undercover personnel should remember that most questions about their cover story are bluffs, and they should remain calm and confident, discounting the challenges presented without appearing scared, intimidated, or paranoid.

Infiltration

After a cover story is established, a methodical process of infiltration must take place to uncover criminal wrongdoing and its associated evidence. During infiltration, a relationship is established between the officer and a suspect. Frequently, an officer finds it difficult to meet or establish any rapport with the suspect without the help of an informant. In some cases, however, informants may cause more trouble for the officer and the investigation than they are worth; therefore, their use should be carefully considered. Infiltration requires

LEARNING OUTCOMES 9 — Explain methods of infiltration and the risks involved in undercover operations.

inventiveness and originality on the officer's part because he or she might have to create his or her own opportunity to speak with the suspect.

After contact has been made between the officer and the suspect, the suspect's confidence must be gained as soon as possible. An officer can best accomplish this by learning the interests of the suspects (for example, jobs, the opposite sex, local bars, motorcycles, cars, drugs) that the officer can then discuss. Context must be regularly attempted throughout the investigation to maintain rapport with the suspect.

When working without an informant, it might be necessary to canvass a target area. The undercover officer can expedite the investigation by revealing intelligence on target suspects and locations, concentrating on areas with high levels of crime that might provide investigative leads. Typical starting places might be bars, nightclubs, or taverns, which can be excellent sources of intelligence for undercover officers. Much can be learned just by being present at these locations; generally people do not have a reasonable expectation of privacy when "openly" conversing in public in such places as a bar. The undercover agent can simply overhear otherwise private or guarded information about the suspects' names, types of criminal activities, places of employment, and vehicles they drive. After the officer learns such information and it appears that the information might be useful in showing criminal activity, it should be properly documented in intelligence reports. The lack of such properly generated intelligence reports accounts for the loss of much valuable criminal information to the unit.

Risks in Undercover Assignments

For investigators assigned to undercover roles, two principal problems can be identified that may pose problems for both the investigator and his or her agency. The first is the problem of maintaining the "criminal" identity, and the second area is the process of reintegration back into normal investigative duties. The maintenance-of-identity problems are those that are associated with adopting and living a double life in a new environment.

Stress in Relationships

Undercover work is one of the most stressful jobs that a police officer can undertake.[13] The greatest cause of stress for investigators working undercover is the requirement that they distance themselves from friends, family, and their normal environment. This simple isolation can result in the onset of depression and anxiety. There are no data on the divorce rates of undercover agents, but considerable tension in relationships has been known to develop. This can result from a need for secrecy and an inability to share work problems, the unpredictable work schedule, personality and lifestyle changes, and the length of separation. These factors can all result in problems for relationships.[14]

Stress from Uncertainty

Stress can also result from an apparent lack of direction of the investigation or not knowing when it will end. The amount of elaborate planning, risk, and expenditure can also place pressure on an agent to succeed, which can cause considerable stress.[15] The stress that an undercover agent faces is considerably different from that faced by investigators who are not assigned to undercover assignments and whose main source of stress results from pressures by the administration and the general bureaucracy of police work.[16] Because the undercover agent is removed from the bureaucracy, it may result in another problem. These officers have an increased likelihood of corruption because they do not have the usual controls of a uniform, badge, constant supervision, a fixed place of work, or (often) a set assignment, and because they have continual contact with the criminal underworld (members of the opposite sex, pressure and manipulation from criminal suspects, alcohol, availability of illicit drugs, and opportunities to earn or seize large amounts of illicit money).[17]

Development of Alcohol or Drug Abuse

This stress may be instrumental in the development of drug or alcohol abuse in some agents. These agents are more prone to the development of an addiction because they experience greater stress than other police, they are isolated, and drugs are often very accessible.[18] Police, in general, have very high alcoholism rates compared with people in most occupational groups, and stress is cited as a likely factor.[19] The environment that agents work in, including taverns, bars, and private residences of criminal suspects, often involves considerable exposure to the consumption of alcohol, which in conjunction with the stress and isolation may result in alcoholism.[20]

Feelings of Personal Guilt

There can also be some guilt associated with working undercover because of the need to essentially betray the trust of those (criminal suspects) who have come to trust you. According to Marx, this can cause anxiety or even, in very rare cases, sympathy with those being targeted.[21] This is especially true with the infiltration of political groups because often agents share similar characteristics, such as class, age, ethnicity, or religion, with those they are infiltrating. This could even result in the conversion of some agents.[22]

Problems of Reintegration

The lifestyle led by undercover agents is very different than that of other areas in law enforcement, and it can be quite difficult to reintegrate back into normal duties. Agents work their own hours, they are removed from direct supervisory monitoring, and they can ignore the dress and etiquette rules.[23] So the resettling back into the normal police role requires the shredding of old habits, language, and dress. After working such free lifestyles, agents may have discipline problems or exhibit neurotic responses. They may feel uncomfortable and take a cynical, suspicious, or even paranoid worldview and feel continually on guard.[24]

Becoming a DEA Special Agent

DEA Special Agents are a select group of men and women from diverse backgrounds whose experience and commitment make them the premier federal drug law enforcement agents in the world. Applicants must be at least 21 years of age and no older than 36 at the time of their appointment.

Salary

DEA Special Agents are generally hired at the GS-7 or GS-9 level, depending on education and experience. The salary includes federal Law Enforcement Officer base pay plus a locality payment, depending on the duty station. Upon successful graduation from the DEA Training Academy, 25% availability pay will be added to the base and locality pay. After graduation, the starting salaries are approximately $49,746 for a GS-7 and $55,483 for a GS-9. After four years of service, Special Agents are eligible to progress to the GS-13 level and can earn approximately $92,592 or more per year.

Education

The most competitive candidates possess a bachelor's or master's degree, along with a grade point average (GPA) of 2.95 or higher. Special consideration is given to candidates with degrees in criminal justice/police science or related disciplines; finance, accounting, or economics; foreign languages (with fluency verified) in Spanish, Russian, Hebrew, Arabic, dialects of Nigerian languages, Chinese, Japanese; computer science/information systems; and telecommunications, electrical engineering, and mechanical engineering.

Depending on scheduling and candidate availability, the DEA's hiring process may take 12 months or longer. Hiring involves a multistep process that includes the following phases:
- Qualifications review
- Written and oral assessment and panel interview
- Urinalysis drug test
- Medical examination
- Physical task test
- Polygraph examination
- Psychological assessment
- Final hiring decision

Mobility

Mobility is a condition of employment. Special Agents are subject to transfer throughout their career based on the needs of the agency.

Drug Use Policy

The DEA is charged with enforcement of the Federal Controlled Substances Act; therefore, all applicants must fully disclose any drug use history during the application process. Applicants whose drug use history is outside of acceptable parameters will not be considered for employment. All DEA employees are subject to random urinalysis drug testing throughout their careers.

Background Investigation (BI)

A BI is one of the final steps in the application process that seeks to discern a comprehensive snapshot of applicants. The investigation provides information on applicants' personal history, education and work experience, personal and professional references, as well as other necessary checks. The time it takes to complete the BI is dependent on the type and scope of investigation being conducted.

The Physical Task (PT) Test

The PT test determines if potential candidates can withstand the rigors of Special Agent training. Candidates must be in excellent physical condition to pass this test.

If a candidate fails the first PT test administered in the field, a second test must be successfully taken within 30 days. A second failure will cause the candidate's application process to be discontinued. Candidates are encouraged to train to ensure that they are prepared to successfully complete this test.

Training

All applicants must successfully complete all phases of the hiring process and remain most competitive to receive a final offer of employment. For more information, contact your nearest DEA field division recruitment office. Scheduling times and locations are handled by the local recruitment coordinators. Special Agent candidates are required to successfully complete a 16-week Basic Agent Training (BAT) program at the DEA Training Academy in Quantico, Virginia.

Through this program, instruction and hands-on training are provided in undercover, surveillance, and arrest techniques; defensive tactics and firearms training; and the basics of report writing, law, and drug identification and recognition. In addition, applicants participate in a rigorous physical fitness program.

Duty Station

Between the 8th and 12th weeks of the training, applicants are provided with final duty station assignments. Mobility is a condition of employment. Assignments are made based upon the DEA's current operational needs.

The Antisnitch Movement

Informers have always been a key investigative tool but at the same time have been viewed as a necessary evil. In some cases, if a drug dealer needs to make a deal with law enforcement, he or she will tell on friends or family alike if necessary. It may not be right, but it's the only answer for some people. In some cases, criminal informers who are allowed to remain free commit more crimes, return to crime after serving a short prison sentence, frame other people for crimes they didn't commit, or tell prosecutors anything they want to hear.

It was strange enough for prosecutors and police to see the T-shirt with a traffic-sign message of "STOP SNITCHING," but one of those T-shirts was about to show up in court with a matching baseball cap. Worse yet, the wearer was a prosecution witness for Pittsburgh's Prosecutor Lisa Pellegrini. In March of 2006, Rayco "War" Saunders—ex-con, pro boxer, and walking billboard for an antisnitch movement—sparked a coast-to-coast debate involving everyone from academics to police to rappers. Pellegrini, while thinking "witness intimidation," told Saunders to lose the hat and reverse the shirt. Saunders, claiming First Amendment rights, refused. He left the courthouse, shirt in place. The case was dismissed. The attitude of "don't be a snitch" is common throughout many communities and, in some cases, even condoned. While the Mafia's traditional blood oath of silence, "Omerta," has been broken by turncoat after turncoat, in some inner-city neighborhoods, the call to stop snitching is galvanizing. Some say it's an attempt by drug dealers and gangsters to intimidate witnesses, but others say it's a legitimate protest against law enforcement's overreliance on criminal informers.

Monkey Business Images/Shutterstock.com

Take the case of Busta Rhymes, the hip-hop star who refused to cooperate with police investigating the slaying of his bodyguard, Israel Ramirez, on February 5, 2006, outside a Brooklyn studio where Rhymes was recording a video with other rap performers. Police claimed that although Rhymes and as many as 50 others may have witnessed the shooting, no one came forward—reminiscent of the echo of silence that followed the unsolved murders of rappers Tupac Shakur, The Notorious B.I.G., and Run-DMC's Jam Master Jay.

Sources: Hampson, R. (2006, March 29). Anti-snitch campaign riles police, prosecutors. *USA Today*, 1A–2A; Scolville, D. (2007). How to develop informants. *Police. The Law Enforcement Magazine*. Retrieved from http://www.policemag.com/-Articles/2007/08/How-to-Develop-Informants.aspx.

One of the undercover investigator's most useful tools is the informant:

1. Using the chapter material and the preceding case, what is the role in undercover work with respect to managing informants?

2. Given the two preceding examples, what are your thoughts on why society does not support informing about criminal activity (be specific)?

Identify informants and their various uses.

The word "informant" could best be defined as "anyone who provides information of an investigative nature to law enforcement." Informants can be classified into four general groups: *average citizens*, *fellow law enforcement officers*, *mentally ill persons*, and *criminals or their associates*. Criminal informants are people who are currently, or have been, associated with a particular criminal element and are in a position to supply information about criminal activity.

1. What public forums are used/have been used to help law enforcement officials locate criminals?

2. What is meant by proactive law enforcement?

3. How are informants classified?

4. Why do criminals or their associates make good informants?

5. What variables make the use of informants problematic?

6. How can an informant assist law enforcement officials? What services can informants provide investigators?

7. What motivates informants to aid in police investigations?

informant Anyone who provides information of an investigative nature to law enforcement authorities.

credibility One's ability to be believed.

motivations Reasons why someone does something.

Explain how to properly document and process an informant.

All candidates for informants should be fingerprinted, photographed, and interviewed by investigators before being used as an informant. Interviews should reflect the informant's true name and any aliases, address, employment history, and so on. Criminal records, if any, should be verified. All procedures should be contained in an official informant file for each person (indexed by number, which should be used in all subsequent references to the informant).

1. What procedures are used to document informants?

2. During an informant interview, what pertinent information should be obtained by law enforcement agencies?

3. What key questions should be asked during the interview?

4. How can law enforcement agencies verify the criminal records of informants?

Explain how to maintain control of an informant during an investigation.

The investigator who develops an informer is the one who is assigned to him or her. Although informants should be asked frequently for their opinions, each suggestion should be considered carefully. Additionally, investigators must be careful not to promise anything they cannot deliver (for example, money, a reduced charge, relocation of the informant's family, police protection).

1. What is the cardinal rule when it comes to working with informants?

2. What is the best way to control informants?

3. Why is it important for investigators to develop and maintain rapport with informants?

4. Why is it important for the informant to understand the issue of entrapment?

5. Who should have the most interactions with informants? Why?

entrapment When an undercover officer convinces a criminal suspect to commit a crime he or she was not predisposed to commit.

Summarize the legal framework for informant management.

Because investigators and their informers work together closely, an officer can become caught up in an informant's personal problems. During initial meetings, officers should stress that any criminal activity on the part of the informant will not be tolerated. Informants should be considered the "property" of the department and should be sufficiently documented. This avoids any allegations of misconduct on the part of investigators if seen with known criminals.

1. What are areas of concern when working with informants?

2. What precedent was established by the Supreme Court's review of the case of *Alabama* v. *White*?

3. What two criteria must be met before an informant's information can provide probable cause?

4. What is the potential danger of informants being the opposite sex of their control officer/investigator? How can agencies alleviate this potential problem?

5. When it is permitted to pay informants for information?

LEARNING OUTCOMES 5

Summarize the usefulness of undercover investigations.

Undercover operations have been used by police agencies for decades and are an important part of the criminal investigation function but one that is highly specialized. Undercover work and surveillance are viable options for police investigators because they provide considerable information that is not otherwise available through traditional investigative methods.

1. Why would undercover operations be considered a double-edged sword?
2. Why don't all law enforcement agencies practice undercover operations?

3. What are some problems associated with undercover work?
4. What entity reviews large-scale undercover operations before they are initiated?
5. What is selective enforcement?
6. Why do police agencies engage in selective enforcement?
7. What are potential problems with selective-enforcement policing?

LEARNING OUTCOMES 6

Describe types of undercover operations.

Undercover assignments are performed in either the short term or long term. Short-term undercover operations are normally considerably safer for the officer than those that are longer. Although no two cases are exactly the same, there are certain elements common to each undercover operation. After the introduction, there is a short period of "bobbing, weaving, and circling."

1. What resources are necessary to operate a successful undercover investigation?
2. What are the advantages associated with short-term undercover operations?
3. What are the advantages associated with deep-cover undercover operations?

4. What are the common elements of undercover operations?
5. What type of officer makes the ideal candidate for an undercover agent?

deep cover Working undercover for extended periods of time.

buy-bust When an undercover agent makes a purchase of illicit narcotics and the suspect is immediately arrested.

buy-walk When an undercover agent makes a purchase of illicit narcotics and the suspect is allowed to leave for the purposes of continuing the investigation.

seed money Money required to initiate an undercover drug transaction.

LEARNING OUTCOMES 7

Describe the undercover working environment.

A prerequisite for assuming an undercover role is to establish a cover story. The cover story should fit with the area and people involved with the investigation. Whatever story is chosen, the officer should be provided with supporting credentials to corroborate the cover story. The officer's appearance and mannerisms should also fit the cover story.

1. What is the downside to undercover operations?

2. How do officers prepare for an undercover operation?
3. What are the keys to developing a viable cover story?
4. What are the benefits of undercover operations?
5. What are examples of supporting credentials used to corroborate a cover story?

cover story A fictitious story contrived by an undercover investigator to explain his or her presence as a drug buyer to criminal suspects.

LEARNING OUTCOMES 8

Explain how to protect the undercover officer's "cover."

Different criminals use different methods to expose undercover police agents. Undercover officers should remember that most questions about their cover story are bluffs, and they should remain calm and confident, discounting the challenges presented without appearing scared, intimidated, or paranoid. After a cover story is established, a methodical process of infiltration must take place to uncover criminal wrongdoing and its associated evidence.

1. What methods are recommended for establishing a cover story?

2. How can officers safeguard their undercover identity?
3. In what ways do criminals attempt to expose possible police infiltration?
4. What are typical problems encountered by undercover agents?
5. How has the antisnitching movement affected law enforcement?
6. What have the criminal justice system and law enforcement done to combat the antisnitching movement?

LEARNING OUTCOMES 9

Explain methods of infiltration and the risks involved in undercover operations.

Methods of infiltration include establishing a cover story and establishing a relationship with the criminal suspect for the purpose of infiltration. Risks are inherent in infiltration because the officer must act as a criminal without breaking the law him- or herself. Officers are typically vulnerable as they are working alone or with minimal direct supervision. After working in an undercover capacity, it is also sometimes difficult for officers to reintegrate back into normal investigative duties.

1. What is the process of infiltration?

2. How does the lifestyle of an undercover officer differ from those in other areas of law enforcement?

3. In what ways can a rapport be built with criminals in the street?

4. How can an officer safeguard against becoming involved in criminal activity?

5. What are the problems in reintegration of an undercover officer back into normal investigative duties?

Additional Links

www.policemag.com

The site of Police: The Law Enforcement Magazine offers blogs, news, jobs, archives, podcasts, and a bookstore. The issues discussed include columns written by police, firearms experts, and legal experts. The site also includes articles written by law enforcement journalists.

www.justice.gov/dea

The U.S. Drug Enforcement Administration (DEA) site includes a pressroom with news releases, speeches and testimony, a careers link, drug information resources, and links for drug prevention, legislative resources, publications, and law enforcement.

www.fbi.gov

The official site of the Federal Bureau of Investigation (FBI) provides a link to the National Crime Information Center (NCIC; see www.fbi.gov/about-us/cjis/ncic). The NCIC page includes history and milestones, statistics, and NCIC files.

"The crime of homicide represents one of society's most serious crimes and one to which the greatest amount of resources are committed by the community."

Death Investigations

1 Summarize legal characteristics of homicide.

2 Describe how a homicide investigation is conducted.

3 Explain how time of death is estimated.

4 Explain the use of gunshot wounds as evidence in death investigations.

© kiuikuu/Fotolia

INTRO WHEN A MOTHER KILLS

In May 2014, 53-year-old Julie Schenecker, a former military linguist and longtime U.S. Army officer's wife, was convicted of first-degree murder when jurors rejected her argument that she was legally insane when she shot and killed her 13-year-old son and 16-year-old daughter three years earlier.

The criminal complaint against Schenecker showed that she killed her daughter, Calyx, and son, Beau, in January 2011 while her husband, Col. Parker Schenecker, was on a 10-day deployment to the Middle East.

Schenecker's lawyers argued that she was so affected with bipolar disorder and depression that she didn't know right from wrong. Under Florida law, the inability to tell right from wrong is one of the criteria for a plea of not guilty by reason of insanity. Prosecutors, however, told the jury that Schenecker wrote in her journal that she wanted to kill herself and wanted to be cremated with her children with their ashes mixed together. She mentioned that she was going to try to move her son's body into her bed and wanted to die next to him.

At trial, six mental health experts who testified said Schenecker was mentally ill, but three prosecution experts said she was legally sane when she shot her children. Prosecution experts further testified that Schenecker was calculating and deliberate when she bought the .38-caliber handgun along with more-lethal hollow bullets just days before the killings. In addition, in her journal, she lamented the three-day wait for a background check, writing that she had planned a weekend massacre.

Tampa Police officers escorting Julie Powers Schenecker from the Tampa Police station to the Orient Road Jail in January 2011.

DISCUSS The case of Julie Schenecker is but one of a number of disturbing cases where mothers have murdered their children. Discuss the challenges that are presented to a criminal investigator when investigating such a case.

▶ *The Extent of Homicide*

Murder continues to be one society's highest-priority crimes. Properly conducted investigations that lead to the arrest of a homicide suspect not only brings the perpetrator to justice but also protects communities and provides closure for the victim's family. The extent of homicide is instructive. For example, in 2012 the Federal Bureau of Investigation (FBI) reported that an estimated 14,827 persons were murdered in the United States. There were 4.7 murders per 100,000 people.[1] These statistics demonstrate the importance of properly conducted criminal investigations.

The Homicide Investigator's Guiding Principle

Few things in our democracy are as important as ensuring that citizens have confidence in their institutions in a crisis. For many individuals the death of a loved one is just such a crisis. Ensuring that the proper steps and procedures are taken at the scene of that death to reassure

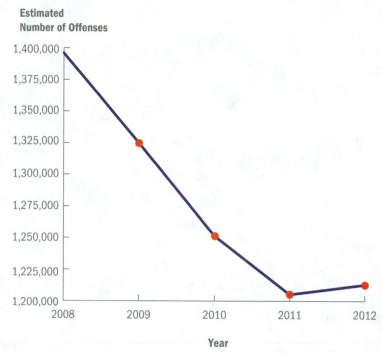

Violent Crime Offenses.

family members that the death was a natural one, a suicide, or a homicide is a key element in maintaining citizen confidence in local officials and bringing closure to family members and loved ones.

How local death investigators do their job is crucial to family members who are mourning a loss today and who may be seeking justice tomorrow. Most of us cringe at the idea of death investigations where important steps were omitted that might have led to arrests and ultimately convictions in those deaths. Justice denied breeds contempt for the institutions created to ensure that justice is done.

Murder and Wrongful Death

Murder is the unlawful killing of one human being by another. *Uniform Crime Reports* (UCR) statistics on murder describe the early incidence of all willful and unlawful homicides within the United States; included in the count are cases of non-negligent manslaughter that have been reported to or discovered by the police. Not included are suicides, justifiable homicides (e.g., self-defense), deaths caused by negligence or accident, and murder attempts. In 2012, an estimated 14,827 murders came to the attention of police departments across the nation.[2] First-degree murder is a criminal **homicide** that is planned (see Figure 9–1). Second-degree murder is an intentional and unlawful killing but one that is generally unplanned and that happens "in the heat of passion."

According to statistics, young adults between 20 and 24 were the most likely to be murdered. The perpetrators of murder were also most common in the same age group. Statistics show that firearms are the weapon used most often to commit murder. For example, in 2012 guns were used in 69.3 percent of all killings.[3] Handguns outnumbered shotguns almost 15 to 1 in the murder statistics, with rifles used almost as often as shotguns.[4] Knives were used in approximately 12.5 percent of all murders. Finally, only 12.2 percent of all murders in 2012 were perpetrated by offenders classified as "strangers."[5] The largest category of killers was officially listed as "acquaintances."

Legal elements of the crime of homicide vary from one state to another but do exhibit some commonalties.

MURDER

- *First degree.* A person commits the crime if he or she knowingly causes the death of another person after deliberation on the matter.
- *Second degree.* A person commits the crime if he or she knowingly causes the death of another person while committing a criminal act and not acting under the influence of sudden passion.

MANSLAUGHTER

- *Involuntary.* A person commits the crime if he or she recklessly causes another person's death.
- *Voluntary.* A person commits the crime if he or she causes the death of another person by being certain of taking the victim's life and acting in the heat of passion.

FIGURE 9–1 Elements of Homicide.

▶ Dynamics of the Homicide Unit

The police homicide unit is probably one of the more celebrated investigative units in the law enforcement organization. This is because, in part, solving the crime of murder is one of society's highest priorities. This, in and of itself, places considerable pressure on homicide detectives to clear their cases by making an arrest. Of the many challenges involved in doing so, investigators must be certain that their actions are consistent with accepted investigative procedure and the constraints of U.S. Constitution.

Although homicide command staff officers are typically confident about the abilities of their detectives, in many cases there are concerns about how homicide units can raise clearance rates. As a general rule, the success for a homicide unit is measured by its clearance rate. The clearance rate is the standard measurement index used by the FBI's Uniform Crime Reporting system, and is based on the number of arrests made for a given offense. However, some units use a different measurement of success by referring to their conviction rate as opposed to the number of arrests.

The clearance rate is a readily available statistic and is directly impacted by the homicide unit. On the other hand, a number of indirect, non-homicide-unit-related variables can affect the conviction rate, if the actual percentage can even be determined. These variables include jury selection, testimony by witnesses, the ability of the prosecutor to successfully present a case to a jury, and the extent to which quality evidence has been obtained and is made available to the jury.

Selecting the Right Detective

The process for selecting a homicide detective varies from one law enforcement organization to another and typically is influenced by departmental policies and union rules. For many departments, both the formal oral interview and the recommendations of the homicide supervisor are the preferred methods of selection as opposed to written exams.

Statistics in this regard are instructive. A study conducted by Timothy Keel and published in the FBI's *Law Enforcement Bulletin* notes that over 80 percent of law enforcement organizations do not consider an appointment to the homicide unit as a promotion; over 70 percent thought of it as an elevated position.[6] In examining a particular candidate for a homicide assignment, 64 percent of departments expected that person to have prior investigative experience in some other unit, and 55 percent preferred that the candidate have prior investigative experience.[7] According to Keel, many law enforcement administrators identify desired traits as interview and interrogation skills, dedication, experience, patience, common sense, tenacity, persistence, and organizational skills. A department with a higher-than-average clearance rate revealed that the average time detectives had spent in their department was 17.18 years.[8] In addition, the average time spent in uniform patrol was 6.71 years; an investigative unit, 9.66 years; and the homicide unit, 6 years. The average age of the detectives was 42.25 years, and their average years of education totaled 14.81.[9]

Caseload Management

In most cases, homicide units will work more than just homicide cases. Examples are police-involved shootings and in-custody deaths.

Another contemporary issue facing police supervisors is the rotation of homicide investigators out of the homicide unit after a period of time. Although a rotation policy may have some benefits from a management perspective, law enforcement administrators considering implementing such a policy should proceed cautiously. This is because the training and acquired skills of a homicide detective are a valuable resource for the department and re-training investigators is a costly and lengthy process.

Another issue in management of the homicide unit is caseload. Most homicide supervisors would like to have more detectives to investigate each case. But fighting for limited resources and demonstrating the need for additional detectives is difficult without some accepted understanding of what should comprise a detective's annual caseload. Researcher Timothy Keel found that a homicide detective handles an average of five cases annually as a primary investigator,[10] which appears to be the maximum caseload in order for the investigator to be effective. For example, statistics show that departments with detectives who handled fewer than five cases per year as a primary investigator had a 5.4 percent higher clearance rate than those with detectives who had higher caseloads.[11]

Investigative Tools

Detectives often use specialized tools to assist them in investigations. Utilization of the right investigative tool can result in a homicide investigator improving his or her clearance rate. For example, research shows that almost 93 percent of the departments reported that a polygraph was available for use, and 34.5 percent used a computer voice-stress analyzer.[12] Almost 90 percent of departments studied used bloodstain-pattern analysis, and those departments had a 4.8 percent higher clearance rate.[13] One-half of the respondents used criminal investigative analysis (criminal profiling), and those departments had a 5.7 percent higher average clearance rate.[14]

Cold Case Squads

Of course detectives want to solve each and every case, but in spite of their best efforts many remain unsolved. In addition to causing the case detective considerable frustration, unsolved cases deprive families of closure and the community of a sense of justice. Sometimes, a new look at a cold case and a fresh analysis of the evidence can result in new leads and possible case closure.

The creation and use of cold case squads (CCS) have become more widespread as commanders of homicide units realize the potential of such a division. Research shows that of departments with clearance rates above the national average, over 80 percent had some type of CCS.[15] The advances in forensic science over the past 20 years have made case closure more likely for all homicide investigators.

The objective of a CCS is to identify and arrest an offender, removing a violent or dangerous person from the street and giving the victim's family a sense of closure and justice. Also, from an administrative standpoint, there is an advantage for having a CCS in that a department receives credit for a clearance in the year the clearance (arrest) is made, in spite of the year the homicide actually occurred. Statistically, this increases the department's overall clearance rate.

▶ The Homicide 911 Call

A frantic young man called 911: "Get an ambulance to 168 Birch. My friend's been shot!"

On another occasion, the father of a 1-year-old boy reported, "Yes, ma'am . . . my, my son can't breathe." These examples beg the question, "Do 911 homicide calls contain clues that could help investigators identify the killer?" The answer is, quite possibly. In these two examples, the first caller demanded immediate medical assistance for his friend and did not commit

---

A CLOSER LOOK

Keys to a Successful Homicide Unit

- No more than five cases per year as primary for each detective
- Minimum of two, two-person units responding initially to the crime scene
- Case review by all involved personnel within the first 24 to 72 hours
- Computerized case management system with relational capacity
- Standardized and computerized car stop and neighborhood canvass forms
- Compstat-style format

- Effective working relationships with medical examiners and prosecutors
- No rotation policy for homicide detectives
- Accessibility to work overtime when needed
- Cold case squads
- Investigative tools, such as polygraph, bloodstain-pattern analysis, criminal investigative analysis, and statement analysis
- Homicide unit and other personnel work as a team

Source: Keel, T. G. (2008, February 8). Homicide investigations: Identifying best practices. *FBI Law Enforcement Bulletin, 77*(2), p. 4.

the crime. In the second instance, the father politely reported his child's condition, never asking for help for his son or expressing any urgency. He had shaken the boy, who later died.

Analyzing the Call

The homicide 911 call can provide invaluable clues to investigators because the caller, in fact, may have committed the crime. It is not unusual for homicide offenders to contact 911 without revealing their involvement in the murder. In these cases, the dispatcher simply asks, "What is your emergency?" and the caller typically responds with spur-of-the moment verbal and vocal clues. For this reason, it is fortunate that 911 calls are recorded. Therefore, investigators have access to a transcript, the actual call, and, thus, important evidence. This evidence allows them to examine both the words of the caller and his or her tone of voice, which can also provide investigators with interviewing strategies to help solve the homicide case.

When analyzing a 911 homicide call, the investigator's primary question should be, Was the caller requesting assistance? If not, why not? Was the individual simply reporting a crime? Research shows that almost twice as many innocent callers (67%) asked for help for the victim than did guilty callers (34%).

The relevance of the information provided by the caller is also important. For example, in a study conducted by Adams and Harpster (2008), research showed that during the dispatchers' questioning of 911 homicide callers, very few of those later shown to be guilty actually lied to the dispatcher unless forced to. Instead, they deceived by omitting information rather than by lying about their role in the crime. In lieu of offering the complete truth, such as "I did it," many provided rambling information, instead of concise points; confusing, rather than clear, details; and extraneous information, instead of relevant facts.[16] These details, although irrelevant to the dispatchers' questions, are sometimes related to the criminal act itself.

Consider the following example, which occurred when a father called 911 concerning his son:

- Dispatcher: 911. What is your emergency?
- Guilty caller: "I have an unconscious child who is breathing very shallowly."

In this case, the father took personal possession of a problem ("I have") and referred to his problem (his dying son) as "an unconscious child." When the paramedics arrived at the residence, the child already had died. The father had assaulted his son, causing cerebral hemorrhaging. Adams and Harpster reported that in 12 percent of the 911 calls studied, callers took personal possession of the problem.[17] All were guilty of the homicide.

In summary, the significance of the homicide 911 call should cause investigators to consider numerous possible clues that are recorded in the call itself. By examining 911 homicide calls, investigating officers can gain vital clues. While listening to a call and analyzing the transcript, the investigator should ask three critical questions:

1. What was the call about?
2. Who was the call about?
3. How was the call made?

Asking those three questions, along with a careful analysis, can give investigators insight as to a possible suspect. If the caller appears guilty of or knowledgeable about the homicide, investigators can immediately plan a strategy for interviewing the individual and conducting the subsequent homicide investigation.

Legal Characteristics of Homicide

Criminal investigators encounter wrongful death in many ways. Some victims are killed by accident, others in the heat of passion, and still others for profit. Therefore, it is incumbent on the professional investigator to be clear as to what laws best describe the alleged crime. Under law, categories of homicide are generally divided into two distinct classifications: murder and manslaughter. Murder is considered the most serious of all statutory crimes and is defined as the purposeful, premeditated, and unlawful taking of the life of a human being by another person. Persons found guilty of murder receive the harshest of sentences, which may include life imprisonment

LEARNING OUTCOMES 1 — Summarize legal characteristics of homicide.

or the death penalty. Many states classify murder in different degrees, typically first and second. For example, first-degree murder is considered the most serious and includes, as one of the elements, premeditation and preplanning. Second-degree murder is a lesser offense but requires that the person "attempted" to kill his or her intended victim (for example, a domestic argument that erupts into a physical altercation resulting in the death of one of the parties).

Manslaughter is the deliberate killing of another person and is typically classified into two subcategories: voluntary and involuntary. *Voluntary manslaughter* generally refers to the killing of another person out of an act of passion but lacks premeditation. For example, a man arrives at his home to find his wife with another man. The husband then loses his temper and immediately shoots the man. The key element here is that the scene must erupt into passion and must be followed immediately by the act of murder without premeditation or "cool reflection" about the incident.

Involuntary manslaughter usually refers to the accidental or nonintentional death of another human being, with severe negligence. Examples of involuntary manslaughter include a motorist who is exceeding the speed limit by 30 miles per hour and hits a child playing in the street. If the driver were traveling at the speed limit, he or she would have been able to stop in time to miss the child. Other examples of involuntary manslaughter include the reckless handling of a firearm that results in someone's death, and leaving dangerous poisons or drugs in reach of children.

The Preliminary Investigation

Homicide investigations are usually reactive in nature and are typically initiated by a telephone call to a local law enforcement

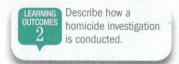

LEARNING OUTCOMES 2 Describe how a homicide investigation is conducted.

agency notifying them of some aspect of the offense. Such calls may be a simple request for assistance by an injured person, a call stating "shots were fired," or a report of some form of violence that was observed (for example, a man or woman being beaten). Rarely, however, does this initial call contain enough information to determine exactly what is occurring or what has occurred. Investigators on the scene typically learn such details.

The first officer to respond to a suspected homicide call is generally a patrol officer who arrives a short time after the call is received.

After these fundamental steps are dealt with, the officer must become what could be termed **scene-conscious**. That is, he or she must become aware of the crime-scene situation and be prepared to take certain immediate actions, the focus being identifying any aspects of the scene that might be subject to chemical change, change by dissipation, or change because something was moved.

Protecting the Crime Scene

After the preliminary duties have been performed, the responding officer must protect the crime scene from unauthorized persons who may move, destroy, or otherwise contaminate evidence. It is important for civilians and unauthorized police personnel alike to be denied entrance to the scene. Experience has shown that probably no aspect of the homicide investigation is more open to error than the preservation and protection of the crime scene.[18] Death scenes can be expected to produce an abundance of evidence. All such evidence will enable the investigators to determine the manner of death, weapons used, time of death, and other pertinent information.

Taking Notes at the Scene

Complete notes are critical during the early stages of the homicide crime-scene investigation. Because details are of such vital importance, both the investigating and responding officers should take notes. In fact, these notes could later become decisive evidence in the prosecution of the suspect(s). Crime-scene notes in a homicide investigation should include the following:

- Names of officers on the scene
- Names and addresses of witnesses at the scene
- Name and address of the person notifying the police
- Manner of entry/exit of the perpetrator of the crime
- Description of weather conditions

As indicated earlier, investigators should also be prepared to draft a sketch of the scene. The sketch should show all critical aspects of the homicide crime scene, such as the location and position of the body; location of any weapons; and positions of furniture, clothing, and other types of evidence. The sketch will prove to be of value later in the investigation when reports are being finalized and in preparing for court.

Identifying the Victim

Homicide crime scenes can vary greatly from one case to the next. For example, in one case, the body might be charred as a result of a fire designed to cover up evidence. In another, the body might have been chopped up and parts distributed over a broad geographical area. In other cases, bodies have been recovered in lakes and rivers and offer little or no immediate clues as to their identity. In all circumstances, the body must be identified.

▶ Estimating the Time of Death

If the wrongful death appears to have been a homicide, all areas around the body become important in determining the time of death. The time of death in a homicide case, particularly when there are no witnesses, is one of the most critical variables in its investigation. It may convict a murderer, break an alibi, or even eliminate a suspect. Time may come into play if the deceased had an appointment with someone around the time of his or her death. In addition, in cases of exclusive opportunity, in which only certain persons are present with the victim, husbands or wives, boyfriends or girlfriends, and so on, may become likely suspects.

LEARNING OUTCOMES 3 Explain how time of death is estimated.

The actions taken at the time of arrival may have a critical bearing on the subsequent course of the investigation. Some of the most critical of these are featured in this section. Responding officers might encounter any of the following:

- A person who directs the officer to the crime scene
- A crime scene that might be in an isolated place that is untouched and easily safeguarded
- A crime scene that might be filled with people milling around, acting confused, shouting, or crying
- A killer who might either still be on the scene or who may have just exited
- A victim who may be dead or may still be alive but in need of medical attention
- A crime scene in a public place that may be difficult to secure

In all situations, the first officer on the scene has several principal concerns:

- Determine if the victim is dead or alive.
- Contact medical help for the victim if needed.
- Apprehend the perpetrator if still present on the scene.
- Make the appropriate notifications if the perpetrator has left the scene.
- Safeguard the crime scene.
- Detain any witnesses.

Changes in the Body: Decomposition

Simply stated, death occurs when vital functions of the body are halted. These include functions of breathing and circulation. In addition, investigators should observe other changes (see Figure 9–2).

After death occurs, human decomposition takes place in five stages. The process of tissue breakdown may take from several days up to years. At all stages of decomposition, insect activity occurs on the body, as detailed next.

Stage 1: The Fresh Stage

- First few days after death
- No physical signs of decomposition
- Body enters algor mortis
- VOCs are produced
- Insects lay eggs on body

Stage 2: The Putrefaction Stage

- Odor, color changes, and bloating
- Marbelization of skin
- Color changes to green and then to brown
- Skin becomes fragile and body hair is easily removed
- Continued insect activity

Stage 3: The Black Putrefaction Stage

- 10-20 days after death
- Body cavity ruptures and gases escape
- Body color darkens from greenish color
- Insect activity greatly increases
- Bones become apparent

Stage 4: The Butyric Fermentation Stage

- Body begins mummification/dries out
- Adipocer (grave wax) formation
- All internal organs lost to insect activity

Stage 5: The Dry Decay Stage

- No soft tissue remains
- Skeletonization occurs
- Longest of the decomposition processes

FIGURE 9–2 Stages of Decomposition.

Stage 1: The Fresh Stage

The fresh stage of decomposition occurs during the first few days after the death. There are no physical signs of decomposition during this time. However, homeostasis of the body has ceased, allowing cellular and soft tissue changes to occur because of the process of autolysis, the destruction of cells and organs due to an aseptic chemical process. At this point, the body enters *algor mortis*, the cooling of the body's temperature to that of its surroundings.

When the body's cells reach the final stage of autolysis, an anaerobic environment is created, that is, an environment in which oxygen is not present. This allows the body's normal bacteria to break down the remaining carbohydrates, proteins, and lipids. The products from the breakdown create acids, gases, and other products that cause production of volatile organic compounds (VOCs) and putrefactive effects. VOCs are produced during the early stages of human decomposition.[19]

Substances produced during the fresh stage of decomposition attract a variety of insects. *Diptera* insects begin to lay their eggs on the body during this stage, especially members of the Calliphoridae family of insects.[20] If the body is on the ground or buried in soil, there is also considerable insect activity by the insects that live in the soil around the body. The reasoning for this is simple: A dead human body serves as an excellent source of decaying matter to feed on and, as such, a hospitable environment.

Stage 2: The Putrefaction Stage

Odor, color changes, and bloating of the body during decomposition are the results of putrefaction. The lower part of the abdomen turns green due to bacteria activity in the cecum. Bacteria break down hemoglobin into sulfhemoglobin, which causes the green color change. A formation of gases enters the abdomen, which forces liquids and feces out of the body. The gases also enter the neck and face, causing swelling of the mouth, lips, and tongue. Due to this swelling and misconfiguration of the face, identification of the body can be difficult.

Bacteria also enter the venous system, causing blood to *hemolyze*. This leads to the formation of red streaks along the veins. This color soon changes to green through a process known as *marbelization*. It can be seen on the shoulders, chest area, and thighs. The skin can develop blisters containing fluid. The skin also becomes fragile, leading to skin slippage, making it difficult to move a body. While in this condition, body hair comes off easily. The color change of the discoloration from green to brown marks the transition of the early stage of putrefaction to the advanced decompositional stages.

During the putrefaction stage of decomposition, the majority of insect activity again comes from members of the Calliphoridae family (included are Formicidae, Muscidae, Sphaeroceridae, Silphidae, Lepidoptera, Hymenoptera, Sarcophagidae, Histeridae, Staphylinidae, Phalangida, Piophilidae, Araneae, Sepsidae, and Phoridae). As with the fresh stage of decomposition, if the body is on the ground or buried in soil, there is also considerable insect activity by soil-inhabiting arthropods.[21]

Stage 3: The Black Putrefaction Stage

After the body goes through the bloating stage, it begins the black putrefaction stage. At this point, the body cavity ruptures, the abdominal gases escape, and the body darkens from its greenish color. These activities allow for a greater invasion of scavengers, and insect activity increases greatly. This stage ends as the bones become apparent, which can take anywhere from 10 to 20 days after death depending on the region and temperature. This period is also dependent on the degree to which the body is exposed.

During the black putrefaction stage of decomposition, insects that can be found living in the body are Calliphoridae larvae, Staphylinidae, Histeridae, Gamasid mites, Ptomaphila, Trichopterygidae, Piophilid larvae, parasitic wasps, Staphylinid larvae, Trichopterygid larvae, Histerid larvae, Ptomaphila larvae, Tyroglyphid mites, Tineid larvae, and Dermestes larvae.[22] Some insects can also be found living in the soil around the body, such as Isopoda, Collembola, Dermaptera, Formicidae, Pseudoscorpiones, Araneae, Plectochetos, Acari, Pauropoda, Symphyla, Geophilidae, and Protura. The types of insects differ based on where the body is, although Diptera larvae can be found feeding on the body in almost all cases.[23]

It is important to note that the identification of insects has proven to be one way that the time of death can be determined. Examining the larvae of insects found on the body accomplishes this. Investigators should consider contacting an entomologist (insect expert) for advice at this stage of the investigation. This technique studies the various stages of growth of each larva before it develops into an adult insect. Houseflies, for example, deposit eggs on the remains of the corpse, usually in the area of the eyes, mouth, nostrils, and wounds. The eggs then become maggots and feed on the body. Typically, the time span for the hatching of the maggot is 24 hours.

The developmental stage depends on the type of insect in question. An entomologist can identify the specific insect and determine an estimated time span for its development as well as the season in which the death occurred. The recommended procedure is for all insects to be placed into alcohol for preservation.

Stage 4: The Butyric Fermentation Stage

After the early putrefaction and black putrefaction phases have taken place, the body begins mummification, in which the body begins to dry out. The human carcass is first mummified and then goes through adipocere formation. Adipocere (grave wax) formation is the loss of body odor and the formation of a cheesy appearance on the cadaver. Mummification is considered a postactive stage because there is less of a definite distinction between changes, and these changes are indicated by reduced skin, cartilage, and bone. Mummification is also indicated when all of the internal organs are lost due to insect activity.[24]

Stage 5: The Dry Decay Stage

When the last of the soft tissue has been removed from the body, the final stage of decomposition, skeletonization, occurs. This stage encompasses the deterioration of skeletal remains and is the longest of the decomposition processes. Skeletonization differs markedly from the previous stages, not only in length but also in the deterioration process itself.

The strength and durability of bone stems from the unique protein–mineral bond present in skeletal formations.

Consequently, changes to skeletal remains, known as *bone diagenesis*, occur at a substantially slower rate than stages of soft tissue breakdown. As the protein–mineral bond weakens after death, however, the organic protein begins to leach away, leaving behind only the mineral composition. Unlike soft tissue decomposition, which is influenced mainly by temperature and oxygen levels, the process of bone breakdown is more highly dependent on soil type and pH, along with the presence of groundwater. However, temperature can be a contributing factor: Higher temperature leads the protein in bones to break down more rapidly. If buried, remains decay faster in acidic-based soils than in alkaline soils. Bones left in areas of high moisture content also decay at a faster rate. The water leaches out skeletal minerals, which corrode the bone, leading to bone disintegration.[25]

The Forensics of Decomposition

Various sciences study the decomposition of bodies. These sciences fall under the general topic of forensics because the usual motive for study of the decomposition of human bodies is to determine the time and cause of death for legal purposes:

- *Forensic pathology* studies the clues to the cause of death found in the corpse as a medical phenomenon.

- *Forensic entomology* studies the insects and other vermin found in corpses; the sequence in which they appear, the kinds of insects, and where they are found in their life cycle are clues that can shed light on the time of death, the length of a corpse's exposure, and whether the corpse was moved.[26]

- *Forensic anthropology* is the branch of physical anthropology that studies skeletons and human remains, usually to seek clues as to the identity, race, and sex of their former owner.[27]

The University of Tennessee Anthropological Research Facility (better known as the "Body Farm") in Knoxville, Tennessee, has a number of bodies laid out in various situations in a fenced-in plot near the medical center. Scientists at the Body Farm study how the human body decays in various circumstances to gain a better understanding of decomposition.[28]

The speed at which decomposition occurs varies greatly. Factors such as temperature, humidity, and the season of death all determine how fast a fresh body will skeletonize or mummify. A basic guide for the effect of environment on decomposition is given as Casper's law (or ratio): If all other factors are equal, then when there is free access of air, a body decomposes twice as fast than if immersed in water and eight times faster than if buried in earth.

The most important variable is a body's accessibility to insects, particularly flies. On the surface in tropical areas, invertebrates alone can easily reduce a fully fleshed corpse to clean bones in less than two weeks. The skeleton itself is not permanent; acids in soils can reduce it to unrecognizable components. This is one reason given for the lack of human remains found in the wreckage of the *Titanic*, even in parts of the ship considered inaccessible to scavengers. Freshly skeletonized bone is often called "green" bone and has a characteristic greasy feel. Under certain conditions (normally cool, damp soil), bodies may

Factors Affecting Decomposition

The rate and manner of decomposition in an animal body are strongly affected by a number of factors. In roughly descending degrees of importance, they are the following:

- Temperature

- The availability of oxygen

- Prior embalming

- Cause of death

- Burial and depth of burial

- Access by scavengers

- Trauma, including wounds and crushing blows

- Humidity or wetness

- Rainfall

- Body size and weight

- Clothing

- The surface on which the body rests

- Foods and objects inside the specimen's digestive tract (e.g., bacon opposed to lettuce)

Think About It...

"How Long Is Too Long?" Thankfully, there are more realistic crime shows on TV these days that show the difficulty investigators have in dealing with death investigations. Just like with the "CSI Effect," which has caused misperceptions among the public about crime-scene investigation, the public has generally misunderstood the nuances of the various stages of body decomposition and the artful science associated with trying to make a correct judgment during an investigation. Understanding the various stages of decomposition, and especially the forensic science associated with aiding investigations, is crucial to good police work of this type. What are some of the areas of forensics that can aid in understanding the decomposition of bodies?

Human Skeletal Remains.

Bork/Shutterstock.com

undergo saponification and develop a waxy substance called adipocere, described earlier, caused by the action of soil chemicals on the body's proteins and fats. The formation of adipocere slows decomposition by inhibiting the bacteria that cause putrefaction.

In extremely dry or cold conditions, the normal process of decomposition is halted—by either lack of moisture or temperature controls on bacterial and enzymatic action—causing the body to be preserved as a mummy. Whereas frozen mummies commonly restart the decomposition process when thawed, heat-desiccated mummies remain as is unless exposed to moisture.

Other Visual Evidence of Decomposition

Body Color

After the victim dies, circulation of blood through the arteries and veins ceases. As the body settles, color in the lips and nails disappears as the blood settles into the lower capillaries of the body. The blood then changes from red to a dark purplish color as it loses its oxygen. This is the beginning of lividity, which we discuss later.

Changes in Eyes

The eyes are the most sensitive part of the human body and, in death, do not react to light, touching, or pressure. In addition, the eyelids may remain open; the pupils may become irregular in size and shape and typically become milky and cloudy in color within 8 to 10 hours of death.

Temperature of the Body

In life, a person's body maintains a body temperature of 98.6°F. Even after death, there may not be a loss of body heat because the body will tend to adapt to the temperature of its environment. The rate of cooling can, however, be a primary determinant as to the time of death. For example, a corpse will feel cool to the touch from 8 to 12 hours after death and will remain the same temperature as its surroundings for about 24 hours after death. Several factors can contribute to the rate at which a body loses heat. The greater the difference between the body and the environment, the faster the body will cool down.

Water and air temperature are the most important contributing factors. The temperature of the body before death can influence its temperature after death occurs. Predeath conditions such as stroke, sun stroke, and strangulation generally result in a higher body temperature at the time of death. One reliable method for determining body temperature is to insert a thermometer into the rectum of the deceased (do not insert a thermometer into the wound). The medical examiner will usually place a thermometer in the victim's liver. Body temperature can also be raised by the victim's excessive body fat or heavy clothing. A formula for determining the estimated time of death is shown in Box 9–1.

Rigor Mortis

Rigor mortis—the process of stiffening, or the contraction of body muscles after vital functions cease—is generally considered a poor indicator of time of death. As a rule, rigor mortis sets in two to four hours after death, but many variables may

BOX 9-1 🛡

The International Association of Chiefs of Police (IACP) offers a working formula to determine the estimated time of death when it is thought to be less than 24 hours:

$$\frac{98.6 \text{ (normal temp.) } 2 \text{ (rectal temp.) no. of hours since death}}{1.5 \text{ (avergae rate of heat loss)}}$$

contribute to "rigor." Contrary to popular belief, rigor mortis starts at the same time throughout the entire body. However, it is first observed in the jaws and neck.[29] It then tends to progress in the head-to-foot direction. At the time of completion, typically 8 to 12 hours after death, the torso, jaws, neck, and upper and lower extremities are "stiff as a board." Once in this state, the body resists any change in position.

Postmortem Lividity

As indicated earlier, when a body's vital functions cease, blood settles to the bottom side of the body because of gravity. A purplish **lividity** stain forms on the skin of the body closest to the surface on which it is lying (see Figure 9–3). So if a body is lying on its stomach and the lividity stain is on its back, the body has probably been turned over. Postmortem lividity may appear anywhere between one-half hour to four hours after death. It is sometimes valuable in determining whether or not a body has been moved, depending on the state of the lividity. If it is determined that the body has been moved, the officer must ask why—perhaps another police officer turned over the body. Generally speaking, however, after lividity has set in for 12 hours, the body will not diminish in color and will remain unchanged.

▶ Gunshot Wounds as Evidence

Several factors can affect the type of wound inflicted by a firearm. Such wounds may resemble a stab wound at first, but certain physical characteristics may vary, depending on the caliber of the weapon used, the distance between the shooter

FIGURE 9–3 **Body Showing Marbelization, Blisters, and Postmortem Lividity.**
Source: Courtesy of Mike Himmel and the Missouri State Highway Patrol.

Think About It…

Understanding the connection between rigor mortis and postmortem lividity is important in helping to identify and corroborate details associated with how death occurred. Additionally, if done correctly, understanding this relationship can be a key to identifying details about the crime in connection with a death as well. What are some advantages of connecting understanding of rigor mortis and postmortem lividity during an investigation?

and victim, and whether the lethal bullet had ricocheted off another object. To understand the firearm wound best, let's discuss the effect that a firearm

LEARNING OUTCOMES 4 — Explain the use of gunshot wounds as evidence in death investigations.

has on the human body. Vernon Geberth states that when a firearm is discharged, several things can occur:[30]

- Fire or flames are emitted from the barrel.
- Smoke follows the flame.
- The bullet emerges from the barrel.
- Additional smoke and grains of both burned and unburned gunpowder follow the bullet out of the barrel.
- The material spreads outward from the barrel as it is emitted.
- If the firearm is close to the targeted surface, much of this material will be deposited on it.

In addition, if the surface is farther away, less of the material will be deposited. Depending on the material or clothing present on the body, it is sometimes possible to predict the distance between the firearm and the victim (see Figure 9–4).

FIGURE 9–4 **The Value of Bloodstain Evidence.**
Source: Courtesy of Mike Himmel and the Missouri State Highway Patrol.

In the case of a contact wound, where the muzzle of the weapon was held against the body when discharged, certain residue will be present. Soot is always present in such wounds, with powder particles identified in at least half of cases.[31] These particles are often difficult to readily identify, however, and may require expert analysis.

Assessing the Severity of Gunshot Wounds

When assessing the likely severity of gunshot wounds, there are numerous variables considered either singly or in concert, which include the following:

- *The specific type of weapon used.* As a rule, rifles are more destructive than handguns. For example, a close-range abdominal wound inflicted by a 7.62 NATO rifle will be much more severe than one inflicted by a 9mm revolver from the same distance.

- *The weapon's caliber.* A .22 caliber bullet is considerably smaller than a .45 caliber bullet. Accordingly, a wound from a small-diameter bullet will typically be less severe than a wound inflicted by a larger-diameter bullet with like velocity. The cartridge designation is generally an approximation of bullet diameter and is of value to persons who are knowledgeable about guns in estimating other characteristics (for example, velocity, weight, design).

- *The bullet's design and velocity.* Bullets that expand cause more damage than those that do not. Nonexpanding bullets that are flat or blunt-nosed cause more damage than bullets with a pointed tip. This is because pointed bullets can push tissue aside. Furthermore, a heavier bullet will penetrate more deeply than a lighter bullet traveling at the same velocity.

- *The range at which the victim was shot.* In almost all cases, wounds inflicted from a distance of 16 feet will be more serious than those fired from a range of 1,600 feet if all other variables are equal. The velocity of a bullet and its potential for damage are progressively reduced as it travels from the firearm's muzzle.

- *The path of the wound.* The initial entry of a bullet is generally a poor guide because it is only a single point.

- *The number of wounds.* Frequently, gunshot wound victims sustain multiple hits. For example, being hit once is less severe than suffering four separate wounds. In comparison, an individual buckshot pellet is fairly small, but because victims are usually hit by a large number of pellets at the same time, the degree of injury is severe, particularly when the person is shot at close range.[32]

Even nonfatal gunshot wounds frequently have severe and long-lasting effects, even after the victim has made a successful recovery.[33] Typically, the consequences involve some form of major disfigurement or permanent disability. As a rule, all gunshot wounds are considered medical emergencies that require immediate hospital treatment.

Gunshot wounds consist of two basic types: entrance and exit wounds. Determining whether the wound in question is an entrance or an exit wound can have an overwhelming effect on the outcome of the case. Although the medical examiner makes this determination, in many cases he or she might not come to the crime scene, and the initial determination will be made by the investigator.

Entrance Wounds

Generally, the wound where the projectile entered the body is smaller than the exit wound, but there have been well-documented exceptions to this. The hole will usually be a neat, clean hole with an abrasion mark around it accompanied by a blackish-gray ring around the edges. Minimal bleeding will typically be observed.

Exit Wounds

An exit wound is usually a larger wound than the entrance wound, with a ragged or torn appearance. The exit wound usually has a larger amount of blood around it than the entrance wound.

Smudging

Smudging is usually a ring that results from gunpowder being deposited around the wound. It has a dirty appearance and can usually be wiped off. The significance of smudging is that it indicates that the victim was close to his or her assailant, although the firearm was not actually touching the skin.

Tattooing

Tiny pinpoint hemorrhages may result from the discharge of unburned powder being deposited into the skin. Called *tattooing*, these marks cannot be wiped away. One issue of critical importance in investigating gunshot wounds is the determination of whether or not the victim was murdered or died from suicide. The presence (or absence) of powder burns not only helps in making this determination but also helps the investigator decide the distance between the victim and the firearm.

The Role of Gunshot Residue

For decades, gunshot residue (GSR) has been considered evidence that a specific person fired a handgun (see Figure 9–5). But in recent years, GSR has been somewhat discredited and its usefulness limited, if not disregarded. To best understand the role of GSR in death and shooting investigations, it is instructive to understand the operation of a handgun.

If one inspects the back of a bullet larger than a .22, a small circle in the center (known as "centerfire") can be seen. This is a short, sealed cylinder containing primer. When the trigger is pulled, the hammer of the gun strikes this cylinder, and the shock of that blow causes the primer to explode. This explosion blows out into the large chamber of the casing, where the gunpowder is, causing the gunpowder to catch fire. The burning of the gunpowder is what expels the bullet away from the casing, down the barrel of the gun, and out the open end.[34]

FIGURE 9–5 Slow-Motion Photo of a Firearm Discharge and the Dispersion of Gunshot Residue.
Source: Courtesy of Forensic Technology, Inc.

Tiny particles of this primer material (GSR) are also expelled from the front of the gun. They can also "leak" from the breechblock area when the gun is fired, either from the open back of the chamber in revolvers or when the chamber opens and the cartridge is ejected in automatics. As a result, GSR can settle on the hand of the shooter.

Primer is generally made up of barium nitrate and antimony sulfide; however, most .22 ammunition does not have antimony, and rare brands have neither antimony or barium.[35] Primer also contains lead styphnate, but because lead is commonly found in the environment, the presence of it on a person's hands is not considered significant. Therefore, most GSR detection techniques concentrate on barium and antimony.[36]

Most gunpowder used today is "double base," which means it is a combination of nitroglycerin and cellulose nitrate (commonly and incorrectly known as nitrocellulose).[37] GSR tests used to range from the now-discredited "paraffin test," which essentially tested for the nitrates from the gunpowder, to "atomic absorption" (see Figure 9–6).

Atomic absorption involves swabbing the suspect's hands with cotton swabs and then soaking them in an acid solution. The solution is exposed to high temperatures, and a light reads the absorption rate of the atomized solution. This is a time-consuming and time-limited process because the swabs have to first be "digested," then spun, and then diluted with deionized water (in different concentrations for barium and antimony) in tiny sample cups that are placed in an automated machine, a spectrometer.[38]

Atomic absorption only shows that the element is present but not in what form. Moreover, barium and antimony can also be found in other sources such as firecrackers, paint, and some industrial settings. Accordingly, locating these elements on a suspect's hands does not prove that he or she fired a gun or even that he or she handled a gun. Rather, it is only an "indication" that he or she was in the general area of a fired gun.[39]

GSR is composed of extremely tiny particles that can be easily removed from the skin. For example, all the shooter has to do is wash his or her hands thoroughly; also, normal human movement and activity can remove the particles as well. To a great extent, this is the reason why deceased victims' hands are bagged in paper (not plastic as is often depicted in television shows)—to preserve the GSR particles. Most labs will not test samples collected from living persons more than six hours after the shooting. This doesn't apply to deceased persons because they're not moving around or using their hands after death.[40]

Gas Gunshot.

Csabacz/Shutterstock

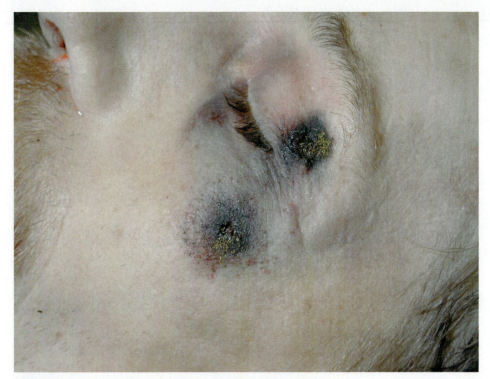

FIGURE 9–6 **Dual Gunshot Wounds to the Head with Stippling.**
Source: Courtesy of Mike Himmel and the Missouri State Highway Patrol.

From this comes the determination that although the presence of GSR doesn't prove someone did fire a gun, the absence of GSR doesn't prove they didn't. As such, attorneys and forensic scientists disagree on the usefulness of GSR evidence. For example, prosecutors often say that GSR on the defendant's hands proves that he or she is the killer. On the other hand, defense attorneys argue that the absence of GSR on the defendant's hands proves that he or she is not the killer. Consequently, in recent years, the legal community has become increasingly disenchanted with circumstantial evidence and more interested in evidence that provides a higher degree of scientific certainty, such as DNA. For this reason, numerous crime laboratories across the nation have discontinued GSR analysis.[41]

In summary, the practical use of GSR is limited because it fails to prove, with certainty, that a suspect fired a weapon. Its use, however, can be corroborative if considered with other evidentiary factors.

Defense Wounds

Defense wounds are characteristic of a struggle between a victim and an assailant. Such wounds may appear on the body of the victim and may take many forms. For example, in a fatal stabbing, slashing wounds on the hands of the victim may indicate that the victim grabbed the knife during a struggle, only to have it pulled back by the killer. These wounds are usually deep and concentrated on the palms and the undersurface of the fingers. Other indicators of a struggle are bruises on the forearms of the victim of a beating, indicating that the victim was attempting to defend him- or herself from attack by the assailant. In addition, a victim of a shotgun killing might have a shot from the shotgun blast embedded in his or her hands or forearms.

Think About It…

The importance of gunshot residue (GSR) has been thought of differently over time with respect to investigations. Simply put, even though technology abounds that can help identify whether or not someone might have recently fired a gun, proving that a particular suspect fired a particular gun is not an easy task. This obviously is something to consider when stereotypes about GSR thrive in TV crime shows. What technology exists to aid in analyzing GSR?

Kevin L Chesson/ Shutterstock.com

Gun Residue Test.

Shotgun Wounds

Second only to the handgun, the most common weapon with which officers are confronted is the shotgun. A shotgun shell may project anywhere from 200 small pellets (birdshot) to nine larger (buckshot) to one large lead projectile called a *slug* (see Figures 9–7 and 9–8). The shotgun remains one of the most effective killing weapons because of its capability for massive tissue destruction. It remains a choice of many criminals because

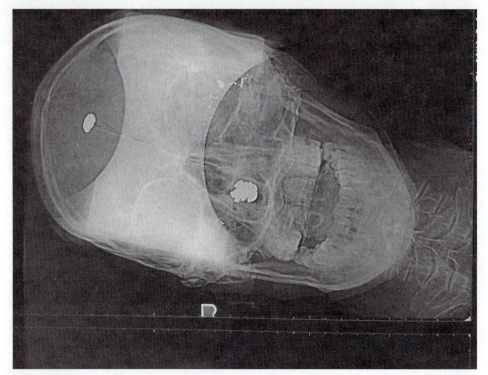

FIGURE 9–7 **X-ray of a Shooting Victim Showing Locations of Bullets in Skull.**
Source: Courtesy of Mike Himmel and the Missouri State Highway Patrol.

FIGURE 9–8 **One of Two Bullets Recovered from the Skull of a Shooting Victim.**
Source: Courtesy of Mike Himmel and the Missouri State Highway Patrol.

all that is required, in many cases, is simply pointing the weapon in the general direction of the victim, and, after discharge, some contact is typically made.

In addition, the appearance of the shotgun commands respect from all who face it, making it an effective tool of intimidation. From an evidentiary standpoint, the shotgun wadding usually remains in the skin of the victim if discharged within 10 feet. Shotgun wadding can tell the investigator three things:

1. The type of shot used

2. The gauge of gun used

3. Possible evidence to help identify the gun used

The Investigation of the "BTK" Killer

Dennis Lynn Rader (born March 9, 1945) is a serial killer who murdered at least 10 people in Sedgwick County, Kansas, between 1974 and 1991. He was known as the BTK killer, which stands for bind, torture, and kill, an apt description of his modus operandi. Rader casually described his victims as his "projects" and at one point likened the murders of his victims to killing animals by saying he "put them down." He created a "hit kit" of items he would use during murders (for example, guns, tape, rope, and handcuffs). Rader developed a pattern for his murders by wandering the city, finding a victim, and stalking the victim to learn the individual's pattern in order to maximize his attack. He would strangle his victims until they lost consciousness, then let them revive, then strangle them again—repeating the pattern over and over again, forcing them to experience near-death situations, and becoming sexually aroused at the sight of their struggles. Finally, Rader would strangle them to death. Rader sent taunting letters to police and newspapers, including a letter stashed at the library and another sent to the media.

All of Rader's communications were poorly written, with many misspellings and incorrect grammar usage. In March 2004, a series of 11 communications with BTK led directly to his arrest in February 2005. In June, a package was found taped to a stop sign in Wichita containing graphic descriptions of some BTK murders. In July, a package was dropped into the return slot at the downtown public library containing more bizarre material, including the claim that he, BTK, was responsible for the death of a 19-year-old. On February 16, 2005, Rader sent a floppy disk to Fox TV station KSAS in Wichita. Police forensic analysis quickly determined that the disk had been used by the Christ Lutheran Church in Wichita; the analysis also recovered

© kilukilu/Fotolia

the name Dennis. An Internet search determined that Rader was president of this church; Rader was arrested on February 25. Additionally, the police investigation was benefitted by police surveillance of Rader, a warrant for the medical records of Rader's daughter Kerri, and a test of a tissue sample seized. At the time of arrest, Rader was stopped while driving near his home and taken into custody by law enforcement officials, including a Wichita Police bomb unit truck, two SWAT trucks, and FBI and Alcohol, Tobacco, and Firearms (ATF) agents. He confessed after two hours of interrogation.

Sources: Ono, D. (2005, August 17). Who is the BTK killer? Wichita family man and church leader—and a psychopathic murderer. msnbc .com. Retrieved from http://www.msnbc.msn.com/id/8929452/ns/ us_news-crime_and_courts/t/who-btk-killer/.

Wrongful death investigations are among the highest priority in the criminal investigation field:

1. Using the chapter material and the preceding case, how do you think the police used death investigation techniques to aid in the identification and capture of the BTK killer?

2. Given this case, what are your thoughts on the importance of how police communicate with potential suspects and the public during an investigation?

LEARNING OUTCOMES 1

Summarize legal characteristics of homicide.

Criminal investigators encounter wrongful death in many ways. Some victims are killed by accident, others in the heat of passion, and still others for profit. Therefore, it is incumbent on the professional investigator to be clear as to what laws best describe the alleged crime.

1. What were some of the problems associated with the JonBenét Ramsey murder investigation?

2. What are the two distinct categories of homicide? How do they differ?

3. What is the difference between first- and second-degree murder?

4. What distinguishes voluntary manslaughter from involuntary manslaughter?

5. What are the common legal elements of homicide?

murder The purposeful, premeditated, and unlawful taking of human life by another person.

homicide The unlawful killing of one human being by another.

manslaughter The deliberate killing of another person, characterized by either voluntary or involuntary classifications.

LEARNING OUTCOMES 2

Describe how a homicide investigation is conducted.

The first officer to respond to a suspected homicide call is generally a patrol officer. The responding officer must protect the crime scene from unauthorized persons, and begin note taking. Investigators should also be prepared to draft a sketch of all critical aspects of the homicide crime scene. The sketch will prove to be of value later in the investigation when reports are being finalized and in preparing for court.

1. What are the principal concerns of the first officer arriving at the scene of a possible homicide?

2. What steps are taken to protect a homicide crime scene?

3. What can investigators determine about a homicide based on the evidence found at the scene?

4. What should be included in the crime-scene notes of a homicide?

5. Why are complete, accurate notes critical during the early stages of a homicide investigation?

6. What are the major components/elements of a preliminary homicide investigation?

scene-conscious When the crime-scene investigator becomes aware of the crime-scene situation and is prepared to take certain immediate actions.

LEARNING OUTCOMES 3

Explain how time of death is estimated.

The time of death in a homicide case is one of the most critical variables in its investigation. All areas around the body become important in determining the time of death. After death occurs, human decomposition takes place in five stages. The rate and manner of decomposition are strongly affected by a number of factors. The process of tissue breakdown may take from several days up to years.

1. Why is time of death a critical variable in a homicide investigation?

2. Why is rigor mortis a poor indicator of time of death?

3. What happens in the putrefaction stage that makes it difficult to identify the body?

4. What factors affect decomposition?

5. How can an entomologist aid investigators in determining a cause of death?

6. What visual evidence indicates decomposition?

rigor mortis The process of the stiffening or contraction of the muscles of a deceased person after the vital functions cease.

lividity A bloodstain on the body of a deceased person.

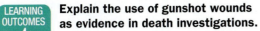

LEARNING OUTCOMES 4

Explain the use of gunshot wounds as evidence in death investigations.

One issue of critical importance in investigating gunshot wounds is the determination of whether or not the victim was murdered or died from suicide. The presence (or absence) of powder burns not only helps in making this determination but also helps the investigator decide the distance between the victim and the firearm.

1. What variables are considered when assessing the severity of gunshot wounds?

2. What are the basic types of gunshot wounds?

3. What are the characteristics of the two types of gunshot wounds?

4. What can the presence of smudging tell an investigator?

5. What information can be obtained from the presence of tattooing?

6. What are the indicators of a struggle?

7. What can investigators learn from shotgun wadding?

Additional Links

http://web.utk.edu/~fac/
This is the website of the University of Tennessee Anthropological Research Facility. The site's quick links include news, what's new, courses, and an overview of forensic anthropology. Other links include research, a data bank, publications, and FAQs.

www.fbi.gov/wanted
This FBI site features photos and information of the most wanted criminals. Links on this site include Wanted Fugitives, Missing Persons, and other federal fugitive programs. The site also includes information on most wanted terrorists, crime alerts, cybercrimes, violent crimes, and crimes against children.

http://thename.org
This is the official site of the National Association of Medical Examiners. The site includes FAQs, downloadable information, publications, library and archives, news links, membership information, and position papers, as well as links to other sites such as forensic and medical journals, forensic training, law, public health, and missing people.

www.theiacp.org
This is the official site of the International Association of Chiefs of Police. The site includes publications, training resources and information, links to blogs, a jobs link, podcasts, legislative action, and police services.

10

"The crime of robbery represents one of society's most violent crimes."

Robbery

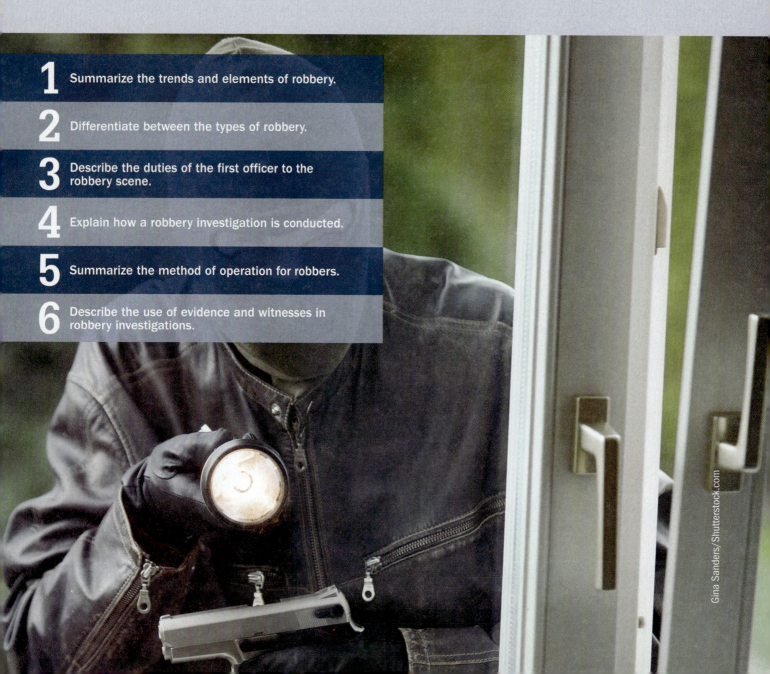

1 Summarize the trends and elements of robbery.

2 Differentiate between the types of robbery.

3 Describe the duties of the first officer to the robbery scene.

4 Explain how a robbery investigation is conducted.

5 Summarize the method of operation for robbers.

6 Describe the use of evidence and witnesses in robbery investigations.

Gina Sanders/Shutterstock.com

THE UNPREDICTABILITY OF BANK ROBBERY

On May 2, 2014, Russell Cooper, a 77-year-old Florida man using a walker, entered the PNC Bank in Boynton Beach, Florida and demanded $130. Cooper was at the bank to ask a manager why he couldn't access his bank account. The manager told him his account had been closed due to "the consistent lack of funds," Cooper became "agitated," walked around the bank manager's desk and pulled out a pocketknife and ordered the manager to escort him to a bank teller window to get the money. Once the $130 was given to him, Cooper told the manager he was taking him as a hostage and threatened to "slit his throat." When the police arrived, the manager was able to escape from Cooper. According to police reports, when confronted by a police officer, Cooper held up the pocketknife and said, "I'm not dropping it. I'm going stick it in your (expletive) gut," As Cooper held the knife he continued to walk toward police officers and was stopped with a Taser.

DISCUSS Discuss the nature of bank robbery and whether or not the police response to an elderly bank robber should be different than for a more traditional younger offender.

The bank robbery just discussed demonstrates that there is no "typical" bank robbery and that suspects aren't necessarily of a young age. Cooper's advanced age and physical disability did not spare him from facing serious criminal charges, which included armed robbery and kidnapping.

▶ *Understanding Robbery*

LEARNING OUTCOMES 1 Summarize the trends and elements of robbery.

Robbery is a personal crime involving a face-to-face confrontation between the victim and a perpetrator. It is often confused with burglary, which is primarily a property crime. Weapons may be used in robberies or strong-arm robbery may occur through intimidation. Purse snatching and pickpocketing are not classified as robbery by the *Uniform Crime Reports* (UCR) program but are included under the category of larceny-theft.

According to statistics, in 2012 individuals were the most common target of robbers. Banks, gas stations, convenience stores, and other businesses were the second most common targets, with residential robberies accounting for only 16.9 percent of the total (see Figure 10–1). In 2012, 354,520 robberies were reported to the police.[1] Of that number, 43.5 percent were highway robberies, meaning that the crime occurred outdoors, most commonly as the victim was walking in a public place. Guns were used in 41 percent of all robberies and knives were used in 7.8 percent. Armed robbers are dangerous, as guns are actually discharged in 20 percent of all robberies.[2]

Consequences of Robbery

In the sense that most robbers are motivated by economic gain, robbery could be considered a property crime. However, judged

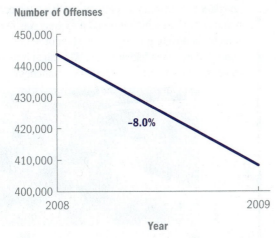

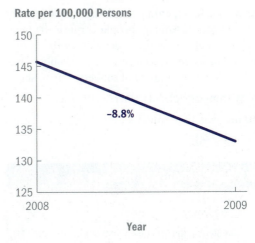

Number of Offenses

−8.0%

Rate per 100,000 Persons

−8.8%

Robbery Trends 2008–2009.

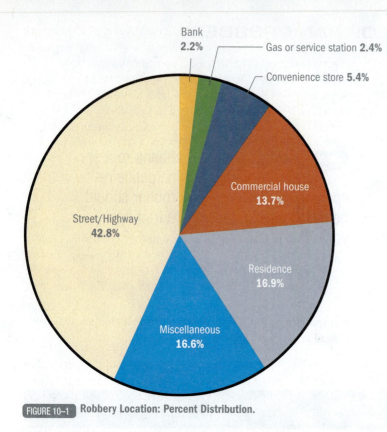

Bank **2.2%**

Gas or service station **2.4%**

Convenience store **5.4%**

Commercial house
13.7%

Street/Highway
42.8%

Residence
16.9%

Miscellaneous
16.6%

FIGURE 10–1 Robbery Location: Percent Distribution.

by the value of property taken in robberies, it is not a particularly serious crime. The loss sustained in most robberies is less than $100. It is, of course, the violent nature of the crime that makes it a crime against persons and a serious violation of criminal law. Among the other consequences of the crime, robbery creates a sense of widespread anxiety and defensive behavior. For example, an elderly couple was robbed at gunpoint one summer evening in the parking lot of their favorite restaurant. Although less than $75 was taken and no one was physically hurt, they chose not to return to the restaurant for fear of falling victim to robbers a second time. Other types of defensive behavior include carrying a weapon and moving to the suburbs to avoid the likelihood of becoming a victim of a robbery.

Elements of Robbery

State laws are very specific regarding the definition of robbery (see Box 10–1). As indicated, many people confuse the term *robbery* with *burglary*, but clearly some elements of the crimes differ considerably. For example, as a general rule robbery has four main elements: A person is guilty of robbery if he or she:

- Takes property from its rightful owner;
- Acts without the owner's permission;

BOX 10–1 ⬛ Legal Elements of Robbery

- Forcibly stealing property
- Using force or threatening the immediate use of physical force against another person

- Intends to steal property; and
- Uses force or intimidation against the owner.

A person must have specific intent to commit robbery. If the individual is just borrowing property or playing a joke, it's not robbery. The force or intimidation must be directly related to taking of property for the act to be robbery. It can't take place after the property is taken; the force or intimidation must be immediate. There's no robbery if the threat is for future violence.[3]

Furthermore, an apartment dweller might claim that his apartment was "robbed" when in actuality it was burglarized. Accordingly, a person might claim she was the victim of robbery when, in fact, she was the victim of a larceny. The distinction between these offenses is evident in the elements of the crime. In any case, the elements must be present for criminal charges of robbery to be brought against a suspect.

The elements of robbery vary depending on certain attributes of the crime. These attributes may include inflicting serious physical injury on the victim or being accompanied by an accomplice during commission of the crime. Because of these differences, many states have chosen to divide robbery into first, second, and third degrees, depending on the seriousness of the act.

▶ Types of Robbery

Attempts have been made to classify and explain the character and dynamics of robbery. In a study conducted in London, McClintock and Gibson found that robbery follows one of five patterns:[4]

Think About It…

Aren't All Robberies Just Robberies? With movies like *Dirty Harry* and popular TV shows such as *America's Most Wanted* and *Crime Scene Investigation (CSI)*, it is easy to understand why many might think that most robberies are of banks. Because bank robberies only make up a small percentage of robberies, there must be more to what robbery is actually about. This is why police always try to consider various robbery patterns. Police often consider nuances such as whether or not a robbery was in an open area or on private property, or whether or not the victim had control of merchandise or funds. Why might it be important to consider patterns associated with robberies?

Judex/Shutterstock.com

Car Robbery.

1. *Robbery of persons employed in positions placing them in charge of money or goods.* Examples are robberies of banks, stores, offices, jewelry stores, or other sites where money changes hands. The instance of these types of robberies has decreased in recent years.

2. *Robbery in open areas.* This includes muggings, street robberies, and purse snatchings. Crimes of this nature constitute an estimated 30 percent of violent crimes.

3. *Robbery on private premises.* This represents crimes in which robbers break into homes and rob residents.

4. *Robbery after preliminary association of short duration.* These types of robberies typically occur as a consequence of a chance meeting in a nightspot or party or after a sexual encounter.

5. *Robbery after previous association of some duration between victim and offender.* These are considerably less common than stranger-to-stranger robberies, which account for an estimated 75 percent of robberies (see Figure 10–1).[5]

In accordance with the preceding typologies, the following examples of common robberies should be considered. Notice the addition of crimes such as school and vehicle robberies.

Commercial Robberies: Stores and Banks

The **commercial robbery** typically occurs at the end of a workweek during the evening and very early morning hours. Typical targets of the commercial robber are stores and businesses located close to major thoroughfares, such as main streets, highways, and interstates. Such locations offer the offender a quick and easy means of escape. In addition, stores employing only one or two employees make prime targets for a bandit.

Because many robberies are committed by persons with criminal records, their methods of operation (MOs) can sometimes be established easily. After it has been identified, the MO can be compared with other robberies with similar MOs to identify a suspect. Convenience stores, which are the target for an estimated 6 percent of all commercial robberies, represent a growing target for robbers. The growing numbers of such businesses have contributed to their victimization by robbers. Many stores have a policy of keeping only a minimal amount of cash on the premises to deter would-be robbers. Others use video cameras to record business transactions and customers in the store.

Bank robbery represents a much greater property loss than other types of robbery but accounts for only an estimated 2 percent of all robberies.[6] Bank robberies are both state and federal crimes; therefore, they fall under the jurisdiction of local, state, and federal law enforcement. The FBI is summoned in these cases because any banking institution federally insured by the Federal Deposit Insurance Corporation (FDIC) falls under federal jurisdiction. These include federal banks, federal credit unions, and federal savings and loan companies. Typically, the investigation of such offenses involves the collective talents and resources of investigators in each jurisdiction.

The most common method of bank robbery is a threat with a visible firearm, most typically a handgun. Most of the remaining robberies are perpetrated with a demand note passed to the teller. In this case, the note can be a valuable piece of evidence if the robber fails to ask for its return. In addition, in the majority of bank robberies the perpetrator acts alone in the facility, but accomplices may be waiting in an escape vehicle outside. At times, lookouts are also used to spot police cruisers.

One of the best tracing clues in a robbery is the vehicle used in the escape. Such clues vary from one offense to another. For example, the professional robber's getaway vehicle may be rented or stolen and may have stolen license plates. This enables the suspects to ditch the vehicle or the plates after they have left the area of the robbery. Conversely, an amateur robber often uses his or her own vehicle. Bank robbery has changed in recent years due to an increase in the number of branch banks, which tend to be located in such a way as to be highly vulnerable to robbers.

Street Robberies

The most common type of robbery is the one committed on public streets and alleyways. Most street robberies (also called *muggings*) are committed with a weapon, typically a handgun, and usually take place at night. Additionally, both the robber and victim are usually on foot. Suspects in street robberies are apt to be teenagers, usually young men. The unarmed **street robbery** is also common in many cities. In this case, the victim is approached by two or more attackers who, through their numbers, intimidate the victim, reducing his or her willingness to resist. Those who are most likely to become victims of street muggers are elderly individuals and people who are drunk in public. Both categories of victims pose no immediate threat to robbers, are slow to react, and will probably not offer resistance. The unarmed robber relies on opportunity rather than a strategic plan in selecting a victim. The most likely victim is one who walks alone on a secluded street after dark.

Residential Robberies

The **residential robbery** is one of the most terrifying types of robberies because an armed intruder breaks into a home and holds residents at gun- or knifepoint. Often, these crimes begin as burglaries but "convert" to robberies after the intruder discovers that there is someone home and chooses to use violence as a means of completing the theft. One common type of residential robbery is when someone who has a right to be in the house, such as an invited guest, commits the crime. Indeed, according to the National Institute of Justice (NIJ), 54 percent of all residential robberies are committed by acquaintances (see Figure 10–2).[7]

School Robberies

The NIJ concludes that an estimated 3.2 percent of noncommercial robberies occur in schools every year. This averages out to be an estimated one million school-related robberies annually. Accordingly, the victimization rate for youths aged 12 to 19 is about 1 percent per year. A **school robbery** fails to meet the stereotypic type of robbery in that it is not a stickup or a mugging but, for the most part, is an instance of petty extortion or

- About 1 in 12 victims experiences serious injuries such as rape, knife or gunshot wounds, broken bones, or being knocked unconscious.
  - Most robberies are committed by two or more people.
    - About half of all completed robberies involve losses of $82 or less; 10 percent involve losses of $800 or more. Most theft losses are never recovered.
      - Offenders display weapons in almost half of all robberies.
        - Robbers use guns in about 40 percent of robberies.
          - Offenders using weapons are more likely to threaten than actually attack their victims.
            - In almost 9 of 10 robbery victimizations, the robbers are male.
              - More than half of all robbery victims are attacked. Female robbery victims are more likely to be attacked than are male victims.
                - Victims aged 65 and older are more likely to be attacked than younger victims.

FIGURE 10–2 Characteristics of Robbery.

a "shakedown" of students or teachers. Ironically, few of these robberies have resulted in property loss. The average dollar loss is typically less than $1.[8]

Vehicle Robberies

On October 5, 1997, an armored car with $17 million in cash was stolen from its Loomis Wells Fargo and Company warehouse. After a five-month police search, a 28-year-old former Loomis employee, David Scott Ghantt, was arrested in Cozumel, Mexico, together with six others. At the time of Ghantt's arrest, about $14 million was still missing. The police were tipped off because someone noticed that one of the suspects had moved from a trailer park to a $650,000 home, purchased a BMW automobile, and paid for breast implants for his wife—all with cash.

One year earlier, the largest armored car heist in U.S. history occurred in Jacksonville, Florida, where an employee pulled a gun on two coworkers and stole $18.8 million in cash. The robber, Philip Noel Johnson, was arrested five months later as he was attempting to cross the Mexican border. In that theft, all but about $186,000 was recovered from a mountain home in North Carolina (For a better understanding of types of robbers, see Conklin's Robber Typology in Figure 10–3).

The victim of the vehicle robbery is often the driver of the vehicle, as illustrated in the previous example. Such vehicles often include delivery vehicles, taxicabs, buses, and so on, while the people involved make easy targets for the robber because they frequently work alone and in sparsely populated areas of town. A delivery vehicle, for example, is most vulnerable when it is arriving for a delivery or after a delivery has been made. Sometimes the robbers opt for the cash given to the driver after a delivery has been made.

Taxi drivers are vulnerable because they are required to work alone and cruise all areas of town. The most common MO for a taxi robbery is for the driver to be asked to drive to an address in a secluded part of town, where the robber makes his or her move. A preventive measure taken by some taxi companies is the placement of a protective shield between the driver and passenger seats. Robberies of buses generally occur during layoff points where there are few passengers. A new trend in vehicle robberies emerged in Miami, Florida, in 1991—the **smash-and-grab robbery**. The robbers stake out streets and exit ramps from airports, and when automobile drivers come to a stop at a street light, the robbers approach the car, break the window, and hold up the driver at gunpoint.

▶ The First Officer on the Scene

After receiving a radio call, the first officer's initial responsibility is to arrive at the scene as quickly and safely as possible. Of the two, safety

LEARNING OUTCOMES 3
Describe the duties of the first officer to the robbery scene.

A CLOSER LOOK

Brazen Bank Robbers

In 1995, a pair of holdup men who were thought to have robbed at least 18 midwestern banks were also playing a kind of cat-and-mouse game with the FBI. They wore FBI logos during their holdups, used agents' names when they rented their getaway cars, and wrote letters to the newspapers making fun of the FBI. The "Midwestern Bank Bandits," as they called themselves, concentrated on banks in Kansas, Iowa, Wisconsin, Nebraska, Ohio, and Kentucky. The pair adopted a clear method of operation:

- They spent no more than five minutes in a bank.
- They prohibited tellers from touching cash so the tellers couldn't rig a moneybag with a dye bomb. Instead, they leaned over the counter and grabbed the cash themselves.

- They purchased old used cars before each robbery and signed FBI office chiefs' names on the titles.
- They sometimes wore clothing bearing the logos of the FBI and the Bureau of Alcohol, Tobacco, and Firearms (ATF).
- They sometimes slowed their pursuers by leaving behind such items as a package they said contained explosives, a grenade pin, or a taut string tied to the glove compartment door of their getaway car, giving the appearance of a booby trap.

Conklin developed a well-known typology of robbers. Rather than focusing on the nature of robbery incidents, Conklin organized robbers into the following types:

- *Professional robber.* The professional robber is characterized as having a long-term commitment to crime as a source of livelihood, planning and organizing crimes before committing them, and pursuing money to support a particular lifestyle. Professionals may be robbers exclusively or may be involved in other types of crime as well. The professional robber recognizes robbery as a type of crime that is quick, direct, and profitable. The "pro" might typically effect three or four "big scores" a year to support him- or herself, all well planned, and sometimes while working in groups with specifically assigned tasks for all group members.
- *Opportunistic robber.* The opportunist will steal to obtain small amounts of money when he or she identifies what seems to be a vulnerable target. Examples of opportunist targets are cab drivers, drunks, and elderly people. The opportunist is typically a younger perpetrator who does not plan the crime well (for example, use of weapons, getaway car). Typically, he or she operates in the environment of a juvenile gang.
- *Drug-addict robber.* The drug-addict robber robs to support his or her drug habit. Unlike the professional, he or she has a low commitment to robbery because of its danger but a high commitment to theft because it supplies much-needed funds. Although the addict is less likely to use a weapon, he or she is more cautious than the opportunist. When desperate for funds, however, he or she will be less careful in selecting victims and carrying out the crime.
- *Alcoholic robber.* Excessive consumption of alcohol may cause some persons to enter into robbery as a criminal alternative. Alcoholic robbers plan their crimes randomly and give little consideration to victim selection, escape, or circumstances under which the crime will be committed.

FIGURE 10–3 **Types of Robbers.**

Think About It…

"My Home Is My Castle. . . ." One of the most frightening crimes is that of residential robbery, that is, coming into someone's home prepared to use force to steal from the owner(s). Because many residential robberies involve people known to the homeowners, the security company commercials showing strangers with mean looks and crowbars smashing through doors to take items by force are not necessarily accurate. Make no mistake, though, there are strangers who target residences for such violent crime. Why should police consider who might have had a legitimate reason to be in the house recently when investigating residential robberies?

Gina Sanders/Shutterstock.com

Burglary Investigations Typically Start with Identifying the Point of Entry. Here a Burglar Forces His Way into a Residence Using a Crowbar.

should be emphasized more than swiftness. The decision to use equipment such as emergency lights and a siren is left to the officer's judgment and may depend on several considerations. Factors influencing the decision to use emergency equipment include the following:

- Distance to be traveled to the crime scene
- Amount of traffic
- Time of day of the call
- Inability to clear traffic
- Need to halt assault of a victim

Next, the officer should summon assistance and be prepared to wait for backup before attempting to enter the robbery location. When approaching the scene, he or she should be on the lookout for fleeing subjects and persons sitting in parked cars. These might be accomplices or lookouts working with the robber. Police vehicles should be parked a reasonable distance from the robbery location. After removing the keys from the patrol car, the officer should take a shotgun and approach the location cautiously on foot.

The first officer on the scene should cover the most likely exit from the robbery location. After assessing the situation, it is his or her job to direct other responding officers to cover other escape routes. If possible, a determination should be made as to whether or not the robbery is still in progress before officers enter the building.

If the robbery is still in progress, entry into the structure should not be authorized. It is likely that robbers might exit the structure on their own, especially if they are unaware that the police are at the location. If the suspect sees the police, the officer should make every attempt to convince him or her to surrender. If it cannot be determined whether or not a crime is still in progress, officers covering the front should enter together. Under no circumstances should the first-arriving officer enter the location without assistance. Once on the scene, the officer should apprehend the suspect if possible. First aid should then be rendered if victims have been injured. Finally, witnesses should be located and questioned.

▶ The Preliminary Investigation

When responding to calls in which the robbers have already left the scene, officers must prioritize the care of any injured parties. In addition, they must keep in mind that the robbery scene is a crime scene, where valuable evidence may be present. Therefore, possible locations

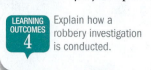

LEARNING OUTCOMES 4

Explain how a robbery investigation is conducted.

A CLOSER LOOK

The "Typical" Robbery

The most common type of robbery is of the individual. And the most common place for it is on your way to and from your car. Nearly half of all robberies occur on the streets and in parking lots. Another 14 percent happen in locations like subway and train stations, indoor ATMs, and other locations. It is always important to recognize when you are entering a "fringe area," where the likelihood of being robbed increases.

There is more than a 60 percent chance that you will face a weapon when robbed. That is, however, a statistical norm across all types of robberies. The odds of facing a weapon go up significantly if you are being robbed by only one person. Strong-arm tactics tend to be the domain of the pack; the individual mugger tends to prefer weapons— and guns are the most common.

Weapons

Although all robberies are felonies, the use of a weapon tends to bring about stiffer penalties. Although all robberies are considered violent crimes, it is common for states to upgrade the class of felony if a weapon is used in the commission of a robbery. That means the person who is robbing you is risking a much greater prison sentence if he or she is caught and convicted.

The weapon of choice is a gun. It is fast and easy to get, and because most robberies happen at point-blank range, it requires very little training to hit the target. All the robber has to do is point in the general direction and pull the trigger until either he or she runs out of bullets or the victim has been injured. Guns are used in up to 40 percent of all robberies, and knives and other weapons are used in another 20 percent. Again, these numbers are a national average that incorporates every kind of robbery.

Needless to say, guns, knives, and other weapons make up 100 percent of all *armed* robberies. Weapons are also the norm for robberies of establishments.

Strong Arm

Many people do not realize that 40 percent of all robberies are committed by strong-arm tactics. That doesn't sound too bad until you realize that this means the victim is being mugged by a wolf pack. A varying number of individuals surround the victim and then either threaten or proceed to pilfer his or her possessions. That

means that ten or so people proceed to assault the victim, and often after he or she is on the ground, they continue to kick and stomp him or her.

Furthermore, most states recognize both an extreme disparity of force and the shod human foot on a downed individual as legal justification for the victim to use lethal force to protect him- or herself from immediate death or serious bodily injury—both of which can, and often do, occur during a strong-arm robbery. It doesn't matter if they don't have weapons—ten people stomping a person can kill or hospitalize him or her for months just as well as one person with a weapon.

Packs of young criminals roaming or loitering in an area are a serious danger sign, one that should be avoided at all costs. People should not walk into their midst. Doing so would be literally walking into the lions' jaws.

What makes these kinds of robberies even more difficult is how often they will be explained away as "we were just messin' witcha." And because no weapons have been displayed, it is difficult for prosecutors to prove intent in such cases. Until the robbery has actually occurred, there is no clear-cut crime even if the group is displaying or menacing with a weapon.

Home Invasion Robbery

Home invasion robberies have become common in the past decade. In areas where automatic garage doors are standard, a tactic often used is to follow the victim home and then either pull into the garage or jump out of the car and rush the person before the garage door closes.

In other areas, entry through the front door is common. Whether this is achieved by simply ringing the doorbell and crashing the door when the person answers it, through deceit (for example, "My car broke down; can I use your phone?"), or just kicking in the door depends on the robbers.

Although an individual can perform a home invasion, these types of robberies tend to be the domain of packs and gangs, which tend to be armed as well. This is because they expect there to be multiple people at home.

Fortunately, many of the best protections against a home invasion robbery will also keep your home safe from burglars.

Source: Federal Bureau of Investigation. (2010). *Crime in America, 2009. Uniform crime reports.* Washington, DC: U.S. Government Printing Office.

---

of fingerprints and other evidence should be protected. Next, witnesses should be located and statements taken regarding descriptions of the suspects and their vehicles so that a "flash" description can be broadcast.

When obtaining description information from witnesses, officers should first separate them to minimize discussion about the robbery and provide officers with separate suspect description sheets. It is important during this stage of the investigation to get descriptions while the witnesses' recollection of the crime is still fresh. Officers should remember that although speed is crucial at this stage of the preliminary investigation, so is accuracy. A second broadcast is required after further questioning of the witnesses is conducted. The purpose is to correct any errors broadcast in the original transmission and to provide district officers with additional details. The correct form of broadcast is typified by the following example:

> *Robbery.* Seventh Heaven Convenience Store, 308 Granada, at 2330 hours by two suspects.
>
> *Suspect 1.* Male, white, 18 to 25 years of age, 6 feet 2 inches, 210 pounds, long brown hair, full beard, sunglasses, wearing black "Poison" T-shirt and faded blue jeans and white tennis shoes. Suspect in possession of proceeds from robbery: brown paper bag containing approximately $350 cash.
>
> *Suspect 2.* Female, white, 20 to 22 years of age, 5 feet 4 inches, 120 pounds, wearing red tank top and blue jean shorts, dirty white tennis shoes. Suspect has long brown hair pulled back and is armed with a small semiautomatic handgun, possibly .32 caliber.
>
> *Escape.* Both suspects were last seen driving east on Broadway in an older model light tan Ford Mustang, Texas license, with the first two digits believed to be "RW." The paint on the car is faded, and its top is rusted.

The supplemental broadcast should contain as much important information as possible, and when significant information is unavailable, its omission should be so stated. For example, in the preceding scenario, it is not mentioned whether either suspect had a coat. Stating that details are not available at the time of the broadcast will let officers know that there is a possibility that the suspects might, in fact, be wearing coats. The intent here is to eliminate unnecessary inquiries from the field regarding such items.

The Neighborhood Canvass

Typically, a robbery investigation takes weeks or even months to complete. A logical starting place, however, is a canvass of the area surrounding the location of the robbery. Specifically, investigators should consider the suspect's most likely escape route and question residents and business owners in the area. In addition, while the canvass is in progress, officers should look for evidence discarded by the suspect during his or her escape. Because many citizens are apprehensive about the presence of officers at their residence, investigators should immediately state their intended purpose to place the citizens at ease. It is also important for the officer to stress the significance of all information, regardless of how meaningless it appears to the citizens. Specific questions include whether the citizens observed anyone meeting the description of the suspect or the getaway vehicle. Additionally, it should be determined if anyone heard anything of interest to the officer, such as a car door slamming, gunshots, or tires screeching.

The **neighborhood canvass** is also critical in the event that the robber is hiding somewhere close to the robbery location. Therefore, investigators should look in parked cars, dumpsters, and alleyways for the hidden suspect. In addition, local motels or hotels in surrounding towns and car rental companies should also be checked. When speaking to residents in the area of the robbery, it is advantageous to have a sketch of what the suspect looks like. The sketch could also be circulated throughout the community, and a "tip line" for anonymous information could be established.

▶ *The Robber's Method of Operation*

In Southern California, the "Blue Note Bandit" issued demands to bank tellers on blue paper. In San Diego, the "Geezer Bandit"—who appeared to be well into his golden years—displayed a semi-automatic weapon. In Arizona, a goateed man in sunglasses issued ominous notes that read, "No Tricks." In Dallas during 2009, heavily armed men in body armor terrorized bank employees and customers in 21 takeover-style heists.

LEARNING OUTCOMES 5 — Summarize the method of operation for robbers.

Bank robbery methods are as novel and varied as the monikers used to label them. But in the end, the most common approach is to step up to a teller and make a demand verbally, with a written note, or both.

In 2008, a violent serial gang terrorized the Dallas area for a period of six months, pulling off 21 bank jobs. The so-called

---

Typical MO Information for Robbery

- Type of location robbed
- Time and day of week
- Type of weapon used
- Use or threatened use of force
- Verbal statements made
- Vehicle used
- Object(s) stolen
- Number of suspects
- Use of disguises
- Other peculiarities

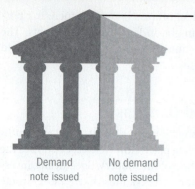

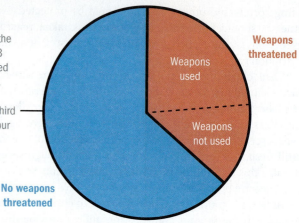

In 2008, the most recent full-year data available, demand notes were issued in 3,833 of the 6,700 bank heists during the year. Verbal demands occurred in 3,683 bank jobs, although some were combined with the demand notes (FBI.gov, 2010).

Weapons were threatened in roughly a third of robberies and used in about one in four bank jobs, the statistics show.

Demand note issued   No demand note issued

Weapons used

Weapons threatened

Weapons not used

No weapons threatened

"Scarecrow Bandits"—named for the floppy hats and plaid shirts they wore in early robberies—were arrested in June 2008 after a foiled bank robbery led to a high-speed chase. Subsequent investigation revealed that the defendants were well organized in their operations, communicating with cell phones and walkie-talkies and spending no more than two or three minutes inside each bank.

The "Geezer Bandit" is still sought in connection with a string of six robberies in the San Diego area as of the preparation of this text. The suspect's geriatric appearance and the catchy label given to him by local authorities have drawn national attention to the case. The labels for bank robbers are thought to be a positive because more media attention leads to more tips and investigative leads.

Today, there exists a greater risk for those willing to rob a bank. These criminals know that cameras are present and that employees are trained to recognize faces. They also know that the police and the FBI are going to respond and investigate. Yet, many are willing to take that chance.

Studies have shown that many people who commit a robbery are often repeat offenders, or recidivists. Therefore, it is important to document the techniques and **method of operation (MO)** used by the suspect. An MO focuses on the behavior of the criminal during the commission of a crime. For example, the location of the robbery, such as a bank or convenience store, may identify certain groups of suspects. Other factors include the type of weapon used; the dress of the robber(s); and the amount of money, merchandise, drugs, and so on taken.

In addition to the age, gender, height, and race of a suspect, it is important to document specific behavior during a crime. Such behavior might indicate nervousness (or calmness) or could indicate that a person was under the influence of drugs at the time.

The treatment of the victim(s) could also have a bearing on the investigation. For example, was violence used? If so, what were the injuries? Was the victim kicked, beaten, shot, or struck with the weapon? Other actions might also be significant:

- Did the suspect cut the telephone wires?
- Were the victims locked up?
- Were the victims tied up or gagged?

Investigators should remember that because of a lack of abundant physical evidence, robbery scenes may suggest other types of evidence. MOs in connection with any available physical evidence may help identify the perpetrator and ultimately prove a case.

▶ *Physical Evidence*

The crime scene should be processed as soon as possible after physical evidence has been identified. Evidence in robberies may take several forms, including fingerprints, **binding material**, and fired cartridges. The value of fingerprints at a robbery crime scene is immense, so it is essential to conduct a thorough search of all surfaces in or near the scene that the robbers might have touched. These surfaces include countertops, doors and door handles, cash registers and computers, and any furniture encountered by the suspects. In particular, if the robbers handled any paper products (for example, notes to bank tellers), such surfaces are particularly good for preserving latent prints and should be protected and processed.

LEARNING OUTCOMES 6 — Describe the use of evidence and witnesses in robbery investigations.

Binding material, if located, may include strips of tape, such as duct or masking tape; cloth strips; wire; rope; or any material used to incapacitate the victim. In the event that rope is used as a restraining device, care should be taken not to destroy any knots. These can be used to link the suspect with any specialized technique of tying knots. Such items can be used as comparison items in the event that similar material is later found in the possession of suspects.

Shell casings or cartridges may also provide important evidence of a robbery. Such items may bear latent prints of perpetrators or identify the type of weapon used for the crime. In fact, rifling (impressions) on the sides of casings may be used in linking a specific gun with a crime.

In the case of bank robberies, some banks may use bait money to aid in capturing the robbery suspect. When used, bait money is placed in a specially designated bin in a teller's cash drawer. This cash has had its serial numbers prerecorded so that

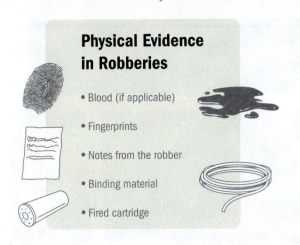

Physical Evidence in Robberies

- Blood (if applicable)
- Fingerprints
- Notes from the robber
- Binding material
- Fired cartridge

Think About It...

Understanding the Scene . . .
The importance of physical evidence when investigating a robbery cannot be overstated. Given that society abhors robbery based on the violence associated with it, physical evidence not only of what was used to steal from the victim but also of any threatening or harming of a victim is important. What types of physical evidence might be important to a robbery investigation?

Bullet Casing in Evidence Bag.

it can be identified if it is later found in a suspect's possession. In other cases, when bait money is removed from a drawer, a silent alarm will be set off, notifying local police that a robbery is in progress.

The Role of Witnesses

Because of the violent nature of the crime of robbery and the imminent threat of injury, witnesses are not likely to remember many specific details of a robbery. It is important, however, that officers attempt to gather as much information as possible from any witnesses. It is vital that witnesses be separated so that their individual perceptions of what happened won't influence other witnesses. Experience has shown that an exchange of dialogue between witnesses might unconsciously alter the way in which some witnesses "recall" an event. After the witnesses have been separated, interviews should be conducted regarding both the event and details about the robber(s).

People at the scene of a robbery will be afraid, confused, and even angry. Because of the emotionally charged environment, officers should expect to receive somewhat different interpretations of what occurred from the witnesses because no two people will perceive a situation in exactly the same way. In fact, if the stories are too similar, the investigator should question the truthfulness of the witnesses' stories. The details regarding perpetrators should be as specific as possible. Information should be sought regarding specifics, such as scars, tattoos, jewelry worn, and other particulars about the suspects. Leading questions asked by the investigator might help draw out these details. Leading questions include the following:

- What did you notice most about the robber's appearance?
- What were the most noticeable features about the robber's face?
- Was there anything unique or unusual about the robber's manner of speech?

Such questions encourage witnesses to stop and think about specific details regarding a crime.

A New Reality in Robberies—Pharmaceuticals

In today's society, retail establishments are more and more likely to become the target of those choosing to steal by force in order to obtain a goal (for example, money or drugs). On June 19, 2011, four people were killed inside a pharmacy located in Long Island, New York, as what police say was the result of a robbery. Pharmacy employees as well as some customers were victims of what police say was probably one suspect. What makes this violence so horrific is that the victims were killed "execution-style," by being shot at close range in the head.

This is a good example of how complicated robberies can be in the sense that it is often not initially clear what the motivation for the crime might have been. In this case, even though police have not officially stated it, theft of pharmaceutical drugs is a growing issue nationwide, and there is always the possibility that this might have been the motivation. However, obtaining money or even someone deciding to kill an acquaintance at the pharmacy must also be considered among other possible motivations. Finally, this case is a good example in that it helps make clear why society tends to treat robbery so punitively as a crime; the possibility of violence in using force is an

Gina Sanders/Shutterstock.com

unpredictable reality that can result in the injury or death of innocent people over mere material items.

Source: CNN Wire Staff. (2011, June 19). Four dead in New York area pharmacy shooting. CNN.com. Retrieved from http://www.cnn.com/2011/CRIME/06/19/new.york.pharmacy.shooting/index.html?iref=allsearch.

The investigation of serial homicide cases represents one of the greatest challenges to criminal investigation:

1. Robbery is a personal crime involving a face-to-face confrontation between the victim and a perpetrator. Weapons may be used in robberies or strong-arm robbery may occur through intimidation. Using the chapter material and the case study, do you think the police should automatically presume the robbery in this case was motivated by the desire to obtain drugs? Explain your answer.

2. Given this case, what are your thoughts on the importance of how police consider the elements of robbery during an investigation?

CHAPTER 10   Robbery

LEARNING OUTCOMES 1

Summarize the trends and elements of robbery.

Robbery is a personal crime and involves face-to-face contact between the victim and offender with the primary motivation connected to obtaining money. Many people confuse the term *robbery* with *burglary*, but some elements of the crimes differ considerably. Many states have chosen to divide robbery into first, second, and third degrees, depending on the seriousness of the act.

1. What are the advantages of robbery compared to other types of crime?

2. What is the difference between robbery and burglary?

3. How does the FBI's Uniform Crime Report define robbery?

4. What are the emotional and psychological consequences of robbery?

5. What are the elements of robbery?

LEARNING OUTCOMES 2

Differentiate between the types of robbery.

According to one study, robbery follows one of five patterns. The commercial robbery targets stores and businesses; most street robberies are committed with a weapon; the residential robbery often begins as a burglary but turns to robbery when the intruder uses violence in the theft; a school robbery is petty extortion or a "shakedown"; and the victim of the vehicle robbery is often the vehicle's driver.

1. According to London, McClintock, and Gibson, what are the patterns of robbery?

2. What cautions do convenience stores take to deter potential robbers?

3. From a legal perspective, what are the elements of robbery?

4. What are the most common methods used in bank robberies?

5. Who are the most likely targets of street robberies? Why?

6. What are three key characteristics of robbery?

7. What characteristics distinguish the professional robber from the opportunistic robber?

8. What is the most common type of robbery committed?

commercial robbery   Robbery of stores and businesses located close to major thoroughfares such as main streets, highways, and interstates.

bank robbery   The unlawful taking of money or other assets from a bank through the use of face-to-face contact between suspect and victims.

street robbery   Robbery committed on public streets and alleyways.

residential robbery   Robbery when an armed intruder breaks into a home and holds the residents at gun- or knifepoint.

school robberies   Instances of petty extortion or "shakedowns" of students and teachers in public schools.

smash-and-grab robbery   A type of robbery in which the robbers approach a car, break the window, and hold up the driver at gunpoint.

LEARNING OUTCOMES 3

Describe the duties of the first officer to the robbery scene.

After receiving a radio call, the first officer's initial responsibility is to arrive at the scene as quickly and safely as possible. When approaching the scene, he or she should be on the lookout for fleeing subjects and persons sitting in parked cars. These might be accomplices or lookouts working with the robber. Once on the scene, the officer should apprehend the suspect if possible.

1. What factors influence the decision to use emergency equipment when en route to a robbery scene?

2. What are the responsibilities of the first officer on the scene of a robbery?

3. Under what circumstances is it advisable for the arriving officer to enter the location of a robbery?

Explain how a robbery investigation is conducted.

When responding to calls in which the robbers have already left the scene, officers must follow proper investigative procedures. A robbery investigation may take weeks or even months to complete. A good place to begin the investigation is a canvass of the area, particularly the most likely escape route. The canvass is also critical in the event that the robber is hiding somewhere close to the robbery location.

1. What are the first steps officers should take when arriving at a robbery scene?

2. What information is included in a flash description?

3. When conducting a neighborhood canvass, where should investigators look if the suspect is hiding/still in the area?

4. What typical MO information is needed when investigating robberies?

5. What is the most common type of robbery?

6. What information is included in a second broadcast? Why is a second broadcast important?

neighborhood canvass A door-to-door search of the area of a crime to identify witnesses.

Summarize the method of operation for robbers.

Robbery methods are as novel and varied as the people who commit them. However, studies have shown that many people who commit a robbery are often repeat offenders. Because of this fact, it is important to document specific behavior during a crime. Methods of operation (MOs) may help identify the perpetrator and ultimately prove a case.

1. What is the most common method of operation used in bank robberies?

2. Why are the labels often given to bank robberies considered positive from an investigative point of view?

3. Why is it imperative to properly document techniques and methods used by robbery suspects?

4. What factors assist investigators with identifying certain groups of robbery suspects?

5. How does the treatment of the victim(s) affect the investigation?

method of operation (MO) The behavior of the criminal during the commission of the crime.

Describe the use of evidence and witnesses in robbery investigations.

The crime scene should be processed after physical evidence has been identified. A search of all surfaces in or near the scene that the robbers might have touched must be conducted. Officers should attempt to gather as much information as possible from witnesses, and should expect to receive different interpretations of what occurred from the witnesses because people perceive situations differently.

1. What types of physical evidence may be present at a robbery scene?

2. What does the presence of shell casings tell investigators about a robbery?

3. Why should investigators interview witnesses of a robbery separately?

4. What information from witnesses should be sought regarding perpetrators?

5. What questions should interviewers ask witnesses about perpetrators?

6. How do some banks help to simplify bank robbery investigations?

binding material Material used to incapacitate a victim during the course of a robbery.

Additional Links

www.nij.gov
This is the official site of the National Institute of Justice, the research, development, and evaluation agency of the U.S. Department of Justice. The mission of the NIJ is to improve knowledge and understanding of crime and justice through science. The site's main menu contains links for funding, publications, events, training, and multimedia, including audio and video presentations. Quick links include topics A–Z, which contain information on corrections, courts, crimes and prevention, law enforcement, and technology and tools, to name a few.

www.fbi.gov
This is the official site of the FBI. For those interested in learning more about the various cases noted in the chapter, the site has a search engine to find press releases and other information about the cases. The Geezer Bandit, Midwestern Bandit, and Scarecrow Bandit cases are all archived on the site. A search using the term "bank bandits" reveals even more intriguing cases.

11

Assault and Related Offenses

"Assault investigations are one of the most common types of criminal investigations."

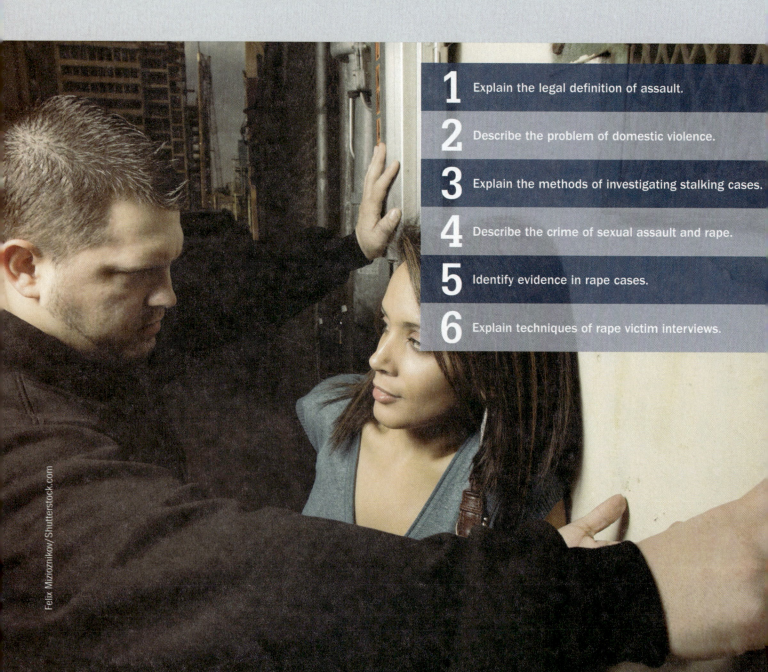

1 Explain the legal definition of assault.

2 Describe the problem of domestic violence.

3 Explain the methods of investigating stalking cases.

4 Describe the crime of sexual assault and rape.

5 Identify evidence in rape cases.

6 Explain techniques of rape victim interviews.

INTRO AN UNSETTLING ENCOUNTER

In April 2014, 27 year-old Jarred Ashley Workman met a 14-year-old girl online. They chatted using social media for about a month and then agreed to meet in the woods near the teen's home in the Love Valley, North Carolina, area. He then sneaked into the girl's bedroom without her family's knowledge. Workman hid in her closet for five days and ran away when the girl's mother went to put some of her daughter's clothes away.

According to the investigation, during the day, Workman was hiding either in her closet or in her bedroom, and when she would come home from school or other activities, he would come out in the evenings. In the five-day span from April 27 to May 2, Workman allegedly had sex with the teen several times. In North Carolina, the age of consent for sexual activity is 16, as it is in 33 other states and the District of Columbia.

After Workman fled, investigators tracked him through the woods behind the victim's house. His trail ran cold along North Carolina 115, where he probably got a ride from an unsuspecting motorist. But the suspect dropped his wallet and cell phone along the way, enabling investigators to identify Workman. Workman soon turned himself in to Iredell County sheriff's deputies. He had several prior arrests and was charged with 11 counts of statutory rape and five counts of statutory sex.

This case illustrates not only the crime of statutory rape but also the unsettling manner in which some child predators locate and stalk their victims. Rape is an assault! Other acts of violence are also assaults under legal definitions and will be discussed in this chapter.

DISCUSS Can you think of what police can do to prevent the frequency of assaults?

The crime of rape, as just mentioned, is generally classified as a sexual assault. You will see that many types of assault exist under law.

The pattern of assault (e.g., a physical assault) is similar to that of homicide. One might say that the difference between the two is that in an assault, the victim survives. Assaults can occur in many ways: a rock is thrown by one teen at another, a wife breaks a bottle over her husband's head during a domestic squabble, a drug dealer beats up a customer who steals his drugs. These are all forms of assault. Many "traditional" crimes are also accompanied by assaults against victims. For example, robbery, drug dealing, sexual assault (rape), and loan sharking all frequently contain some aspect of the crime of assault.

Studies of assault cases have revealed that most victims of assault (two-thirds to three-fourths of cases) are acquainted with their attacker. In addition, it is common for such victims to choose not to file charges against their attackers. If charges are filed, many victims later choose not to follow through with prosecution, particularly if the parties are related or are close friends. Such realities can make investigation of these types of crime difficult and frustrating.

▶ Legal Classifications of Assault

Although states often define *assault* differently, some general definitions will be considered. The terms *assault* and *battery* were formerly used to distinguish between threats and actual contact between suspect and victim. Today, many revised state statutes categorize threats and actual physical contact as **simple assault** and **aggravated assault**. These are defined as follows.

LEARNING OUTCOMES 1 Explain the legal definition of assault.

Simple Assault

- *Threats by one person to cause bodily harm or death to another.* Investigators must identify evidence to show specific intent to commit bodily injury; an injury received as a result of an accident is not an assault. A suspect's words and actions or any injuries to the victim may demonstrate intent. The injury must be to another party; injury to property or self-inflicted injury, regardless of its seriousness, is not assault.

- *Purposely inflicting bodily harm on another.* Bodily harm or injury and simple assault need not cause severe physical pain or disability. The degree of force necessary in simple assault may range from a push or a slap to slightly less than that required for the great bodily harm that is characteristic of aggravated assault.

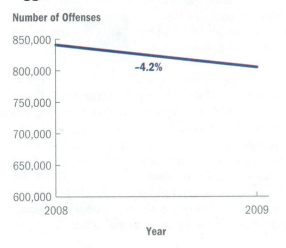

Aggravated Assault Trend 2009

Number of Offenses

-4.2%

Year

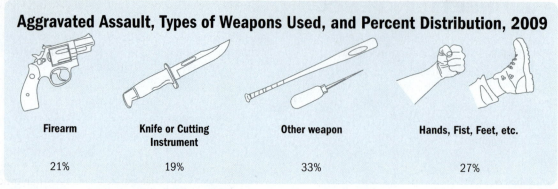

Aggravated Assault, Types of Weapons Used, and Percent Distribution, 2009

Firearm	Knife or Cutting Instrument	Other weapon	Hands, Fist, Feet, etc.
21%	19%	33%	27%

Source: FBI, Crime in the United States, 2010.

Legal Elements of Simple Assault

☑ Threats by one person to cause bodily harm or death to another

☑ Purposely inflicting bodily harm on another

Legal Elements of Aggravated Assault

☑ High probability of death

☑ Serious, permanent disfigurement

☑ Permanent or protracted loss or impairment of the function of any body part or organ or other severe bodily harm

Aggravated Assault

Aggravated assault includes the elements of simple assault plus an element relating to the severity of the attack. Aggravated assault is usually committed with a weapon or by some means likely to produce great bodily harm or death.

- *High probability of death.* The assault is considered aggravated if it is committed by any means so severe that any reasonable person would think it would result in a high probability of death. For example, a strike to the head sufficient to cause unconsciousness or coma, a gunshot or knife wound that causes heavy bleeding, or burns inflicted over a large area of a person's body would be considered aggravated assault.

- *Serious, permanent disfigurement.* Permanent disfigurement includes such things as loss of an ear or part of the nose or permanent scarring of the face or other parts of the body that are normally visible. It cannot be a temporary injury that will eventually heal and not be evident.

- *Loss or impairment of body members or organs.* Regardless of the part of the body affected, a charge of aggravated assault is supported by the loss or permanent impairment of body members or organs or by maiming.

Only one of these additional elements is needed to show aggravated assault, although two or all three are sometimes present. Some states do not require that there be permanent or protracted injury or loss if the weapon used in the assault is a dangerous weapon that causes fear of immediate harm or death. As with simple assault, the act must be intentional, not accidental.

In 2012, 760,739 cases of aggravated assault were reported to law-enforcement agencies in the United States.[1] According to statistics, assault reports were most frequent during the summer months and the least frequent in February, November, December, and January. The majority of aggravated assaults were committed with blunt objects or objects near at hand, and hands, feet, and fists were also commonly used (27 percent).[2] Less frequently used were knives (19 percent) and firearms (22 percent). Because those who commit assaults are often known to their victims, aggravated assaults are relatively easy to solve. About 56 percent of all aggravated assaults reported to the police in 2012 were cleared by arrest.[3]

▶ *Domestic Violence*

Responding to domestic violence calls is one of the most unpleasant duties for police officers. In some cases, officers not trained properly for this type of duty may have preconceptions or biases that it is simply a "family matter" and not a real policing issue. However, domestic assault calls are often dangerous for the police. This is because the highly emotional atmosphere accompanying domestic abuse situations, the raw violence often

LEARNING OUTCOMES 2 — Describe the problem of domestic violence.

displayed, the family lives destroyed, and the victim's frequent hesitancy to prosecute or seek shelter all place a heavy burden on the officers sent to such disturbances. Still, an appropriate and effective police response to all domestic calls is warranted.

Response to such calls may be initiated by the dispatcher, who can save hours of legwork by exploring with the victim his or her frame of mind and that of the alleged attacker. From that point on, responding officers' actions are critical. What responding officers do upon arrival often determines what

Think About It…

Aggravatingly Simple . . . It is very common for people to not consider the difference between a simple assault and an aggravated assault. The reality is that investigators must work diligently to find evidence so that prosecutors can actually charge suspects in such cases. This can be difficult when you factor in that when police respond to a call, they must also simultaneously deal with potential panic, anger, frustration, curiosity, and many other realities that can impact their ability to gather evidence quickly or reliably. What are the differences between a simple assault and an aggravated assault?

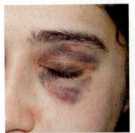

Courtesy of Mike Himmel

This Photo Shows a Pattern of Bruising of a Victim's Eye. Because Coloration of the Bruising Will Change in the Hours Following the Assault, Investigators Should Take Incremental Photos in the Days Following the Initial Assault.

happens in court, whether an effective arrest will be conducted, and whether or not proper evidence will be collected. Domestic violence calls are complicated in that they may unfold into simple battery, assault, kidnapping, trespassing, murder, stalking, terroristic threats, spousal rape, or many other types of criminal violations. Police investigators should never assume that the parties involved in a domestic dispute are merely involved in a minor squabble.

Typically, patrol officers respond to domestic violence calls. When that occurs, officers should not park their patrol car within view of the location to which they are responding. Doing so may allow the suspect to see the officers coming and to become even more enraged at the thought of going to jail. This could result in the infliction of additional injuries to the victim or provide the suspect with time to gather weapons with which officers could be assaulted.

After officers have entered the location of the domestic violence call and have secured the area, the investigation begins. The first rule is to interview the suspect and victim separately. Upon first contact with the suspect, the *Miranda* warning should not be read to the suspect. At this point, until a determination has been made as to the nature of the dispute and the relationship between the suspect and victim, the suspect is not under arrest for domestic violence. The parties are simply under detention for investigation because police officers have reasonable suspicion to detain them. This is a critical point in the investigation. Because of their agitated emotional state, many

domestic violence suspects make spontaneous admissible statements that can be used against them later in court. The officers should reduce the level of tension at the scene by separating and talking to the participants. The officers must also consider the safety of the participants and any children present.

Any evidence that would lead an officer to make an arrest in any other situation also applies to spousal abuse situations. Most states allow arrests based on probable cause. In line with the probable cause standard, police officers should arrest all abusers who are not acting in self-defense and issue an arrest warrant even if the offender is absent. Finally, officers should be careful not to detain a potential abuser any longer than other offenders.

Twenty states now mandate that police make an arrest in domestic violence incidents if there is a protective or restraining order against the attacker. A number of states make it mandatory for an officer to make an arrest if there is probable cause, even without an assigned complaint by the victim. In Nevada, for example, if the police have sufficient reason to believe that a person, within the preceding four hours, committed an act of domestic violence or spousal battery, they are required to arrest the person if there are no mitigating circumstances.

Officers should not base their decisions regarding arrest on their perception of the willingness of the victim or witness to testify. The victim need not sign a complaint. If the assault was a mutual assault (that is, both people involved committed assault), officers must try to determine the **primary physical aggressor** and arrest that person. Some factors to consider in making this determination include

- Prior domestic violence involving either person
- The relative seriousness of the injuries inflicted upon each person involved
- The potential for future injury
- Whether one of the alleged assaults was committed in self-defense
- Any other factor that helps the officer decide which person was the primary physical aggressor

As with any criminal investigation, evidence must be collected. In domestic violence cases, evidence includes photographs of injuries, victims' statements, prior police reports, doctor or hospital reports, weapons used, damaged clothing or other property, and statements from neighbors and other witnesses. It should be made clear to the victim that an "order of protection" may be obtained from the court to help prevent further assaults.

Legal Approaches to Domestic Violence

In many cities, a high percentage of female victims request that battery charges be dropped or refuse to testify against the abuser after he has been arrested. In response to this, prosecutors in many cities with vigorous prosecution philosophies are increasingly adopting a controversial policy of "no drop." For example, in San Diego, if the victim won't testify, prosecutors use tapes from the woman's 911 calls and testimony from neighbors and police to build a case.

Profiling the Batterer[4]

The profiles of abusive men have been fairly consistent. They tend to be manipulative, persuasive actors. They believe women should be subordinate, although they are often quite dependent on their spouses or girlfriends. They are cons: smart, charming, and cunning. Once they spot vulnerable women, they put on their best behavior and treat women with great respect, but the real anger they feel for women is just below the surface. Many batterers don't beat women out of a fit of rage but rather after some premeditation. In some cases, men have ripped out the telephone wires just before beating their spouses, which prevents the victims from calling 911 for help. Economic considerations are also a reason why battered women stay with their abusive partners. The cruel choice for battered women is often whether to be beaten or to be poor.

Psychologists have likened battering relationships to the Stockholm syndrome, in which hostages, over time, identify with their captors. Entangled in an intimate relationship that often begins as romance, many women come to agree with their partner's view of them as worthless. Often, a batterer goes into a "honeymoon" period just after a beating, persuading his partner that he will reform.

Protection Orders

For many women who have become leery of the criminal justice system but are threatened by their violent partners, **protection orders** are an option. Now used in all 50 states and the District of Columbia, protection orders are often backed up by the threat of jail. In some cases, judges can establish temporary custody for children, forbid telephone threats or harassment, and make the husband pay financial support or leave his home.

A temporary protection order can be issued the same day the woman requests it and can be put into effect for a year or longer. In comparison, a woman can wait for months for a criminal prosecution to come to trial or years for a property settlement from a divorce decree. On the other hand, in some states, protection orders amount to nothing more than a cruel hoax on victims. Husbands or boyfriends have killed women while under protection orders.

▶ Stalking

The crime of stalking generally refers to some form of repeated harassing or threatening behavior. A stalker is someone who intentionally and repeatedly follows and tries to contact, harass, or intimidate another person. The Violence Against Women Grants Office adds, "Legal definitions of stalking vary widely from state to state. Though most states define stalking as

LEARNING OUTCOMES 3 — Explain the methods of investigating stalking cases.

the willful, malicious, and repeated following and harassing of another person, some states include in their definitions such activities as lying in wait, surveillance, nonconsensual communication, telephone harassment, and vandalism."[5] Other experts have asserted that although statutes vary from one state to another, most define stalking as a course of conduct that would place a reasonable person in fear for his or her safety and that the stalker attempted to and did in fact place the victim in fear.

Legal definitions of stalking vary widely from state to state, but the term generally refers to harassing or threatening behavior that a person engages in repeatedly, such as following a person, appearing at a person's home or place of business, making harassing telephone calls, leaving written messages or objects, or vandalizing a person's property. These actions may or may not be accompanied by a credible threat of serious harm, and they may or may not be precursors to an assault or murder.

Stalking Statistics

Using a definition of stalking that requires victims to feel a high level of fear, the NVAW survey found that 8 percent of women and 2 percent of men in the United States have been stalked at some time in their lives. Based on U.S. Census estimates of the number of women and men in the United States, 1 of every 12 U.S. women (8.2 million) has been stalked at some time in her life and 1 of every 45 U.S. men (2 million) has been stalked at some time in his life.

Although stalking is a gender-neutral crime, women are the primary victims of stalking and men the primary perpetrators. Seventy-eight percent of stalking victims identified by the NVAW survey were women, and 22 percent were men. Thus, four out of five stalking victims are women. Overall, 87 percent of the stalkers as defined by victims were male.

Statistics addressing the frequency of stalking are concerning. For example, the National Violence Against Women Survey (NVAWS) revealed that the stalking of a woman often ends up in a physical or sexual assault of the person who is stalked. Moreover, when this occurs, women are more likely than men to be injured (29 percent versus 22 percent, respectively).

As noted, the act of stalking might involve following a person or appearing at the person's home or place of business, making harassing phone calls or leaving written messages or objects on the victim's property.[6] Most stalking laws require that the perpetrator make a credible threat of violence against the victim or members of the victim's immediate family.

Who Stalks Whom?

Experts say that the motive for stalking can be romantic jealousy—gay men are the most likely victims of male-on-male stalking. But male stalking is often linked to the high-profile positions that the targets hold in society. For example, students stalk professors, attractive celebrities are pursued by lonely men looking for famous buddies, and business and political leaders can become objects of hate when consumer complaints turn

Documentation of victim interviews. Has the victim

- moved to a new location?

- obtained a new phone number?

- put a tap on the phone?

- told friends, coworkers, or family members of the harassment?

- given photos of the defendant to security?

- asked to be escorted to the parking lot and work site?

- changed work schedule or route to work?

- stopped visiting places previously frequented?

- taken a self-defense course?

- purchased pepper spray?

- bought a gun?

- installed an alarm system?

ugly. Researchers say that men stalk other men for primarily the same reasons that they stalk women: a complex mix of mental and personality disorders that can include schizophrenia, drug dependency, narcissism, and antisocial behavior. Some of the problems with male stalking are that men are more reluctant than women to report being stalked and can have trouble getting police to take them seriously. Furthermore, public services for stalking victims, such as spouse-abuse shelters, are still oriented to the most frequent targets—women.

Although only a small percentage of stalking victims are actually physically attacked, psychological and social consequences

Think About It…

"Can You Prove I Was Stalking Her?" There is a fine line between a dedicated fan and a stalker, if you were to ask a celebrity. Celebrities often hire teams of security simply to help protect them from those who would simply show up or send potentially malicious or "unusual" communications. The reality is that one does not need to be a celebrity for someone to want to have inappropriate contact such as harassment, intimidating calls/visits, and so forth. Based on this chapter, what are some interesting details with respect to "who stalks whom"?

Steven Frame/Shutterstock.com

Some Stalkers Watch Their Victims from a Distance, as Depicted in This Photo of a Stalker Watching from a Vehicle.

are also common. About one-third of women and one-fifth of men who have been stalked sought psychological counseling as a result of their victimization. More than one-fourth of stalking victims said their victimization caused them to lose time from work. This included attending court hearings, meeting with psychologists or other mental health professionals, meeting with attorneys, and avoidance of contact with the assailants. For those victims who are stalked, the behavior lasts only a relatively short period of time—about two-thirds of all stalking cases last a year or less.

Responses to the questions during a victim interview can indicate the victim's state of mind to help prove that element of the crime. In 1996, a federal law prohibiting interstate stalking was also enacted. Such legislation makes stalking a specific crime and empowers law enforcement to combat the stalking problem. Antistalking laws describe specific threatening conduct and hold the suspect responsible for proving that his or her actions were not intended to frighten or intimidate the victim.

▶ Sexual Assault

One doesn't have to read far in the newspapers to find yet another incident involving criminal sexual misconduct. Because of intense media (and public) interest, such cases tend to raise the consciousness of society regarding the plight of both victims and their perpetrators. Generally speaking, most sex crimes, rape in particular, are thought to be grossly underreported by victims. In fact, an estimated 50 percent of all sexual assaults are believed to go unreported to authorities. Perhaps this could be attributed to the intense personal nature of such offenses and because victims are too embarrassed or humiliated to report the incident. Indeed, studies have revealed that many victims would rather just forget such crimes than go through the agony of reliving them through police interviews and courtroom testimony. In addition, many perpetrators have turned out to be the friends, relatives, and acquaintances of the victims, creating an even greater disincentive for bringing about formal charges.

LEARNING OUTCOMES 4 Describe the crime of sexual assault and rape.

Although many different types of sex-related crimes exist, this chapter focuses on the crime of rape. Let's take a broader look at some of the most common types of rape that one might consider as an investigative priority. These include forcible rape and acquaintance rape.

Forcible Rape

The terms *rape* and *forcible rape* are often applied to a wide variety of sexual attacks, including same-sex rape and the rape of a male by female. Under the *Uniform Crime Reports* (UCR) program of the Federal Bureau of Investigation (FBI), the term *forcible rape* generally refers to "the carnal knowledge of a person forcibly and against their will." More specifically, forcible rape is identified by the UCR program as, "penetration, no matter how slight, of the vagina or anus with any body part or object or

Trends

oral penetration by a sex organ of another person, without the consent of the victim."

The UCR statistics show 84,376 reported forcible rapes in 2012.[7] This is a slight decrease from the number of offenses reported the previous year. Reports of rape, however, have sometimes increased even in years when reports of other violent crimes have been on the decline. Statistics show that the greatest number of forcible rapes occurring in 2012 were reported in the hot summer months and, conversely, the lower numbers were recorded in January, February, November, and December.[8]

Conventional wisdom holds that forcible rape is often a planned violent crime that serves the offender's need for power rather than sexual gratification. The "power thesis" has its origins in the writings of Susan Brown Miller, who argued in 1975 that the primary motivation leading to heterosexual rape is the rapist's desire to "keep women in their place" and to preserve gender inequity through violence."[9]

As a rule, most rates are committed by acquaintances of the victim and often betray a trust for friendship. Date rape, which falls into this category, appears to be far more common than previously believed. Currently, there is a growing number of rapes reported with the use of Rohypnol, the "date rape drug." Rohypnol is available on the black market; it dissolves easily in drinks and can leave anyone who consumes it unconscious for hours, making them vulnerable to sexual assault.

Forcible Rape Trend 2009

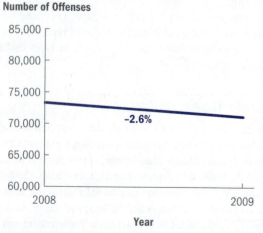

Number of Offenses

-2.6%

Year

Source: FBI, Crime in the United States, 2010.

Legal Aspects of Rape

According to common law, there are three elements to the crime of **rape** when the female is over the age of consent:

1. Carnal knowledge (penetration)
2. Forcible submission
3. Lack of consent

Penetration, as an essential element of rape, means generally that the sexual organ of the male entered the sexual organ of the female. Court opinions have held that penetration, however slight, is sufficient to sustain a charge of rape. There need not be an entering of the vagina or rupturing of the hymen; entering of the vulva or labia is usually all that is required. It is important during the victim interview that investigators clearly establish that penetration occurred with the penis. Penetration of a finger is not rape, although it is, of course, another form of assault.

In many states, the victim must have resisted the assault and her **resistance** must have been overcome by force. The amount of resistance that the victim is expected to have displayed depends on the specific circumstances of the case. The power and strength of the aggressor and the physical and mental ability of

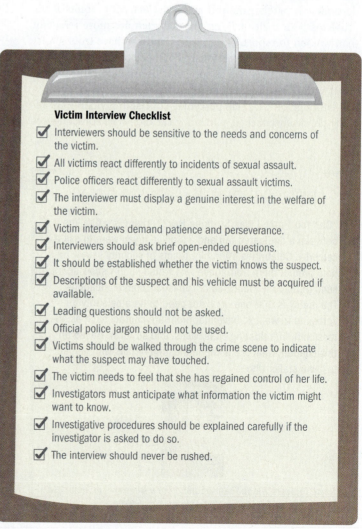

Victim Interview Checklist

☑ Interviewers should be sensitive to the needs and concerns of the victim.

☑ All victims react differently to incidents of sexual assault.

☑ Police officers react differently to sexual assault victims.

☑ The interviewer must display a genuine interest in the welfare of the victim.

☑ Victim interviews demand patience and perseverance.

☑ Interviewers should ask brief open-ended questions.

☑ It should be established whether the victim knows the suspect.

☑ Descriptions of the suspect and his vehicle must be acquired if available.

☑ Leading questions should not be asked.

☑ Official police jargon should not be used.

☑ Victims should be walked through the crime scene to indicate what the suspect may have touched.

☑ The victim needs to feel that she has regained control of her life.

☑ Investigators must anticipate what information the victim might want to know.

☑ Investigative procedures should be explained carefully if the investigator is asked to do so.

☑ The interview should never be rushed.

the victim to resist vary in each case. The amount of resistance expected in one case will not necessarily be expected in another situation.

It can be expected that one woman would be paralyzed by fear and rendered mute and helpless by circumstances that would inspire another to fierce resistance or that a woman may be rendered incapacitated by drugs such as Rohypnol or GHB.[10] For the most part, there must be resistance on the part of the woman before there can be a foundation for a rape charge.

The kind of fear, however, that would render resistance by a woman unnecessary to support a case of rape includes a fear of death or serious bodily harm, a fear so extreme as to preclude resistance, or a fear that would render her incapable of continuing to resist. On the other hand, consent prior to penetration may remove the criminal character of rape from the subsequent intercourse. Of course, it is problematic in some cases to determine whether the consent was voluntary or coerced or whether resistance was possible or even prudent on the part of the victim. As one state ruled, "There is no definite standard fixed for the amount of resistance required in rape cases. Resistance is not necessary where it would endanger the complainant's safety or when she is overcome by superior strength or paralyzed with fear."[11] This ruling may reflect the position of some state courts, although other states require more demonstrable evidence of resistance to rape. In any event, most recognize that there is a wide difference between consent and submission by force or threat of force: Consent may involve submission, but submission does not necessarily imply consent.

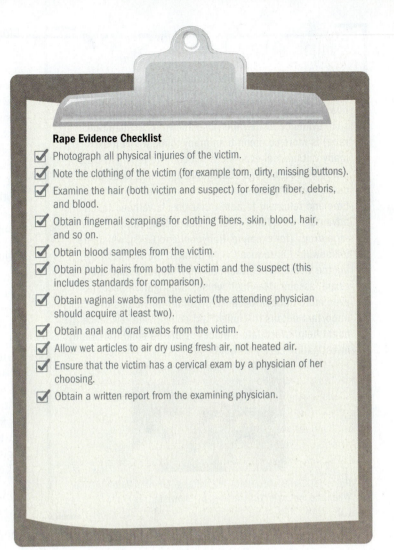

Rape Evidence Checklist

- ☑ Photograph all physical injuries of the victim.
- ☑ Note the clothing of the victim (for example torn, dirty, missing buttons).
- ☑ Examine the hair (both victim and suspect) for foreign fiber, debris, and blood.
- ☑ Obtain fingernail scrapings for clothing fibers, skin, blood, hair, and so on.
- ☑ Obtain blood samples from the victim.
- ☑ Obtain pubic hairs from both the victim and the suspect (this includes standards for comparison).
- ☑ Obtain vaginal swabs from the victim (the attending physician should acquire at least two).
- ☑ Obtain anal and oral swabs from the victim.
- ☑ Allow wet articles to air dry using fresh air, not heated air.
- ☑ Ensure that the victim has a cervical exam by a physician of her choosing.
- ☑ Obtain a written report from the examining physician.

▶ Evidence in Rape Cases

LEARNING OUTCOMES 5 — Identify evidence in rape cases.

As with all investigations, the identification, collection, and preservation of evidence are the primary responsibility of the investigator. Rape cases are somewhat unique in that evidence may present itself in three general areas:

1. On the crime scene
2. On the victim
3. On the suspect (or at locations occupied by the suspect)

If the incident was fairly recent, a flash description of the suspect or his vehicle should be given to the dispatcher for possible broadcast. After the crime-scene investigation is under way, the investigator should determine if there is any physical evidence to be collected. Typically, the rape victim will scratch the skin or tear the hair of her attacker, and evidence may be present under her fingernails. For example, a single strand of hair may reveal the gender, race, and age of the attacker. Such evidence is seizable by investigators and extremely valuable in court.[12]

The clothing of the victim can also provide valuable information (for example, stains, blood, soil, grass stains, trace evidence). As early as possible, clothing should be collected from the victim and preserved for laboratory analysis. Other types of evidence that should be considered are bed sheets, mattress, towels and washrags, discarded facial tissues, robes, and sofa or chair cushions. The investigator is limited only by his or her imagination when considering the types and locations of such articles.

Investigative Procedures: The Crime-Scene Investigation

An officer's first duty at the scene of a rape is to aid the victim and obtain medical attention immediately, if required. If the attack was brutal and the victim is suffering from wounds, briefly question the victim about the attack if she is able to speak. Questions relating to what happened and where the attack took place, as well as a description of or information about the assailant are pertinent basic facts. This initial attempt to secure information should be made whenever possible while awaiting the arrival of an ambulance or during transport to medical facilities. In

Date Rape in College The importance of physical evidence when investigating a sexual assault is that numerous factors can impact an investigator's ability to collect such evidence. Date rape (also known as acquaintance rape) is more common than many think, which makes many victims feel even more reluctant to report it. Date rape involving college students is a growing issue because many students are away from home for the first time and reluctant to admit that they have been taken advantage of. Adding to this issue is the reality of date rape drugs (for example, Rohypnol and GHB), which are unknowingly introduced via a drink to the victim, causing the victim to be essentially in a stupor during the sexual assault. Making it worse, investigation becomes even more difficult because it is hard for victims to recall important details that might aid police. What evidence might help investigators piece together a solid date rape investigation case and why?

Rohypnol Can Be Discreetly Placed in a Potential Victim's Drink When the Victim Is Not Looking, as Shown in This Photo.

turn, the dispatcher should be contacted immediately with this information.

Usually upon arriving at a rape scene, officers will find the victim of a sexual assault under severe emotional stress ranging from hysteria to deep depression. She may be sobbing uncontrollably, excited to the point of incoherence, or in a state of shock. In cases in which the victim was drugged, she may be confused and unsure of what happened to her. When encountering any of these situations, officers must comfort the victim and reassure her that she will be all right and that she has nothing more to fear. A victim in this mental state may best be comforted by another woman such as a female officer, a family member, a friend, or a victim advocate. Such individuals should be summoned as quickly as possible if not objectionable to the victim.

The crime scene should be secured and a search for physical evidence begun as soon as possible. Quite often, the victim will pull the assailant's hair, tear his clothes, or scratch his face and accumulate skin tissue or bloodstains under her fingernails. The victim's clothing can also provide valuable information. This should be collected and forwarded to the crime laboratory with other trace evidence for analysis.

Clothing

When a rape occurs in the home, the victim should be requested by the responding officer not to change her clothing, shower, or touch anything in the area until officers arrive at the scene to give her instructions. Responding officers should assume custody of all the clothing worn at the time of the attack so they may be examined for blood or seminal stains, hair fibers, and other physical trace evidence that may lead to the identification, apprehension, and conviction of a suspect. If the location of the crime makes the immediate recovery of the clothing impractical, the victim should be informed that an officer will collect her garments at the hospital for transfer to the crime laboratory.

Semen

Seminal traces may be located by ultraviolet radiation because of their fluorescent qualities. Semen is highly proteinaceous serum normally containing a great number of spermatozoa. These traces are usually found on underclothing of the victim, the suspect, or both and may also be located on bedding, mattresses, towels, automobile cushions, and similar types of materials found at or near the crime scene or in the possession of a suspect. Ultraviolet light or an acid phosphatase color test is helpful in identifying semen on these and other surfaces. Vaginal secretions and some other material will react to the latter test but not at the same speed as semen (See Figure 11–1a of vaginal swabs and Figure 11–1b of a hair collection kit).

Hair

It is fairly common to find a reciprocal transfer of evidence in crimes involving bodily contact. As such, it is not unusual to find hair of the offender transferred to the body or clothing of the victim and, in turn, to discover some of the victim's hair on the suspect.

Recovered hair is usually subjected to microanalysis at the crime laboratory. The results of this examination can generally narrow the search for a suspect. A single strand of hair may identify the race, sex, approximate age, and true color of the hair of its host. The analysis can also determine the portion of the body that the hair is from, such as the scalp, chest, arm, leg, or pubic region.

Investigative Procedures: The Forensic Examination

The forensic examination is arguably the most critical component in the aftermath of a sexual assault. The exam has two main goals: to treat the assault survivor for medical injuries and to collect evidence that may lead to the arrest, prosecution, and conviction of the offender. Exams are usually conducted by a sexual assault forensic examiner, or SAFE—a medical professional who has received specialized education and has fulfilled clinical requirements to perform medical forensic examinations. SAFEs can be nurses (often called sexual assault nurse examiners, or SANEs), doctors, or even physician assistants. Rape victims should receive medical attention and undergo an examination as soon as possible after the incident.

NATIONALLY RECOGNIZED SEXUAL ASSAULT FORENSIC EXAMINATION CHECKLIST

Check all items as provided during the sexual assault forensic exam.

☐ Utilized appropriate evidence collection kit (city, county, or state forensic lab)

☐ Completed screening exam for Emergency Medical Condition

☐ Activated bedside advocacy

☐ Activated interpreter

☐ Interventions for disabilities

☐ Obtained history of assault (including narrative)

☐ Obtained history of drug-facilitated sexual assault (if indicated)

☐ Obtained consent for evaluation and treatment

☐ Obtained consent for evidentiary SAFE exam

☐ Obtained consent for photography

☐ Obtained consent for drug screening (if drug-facilitated assault indicated)

☐ Obtained consent for release of information to all appropriate agencies

☐ Obtained consent for law enforcement activation (per patient request)

☐ Collected urine for drug facilitated sexual assault

☐ Collected underwear worn during or immediately after the assault

☐ Collected clothing, as forensically indicated, in brown paper bags, sealed and labeled

☐ Obtained swabs and smears from all areas that victim states were bitten or licked

☐ Obtained swabs and smears from appropriate areas as identified using an alternative light source

☐ Collected blood standard (if forensically indicated)

☐ Utilized crime scene investigators for bite mark impressions (if forensically indicated)

☐ Collected oral swab for DNA Standard (if forensically indicated)

☐ Collected oral swabs and smear (if orally assaulted)

☐ Collected anal swabs and smear (if forensically indicated)

☐ Collected vaginal swabs and smear (if forensically indicated)

☐ Collected cervical swabs and smear (if forensically indicated)

☐ Collected penile swabs and smear (if forensically indicated)

☐ Collected head hair standard (if forensically indicated)

☐ Collected pubic hair standard (if forensically indicated)

☐ Completed toluidine dye exam (if forensically indicated)

☐ Completed Xrays (if indicated)

☐ Completed CTs (if indicated)

☐ Collected unknown sample(s) (if forensically indicated)

☐ Collected fingernail scrapings (if forensically indicated)

☐ Photography (with colposcope or digital)

☐ Genital photography by forensic examiner

☐ Nongenital photography by forensic examiner

☐ Fewer than ten photos

☐ More than ten photos

☐ Forensic evidence storage/log (as indicated)

☐ Completion of DHSS Adult Female, Adult Male, or Child Sexual Assault Exam Form

☐ Confidential forensic patient file separate from general hospital medical records

☐ Forensic exam conducted by forensically trained physician or health care provider such as Sexual Assault Nurse Examiner (SANE)

Source: U.S. Department of Justice. National Protocol for Sexual Assault Medical Forensic Examinations.

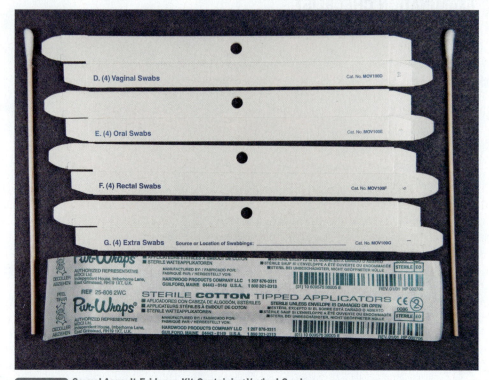

FIGURE 11–1a **Sexual Assault Evidence Kit Containing Vaginal Swabs.**
Source: Courtesy of Mike Himmel and the Missouri State Highway Patrol.

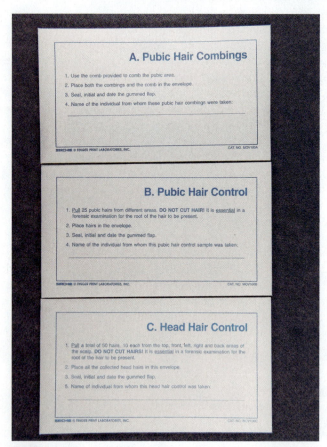

FIGURE 11–1b **Photo of Pubic and Head Hair Evidence Collection Kits.**
Source: Courtesy of Mike Himmel and the Missouri State Highway Patrol.

▶ *Investigative Procedures: The Interview*

Although the victim interview is one of the key components of a rape investigation, it can also be one of the more difficult functions for a criminal investigator. The difficult and, in many ways, specialized nature of these interviews has been a major reason for the introduction and use of rape crisis specialists to assist in these cases. Most agencies do not have such specialized personnel resources, but many agencies have found it helpful to utilize female officers individually or in conjunction with a male officer for such interviews. Female officers, even without specialized training, are generally effective in mitigating some of the anxiety and apprehension

LEARNING OUTCOMES 6 Explain techniques of rape victim interviews.

that rape victims have concerning the interview process and related investigatory activities. Significant additional benefits can be realized for both the victim and the criminal investigation if the same female officer can be assigned to assist the victim throughout the investigation and prosecution of the case.

Most rape investigations should incorporate a preliminary and subsequent in-depth interview with the victim. The initial interview conducted at the crime scene should be limited to gathering basic facts about the crime sufficient to identify the victim and to describe and locate the offender on a timely basis. The investigative goal of the police officer in interviewing a rape victim is to determine if and how the crime occurred. It is from the statements made by the victim to the officer that the essential elements of the offense and the direction of the investigation are established. The prosecutor and eventually the court must be given a well-balanced account of the offense describing the actions of the offender, any accomplices, and the victim. It is the investigator's responsibility to provide the court with the explanation and clarification it seeks. Part of the story may be obtained from the analysis of physical evidence, but the eyewitness account of the victim or other persons fills in the missing portions of the picture presented to the court.

Because the interview process may be considered a routine operation, the police officer may, if not careful, project a feeling of lack of concern for the victim as a person. The danger is that the victim may be left with the impression that she is being treated as an object of physical evidence rather than as a human being. This eventuality must be avoided for its own sake as well as for the good of the investigation. It is by the personal and sensitive communication of the interview that the victim's cooperation is gained and her emotional well-being maintained. If the officer treats the victim impersonally, her confidence will be shattered, the interview will be unsuccessful, and the victim may suffer further emotional stress. The following points should be kept in mind when conducting the in-depth interview.

Officer Attitude   When interviewing a rape victim, the officer must realize that, from the victim's viewpoint, what has occurred is a violent and perverted invasion of her "self." Furthermore, the officer must be constantly aware of personal sexual attitudes and prejudices as well as the subtle and not-so-subtle ways in which they emerge. Special care should be exercised so that the rape victim is not placed in the position of perceiving herself as being guilty because of the personal nature of the crime and the social stigma attached to it. Maintaining professionalism throughout the interview will help the officer obtain an accurate report of the crime without causing the victim to experience unnecessary anxiety.

Physical Setting   It is unreasonable to expect a rape victim to respond to detailed questioning while she is uncomfortable or in physical pain. The victim may have been beaten as well as raped. If the rape has occurred outdoors, the victim and her clothing will probably be soiled. Sometimes the victim has been urinated on or has been forced to commit oral sodomy. Under conditions such as these, the preliminary interview should be brief, and the in-depth follow-up interview should be conducted after the victim has been medically examined and treated and her personal needs, such as washing and changing clothes, have been met.

Officers often interview a rape victim at the hospital or other medical facility where the victim is being treated. Most hospitals meet the basic requirements of appropriate physical setting for an interview. The physical surroundings of most hospitals provide desired privacy and a professional care environment that can restore confidence in the victim.

Outside the hospital, the interview should take place in a comfortable setting where there is privacy and freedom from distraction. A crowded office or similar location where the interview is subject to interruption is inappropriate. The reluctance of a rape victim to discuss intimate details of the crime will generally increase if there are other people present. This may include persons who would be close to the victim under otherwise normal conditions, such as a husband or boyfriend.

Opening Remarks   The opening remarks represent a critical point at which an officer must gain the victim's confidence and let her know that a major part of the officer's function is to help and to protect her. The officer should make clear his or her sympathy for and interest in the victim. By doing this, the officer contributes to the immediate and long-term emotional health of the victim and lays the foundation of mutual cooperation and respect on which an effective interview is built.

Ventilation Period   After the opening remarks, the officer should allow the victim to direct the conversation into any area of concern to her. This "ventilation" period gives the victim an opportunity to relieve emotional tension. During this time, the officer should listen carefully to the victim and provide answers to questions as appropriate and reassurance when necessary.

Investigative Questioning   After a ventilation period, the victim should be allowed to describe what occurred in her own words and without interruption. As the victim provides details about the rape, she will also relate a great deal about herself. Her mood and general reaction, her choice of words, and her comments on unrelated matters can be useful in evaluating the facts of the case. It is important in such an interview that the police officer be humane, sympathetic, and patient. He or she should also be alert to inconsistencies in the victim's statements. If the victim's story differs from the originally reported facts, the officer should point out the discrepancies and ask her to explain them in greater detail. The officer should phrase questions in simple language, making sure that she understands the question.

Concluding the Interview   As a result of having been raped, many victims suffer long-term emotional problems. Because of this, it is appropriate for the officer conducting the interview to determine whether the victim has sought assistance for any such problems. It is generally advisable to inform the victim that emotional reactions to rape are common and that counseling is advisable. Victims who are not familiar with available community resources to assist in these matters should be provided with information on referral agencies.

THE CASE

Date Rape in Connection with a University Employee

Date rape is a fear that many have under normal circumstances. The fact that people are sometimes in situations where they need something immediately (for example, a place to live), can make the prospect of being alone with people we know, but not that well, scary. Mahmood Kalantar was an engineering professor at Rappahannock Community College in Virginia. He was indicted in May of 2011 on one count of felony rape of a woman within a rental property he owned. The allegation made to police is that in April 2011 a woman visited the property that was being shown by Kalantar. According to the police report, the woman attempted to leave the house and Kalantar grabbed her, threw her on the ground, and repeatedly assaulted her sexually. When she escaped, she reported the incident to police and consented to a medical examination. The case is still pending in court while Kalantar is free on $75,000 bond.

Felix Mizioznikov/Shutterstock.com

Sources: Daily Press. (2011, June 22). Rape case court date pushed back: Case continued at request of defense. Retrieved from http://articles.dailypress.com/2011-06-22/news/dp-tsq-mid-rape-case-continuance-062320110622_1_search-warrant-trial-date-gloucester-woman; Sampson, R. *Acquaintance rape of college students*. Problem-Oriented Guides for Police Series Number 17. Washington DC: U.S. Department of Justice. Office of Community Oriented Policing Services. Retrieved from http://www.cops.usdoj.gov.

Assaults and sexual assault are crimes that can escalate into murder:

1. Using the chapter material dealing with the sexual assault/rape investigative checklist, what evidence do you think the police might focus on in this case?

LEARNING OUTCOMES 1

Explain the legal definition of assault.

Assault and *battery* were formerly used to distinguish between threats and actual contact between suspect and victim. Today, many states categorize threats and physical contact as simple assault and aggravated assault, respectively. Some states do not require permanent or protracted injury or loss if the weapon used is a dangerous one that causes fear of harm or death.

1. What is the primary difference between simple and aggravated assault?

2. What kind of evidence can be used to demonstrate intent in a simple assault case?

3. What element/characteristic do simple assault and aggravated assault have in common?

4. What factors make investigating assault cases difficult?

5. Identify the best evidence in sexual assault cases.

simple assault Threats by one person to cause bodily harm or death to another or purposely inflicting bodily harm on another.

aggravated assault A personal crime associated with a high probability of death; serious, permanent disfigurement; permanent or protracted loss or impairment of the function of any body member or organ; or other severe bodily harm.

LEARNING OUTCOMES 2

Describe the problem of domestic violence.

Typically, patrol officers respond to domestic violence calls, and what responding officers do upon arrival often determines what happens in court, whether or not proper evidence will be collected, and whether an effective arrest will be conducted. Domestic violence cases can be hampered by the reluctance of female victims to testify against the abuser or their desire to drop charges.

1. What factors make domestic disputes potentially dangerous for law enforcement officers?

2. What factors are considered when determining whether an arrest should be made in a domestic violence case?

3. What are examples of evidence collected in domestic violence cases?

4. When women refuse to testify against an abuser who has been arrested, what recourse do a prosecutor and the courts have?

5. What issues must be first and foremost in the minds of the first officers arriving at the scene of a domestic dispute?

primary physical aggressor If the police have sufficient reason to believe that a person, within the preceding four hours, committed an active domestic violence or spousal battery, the officer is required to arrest a person. This person is known as the primary physical aggressor.

protection order A legal document that orders one person to stay away from another.

LEARNING OUTCOMES 3

Explain the methods of investigating stalking cases.

Although statutes vary from one state to another, most define stalking as a course of conduct that would place a reasonable person in fear for his or her safety. The majority of stalking victims are not physically attacked, but they do suffer psychological trauma. Many antistalking laws describe specific threatening conduct toward the victim.

1. What actions on the part of the victim can be used as evidence in a stalking case?

2. In states with antistalking laws, the burden of proof falls on which participant in the case?

3. Who are the primary victims of stalking?

4. Who are the primary perpetrators of stalking?

5. What problems are encountered when the victims of stalking are men?

6. What psychological and social consequences are associated with stalking?

7. What elements are included in many state definitions of the crime of stalking?

8. What are the causes of stalking?

LEARNING OUTCOMES 4

Describe the crime of sexual assault and rape.

There are three elements to the crime of rape when the female is over the age of consent. In many states, the victim must have resisted the assault and her resistance must have been overcome by force. The amount of resistance the victim displayed depends on the circumstances of the case. For the most part, there must be resistance on the part of the woman before there can be a foundation for a rape charge.

1. Why do many sexual assaults go unreported?

2. How does the definition of rape impact its reporting to law enforcement agencies and its overall rate of occurrence in statistical terms?

3. What are the three elements of the crime of rape when a female is over the age of consent?

4. What are the general exceptions to the rule of resistance in rape cases?

5. In rape cases, how is the concept of resistance determined?

rape Unlawful sexual intercourse, achieved through force and without consent.

resistance Physical or psychological unwillingness to comply.

LEARNING OUTCOMES 5

Identify evidence in rape cases.

Rape cases are somewhat unique in that evidence may present itself in three general areas. After the investigation is under way, the investigator should determine if there is any physical evidence to be collected. In terms of potential evidence, an investigator is limited only by his or her imagination when considering the types and locations of such articles.

1. What are the three areas in a rape case where evidence may be discovered?

2. During a rape investigation, what types of evidence should be considered by the investigator?

3. What are the duties of an officer at the scene of a rape?

4. What is the most critical component of an investigation following a sexual assault, and why is this component so critical? What are the goals of this component of the investigation?

LEARNING OUTCOMES 6

Explain techniques of rape victim interviews.

Most rape investigations should include a preliminary and subsequent in-depth interview with the victim. The preliminary interview conducted at the crime scene should be limited to gathering basic facts to identify the victim and to describe and locate the perpetrator in a timely manner. In-depth interviews should take place in a comfortable setting where there is privacy and freedom from distraction.

1. What role can a female officer play in a rape investigation?

2. What makes the victim interview in a rape investigation difficult for the criminal investigator?

3. What is the investigative role of the officer interviewing a rape victim? Why is this role a vital one?

4. How can an officer's attitude impact the interview process?

Additional Links

www.fbi.gov
The Uniform Crime Reporting Handbook can be found at this official site of the Federal Bureau of Investigation.

www.ncjrs.gov; http://samfe.dna.gov
For those interested in learning more about the National Protocol for Sexual Assault Medical Forensic Exam, visit these sites. The document can also be accessed under publications on the U.S. Department of Justice website.

www.Time.com; www.health.howstuffworks.com
For an overview of the Stockholm syndrome, see *Time* magazine's site as well as the howstuffworks site. The howstuffworks information is published in conjunction with Discovery Health.

www.ovw.usdoj.gov
This is the official site of the U.S. Department of Justice's Office on Violence Against Women. The site includes quick links to a variety of topics and data, including the grants program, as well as publications, press room, and other resources. It also includes a careers link that contains information on student opportunities and internships.

"The timely and thorough investigation of missing persons is one of the most important roles of a criminal investigator."

12

Missing and Abducted Persons

1 Summarize the complexity of the nation's missing persons problem.

2 Identify the different types of missing person cases.

3 Identify the investigative response to missing person cases.

4 Explain the role of the responding officer in missing person cases.

5 Explain the role of the criminal investigator in missing person cases.

WHEN A KIDNAPPED VICTIM IS FOUND 10 YEARS LATER

In May 2014, a woman told Santa Anna, California, police that she was kidnapped in 2004 by her mother's ex-boyfriend when she was 15 years old. She said that her abductor, Isidro Garcia, held her hostage for 10 years, during which time he married her and fathered a child with her. The victim (whose name was initially withheld) stated that Garcia drugged her by giving her pills and then drove her to a house in Compton where he held her in a locked garage.

Garcia moved them frequently and forced her to marry him in 2007—and they had a child in 2012, police said. The victim, 25 years old when the story surfaced, came

Photo of Isidro Garcia following his 2014 arrest for allegedly kidnapping a 15-year-old, keeping her in captivity for 10 years, and fathering a child with her.

SAPD/Splash News/Newscom

forward after contacting her sister via Facebook. The girl's mother reported her missing to police in August 2004.

Investigators learned that the victim arrived with her mother and sister from Mexico illegally in February 2004 and spoke no English. Six months later she was kidnapped. Garcia knew the victim's mother. Police records showed that he fought with her mother in August 2004 and left, taking the 15-year-old girl with him. She told investigators he gave her pills that knocked her out, and that she awoke in a garage in Compton. Garcia was arrested and held on $1 million bail. He was 41 years old at the time of his arrest.

The case is eerily similar to the 1991 kidnapping of Jaycee Dugard. Dugard was kidnapped by Phillip Craig Garrido when she was 11 years old. It wasn't until 2009 that Dugard was discovered in Garrido's home in South Lake Tahoe, California—18 years after her abduction. During the time she was in captivity, she gave birth to two of Garrido's children—both girls, who were 11 and 15 years old at the time Dugard was found.

DISCUSS How can a child go missing for over a decade before being found? Is there anything law enforcement could be doing better to locate victims of child abduction?

▶ *Understanding the "Big Picture"*

LEARNING OUTCOMES 1 Summarize the complexity of the nation's missing persons problem.

All too often we hear of yet another missing person in the United States. For example, in addition to stories like those discussed earlier in this chapter, we must remember the disappearance of Natalie Holloway. Holloway was a 19-year-old student who disappeared on May 30, 2005, during a high school graduation trip to Aruba. She has not been located as of the preparation of this book.

The incidence of missing children is alarming. For example, as of December 2010, the National Crime Information Center (NCIC) of the Federal Bureau of Investigation (FBI) contained 85,820 active missing person records. Of those, juveniles under the age of 18 accounted for 38,505 (44.9 percent) of the records and 10,248 (11.9 percent) were juveniles between the ages of 18 and 20.

Missing person cases include both children and adults. While this chapter addresses both categories, it focuses primarily on the thousands of children who are discovered missing each year. The magnitude of the missing and abducted problem is complex, multifaceted, and disturbing. For example, there are different types of missing children cases, including family abductions; endangered runaways; nonfamily abductions; and lost, injured, or otherwise missing children. National estimates for the number of missing children are from incidence studies

conducted by the U.S. Department of Justice's Office of Juvenile Justice and Delinquency Prevention.

Statistics show that there are an estimated 100 cases per year in the United States in which a child is abducted and murdered. The victims of these cases are "average" children leading normal lives and living with normal families, that is, typical low-risk victims. The vast majority of them are girls (76 percent), with the average age being slightly older than 11 years of age. In 80 percent of cases, the initial contact between the victim and killer is within 1/4 mile of the victim's residence.[1]

Profiling the Abductor: Stranger versus Non-Stranger

According to the National Center for Missing and Exploited Children (NCMEC), every year, more than 200,000 children are abducted by family members.[2] An additional 58,000 are taken by non-relatives with primarily sexual motives. However, only 115 reported abductions represent cases in which strangers abduct and kill children, hold them for ransom, or take them with the intention to keep them, such as in the Jaycee Dugard case.[3]

Media news outlets have portrayed that abductors primarily consist of strangers or registered sex offenders (RSOs),

MISSING

In 2009, the National Center for Missing and Exploited Children reported the following instances of missing and abducted children:

- 797,500 children (younger than age 18 years) were reported missing in a one-year period of time studied. This is an average of 2,185 children being reported missing each day.

- 203,900 children were the victims of family abductions.

- 58,200 children were the victims of nonfamily abductions.

- 115 children were the victims of "stereotypical" kidnapping. (These crimes involve someone the child does not know or someone of slight acquaintance who holds the child overnight, transports the child 50 miles or more, kills the child, demands ransom, or intends to keep the child permanently.)

Source: J. Wolak, K. Mitchell, and D. Finkelhor (2006). On-line victimizations of youth. Washington, D.C.: Office of Juvenile Justice Programs. National Center for Missing and Exploited Children.

Children Who Are Killed

Considering the previous discussion, the relationship between the victim and the killer varies with the gender and age of the victim. According to NISMART, whereas the youngest girls, one to five years old, tended to be killed by friends or acquaintances (64 percent), the oldest young women, 16 to 17 years old, tended to be killed by strangers (also 64 percent). The relationship between the killer and victim is different for the male victims. The youngest male victims (one to five years old) were most likely to be killed by strangers (also 64 percent), as were teenage boys (13 to 15 years old, and 16 to 17 years old, 58 percent).[7]

The average age of killers of abducted children in the NISMART study was around 27 years old. They were predominantly unmarried (85 percent) and half of them (51 percent) either lived alone (17 percent) or with their parents (34 percent). Half of them were unemployed, and those who were employed worked in unskilled or semi-skilled labor occupations. Therefore, the killers can generally be characterized as "social marginals."

Almost two-thirds of the killers (61 percent) in the NISMART study had prior arrests for violent crimes, with slightly more than half of the killers' prior crimes (53 percent) committed against children. The most frequent prior crimes against children were rape (31 percent of killers) and other sexual assault (45 percent of killers). Sixty-seven percent of the child abduction murderers'

which has proven invalid based on research. When a child is reported missing, members of the media advise parents to check sex offender registries to prevent their child from possible abduction or sexual victimization. According to the FBI, however, statistics show that RSOs are a minimal part of the problem.[4] In 2009, an RSO was the abductor in only 2 percent of child abduction cases; in 2010, this figure dropped to 1 percent.[5]

Although parents teach their children to stay away from strangers, most neglect to teach them not to allow anyone, even someone they know, to take them without parental consent. Additionally, children frequently are instructed to obey elders without question, adding to their vulnerability to offenders known to the child victim.

A kidnapping is the type of abduction that is most harmful to the child, both psychologically and physically. Many child abductions also involve some type of sexual abuse. An earlier study funded by the Justice Department's Office of Juvenile Justice and Delinquency Prevention (OJJDP) provided additional insight on the child abduction problem. This 1997 survey examined 600 abduction cases across the nation. The findings were very similar to those of the **National Incidence Studies of Missing, Abducted, Runaway and Thrown-Away Children (NISMART) project**.[6] See Box 12–1 for definitions of runaway and thrown-away children.

BOX 12–1 🛡 Defining Runaway/Thrown-Away Children

A runaway child episode is one that meets any one of the following criteria:

- A child leaves home without permission and stays away overnight.

- A child 14 years old or younger (or older and mentally incompetent) who is away from home chooses not to come home when expected to and stays away overnight.

- A child 15 years old or older who is away from home chooses not to come home and stays away two nights.

A thrown-away child episode is one that meets either of the following criteria:

- A child is asked or told to leave home by a parent or other household adult, no adequate alternative care is arranged for the child by a household adult, and the child is out of the household overnight.

- A child who is away from home is prevented from returning home by a parent or other household adult, no adequate alternative care is arranged for the child by a household adult, and the child is out of the household overnight.

Source: NISMART. (2014). Conceptualizing the problem. Retrieved from https://www.ncjrs.gov/html/ojjdp/nismart/04/ns2.html.

A unique pattern of distance relationships exists in child abduction murders. The initial contact site is within 1/4 mile of the victim's last known location in 80 percent of cases.

Conversely, the distance between the initial contact site and the murder site increases to distances greater than 1/4 mile (54 percent). The distance from the murder site to the body recovery site again decreases to less than 200 feet in 72 percent of cases.

Distance Pattern in Child Abduction Murders.

nonfamily abductions and family abductions is in the treatment of the victim. In 99 percent of nonfamily abductions, the child is returned alive. In nonfamily abductions, a safe return occurs only 57 percent of the time. Ominously, the child suffers a sexual or physical assault in an astounding 86 percent of stereotypical kidnappings. These findings powerfully emphasize the extreme danger of these events and the urgency of police interaction as soon as possible.

Stereotypical kidnappings, in which a child is abducted and either assaulted or held for ransom, is a crime that first appeared in the United States in the late nineteenth century. During the 1920s, it became entrenched in the public consciousness when a series of child abduction cases terrified parents across the country.

prior crimes were similar in method of operation (MO) to the child abduction murder.

Commonly, the killers in the NISMART study were at the initial victim–killer contact site for a legitimate reason (66 percent). They either lived in the area (29 percent) or were engaging in some normal activity. Most of the victims of child abduction murder were victims of opportunity (57 percent). Only in 14 percent of cases did the killer choose his victim because of some physical characteristic of the victim. The primary motivation for the child abduction murder was sexual assault. After the victims were killed, 52 percent of the bodies were concealed to prevent discovery. In only 9 percent of cases was the body openly placed to ensure its discovery. NISMART also noted that once the murder investigation had begun, the name of the killer was known to the police within the first week in 74 percent of cases.[8]

Abductor Characteristics and Factors

The Elizabeth Smart kidnapping emphasizes several characteristics that child abductors seem to have in common. First, they most often have a prior visual sighting of the victim, and the initial contact is frequently made at or near the home. Second, the motivation for the crime is often sexual in nature. The victim is usually a girl younger than 14 years old, and the suspect is usually an unemployed white male with a criminal record. Although the alleged kidnapper in the Smart case, Brian Mitchell, was 20 years older than the NISMART average, he fit the profile reasonably well. Elizabeth Smart could be considered a very lucky victim. That's because girls her age who are abducted under similar circumstances stand a very good chance of being killed.

The duration of a kidnapping episode is usually less than 24 hours (90 percent). Only fewer than 10 percent last longer than one day. Nonfamily abductions (stereotypical kidnappings) show the same patterns, although 30 percent of them last less than three hours. The most dramatic difference between

▶ Types of Missing Children Cases

In general, missing children cases fall into three basic categories: nonfamily abduction, family abduction, and runaway (or lost).

The **nonfamily abduction** case, in which a child is removed without authorization from his or her family by force or trickery, is the most complex and dangerous type of missing child case. In this situation, time is of the essence because the child is considered to be in great danger. Many experts believe that the first few hours after an abduction are the most dangerous for children.

Also included in this category are abductions of newborns and infants from health care facilities, malls, grocery stores, and public transportation facilities, as well as other public places where the mother's or childcare provider's attention may be diverted. Although the snatching of newborns is not a crime of epidemic proportions, naturally, it causes tremendous trauma for the parents or guardians. The offender almost always is a woman and generally does not harm the baby because she usually abducts the child in order to have a baby of her own.

The second type of case is the **family abduction**, which generally occurs in conjunction with divorce and separation. In this type of case, the noncustodial parent removes the child from the care of the custodial parent and may flee to another state or even another country with the child. The child may be at risk with the noncustodial parent. There have been recent cases across the nation in which the child of a family abduction was murdered by the noncustodial parent, who then committed suicide. Family abductions are often very complex cases involving court orders, child protection services, and hidden agendas, as well as raw emotions and sometimes extreme possessiveness toward the children on the part of one or both parents.

The third type of missing child case involves the **runaway or lost child**, who could be in great danger depending on such factors as age, maturity, and intelligence. The voluntary runaway child is the most common missing child case encountered by law enforcement officers.

Abductions via the Internet

Some child abductions have been connected to the Internet as a result of the easy access both the child and predator have to this worldwide communications network. Susceptible preteens and teens are sometimes lured into false friendships in Internet "chat rooms" and then kidnapped from a prearranged meeting place. In other cases, the abductor may send the child money and a bus ticket to meet in another state. Children and teens who get involved in chat room conversations on the Internet have no way to know exactly who they're talking to. One of the many attractions of chat rooms is the anonymity they provide. People can be anyone they choose to be online, where real identities are hidden and fictitious names and personalities emerge.

In one case, a preteen boy was lured to San Francisco by an adult male pedophile with a large collection of child pornography. The youth told his friends at school and showed them the bus ticket and money he was sent. His friends revealed this information to the police only after the boy was reported missing. A nationwide search was initiated, and they were questioned.

How do investigators determine if a missing child case involves an Internet lure? A computer in a child's room or home with an Internet connection can steer the investigation in this direction, especially if the parents or guardians reveal that the child spent a lot of time "online" and talked about new friends made via "chat rooms." Another clue is the sudden disappearance of the child for no apparent reason (for example, there was no recent fight between the child and parents, yet the child was gone one day when the parents returned from work). In a case like this, the investigator should check to see whether the child took any favorite possessions, a suitcase, a duffle bag or backpack, clothes, or money. Missing possessions indicate a runaway, but runaways are not always what they appear to be.

Recovering Endangered Children

With the goal of effectively recovering endangered children, how do authorities decide if a missing child fits the criteria specified for broadcast? The U.S. Department of Justice, the organizing agency nationwide, recommends that law enforcement agencies

- reasonably believe that an abduction has occurred.
- believe that the child is in imminent danger of serious bodily injury or death.
- have enough descriptive information about the victim and the abduction to issue an Amber Alert to assist in the recovery of the child.
- know that the abducted child is 17 years of age or younger.
- have entered the child's name and other critical data elements, including flagging it as a child abduction, into NCIC.

Other clues to the child's disappearance can be found on the computer itself. The computer may yield electronic mail (e-mail) saved on the hard drive, a disk, or a printout. The child may have left notes in schoolbooks that can provide clues, such as the online friend's address, phone number, or e-mail address. Before searching computers for data and evidence, the investigator should consult with the department attorney as well as agency computer specialists because complex investigations involving computer systems and online access services present unique technical, operational, and legal problems.

Because of the threat Internet predators pose, there have been efforts to use the Internet as a resource to prevent child abduction or to help the families of those who have been abducted. Many organizations have set up websites where users can go to gain knowledge or contribute help to stopping child abduction. Among these are the organizations Enough is Enough and National Center for Missing and Exploited Children, which have partnered with the online community MySpace to help keep the Internet a safe place for children. MySpace also features pages and groups dedicated to helping find missing children.[9]

Code Adam

Code Adam is a "missing child" program that was implemented in the United States and Canada. The program was initially created in 1994 by Walmart retail stores. It is named in memory of Adam Walsh, the 6-year-old son of John Walsh (the host of Fox Network's *America's Most Wanted*). In 1981, Adam was abducted from a Sears department store in Florida and was later found brutally murdered. Today, many department stores, retail shops, shopping malls, supermarkets, amusement parks, and museums participate in the Code Adam program. In 2003, Congress enacted legislation that currently mandates that all federal office buildings use the program.[10]

Walmart, along with the NCMEC and the departments of several state attorney generals, have offered to assist in training workshops for other companies to implement the program. Researchers, however, point out that the fear of child abduction is out of proportion with its incidence. Specifically, they point to the long-term persistence of retail kidnapping narratives in urban legends to highlight how parents had been sensitized to this issue for generations before the Adam Walsh incident.[11]

Think About It...

Should Violent Criminals Also Be Registered? ... Almost two-thirds of the killers of abducted children had prior arrests for violent crimes. Knowing this statistic, do you think people convicted of violent crimes should have to register their addresses with local law enforcement, just as sex offenders do?

© Craig Steven Thrasher/Alamy

Missing Person Poster.

Megan's Laws and Jessica's Law

Megan's Laws

Megan's laws is an informal name for laws in the United States requiring law enforcement authorities to make information available to the public regarding registered sex offenders. Individual states decide what information will be made available and how it should be disseminated. Commonly included information includes the offender's name, picture, address, incarceration date, and the nature of the crime. The information is often displayed on free public websites but can also be published in newspapers, distributed in pamphlets, or distributed through various other means.

At the federal level, **Megan's law** is known as the Sexual Offender (Jacob Wetterling) Act of 1994 and requires persons convicted of sex crimes against children to notify local law enforcement of any change of address or employment after release from custody (prison or psychiatric facility). The notification requirement may be imposed for a fixed period of time—usually at least 10 years—or permanently. Some states may legislate registration for all sex crimes, even if no minors were involved. It is a felony in most jurisdictions to fail to register or fail to update information.

Megan's laws provide two major information services to the public: sex offender registration and community notification. The details of what is provided as part of sex offender registration and how community notification is handled vary from state to state, and in some states, the required registration information and community notification protocols have changed many times since Megan's laws were passed. The Adam Walsh Child Protection and Safety Act supplements Megan's laws with new registration requirements and a "three-tier" system for classifying sex offenders according to their risk to the community.

Jessica's Law

Jessica's law is the informal name given to a 2005 Florida law, as well as laws modeled after the Florida law in several other states, designed to punish sex offenders and reduce their ability to reoffend. Forty-two states have introduced such legislation since Florida's law was passed, and a version of Jessica's law has been introduced on the federal level, known as the Jessica Lunsford Act.

The law is named after Jessica Lunsford, a young Florida girl who was raped and murdered in February 2005 by John Couey, a previously convicted sex offender. Public outrage over this incident spurred Florida officials to introduce this legislation. Among the key provisions of the (Florida) law are a mandatory minimum sentence of 25 years in prison and lifetime electronic monitoring of adults convicted of lewd or lascivious acts against a victim younger than 12 years old. In Florida, sexual battery or rape of a child younger than 12 years old is punishable only by life imprisonment with no chance of parole.

Sources: Levenson, J. S., & Cotter, L. P. (2005). The effect of Megan's Law on sex offender reintegration. *Journal of Contemporary Criminal Justice, 21*(1), 49–66. doi:10.1177/1043986204271676; Levenson, J. S., D'Amora, D. A., & Hern, A. L. (2007). Megan's Law and its impact on community re-entry for sex offenders. *Behavioral Sciences & the Law, 25*(4), 587–602. doi:10.1002/bsl.770; Welchans, S. (2005). Megan's Law: Evaluations of sexual offender registries. *Criminal Justice Policy Review, 16*(2), 123–140. doi:10.1177/0887403404265630; Wilson, D. (2009, March 21). Appleton attorney fights "Jessica's Law" on mandatory sex offender sentencing. *Post-Crescent*; Florida Statute 800.04; Florida Statute 947.1405.

Companies that do implement the program generally place a Code Adam decal at the front of the business. Employees at these businesses are trained to follow these six steps, according to the National Center for Missing and Exploited Children:

1. If a visitor reports that a child is missing, a detailed description of the child and what he or she is wearing is obtained. Additionally, all exterior access to the building is locked and monitored; anyone approaching a door is turned away.

2. The employee goes to the nearest in-house telephone and pages Code Adam, describing the child's physical features and clothing. As designated employees monitor front entrances, other employees begin looking for the child.

3. If the child is not found within 10 minutes, law enforcement is called.

4. If the child is found and appears to have been lost and unharmed, the child is reunited with the searching family member.

5. If the child is found accompanied by someone other than a parent or legal guardian, reasonable efforts to delay their departure will be used without putting the child, staff, or visitors at risk. Law enforcement will be notified and given details about the person accompanying the child.

6. The Code Adam page will be canceled after the child is found or law enforcement arrives.

Six Steps of Code Adam.

▶ *The Investigative Response*

LEARNING OUTCOMES 3 Identify the investigative response to missing person cases.

From an investigative standpoint, child kidnapping is one of the most emotionally charged and difficult criminal cases for law enforcement officers. Time is the merciless enemy. In 1997, the U.S. Office of Juvenile Justice Delinquency and Prevention (OJJDP) reported that most children (74 percent) who are murdered during stranger kidnappings are killed within the first few hours of the event. Therefore, it is imperative that investigators use every tool available to them, including the awesome power of the media.

By its very nature, abduction must take priority over many types of cases. Research has indicated that strangers who commit the offense with the intention of fulfilling a sexual desire often murder their victims within three hours.[12] In contrast, a noncustodial parent may take the child to use as a weapon against his or her former significant other. In either situation, time may be very short. The person responsible for the investigation must be called immediately to the scene. No agency would assign a homicide investigator a case the next morning and then reconstruct the incident from police reports.

Abductions can be even more complex than some murders. As with all violent suspects, law enforcement officers use proven methods to locate them. All of these and more also come into play during the investigation of an abduction.

As with any other investigations, however, the best efforts by police may not lead to a quick resolution of a case. If the incident is a stranger abduction, law enforcement administrators must be prepared for the anger of the family to be redirected toward their agency. These family members are hurt and, especially if the victim is not recovered, need closure. When this is lacking, they react like any other human being and find somewhere to refocus their anger. Departmental procedures prepared in advance can help investigators cope with such difficulties and reassure the family that authorities are doing all they can.[13]

Noncustodial parental abductions can prove equally dangerous to a child. Often, the suspect takes the child and starts another life outside the investigating agency's jurisdiction. Again, investigators need to recognize and use the methods they would in any other criminal investigation. In most states, a noncustodial parental abduction is a felony.

Early in the investigation, agencies may want to request an off-line search from NCIC. Usually, abductions are planned, and within minutes of the act the suspect may have left the jurisdiction with the child. Often, the abductor may drive too fast, leading to a stop on a traffic violation. The custodial parent may not even know that an abduction has occurred before the suspect has fled the state. An off-line search can show the location of the stop, thereby giving investigators an indication of the abductor's possible destination.

In 2005, this tactic worked for an investigator in Indianapolis, Indiana. A mother was allowed to make an unsupervised visitation with her child, a ward of the state because of the woman's history of drug abuse and neglect. When the mother did not return as scheduled, a child protective services worker made a police report. Officers had no idea which direction the woman would go. An off-line search revealed that an officer in Missouri had stopped her for a traffic violation only a few hours after she had picked up the child for the visit and before the Indianapolis police received the report of the missing child. Through a variety of tools, including federal assistance agencies, the Indianapolis investigator tracked the woman to Long Beach, California, where detectives located the suspect and her children living in a van under a bridge. Extradited to Indianapolis, she was prosecuted and convicted on the felony charge. The judge in the case felt that she would continue to be a danger to her children and sentenced her to a prison term.[14]

The Initial Call for Assistance

The initial response to a missing child call is perhaps the most crucial component of the investigation. The manner in which patrol officers respond to the initial call often determines whether the child is found quickly and returned home safely, remains missing for months or years, or is never found.

In most law enforcement agencies, the patrol officer is the first responder to missing child calls. Therefore, all patrol officers need to be trained to respond to such calls efficiently, compassionately, and professionally— paying particular attention to safeguarding evidence, quickly obtaining as much information as possible about the child and the circumstances, interviewing

witnesses, and at the same time calming and reassuring the parents or guardians of the missing child. But before the patrol officer even arrives on the scene, information about the missing child should be relayed from the dispatcher to the responding officers. Dispatch operators, working with a standard list of predetermined questions, should gather pertinent information from the caller and relay it to the responding officers. After the dispatch operator has calmed the caller, basic facts and information, including a brief description of the missing child and information about a possible abductor(s), can be gathered to help the responding officers.

▶ *Responding Officer Responsibilities*

The patrol officer initially establishes the seriousness of the complaint about a missing child, safeguards the scene, gathers crucial facts, and conducts preliminary interviews of witnesses. For this reason, patrol officers must learn to become as thorough as they can in responding to missing child reports. Assumptions about such cases must be avoided or officers may overlook crucial information and evidence.

LEARNING OUTCOMES 4 — Explain the role of the responding officer in missing person cases.

To initiate a successful missing persons investigation, the first responder must focus on quickly gathering factual information and safeguarding potential evidence. This is particularly the case with regard to missing children, whether they may be abducted, runaway, or lost. This may also be true of some elderly persons or others who, because of physical or mental disability or reduced functioning, are not fully capable of taking care of themselves. The elderly, especially those suffering from Alzheimer's disease or similar problems, present specific concerns as the subjects of missing persons reports. Open terrain searches for missing persons in general also require adherence to professionally recognized search management principles. Some of the most widely accepted principles of searching for missing persons are discussed later in this chapter.

The patrol officer who responds to the call is best suited to obtain the details of the initial account, particularly because the

Even before charges are filed, however, the law enforcement agency can enter the child, the suspect, and the suspect's vehicle into NCIC. If the department cross-references all of the information, it will alert officers in other jurisdictions, who may stop the suspect on a traffic violation and possibly recover the child. The custodial parent then can make arrangements to retrieve the child. After the felony warrant is on file and if investigators believe the suspect has fled their jurisdiction, the FBI can help obtain a warrant for unlawful flight to avoid prosecution. This enables a wide variety of federal resources to come into play, including the Federal Parent Locator Service, which coordinates with such agencies as the Internal Revenue Service, the U.S. Social Security Administration, and the U.S. Department of Agriculture to monitor the issuance of checks; it also notifies law enforcement if the suspect registers for or receives any type of public assistance.

Law Enforcement Actions for a Child Abducted by a Parent.

officer patrols the area or neighborhood and is likely to notice any unusual activities or suspicious persons. The officer should respond to the call promptly, as the time factor is often crucial, especially in cases involving abductions by strangers.

In 1994, the NCMEC developed a checklist for first responders in missing children cases, listing tasks an officer should complete to ensure a successful investigation.[15] These steps are general, but they do provide a framework for the officer's actions.

The 16 Steps of Investigation

Sixteen tasks commonly associated with the responsibilities of the first responder are identified in this chapter. However, it is recognized that in the real world, many tasks of first responders, supervisors, and investigators are not distinctly or conveniently divided between these respective agency personnel. The following 16 steps are those that should nominally be taken by officers. It should be understood that not every step may pertain to all situations, nor do the steps need to be addressed in the exact order in which they are presented here.

Step 1: Interview Parents or the Person Who Made the Initial Report to the Emergency Operations Center (EOC)

This interview should be conducted in an area where interruptions are minimal and that is, preferably, private. The purpose of the interview is to obtain a complete description of the missing child, circumstances of how the child came to be missing, and information necessary to make an initial definition and assessment of the type of case.

Case example: The complainant may be the operator of a preschool who reports that the child was approached by a man whom the child called "Daddy." The man then put the child in a car and left without speaking to any of the adults at the school. One of the teachers, however, obtained the license tag number of the car. Further questioning of the complainant reveals that the child's parents are divorced and engaged in a bitter custody dispute, although the court has awarded custody to the mother. The officer can make a preliminary assessment that this is a family abduction that may not warrant calling in additional personnel. *Consider another case example*: The mother of a five-year-old girl calls from the mall to report that her daughter is missing; the line of questioning and initial actions of the responding officer should be very different from the school scenario because all initial signs point to a possible abduction by a stranger.

Step 2: Verify That the Child Is in Fact Missing

Here the officer needs to make certain that the child cannot be located on the premises or nearby. In the preschool case just described, 3 teachers and 40 children (ranging in age from two to five) saw the missing boy (aged three) run and greet his father and then leave in the car. At the mall, a search of the grounds by security officers failed to turn up the missing five-year-old girl. However, when the patrol officer asked the mother if she had checked her vehicle in the parking lot, the mother said no. The officer went with the mother to the parking lot and found the

girl asleep on the back floor of the family van, which had been left unlocked. The little girl said she was tired and went to take a nap without telling her mother because "Mommy was talking to the lady about the furniture, and Mommy told me not to interrupt when grown-ups are talking to each other. So I just came to the van to take a nap." Case closed.

Step 3: Verify the Child's Custody Status

With divorce so prevalent in the United States and custody battles a common denominator in the lives of many children, the patrol officer should ask the parent if there has been a divorce or separation and, if so, which parent has primary legal custody. If there has been a marital breakup, the officer should raise the issue of a possible abduction of the child by the **noncustodial parent**. Another area of inquiry involves possible emotional problems affecting the child; if the child is taking the parental breakup badly and falsely assuming blame, then he or she may have run away.

Step 4: Identify the Circumstances of the Disappearance

Did the child disappear from home or from the residence of a relative or friend? Is the child missing after a visit with a noncustodial parent? Is the child missing from a public place, such as a shopping mall, park, amusement center, or school playground? Was the child seen talking to a stranger? Did the child disappear while the parent or guardian's attention was focused elsewhere, such as paying for a purchase or loading groceries into a vehicle? The NCMEC lists several unusual circumstances that alert the first responding patrol officer to "pull out all the stops" by requesting additional personnel, supervisory and investigative assistance, and any special support units that may be needed, such as K-9 and helicopters. The need for other resources, such as assistance from other law enforcement agencies, fire department search and rescue teams, neighborhood watch teams, and others, can be determined by a field supervisor. When one or more of these circumstances is present, the patrol officer should take immediate action and call for mobilization of additional resources.

Step 5: Determine When, Where, and by Whom the Missing Child Was Last Seen

For example, if the child disappeared while the parent or guardian was paying for groceries, did any of the cashiers, store employees, or other shoppers see the child leave the store with anyone? If the child disappeared while walking to school, did any residents or delivery persons on the child's route witness the child getting into a vehicle? Interview everyone who may have been in a position to see the child.

Step 6: Interview the Individuals Who Last Had Contact with the Child

It is especially important to interview the child's friends if the child is a preteen or teenager. Friends of older children often know more about the child's attitudes, emotions, and plans than the parents or guardians. Perhaps friends will reveal that the child is having trouble with his father and is staying with another friend. A teacher may reveal that the child's noncustodial parent came to the school to get permission to remove the child from school because the child was being taken to a dental appointment.

Step 7: Identify the Child's Zone of Safety for His or Her Age and Developmental Stage

Try to determine how far the child could travel from the spot where last seen before he or she would most likely be at risk of being injured or exploited. This perimeter should define the first immediate search zone under many circumstances.

Step 8: Make an Initial Determination of the Type of Incident

Based on the available information, determine whether the incident appears to be a nonfamily abduction; family abduction; endangered runaway; or lost, injured, or otherwise missing person. This initial classification will help the officer begin investigative actions. To make the initial classification, the officer should analyze the information already gathered. However, officers must be extremely cautious in **labeling**, or classifying, a missing child case, because the classification process will affect the way initial evidence or information is gathered.

Step 9: Obtain a Detailed Description of the Missing Child, Suspected Abductor(s), Vehicles, and the Like

If several people are at the scene, each person should be interviewed separately by the officer to obtain descriptions of a possible suspect and vehicle. Witnesses should not be interviewed in the presence of other witnesses because there is a tendency on the part of some to "go along"—either consciously or unconsciously—with a description given by another witness. As most officers know, the perception and recall of witnesses can be faulty, and when they use each other to fill in missing details in their memories, important details may be lost.

Step 10: Relay Detailed Descriptive Information to the EOC for Relay to Other Law Enforcement Agencies and Information Referral Sources

Supervisors, in consultation with the public information officer or agency chief executive, may decide at this time to provide descriptive information to the news media to generate assistance from the public in locating the missing child or encouraging any witnesses to come forward.

Step 11: Ensure That Any Remaining Persons at the Scene Are Identified and Interviewed and Information Is Properly Recorded

To aid in this process, take pictures or videotape everyone present, if possible. Note the name, address, and home or business telephone numbers of each person. Determine each person's relationship to the missing child, if any. Note information that each person may have about the child's disappearance. Determine when or where each person last saw the child. Ask each one, "What do you think happened to the child?" Obtain the names, addresses, and telephone numbers of the child's friends and other relatives and friends of the family.

Step 12: Continue to Update the Emergency Dispatcher and Other Appropriate Department Personnel

Periodically update the public information officer or department spokesperson. If there is no media relations officer or supervisor on the scene handling these duties, the senior officer at the scene may be asked to provide periodic updates to media personnel. Under such circumstances, the officer must follow the agency's media relations policies and procedures, being careful not to release information that could jeopardize an investigation, falsely accuse individuals, or inadvertently implicate anyone in a crime.

Step 13: Obtain and Record Permission to Search Houses or Buildings

This includes any locations where the incident took place or where entry is required to conduct the investigation. To search a house or apartment, obtain the permission of the owner or renter. In the case of a building, such as a shopping mall or store, obtain the manager's permission or the permission of any private security firm working on the premises. Be sure to search any surrounding areas, including vehicles, parking lots, storage sheds, garbage containers, truck trailers at loading docks, warehouse areas behind stores, construction sites, shrubbery, culverts, and other places of concealment.

Even if the child was reported missing from a public place, such as a shopping mall, it is highly advisable to seek permission for a thorough search of the child's home. In some recent cases, the child was murdered in the home, leaving bloodstain evidence, and after disposing of the body the parents or guardians drove to a public place (for example, mall, gas station), called the police, and reported that the child had been abducted from that location. By not searching the home, vital evidence of a crime can be lost.

Step 14: Secure and Safeguard the Crime Scene

This includes securing the area where the incident took place or the location at which the child was last seen as a crime scene in order to safeguard vital evidence. The patrol officer must take control of the immediate area where the incident occurred and establish an appropriate perimeter to avoid destruction of vital evidence.

Step 15: Obtain Photos, Videotapes, and Any Other Identifying Information on Suspects

In particular, any photos of the suspect should be relayed to the shift commander as soon as possible. In some cases, the first responder may be able to secure photos or videos.

Step 16: Prepare Reports and Make All Required Notifications

Ensure that information about the missing child is entered into the FBI's NCIC Missing Persons File and that any information on a suspected abductor is entered into the NCIC Wanted Persons File.

The Importance of the Neighborhood Canvass

In 2012, the FBI reported that in 76 percent of child abduction murders, the victim was killed within 3 hours of the reported abduction, and in 89 percent of child abduction murders, the victim was killed within 24 hours.[16] These statistics illustrate the importance of getting the investigation under way immediately after a child is reported missing. A neighborhood canvass is one such method. Research shows that the majority of successfully resolved child abduction cases included a neighborhood canvass.[17]

At times, law enforcement personnel overlook or fail to prioritize the importance of this investigative measure. Yet, according to the FBI's Behavioral Analysis Unit's (BAU) Child Abduction Response Plan (CARP), the neighborhood canvass is, perhaps, the most vital step in missing children cases.[18]

A neighborhood canvass may cover the area around the victim's residence or last known location—the most recent place

the victim was sighted after the initial abduction. A proper neighborhood canvass provides information about the physical location and people who live nearby. Thorough searches of the victim's neighborhood and last known location, in combination with interviews, help investigators develop possible suspects and establish a timeline for the missing child. According to BAU's CARP, in many cases, the offender resided, worked, frequently visited, or otherwise spent time in the immediate area of the abduction.[19] If executed quickly and properly, a neighborhood canvass can provide crucial information about potential suspects.

A thorough neighborhood canvass allows investigators to search for the missing child while identifying and interviewing all individuals near the victim's abduction site or last known location during the critical period that follows a child's disappearance. In the hours immediately following an abduction, investigators must begin the canvass promptly. This is because there typically is a two-hour delay in missing children being reported to authorities.[20] During this process, officers should interview every resident and visitor from the neighborhood in question.

Furthermore, any missing child case poses numerous possibilities for the cause of the victim's disappearance aside from abduction. The victim could be a runaway, lost child, "throwaway" child, or victim of accidental death. Moreover, the abduction could have been entirely fabricated to cover up a family member's crime against the victim or other such domestic issue. Evaluating the previously discussed items will eliminate some possibilities of how the child disappeared, reveal the options that remain, and help investigators decide which leads they need to pursue.

▶ The Investigator's Role

Many of the duties of the investigator in a missing or abducted child case are the same as those used in conducting almost any type of investigation. Indeed, some have been referenced in chapters related to the first responding officer and supervisory responsibilities.

LEARNING OUTCOMES 5 — Explain the role of the criminal investigator in missing person cases.

Moving Forward with the Investigation

Investigators can take eight basic steps to help ensure a successful outcome in a missing or abducted child case. These procedures are geared more toward nonfamily abduction cases and situations in which a child disappears and could be in danger. Family abduction and runaway (or lost) child investigative procedures are covered in depth in the NCMEC's manual.

Step 1: Obtain a Detailed Briefing from the First Responding Officer and Other On-Scene Personnel

The investigator should debrief the first responding officer before conducting any interviews with family members of the missing child or witnesses who may have been identified in the early stages of the case. A thorough debriefing of the first responder will help the investigator analyze the information in order to formulate an approach to upcoming interviews of family members and witnesses.

Step 2: Verify the Accuracy of All Descriptive Information

The verification process should include all other details developed during the preliminary investigation. At this point, the investigator should begin interviewing the missing child's family members and possible witnesses to determine the facts and sort out any conflicting information obtained by the first responder and other officers on the scene.

Step 3: Obtain a Brief Recent History of Family Dynamics

This process will help the investigator hypothesize about various possibilities involving the disappearance of the child. Was the family the truly loving, close-knit family the mother tearfully described to the first responder? Or were there previous police calls to the residence for domestic disturbances? Has the child's school reported the family to social service agencies for possible abuse of the child? Is there a large life insurance policy on a four-year-old child? If so, why? Is the missing little girl an "ugly duckling" with a learning disability while the mother is the glamorous "prom queen" type with a live-in boyfriend who spends all his money on drugs and alcohol? Answers to such questions, often obtained from neighbors, friends of the child, and other family members, can offer invaluable insights to what may have happened to the child and where the child may now be located.

Step 4: Explore the Basis for Conflicting Information

Information offered by witnesses and other individuals may not coincide. Thus, the investigator needs to conduct in-depth fact-finding interviews with all witnesses, friends, and relatives of the child and the child's parents or guardians necessary to resolve those conflicts. It is at this point that the investigator may consider asking the parents or guardians to submit to a polygraph examination.

Step 5: Review and Evaluate All Available Information and Evidence

At this point, an information management system becomes a critical tool in the investigative process. The investigator should designate another investigator, a crime analyst, or a patrol officer to serve as the case information manager, centralizing all data as they are gathered, making comparisons, and keeping track of leads and tips. Appointing one person to be in charge of all information pertaining to the case helps ensure that valuable data will not become misdirected and possibly lost.

Step 6: Develop an Investigative Plan for Follow-Up

By evaluating evidence and the information gathered from interviews of police officers, witnesses, the child's parents or guardians, and others, the investigator can prepare a follow-up plan, which may include the following tasks:

1. Conduct more in-depth interviews with specific people who have been questioned previously.

Cell Phone Tracking

Cell phones are constantly scanning for the nearest network connection. Using triangulation—measuring the time it takes for the signal to travel from the phone to three cell towers—authorities can locate a cell phone within about 500 feet.

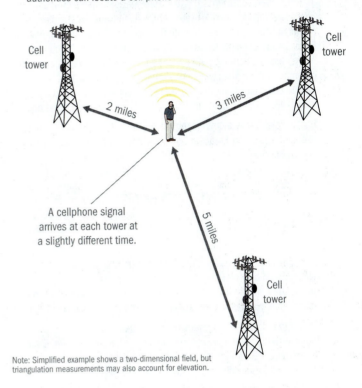

Note: Simplified example shows a two-dimensional field, but triangulation measurements may also account for elevation.

2. Set up lead-tracking policies and procedures.

3. Gather more complete background information on the missing child, parents or guardians, and possible suspects.

4. Reevaluate the scene and conduct a more detailed search.

5. Canvass the neighborhood to locate potential witnesses and information.

6. Search the child's home even if the child is missing from another location.

7. Obtain search warrants when consent for a search is denied.

8. Administer polygraph examinations to the parents or guardians if officers and investigators suspect they are not telling the truth or something seems awry.

9. Contact social service agencies and the child's school to determine whether the child's family was the subject of abuse investigations or had other problems that may be significant to the progress of the investigation.

Step 7: Determine What Additional Resources and Specialized Services Are Required

At this point, the investigator's assessment of the type of incident (for example, abducted child, possible abduction, family abduction, lost child, or runaway) should help determine what additional assistance may be needed both from within the

The 2003 Child Protection Act (Amber Alerts)

In September 2006, Vinson Filyaw, a 26-year-old unemployed construction worker, approached 14-year-old Elizabeth Shoaf as she stepped off her school bus in Lugoff, South Carolina. Posing as a police officer, Filyaw used handcuffs to restrain Elizabeth and dragged her back to a bunker located near his rural trailer home. Filyaw told Elizabeth that the entrance to the bunker was booby-trapped and warned her that if she tried to escape or if anyone tried to rescue her, a bomb would detonate. While Filyaw had Elizabeth in his custody, he sexually assaulted her.

For 10 days, family members, police, and volunteers conducted a sweeping search for Elizabeth but found few clues. Elizabeth engineered her own remarkable rescue by snatching Filyaw's cell phone as he slept and sending a text message to her mother describing the location where she was being held. Investigators using cell phone tracking technology traced the call to Filyaw's cell phone. Investigators deduced that Elizabeth's kidnapper was, in all likelihood, a known sex offender who was suspected of a sexual assault against a 12-year-old relative.

Using the signal from a nearby cell tower to triangulate her location, authorities began scouring the area and were able to rescue her. Police also seized a cache of pornography, canned goods, cheap generic cigarettes, homemade hand-grenades, and incendiary devices fashioned out of black powder from fireworks. They did not, however, find Filyaw.

After a failed attempt to hijack a car to make his escape, Filyaw was found walking along the side of Interstate 20. He was charged with kidnapping, first-degree sexual assault, impersonating a police officer, and possession of incendiary devices.

This case illustrates the seriousness and reality of child abductions and points to the need for community and police cooperation in the investigative phase. It also shows the importance of Amber Alerts and how they provide much-needed and timely information regarding child abductions.

In April 2003, President George W. Bush signed into law the so-called Child Protection Bill, which encourages states to establish **Amber Alert** systems to quickly post information about child abductions. The measure was hailed as an important milestone in the protection of America's children because when a child is reported missing, the case becomes a matter of the most intense and focused effort by law enforcement.

The law also enhanced penalties for youth abductions and child sex crimes, boosted funding for missing and exploited children programs, and increased penalties for those convicted of child pornography, including images created digitally.

The Amber Alert system makes use of radio, television, roadside electronic billboards, and emergency broadcast systems to disseminate information about kidnapping suspects and victims soon after the abduction of a child younger than age 18 years is reported. In such cases, authorities say, the child could be killed or seriously injured a short time after being kidnapped.

The alerts, named after a 9-year-old Texas girl, Amber Hagerman, who was kidnapped and killed in 1996, are in effect in 41 states at the time of this writing. Amber's mother, Donna Norris, attended the bill-signing ceremony along with Jacqueline Marris and Tamara Brooks, the survivors of two high-profile kidnapping cases who were rescued in the first use of the system in California when they were teenagers, and Utah teen Elizabeth Smart, whose father, Ed Smart, called for a national Amber Alert system after her recovery in March 2003.

One of the primary purposes of the new law is to encourage states to develop Amber Alert systems of their own. Attorney General John Ashcroft stated that the bills aim to create a "seamless" system across the country. After the signing of the bill, an Amber Alert coordinator was appointed at the Justice Department to assist states and the office was designated $10 million for the establishment of the initiative.

Think About It…

Warning the Public through "Amber Alert" Technology The Amber Alert system has been of great use to find missing children, but many people do not know that the technology used to implement the Amber Alert system has also aided in providing a mechanism to warn the public of serious weather and other important messages that need to be spread quickly. In what other scenarios might the technology used for the Amber Alert system be used to spread the word quickly to the public?

Amber Alert.

© Spencer Grant/Alamy

department and from outside agencies. For example, the investigator may have been told by a relative of the child that the child's parents appeared in family court to answer child neglect charges. The investigator can save time by asking the police juvenile officer to follow up this lead with the family court and social service agency assigned to the family's case. The juvenile officer could also contact teachers where the missing child attends school and might even interview parents of the child's playmates.

Step 8: Execute an Investigative Follow-Up Plan

The procedures initiated by the investigator depend on the type of case—runaway, family kidnapping, suspected abduction by a stranger, or lost child. Although the procedures are similar to those involved in investigating other major cases, investigators should be aware that the missing or abducted child case may bring the added factor of emotional stress and that the degree of stress will vary depending on the circumstances of the case.

The Abduction of Elizabeth Smart

In 2002, 14-year-old Elizabeth Smart was abducted at gunpoint from her home in Salt Lake City. After a considerable amount of publicity and a search conducted by literally thousands of police and volunteers, investigators were unable to develop solid leads in the case. It wasn't until Elizabeth's own younger sister recalled a workman who visited the Smart home in 2001 that a suspect was developed.

On March 12, 2003, almost nine months after she was abducted, Brian David Mitchell, 49, was arrested and charged with kidnapping. Elizabeth was found in his custody and safely returned to her parents. During her captivity, she was allegedly sexually assaulted several times. Later, it was discovered that her mother, Lois Smart, had picked Mitchell off the street in downtown Salt Lake City in 2001 and brought him home to do some minor chores. Mitchell had spent several hours raking leaves and repairing the roof. During that time, he also observed Elizabeth, who was home at the time.

Sfrane/Fotolia

Sources: CNN News. (2002, June 18). Interview with Jake and Kathleen Garn. Retrieved from http://transcripts.cnn.com/TRANSCRIPTS/0206/18/ltm.01.html; Cosgrove-Mather, B. (2004, May 24). Elizabeth Smart, one year later. CBS News. Retrieved from http://www.cbsnews.com/stories/2004/03/03/national/main603816.shtml; Smart, T. (2005). *In plain sight: The startling truth behind the Elizabeth Smart investigation.* Chicago: Chicago Review Press.

Missing and abducted persons represent one of the greatest challenges to criminal investigators:

1. If you were the lead investigator in this case, what do you think would have been important in considering the possibility of either friends, family, or acquaintances being involved in Elizabeth Smart's disappearance?

LEARNING OUTCOMES 1

Summarize the complexity of the nation's missing persons problem.

There are different types of missing children cases, including family abductions; endangered runaways; nonfamily abductions; and lost, injured, or otherwise missing children. Statistics show that there are 100 cases per year in the United States in which a child is abducted and murdered. In 99 percent of nonfamily abductions, the child is returned alive. In kidnappings, a safe return occurs only 57 percent of the time.

1. What makes missing persons cases especially difficult for investigators to solve?

2. What is the primary motivation for the child abduction murder?

3. What characteristics are common among child abductors?

4. What is the major difference between nonfamily abductions and kidnappings?

5. What are the elements of a stereotypical kidnapping?

6. What were some of the unique aspects of the Jaycee Dugard case?

National Incidence Studies of Missing, Abducted, Runaway and Thrown Away Children (NISMART) project Studies undertaken in response to the mandate of the 1984 Missing Children Assistance Act that requires the Office of Juvenile Justice and Delinquency Prevention (OJJDP) to conduct periodic national incidence studies to determine the actual number of children reported missing and the number of missing children who are recovered for a given year.

LEARNING OUTCOMES 2

Identify the different types of missing person cases.

In general, missing children cases fall into three basic categories: nonfamily abduction, family abduction, and runaway (or lost). Some abductions have been connected to the Internet due to the easy access both the child and predator have to this network. Susceptible preteens and teens are sometimes lured into false friendships in Internet "chat rooms" and then kidnapped from a prearranged meeting place.

1. What are the differences in the three types of missing children cases?

2. What makes family abduction cases complex and volatile?

3. Who is most likely to be the abductor in nonfamily abductions?

4. What kind of evidence is useful in potential Internet abduction cases?

5. What is the most common missing child case?

nonfamily abduction When a child is removed from his or her family through force or trickery.

family abduction An abduction related to a domestic or custody dispute.

runaway or lost child A category of missing children that is the most commonly encountered by law enforcement.

Code Adam An internationally recognized "missing child" safety program in the United States (and Canada) originally created by Walmart retail stores in 1994.

Megan's law An informal name for laws in the United States requiring law enforcement authorities to make information available to the public regarding registered sex offenders, created in response to the 1994 murder of Megan Kanka.

Jessica's law Named after child victim Jessica Lunsford, the informal name given to a 2005 Florida law, as well as laws in several other states, designed to protect potential victims and reduce a sexual offender's ability to re-offend.

LEARNING OUTCOMES 3

Identify the investigative response to missing person cases.

Generally, the patrol officer is the first responder to missing child calls. But before the patrol officer arrives on the scene, information about the missing child should be relayed from the dispatcher to the officers. Dispatchers should gather pertinent information, including a brief description of the missing child and information about a possible abductor(s), from the caller and relay it to the responding officers.

1. What federal non–law enforcement agencies are helpful to investigators in missing children cases?

2. Why is the initial response considered a crucial component of the investigation?

3. What specialized training should patrol officers receive to help them be more effective first responders?

4. How can the media be used to assist investigators in kidnapping cases?

5. How can an off-line search be used as part of an investigation?

LEARNING OUTCOMES 4

Explain the role of the responding officer in missing person cases.

The patrol officer initially establishes the seriousness of the complaint about a missing child, safeguards the scene, gathers crucial facts, and conducts preliminary interviews of witnesses. The patrol officer who responds to the call is best suited to obtain the details of the initial account, particularly because the officer patrols the area or neighborhood and is likely to notice any unusual activities or suspicious persons.

1. What unusual circumstances surrounding a missing person case should prompt a responding officer to call for the mobilization of additional resources?

2. What additional resources on the part of law enforcement officials are useful in solving missing and abducted child cases?

3. Why is it important for a responding officer not to mislabel a missing child case?

4. What does an officer do to verify that a child is missing?

5. Of the 16 steps that should be taken by a responding officer, in your opinion which 3 are most critical to ensure a thorough and proper investigation?

6. What specific steps can law enforcement agencies take to publicize the case as well as receive tips from the public and obtain assistance with a widespread search?

noncustodial parent A parent who does not have legal custody of his or her child.

labeling Classifying a missing child case.

LEARNING OUTCOMES 5

Explain the role of the criminal investigator in missing person cases.

Investigative officers can take several basic steps to help ensure a successful outcome in a missing or abducted child case. The procedures initiated by the investigator depend on the type of case—runaway, family kidnapping, suspected abduction by a stranger, or lost child. Investigators should be aware that the missing or abducted child case may bring added emotional stress that depends on the circumstances of each case.

1. What are the basic steps investigative officers can take to help ensure a successful outcome in a missing child case?

2. What are the most critical components of the investigator's follow-up plan in abduction and missing child cases?

3. What role does the juvenile officer play in the investigation of abducted or missing children?

4. Why were the development of the Child Protection Act and the Amber Alert considered important milestones?

5. How does the Amber Alert system establish cooperation between the community and police in the investigative process?

6. What elements of the Amber Alert help law enforcement officials in their investigation of abducted children?

Amber Alert A system that quickly posts information about child abductions.

Additional Links

www.missingkids.com
This is the site of the National Center for Missing and Exploited Children. The site includes a quick search for missing children; visitors can report child pornography or suspected child sexual exploitation incidents. The site includes a cybertip line and resources for parents and guardians, media, childcare providers, and law enforcement.

www.ojjdp.gov
This is the site of the Office of Juvenile Justice and Delinquency Prevention. Links include news, statistics, publications, programs, and tools. The tools link includes a section with useful research data for students.

www.amberalert.gov
The website for the Amber Alert program includes relevant fact sheets, press releases, videos, training, and toolkits for raising awareness about the problem of child abductions.

www.acf.hhs.gov
The microsite of the U.S. Department of Health and Human Services is the home of the Federal Parent Locator Service (FPLS), which aids in finding participants in child support cases, collection of child support payments, and enforcement of child support orders. The site includes statistics, FAQs, and a library. It contains information pertinent to the public, courts, federal and state agencies, and financial institutions.

13

"The investigation of child physical and sexual abuse requires a multidisciplinary investigative approach."

Crimes against Children: Child Abuse and Child Fatalities

1 Summarize the scope of the problem of child abuse.

2 Explain the role of Child Protective Services (CPS) and the police in crimes against children.

3 Describe the problem of child physical abuse.

4 Describe the problems of battered child syndrome, shaken baby syndrome, Munchausen's syndrome by proxy, and sudden infant death syndrome.

5 Summarize the scope and prevalence of child sexual abuse.

6 Explain the significance of the forensic interview.

7 Summarize the various problems associated with child exploitation.

WHEN CHILDREN PAY THE ULTIMATE PRICE

On July 12, 2012, police responded to a 911 call from a citizen who reported a neighbor who was grabbing his daughter by the ankle and dragging her across a gravel driveway. The investigation revealed that Melvin Morse, a Delaware pediatrician, along with his wife, were physically abusing their daughter by "waterboarding" her on a number of occasions. Morse, who was co-author of a book about the near-death experiences of children, was arrested and charged with first-degree reckless endangering of a child.

Morse's 11-year-old daughter told detectives and social workers that her father had disciplined her by what he called "waterboarding" at least four times between May 2009 and May 2011. She said he would hold her face under running water, causing the water to pour over her face and fill her nostrils. The incidents allegedly took place at the kitchen sink, bathroom sink, and bathtub faucet, according to court records. The girl's younger sister was also interviewed and told social workers she saw this happen to her sister, but that "it has never been done to her because she is too young for it," the newspaper reported. Both children were placed in the care of the Delaware Division of Family Services.

DISCUSS In a democratic society, is it possible for child abuse investigations to be more proactive to prevent the pain and suffering of children?

► *The Abuse of Children*

The Morse case illustrates only one example of a **child abuse** case. Sadly, there are many such cases. The numbers of child abuse cases, of course, reflect only those cases that come to the attention of the police. Statistics show that many more cases exist. In fact, every year in the United States, tens of thousands of children die from a variety of causes, including illness, diseases, accidents, suicides, and homicides. Each death is a heartbreaking event for the child's family and a tragic loss for society.

LEARNING OUTCOMES 1 — Summarize the scope of the problem of child abuse.

Why Does Child Abuse Occur?

There is no single known cause of child abuse nor is there any single description that captures all families in which children are victims of abuse and neglect. Child abuse occurs across socio-economic, religious, cultural, racial, and ethnic groups. Although no specific causes definitively have been identified that lead a parent or other caregiver to abuse or neglect a child, research has recognized a number of risk factors or attributes commonly associated with maltreatment.

Research shows that children within families and environments in which these factors exist have a higher probability of experiencing maltreatment. However, while certain factors often are present among families where maltreatment occurs, this does not mean that the presence of these factors will *always* result in child abuse or neglect. Factors that may contribute to maltreatment in one family may not result in child abuse and neglect in another family. For example, several researchers note the relation between poverty and maltreatment, yet it must be noted that most people living in poverty do not harm their children. Professionals who intervene in cases of child maltreatment must recognize the multiple, complex causes of the problem and must tailor their assessment and treatment of children and families to meet the specific needs and circumstances of the family. According to the U.S. Department of Health and Human Services, child abuse is most likely to occur when parents are struggling with:

- Stress—Pressures from money problems, everyday frustrations, illness, or heavy responsibilities can result in severe levels of stress.

- A painful childhood—Adults who were mistreated as children may, without meaning to, continue the pattern of abuse with their own children.

- Alcohol or other drugs—Substance use and abuse can blind a parent to a child's needs or may reduce inhibitions and tolerance levels so that parents may be more likely to lash out.

- Isolation—Without friends or relatives nearby, parents can feel overwhelmed by the demands of raising a child.

- Inexperience with children or unrealistic expectations—If parents don't know what to expect from children, they may expect too much. Besides lacking the parenting skills necessary to raise a child, some parents may have no models of successful family relationships from which to learn.

- Immaturity—Very young, insecure parents often can't understand their child's behavior and needs.

- Unmet emotional needs—Parents may expect children to take care of them and to satisfy their need for love, protection, and self-esteem.

The Connection between Child Abuse and Father Absence

According to the U.S. Department of Health and Human Services, children living with single parents may be at higher risk of experiencing physical and sexual abuse and neglect than children living with two biological parents. Single-parent households are substantially more likely to have incomes below the poverty line. Lower income, the increased stress associated with the sole burden of family responsibilities, and fewer supports are thought to contribute to the risk of single parents maltreating their children. Research also shows:

- The rate of child abuse in single-parent households is 27.3 children per 1,000, which is nearly twice the rate of child abuse in two-parent households (15.5 children per 1,000).

- An analysis of child abuse cases in a nationally representative sample of 42 counties found that children from single-parent families are more likely to be victims of physical and sexual abuse than children who live with both biological parents. Compared to their peers living with both parents, children in single parent homes had:

    - a 77 percent greater risk of being physically abused,

    - an 87 percent greater risk of being harmed by physical neglect,

    - a 165 percent greater risk of experiencing notable physical neglect,

    - a 74 percent greater risk of suffering from emotional neglect,

    - an 80 percent greater risk of suffering serious injury as a result of abuse, and

    - a 120 percent greater risk of experiencing some type of maltreatment overall.

- A national survey of nearly 1,000 parents found that 7.4 percent of children who lived with one parent had been sexually abused, compared to only 4.2 percent of children who lived with both biological parents.

- Using data from 1,000 students tracked from seventh or eighth grade in 1988 through high school in 1992, researchers determined that only 3.2 percent of the boys and girls who were raised with both biological parents had a history of maltreatment. However, a full 18.6 percent of those in other family situations had been maltreated.

- A study of 156 victims of child sexual abuse found that the majority of the children came from disrupted or single-parent homes; only 31 percent of the children lived with both biological parents. Although stepfamilies make up only about 10 percent of all families, 27 percent of the abused children in this study lived with either a stepfather or the mother's boyfriend.

Source: U.S. Department of Health and Human Services. Child Welfare Information Gateway (2014). A coordinated response to child abuse and neglect. Retrieved from https://www.childwelfare.gov/pubs/usermanuals/foundation/foundatione.cfm.

Child Fatalities: The Nature of the Problem

When a child's death is sudden and unexpected, the tragedy is compounded if law enforcement is unable to conduct a proper investigation. If the investigation is flawed, two outcomes—neither acceptable—are very real possibilities. First is that an innocent person will be suspected or accused of either a crime that did not occur or a crime for which the person has no responsibility. Second, a real crime will remain undetected or unsolved and the person responsible for the fatal maltreatment of the child will never be identified or brought to justice.

Although the vast majority of child deaths are related to natural causes or accidents, all sudden and unexpected child deaths must be properly investigated. Every day, at least four children in the United States die from maltreatment. Only by thoroughly investigating all sudden and unexpected child deaths can society be certain that maltreatment is not involved. Professionally conducted investigations of child fatalities ensure that innocent people are not falsely accused of wrongdoing and guilty people are not allowed to escape arrest and prosecution and possibly go on to harm another child.

Awareness of some basic dynamics in issues is critical to effective investigations of child fatalities. Research and experience have shown that children are most at risk of dying of maltreatment during the first four years of life. In fact, 40 percent of children who are victims of fatal maltreatment are infants (younger than one year old), and 75 percent are younger than five years old.[1] The Centers for Disease Control and Prevention (CDC) report that the chances of being murdered are greater on the day of birth than at any other point in a person's life.

Caring for children during their preschool years can be very stressful for parents and other caretakers. Faced with a young child's persistent problems with sleeping, feeding, and toilet training, a caretaker may lose control and assault the child in anger or may cause injury while punishing the child. Some inexperienced caretakers have unrealistic expectations about what is appropriate child behavior and what children are even capable of doing in the early stages of their development. In these cases, caretakers can become angry because they view a child's crying or bedwetting as an act of defiance rather than being normal behavior for a young child. The deadly combination of an angry adult and a physically vulnerable child can result in fatal or life-threatening injuries to the child. For the most part, child fatalities can be categorized as either acute or chronic maltreatment. These are discussed next.

Acute Maltreatment

Acute maltreatment means that the child's death is directly related to injuries suffered as a result of a specific incident of abuse or act of negligence. In such cases, the child has not been previously abused or neglected.[2]

In cases involving acute physical abuse, the caretaker may have fatally assaulted the child in either an inappropriate response to the child's behavior or in a conscious act to hurt the child. Offenders of cases of **shaken baby syndrome (SBS)**, in which a child's brain is injured from violent shaking, often cite the child's crying as the "triggering event."[3]

In cases of acute neglect, a caretaker's one-time failure to properly supervise the child may result in a fatal injury. A common example is a fatal drowning that occurs when an infant is briefly unsupervised in a bathtub. Children have also sustained fatal gunshot wounds when caretakers fail to properly secure loaded firearms. Some states have statutes that specifically assign criminal responsibility to an individual who makes a firearm accessible to a child, either intentionally or through failure to properly secure the weapon. The penalty for this crime may be increased if the child's possession of a firearm results in either injury or death to the child or another person.[4]

Chronic Maltreatment

In **chronic maltreatment** cases, the child's death is directly related to injuries caused by neglect occurring over an extended period of time. Battered child syndrome is an example of chronic physical abuse (discussed later in this chapter). Although the direct cause of death in a battering case is usually a specific injury (often brain trauma), numerous indications of former maltreatment—old and new injuries and possible signs of neglect—are also typically present. Depriving a child of food for a significant period of time is a common form of chronic physical neglect. In cases of chronic abuse or neglect, a history of the child's previous maltreatment often will appear in either Child Protective Services (CPS) or medical records. In fact, research shows that 38 percent of all children who died of abuse or neglect had prior current contact with a CPS agency.[5]

Child Abuse and the Law: The Doctrine of *Parens Patriae*

The basis for intervention in child maltreatment is grounded in the concept of **parens patriae**, a legal term that asserts the government's role in protecting the interests of children and intervening when parents fail to provide proper care. The legal framework regarding the parent–child relationship balances the rights and responsibilities among parent, child, and state, as guided by federal statutes. It has long been recognized that parents have a fundamental liberty interest, protected by the Constitution, to raise their children as they choose. This parent–child relationship grants certain rights, duties, and obligations to both parent and child, including the responsibility of the parent to protect the child's safety and well-being. If a parent, however, is unable or unwilling to meet this responsibility, the state has the power and authority to take action to protect a child from significant harm.

Several U.S. Supreme Court cases have defined when it is constitutional for the state to intervene in family life. Although the Court has given parents great latitude in the upbringing and education of their children, it has held that the rights of parenthood and the family have limits and can be regulated in the interest of the public.

The Court has further concluded that the state, in its role as *parens patriae*, may restrict the parent's control by regulating or prohibiting the child's labor, requiring school attendance, and intervening in other ways to promote the child's well-being. This doctrine has evolved into the principle that the community, in addition to the parent, has a strong interest in the care and nurturing of children, who represent the future of the community. When basic needs of children are not met or when their rights have been violated, as with cases of child maltreatment, the state has an obligation to intervene to assist the affected individuals.

▶ The Role of Child Protective Services and the Police

Unlike other types of criminal investigations such as arson, an unusual aspect of child fatality cases is the involvement of an agency other than law enforcement in the investigation. Typically, CPS has legal authority to be involved in the investigation of a child's death if a parent or other member of the household is suspected. It should be noted, however, that the CPS role is very different from the law enforcement role.[6]

LEARNING OUTCOMES **2** Explain the role of Child Protective Services and the police in crimes against children.

The role of CPS is to determine whether maltreatment was involved in the child's death, identify the responsible party, and then take appropriate action to protect any surviving siblings. CPS does not determine whether anyone committed a crime, and CPS

CASE EXAMPLE OF MALTREATMENT: Child Neglect

Robert and Carlotta are the parents of a 9-month-old son named Ruiz. Robert and Carlotta used various drugs together until Robert was arrested and sent to prison for distributing cocaine. Since Robert's arrest, Carlotta has been living with different relatives and friends. Recently, she left her son with her sister who also has a history of drug use. Her sister then went to a local bar and left Ruiz unattended. After hearing the baby boy cry for over an hour, the neighbors called the police. When Carlotta arrived to pick up Ruiz, the police and the CPS worker were also there. It appeared that she had been using drugs.

Source: U.S. Department of Health and Human Services. (2014). Retrieved from http://www.hhs.gov/.

personnel are not trained in the techniques of criminal investigation, evidence collection, or the interrogation of suspected offenders. It is therefore important that law enforcement and CPS communicate and coordinate their efforts during the course of the investigation. One coordinated investigation is always preferable to two separate investigations. In fact, at least 30 states have either mandated or authorized implementation of multidisciplinary teams to investigate child maltreatment.[7]

The role of the criminal investigator is to determine whether a crime has been committed and who is responsible. Accomplishing this involves analyzing old and new injuries revealed by an autopsy and by a review of the child's medical history, thoroughly investigating the death scene, collecting and examining evidence, interviewing witnesses, and interrogating suspects.

Although it is important that law enforcement and CPS coordinate their efforts, it is imperative that the police assume the leadership role in the investigation. This is necessary because of the legal and practical issues involved in obtaining evidence and confessions. Only a police investigator has the training, expertise, and legal mandate to execute search warrants, collect and evaluate evidence, interrogate suspects, and file criminal charges.

If the CPS investigator prematurely confronts a parent suspected of fatal child abuse, the police investigator will find it more difficult, if not impossible, to successfully interrogate that same individual at a later time. It must be remembered that both police and CPS investigators are acting under statutory

The search of the scene should include the following:

- Ensure that scale diagrams are made of the layout and that photographs, a video, or both are taken. Photographs should show the general location and progress to specific items of interest.

- Consider as evidence prescription or over-the-counter medicine the child was taking and other medicine or substances the child may have ingested. If it is not practical to remove such medicine from the scene because someone else in the household needs it, document the information on the label.

- If it appears that the child may have died of malnourishment, the investigator may want to take an inventory of the amount of baby food or formula that is present. Whatever is found should be documented and photographed.

- If evidence that the caretaker has been abusing alcohol or other substances is located, this evidence should also be carefully documented.

- Trash cans inside and outside the residence should also be searched for possible evidence such as bloodstained clothing; items used to clean up blood, vomit, urine, or feces; and implements used to injure the child, such as wooden spoons, belts, and electrical extension cords.

Source: Pence, D., & Wilson, C. (1994). *Team investigation of child sexual abuse.* Thousand Oaks, CA: Sage Publications.

requirements. Only if these two entities coordinate their efforts and use their respective resources will the investigation succeed.[8]

Evidence from the Autopsy

In cases involving a child fatality, the autopsy will determine the official cause of death (for example, blunt force trauma, drowning) and manner of death (for example, natural, accidental, homicide, suicide, undetermined). The criminal investigator should observe the autopsy if at all possible. The information learned from the autopsy will better prepare the investigator for subsequent interviews and interrogations.

The pathologist can provide information about the child's injuries, including those related to the death and those previously inflicted, and about the child's general state of health before death. It is important to ask for details to explain whether a single event or multiple factors caused or contributed to the death.[9]

In turn, the investigator can tell the pathologist what he or she has learned from interviews and record checks. In many cases, the pathologist's knowledge can offer an opinion regarding the possibility that the child's injuries occurred in the manner described by witnesses. The pathologist may also be able to estimate the time of death based on the child's stomach contents and investigative notes about the child's last meal.[10]

The Child Fatality Review Board

In 1987, the death of a 7-year-old Ohio boy at the hand of his mother's live-in boyfriend raised many questions about the

Think About It…

Protecting the Kids In popular court and crime shows on TV, the acronym *CPS,* or the term *Child Protective Services,* is often part of the discussion surrounding problematic parenting. Many viewers might not realize that the role of CPS is not simply to remove kids from problematic homes; CPS personnel specifically work with investigations dealing with abuse and/or deaths of children, as well as those dealing with the protection of children. They play an important role in that CPS often have the most detailed records regarding abused children, which might cover everything from birth information to education to residences to medical records. If you were an investigator working with CPS on a case, why do you think it would be useful to have such a partner during the investigation?

Pixel Memoirs/Shutterstock.com

procedures and practices used by the area's agencies that were established to protect and serve children. Newspaper articles brought into question the roles and responsibilities of the various organizations that had dealt with the family prior to the youngster's death and why a closer working relationship did not exist among them.[11] These questions were directed at the local children's social service, the schools, and the police because all had contact with the family prior to the child's death. But, unfortunately, the information that each possessed was either not available or only so in small amounts to the other agencies involved.

Child fatality review boards have become commonplace in the United States. These are typically governed by each county's Department of Health, and the purpose of such boards is to reduce the incidence of preventable child deaths.

Following the tragic death of the young boy in the Ohio case, a review board was formed. The board, made up of representatives from local child-serving agencies, public health officials, medical practitioners, the medical examiner, prosecutors, and law enforcement personnel, began with two main goals:

1. To review all child deaths and near deaths due to child abuse and neglect, to assess each involved-agency's system performance, to make recommendations for the improvement of intra- and interagency performance, and to reduce the number of preventable deaths in the county; and

2. To present to the community a statement of the committee's analysis and findings.[12]

The multi-agency concept of a child fatality board originated in Los Angeles, California, in 1978. This investigative initiative has allowed different agencies within the criminal justice system to benefit by exchanging information and improving performance relating to the protection of children. Since its beginning, the child fatality review process now exists in all 50 states and has expanded from a core membership to include representatives from education, other health-related agencies, the court, and prosecutors. Such boards can also review not only deaths from abuse and neglect but also those as a result of natural causes, accidents, and suicides.

► Child Physical Abuse

In addition to child fatalities, child physical abuse remains a serious problem. As with the investigation of child fatalities, the investigative response to child physical abuse must be timely and thorough. *Child abuse* is a generic term that incorporates a variety of purposeful acts resulting in injuries to a child. Probably the most dramatic of these

LEARNING OUTCOMES 3 — Describe the problem of child physical abuse.

and the most often reported to the police is physical child abuse that results in death or serious injury. However, child abuse is far more pervasive and often more subtle. For example, as stated earlier, physical battering may be the result of a parent's momentary fit of anger, or it may be part of an ongoing abusive situation. In the case of sexual abuse situations within families, offenses are more frequently calculated and may form a long-term pattern of sexual abuse. Physical neglect of a child's needs

Child Victims of Physical Abuse Can Range from Very Young to Youths in Their Teens, as Shown Here.

Squidmediaro/Fotolia

for nourishment or medical care, reckless disregard for his or her safety, and failure to provide food or medical care are all elements of the child abuse and neglect problem.

The physical effects of child abuse are only part of a child's injuries. The psychological and emotional impacts of abuse frequently have long-term consequences for the child. Many children blame themselves for the abuse, adopting the feeling that they are bad and deserve the abusive treatment. Others may adopt the long-lasting perception that violence is a natural, even acceptable, component of family life and interpersonal relationships. As a consequence, many abused children carry to the next generation the same type of treatment that they endured. Other children translate physical abuse into later criminal violence. The fact that so many violent offenders have histories of child abuse and neglect is testimony to the fact that child abuse is often an intergenerational phenomenon. As such, it is important not only for the current victim but also for future generations to identify child abuse whenever possible and to bring appropriate enforcement and treatment to the problem.

Emergency Room Personnel and Medical Examiners

In the worst-case scenario—the death of a child—a medical examiner may be the primary source of contact for investigative purposes. Police departments in general and investigative personnel in particular must develop a good working relationship with the medical examiner's office. In these and related circumstances, a collaborative relationship generally proves to be far more productive than either the police or medical personnel working independently. The investigative officer should be present at the autopsy or at the initial examination of the body and should brief the examining physician on the circumstances of the alleged accident if information is available. This also holds true for emergency room physicians who treat a child after a presumed serious but nonfatal accident. In both cases, physical examinations may reveal certain types of injuries that confirm or suggest abuse. These include the following:

1. *External signs.* Some injuries have identifiable patterns that can be linked to specific objects used in an attack. For example, one may be able to identify bite or scratch

Age Group

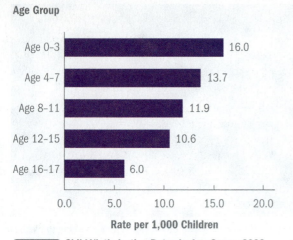

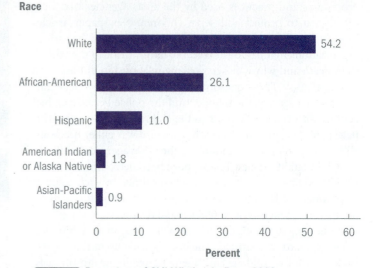

Race

FIGURE 13-1 Child Victimization Rates by Age Group, 2002.
Source: U.S. Department of Health & Human Services, Administration for Children and Families. (2003).

FIGURE 13-2 Percentage of Child Victims by Race, 2002.
Source: U.S. Department of Health & Human Services, Administration for Children and Families. (2003).

marks; coat hanger or hot iron impressions; fingertip marks caused by tight gripping; straight, curved, curvilinear, or jagged lesions that may indicate whipping by specifically shaped objects; and scald or peculiar burn marks.

In all cases of suspected abuse, injuries should be photographed in color to assist in establishing the extent of damage and the age of injuries at later trial presentation.

2. *Internal signs.* As noted, some injuries are not characteristic of childhood activities and common accidents. For example, it is very unlikely that pre-toddlers would be able to break a major bone, such as a thigh or upper arm bone, or other smaller bones given the children's lack of mobility and the inherent difficulty in breaking the bones of young children. Some fractures will be apparent externally. Others, particularly older fractures, require radiologic examination to be identified. The nature of some fractures provides almost indisputable evidence of abuse. These include spiral fractures, indicating vigorous handling, shaking, or twisting, and fractures to the rear and upper part—the occipital and varietal bones, respectively—of the skull, suggesting that the child was swung by the feet into a solid object or suffered a blow to the head. Subdural hematomas, without evidence of contusions on the scalp, or skull fractures may suggest violent shaking of an infant, causing whiplash of the child's head and subsequent internal injuries (see Figure 13–1).

As with any assault case, evidence is a primary objective. Bruises, bloody clothes, dramatic changes in a child's behavior,

and statements from possible witnesses are all important. Special care must be afforded in the interview of a child victim because children are imaginative and highly susceptible to suggestion. Because of this, the use of specially trained child interviewers is recommended to secure a competent statement from the child victim (see Figure 13–2).

▶ Battered Child Syndrome

Battered child syndrome, defined as the collection of injuries sustained by a child as a result of repeated mistreatment or beating, is a tragic and disturbing phenomenon. Unfortunately, it is a crime that is often successfully hidden by its perpetrators. Law enforcement has an important role to play in uncovering cases of battered child syndrome and gathering evidence for successful prosecution. Investigators must have a working knowledge of battered child syndrome and what it means to an investigation. If the child's injuries indicate intentional trauma or appear to be more severe than could reasonably be expected from an accident, battered child syndrome should be suspected (see Figure 13–3). In such cases, an investigator must do more than collect information

LEARNING OUTCOMES 4 Describe the problems of battered child syndrome, shaken baby syndrome, Munchausen's syndrome by proxy, and sudden infant death syndrome.

CASE EXAMPLE OF MALTREATMENT: Physical Abuse

During a violent fight between her mother and her mother's boyfriend, eight-year-old Kerry called 911. She told the operator that her mother's boyfriend always hit her mommy when he came home drunk. In addition, Kerry said she was worried about her five-year-old brother, Aaron, because he tried to help their mom and the boyfriend punched him in the face. As a result, Aaron fell, hit his head on the coffee table, and had not moved since. The operator heard yelling in the background and the mother screaming, "Get off the phone!" When the police and paramedics arrived, Aaron was unconscious and the mother had numerous bruises on her face.

Source: U.S. Department of Health and Human Services. (2014). Retrieved from http://www.hhs.gov/.

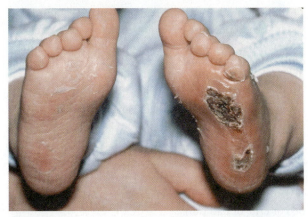

Burns on an Infant's Feet Are Evidence of Child Abuse.
Source: SPL/Photo Researchers, Inc.

about the currently reported injury. A full investigation requires interviewing possible witnesses about other injuries that the child may have suffered, obtaining the caretaker's explanation for those injuries, and assessing the conclusions of medical personnel who may have seen the victim before.

Steps in Investigating Battered Child Syndrome

Investigators confronted with the case of possible child abuse or child homicide must overcome the unfortunately frequent societal attitude that babies are less important than adult victims of homicide and that natural parents would never intentionally harm their own children. When battered child syndrome is suspected, the investigator should always do the following:[13]

- Collect information about the "acute" injury that led the person or agency to make the report.
- Conduct interviews with medical personnel who are attending the child.
- Review medical records from a doctor, clinic, or hospital.
- Interview all persons who had access to or custody of the child during a time in which the injury or injuries allegedly occurred. Caretakers should always be interviewed separately; joint interviews can only hurt the investigation.
- Consider any statements the caretakers made to anyone concerning what happened to the child to require medical attention.
- Conduct a thorough investigation of the scene where the child was allegedly hurt.

Justifications for Officers Making an Arrest

☑ Injury to the child is severe.
☑ Evidence of a serious crime exists.
☑ It seems likely that the suspect will flee the scene.
☑ There is a disturbance of the peace.
☑ The suspect seems to pose a danger to others.

Interviews with Medical Personnel

It is important for the investigator to contact all medical personnel who had contact with the family, such as doctors, nurses, admitting personnel, emergency medical technicians (EMTs), ambulance drivers, and emergency room personnel.[14]

- Talk with those who provided treatment for the child about the diagnosis and what treatments were used. The attending physician will often be able to express at least an opinion of whether the caretaker's explanation did or did not "fit" the severity of the injury. However, failure to obtain an opinion from the attending physician should not end the investigation.
- Speak with any specialists who assisted the attending physician.
- Have someone knowledgeable about medical terms translate them into layperson terms so that the exact nature of the injuries is clear.
- Obtain available medical records concerning the injured child's treatment, including records of any prior treatment. (Note: If only one caretaker is suspected of abuse, the nonabusive caretaker may need to sign a release of the records. If both are suspected, most states have provisions that override normal confidentiality rules in the search for evidence of child abuse. Procedures for obtaining these records must be confirmed in each state.)
- Interview the child's pediatrician about the child's general health since birth, and look for a pattern of suspected abusive injuries.

It is absolutely vital that photographs of the child be taken as soon as possible after he or she has been brought to the treatment facility. Most clinics and hospitals have established procedures for photographing injuries in obvious cases of abuse, but when the injuries are more subtle, they may overlook the need for photographs. The investigator should make sure that

Think About It…

Battered Child Syndrome It can be difficult for a child to actually have his or her abuse either identified or stopped. What becomes difficult for law enforcement personnel is that if an officer makes a judgment to make an arrest based on suspicion of repeated abuse, he or she must be careful to be as sure as possible that abuse is occurring, as a false arrest on such a charge could be extremely damaging to an individual's reputation. Discuss the justifications for an officer making an arrest when dealing with a suspected case of battered child syndrome.

A Physical Arrest, as Shown Here, Is Sometimes the Most Effective Response to Suspected Child Abuse.

Jack Dagley Photography/Shutterstock.com

medical personnel take and preserve photographs or that the investigating team takes them.

Consultation with Experts

Identifying experts is important to the child abuse investigator. If the investigator does not have a basic knowledge of the causes of young children's injuries, experts should be consulted. Attending training conferences can provide the investigator with a great deal of basic knowledge and help establish a network of experts.

Interviews with Caretakers

A major trait of abuse by caretakers is either complete lack of an explanation for critical injuries or explanations that do not account for the severity of the injuries. The investigation must not be dictated solely by caretakers' early explanations because after they learn that their excuses don't match the medical evidence, they will come up with new ones.

In child homicide cases, for example, investigators will learn quickly about "killer couches," "killer stairs," and "killer cribs." Abusers freely use these terms in their explanations of the child's death. However, studies show that children do not die from falls from simple household heights; they usually do not even suffer severe head injuries from such falls.

In nearly every case of actual abuse, caretakers will not be consistent in their explanations of the injuries over time. Sometimes the changes are apparent from statements that abusers have made to others. Additional interviews may be needed to document the changes in explanations and to follow up on additional information that the investigation uncovers.

The Crime-Scene Investigation

Caretakers' changes in explanations often mean that investigators must visit the home or the scene of the injury more than once. The ideal time to obtain crime-scene evidence is immediately after the child's injury is reported and before the caretakers have an opportunity to tamper with the scene. If the caretakers do not consent to a search of the scene, a search warrant may be necessary. The strongest evidence of the need for a search warrant is the medical evidence supporting what probably happened to the child and the caretakers' inconsistent or absent accounts of the events.

Whatever explanation caretakers offer for a child's injury or injuries, it is vital that the investigator secure physical evidence. He or she must be thorough in obtaining photographic evidence of the location where the injury took place because physical evidence and records must be preserved, for example:[15]

- The crib from which the child allegedly fell.
- The child's "environment," including bedding on the bed or in the crib and on other beds in the home.
- Any toys or objects on which the child allegedly landed.
- In cases in which the child was apparently burned, a record of any sinks, bathtubs, and pots or pans containing water.

In addition to testing the temperature of the standing water, the temperature of water from the water heater and from each tap should be tested. The temperature setting of the water heater should also be checked. This may help disprove an allegation that the child accidentally turned on the hot water. Other sources of heat in the home should be documented, regardless of the caretakers' initial explanation of what burned the child.

- A complete photographic or videotape record of the home or other location in which the injuries allegedly occurred, focusing on areas that the caretakers have already identified as the site of the particular trauma (for example, stairs, bed or crib, or bathtub).

▶ Shaken Baby Syndrome

Shaken baby syndrome (SBS) is a form of child abuse that occurs when an abuser violently shakes an infant or small child, creating a whiplash-type motion that causes acceleration–deceleration injuries. The injury is estimated to affect between 1,200 and 1,600 children every year in the United States.[16] In shaken baby cases, it is common for there to be no external evidence of trauma.[17] Injuries from impacts with hard objects may accompany SBS; this combination of shaking with striking against a hard object is sometimes termed *shaken impact syndrome* or *shaken/slam syndrome*.

The classic medical symptoms associated with infant shaking

- Retinal hemorrhaging (bleeding in the back of the eyeball), often bilaterally (in both eyes).
- Subdural or subarachnoid hematomas (intracranial bleeding, most often in the upper hemispheres of the brain, caused by the shearing of the blood vessels between the brain and the dura mater of the arachnoid membrane).
- Absence of other external signs of abuse (for example, bruises), although not always. Symptoms include breathing difficulties, seizures, dilated pupils, lethargy, and unconsciousness.

Victims of SBS are aged three years and younger. Typically, most child victims are younger than 18 months. The motion required to injure a child often results in bleeding inside the head and may cause irreversible brain damage, blindness, cerebral palsy, hearing loss, spinal cord injuries, seizures, learning disabilities, and even death. The incidence of the syndrome can be traced historically from the mid-1500s and was officially named and defined in 1974.

According to all credible studies in the past several years, retinal hemorrhaging in infants is, for all practical purposes, conclusive evidence of SBS in the absence of a good explanation. Good explanations for retinal hemorrhaging include the following:

- A severe auto accident in which the baby's head either struck something with severe force or was thrown about wildly without restraint
- A fall from several stories onto a hard surface, in which case there are usually other signs of trauma, such as skull fractures, swelling, and intracranial collection of blood

Simple household falls, cardiopulmonary resuscitation (CPR), and tossing a baby in the air in play are not good explanations for retinal hemorrhaging. There simply is not enough force involved in minor falls or play activities to cause retinal hemorrhage or the type of severe life-threatening injuries seen in infants who have been shaken.

In most cases of SBS, there is no skull fracture and no external sign of trauma. The typical explanation given by caretakers is that the baby was "fine" and then suddenly went into respiratory arrest or began having seizures. Both of these conditions are common symptoms of SBS.

The shaking necessary to cause death or severe intracranial injuries is never an unintentional or nonabusive action. Rather, such injuries are caused by a violent, sustained action in which the infant's head, which lacks muscular control, is violently swept forward and backward, hitting the chest and shoulders. The action occurs right in front of the shaker's eyes. Experts say that an observer watching the shaking would describe it as "as hard as the shaker was humanly capable of shaking the baby" or "hard enough that it appeared the baby's head would come off." In almost every case, the baby begins to show symptoms such as seizures or unconsciousness within minutes of the injury. The baby may have difficulty breathing, or his or her breathing may stop completely.

SBS occurs primarily in children 18 months of age or younger. It is most often associated with infants younger than one year old because their necks lack muscle control and their heads are heavier than the rest of their bodies. An infant cannot resist the shaking, but a toddler can, to some extent. Although the collection of injuries associated with SBS is sometimes seen in toddlers, it is rare and is always a sign of extremely violent and severe action against the child.

Indications of Munchausen Syndrome

Caution is required in the diagnosis of fabricated or induced illness (FII). Many of the items below are also indications of a child with organic but undiagnosed illness. An ethical diagnosis of Munchausen syndrome must include an evaluation of the child, the parents, and the family dynamics. Diagnoses based only on a review of the child's medical chart can be rejected in court. An adult care provider who is abusing the child often seems comfortable and not upset over the child's hospitalization. Medical professionals need to monitor that adult's visits to the child while in the hospital in case that adult does things to make the child sicker. In addition, in most states medical professionals have a duty to report such abuse to legal authorities.

- A child who has one or more medical problems that do not respond to treatment or that follow an unusual course that is persistent, puzzling, and unexplained
- Physical or laboratory findings that are highly unusual, discrepant with history, or physically or clinically impossible
- A parent who appears to be medically knowledgeable or fascinated with medical details and hospital gossip, appears to enjoy the hospital environment, and expresses interest in the details of other patients' problems
- A highly attentive parent who is reluctant to leave the child's side and who him- or herself seems to require constant attention
- A parent who appears to be unusually calm in the face of serious difficulties in the child's medical course while being highly supportive and encouraging of the physician, or a parent who is angry, devalues staff, and demands further intervention, more procedures, second opinions, and transfers to other, more sophisticated facilities
- A parent who may work in the health care field him- or herself or profess interest in a health-related job
- Signs and symptoms of a child's illness that do not occur in the parent's absence (hospitalization and careful monitoring may be necessary to establish this causal relationship)
- A family history of similar or unexplained illness or death in a sibling
- A parent with symptoms similar to the child's medical problems or an illness history that itself is puzzling and unusual
- A suspected emotionally distant relationship between parents; a spouse who often fails to visit the patient and has little contact with physicians even when the child is hospitalized with serious illness
- A parent who reports dramatic, negative events, such as house fires, burglaries, or car accidents, that affect him or her and the family while the child is undergoing treatment
- A parent who seems to have an insatiable need for adulation or who makes self-serving efforts for public acknowledgment of his or her abilities

These indicators may or may not provide the need for further investigation but should be taken seriously until the allegations have been proven invalid.

Sources: Elder W., I. C. Coletsos, and H. J. Bursztajn. (2010). In F. J Domino (Ed). *Factitious disorder/Munchausen syndrome. The 5-minute clinical consult,* 18th edition. Philadelphia: Wolters Kluwer/Lippincott.
Vennemann B., M. G. Perdekamp, W. Weinmann, et al. (2006). A case of Munchausen syndrome by proxy with subsequent suicide of the mother. *Forensic Science International.*158(2-3):195–199.

► Munchausen Syndrome by Proxy

Munchausen syndrome is a psychological disorder in which a patient fabricates symptoms of disease or injury in order to undergo medical tests, hospitalization, or even medical or surgical treatment. To command medical attention, patients with Munchausen syndrome may intentionally injure themselves or induce illness in themselves. In cases of **Munchausen syndrome by proxy**, parents or caretakers with Munchausen syndrome attempt to bring medical attention to themselves by inducing illness in their children. The parent then may try to resuscitate or have paramedics or hospital personnel save the child. The following scenarios are common occurrences in these cases:[18]

- A child's caretaker repeatedly brings the child in for medical care or calls paramedics for alleged problems that cannot be documented medically.

- The child experiences "seizures" or "respiratory arrest" only when the caretaker is there, never in the presence of neutral third parties or in the hospital.

- When the child is hospitalized, the caretaker turns off the life-support equipment, causing the child to stop breathing, and then turns everything back on and summons help.

- The caretaker induces illness by introducing a mild irritant or poison into the child's body.

► Sudden Infant Death Syndrome

Sudden infant death syndrome (SIDS) is the diagnosis given for the sudden death of an infant one month to one year of age that remains unexplained after a complete investigation, which includes an autopsy, an examination of the death scene, and a review of the victim's medical and family history. SIDS is a recognized medical disorder. Infants who succumb to the syndrome appear healthy before the incident, even to a physician. At this time, there is no strong evidence to suggest that SIDS can be stopped, because the first and only symptom is death. SIDS appears to occur after an infant has been put down for sleep. Victims may have been down for sleep for as little as 10 minutes.

Investigative Guidelines

- ☑ Consult with all possible experts, including psychologists.
- ☑ Exhaust every possible explanation in the cause of the child's illness or death.
- ☑ Find out who had exclusive control over the child when the symptoms of the illness began or at the time of the child's death.
- ☑ Find out if there is a history of abusive conduct toward the child.
- ☑ Find out if the nature of the child's illness or injury allows medical professionals to express an opinion that the child's illness or death was neither accidental nor the result of a natural cause or disease.
- ☑ In cases of hospitalization, use covert video surveillance to monitor the suspect. Some cases have been solved in this fashion.
- ☑ Determine whether the caretaker had any medical training or a history of seeking medical treatment needlessly. Munchausen syndrome by proxy is often a multigenerational condition.

Some general risk factors for SIDS have been identified. These include the following:
- Mother younger than 20 years of age
- Late or no prenatal care
- Premature infants
- Low-birth-weight infants
- Drug and alcohol use during pregnancy
- Smoking (mothers who smoke during and after pregnancy triple the risk of SIDS in their infants)

Source: Protective and Family Services, State of Texas. Available at http://www.dfps.state.tx.us/child_care/information_for_child_care_professionals/sbs_sids.asp.

Studies show that there are no apparent signs of a struggle or suffering. Although SIDS is associated with an infant's sleep time and often occurs in the crib, the event may occur anywhere the infant is sleeping. SIDS events have occurred in infant seats, car seats, strollers, and in the parents' bed.

SIDS is not a positive finding; rather, it is a diagnosis made when there is no other medical explanation for the abrupt death of an apparently healthy infant. When a baby dies from shaking, intracranial injuries, peritonitis (inflammation of the peritoneum, the membrane that lines the abdominal cavity), apparent suffocation, or any other identifiable cause, SIDS is not even considered a possibility. SIDS rarely occurs in infants older than age 7 months and almost never is an appropriate diagnosis for a child older than 12 months.

Research shows that SIDS can occur at any time between one month of age and one year of age; however, 91 percent of SIDS deaths occur before the age of six months, with the highest concentration occurring between two months and four months of age. The syndrome affects all races and socioeconomic groups. Environmental, behavioral, and physical influences may put some infants at greater risk for SIDS, and conversely, many SIDS victims meet no specific risk factors.

SIDS cases must be approached with great sensitivity. However, before SIDS can be determined to be the cause of death, investigators must ensure that every other possible medical explanation has been explored and that there is no evidence of any other natural or accidental cause for the child's death.

An investigator's suspicions should be aroused when multiple alleged SIDS deaths have occurred under the custody of the same caretaker. Statistically, the occurrence of two or three alleged SIDS deaths in the care of the same person strongly suggests that some degree of child abuse was involved. Whenever there is evidence that the child who has died was abused or that other children in the family have been abused, SIDS is not an appropriate finding.

► Sexual Abuse of Children

The abuse of children can take many forms. In addition to the possible physical danger posed by an abusive caregiver or parent, a child can also be traumatized by being sexually abused. Consider the 1995 case in which an 11-year-old testified that she was molested during sexual orgies supposedly staged by a Pentecostal preacher in Wenatchee, Washington. The child also

FIGURE 13–4 John J. Geoghan in Court.
Source: AP Photo/John Blanding, Pool.

Charges were brought in Cambridge, Massachusetts, concerning accusations of a molestation that took place in 1991. Geoghan was defrocked in 1998. In January 2002, he was found guilty of indecent assault and battery for grabbing the buttocks of a 10-year-old boy in a swimming pool at the Waltham Boys and Girls Club in 1991. Geoghan was sentenced to 9 to 10 years in prison.

Numerous civil lawsuits resulted from Geoghan's actions because lawyers argued that the archdiocese had transferred him from parish to parish despite warnings of his behavior. On August 23, 2003, while in protective custody at the Souza-Baranowski Correctional Center in Shirley, Massachusetts, Geoghan was trapped in his cell, strangled, and stomped to death by another inmate, Joseph Druce.

testified that her foster father, who happened to be Detective Bob Perez, lead police investigator in the case, also physically abused her. Prosecutors charged 28 persons in the case, claiming that they forced 50 children to have sex with each other and with adults in two "sex rings." Nineteen people either pleaded guilty or were convicted in the case; only one person was acquitted. In yet another case, the Boy Scouts have dismissed more than 1,800 scoutmasters suspected of molesting children between 1971 and 1991; some of those dismissed may have moved to other troops to continue their abuse.[19]

LEARNING OUTCOMES 5 Summarize the scope and prevalence of child sexual abuse.

In recent years, the problem of child sexual abuse has generated increased attention and is becoming more openly discussed than ever before. Child abuse can take a number of insidious forms. An example is the case of Catholic priest John J. Geoghan (Figure 13–4), who was a key figure in the Roman Catholic sex abuse cases that rocked the Boston Archdiocese in the late 1990s and early 2000s. Geoghan's case eventually led to the resignation of Boston's archbishop, Cardinal Bernard Francis Law, on December 13, 2002.

Over a 30-year career in six parishes, Geoghan was accused of sexual abuse involving more than 130 children.

Statistics also point out that child sexual abuse is a growing problem. Although it is difficult to estimate the incidence of child sexual abuse, stories of abuse such as those discussed previously illustrate the seriousness of the problem. In one study by Diana Russell, women in the San Francisco area were surveyed, and Russell found that 38 percent had experienced intrafamilial or extrafamilial sexual abuse by the time they reached age 18 years.[20] A more recent survey of Minnesota students in grades 6, 9, and 12 revealed that about 2 percent of the boys and 7 percent of the girls had experienced incest, and 4 percent of males and 13 percent of females had experienced extrafamilial sexual abuse. Although the percentage of abused girls is smaller than that found by Russell, research by Glenn Wolfner and Richard Gelles indicates that up to one in five girls suffers sexual abuse.[21]

Although these results are alarming, it is probable that they still underestimate the true incidence of child sexual abuse. It is difficult to get people to respond to questions about child sexual abuse, and many victims either are too young to understand their abuse or have repressed their memory of such incidents. Of course, children may be inhibited because parents are reluctant to admit that abuse occurred. In one study, 57 percent of children referred to a clinic because they had sexually transmitted diseases claimed not to have been molested despite irrefutable evidence.[22]

CASE EXAMPLE OF MALTREATMENT: Sexual Abuse

Jody, age 11, said that she was asleep in her bedroom and that her father came in and took off his robe and underwear. She stated that he got into bed with her and pulled up her nightgown and put his private part on her private part. She stated that he pushed hard and it hurt. Jody said that the same thing had happened before while her mother was at work. Jody stated that she told her mother, but her father insisted that she was telling a lie.

Source: U.S. Department of Health and Human Services. (2014). Retrieved from http://www.hhs.gov/.

As with the previous categories of sexual criminal activity, much misunderstanding exists regarding the sexual abuse of children. This category of offense includes the following:

- *Exploitation.* The use of children for illegal activities such as prostitution and pornography.
- *Incest.* Sexual relations between children and their parents.
- *Child sexual abuse.* The sexual molestation of children, as well as seduction and statutory rape.

The Child Protection Act of 1984 describes child pornography as a highly organized business that focuses on runaways and homeless youth and that operates on a national basis. The act provides for increased penalties for adults involved in child pornography and points out that it is injurious to the physical and emotional well-being of the child. In addition to this act, most states have passed legislation addressing child abuse and the sexual exploitation of children.

▶ The Forensic Interview

For the most part, the child abuse investigation begins with information provided by the child victim. Obtaining this information is a vitally delicate task that normally requires a forensic interview of the child to determine whether he or she has been

LEARNING OUTCOMES 6 — Explain the significance of the forensic interview.

abused. In the case of a criminal investigation, the forensic interview can be conducted by a law enforcement officer or a member of child welfare or CPS, provided he or she is properly trained to do so. As such, child abuse investigations typically represent a collaborative effort between law enforcement and social service professionals.

In addition to yielding the information needed to make a determination about whether abuse or neglect has occurred, forensic interviewing provides evidence that will stand up in court if the investigation leads to criminal prosecution. Properly conducted forensic interviews are legally sound in part because they ensure the interviewer's objectivity; use nonleading, nonsuggestive techniques; and emphasize careful documentation of the interview. Generally, the forensic interview is used only during the assessment portion of a child abuse investigation and involves only the children who are the subject of the investigation.[23]

Why Are Forensic Interviews Needed?

The reason forensic interviews are needed is because most perpetrators deny the abuse and most acts of maltreatment are not witnessed; the victim's statement is critical evidence in child abuse cases. Yet developmental issues, such as children's varying abilities to recall events and use language, as well as the trauma they may have experienced, complicate efforts to obtain information about the abuse. The forensic interview is designed to overcome these obstacles.[24] The goal of the forensic interview is to obtain a statement from a child in an objective, developmentally sensitive, and legally defensible manner.[25]

In many jurisdictions, the backgrounds and professions of the persons who conduct forensic interviews vary from community to community and from investigation to investigation. Sometimes these interviews are conducted only by child welfare workers or law enforcement investigators in the field; sometimes another secondary forensic interview is conducted by a therapist or other specially trained professional in a controlled, child-friendly environment.

The Initial Interview

In most jurisdictions, state child welfare investigators conduct the initial forensic interview because state laws often require that after a report is received that a child has been physically, emotionally, or sexually abused, there must be immediate face-to-face contact with the child. During this meeting, which must typically occur within 24 hours after the report is made, child welfare workers assess risk and determine whether steps need to be taken to ensure the child's immediate safety. When police investigators discover a possible child abuse case, they can contact state child welfare workers and then observe the interview.[26]

The location of the interview is an important consideration when establishing the proper atmosphere for the child interview. Not only should the interview room be specifically designed—comfortable, quiet, and free from distractions—but there should also be only one interviewer responsible for interviewing the child.

In joint investigations, such as those involving police investigators and child service workers, both may be present, but only one should be in the primary interviewer role. Moreover, to protect the child from outside influence, no person having a direct relationship with him or her can be present, even for support. A trained victim advocate may accompany the child during the interview. The interview room needs to be equipped with nonintrusive video and audio equipment, and all interviews must be recorded. Such recordings document the interviewer's technique and capture the child's demeanor and statements.

The initial forensic interview can be influenced by a number of factors. These include the specific circumstances being investigated (for example, the child may need to be referred for a medical examination, which is often accompanied by a secondary forensic interview); the investigating officer's proximity to and ability to access forensic interviewing resources, such as a local Child Advocacy Center (CAC); the protocols and procedures adopted by each agency; and the interviewer's skill and comfort level.

To ensure facts are gathered in a way that will stand up in court, forensic interviews are carefully controlled. For example,
- the interviewer's statements and body language must be neutral.
- alternative explanations for a child's statements are thoroughly explored.
- the results of the interview are documented in such a way that they can bear judicial scrutiny.

One of the objectives of forensic interviewing is to reduce the number of times children are interviewed. The concern is contamination of the child's memory of the incident(s) being investigated. Research and clinical experience indicate that the more times a child—especially a young child—is interviewed about alleged abuse, the less reliable and legally defensible that child's testimony may become.[27]

Lauren Flick, a psychologist who has conducted more than 3,000 child interviews, describes contamination this way:

> If I am the first person to talk to a child about an event, that event is like a design on the bottom of a swimming pool filled with clear water—it is easy to read. But each conversation this child has with someone about the alleged abuse clouds the water. If he has talked with his principal, parents, a police officer, etc., it can be very hard or impossible to discern the design at the bottom of the pool.[28]

The Secondary Forensic Interview

More in-depth forensic interviews sometimes occur after the initial stages of an investigation. These are usually conducted by specially trained psychologists or professionals with graduate-level education in the areas relevant to this type of interviewing. Furthermore, these interviews usually take place at centers that facilitate the interview process—therapists and doctors sometimes have such facilities, as do most providers of child medical evaluations.

CACs are also excellent resources for forensic interviewing. CACs offer comfortable rooms with children's furniture, toys, interviewing props, and other aids for observing and documenting interviews. Law enforcement and child welfare agencies are encouraged to work with CACs to avoid delays that can be detrimental to the overall success of the investigation.

Techniques of Forensic Interviewing

Because forensic interviews can play a pivotal role in investigations of sexual and emotional abuse of children, criminal investigators need to know how they are conducted. There are many ways to conduct the forensic interview, and there is no single model or method endorsed unanimously by experts in the field. Some of the many forensic interviewing models in use today include the child cognitive interview, step-wise interview, and narrative elaboration. Similar to many of the others in existence, these three interview types have been shown to be more effective in helping children recall information than standard interviewing techniques used with adults.

Despite the different styles of interviews, there are some basic elements common to most forensic interviews. These include phases such as introduction, rapport building, developmental assessment (including learning the child's names for different body parts), guidelines for the interview, competency assessment (during which, among other things, it is determined if the child knows the difference between lying and telling the truth), narrative description of the event or events under investigation, follow-up questions, clarification, and closure.[29]

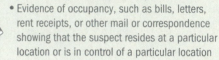

Physical Evidence in Child Sexual Molestation Cases

- Camera or video equipment used for taking photographic images of the victim engaged in sexual acts with the offender
- Notebooks, diaries, papers, or anything else linking the offender to the victim
- Negatives or undeveloped film that depict the victim (or other juveniles)
- Magazines, books, or movies depicting juveniles in sexual situations
- Newspapers, magazine clippings, or other publications listing phone numbers with other sexual interests that might tend to identify juveniles involved with the suspect
- Evidence of occupancy, such as bills, letters, rent receipts, or other mail or correspondence showing that the suspect resides at a particular location or is in control of a particular location
- Any items of physical evidence belonging to the victim or used by the subject in sexual acts

Investigating the Molester

It is important for any investigator to understand, as fully as possible, the methods used by child sex offenders. When an investigator understands the molester's desires and intentions, he or she can more adequately seek out the proper evidence for prosecution. For example, investigations have shown that child molesters frequently collect pornography and child erotica. Such items aid the prosecution in establishing the intent or motive of some offenders. Pornography fuels the desires that child molesters harbor for sexual contact with children.[30] Studies have also shown that child sexual assault is frequently a premeditated act; that is, offenders might only casually consider a particular course of action (fantasizing) without a specific plan or act, or they might take a more overt action in stalking and abducting their victims.

Premeditation and Intent

The circumstances of any given incident can show premeditation on the part of the molester. For example, in one such case,

Characteristics of Child Victims

☑ In the 8- to 16-year-old age group
☑ Unsupervised
☑ From unstable home environments
☑ From low- or average-income families
☑ Subject to abrupt changes in moods
☑ Not necessarily delinquent
☑ In possession of more money than normal, new toys, new clothes, and so on (gifts from the molester)
☑ Withdrawn from family and friends

The Pedophile/Child Molester

☑ Has access through family
☑ Lures the child, or tricks the child into sex acts; sometimes pressures the child into sexual activity
☑ Gives gifts or rewards to the child
☑ Cautions his or her victims against disclosure
☑ Frequently explains that the activity must be kept a "secret" between the offender and the child
☑ Gives the child attention, acceptance, recognition in exchange for sex
☑ Often targets children with disabilities who are loners
☑ May target the child of a single parent who may have no male figure in the immediate family
☑ May be a child rapist (forcible)
☑ Overpowers and controls the child much as do adult rapists
☑ Uses physical force or threats
☑ Is part of a small minority of sex offenders of children

a man boarded a transit bus loaded with children. The offender was seated next to a young girl approximately 10 years old, and during the bus ride the man's arm came to rest on the child's inner thigh or upper leg. Subsequent investigation revealed that the same man was frequently among a group of children at the time a local school let out and had no business being there. Here he also used his "hand trick" that he used on the bus.[31]

As this case illustrates, premeditation may be demonstrated through comparing different situations in which the same suspect was involved and establishing a mode of operation. As indicated, investigators should remember that molesters frequent places where there are children in their target group. This will help establish the molesters' intents and might also help establish probable cause to stop, detain, identify, and possibly arrest offenders.

Think About It…

Asking the "Right" Questions Forensic interviewing is a meticulous process that should be carried out only by those properly trained to do so.

Courtesy of Michael D. Lyman, Ph.D.

Child Interview.

Stereotypes about interviewing abound with respect to investigations dealing with victims, so it is important to know what question to ask and how to ask them. Some people are surprised to learn that forensic interviewers are not only law enforcement professionals but also social work professionals, medical professionals, and professionals belonging to other relevant fields. Discuss the difference between an initial forensic interview and a secondary forensic interview.

In conclusion, both the medical and legal professions have made great strides in identifying nonaccidental trauma inflicted on children and the suspected sexual abuse of children. This progress accounts for what appears to be an increase in the number of identified child abuse homicides. Sadly, however, there will always be some children who die of abuse that is never discovered. Children deserve investigators' best efforts to turn over every stone in cases involving any suspicion of abuse of children.

▶ Child Exploitation

In January 2014, Mount Pleasant, New York, Police Chief Brian Fanelli was charged with possession of child pornography following a raid by federal agents. The raid resulted in agents seizing Fanelli's home computers, which were filled with files of preteen girls in various sexual poses. Fanelli told investigators he first began viewing pornographic images as research for elementary and middle school classes he was teaching about the dangers of sexual abuse. But shortly thereafter he began viewing child pornography for personal interest, according to the federal complaint. Agents discovered more than 120 pornographic files on two computers taken from Fanelli's home, with photos and videos of the girls, some as young as seven years old. Fanelli's arrest resulted from his sharing of the downloaded files with undercover federal agents.

LEARNING OUTCOMES 7 Summarize the various problems associated with child exploitation.

Legal Implications

It is a federal crime to knowingly possess, manufacture, distribute, or access with intent to view child pornography (18 U.S.C. §2252[b]). In addition, all 50 states and the District of Columbia have laws criminalizing the possession, manufacture, and distribution of child pornography. As a result, a person who violates these laws may face federal and/or state charges.

The National Center for Missing and Exploited Children acknowledges the definition of child exploitation as defined under federal law. For example, federal law (18 U.S.C. §2256[8]) defines child pornography as any visual depiction, including any photograph, film, video, picture, or computer/computer-generated image or picture, whether made or produced by electronic, mechanical, or other means, of sexually explicit conduct, where the:

- Production of the visual depiction involves the use of a minor engaging in sexually explicit conduct,

- The visual depiction is a digital image or computer/computer-generated image that is, or is indistinguishable from, that of a minor engaging in sexually explicit conduct, or

- The visual depiction has been created, adapted, or modified to appear that an identifiable minor is engaging in sexually explicit conduct.

Federal law (18 U.S.C. §1466A[a]) also criminalizes knowingly producing, distributing, receiving, or possessing with intent to distribute a visual depiction of any kind, including a drawing, cartoon, sculpture, or painting, depicting:

- A minor engaging in sexually explicit conduct that is obscene, or

- An image that is, or appears to be, of a minor engaging in graphic bestiality, sadistic or masochistic abuse or sexual intercourse, including genital-genital, oral-genital, anal-genital, or oral-anal, whether between people of the same or opposite sex, that lacks serious literary, artistic, political, or scientific value.

Additionally, sexually explicit conduct is defined under federal law (18 U.S.C. §2256[2][A]) as actual or simulated sexual intercourse, including genital-genital, oral-genital, anal-genital, or oral-anal, whether between people of the same or opposite sex; bestiality; masturbation; sadistic or masochistic abuse; or lascivious exhibition of the genitals or pubic area of any person.[32]

Recent History

According to the U.S. Department of Justice, by the mid-1980s, the trafficking of child pornography within the United States was almost completely eradicated through a series of successful campaigns waged by law enforcement. Producing and reproducing child sexual abuse images was difficult and expensive. Anonymous distribution and receipt was not possible, and it was difficult for pedophiles to find and interact with each other. For these reasons, child pornographers became isolated individuals because the purchasing and trading of such images was extremely risky.

Unfortunately, the child pornography market exploded in the advent of the Internet and advanced digital technology. The Internet provides ground for individuals to create, access, and share child sexual abuse images worldwide at the click of a button. In present day, child pornography images are readily available through virtually every Internet technology, including websites, e-mail, instant messaging/Internet chat query (ICQ), Internet relay chat (IRC), newsgroups, bulletin boards, peer-to-peer networks, and social networking sites. Child pornography offenders can connect on Internet networks and forums to share their interests, desires, and experiences in abusing children in addition to selling, sharing, and trading images.

In addition, online communities have promoted communication between child pornography offenders, both normalizing their interest in children and desensitizing them to the physical and psychological damages inflicted on child victims. Online communities may also attract or promote new individuals to get involved in the sexual exploitation of children.

According to the National Center for Missing and Exploited Children, more than 2 million reports of child sexual exploitation have been made since 1998. Commercial sexual exploitation of children occurs when individuals buy, trade, or sell sexual acts with a child. Sex trafficking is "The recruitment, harboring, transportation, provision, or obtaining of a person for the purposes of a commercial sex act."[33]

Victims of Child Pornography

It is important to distinguish child pornography from the more conventional understanding of the term *pornography*. **Child pornography** is a form of child sexual exploitation, and each image graphically memorializes the sexual abuse of that child. Each child involved in the production of an image is a victim of sexual abuse.

Although some child sexual abuse images depict children in great distress and the sexual abuse is self-evident, other images may depict children that appear complacent. However, just because a child appears complacent does not mean that sexual abuse did not occur. In most child pornography cases, the abuse is not a one-time event, but rather ongoing victimization that progresses over months or years. It is common for producers of child pornography to groom victims, or cultivate a relationship with a child and gradually sexualize the contact over time. The grooming process fosters a false sense of trust and authority over a child in order to desensitize or break down a child's resistance to sexual abuse. Therefore, even if a child appears complacent in a particular image, it is important to remember that the abuse may have started years before that image was created.

Furthermore, victims of child pornography suffer not just from the sexual abuse inflicted upon them in producing child pornography, but also from knowing that their images can be traded and viewed by others worldwide. Once an image is on the Internet, it is irretrievable and can continue to circulate forever. The permanent record of a child's sexual abuse can alter his or her life forever. Many victims of child pornography suffer from feelings of helplessness, fear, humiliation, and lack of control given that their images are available for others to view in perpetuity.

Child Prostitution

Federal law prohibits the prostitution of children, both with respect to individuals who offer children for sex in exchange for money or other considerations, and with respect to individuals who would pay to have sex with a child. Those who sell children for sex are commonly referred to as traffickers or "pimps," whereas the purchasers or customers are commonly known as "johns." Children involved in this form of commercial sexual exploitation are victims. Under federal law, children cannot consent to being prostituted.

Numerous different phrases are used to describe the prostitution of children, including *sex trafficking*, *a severe form of human trafficking*, or the *commercial sexual exploitation of children*. Whatever the name, the dynamic is the same: the sale of children for sex. Sex trafficking is a lucrative industry, and criminals sell children just as they would traffic drugs or other illegal substances. The prostitution of children is a serious crime, and convicted offenders face severe statutory penalties.

Federal law in the United States notes that a child does not need to be moved across international or even state borders to be considered a victim of commercial sexual exploitation. Pimps and traffickers sexually exploit children through street prostitution and in adult strip clubs, brothels, sex parties, motel rooms, hotel rooms, and other locations throughout the

United States. Many recovered American victims are runaways or "throwaway youth" who often suffer from a history of physical abuse, sexual abuse, and family abandonment issues. Pimps see this population as an easy target because the children are generally vulnerable, without dependable guardians, and suffer from low self-esteem. Child victims of prostitution come from all backgrounds in terms of class, race, and geography (i.e., urban, suburban, and rural settings).

Often in domestic sex trafficking situations, a pimp will cause a child victim to feel dependent on him for life necessities and survival. For example, a pimp will lure a child with food, clothes, attention, friendship, love, and a seemingly safe place to stay. After cultivating a relationship and engendering a false sense of trust with the child, the pimp will begin engaging the child in prostitution. It is also common for pimps to isolate victims by moving them far away from friends and family, altering their physical appearance, or continuously moving victims to new locations. In many cases, the pimps are so adept at controlling and manipulating the victims that the children are incapable of leaving the situation on their own.

Technological advances, in particular the Internet, have facilitated the commercial sexual exploitation of children by providing a convenient worldwide marketing channel. Individuals can now use websites to advertise, schedule, and purchase sexual encounters with minors. The Internet and web-enabled cell phones also allow pimps and traffickers to expand their clientele base.

Child Exploitation Offenders

Each year, Americans are convicted of committing this crime against children. While some offenders are pedophiles who preferentially seek out children for sexual relationships, others are situational abusers. These individuals do not consistently seek out children as sexual partners, but do occasionally engage in sexual acts with children when the opportunity presents itself. Children from developing countries are seen as easy targets by American perpetrators because they are often disadvantaged by unstable or unfavorable economic, social, or political conditions, or their home country lacks effective law enforcement against this crime. However, incidents of the extraterritorial sexual exploitation of children involving American perpetrators are reported and occur all over the world, including less developed areas in Southeast Asia and Central and South America, to more developed areas in Europe.

Some perpetrators rationalize their sexual encounters with children with the idea that they are helping the children financially better themselves and their families. Other perpetrators are drawn toward this crime because they enjoy the anonymity that comes with being in a foreign land. Racism, gender discrimination, and cultural differences are among other justifications. However, the reason for travel makes no difference under the law; any American citizen or resident who engages in sexual conduct with a minor in a foreign land is subject to federal prosecution.

Sexual Abuse of Children within the Catholic Church

For years, what were initially allegations of sexual abuse of children by Catholic priests were vehemently denied and officially ignored by the church. In fact, many in the public simply could not imagine these allegations to be truthful. Today, there are enough documented cases of this abuse being real that even the church has become involved after several criminal investigations and lawsuits.

Recently in the state of Washington, Catholic bishops voted and passed various revisions to a charter by listing child pornography as the same as sexual abuse. Bishop Blase Cupich was quoted as saying, "We learned the hard way the advice we got from psychology that people could be rehabilitated was bad advice . . . they re-offended. You cannot take that risk." Some in the public are saying that this action is simply not enough to address the issue of sexual abuse within the church, citing the fact that the church has merely reassigned priests accused of sexual abuse in the past to new locations, providing opportunities for continued abuse. This case is important in that it demonstrates, as the chapter does, that the responsibility to address sexual abuse, even in investigations, does not fall solely on law

Pixel Memoirs/Shutterstock.com

enforcement; it requires a public willingness to seriously address the issue as well.

Source: Porterfield, Elaine. (2011, June 16). U.S. Catholic bishops approve shifts in abuse policy. *Reuters.* Retrieved from http://www.reuters .com/article/2011/06/16/us-usa-bishops-abuse-idUSTRE75F69Q20110 616?feedType=RSS&feedName=domesticNews.

The investigation of crimes against children is one of society's most urgent and important priorities:

1. If you were the lead investigator in a sexual abuse case involving a religious person, what steps do you think you might take to deal with public pressure and possible denial that a member of the clergy could commit such a crime?

LEARNING OUTCOMES 1

Summarize the scope of the problem of child abuse.

Every year in the United States, thousands of children die from a variety of causes, including homicides. At least four children in the United States die from maltreatment each day. Professionally conducted investigations of child fatalities ensure that innocent people are not falsely accused and guilty people are not allowed to remain free and possibly harm another child.

1. How does the case example at the beginning of this chapter illustrate the complex nature of child abuse cases?

2. In terms of child abuse cases, what are the likely results of a flawed investigation?

3. What elements make child abuse cases complex and potentially problematic for law enforcement?

4. How are child fatality cases categorized?

5. What are the differences between the two ways child fatality cases are categorized?

6. Why is it important to have experienced, emotionally stable caretakers for children during their preschool years?

child abuse The physical, sexual, or emotional abuse of children.

acute maltreatment When a child's death is directly related to injuries suffered as a result of a specific incident of abuse or act of negligence.

shaken baby syndrome (SBS) A medical term for murder of infants who are violently shaken.

chronic maltreatment Occurs when a child's death is directly related to injuries caused by maltreatment or neglect occurring over an extended period.

parens patriae Latin for "parent of the nation." Under law, it refers to the public policy power of the state to intervene against an abusive or negligent parent, legal guardian, or informal caretaker and to act as the parent of any child or individual who is in need of protection.

LEARNING OUTCOMES 2

Explain the role of Child Protective Services and the police in crimes against children.

At least 30 states have either mandated or authorized implementation of multidisciplinary teams to investigate child maltreatment. CPS does not determine whether anyone committed a crime; it determines if maltreatment occurred. The criminal investigator determines whether a crime has been committed and who is responsible. Law enforcement and CPS must communicate and coordinate efforts.

1. What role does CPS play in the investigation of child fatality cases?

2. Why is it necessary for law enforcement agencies to take the lead when investigating cases jointly with CPS?

3. What kind of evidence is collected in cases involving child fatalities and abuse?

4. What important information can be obtained from an autopsy?

5. How can CPS investigators hinder law enforcement work in child fatality cases?

LEARNING OUTCOMES 3

Describe the problem of child physical abuse.

Child physical abuse remains a serious problem involving a variety of acts resulting in injuries to a child. The crime most often reported to the police is physical child abuse that results in death or serious injury. However, child abuse is far more pervasive and often more subtle. The physical effects of child abuse are only part of a child's injuries.

1. What are the elements of child abuse and neglect?

2. What are the psychological and emotional impacts of child abuse?

3. What is meant by the phrase "child abuse is an intergenerational phenomenon"?

4. When conducting physical examinations on suspected victims of physical child abuse, what types of injuries can confirm or suggest abuse to the medical examiner?

5. What kinds of evidence should be collected during physical child abuse investigations?

Describe the problems of battered child syndrome, shaken baby syndrome, Munchausen's syndrome by proxy, and sudden infant death syndrome.

Uncovering cases of battered child syndrome and gathering evidence for successful prosecution can be difficult for law enforcement because it is a crime that is often hidden by its perpetrators. Shaken baby syndrome (SBS) affects 1,200 or more children every year in the United States. In cases of Munchausen syndrome by proxy, parents or caretakers with Munchausen syndrome attempt to bring medical attention to themselves by inducing illness in their children. Caution is required in the diagnosis of fabricated or induced illness. Sudden infant death syndrome (SIDS), also known as "crib death," is the sudden death of an infant that is not predicted by medical history and remains unexplained after a thorough forensic autopsy and detailed death-scene investigation

1. Under what circumstances are officers justified in making an arrest in suspected cases of battered child syndrome?

2. What investigative steps should an investigator take when faced with a suspected case of battered child syndrome?

3. What physical evidence is necessary and useful when investigating a potential case of battered child syndrome?

4. What injuries result from SBS?

5. What makes investigating cases of Munchausen syndrome by proxy problematic and complex?

6. Why are infants and newborns more susceptible to SBS than toddlers and older children?

7. What characteristics make SIDS different from all the other syndromes discussed in the chapter?

8. Why is it necessary to interview a child's pediatrician as well as obtain all available medical records when investigating various syndromes related to child physical abuse?

battered child syndrome A clinical term referring to the collection of injuries sustained by a child as a result of repeated mistreatment or beating.

Munchausen syndrome by proxy A clinical term referring to when a parent or caretaker attempts to bring medical attention to him- or herself by inducing illness in his or her children.

sudden infant death syndrome (SIDS) A diagnosis made when there is no other medical explanation for the abrupt death of an apparently healthy infant.

LEARNING OUTCOMES 5

Summarize the scope and prevalence of child sexual abuse.

A survey of Minnesota students in grades 6, 9, and 12 revealed that about 2 percent of the boys and 7 percent of the girls had experienced incest, and 4 percent of males and 13 percent of females had experienced extrafamilial sexual abuse. Other research indicates that up to one in five girls suffers sexual abuse before age 18. Experts suggest that the statistics underestimate the true incidence of child sexual abuse.

1. Why is it difficult for authorities to understand the actual prevalence of child sexual abuse?

2. What are the three categories of child sexual abuse?

3. Why was the adoption of the Child Protection Act a significant development for children, children's advocates, and law enforcement?

LEARNING OUTCOMES 6

Explain the significance of the forensic interview.

The forensic interview is used during the assessment portion of a child abuse investigation and involves only the children who are the subject of the investigation. The goal of the interview is to obtain a statement from a child in an objective, developmentally sensitive, and legal manner. Furthermore, one of the objectives of forensic interviewing is to reduce the number of times children are interviewed.

1. Why is the forensic interview especially important in child abuse cases?

2. What are key tips in ensuring facts gathered in the forensic interview can withstand judicial scrutiny?

3. Why are all forensic interviews with children recorded?

4. What factors influence the general direction and outcome of forensic interviews?

5. Who typically conducts secondary forensic interviews? Why?

6. What are the basic elements of forensic interviews?

7. What are examples of physical evidence in child molestation cases?

LEARNING OUTCOMES 7

Summarize the various problems associated with child exploitation.

The National Center for Missing and Exploited Children acknowledges the definition of child exploitation as defined under federal law. For example, federal law (18 U.S.C. §2256[8]) defines child pornography as any visual depiction, including any photograph, film, video, picture, or computer/computer-generated image or picture, whether made or produced by electronic, mechanical, or other means, of sexually explicit conduct, where the:

- Production of the visual depiction involves the use of a minor engaging in sexually explicit conduct,
- The visual depiction is a digital image or computer/computer-generated image that is, or is indistinguishable from, that of a minor engaging in sexually explicit conduct, or

- The visual depiction has been created, adapted, or modified to appear that an identifiable minor is engaging in sexually explicit conduct.

1. Explain the problem of child pornography and why it is a growing concern

2. Describe how child prostitution rings operate.

3. Identify the characteristics of a child exploitation offender.

child pornography Pornography that involves a child. It may be simulated child pornography or produced with the direct involvement of the child; also known as child sexual exploitation. Abuse of the child occurs during the sexual acts that are recorded in the production of child pornography.

Additional Links

www.cdc.gov
This is the site of the Centers for Disease Control and Prevention (CDC). The site contains extensive information and resources on child abuse/maltreatment. Visitors can also search for specific topics on the site. Searches for sudden infant death syndrome, battered child syndrome, Munchausen syndrome by proxy, and shaken baby syndrome result in a host of links and articles. There are links for researchers, media, businesses, students and educators, and individuals interested in a variety of topics related to the health and safety of children.

"Crimes of theft are the most common types of crime and as such consume a considerable amount of investigative resources."

14

Theft-Related Offenses

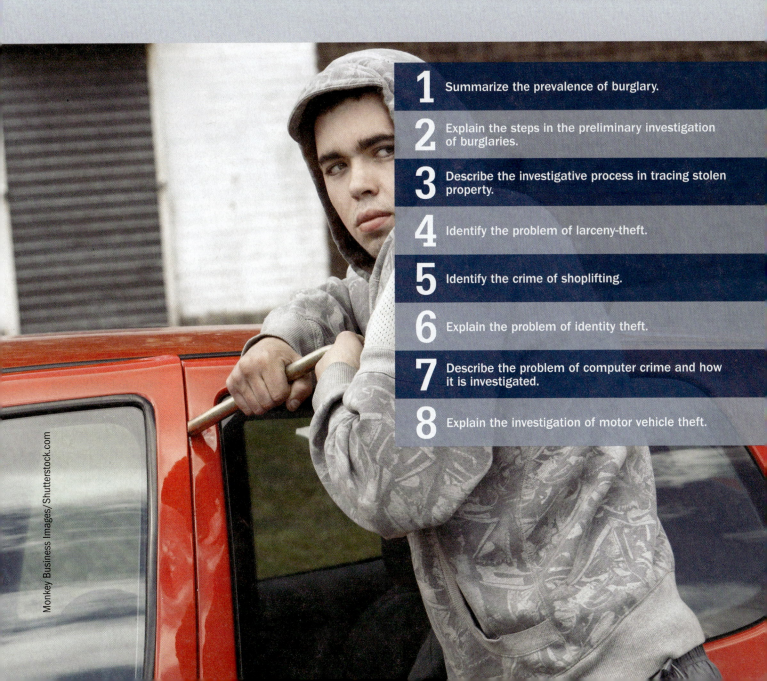

1 Summarize the prevalence of burglary.

2 Explain the steps in the preliminary investigation of burglaries.

3 Describe the investigative process in tracing stolen property.

4 Identify the problem of larceny-theft.

5 Identify the crime of shoplifting.

6 Explain the problem of identity theft.

7 Describe the problem of computer crime and how it is investigated.

8 Explain the investigation of motor vehicle theft.

Monkey Business Images/Shutterstock.com

INTRO THE STRENGTH OF A SURVIVOR

On May 3, 2011, 27-year-old Erick Rodrigo Carranza and 18-year-old Junior Alexis Velasquez broke into a Harris County, Texas, home in what appeared to be an attempted burglary. Once inside, however, they encountered 76-year-old Henry Schmidt. The intruders bound Schmidt's arms with duct tape and wrapped him up in a blanket so they could ransack his home.

Schmidt managed to roll himself into the kitchen during the night, only to be taken back to the bedroom when the two intruders returned the next morning. They then spent about two hours cleaning the house in an attempt to eliminate evidence before leaving with more of Schmidt's belongings.

Schmidt, although dehydrated and with little strength left, then resumed his struggle to free himself. After several hours, he was eventually able to free his arms from the quilt. His wrists still taped together, Schmidt crawled on his elbows to the kitchen. There he pried open the re-frigerator and knocked some grapes to the floor to eat.

Then, again using his elbows, he worked his way to a rear entrance and used his feet to slide the door open. Schmidt crawled outside on his elbows and rolled some 100 feet down a concrete drive to the road. Some two hours passed before a motorist finally stopped, freed him, and summoned help.

Paramedics transported Schmidt to a hospital, where he was treated for his injuries. The criminal suspects were later identified and arrested.

DISCUSS **Although it is amazing how Mr. Schmidt survived his ordeal, is there anything that could have been done by police to identify and capture these criminals before they victimized Mr. Schmidt?**

The crime of **burglary** is generally considered a covert crime in which the criminal works during the nighttime, outside the presence of witnesses. The burglar has often been portrayed in the media as a cunning masked person who is quick to elude police. In actuality, burglars are represented by virtually every creed, gender, and color and may indeed be skillful in their techniques, but they may also be bungling amateurs. In fact, it is estimated that opportunists commit most burglaries. Burglary for the most part is a **property crime**. The crime differs from robbery because burglars are more concerned with financial gain and less prepared for a violent altercation with the victim.

Burglar Making Forced Entry into a Residence.

Kadmy/Fotolia

Their goal is to steal as much valuable property as possible and sell what they steal (usually to a *fence*, a person who has connections to dispose of the property before police can discover it).

The *Uniform Crime Reports* (UCR) program of the Federal Bureau of Investigation (FBI) uses three classifications of burglary: forcible entry, unlawful entry or no force used, and attempted forcible entry. In most jurisdictions, force need not be used for a crime to be classified as burglary. Unlocked doors and open windows are invitations to burglars, and the crime of burglary consists not so much of a forcible entry as it does the intent of the offender to trespass and steal.

Many people fear nighttime burglary of their residence. They imagine themselves asleep in bed when a stranger breaks into their home, resulting in a violent confrontation. Although such scenarios do occur, daytime burglaries are more common. Many families now have two or more breadwinners, and because children are in school during the day, some homes—and even entire neighborhoods—remain unoccupied during daylight hours. This shift in patterns of social activity has led to growing burglary threats against residences during the daytime.

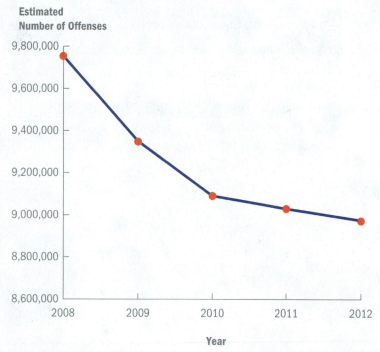

Estimated Number of Offenses

Property Crime Offenses.

The Frequency of Burglary

Although it may involve personal and sometimes violent confrontations, burglary is primarily property crime. Burglars are interested in financial game and usually fence (illegally sell) stolen merchandise, recovering only a fraction of its cash value. Approximately 2.1 million burglaries were reported to the police in 2012.[1] Dollar losses to burglary victims totaled $4.7 billion, with an average loss per offense of $2,230.[2]

In the UCR program, three classifications of burglary have been identified: (1) forcible entry, (2) unlawful entry where no force was used, and (3) attempted forcible entry. As noted, unlocked doors and windows are invitations to burglars, and the legal essence of burglary consists not so much of forcible entry as it does of the intent to trespass and steal. In 2012, 60.5 percent of all burglaries were forcible entries, 33.2 percent were unlawful entries, and 6.3% were attempted forcible entries.[3] The most dangerous burglaries are those in which a household member was home; such burglaries constituted about 10 percent of all burglaries. The clearance rate for burglary is generally low. In 2012, the clearance rate for burglary was only 12.4 percent. Typically, burglars do not know their victims, and in cases where they do, they conceal their identities or commit their crimes when the victim is not present.[4]

The Preliminary Investigation

The patrol division is usually the first to respond to a burglary call. The first action officers should take is to determine whether a crime is currently in progress. If so, an ample number of officers should be dispatched to prevent the escape of the suspect(s). Officers approaching the burglary location should do so quietly without warning emergency lights or siren. En route, officers should also be on the lookout for persons fleeing the scene. It is also important for each officer to know exactly which fellow officers are responding to the call. As a rule, the first officer to receive the call will assume responsibility for placement of assisting officers.

After arriving, great care should be taken not to slam car doors, to turn down police radios, and to avoid the jangling of keys while approaching the residence. In addition, officers should approach the residence on both the front and back sides in case the suspect attempts to flee (see Figure 14–1).

Indications of Burglary

At the scene, certain reliable indicators that a burglary has been (or is being) committed can be observed, for example, open doors or windows or pry marks on doors and windows (see Figure 14–2). Sometimes a burglar who makes his or her entrance through a window will remove the glass. This makes it difficult for the officer to detect a break-in with only a superficial glance. So when checking glass, the officer should look for a reflection with the use of a flashlight. Sometimes burglaries can be detected by spotting debris on the floor from shelves or counters. Also, debris can be found around desks and cabinets. Other indicators include vehicles parked near the suspect location for no apparent reason or trucks parked close enough to a building to permit access to a roof or to conceal a window or door. In the case of a building burglary, a burglar alarm is another indicator of possible entry. Although wind, stormy conditions,

Inside lights remain off at night, indicating no one is home.

Newspapers collect on driveway or yard, indicating that owners are away.

Shrubs are not trimmed.

Area around the home is not properly lighted.

House keys are located around the home.

Windows or doors are left unlocked.

No vehicles located in the driveway or in front of the home, indicating that owners are away.

FIGURE 14–1 What Makes a House an Attractive Target to a Burglar?

FIGURE 14–2 Pry Marks Such as These Are Often Evidence of a Forcible Entry.

or malfunctions can set off some alarms, the responding officer should not assume anything. Every alarm situation should be responded to as though it were a burglary in progress.

Yet another sign of a burglary in progress is a person serving as a lookout. Lookouts may be on, in, or near buildings or sitting in cars. Burglars have been known to use such tactics as parking a car a few feet down the street, raising the car's hood, using citizens-band walkie-talkies, or just blowing the horn as a signal that police are approaching.

▶ Tracing Stolen Property

LEARNING OUTCOMES 3 — Describe the investigative process in tracing stolen property.

After a successful burglary has occurred, the thief will probably seek to get rid of the stolen property as soon as possible. To this end, a **fence** is used. The fence is a person who buys and sells stolen property with criminal intent.

The Fence

Fencing operations can range from professional to highly unorganized. For example, a nonprofessional fence might simply take a trunk full of stolen property in his or her vehicle to a location such as a factory parking lot, where workers on break can come for "good deals." A professional fence may operate from an otherwise legitimate business such as a pawn shop or used furniture store. People operating in this fashion don't necessarily consider themselves criminals yet seldom question the lawful ownership of the property they receive. From this fixed location, the fence purchases property on a random basis from thieves in the area. This arrangement tends to foster a degree of dependency between the thief and the fence, with each needing the services of the other.

Proving the Receipt of Stolen Property

Establishing proof of a fencing operation is a grueling and time-consuming task. However, a fence is most vulnerable during the possession and storage of stolen property. Although many arrests result from lengthy investigations, many also are made when suspected stolen property is identified. This is sometimes necessary when there is a risk of losing the property and confiscation is required. As a first rule of thumb, the property in question must be identified as stolen, a task that is more difficult than it may at first seem. For instance, many suspected thieves are in possession of property that bears no identification numbers. Without some type of identification number, positive identification is extremely difficult.

In addition, many companies fail to maintain adequate inventory control. Poorly kept records also make it difficult to trace property even when identification numbers are present. Another category of untraceable goods is **fungible goods**, items such as tools, liquor, and clothing that are indistinguishable from others like them. In the absence of some type of identifying numbers, such items are virtually untraceable. To convict a thief for a property offense in this category, investigators must prove that the suspect received stolen property. Laws addressing stolen property also include possession, concealment, and sale of stolen property. Because evidence in this category is sometimes difficult to obtain, investigators might have to rely on circumstantial evidence for prosecution.

One method of showing possession of stolen property is to locate the property on the premises of the suspect. This finding,

Investigative Techniques in Burglary Cases

☑ Determine the point of entry.

☑ Check to see if a window or door was forced open.

☑ What type of tool was used?

☑ Are there tool marks?

☑ Is there evidence of lock picks?

☑ Look for footprints, tire tracks, and so on.

☑ Look for other trace evidence such as cigarette butts, fibers, hair, pieces of broken tools, and so on.

☑ Sketch the scene.

☑ Interview victims and witnesses.

☑ Make a list of property taken (include serial numbers).

☑ Make a list of all persons on the crime scene.

Circumstantial Evidence

Other than the evidence discussed previously, investigators might need to rely on circumstantial evidence to prove receipt of stolen property. Such evidence is described as follows:

- Did the suspect pay for the merchandise with a check or cash?
- Was the property purchased for considerably less than the normal retail price?
- Does the suspect have a receipt for the property?
- Were the stolen items isolated from other items in storage?
- Is there property from several different thefts present at the location?

After property has been retrieved, a determination should be made as to how it got there. The owner of the property should examine it and make a positive identification. In many cases, a secondhand store or pawn shop owner can make a positive identification of a fence.

however, may not be sufficient to prove "criminal intent." It is helpful to show that the stolen goods are in close proximity with personal goods owned by the suspect. This will avoid the defense that the stolen goods were in the possession of someone else living at the same residence.

▶ Larceny-Theft

In 2002, 25-year-old Ted Roberts and 22-year-old Tiffany Fowler were arrested in Orlando, Florida, and charged with stealing moon rocks from the Johnson Space Center in Houston, Texas. Roberts had been working as a student intern at the center, and Fowler was a Space Center employee. Officials realized that the lunar samples, along with a number of meteorites, were missing when they discovered that a 600-pound safe had disappeared from the Houston facility. They had been alerted to the loss by messages placed on a website run by a mineralogy club in Antwerp, Belgium, offering "priceless Moon rocks collected by Apollo astronauts" for sale for up to $5,000 per gram. Roberts and Fowler were arrested by federal agents pretending to be potential buyers for the moon rocks.

LEARNING OUTCOMES 4
Identify the problem of larceny-theft.

According to the FBI, larceny-theft is the most commonly committed crime of personal gain. The FBI's UCR program defines larceny-theft as the unlawful taking, carrying, leading, or riding away of property from the possession or constructive possession of another (see Box 14–1). Examples are thefts of bicycles, thefts of motor vehicle parts and accessories, shoplifting, pocket picking, or the stealing of any property or article that

is not taken by force and violence or by fraud. Attempted larcenies are included. Embezzlement, confidence games, forgery, check fraud, and similar crimes are excluded.[5]

Larceny-theft is one of the eight Index crimes according to the UCR. Generally, the two terms *larceny* and *theft* are considered synonymous. In some states, criminal law recognizes simple larceny (for example, shoplifting) and grand larceny (for example, auto theft). In most cases, what distinguishes one form of larceny from another is the dollar amount of the items stolen. In most states there is a specific dollar amount that distinguishes larceny from theft. For example, when anything stolen is valued under $200, the charge is simple larceny, whereas stolen property valued in excess of that figure is grand larceny.

Fraud-Forgery

Countless people each year fall victim to fraudulent acts—often unknowingly. Fraud is a broad term that refers to a variety of offenses involving dishonesty or "fraudulent acts." Generally, fraud is the intentional deception of a person by another made for monetary or personal gain.

Fraud offenses include some sort of false statement, misrepresentation, or deceitful conduct. The motivation for fraud is to gain something of value (usually money or property) by misleading or deceiving someone into thinking something that the fraud perpetrator knows to be false.

Laws against fraud vary from state to state and can be criminal or civil in nature. Criminal fraud requires criminal intent on the part of the perpetrator and is punishable by fines or imprisonment. In comparison, civil fraud applies more broadly to circumstances where bad faith is usually involved and where the penalties are meant to punish the perpetrator and put the victim back in the same position as before the fraud took place.

Although the exact wording of fraud charges varies among state and federal laws, essential elements needed to prove a fraud claim include:

1. A misrepresentation of material fact;
2. By a person or entity who knows or believes it to be false;

BOX 14–1 🛡 Elements of Larceny-Theft

A person commits the crime of larceny-theft if he or she
• takes and carries away
• the personal property
• of another
• without consent and with the intent to steal.

Source: Federal Bureau of Investigation. (2008). *Crime in the United States—2007.* Washington, DC: U.S. Government Printing Office.

Think About It…

Tracing Stolen Property It is sometimes difficult for criminals to move or get rid of merchandise they have stolen. One reason is that finding someone (a fence) to purchase those goods from the criminal opens that fence to possible investigation and therefore risk if he or she accepts possession of the goods. If you were an investigator working on a stolen property case involving a gun collector, what types of information might be important to your investigation?

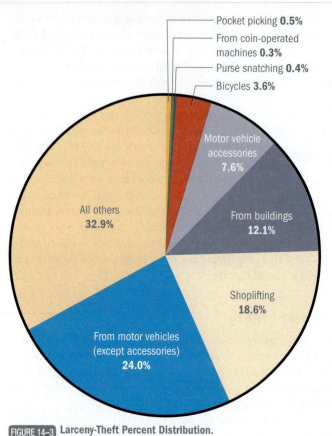

Pocket picking **0.5%**

From coin-operated machines **0.3%**

Purse snatching **0.4%**

Bicycles **3.6%**

Motor vehicle accessories **7.6%**

All others **32.9%**

From buildings **12.1%**

Shoplifting **18.6%**

From motor vehicles (except accessories) **24.0%**

FIGURE 14–3 **Larceny-Theft Percent Distribution.**
Source: U.S. Department of Justice (2013), Crime in the United States—2012.

3. To a person or entity who justifiably relies on the misrepresentation, and;

4. Actual injury or loss resulting from his or her reliance.

There are numerous types of fraud, several of which occur through the mail, Internet, phone, or by wire. Common types include:

- Bankruptcy fraud
- Tax fraud (tax evasion)
- Identity theft
- Insurance fraud
- Mail fraud
- Credit/debit card fraud

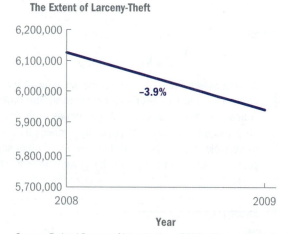

The Extent of Larceny-Theft

–3.9%

6,200,000

6,100,000

6,000,000

5,900,000

5,800,000

5,700,000

2008   2009

Year

Source: Federal Bureau of Investigation. (2010). Crime in the United States—2009

The following offenses are examples of larceny:

- Pocket picking
- Breaking into coin machines
- Purse snatching
- Shoplifting
- Stealing bicycles
- Stealing motor vehicles
- Stealing valuables left in unattended buildings
- Stealing motor vehicle accessories

- Securities fraud
- Telemarketing fraud
- Wire fraud

Penalties for fraud offenses can include criminal penalties, civil penalties, or both. Most criminal fraud offenses are considered felony crimes and are punishable by jail, fines, probation, or all of the above. Civil penalties may include restitution or payment of substantial fines.

Forgery

The crime of forgery generally refers to the making of a fake document, the changing of an existing document, or the making of a signature without proper authorization. Forgery involves a false document, signature, or other imitation of an object of value used with the intent to deceive another person. Persons who commit forgery are often charged with the crime of fraud (discussed earlier).

Documents that can be the object of forgery include contracts, identification cards, and legal certificates. Most states require that forgery be done with the intent to commit fraud or larceny-theft.

The most typical form of forgery is signing someone else's name to a check, but objects, data, and documents can also be

According to the FBI, in 2009 there were an estimated 5,944,792 larceny-thefts nationwide. From 2008 to 2009, the rate of larceny-thefts declined 3.9 percent. Larceny-thefts represent a considerable percentage of property crimes. For example, in 2009 they accounted for an estimated 67.9 percent of property crimes. The FBI reports that the average value of property taken during larceny-thefts was $864 per offense. When the average value was applied to the estimated number of larceny-thefts, the loss to victims nationally was nearly $5.5 billion. The largest portion of reported larcenies, 36.3 percent, were thefts of motor vehicle parts, accessories, and contents.

forged. Legal contracts, historical papers, art objects, diplomas, licenses, certificates, and identification cards can also be forged. Technically, currency and consumer goods can be forged, but that offense is usually referred to as counterfeiting.

Check Fraud

Despite readily available electronic banking, one low-tech device is increasingly popular: the checkbook. Just as check writing has boomed, so has check fraud. According to the American Bankers Association, check fraud is a growing concern, costing banks $12.2 billion in 2006.[6] In addition to its impact on banks is its effect on consumers. For example, check fraud leads to higher fees for bounced checks, and when a person is a victim of check fraud, dealing with it can impose a severe hardship in reconciling and closing an account and dealing with creditors seeking payment for merchandise purchased with bogus checks. Why is there an increase in check fraud? The American Bankers Association responds with several reasons:

- The proliferation of personal computers and high-quality copiers, which make it easier and less expensive to forge copies of checks

- Checking account customers who don't safeguard their account numbers

- Competition for business, which discourages some banks from stepping up procedures to detect and combat fraud because it might inconvenience customers

Criminals realize that check forgery is lucrative and that, because it is a nonviolent crime, their chances of being prosecuted are unlikely. Bands of criminals often travel from region to region targeting different banks and payroll accounts. After infiltrating an employer and forging documents, they can walk off with as much as $300,000 per day.

Forgery of a victim's personal check involves acquiring both the check and a form of identification of the victim. The criminal must then be able to forge the victim's name on the check successfully enough that it closely resembles the original. In addition to the signature, the amounts of checks can sometimes be altered to larger amounts. This can be accomplished in several ways. For

Tom Lynn/Getty Images

Policemen Guard a Recovered Stradivarius Violin.

A CLOSER LOOK

The Nigerian Letter or "419" Fraud

Nigerian letter frauds combine the threat of impersonation fraud with a variation of an advance fee scheme in which a letter mailed from Nigeria offers the recipient the "opportunity" to share in a percentage of millions of dollars that the author—a self-proclaimed government official—is trying to transfer illegally out of Nigeria. The recipient is encouraged to send information to the author, such as blank letterhead stationery, bank name and account numbers, and other identifying information, using a fax number provided in the letter. Some of these letters have also been received via e-mail through the Internet. The scheme relies on convincing a willing victim, who has demonstrated a "propensity for larceny" by responding to the invitation, to send money to the author of the letter in Nigeria in several installments of increasing amounts for a variety of reasons.

Payment of taxes, bribes to government officials, and legal fees are often described in great detail with the promise that all expenses will be reimbursed as soon as the funds are spirited out of Nigeria. In actuality, the millions of dollars do not exist, and the victim eventually ends up with nothing but loss. Once the victim stops sending money, the perpetrators have been known to use the personal information and checks that they received to impersonate the victim, draining bank accounts and swelling credit card balances. Although such an invitation impresses most law-abiding citizens as a laughable hoax, millions of dollars in losses are caused by these schemes annually. Some victims have been lured to Nigeria, where they have been

imprisoned against their will along with losing large sums of money. The Nigerian government is not sympathetic to victims of these schemes, as the victims actually conspire to remove funds from Nigeria in a manner that is contrary to Nigerian law. The schemes themselves violate Section 419 of the Nigerian criminal code, hence the label "419" fraud.

Tips for Avoiding Nigerian Letter or "419" Fraud

- If you receive a letter from Nigeria asking you to send personal or banking information, do not reply in any manner. Send the letter to the U.S. Secret Service, your local FBI office, or the U.S. Postal Inspection Service. You can also register a complaint with the Federal Trade Commission's Complaint Assistant.

- If you know someone who is corresponding in one of these schemes, encourage that person to contact the FBI or the U.S. Secret Service as soon as possible.

- Be skeptical of individuals representing themselves as Nigerian or foreign government officials asking for your help in placing large sums of money in overseas bank accounts.

- Do not believe the promise of large sums of money for your cooperation.

- Guard your account information carefully.

Source: Federal Bureau of Investigation. (2014). Common fraud schemes. Retrieved from http://www.fbi.gov/scams-safety/fraud.

Source: Bennett, W., and Hess, K. (2001). Criminal investigation (6th ed.). Belmont, CA: Wadsworth.

example, the amount of $10 can be altered to read $100 simply by adding a zero onto the designated amount and then altering the written portion. Forgery of government checks is another growing problem in many parts of the country. Many such checks, such as welfare and unemployment payments, are mailed in groups at regular intervals and are sometimes stolen directly from mailboxes.

Banking institutions often consider the government check as legitimate because of its "official" appearance. Therefore, its legitimacy often goes unquestioned. Once passed, the forged government check may go undetected for months before the crime is discovered. Another method of forgery includes the use of fictitious checks drawn from the account of a nonexistent firm or person. These schemes, called **check kiting**, are commonly encountered by law enforcement authorities. Kiting consists of drawing cash on accounts made up of uncollected funds. By using two different banking institutions, the kiter may use funds from one bank to cover checks drawn on another. Each time the bank pays out funds against the account balance, the kiter has been successful in cheating the bank out of its own funds.

Embezzlement

Embezzlement is a low-profile crime that typically consists of employees of organizations stealing large amounts of money over a long period of time. Embezzlement is also extremely difficult to detect. Those who are successful in the embezzling of funds can cause extensive fiscal damage to victim organizations, frequently resulting in their financial ruin.

Embezzlement is usually defined under individual state statutes dealing with grand theft. Generally speaking, however, it can be described as a fraudulent appropriation of property by a person to whom that property has been entrusted.

The element of trust is critical in establishing the crime of embezzlement. For example, a bank teller has the lawful right to

handle a bank's cash. Secretly taking quantities of that cash for his or her own personal use, however, is a form of possession that is contrary to the trust relationship with the bank.

Investigating Embezzlement

A primary element of the crime of embezzlement is the element of trust. So, to investigate this type of crime, the investigator must show that the suspect first accepted the property in the scope of employment and then misappropriated it for his or her own use. Intent is relatively easy to demonstrate in these cases, however, because it usually requires some form of concealment or secrecy, such as altering business records. The investigation of embezzlement allegations is a tenacious and time-consuming task because paper trails are sometimes difficult to follow. Yet the investigator must be able to explain fully to a prosecutor, judge, and jury how the crime was committed and offer convincing evidence to support the findings of the case. This task can be especially perplexing when dealing with a company whose record-keeping practices are already haphazard.

Because many embezzlement cases require a degree of accounting expertise, investigators lacking such expertise may become frustrated, and the successful outcome of the case may then be jeopardized. The most common way of overcoming this obstacle is for the investigator to solicit the victim's help in providing technical support during the investigation.

▶ *Shoplifting*

Shoplifting is a common form of theft involving the taking of goods from retail stores. In fact, it has grown into one of the biggest concerns in the area of retail business. Statistics bear this out: Shoplifting incidents have grown dramatically in the past 20 years, and some retailers expect an annual increase of 10 to 15 percent. Some studies have even suggested that one of every nine retail customers steals from department stores. More-  over, the increasingly popular discount stores such as Walmart, Kmart, and Target employ a minimum of retail sales help and rely heavily on highly visible merchandise displays to attract purchasers.

LEARNING OUTCOMES 5 — Identify the crime of shoplifting.

According to the *Economic Crime Digest*, shoplifting is the form of theft that occurs most frequently in business and accounts for some of the greatest losses: an estimated $16 billion a year. The FBI reports that shoplifting acts number some 1 million yearly and have increased 30 percent since 1985. Because shoplifting is a kind of larceny-theft, it has basically the same elements of larceny-theft as discussed earlier.

Modern retail stores market their wares by allowing potential customers to examine them while on display. Computers may be tinkered with, clothes may be tried on, and television sets may be adjusted to demonstrate the clarity of the picture and the function

Crime-Prevention Key: Avoiding Becoming a Victim of Check Fraud

☑ Don't give your checking account number or the numbers at the bottom of your checks to people you don't know, including people who say they are from your bank. They have no business requesting such information.

☑ Reveal checking account information only to businesses you know are reputable.

☑ Guard your checkbook. Report lost or stolen checks immediately.

☑ Properly store or dispose of canceled checks.

☑ Report any inquiries or suspicious behavior to your banker, which will take steps to protect your account and to notify authorities.

☑ Do not leave your ATM receipt at the ATM because these receipts contain your account information. Dispose of it safely and securely.

Photo Showing How Some Shoplifters Can Conceal Stolen Merchandise.

of other features. The list goes on. Because stores often provide carts for the transportation of goods that the customer may wish to purchase, the courts have held that they have a lawful right to possess those goods for limited purposes. Concealment of goods by customers, however, is not allowed by businesses or the courts. Accordingly, the merchandise is offered for sale, and if a customer chooses not to purchase the merchandise, it must be returned to the display shelves in good condition.

Generally speaking, the shoplifter can be characterized as either professional or amateur. Whereas a professional shoplifter will steal goods for resale or bartering, an amateur steals merchandise for his or her own use. Records show that the majority of shoplifters fall into the amateur category. The professional shoplifter, however, represents a much greater problem for investigators. Professionals often work in groups of three or four and often victimize several shopping areas at a time. They are commonly trained on what items to steal, how to conceal them (for example, wearing special clothing to help them conceal merchandise), and where to take the merchandise for resale after the theft. Investigations have revealed women who appear to be pregnant but who are wearing a specially made receptacle for small items. In another case, a heavyset woman had been stealing small television sets by concealing them in a prerigged harness that was located between her legs.

A classic study of shoplifting was conducted by Mary Owen Cameron, who found that about 10 percent of all shoplifters were professionals who derived the majority of their income from shoplifting.[7] Sometimes called *boosters* or *heels*, professional shoplifters resell stolen merchandise to pawn shops or fences at usually one-half to one-fourth the original price. According to Cameron's study, most shoplifters are amateur pilferers, called **snitches**. Snitches are usually respectable persons who do not perceive themselves as thieves yet are systematic shoplifters who steal merchandise for their own use rather than for resale.

Investigative Steps

One problem with shoplifting is that many customers who observe theft are reluctant to report it to managers or security personnel. Many store employees themselves don't want to get involved with apprehending a suspected shoplifter. In fact, an experiment

Think About It…

Theft in Corporate America Many retail experts have instituted more training and technology to deal with the phenomenon of organized retail theft (ORT). ORT has an especially devastating impact on major retail chains in that they are more visible targets and some criminals presume that the impact of their crime on the company or even the public is not serious. One major issue currently is the ORT of baby formula, which is something that is easily transportable and is easier to sell to either other businesses or to private citizens on the street than other types of products. Discuss how snitches can be used to help investigate shoplifting and apply that knowledge to how it might help in an investigation of ORT involving baby formula.

Concealing Stolen Retail Goods under Clothing Is a Common Method of Shoplifting.

by Hartmann and his associates found that customers observed only 28 percent of staged shoplifting acts that were designed to get their attention.[8] In addition, only 28 percent of people who said they had observed an incident reported it to store employees. Another study by Blankenburg showed that less than 10 percent of shoplifting was detected by store employees and that customers seemed unwilling to report even severe cases.[9] Even in stores with an announced policy of full reporting and prosecution, only 70 percent of the shoplifting detected by employees was actually reported to managers, and only 5 percent was prosecuted.

Shoplifting cases can be investigated in one of two ways: reactive or proactive. A reactive investigation will include interviews of witnesses, collection of physical evidence, and conducting of other follow-up functions. A proactive case will probably be handled by in-house security personnel and will focus on the shoplifter who is caught in the act. In the case of proactive investigation, investigators should follow several rules of thumb:

- Be sure that probable cause exists before restraining a suspect.

- Observe the person concealing store merchandise that has not been paid for, not simply concealing "something" that cannot be positively identified as store merchandise.

- Keep the person under observation.

- Before arresting the person, always ask first for a receipt.

Remember, if the person has not yet walked beyond the last pay station, an arrest may not be lawful or appropriate, but confronting the person may still result in reclaiming of the merchandise.

Most shoplifting cases are handled through local police and sheriff's departments and are prosecuted locally as well. When a store is involved with cases such as these, store policy should be considered as well as the opinions of the local prosecuting attorney.

Statistics showing the extent of identity theft are instructive. For example, in 2003, all identity theft victims reported losses of $437,463,950, with a median loss of $228. Internet-related fraud in 2003 accounted for 55 percent of all fraud reports, up from 45 percent the previous year. The most common ID theft complaint related to credit card fraud, followed by phone or utility fraud, bank fraud, employment-related fraud, government document or benefit fraud, and loan fraud.

Source: Federal Bureau of Investigation. (2010). Crime in the United States—2009. CONSUMER SENTINEL CLEARING HOUSE (2004). National and State Trends in Fraud and Identity Theft, January—December 2003

▶ Identity Theft

In 2000, golfer Tiger Woods discovered that his identity had been stolen and that credit cards taken out in his name had been used to purchase $17,000 worth of merchandise, including a 70-inch TV, stereos, and a used luxury car. In 2001, the thief, 30-year-old Anthony Lemar Taylor, who looks nothing like Woods, was convicted of falsely obtaining a driver's license using the name Eldrick T. Woods (Tiger's given name), Wood's Social Security number, and his birth date. Because Taylor already had 20 previous convictions of all kinds on his record, he was sentenced to 200 years in prison under California's three strikes law. Like Woods, most victims of identity theft do not even know that their identities have been stolen until they receive bills for merchandise they haven't purchased.

LEARNING OUTCOMES 6 — Explain the problem of identity theft.

Identity theft, which involves obtaining credit, merchandise, or services by fraudulent personal representation, is a special kind of larceny. According to a recent Federal Trade Commission (FTC) survey, identity theft directly impacts as many as 10 million victims annually, although most do not report the crime.

In 1998 the Identity Theft and Assumption Deterrence Act made identity theft (the use of another's personal information to commit fraud) a federal crime (it is also a crime under most state laws). According to the law, such a crime has been committed whenever anyone "knowingly transfers or uses, without lawful authority, a means of identification of another person with the intent to commit, or to aid or abet, any unlawful activity that constitutes a violation of federal law, or that constitutes a felony under any applicable state or local law."[10]

Identity theft can happen in a variety of ways, and there are a variety of sources from which identity thieves can obtain personal information (see Box 14–2). Such sources are credit card

BOX 14–2 🛡 Types of Identity Theft and Identity Theft Operations

Identity thieves steal personal identifying information, such as names, addresses, dates of birth, Social Security numbers, credit card numbers, and driver's license numbers, and use this personal information to fraudulently obtain cash and credit, goods, services, and other property, including insurance policies. Some of their criminal tactics include opening phony bank accounts or stealing from established ones, obtaining unauthorized credit cards and insurance policies, applying for car or house loans, and leasing apartments with false names.

It seems that there are as many means of committing identity theft as there are of combating it. Now we will examine the different types of identity theft, as well as the tactics and modus operandi of the people responsible for such crimes. Those who commit identity theft are generally after personal and confidential information that can be used for monetary gain, and they gather this information through a variety of means, the most common of which are discussed here:

- Stealing ID cards, credit cards, and bank cards from purses, wallets, or other belongings.

- Stealing bank and credit card statements, preapproved credit card offers, and tax information, all of which can be found in the victim's mail.

- Searching through trash for discarded preapproved credit card offers or bank documents that contain sensitive information.

- Stealing mail by using a change-of-address form to send it to another address.

- Searching a victim's home for personal information, through entry that can be unlawful (such as burglary) or lawful (such as during a visit to a friend's home).

- Obtaining information on the Internet through hacking or through victims' responses to spam or phishing emails.

- Purchasing personal information from companies that collect such information. Oftentimes these entities are criminal in nature, making their profit by obtaining sensitive information and selling it to thieves.

- Pretexting. In a pretexting scheme the thief contacts the victim and requests that he or she provide personal information. Sometimes the thief may claim that the victim has won a prize but needs to provide personal information before it can be received. Other times the thief may claim to have found something belonging to the victim and request that the victim provide personal information so that the item can be returned.

- Shoulder surfing, in which the thief gets close enough to the victim to be able to hear or see sensitive information. For example, the thief may eavesdrop on a cell phone conversation in a public place in which the victim says a credit card or bank account number. Another scenario finds the thief standing close enough to a victim at an ATM or cash register to see the victim key in his or her password.

- Skimming, which is the transfer of data from a valid credit or ATM card to a counterfeit one. One of the ways this can be done is with a handheld electronic device through which a store employee swipes a consumer's credit card during a transaction without the consumer's knowledge. Data from the card is recorded on the device, which is then returned to the thief, who can extract the data.

numbers, Social Security numbers, driver's license numbers, bank account information, and medical records. Once this information has been obtained, thieves put it to fraudulent use, generally for monetary gain. They may also use such information to get a job or medical treatment under someone else's name.

Identity theft in the United States has grown rapidly in recent years, due in large part to ever-improving technology. Computers and other electronic devices are now the preferred method of storing data and personal information, and the Internet has become a major means of communication and commerce. Although beneficial to society, these new ways to exchange information have given criminals an entirely new way to obtain that information. However, use of technology is not the only means by which identity theft is committed. Thieves can get the information they want in many ways, from picking through a victim's trash to paying someone else for the data. The resourcefulness of thieves is unsurprising, given that personal information has become a valuable commodity for criminals, both in this country and elsewhere in the world.

The value of personal information is due in part to it being a gateway to other criminal acts. Fraud (credit card, bank, computer, and Internet) is closely associated with identity theft, as the information a thief gains can lead to substantial profit. This profit can then be used to fund other types of criminal activity, for example, drug trafficking and terrorism.

Because criminals have much to gain from identity theft, and because rapid improvements in technology have allowed them to commit their crimes with greater ease, identity theft is a problem that will likely grow and evolve in years to come, necessitating knowledgeable and resourceful law enforcement personnel to keep it in check.

The Investigative Response

The investigation and prosecution of identity theft cases is dependent on the combined efforts of local, state, and federal agencies, as well as the knowledge and experience of individual investigators. Therefore, one of the most important steps in fighting identity theft is for police personnel to understand what identity theft is, who commits it, and the ways in which it is committed. Police department personnel must also understand how local, state, and federal efforts combine in an effective investigation, and they must be aware of the resources at those levels that are available during such an investigation.

Investigation and prosecution of the case described at the beginning of this section would not have been possible without the coordination of resources among different agencies. Due to its complicated nature, identity theft often requires such cooperation. A case of identity theft in one jurisdiction may have an impact on an investigation in another part of the country. Therefore, strong communication among agencies is an integral part of investigation.

▶ *Computer Crime*

Tyler Clementi was an 18-year-old student at Rutgers University in Piscataway, New Jersey, who jumped to his death from the George Washington Bridge on September 22, 2010.

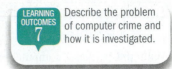

LEARNING OUTCOMES 7 Describe the problem of computer crime and how it is investigated.

Without Clementi's knowledge, on September 19, his roommate, Dharun Ravi, and a fellow student, Molly Wei, used a webcam on Ravi's computer and a computer in Wei's dorm room to view Clementi kissing another man. On September 21, the day prior to the suicide, Ravi notified friends and followers on Twitter to watch via his webcam a second encounter between Clementi and his friend.

Ravi and Wei were indicted for their roles in the webcam incidents, although they were not charged with involvement in the suicide itself. Wei accepted a plea agreement on May 6, 2011, allowing her to avoid prosecution. On March 16, 2012, Ravi was found guilty of 15 counts involving crimes of invasion of privacy, attempted invasion of privacy, bias intimidation, tampering with evidence, and witness tampering. He was given a sentence that included a 30-day jail term.

The death of Tyler Clementi followed another computer-related "cyber-bullying" case involving Megan Meier. Meier was a 13-year-old from Dardenne Prairie, Missouri. Soon after opening an account on MySpace, Meier received a message from Lori Drew, who had assumed a false identify of a 16-year-old boy, Josh Evans.[11] Meier and Josh became online friends but never met in person or spoke. Meier thought he was attractive and began to exchange messages with the fabricated Josh Evans. She was described by family as having had her "spirits lifted."[12]

On October 15, 2006, the tone of the messages changed, with Drew saying (via the account), "I don't know if I want to be friends with you anymore because I've heard that you are not very nice to your friends."[13] Similar messages were sent, some of Megan's messages were shared with others, and bulletins were posted about her. After telling her mother, Tina Meier, about the increasing number of hurtful messages, the two got into an argument over the vulgar language Megan used in response to the messages and the fact that she did not log off when her mother told her to.[14]

After the argument, Megan ran upstairs to her room. According to Megan's father, Ronald Meier, and a neighbor who had discussed the hoax with Drew, the last message sent by the Evans account read: "Everybody in O'Fallon knows how you are. You are a bad person and everybody hates you. Have a shitty rest of your life. The world would be a better place without you."[15] Meier responded with a message reading: "You're the kind of boy a girl would kill herself over." The last few correspondences were made via AOL Messenger instead of MySpace. Megan was found 20 minutes later, hanging by the neck in a closet. Despite attempts to revive her, she was pronounced dead the next day.

Both the Tyler Clementi and Megan Meier cases are sobering reminders that modern-day computer crime is not limited to criminals with a profit motive. Rather, they are evidence that cybercriminals out for revenge or other motives are keenly aware of potential victims who are young and impressionable. Worse yet, such criminals are often able to hide behind false identities while prowling the Internet and avoiding detection by the police.

Understanding the Computer Crime Problem

With the personal computer now in many households and mainframe computers acting as the epicenter of almost all Fortune 500 companies, the problem of computer crime, or **cybercrime**, is now a mainstream social problem. According to one definition, cybercrime is "the destruction, theft or unauthorized use, modification, or copying of information, programs, services, equipment or communication networks."[16]

Some of the fastest-growing crimes in the country are those labeled as cybercrimes, or crimes that take place over the Internet. Disturbingly, the Internet has become a popular hunting ground for child predators of all ages. It allows them to hide their identities and assume the roles of virtually anyone they choose. As a result, such criminals hide in chat rooms and sign up for popular social networking sites where children and teens socialize. Pretending to be teenagers, predators talk kids and teens into meeting with them, and they have been known to rape, molest, and sometimes murder their victims in such encounters.

Perhaps one of the most frightening statistics of all is that in 100 percent of the cases, the victims met up willingly with the attacker, thinking they were meeting someone entirely different. The problem of Internet predators has become so great that many police departments have established dedicated units to investigate such crimes. In this capacity, undercover police also monitor chat rooms and try to attract predators by pretending to be teenage girls or other types of persons that might attract predators; the predators are then arrested. Investigators also discover Internet predators by acting on tips from parents or teens who have encountered or who believe they have come across an online predator.

For obvious reasons, cybercrime has had a relatively short history. Although electronic crime has been somewhat of a problem for the past three decades, it wasn't until the 1970s that a new term entered the public lexicon—**hacker**. Early hackers began using school computers for a number of misdeeds—the least of which was altering grades. By the end of the decade, modems (devices linking computers to telephone lines) and computerized bulletin board services emerged.

Although the first generation of hackers during the 1980s seemed more mischievous than criminal, their emergence was the predecessor for a far more insidious type of computer crime. Many large corporate computers are now "hacked" not as a prank but as a target of large-scale theft. Indeed, computers have provided opportunistic criminals with a new genre in which to ply their crimes, and many of today's criminals are quite computer literate. One early example of cybercrime involved the planting of an unauthorized program known as a Trojan horse, which automatically transferred money to an illegal account whenever a legal transaction was made. To many thieves and hackers, this was akin to striking pure gold.

Computer criminals today have posed as financial advisers or licensed brokers on the Internet to solicit investments in fictitious mutual funds.[17] In some cases, they have attempted to extort money from their victims. In one of the biggest cases of **cyber-extortion**, a computer hacker stole credit card numbers from an online music retailer, CD Universe, and released thousands of them on a website when the company refused to pay $100,000 ransom. In January 2000, *The New York Times* reported that the hacker claimed to have taken the numbers of 300,000 CD Universe customers. The hacker turned out to be a 19-year-old from Russia going by the name of Maxim.[18]

Computer Crime Investigations

Computer crime investigations are dynamic in nature. Therefore, their detection and investigation differ in several respects from the investigation of other, more traditional crimes. These differences include:

- Physical evidence in computer crimes is different from that in traditional crimes.
- The volume of evidence encountered in computer crimes can be burdensome.
- Offenders can commit their crimes with ease.
- Offenders can destroy evidence with ease.

Such investigations require a greater amount of technical expertise by investigators and prosecutors. Despite the contrasts cited earlier, certain approaches of the computer crime investigation remain consistent. For example, such investigations generally require a considerable investment of time, sometimes taking from one month to a full year in duration. This is due, in part, to the fact that identification and analysis of data are necessary to organize information for complicated search warrants. In addition, the investigation of computer crime requires interaction between investigators and victims. Victims, because of their knowledge of computer systems, can aid the investigator in providing technical expertise.

Another commonality in computer crime investigations is that they are largely investigative in nature (i.e., standard investigative procedures can be used), using an estimated 90 percent traditional police work and 10 percent technical skill.[19]

Yet another distinguishing attribute of computer crime investigations is that they are typically proactive in nature. Proactive initiatives include the monitoring of electronic bulletin boards and regular contact with local schools and businesses to help prevent and detect possible crimes being committed with or enabled by computers.

Obtaining Computer Crime Evidence

It is fairly easy to obtain documents in computer crime cases because such documents are easily identified by non-computer experts. These include computer manuals, program documentation, logs, data and program input forms, and computer-printed forms. Ascertaining whether they are complete, originals, or copies can be determined by document custodians.

Requesting specific program documentation may require assistance and knowledge of computer concepts to determine the extent and types of documentation required. In addition, taking possession of other computer media may be more complicated. Magnetic tapes and diskettes, for example, are usually labeled externally. Additionally, a large tape or disk file may reside on more than one reel or cartridge. In this case, assistance may be needed to check the contents of a tape or disk by using a comparable computer. The search for information inside a computer is usually highly complex and most likely will require the aid of an expert. Preparing a search warrant for this task also requires expert advice. In both cases, expert advice can come from the following sources:

- Systems analysts
- Programmers who wrote the programs
- Staff who prepared the data in computer-readable form
- Tape librarians
- Electronic maintenance engineers who maintain the hardware

Advice and help from such people aid the investigator in his or her role in the investigation. When the case goes to court, the same people can offer expert testimony to establish the integrity and reliability of the evidence seized.

Examining Evidence for Criminal Content

Computers can maintain an extremely large amount of information in a small amount of space. A floppy disk is small enough to fit inside a pocket and can easily be hidden in books or taped to the bottom of a keyboard. The contents of a "flash drive" can hold more than enough information to make a case by providing direct evidence or direction to evidence.

If there is printer activity, this information can require a great deal of time to sort through. It is important not to blindly push this potential evidence aside; doing so may very well cost a case. Buried deep inside the amount of paper could be the secret bank account number where the suspects have hidden their assets or their list of past, present, and future victims for rape and murder.[20]

Preserving Computer Crime Evidence

Determining if the evidence can be collected and preserved for future analysis is not as easy as it sounds. Investigators must check their warrants constantly for what they can and cannot seize. If something is found that is needed but is not covered in a search warrant, the wording must be amended before seizure of that item can proceed. Seizing materials not included in a search warrant could cost an investigator the success of an entire investigation.

Some types of computer evidence require special care and attention. Because of this, storage areas must be controlled, and special care must be given to protect the evidence from physical damage. Certain care measures are required for the most common types of computer evidence:

- *Magnetic tape and disks.* These must be handled with care. This type of evidence is also easily destroyed by exposure to magnetic fields such as stereo speakers and printers.

- *Printed computer listings.* No restrictions on storage are required for paper printouts of computerized data except that they should not be stored in direct sunlight. This practice will reduce the chance of fading.

- *Computer.* All types of computers are sensitive—be careful. Even when a computer is turned off, disruption by moving it may occur. If there is a hard drive, it should be "parked" before being moved to avoid destroying information contained on the disk.

- *Additional computer hardware.* Investigators should document the configuration of a computer, what add-on equipment is involved, and how it should be disconnected. This equipment may include telephone modems, auto-dialers, and printers.

Investigators must also remember that the owners of computer-related evidence may have special problems when the evidence is removed from their possession. Such material may be necessary for continuing their legitimate business or other activities. One manner of dealing with this situation is to arrange for copying of the needed material. After this is accomplished, the copy, not the original, is returned to the rightful owner.

▶ Motor Vehicle Theft

Carlos Ponce was one of the longtime leaders of an auto theft ring that operated throughout South Florida and sold stolen cars around the country. Ponce, also known as El Rey de los Carros ("King of the Cars"), ran an interstate auto theft ring that stole luxury cars in South Florida. The ring renumbered the cars using the **vehicle identification number (VIN)** identities of other identical "clone" vehicles and then shipped the vehicles to out-of-state buyers using fraudulent Florida titles. The ring was responsible for stealing hundreds of vehicles, worth an estimated $8 million, from South Florida and using an illicit pipeline—maintained in part from inside a federal prison—to ship the vehicles as far away as Massachusetts and California. In 2006, a Miami-Dade Police investigation known as Operation Road Runner arrested Ponce and 10 of his associates.[21] The Ponce operation illustrates the level of sophistication and organization of some automobile theft operations and reminds us that there are considerable profits for criminals involved in automobile theft.

Since the turn of the century, the advent of the automobile has either directly or indirectly changed the lives of all people.

LEARNING OUTCOMES 8 — Explain the investigation of motor vehicle theft.

According to the FBI, in 2012 there were an estimated 638,964 thefts of motor vehicles nationwide. The estimated rate of motor vehicle thefts was 258.8 per 100,000 inhabitants. Nationwide, nearly $5.2 billion was lost to motor vehicle thefts in 2012, and the average dollar loss per stolen vehicle was $6,505. Statistics show that more than 72 percent of all motor vehicles reported stolen in 2012 were automobiles. Moreover, according to the FBI, only 57 percent of stolen motor vehicles are ever recovered, and those that are recovered are often severely damaged.

Source: Federal Bureau of Investigation. (2013). Crime in the United States, 2012. Washington, DC: U.S. Government Printing Office.

Thief Stealing a Car.

Paolese/Fotolia

BOX 14–3 🛡 **Motor Vehicle Theft Trend, 2012**

Year	Number of Offenses
2010	737,142
2012	638,964
Percent Declined	+1.9

Source: Federal Bureau of Investigation. (2013). *Crime in the United States, 2012.* Washington, DC: U.S. Government Printing Office.

Its impact has inspired both positive and negative uses. Indeed, it has not only enhanced private lives, business, and public service organizations but has also offered criminals innovative ways of transportation to and from their crimes. The value and utility of the motor vehicle have, therefore, become deeply ingrained in today's society.

According to the UCR, the crime of motor vehicle theft includes trains, airplanes, bulldozers, most farm and construction machinery, ships, boats, and spacecraft. Vehicles that are temporarily taken by individuals who have lawful access to them are not thefts. Consequently, spouses who jointly own all property may drive the family car, even though one spouse may think of the vehicle as his or her exclusive personal property. Because most insurance companies require police reports before they will reimburse car owners for their losses, most occurrences of motor vehicle theft are reported to law enforcement agencies. Some of these reports, however, may be false. People who have damaged their own vehicles in solitary crashes or who have been unable to sell them may try to force insurance companies to "buy" them through reports of theft. Motor vehicle theft can turn violent, as in cases of carjacking—a crime in which offenders usually force the car's occupants into the street before stealing the vehicle.

According to the FBI, auto theft is an estimated $7 billion business and continues to grow despite a declining theft rate across the United States. For record-keeping purposes, the UCR defines a motor vehicle as a self-propelled vehicle that runs on the ground and not on rails. This definition includes automobiles, motorcycles, bicycles, trucks, motor scooters, buses, and snowmobiles.

The Extent of Motor Vehicle Theft

Motor vehicle theft is a pervasive problem in the United States. There were an estimated 721,053 thefts of motor vehicles nationwide in 2012 (see Box 14–3). More than $4.3 billion was lost nationwide to motor vehicle thefts, and the average dollar loss per stolen vehicle in 2012 was $6,019.[22] Motor vehicle thefts are common throughout the United States and as a rule require a police report before insurance companies will act on claims. Both police and insurance investigators know that sometimes motor vehicle theft reports are false. Such cases involve persons who attempt to defraud the insurance company or dispose of a vehicle after using it to commit a crime while trying to claim insurance money for it.

Auto theft is big business. Investigations have shown that some large organized groups of car thieves fill orders for contract buyers. Some cars are stolen for shipment out of the country, typically to Mexico. Juveniles often steal cars as a lark or on a dare to joyride. Some thieves intend to keep the car for themselves, but others sell the stolen car to an associate after disguising the vehicle with new paint, plates, and wheels. Stolen vehicles may even be used in other crimes, such as armed robbery or drive-by shootings. Stolen cars are often involved in hit-and-run accidents with injuries, leaving the owners to explain their alibis and prove that they didn't cause the incident and then file a false auto theft report to cover it up.

Experienced car thieves can steal an automobile in less than a minute. Many crude thieves simply smash the driver's-side window to gain entry. In addition, many stolen cars are taken for the value of their parts. Some of the most frequently stolen types of cars have remained constant over the years, suggesting that they are being stolen for parts. According to insurance companies, a $20,000 stolen vehicle can be stripped and sold into $30,000 worth of parts inventory to unscrupulous scrap and auto-body shops. Stolen cars, vans, trucks, and motorcycles cause economic hardship for victims and increase insurance premiums for law-abiding citizens.

Motor vehicles are stolen from a variety of sources, including shopping malls, streets, driveways, parking lots, garages, and car dealerships. Auto theft seems to occur with greater frequency where large groups of cars are parked together for extended periods, such as at airports, shopping centers, colleges, sporting events, fairgrounds, movie complexes, and large apartment complexes.

Motor vehicle thieves target a wide range of popular passenger vehicles, often seeking valuable parts from older-model-year vehicles for sale on the black market. Their preferred targets for theft vary from one year to the next, but many models remain a constant. For example, the Toyota Camry, Honda Accord, and Ford Taurus are particularly attractive targets, along with sport utility vehicles (SUVs), pickup trucks, and mini-vans, according to a recent study by the National Insurance Crime Bureau (NICB), a not-for-profit insurance organization committed to combating vehicle theft and insurance fraud. Box 14–4 notes the models of vehicles most stolen in 2012.

As noted, vehicles may be taken for their parts, especially for those parts that are no longer manufactured and are therefore difficult or expensive to obtain. Individual car components in high demand are "tuners" or "street racers," which are

According to the National Insurance Crime Bureau, in 2012 the most stolen vehicles in the nation were the following:

1.	Honda Accord	58,596
2.	Honda Civic	47,037
3.	Ford Pickup (Full Size)	26,770
4.	Chevrolet Pickup (Full Size)	23,745
5.	Toyota Camry	16,251
6.	Dodge Caravan	11,799
7.	Dodge Pickup (Full Size)	11,755
8.	Acura Integra	9,555
9.	Nissan Altima	9,169
10.	Nissan Maxima	6,947

Source: Courtesy National Insurance Crime Bureau. (2014). Retrieved from https://www.nicb.org/newsroom/news-releases/hot-wheels-2012.

often stolen for illegal export to Central and South America or Europe. Historically, many vehicles have been stolen to remove major parts and sell them to salvage yards or repair shops. Today, another criminal goal has captured the attention of law enforcement authorities: vehicles that are stolen and stripped for valuable accessories, such as seats, expensive radios, custom wheels, and tires.

To help protect their vehicles, experts recommend that motorists always remove the keys from the ignition and vehicle, lock the doors, close the windows, hide valuable items, park in well-lit areas, and use a combination of antitheft devices. Motorists driving theft-prone vehicles need to take additional steps such as installing a visible deterrent such as a steering wheel lock, an alarm, a starter or fuel disabler, and a tracking device.

The Preliminary Investigation

The investigation of a stolen auto typically begins with a report by the victim to the police. As a rule, it is the task of the patrol officer to respond to such complaints and determine the facts and circumstances surrounding the alleged theft. These inquiries should include the following:

- Where was the vehicle last seen?
- Who was the last person to use the vehicle?
- Were the keys left in the ignition?
- Was the vehicle left unlocked?
- Is the victim in arrears on payments?
- Are others allowed to drive the vehicle?
- Was the vehicle equipped with special equipment, such as special wheels, fog lights, or a special sound system?

Answers to these questions allow the officer to determine if a crime has been committed or if another situation is at hand, such as a civil dispute (divorce) or vehicle repossession by a bank or finance company. Other explanations for the disappearance of a vehicle might also exist. For example, the driver might have been intoxicated and may have been involved in a hit-and-run accident. The motor vehicle theft claim might be an effort to cover up the details and avoid suspicion.

True ownership of the vehicle must also be determined early in the investigation. This can be accomplished simply by requesting certain specific information from the victim, such as the title of the vehicle or a copy of the vehicle's insurance policy. Special characteristics of the vehicle should also be noted in the theft report. Details such as cigarette burns on the vehicle's seats, scratches or dents, rusted areas of the vehicle, decals or stickers, and so on will all distinguish the stolen vehicle from others like it on the street.

The Vehicle Identification Number

The VIN is as unique to a motor vehicle as a fingerprint is to a human being. It has no resemblance to other numbers commonly dealt with in criminal investigation, such as one's Social Security number or date of birth. Instead, it is assigned to the vehicle by the manufacturer at the time of production and is designed to distinguish each vehicle from all others. The primary purpose of the VIN is for identification and registration. See Figure 14–4 for a description of how the VIN works.

How the VIN Works

The VIN consists of a combination of letters and numbers. To the average car owner, these combinations mean very little, but to the criminal investigator, they are invaluable in identifying a stolen motor vehicle. To understand the VIN better, let's look more closely at the function of each digit of the 17 numbers. For illustration purposes, we consider the following VIN:

1J3CJ45A0CR335521

The numbers and letters represent the following information:

1	Nation of origin
J	Name of the manufacturer (for example, General Motors, Honda)
3	Specific make of the vehicle (for example, Buick)
C	Type of restraint system
J45	Car line series and body type
A	Engine description
0	Check digit
C	Model year
R	Assembly plant location
335521	Sequential production numbers

With the exception of the check digit, one can easily see the function of each of these characters. The ninth character is called the check digit. It may be a number or a letter; however, it is derived mathematically from the other characters in the VIN to reveal coding and recording errors. Since 1968, U.S. automobile manufacturers have placed a portion of the VIN on other areas of the vehicle, such as the engine and the transmission.

How the VIN Works.

The Altered VIN

Because many vehicles are stolen for the sole purpose of resale, many methods are used by the thief to disguise the true identity of the car. In fact, all outward appearances would indicate that the vehicle is legitimate, so after the VIN alteration has been accomplished, the stolen vehicle can then be sold to an unsuspecting customer.

Tools of the Trade

Vehicles are obtained by many different means by professional thieves. For example, tow trucks are often used to transport a vehicle desired by the vehicle thief. Other common methods are the use of public parking facilities, such as mall parking lots and car rental lots. In these instances, all vehicles are prime targets, especially if they are left with the keys in the ignition. Entry into a vehicle can be accomplished using several tools. Professional thieves become proficient in the use of these tools and use them in a manner in which little, if any, damage is done to the exterior of the vehicle, which could easily be noticed.

Many tools that thieves commonly use also have a legitimate function, which is, however, put to a sinister use by the criminal. When means are devised to counter or deter motor vehicle thefts, criminals inevitably devise methods with which to defeat these means.

Motorcycle Theft and Fraud

As motorcycles have grown in popularity in recent years, they have attracted the attention of thieves who take advantage of more cycles on the road to ply their trade. Many motorcycle models now cost well over $20,000, making them a valuable target for thieves who either sell stolen cycles whole or strip them down in chop-shop-like fashion for parts resale. The motorcycle parts market is especially lucrative in colder-weather climates where a shorter riding season encourages a stolen parts trade.

Motorcycle thieves are resourceful and will often use every part of the motorcycle for resale or reconstruction into another cycle. Motorcycle parts, including frames, can be more easily altered, reused, and camouflaged than can car or truck parts. According to the National Insurance Crime Bureau, this results in a lower recovery rate for stolen cycles than vehicles: approximately 25–30 percent versus 60–65 percent, respectively.[23] Higher-end motorcycles are also highly sought-after luxury items in foreign countries, fostering a lucrative export market for stolen cycles.

In addition to theft, motorcycle fraud is also a major criminal issue. One common scam criminals commit against consumers interested in purchasing a used motorcycle is to assemble a cycle from replica aftermarket parts, and then sell it as, for example, an original Harley. This is known as a "cloned" cycle and the technique is an age-old method for ripping off unsuspecting consumers. False vehicle identification numbers can be easily obtained and applied to cloned cycles. Tightened state titling laws on replica and salvaged cycles have helped discourage motorcycle fraud.

Motor Vehicle Fraud

In years gone by, vehicle thieves were content stealing cars and trucks the old-fashioned way, such as forcing entry and circumventing ignitions. Today, they have new scams for stealing vehicles that are much more difficult to detect. Criminals use fraudulent techniques or "schemes" to steal cars that do not involve smashing windows, disconnecting alarm systems, or racing from the scene of a crime. According to the National Insurance Crime Bureau, in 2014 some of the most common vehicle theft fraud schemes included these:

Owner Give-Ups—The vehicle owner lies about the theft of his

Motor Vehicle Theft: Tools of the Trade

☑ *Slim jim.* This is a thin, easily obtainable piece of metal or aluminum that is notched at both ends. This tool enables easy entry by the thief, who slides the tool in the small crevice between the door and the door frame. After the lock is manipulated, the door is easily opened.

☑ *Slide hammer.* This tool is also referred to as a dent puller or slam puller. After the thief removes the lock cap of the ignition, the slam puller is inserted by screwing the tip into the keyway. Force is then applied to the slide mechanism, away from the steering column, and the lock is removed. The vehicle can then be started by inserting a screwdriver that is twisted just like a car key.

☑ *Ignition extractor.* The lock cap is removed upon getting into the vehicle. The extractor is attached and turned to remove the lock. The vehicle can then easily be started with a screwdriver.

☑ *Force tool.* The force tool is placed over the lock and tapped after removal of the lock cap. The ratchet is turned, thus destroying the locking mechanism.

☑ *Key cutter, codebook, and blank keys.* These tools enable entry into a single-key vehicle and are widely used. After a door lock is pulled, the code number from that lock can be obtained and a new key made. This gives the thief a new key that he or she can use at a time of his or her choosing.

vehicle and then orchestrates its destruction to collect insurance money. He claims his vehicle was stolen, but then it is found burned or heavily damaged in a secluded area, submerged in a lake, or, in extreme cases, buried underground.

30-Day Specials—Owners whose vehicles need extensive repairs oftentimes perpetrate the "30-day special" scam. They will report the vehicle stolen and hide it for 30 days—just long enough for the insurance company to settle the claim. Once the claim is paid, the vehicle is often found abandoned.

Export Fraud—After securing a bank loan for a new vehicle, an owner obtains an insurance policy for it. The owner reports the vehicle stolen to a U.S. law enforcement agency, but in reality it was illegally shipped overseas to be sold on the black market. The owner then collects on the insurance policy, as well as any illegal profits earned through overseas conspirators who sell the vehicle.

Phantom Vehicles—An individual creates a phony title or registration to secure insurance on a non-existent vehicle. The insured then reports the vehicle stolen before filing a fraudulent insurance claim. Oftentimes antique or luxury vehicles are used in this scheme, as these valuable vehicles produce larger insurance settlements.

Motor Vehicle Insurance Fraud

Another way criminals commit crimes with motor vehicles is by through insurance fraud. Criminals who defraud insurance companies not only steal from insurers, but everyone else as well. According to insurance industry studies, 10 percent or more of property/casualty insurance claims are fraudulent.[24] And fraud is the second most costly white-collar crime in America behind tax evasion. Add it all up and insurance fraud costs Americans billions of dollars each year. Not only does fraud cause higher insurance rates, but it also raises our taxes and inflates prices for consumer goods.

Persons who cheat on insurance range from members of organized criminal enterprises, to unscrupulous doctors and lawyers, to dishonest body shop operators, to your neighbors. Regardless of who they are, insurance criminals are motivated by one thing: money.

A Collective Response to Crime

It takes a concerted team effort to fight back against insurance criminals. No individual organization or agency has the resources to single-handedly stop these criminals. But by combining the resources and expertise of thousands of insurers, law enforcement agencies, state fraud bureaus, and the National Insurance Crime Bureau (NICB), insurance fraud can be detected, deterred, and stopped, thus helping to protect American consumers' pocketbooks. The following strategies are involved in the collective response to insurance crime:

- The nation's property/casualty insurers have made significant investments in creating special investigative units, or SIUs, within their companies. These groups are composed of specially trained professionals who investigate suspicious insurance claims and work with law enforcement agencies and the NICB to track down insurance criminals.

- Many states have enacted laws and statutes that contribute to successful fraud deterrence, and most states have fraud bureaus dedicated to fighting insurance fraud.

- The insurance industry also supports the NICB, whose mission is to combat fraud and theft for the benefit of members and the public through information analysis, forecasting, criminal investigation support, training, and public awareness.

A CLOSER LOOK

Possession of Burglary Tools

Ronald is standing in an alley behind a store late at night. A police car arrives, and the officers see Ronald. The officers also see a crowbar, a false key, a lock pick, and a force screw near the area where Ronald is standing. In addition, Ronald has no reasonable explanation for standing in the alley. Under these circumstances, Ronald has probably committed the crime of possession of burglary tools. Although many burglary tools can be purchased in hardware stores, investigators must show that the "intent" was present for the suspect to use them in a burglary. For example, the "reputation" or criminal history of the suspect can offer some evidence to show criminal intent to commit the crime.

Burglary tools may include

- Explosives

- Slim jims

- Any instrument designed for cutting, burning, or opening containers, such as torches or welders

- Portable key cutters

- Key blanks

- Pry bars

- Bolt cutters

- Explosives or chemicals

- Tension wrenches

- Lock picks

Identity Theft and Its Implications . . .

Identity theft is considered by many in the criminal justice field as the "new frontier" of criminality, based on the complexity of the crime and the capability to quickly impact so many potential victims. In June of 2011, Daniel Spitler admitted during a federal plea in court to creating the computer code that enabled him to pull the personal information of over 100,000 users of iPads. He was able to do so allegedly based on a vulnerability that servers at AT&T used to move iPad data via their network. The charges against him are identity theft as well as conspiracy with a person named Andrew Auernheimer.

Spitler is responsible for writing the "iPad 3G Account Slurper" script, in order to pull as much data from iPads as possible. His victims ranged from celebrities to a U.S. Air Force major contractor to high-level financial managers to top-level staff at the White House. Spitler might receive a maximum penalty of five years in federal prison and a $250,000 fine, but this case truly embodies the need for all relevant parties, such as law enforcement, politicians, the public, and the private sector, to take

Monkey Business Images/Shutterstock.com

data security seriously. This is especially important as more and more people use computer technology to handle personal and professional business.

Sources: Goodin, D. (2011, June 23). Man admits writing script that slurped celebrity iPad data. *The Register*. Retrieved from http://www.theregister.co.uk/2011/06/23/ipad_data_hacker_guilty/.

Theft is one of the most commonly occurring crimes:

1. Pretend you are the lead investigator in this case. Based on the section in the chapter dealing with the investigative response to identity theft, what are some realities you would have had to consider?

Summarize the prevalence of burglary.

Burglary is one of the most pervasive crimes law enforcement must handle. According to FBI statistics, in 2009, there were more than 2 million burglaries, which accounted for nearly a quarter of the total property crimes committed that year. Statistics also indicate that victims of burglary lost an estimated $4.6 billion in property in 2009, with an average loss per burglary exceeding $2,000.

1. How does burglary differ from robbery?

2. How does the FBI *Uniform Crime Reports* program classify burglary?

3. When are burglaries most likely to occur?

4. How have changes in patterns of social activity affected trends in burglary?

burglary A covert crime in which the criminal works during the nighttime, outside the presence of witnesses.

property crime A type of crime whereby the criminal is more concerned with financial gain and less prepared for a violent altercation with the victim.

Explain the steps in the preliminary investigation of burglaries.

The patrol division is usually the first to respond to a burglary call. The first thing officers should do is determine whether a crime is currently in progress. At the scene, certain reliable indicators that a burglary has been (or is being) committed can be observed. A sign of a burglary in progress is persons on, in, or near buildings or sitting in cars serving as lookouts.

1. What reliable indicators do investigators use to determine whether a burglary has been or is being committed?

2. What steps should responding officers take when answering a burglary call?

3. What trace evidence should be collected at a burglary scene?

Describe the investigative process in tracing stolen property.

During the investigation, the property must first be identified as stolen. One method of showing possession of stolen property is locating the property on the suspect's premises. After property has been retrieved, a determination should be made as to how it got there. The owner of the property should make a positive identification. A store or pawn shop owner can positively identify a fence.

1. What factors make it difficult for investigators to prove that property is stolen?

2. In burglary cases, what circumstantial evidence helps prove receipt of stolen property?

3. What types of stolen property are considered untraceable? Why?

fence A person who buys and sells stolen property with criminal intent.

fungible goods Items such as tools, liquor, and clothing that are indistinguishable from others like them.

Identify the problem of larceny-theft.

Larceny-theft is perhaps the most commonly committed crime of personal gain. In 2009 these crimes accounted for an estimated 67.9 percent of property crimes. The loss to victims nationally was nearly $5.5 billion. The largest numbers of reported larcenies were thefts of motor vehicle parts, accessories, and contents. Larceny-theft also includes forgery, fraud (check and credit card), and embezzlement.

1. What is the difference between simple and grand larceny?

2. What common crimes fall under the category of larceny?

3. What impact does check fraud have on consumers?

4. Why have check fraud crimes increased?

5. What steps can people take to avoid becoming victims of check fraud?

check kiting Drawing cash on accounts made up of uncollected funds.

embezzlement A low-profile crime involving employees who steal large amounts of money over long periods of time.

LEARNING OUTCOMES 5

Identify the crime of shoplifting.

Shoplifting is a common form of theft that occurs most frequently in business and accounts for an estimated $16 billion in losses a year. Some studies have even suggested that one of every nine retail customers steals from department stores. Shoplifting acts number some 1 million yearly and have increased 30 percent since 1985.

1. How are shoplifters characterized?

2. What are the differences between the two categories of shoplifters?

3. When people successfully shoplift, where are they most likely to sell the stolen merchandise?

4. What factors make it difficult to investigate many shoplifting cases?

5. What are the characteristics of a reactive shoplifting investigation?

6. How does a reactive shoplifting investigation differ from a proactive shoplifting investigation?

7. When it comes to shoplifting investigations, what are the most important rules of thumb that investigators should follow?

shoplifting A common form of theft involving the taking of goods from retail stores.

snitches Amateur pilferers who are usually respectable persons who do not perceive themselves as thieves, yet are systematic shoplifters who steal merchandise for their own use rather than for resale.

LEARNING OUTCOMES 6

Explain the problem of identity theft.

Identity theft is a special kind of larceny that directly impacts as many as 10 million victims annually, although most do not report the crime. Identity theft became a federal crime in 1998 with the passage of the Identity Theft and Assumption Deterrence Act. Because it is usually part of a larger criminal enterprise, identity theft is one of the most serious of all crimes.

1. What is the most common form of identity theft/fraud?

2. What is the main target of identity theft (that is, what is the commodity that identity thieves seek)?

3. Why do experts predict that identity theft will become an even greater problem in the future?

4. What factors have led to the escalation of identity theft in the United States?

5. What are three ways identity thieves acquire the personal information of others?

6. What steps can people take to protect themselves from identity theft?

7. What motives, besides money, fuel identity theft?

identity theft A type of larceny that involves obtaining credit, merchandise, or services by fraudulent personal representation.

LEARNING OUTCOMES 7

Describe the problem of computer crime and how it is investigated.

Cybercrime is "the destruction, theft or unauthorized use, modification, or copying of information, programs, services, equipment or communication networks." Some of the fastest-growing crimes in the country are those labeled as cybercrimes, or crimes that take place over the Internet. Disturbingly, the Internet has become a popular hunting ground for child predators of all ages. It allows them to hide their identities and assume the roles of virtually anyone they choose.

1. Explain the extent of the problem of computer crime.

2. Identify the steps and methods for investigating computer crime.

3. Describe methods for identifying and preserving evidence in computer crimes.

4. In what ways is evidence in computer crimes examined for evidentiary value?

cybercrime Refers to any crime that involves a computer and a network.

hacker A person who seeks information by exploiting weaknesses in a computer system or computer network.

cyber-extortion An individual or group that uses a computer or other electronic device to extort or otherwise force money or services from another.

Explain the investigation of motor vehicle theft.

Motor vehicle thefts are common and as a rule require a police report before insurance companies will act on claims. True ownership of the vehicle must be determined early in the investigation. Special characteristics of the vehicle should be noted in the theft report and will distinguish the stolen vehicle from others like it.

1. What are the consequences of auto thefts for both victims and the general public?

2. Why are automobiles generally stolen?

3. What is the major trend in automobile thefts?

4. What important questions should a patrol officer ask during the preliminary investigation of an alleged automobile theft?

5. What "special" information about a vehicle should be included in the theft report?

6. What specific information does a VIN provide an investigator?

7. What are some of the most common tools used for automobile thefts?

vehicle identification number (VIN) A 17-digit number assigned to each vehicle by the manufacturer at the time of production designed to distinguish each vehicle from all others.

Additional Links

www.nicb.org
The site of the National Insurance Crime Bureau contains links to audio and video clips on theft and fraud. Visitors can also get tips on how to protect vehicles from theft. Links include access to state fraud bureaus, theft prevention organizations, and an online VIN manual.

www.nw3c.org
This is the site of the National White Collar Crime Center, an organization that provides training, investigative support, and research to agencies involved in preventing, investigating, and prosecuting economic and high-tech crime. The site includes a press room, training CDs/DVDs, and downloadable PDF files of brochures, posters, and fact sheets. It also includes links to the Internet Crime Complaint Center.

15

"Since the terrorist attacks on September 11, 2001, there has been an increased focus on the investigation of arson and bombing incidents in the United States."

Arson and Bombings

1 Summarize the scope of the problem of arson.

2 Explain the official definition of the crime of arson.

3 Describe the relationship between police and fire investigators.

4 Explain the techniques of arson investigation.

5 Explain how to investigate bombs and bombers.

THE RESIDENT ARSONIST

Over a 10-month period between May 2013 and March 2014, more than two dozen fires were set in the Southern Towers Stratford apartment building, a high-rise apartment building in suburban Washington, D.C. Authorities arrested 73-year-old Shirley Ann Vigneua, who lived in the complex for 35 years. She admitted to setting 25 fires in the apartment building but did not give a motive for doing so.

Vigneua was caught on video going in and out of an area right at the time a fire was set. She was known to investigators because they had been there many, many times investigating and speaking to residents of the building, and they recognized her in the surveillance video.

The fires under investigation always had been set in public areas such as stairwells, trash rooms, or elevators with matches and paper or cardboard, often at night. Residents faced repeated evacuations of the building,

which has more than 450 apartments. The blazes did about $50,000 in damage, officials said. Because the fires were set in an occupied building, Vigneua was charged with a felony.

Despite the many underlying issues in the Shirley Ann Vigneua case, it is clear that investigators must have knowledge and resources to properly investigate this serious and violent criminal act to bring the perpetrators to justice and protect innocent citizens.

DISCUSS How common is it for a resident of a neighborhood or apartment complex to be responsible for setting potentially fatal fires? What could be a possible motive for doing so?

Arson is perhaps one of the oldest known crimes. It creates a severe threat to human life and costs society billions of dollars per year. Although arson can be defined as the malicious or fraudulent burning of property, it can also be considered a crime against both persons and property. Furthermore, it receives little media attention and is challenging to investigate because evidence is difficult to locate and criminal intent is difficult to prove. Unlike other "sensational" media events such as murder cases and drug raids, arson is generally considered a low-priority crime even by law enforcement agencies. Several explanations can be cited for this:

- Arson is a time-consuming and difficult crime to investigate.
- There is much misunderstanding about the motives behind the crime of arson.
- Few arson cases lead to arrests, and fewer than 20 percent of arrests result in convictions.
- Arson used to be classified as a property crime rather than a crime of violence, as it is today.

▶ Arson Offenses

The Extent of Arson

The United States has one of the highest fire death rates in the industrialized world. According to the National Fire Protection Association, the U.S. fire death rate was 14.9 deaths

LEARNING OUTCOMES 1 Summarize the scope of the problem of arson.

per million people. Between 1994 and 1998, an average of 4,400 Americans lost their lives and another 25,100 were injured annually as the result of fire.[1] Furthermore, about 100 firefighters are killed each year in duty-related incidents. Each year, fire kills more Americans than all natural disasters combined.[2]

According to the *Uniform Crime Reports* (UCR) program, in 2012 there were 21,494 instances of arson reported to the police.[3] The second most common category was arson of vehicles, with 10,609 instances reported. The average dollar loss for each instance of arson in 2012 was $12,796.[4] As with most property crimes, the clearance rate for arson was low, only 20 percent nationally.[5]

Many arson crime scenes are not recognized or treated as such, and much evidence is destroyed. Despite the fact that many of the preceding considerations are no longer considered

Think About It...

What Motivates the Arsonist? Each year, almost 60,000 arsons are reported to law enforcement authorities. What motives might a person have for committing the crime of arson?

Whether It Be the Simple Striking of a Match or the Use of Accelerants, One of the Main Responsibilities of the Arson Investigator Is to Determine the Point of Origin of the Fire.

BOX 15–1 🛡 Elements of Arson

A person knowingly damages a building or property of another by
• starting a fire or explosion, or
• procuring or causing such property to be burned.

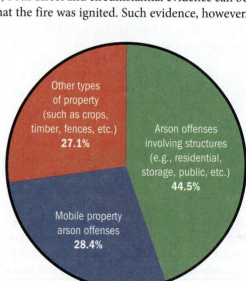

Arson Investigator Interviewing Possible Witnesses to a Suspected Arson.

Lucy Nicholson/Reuters/Corbis

as great a problem as they used to be, arson still accounts for substantial losses to victims. For example, property losses alone are estimated at $5 billion annually.[6]

Because valuable evidence is sometimes destroyed during a blaze, it is often difficult to determine that arson was committed. Other complicating factors include the fact that there are few, if any, witnesses to the crime; physical evidence is difficult to locate; and if the crime is executed properly, it is difficult to determine the fire's point of origin. Finally, often the victim of the fire ends up being the perpetrator of the crime. For these reasons, arson investigation is one of the more difficult criminal investigations.

The Definition of Arson

The UCR program defines arson as any willful or malicious burning or attempt to burn, with or without intent to defraud,

> **LEARNING OUTCOMES 2** Explain the official definition of the crime of arson.

a dwelling house, public building, motor vehicle or aircraft, personal property of another, and so on (see Box 15–1). Only fires determined through investigation to have been willfully or maliciously set are classified as arsons. Fires of suspicious or unknown origins are excluded from this category.

The Police and Fire Alliance

> **LEARNING OUTCOMES 3** Describe the relationship between police and fire investigators.

After a fire has been determined to have a suspicious origin, investigators from the local fire and police departments as well as the victim's insurance company become involved with the case. Problems and confusion sometimes unfold if investigators from these agencies fail to understand the differences in their roles. The traditional role of the fire department is to investigate every fire for cause and origin. Accordingly, 80 percent of the fire protection in the United States is provided by volunteer fire departments.[7] To this end, firefighters are usually trained in the suppression of fire rather than its investigation.

Arson Investigative Techniques

The act of arson has been described as a stealthy, cowardly crime that, by its very nature,

> **LEARNING OUTCOMES 4** Explain the techniques of arson investigation.

leaves very little direct evidence as to the identity of the arsonist. Many arsonists, however, fail to cover their tracks adequately and may therefore leave some type of evidence behind. For example, in many commercial arsons, the suspect leaves a **paper trail** that investigators can follow. This includes financial records, inflated insurance coverage, little or no inventory, and excessive debts. In an ideal situation, the arsonist will either be convicted, through the use of well-documented motives and opportunity, or might be willing to cooperate with authorities in identifying accomplices, motives, and prior victims.

The Preliminary Investigation of Arson

The preliminary investigation of arson begins basically like that of many other crimes, with a thorough examination of the crime scene. Arson does not have an immediate *corpus delicti*. It is therefore the responsibility of the investigator to prove that a specific fire did occur and that it was ignited deliberately. To accomplish this, both direct and circumstantial evidence can be used to show that the fire was ignited. Such evidence, however,

Arson is a pervasive problem throughout the nation. According to the FBI, in 2009, 58,871 arsons were reported to law enforcement. They involved structures (for example residential, storage, public, etc.) and accounted for 44.5 percent of the total number of arson offenses. Mobile property was involved in 28.4 percent of arsons while other types of property (such as crops, timber, fences, etc.) accounted for 27.1 percent of reported arsons. Crime reports show that the average dollar loss due to arson was $17,411, but arsons of industrial/manufacturing structures resulted in the highest average dollar losses (an average of $93,287 per arson). Only the fires that investigation determined to have been willfully set—not fires labeled as suspicious or of unknown origin—are included in these data.

Source: Federal Bureau of Investigation. (2010). Crime in the United States—2009.

Other types of property (such as crops, timber, fences, etc.) **27.1%**

Arson offenses involving structures (e.g., residential, storage, public, etc.) **44.5%**

Mobile property arson offenses **28.4%**

Roles in Arson Investigations

When a suspicious fire is discovered, it is generally while it is being extinguished. The role of firefighter is threefold: (1) to extinguish the fire, (2) to investigate the origin of the fire, and (3) to "detect" the possibility of arson but not to investigate arson. Few fire departments have the legal authority to investigate arson fires, although their assistance in such an investigation is not disputed.

When the fire investigation becomes a question of who committed the crime, the matter then becomes a law enforcement concern. This is critical because after it has been determined that law enforcement should take over the investigation, fire investigators should yield the crime scene to the arson investigators and respond to them in an adjunct role. Immediate obeyance of this principle minimizes confusion and duplication of efforts at the crime scene.

The police investigator has a statutory role in investigating arson because it is a violation of state or federal law. The principal goal of the police investigation in an arson case is to identify the perpetrator(s) of the crime and to identify and secure sufficient evidence to prosecute and convict.

Finally, the role of the insurance investigator is to make a determination as to whether or not the insurance company owes payment for the fire loss. The insurance investigator is not a law enforcement officer. His or her authority to investigate is specified in the insured's contract. This contract refers to many of the provisions of the 1943 New York Standard Policy, which sets forth conditions subscribed to by the insured in the event of a loss.[I] In kind, most insurance companies state that coverage is void if the company's investigation proves arson or fraud.

may not reveal the opportunity or motive of the fire setter. As with most crimes, the motive is important, but the key responsibility of the arson investigator is to connect the suspect with the crime scene regardless of the motive.

Identify the Point of Origin

The first step in an arson investigation is to determine the fire's **point of origin**. This may be the most critical phase of the investigation because it includes the ruling out of natural or accidental causes. The materials used in the setting of the fire, along with the type of material being burned, may show a distinct burn pattern. Hence, it is important to identify the point at which the fire originated because it is here that most of the physical evidence can be located, indicating a fire of incendiary nature. The fire's point of origin may be determined in several ways. The questioning of witnesses could reveal the necessary information. In addition, an inspection of the ruins at the fire scene might reveal valuable evidence.

Finding Accelerants in Arson Investigations

Arson investigators can prove that a fire was set intentionally by finding an accelerant at the scene of a fire. An accelerant is a chemical fuel that causes a fire to burn hotter, spread more quickly than usual, or be unusually difficult to extinguish. The presence of an accelerant in fire debris can be used as evidence of arson.[8]

The most commonly used accelerants are gasoline, kerosene, turpentine, and diesel fuel. These are all organic compounds containing mixtures of hydrocarbon molecules. As accelerants evaporate, the hydrocarbons move into the air above the fire debris, which is called the "headspace."[9]

Various techniques exist to detect accelerants at a fire scene. These range from an experienced fire investigator or a specially trained "sniffer" dog using its sense of smell to detect the characteristic odor of various accelerants in the surrounding air to more complex laboratory methods.

One of the most advanced techniques for detecting accelerants in fire debris is called *headspace gas chromatography*. Gas chromatography involves separating mixtures of gases into their individual components based on the different boiling points of their hydrocarbons. Each gas in the mixture can then be identified because each one produces a distinct chemical fingerprint called a *chromatogram*.[10]

In headspace gas chromatography, solid debris taken from the suspected point of origin of the fire is placed in an airtight vial to prevent any accelerants from evaporating. The vial is then heated, releasing the accelerant's hydrocarbons into the trapped headspace above the debris. A needle is inserted through the cap of the vial to remove a sample of the hydrocarbons and inject them into an instrument called a *gas chromatogram* for separation and analysis.[11]

If an accelerant is used to start a fire, a small amount will likely still be present in the charred debris. Identification of the accelerant can serve as physical evidence to support a charge of arson.

Observe the Span of the Fire

Determining the time **span of the fire** is also of paramount importance. Although the majority of evidence collection is conducted at the crime scene, much can be learned simply by observing the fire. Specifically, the physical characteristics of the fire, such as smoke, direction, flames, and distance of travel, are important. Immediately after the fire is extinguished, samples of debris that might have been the material used for starting the fire should be collected. When the rubble is being cleaned up, investigators should be present to observe any additional evidence that might be uncovered.

Photograph the Scene

Complete photographs of the structure should be taken to help preserve the crime scene for the courtroom. This makes a "record" of the condition of the scene at the time the fire was extinguished. When taking photos, the investigator should focus on the location of rags, large amounts of paper, cans, or empty receptacles that might have been used in setting the fire.

Identify Plants or Trailers

Finally, identifying the areas of **plants** (preparations used to set the fire) and **trailers** (materials used to spread the fire) can reveal important clues to the investigator:

- *Plants* are the preparations used to set the fire. These include newspapers, rags, and other flammable waste material.
- *Trailers* are the materials used in spreading the fire. These include gunpowder; rags soaked in flammable liquid; and flammable liquids such as gasoline, kerosene, and alcohol.

Some arsonists prefer to use delayed-timing devices to allow a time lag between the setting up of the arson and the fire's outbreak. To this end, mechanical devices and chemicals are commonly used. Such devices may well be intact when probing the crime scene for evidence.

Question Witnesses

Witnesses also play an important role in determining causes of the fire and possible suspects. Questions to be asked of the witnesses include the following:

- Who are you and why were you present at the fire?
- What attracted your attention to the fire?

The witnesses' observations of the intensity, color, and direction of the fire may also prove to be of great value. Certainly, the observations of witnesses should only be viewed as information to give the investigator a lead as to where to begin looking for evidence. The actual point of origin, of course, must be determined by a thorough examination of the premises.

Observe Alligatoring

The term **alligatoring** refers to the pattern of crevices formed by the burning of a wooden structure. Resembling the skin of an alligator, this pattern reveals a minimum amount of charring, with alligatoring in large segments, when a fire is extinguished rapidly. As the fire continues to burn, the alligatoring will become smaller, with charring becoming deeper.

In a fire crime scene, liquids tend to flow downward and pool around fixed objects such as furniture. Their trails, however, are relatively easy to trace and provide the investigator with good evidence. An accelerant such as gasoline, kerosene, or alcohol can be traced from the point where it was spilled to the lowest point of flow. At times, unburned amounts of these liquids may be found at low points, where the heat was not intense enough for ignition.

Other Clues

Many things may indicate that a fire of suspicious origin was arson. In one example, many fires were set at the scene, but evidence showed that each was set independently, with no proof of spontaneous combustion. Other clues include the following:

- *Flames.* The color of the flame is noteworthy in the early phases of a fire. For instance, a blue-orange flame represents burning alcohol. Certainly, if this material is not normally stored on the premises, one could assume that it was used as the accelerant in the fire. Information as to the description of the fire can be gained from witnesses who arrived on the scene before investigators.

- *Smoke.* As indicated earlier, smoke can also be of value in determining what substance was used to start a fire. If smoke can be observed at the beginning of a fire, before spreading to other parts of a structure, its color should be noted. For example, black smoke indicates that the material is made with a petroleum base. White smoke, conversely, indicates that vegetable matter is burning, such as straw or hay. If the structure is completely engulfed in flames, it will be difficult to make determinations as to what materials are being burned.

- *Size of the fire.* Depending on certain factors, such as the time element of the fire, the size of the fire might give investigators information to determine an act of arson. For example, structures that are engulfed in flames in a short period might indicate arson. Fire investigators recognize that fires of "natural" origin burn in a definable pattern. Therefore, fires burning quickly or in a direction that is not logical will indicate that an accelerant has been used. In determining the "normal" course or pattern for a fire, the investigator should consider such variables as the ventilation and contents of the structure.

- *Odors.* Distinguishable odors that might indicate a specific fire starter, such as kerosene, gasoline, and alcohol, can be emitted from certain types of fires. These materials ensure that a fire will erupt, and arsonists expect any evidence of these accelerants to be destroyed in the fire. Investigators should therefore try to detect any odors by using their own **olfactory** senses.

Motivations of the Arsonist

As a defense attorney once said, "It is not a crime to have a motive." Indeed, when an investigator is successful in the collection of evidence to show the insured's participation in the crime, along with evidence of a motive showing arson as a reasonable alternative for the arsonist, a prosecutable case may have been developed. After it has been determined that the fire was of incendiary origin, possible motives must be examined to help identify the suspect. Motives for arson include profit, revenge, vandalism, crime concealment, and pyromania.

Arson for Profit

This category represents an estimated 50 percent of all fire-related property damage in the United States and the corresponding increase in the number of arsons reported to officials in recent years.[12] The typical arson-for-profit criminal is a businessperson who sets fire to his or her business or hires a professional arsonist to do the task. Traditionally, this category of arson has proven relatively low risk and high profit for the criminal and has virtually become a business in and of itself.

Economic gain from this type of arson may be either direct or indirect. For example, a home or business owner will see a direct financial gain when the insurance company pays the claim. In comparison, an employee in a warehouse who starts a fire and readily extinguishes it might benefit from a raise or promotion for his or her quick and "responsible" response and effort in saving the business. As indicated earlier, insurance fraud is a common motive for arson, perhaps one of the most frequent. A common method of insurance-related fraud is the purchasing of old, run-down buildings in inner-city areas. Over a period of several months, shrewd businesspersons then sell and resell the property. Each of these transactions raises the value of the property, at least on paper. The properties are then insured for the highest possible dollar amount. Sometimes the target of the arsonist is not the building itself but what it contains. A computer dealer, for example, might remove any valuable computers and software from his or her business and leave behind computers and software that are outdated or in which he or she has invested too much money. After the fire destroys the building, the arsonist simply claims the insurance coverage that covered the burned stock and realizes a "market" return on the stock.

Not all arson-for-profit crimes focus on businesses or are perpetuated by people in big business. Indeed, high car payments or excessive mechanical difficulties with an automobile may compel the ordinary citizen to commit automobile arson to collect on the insurance. This type of criminal activity results in an estimated 1,500 automobile arsons each year.[13]

Arson for profit can take many forms, so in all circumstances, the conditions surrounding suspicious fires must be investigated thoroughly for possible motives. These motives should include the possibility that arson was used to cover up another crime, such as homicide or burglary.

Arson for Revenge

A high percentage of arsons are attributed to revenge, jealousy, and spite. People committing such acts are usually adults who target both individuals and property. Offenders include jilted lovers in personal relationships, disgruntled employees, feuding neighbors, persons who were cheated in business and personal transactions, and persons motivated by racial prejudice. From an investigative standpoint, after revenge has been identified as a possible motive in a fire, the list of suspects can be narrowed greatly. From here, care should be exercised in interview and interrogation techniques to extract sufficient and pertinent information.

Arson for Vandalism

Not much planning or preparation is required for a fire designated as vandalism. In addition, readily available materials are commonly used by arsonists. As discussed later, about 95 percent of the arsons for vandalism are caused by juveniles, owing in large part to peer pressure. Statistics show that most violators in this category are youths from lower socioeconomic groups who choose to commit the crime in the morning or early afternoon.

Motives in juvenile arsonist category differ from case to case but include vandalism and revenge. Typically, however, the motive is profit. Indeed, people who have been unable to contract a professional arsonist have been known to hire juveniles to commit such acts. Certainly, a juvenile fire starter will work for much less than a professional "torch."

Children of many ages have experimented with fire out of curiosity. Some, according to theorists, are abused children and set fires as a call for help. Juvenile fire-setter programs have sprung up across the country to identify these troubled children and to deal with their underlying problems.

Arson for Crime Concealment

It is common for some criminals to try to cover up their crimes through the use of a fire. Murders, burglaries, and other crimes have been concealed through the use of this method. Fire investigators must consider this as an alternative motive for all fires.

Pyromania

A pyromaniac is a person who is a compulsive fire starter. This person is motivated by several aspects of the fire-setting experience. For example, some experts claim that pyromaniacs gain sexual stimulation by starting and viewing fires. In addition, excitation is achieved by the crowds that gather and the emergency vehicles that converge on the scene. Pyromaniacs are impulsive fire setters; their acts are seldom planned. Investigators can only examine the routes or paths that the fires seem to establish. Investigations have revealed that a pyromaniac may have a sordid past, which includes being abused as a child, bed-wetting, and cruelty to animals.

Serial Fire Setters

Serial criminals of any type pose great concerns for communities and law enforcement officials alike. A serial arsonist can be defined as one who sets fires repeatedly. This criminal, however, is at somewhat of an advantage because expertise in fire investigations is not as common as expertise in other crimes. The FBI's National Center for the Analysis of Violent Crime (NCAVC) has conducted research in this area and has concluded that compulsive fire setting can be classified as mass, spree, and serial.

- A *mass arsonist* sets three or more fires at the same location.
- A *spree arsonist* sets fires at three or more separate locations, with no cooling-off period between them.
- The *serial arsonist* sets three or more separate fires with a definite cooling-off period between them. This period may last for days, weeks, or months.

Characteristics of the Fire Setter

- ☑ *Age*: Typically around age 17 years
- ☑ *Gender*: Usually male
- ☑ *Race*: Predominantly white
- ☑ *Intelligence*: Often mentally deficient
- ☑ *Academic performance*: Generally have a history of poor academic performance
- ☑ *Rearing environment*: Often come from unstable home environments within lower socioeconomic groups
- ☑ *Social relationships*: Typically experience difficulties in relationships
- ☑ *Sexual disturbance*: Usually associated with sexual perversion; use fire setting as a sexual substitute
- ☑ *Motive*: Typically have an underlying motive of revenge

Source: Rider, A. O. (1980). The firesetter: A psychological profile. FBI Law Enforcement Bulletin June–Aug: p. 9.

Profiling the Fire Starter

After identifying a possible motive, the investigator may wonder to what extent the fire starter shows a propensity for violence. Surprisingly, David Berkowitz, the "Son of Sam" mass murderer who terrorized New York in 1976 by killing five people and wounding seven others, reported to the police that he was personally responsible for setting more than 2,000 fires from 1974 to 1977.[14] Police reports also showed that Berkowitz set these fires in cars, dumpsters, brush, and vacant and unoccupied stores. In addition, police seized notepads bearing handprinted notes by Berkowitz that gave details on 1,411 fires for the years of 1974, 1975, and 1977, including the dates and times of the fires, the streets, the type of weather, and the fire department code, indicating the type of responding apparatus and property burned. The following questions are therefore raised:

- Does Berkowitz typify the fire starter?
- Are arsonists homicidal?
- Do they keep meticulous diaries of their fires?

According to J. James in his article "Psychological Motives for Arson," gender, age, education, intellectual level, and economic status do not in any way limit the possibility that a person will engage in arson.[15] On the other hand, from a study of large

---

A CLOSER LOOK

Arson for Revenge

Jane (not her real name) is a 27-year-old white woman, well groomed and friendly. Her records indicate below-average intelligence. She was arrested in 1984 and charged with several counts of arson. This was her first incarceration. She set a fire to a vacant farmhouse in 1980, amounting to $30,000 in damages; a barn in 1984, resulting in a $150,000 loss; and a corncrib in 1984, worth $10,800. The fires were motivated by revenge, according to Jane, who claimed that she set fire to the barn because she claimed the owner would not give her some kittens.

The corncrib fire was a result of a long-standing grudge against its owner, who years earlier had removed Jane from the school bus she was driving because of her bad language and behavior. Jane indicated that she was under medication for a heart ailment. While growing up, she had constant conflicts with her parents, who she claimed abused her emotionally and physically. Jane stated that she also had been raped at age 18 years by her father and brother. As with many arsonists, Jane reports problems in establishing and maintaining relationships. While incarcerated, Jane had numerous run-ins with corrections officials for minor nuisance offenses. She is presently in a halfway facility, working on her high school equivalency diploma and holding down a part-time job. Jane's caseworker believes that she will be released sometime soon.

Source: O'Conner, R. (1987). *Practical fire and arson investigation.* Boca Raton, FL: CRC Press.

samples, it does appear that, statistically, persons of certain ages and with certain characteristics are more apt to set fires than are others.

The Role of the Insurance Industry

Because of the severe financial strain arson has placed on the insurance industry, insurance companies are becoming more involved with investigations involving arson. Insurance carriers are usually more than willing to assist local law enforcement and fire officials during the course of an investigation. In fact, independent information offered by an insurance company might prove to be highly valuable in discovering motives and suspects for a crime. Indeed, the crime of arson is one that permits the investigator to work hand in hand with the "victim." In addition, many insurance carriers might even offer financial assistance to fire investigators. This may come in the form of providing heavy machinery for aid in processing the crime scene or by bringing in experts in arson investigations to aid local investigators in the investigation.

Typical problems encountered in arson investigation are shown in Box 15–2.

Insurance company assistance may come in many other forms, such as providing local investigators with financial audits and income tax returns; such information may not be readily available to local investigators. To protect insurance

companies from civil recourse in disclosing some of the information discussed previously, many states have passed laws granting limited civil immunity to insurance companies that assist local arson investigators during the course of an ongoing investigation. This contributes to an increased flow of information from insurance companies to local investigators, which increases the chance of an eventual prosecution of the arsonist and subsequent relief from civil claims liability for the insurance company.

Prosecution of Arson Cases

There exists an old adage: "Without the **fire triangle**—heat, fuel, and oxygen—there can be no fire." Similarly, the successful prosecution of an arson case must include a triangle consisting of police detectives, fire investigators, and a prosecutor. Sadly, in many parts of the United States, prosecution of arson crimes may never occur. Some reasons include the following:

1. There is no one qualified or trained to conduct the investigation.

2. The time required for a thorough arson investigation by police or fire authorities is not available.

3. Prosecuting attorneys are reluctant to file and pursue prosecution. This is the most prevalent reason, because arson cases are difficult to prosecute.

Prosecution of an arson case is time consuming and requires expertise. Courts have ruled that circumstantial evidence, the

---

Heat

Fire Triangle

Fuel — **Oxygen**

Police detectives

Successful Prosecution of Arson Case

Prosecutors — **Fire investigators**

BOX 15–2 🛡 Problems in Arson Investigation

- Locating witnesses
- Locating and preserving physical evidence
- Determining whether the victim is also the suspect
- Coordinating the investigation among police, fire, and insurance agents
- Determining if the fire was arson or had some other cause

A CLOSER LOOK

Identifying the Arsonist Using "N-DEx"

Consider this true scenario: Fire investigators in Concord, New Hampshire, responded to an abandoned warehouse fire. The evidence pointed to arson. Investigators interviewed people watching the fire and included their names in the incident report submitted to the FBI's Law Enforcement Data Exchange or "N-DEx." N-DEx is a recently developed national information-sharing system available through a secure Internet site for law enforcement and criminal justice agencies. One of the witnesses was Gordan Kanseah. The case went unsolved.

Approximately three years later, fire investigators in New York City, New York, arrived at a warehouse fire in which a night watchman had

died. Gordan Kanseah was among the witnesses. Kanseah's name was included in a New York incident report submitted to N-DEx. N-DEx notified both New York and New Hampshire authorities that the same person was a witness to both crimes. N-DEx sent a notification to investigators in Concord and New York that a witness had shown up in multiple arson investigations. This led to a cooperative investigation that resulted in Kanseah's arrest.

Source: Federal Bureau of Investigation. (2011). Law enforcement scenarios. Retrieved from www.fbi.gov/about-us/cjis/n-dex/law-enforcement-scenarios/scenarios8.

A Steel Pipe Bomb Such as This Can Be Relatively Easy to Assemble and Can Cause Death or Serious Physical Injury to Victims.

most common type of evidence in an arson case, has the same probative value as direct evidence, but it is up to the prosecution to weave the web of circumstance.[16] Many prosecutors find this an intimidating and unrewarding task.

A good arson investigator begins with the notion that he or she must collect sufficient circumstantial evidence to convince a jury that the suspect committed the crime. Statistics reveal that most successful arson prosecutors rely on circumstantial evidence.

Proving the arson case "beyond a reasonable doubt" through the use of circumstantial evidence is difficult but not impossible. Prosecutors are frequently reluctant to proceed with charges in an arson case because evidence is fragmented and circumstantial. A trained investigator, however, knows what evidence to look for and is aware of the amount of evidence sufficient to remove reasonable doubt from the minds of prospective jurors.

▶ Investigation of Bombing Incidents

Bombs can be constructed to look like almost anything and can be placed or delivered in any number of ways. Bombs are often made out of common household items regularly found in the kitchen, in the garage, or under the sink. The easiest bomb to construct is the pipe bomb, which is often packed with screws and nails that act as projectiles, similar to a hand grenade. These

LEARNING OUTCOMES 5 — Explain how to investigate bombs and bombers.

are materials that the bomber relies on, partly to help conceal his or her identity. Because they are usually homemade, these bombs are limited in their design only by the imagination of the bomber. So when searching for a bomb, the investigator should simply look for anything that appears unusual.

Investigating Bomb Threats

Bomb threats are delivered in a variety of ways, but most are telephoned in to the target. Occasionally, these calls are through a third party. Sometimes a threat is communicated through writing and recording. There are two general explanations as to why bombers communicate a bomb threat:

1. The caller has definite knowledge or believes that an explosive or incendiary bomb has been or will be placed, and he or she wants to minimize personal injury or property damage. The caller may be the person who placed the device or someone who has become aware of such information.

2. The caller wants to create an atmosphere of anxiety and panic that will, in turn, result in a disruption of normal activities at the facility where the device is supposedly placed.

Whatever the reason, there will certainly be a reaction to it. Through proper planning, however, the wide variety of

When a bomb threat is called in, the following steps should be implemented:
- Keep the caller on the line as long as possible.
- Ask him or her to repeat the message and record every word spoken by the person.
- Ask the caller the location of the bomb and the time of detonation of the device.
- Inform the caller that the building is occupied and the detonation of a bomb could kill or injure innocent people.
- Pay particular attention to background noise such as motors running, music playing, or any other noise that may give a clue as to the location of the caller.
- Listen closely to the voice (male or female), voice quality (calm or excited), accents, and speech impediments.
- Interview the person who received the call for the preceding information.

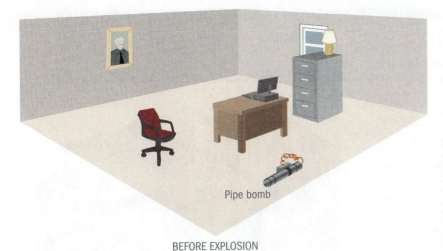

Pipe bomb

BEFORE EXPLOSION

Shock front Fragmentation effect Blast pressure effect

Exploding bomb Secondary fires

FIGURE 15–1 Graphic Representation of Fragmentation, Blast Pressure, and Secondary Forces Produced by an Explosion.

- Wires that appear to be electric should not be cut.
- Be aware of fuses or obvious means of detonation (for example, mercury fuses).
- No containers should be opened without a thorough examination.

No single strategy exists to adequately safeguard officers from all hazards posed by booby traps and explosives. Each case is different and should be evaluated individually, with consideration given to the number of possible suspects (and their backgrounds) and the location of the raid. In any case, keen observation and prudent judgment are still the best investigative precautions.

When a Bomb Is Found

It is important to stress that personnel involved in a search be instructed that their only mission is to search for and report suspicious objects. Under no circumstances should officers attempt to move, jar, or touch a suspicious object or anything attached to it. The actual removal of the bomb should be left to professional bomb disposal personnel. After the suspected bomb has been located, the location and description of the object should be reported to the supervisor or command center. Fire department and rescue personnel should also be notified and placed on standby. If necessary, sandbags or mattresses (never metal shields) should be placed around the suspicious object. Do not attempt to cover the object. Instead, you should do the following:

- Identify the danger area and block it off with a "clear zone" of at least 300 feet, including floors below and above the object.
- Be sure that all doors and windows are open to minimize primary damage from the blast and secondary damage from fragmentation.
- Evacuate the building.
- Do not permit reentry into the building until the device has been removed or disarmed and the building is declared safe for reentry.

Handling the Media

It is important that all inquiries from the news media be directed to one person who is designated as spokesperson. All other persons should be instructed not to discuss the situation with outsiders, especially the news media. The purpose of this provision is to furnish the news media with accurate information and to see that additional bomb threat calls are not precipitated by irresponsible statements from uninformed sources.

uncontrollable reactions can be minimized. The bomb threat caller is the best source of information about a bomb.

Written Bomb Threats

When a written threat is received, all materials should be saved, including envelopes and containers. Remember that paper is an excellent preservative of latent fingerprints. In addition, handwriting, typewriting, and postal markings can provide good investigative leads. Therefore, after the message has been recognized as a bomb threat, further handling of the material should be minimized, and it should be stored in a safe place.

Safety Precautions

In raid or search situations in which explosive devices are expected to be encountered, investigators should be accompanied by an explosives expert. This person can be used to inform officers of what type of device is at hand and how best to proceed safely with the raid. Other precautions include the following:

- Only one officer at a time should approach the suspected booby trap.
- When trip wires are located, both ends of the wire should be checked (some devices use more than one trip wire).

The Case against the Unabomber. . .

Ted Kaczynski, a math-professor-turned-hermit, was charged with 4 of the 16 bombings linked to the Unabomber and faced the death penalty if convicted. After his arrest, he initially pleaded innocent of the charges and was remanded to the Sacramento, California, jail. After his arrest, Kaczynski's Montana cabin was searched by federal agents, who found, among other things, a bomb (which they exploded safely), the original antitechnology manuscript, and his secret identification number. Investigators also found a deposit credited to Kaczynski's account at Western Federal Savings in Helena, Montana, on December 11, 1985, the same day that he was alleged to have planted his first fatal bomb 900 miles away in Sacramento. But the deposit slip was actually dated December 9. The Bureau of Alcohol, Tobacco, Firearms, and Explosives (ATF) determined that a bomb placed at the University of Utah in October 1981 was a hoax. What prosecutors failed to say was that the FBI and postal inspectors disagreed. Also, in a letter to the *New York Times*, the Unabomber described that bomb as a botched operation. Crime-scene investigators found in excess of 20 latent fingerprints, some of which were identified, some of which were not, and none of which were Kaczynski's fingerprints. But the Unabomber's letter boasted about using gloves to avoid leaving fingerprints. In earlier affidavits, FBI analysts had pointed to scores of similarities between Kaczynski's writings and the Unabomber's manifesto and letters, including similarly misspelled words.

Hannamariah/Shutterstock.com

In December 1997, Kaczynski admitted to the FBI that he was in fact the Unabomber and agreed to a plea bargain, pleading guilty to two counts of murder in exchange for a life sentence without the possibility of parole.

Sources: Howard, K. (1995, September 19). Unabomber manuscript is published—public safety reasons cited in joint decision by Post, N.Y. Times. *The Washington Post*, p. A01.

What evidence can be of value collected from the scene or learned from the surviving victims of such an explosion?

1. Pretend you are the lead investigator in this case. Based on the relevant material in the chapter, what about the evidence in this case helped to make clear the identification of Kaczynski as the Unabomber?

CHAPTER 15 — Arson and Bombings

LEARNING OUTCOMES 1

Summarize the scope of the problem of arson.

Arson is a pervasive problem throughout the nation. According to the *Uniform Crime Reports* (UCR) program, in 2012 there were 21,494 instances of arson reported to the police. The average dollar loss for each instance of arson in 2012 was $12,796.

1. Why is arson considered a low-priority crime by law enforcement agencies?
2. What factors can be attributed to the misunderstanding of the crime of arson?
3. What reasons make investigating fires that might be arson difficult?

LEARNING OUTCOMES 2

Explain the official definition of the crime of arson.

Many things may indicate that a fire of suspicious origin was arson—presence of accelerants, color of flames, plants, trailers, smoke, size of fire, odors, evidence of planning and prior knowledge, as well as motivation.

1. What kind of direct and circumstantial evidence can be used to prove arson?
2. What are common examples of plants and trailers?
3. How is compulsive fire setting classified? How are the classifications different?
4. In fires caused by arson, what are the most commonly used accelerants?

LEARNING OUTCOMES 3

Describe the relationship between police and fire investigators.

After a fire has been determined to have a suspicious origin, investigators from the local fire and police departments as well as the victim's insurance company collaborate on the case. When the fire investigation becomes a question of who committed the crime, law enforcement takes charge because firefighters are usually trained in the suppression of fire rather than its investigation.

1. What is the principal goal of the police in arson investigations?
2. What type of assistance does the fire department provide to law enforcement during arson investigations?
3. Who takes the lead role in an arson investigation?
4. What is the primary role of the insurance company in arson investigations?

LEARNING OUTCOMES 4

Explain the techniques of arson investigation.

Discovering the fire's origin is a critical phase because it includes ruling out natural or accidental causes. After the fire is extinguished, samples of debris that might have been the material used for starting the fire should be collected. When the rubble is being cleaned up, investigators should be present to observe any additional evidence that might be uncovered. Witness testimony often yields information as well.

1. How can the physical characteristics of the fire be used to determine if a fire was arson?
2. Why doesn't the prosecution of arson crimes occur often?
3. According to criminal profilers, who is the typical fire starter?
4. What are some key problems in arson investigations?

paper trail Evidence in an arson case that shows motive. This includes financial records, inflated insurance coverage, little or no inventory, and excessive debts.

point of origin The location on an arson scene where the fire originated.

span of the fire Physical characteristics of an arson fire such as smoke, direction, flames, and distance of travel.

plants Preparations used to set an arson fire.

trailers Materials used in spreading an arson fire.

alligatoring The pattern of crevices formed by the burning of a wooden structure.

olfactory Pertaining to smell. A distinguishable odor may indicate a specific type of crime.

fire triangle What a fire needs to burn: heat, fuel, and oxygen.

LEARNING OUTCOMES 5	**Explain how to investigate bombs and bombers.**

Bomb threats are delivered in a variety of ways, including telephoned and written threats. When a bomb threat is called in, investigators respond accordingly. When a written threat is received, all materials should be saved, including envelopes and containers. In raids or searches, investigators should be accompanied by an explosives expert who handles the removal of a bomb if found.

1. What is one of the most popular types of homemade bombs used by bombers?

2. Who serves as the best source of information about a bomb threat?

3. What are three key steps that should be taken when handling a bomb threat?

4. What are the major safety precautions that investigators need to follow in raid or search situations involving bombs?

5. What steps should be taken when a bomb is found?

Additional Links

www.atf.gov
This is the site of the Bureau of Alcohol, Tobacco, Firearms, and Explosives (ATF). Visitors can read the mission and history of the organization. Menu and links include careers, pressroom, publications (newsletters and fact sheets), a most wanted list, and a bomb data center. The site also features ATF for Kids and a search engine.

www.usfa.dhs.gov
This is the site of the U.S. Fire Administration, which is part of the Department of Homeland Security. The goal of the organization is to work for a fire-safe America. Links include publications and data about fires in America, key dates in fire history, fire-prevention campaigns, press releases, statistics, information for students and educators, information about children and fire safety, employment opportunities, a learning resource center, and grants.

http://cyber.eserver.org/unabom.txt; www.newshare.com/Newshare/Common/News/manifesto.html; www.washingtonpost.com/wp-srv/national/longterm/unabomber/manifesto.text.htm
Interested parties who want to read the Unabomber Manifesto in its entirety may do so by visiting one of these sites.

"The problem of international and domestic terrorism has focused new attention on the field of criminal investigation."

Terrorism and National Security Crimes

1 Define *terrorism*.

2 Describe who terrorists are.

3 Describe the various forms of terrorism.

4 Identify notable terrorist incidents.

5 Explain the problem of international terrorism.

6 Identify current threats of mass destruction.

7 Explain the problem of domestic terrorism.

8 Describe the tactics used to destabilize terrorist organizations.

Steve Allen/Shutterstock

INTRO THE INSIDIOUS NATURE OF TERRORISM

On April 15, 2013, two pressure-cooker bombs exploded during the Boston Marathon at 2:49 P.M. eastern time, killing 3 people and injuring 264 others. The bombs exploded about 12 seconds and 210 yards apart, near the finish line on Boylston Street.

The Marathon began on schedule without any signs of a terrorist attack. On two occasions, law enforcement officers swept the area for bombs before the explosions; the second sweep occurred one hour before the bombs went off. People were able to come and go freely, and carry bags and items in and out of the area.

At 2:49 P.M., about two hours after the winner crossed the finish line, but with more than 5,700 runners yet to finish, two bombs exploded on Boylston Street near Copley Square about 210 yards apart, immediately before the finish line. The first exploded outside Marathon Square between 671 and 673 Boylston Street at 2:49:43 P.M. When the first explosion detonated, the race clock at the finish line showed 04:09:43, reflecting the elapsed time since the Wave 3 start time of 10:40 AM. The second bomb detonated at 2:49 P.M., about 13 seconds after the first bomb. The second explosion was one block farther west at 755 Boylston Street. The blasts blew out windows on adjacent buildings but did not cause any structural damage. Sadly, three people were killed and 264 others were seriously injured.

The Federal Bureau of Investigation (FBI) investigated the incident and three days later released photographs and surveillance video of two suspects. The suspects were identified later that day as Chechen brothers Dzhokhar and Tamerlan Tsarnaev. Shortly after the images were released, the suspects killed Officer Sean Collier of the Massachusetts Institute of Technology (MIT) and carjacked a sport-utility vehicle, then became involved in a shootout with Watertown, Massachusetts, police

officers. During the gunfight, a police officer from the Massachusetts Bay Transit Authority (MBTA) was injured but survived. Tamerlan Tsarnaev was shot by police and then run over by his brother Dzhokhar and died. Dzhokhar was injured but escaped.

A record manhunt then ensued, with thousands of law enforcement officers searching a 20-block area of Watertown. During the course of the manhunt, police told residents of Watertown and surrounding areas to remain indoors. In addition, the public transportation system and most businesses were closed down, creating a huge deserted urban area. Shortly after the advisory was lifted, at about 7:00 P.M., Dzhokhar Tsarnaev was discovered by a resident hiding in a boat in his back yard. He was arrested and taken to a hospital shortly thereafter.

During his initial interrogation in the hospital, Dzhokhar said that his brother, Tamerlan, was the architect of the bombing. He also said they were motivated by extremist Islamist beliefs and the wars in Iraq and Afghanistan, and that they were self-radicalized and not associated with any terrorist groups. Dzhokhar further said that he and his brother learned to build explosive devices from an online magazine of the al-Qaeda affiliate in Yemen.

DISCUSS In this case, innocent persons were killed and seriously injured while attending a nationally recognized sporting event. How can such a disaster be avoided in the future? Consider for example, enhanced "Crimestoppers" programs, high-tech surveillance technology, and innovative police training/tactics/operations.

Most acts of terrorism have three basic participants: the perpetrator, the victim, and the audience affected (or the target). Although the perpetrator often is difficult to identify, the victim of the attack is usually the most controversial. The issue of terrorism is clouded because it is commonly viewed as a form of low-intensity, unconventional aggression on the lower end of the warfare spectrum. In this unrealistic view, terrorism is

an act of war rather than a criminal activity, which gives it a purpose and some sense of dignity. However, most people recognize that embassy bombings, political hostage taking, and aircraft hijackings are criminal terrorist acts. Accordingly, they understand that such acts are designed to shock and stun and are outside warfare conventions.

▶ Terrorism Defined

LEARNING OUTCOMES **1** — Define *terrorism*.

Whether domestic or international, terrorism is pervasive throughout the world and remains one of the most complex and difficult issues

facing law enforcement in the twenty-first century. There is no single, universally accepted definition of the word *terrorism*. It is defined in a number of ways by a number of organizations. Simply stated, terrorism is policy intended to intimidate or cause terror.[1] The federal Foreign Relations

Authorization Act defines **terrorism** in terms of four primary elements. The act says that terrorism is

1. Premeditated,
2. Politically motivated,
3. Violent, and
4. Committed against noncombatant targets.[2]

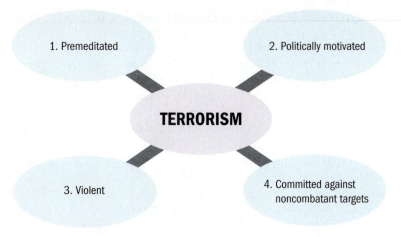

1. Premeditated
2. Politically motivated

TERRORISM

3. Violent
4. Committed against noncombatant targets

Some definitions also include acts of unlawful violence or unconventional warfare, but at present there is no internationally agreed upon definition of terrorism.[3] A person who practices terrorism is generally referred to as a *terrorist*. Acts of terrorism are criminal acts, according to United Nations Security Council Resolution 1373 and the domestic jurisprudence of almost all nations.

Regardless of the origin of its definition, the word *terrorism* is politically and emotionally charged,[4] and this greatly compounds the difficulty of providing a precise definition. A 1988 study by the U.S. Army found that more than 100 definitions of the word *terrorism* have been used.[5] The concept of terrorism is itself controversial because it is often used by states to delegitimize political or foreign opponents and potentially legitimize the state's own use of terror against them.

The history of terrorist organizations suggests that they do not practice terrorism only for its political effectiveness; individual terrorists are also motivated by a desire for social solidarity with other members.[6]

Terrorism has been practiced by a broad array of political organizations to further their objectives. It has been practiced by right- and left-wing political parties, nationalistic groups, religious groups, revolutionaries, and ruling governments.[7]

Acts of terrorism can be carried out by individuals, groups, or states. According to some definitions, clandestine or semiclandestine state actors may also carry out terrorist acts outside the framework of a state of war. However, the most common image of terrorism is that it is carried out by small and secretive cells that are highly motivated to serve a particular cause, and many of the most deadly operations in recent times, such as the September 11 attacks, the London underground bombing, and the 2002 Bali bombing, were planned and carried out by cliques composed of close friends, family members, and other strong social networks.

These groups benefited from the free flow of information and efficient telecommunications and succeeded where others had failed.[8] Over the years, many people have attempted to come up with a terrorist profile to attempt to explain these individuals' actions through their psychology and social circumstances. Others, such as Roderick Hindery, have sought to discern profiles in the propaganda tactics used by terrorists. Some security organizations designate these groups as violent nonstate actors.[9]

Recent research and investigations into terrorist operations have shown that terrorists look, dress, and behave like "normal" people until they execute their assigned mission. Therefore, terrorist profiling based on personality or physical or sociological traits does not appear to be particularly useful. The physical and behavioral description of a terrorist could describe almost any average person.[10]

The Federal Code of Regulations defines terrorism as "the unlawful use of force and violence against persons or property to intimidate or coerce a government, the civilian population, or any segment thereof, in furtherance of social or political objectives" (28 CFR, Section 0.85). In comparison, the Federal Bureau of Investigation (FBI) offers a more compartmentalized definition addressing both domestic and international terrorism:

Domestic terrorism: the unlawful use, or threatened use of force by a group or individual, based and operating entirely within the United States without foreign direction, committed against persons or property to intimidate or coerce a government, the civilian population, or any segment thereof, in furtherance of social or political objectives.

International terrorism: violent acts or acts that are a danger to human life that are a violation of the criminal law of the United States or any state or that would be a criminal violation if committed within the jurisdiction of the United States or any state. These acts appear to be intended to intimidate or coerce a civilian population, influence the policy of a government by intimidation or coercion, or affect the conduct of government by assassination or kidnapping. International terrorist acts occur outside the United States or transcend national boundaries in terms of the means by which they are to be accomplished, the persons they appear intended to coerce or intimidate or the locale in which the perpetrators operate or seek asylum.[11]

The literature of terrorism has been closely associated with the word *guerilla*, which can be defined as "little war."[12] Georges-Abeyie distinguishes the two by suggesting that terrorist groups have a more urban focus, usually attack innocent civilians and property, and operate in small groups or bands of three to five persons.[13]

▶ *Identifying the Terrorists*

The political and social circumstances that lead to the creation of terrorist groups vary widely around the world. Persons who carry out such acts vary in age,

LEARNING OUTCOMES 2

Describe who terrorists are.

race, and cultural background. In 1986, the President's Task Force on Combating Terrorism (PTFCT) reported that an estimated 60 percent of the Third World population is under 20 years of age and half are 15 years or younger. This being the case, a volatile mixture of youthful aspirations coupled with economic and political frustrations tends to create a pool of possible terrorists in those countries. Today's terrorists have a deep-seated belief in the justice of their causes. They are tough and cunning and have little regard for their lives or the lives of others. Terrorists' weaponry often comes from the illegal international arms market and could originate with legitimate arms vendors, which are, to a great extent, unregulated. Through their expansive organizational structure, many terrorists have the ability to acquire timely information on potential targets and the security precautions for these targets. If governmental pressures become more effective against them, terrorists will simply focus on easier targets.

Terrorists can be a part of a large organization or can act with only a few persons who share similar beliefs. Examples of large terrorist organizations include the Palestine Liberation Front (PLF), which has an estimated 300 members operating among three factions. The Abu Nidal Organization (ANO) boasts a membership of 500 and has an international theater of operation. Many terrorist organizations have memberships in the thousands. White points out that most terrorist groups have a membership of fewer than 50 people; under a command element, which usually consists of a few people, the group is divided according to specific tasks.[14] For example, intelligence sections are responsible for accessing targets, support sections provide the means to carry out the assault, and tactical sections actually carry out the terrorist action. Organizationally and operationally, these groups are structured much like other organized crime groups.

Criteria Describing Terrorists

Official definitions determine counterterrorism policy and are often developed to serve it. Most government definitions outline the following key criteria: target, objective, motive, perpetrator, and legitimacy or legality of the act. Terrorism is also often recognizable by a following statement from the perpetrators.

Violence

According to Walter Laqueur of the Center for Strategic and International Studies, "The only general characteristic of terrorism generally agreed upon is that terrorism involves violence and the threat of violence."[15] However, the criterion of violence alone does not produce a useful definition because it includes many acts not usually considered terrorism, such as war, riot, organized crime, and even a simple assault. Property destruction that does not endanger life is not usually considered a violent crime, but some have described property destruction by the Earth Liberation Front and Animal Liberation Front as violence and terrorism.

Psychological Impact and Fear

This means that the attack was carried out in such a way as to maximize the severity and length of the psychological impact. Each act of terrorism is a "performance" devised to have an impact on many large audiences. Terrorists also attack national symbols to show power and to attempt to shake the foundation of the country or society to which they are opposed. This may negatively affect a government while increasing the prestige of the given terrorist organization or the ideology behind a terrorist act.[16]

Perpetrated for a Political Goal

Something that many acts of terrorism have in common is a political purpose. Terrorism is a political tactic, such as letter writing or protesting, that is used by activists when they believe that no other means will effect the kind of change they desire. The change is desired so badly that failure to achieve change is seen as a worse outcome than the deaths of civilians. This is often where the inter-relationship between terrorism and religion occurs. When a political struggle is integrated into the framework of a religious or "cosmic" struggle, such as over the control of an ancestral homeland or holy site such as Israel and Jerusalem, failing in the political goal (nationalism) becomes equated with spiritual failure, which, for the highly committed, is worse than their own death or the deaths of innocent civilians.[17]

One definition that combines the key elements was developed at the George C. Marshall Center for European Security Studies by Carsten Bockstette:

> Terrorism is defined as political violence in an asymmetrical conflict that is designed to induce terror and psychic fear (sometimes indiscriminate) through the violent victimization and destruction of noncombatant targets (sometimes iconic symbols). Such acts are meant to send a message from an illicit clandestine organization. The purpose of terrorism is to exploit the media in order to achieve maximum attainable publicity as an amplifying force multiplier in order to influence the targeted audience(s) in order to reach short- and midterm political goals and/or desired long-term end states.[18]

Deliberate Targeting of Noncombatants

It is commonly held that the distinctive nature of terrorism lies in its intentional and specific selection of civilians as direct targets. Specifically, the criminal intent is shown when babies, children, mothers, and elderly people are murdered or injured and put in harm's way. Much of the time, the victims of terrorism are targeted not because they are threats but because they are specific "symbols, tools, animals or corrupt beings" that tie into a specific view of the world that the terrorists possess. Their suffering accomplishes the terrorists' goals of instilling fear, getting their message out to an audience, or otherwise satisfying the demands of their often radical religious and political agendas.[19]

Disguise

Some terrorists pretend to be noncombatants, hide among such noncombatants, fight from vantage points in the midst of noncombatants, and (when they can) strive to mislead and provoke government soldiers into attacking other people so that the government will be blamed.[20]

Unlawfulness or Illegitimacy

Some official (notably government) definitions of terrorism add a criterion of illegitimacy or unlawfulness to distinguish between actions authorized by a government (and thus "lawful") and those of other actors, including individuals and small groups.[21] Using this criterion, actions that would otherwise qualify as terrorism would not be considered terrorism if they were government sanctioned.

For example, firebombing a city, which is designed to affect civilian support for a cause, would not be considered terrorism if it were authorized by a government. This criterion is inherently problematic and is not universally accepted because it denies the existence of state terrorism; the same act may or may not be classed as terrorism, depending on whether its sponsorship is traced to a "legitimate" government. "Legitimacy" and "lawfulness" are subjective, depending on the perspective of one government or another, and this criterion diverges from the historically accepted meaning and origin of the term (see Box 16–1).[22] For these reasons, this criterion is not universally accepted, and most dictionary definitions of the term do not include it.

▶ Forms of Terrorism

LEARNING OUTCOMES 3 Describe the various forms of terrorism.

In his book *Terrorism: An Introduction*, White suggests that five distinct forms of terrorism can be considered: criminal terrorism, ideological terrorism, nationalistic terrorism, state-sponsored terrorism, and revolutionary terrorism.[23]

Criminal terrorism involves the use of terror for profit or psychological gain. It fails to merit the same attention as does nationalistic violence. Criminal terrorists seem to lack the political sophistication and support of other types of terrorists. Thus, the control of criminal terrorist activity typically becomes a law enforcement matter.

Ideological terrorism is normally an effort to change the current political power. It has been argued that ideological terrorism involves a revolution, but this is not always the case. For example, some governments employ the use of death squads, whose actions might appear to be part of a repressive government, but this could be an extension of revolutionary terrorism.

Nationalistic terrorism is characterized by activity that supports the interests of an ethnic or nationalistic group, regardless of its political ideology. Nationalistic terrorists often align with either Western or Eastern ideologies. This could be viewed in terms of superpower support (food, supplies, weapons, etc.) for nationalistic interests. In other words, we could say that the West tends to supply our terrorists, while the East tends to supply theirs. Stated differently, the goals of democracy are opposed to those of Marxist socialism.[24]

State-sponsored terrorism occurs when governmental regimes use or threaten to use violence

Five Forms of Terrorism

Criminal
Ideological
Nationalistic
State sponsored
Revolutionary

BOX 16–1 🛡 U.S. Terrorism Legislation

- *Biological Weapons Anti-terrorism Act of 1989.* Enacted May 22, 1990; provides for the implementation of the Biological Weapons Convention as well as criminal penalties for violation of its provisions.

- *Executive Order 12947.* Signed by President Bill Clinton January 23, 1995; prohibits financial transactions with any "Specially Designated Terrorist." A "Specially Designated Terrorist" is any person who is determined by the U.S. Secretary of the Treasury under notices or regulations issued by the Office of Foreign Assets Control.

- *Omnibus Counterterrorism Act of 1995.* Prohibits transactions with terrorists; President Clinton described the bill as a "comprehensive effort to strengthen the ability of the United States to deter terrorist acts and punish those who aid or abet any international terrorist activity in the United States" and requested "the prompt and favorable consideration of this legislative proposal by the Congress."

- *US Antiterrorism and Effective Death Penalty Act of 1996.* Pub. L. No. 104-132, 110 Stat. 1214; also known as AEDPA, an act of Congress signed into law on April 24, 1996. The bill passed with broad bipartisan support by Congress (91-8-1 in the U.S. Senate, 293-133-7 in the House of Representatives following the 1990s World Trade Center and Oklahoma City bombings, and signed into law by President Bill Clinton.

- *Executive Order 13224.* Signed by President George W. Bush on September 23, 2001; authorizes the seizure of assets of organizations or individuals designated by the Secretary of the Treasury to assist, sponsor, or provide material or financial support or who are otherwise associated with terrorists (66 Fed. Reg. 49,079).

- *2001 USA Patriot Act (amended March 2006).* Provisions include roving wiretaps, searches of business records (the "library records provision"), and conducting surveillance of "lone wolves"—individuals suspected of terrorist-related activities not linked to terrorist groups.

- *Homeland Security Act of 2002, Pub. L. 107-296.* Created the U.S. Department of Homeland Security and the new cabinet-level position of Secretary of Homeland Security. It is the largest federal government reorganization since the Department of Defense was created via the National Security Act of 1947.

- *Support Anti-terrorism by Fostering Effective Technologies Act (SAFETY Act) of 2002.* A little-known and often misunderstood piece of legislation that can protect an entity from the truly "enterprise-threatening" liability it could face following a terrorist event.

- *Border Protection Anti-terrorism and Illegal Immigration Control Act of 2005.* A comprehensive bill that requires up to 700 miles of fence along the U.S.-Mexico border at points with the highest number of illegal border crossings. It also requires the federal government to take custody of illegal aliens detained by local authorities. This ended the practice of "catch and release," where federal officials sometimes instructed local law enforcement to release detained illegal aliens because resources to prosecute them are not available. It also reimburses local agencies in the 29 counties along the border for costs related to detaining illegal aliens.

- *Real ID Act of 2005.* Sets forth requirements for state driver's licenses and ID cards to be accepted by the federal government for "official purposes," as defined by the Secretary of Homeland Security.

in international relations outside established diplomatic protocol. The term became somewhat popular during the Reagan administration in describing low-level violence used against U.S. diplomatic and military installations. This form of terrorism is typified by such events as the 1979 takeover of the U.S. embassy in Teheran and the bombings aimed against U.S. military personnel in the Middle East. Countries that support such activities are known as terrorist states. Iran, Syria, Afghanistan, Chile, Argentina, El Salvador, and Libya are among the most notorious state sponsors of terrorism.

States (countries) sponsor terrorism for many different reasons. One is to achieve foreign policy objectives that could not otherwise be achieved through political or military means. Sometimes states sponsor terrorism to create or expand their power and influence among ideological movements. Other state-sponsored incidents attempt to stifle domestic opposition through assassination of dissidents abroad. These types of terrorists are easy for a state to disavow. The use of state-sponsored terrorism represents a low-risk, low-budget method of conducting foreign policy. State-supported terrorists can benefit by receiving government assistance in arms or explosives, communications, travel documents, and safe havens for training operatives. Their actions are frequently difficult to trace, so the governments involved can maintain respectability and legitimacy in the international community while secretly financing and supporting terrorist activities to achieve their goals.

Revolutionary terrorism involves persons whose guerrilla-like tactics invoke fear in those holding political power and their supporters. The goal is to overthrow the current power base and replace it with political leaders who share the terrorists' views. Common tactics used by revolutionary terrorists are kidnappings, bombings, and assassinations, all of which are skillfully designed to force the existing government to respond with repressive measures. The terrorist then uses media coverage to attempt to expose the government as being inhumane and in need of being overthrown. Examples of revolutionary terrorism are Mao Tse-tung's takeover of China from Chiang Kai-shek and Fidel Castro's successful takeover of the Cuban government from the Batista regime during the late 1950s.

▶ *Notable Terrorist Incidents*

The World Trade Center and Pentagon terrorist attacks of September 11, 2001, marked a dramatic escalation in a trend toward more destructive terrorist attacks that began in the 1980s. Until the 9/11 attacks, the October 23, 1983, truck bombings of U.S. and French  military barracks in Beirut, Lebanon, which claimed a total of 295 lives, stood as the most deadly act of terrorism. The attacks of 9/11 produced casualty figures more than 10 times higher than those of the 1983 barracks attacks.

The 9/11 attacks also reflected a trend toward more indiscriminate targeting among international terrorists. The vast majority of the more than 3,000 victims of the attacks were civilians. In addition, the attacks represented the first known case of suicide attacks carried out by international terrorists in the United States. The 9/11 attacks also marked the first successful act of international terrorism in the United States since the vehicle bombing of the World Trade Center in February 1993.

FIGURE 16–1 **Second World Trade Center Attack Occurring on September 11, 2001.**
Source: Ken Tannenbaum/Shutterstock.com.

With the death of Osama bin Laden in 2011, the nature of terrorism has changed. Still, the threat of terrorism on U.S. soil is a current and ongoing concern. We need only to look back a few years to see the relentless efforts of terrorists to target U.S. interests at home and abroad. This was demonstrated with the 9/11 attacks, the bombing of the *U.S.S. Cole* in October 2000, and the earlier bombings of two U.S. embassies in east Africa in August 1998, among other plots. Such attacks make terrorism a clear and imminent threat to the United States and pose a number of unique challenges for criminal investigators.

More recently, individuals who have been investigated for possible terrorist links include Richard Reid and Zacarias Moussaoui. Let's now consider investigative leads as well as evidence developed against these terrorist suspects to illustrate terrorism investigation.

On December 22, 2001, Richard C. Reid was arrested after a flight attendant on American Airlines Flight 63 observed him apparently attempting to ignite an improvised explosive in his sneakers while on board a Paris-to-Miami flight. Aided by passengers, attendants overpowered and subdued Reid, and the flight was diverted to Logan International Airport in Boston. Evidence strongly suggests that Reid, who was traveling on a valid British passport, was affiliated with the al-Qaeda network. Reid was indicted on nine counts, including placing an explosive device on an aircraft and attempted murder. The FBI investigation has determined that the explosives in Reid's shoes, if detonated in certain areas of the passenger cabin, could have blown a hole in the fuselage of the aircraft.

Investigators also learned that Reid and another subject, Zacarias Moussaoui, were known associates. Moussaoui came to the attention of the FBI while taking flight-training classes in Minnesota in August 2001. Moussaoui paid more than $8,000 in cash for flight simulator lessons on a 747-400, which far exceeded his training level as a pilot. Moussaoui showed unusual interest in the instructor's comment that airplane cabin doors could not be opened during flight. In addition, his flight instructor was concerned that Moussaoui expressed interest only in learning how to take off and not how to land the 747-400. In preparation for high-fidelity simulator training, he expressed strong interest in "piloting" a simulated flight from London's Heathrow Airport to John F. Kennedy Airport in New York. When the instructor took his concerns to the FBI, Moussaoui was interviewed by special agents from the FBI and the U.S. Immigration and Naturalization Service (INS). He was determined to be an INS overstay and was detained by the INS on August 16, 2001. After his detention, Moussaoui refused to allow a search to be conducted of his possessions, including a laptop computer and a computer disc. Attempts were made to obtain authority to conduct a search of this computer. However, because of the lack of probable cause and lack of predication, neither a criminal nor intelligence search could be conducted. After the 9/11 attack, a criminal search of the computer was conducted. Nothing was located that connected Moussaoui with the events of 9/11; however, information about crop dusting was located on the computer. As a result, crop-dusting

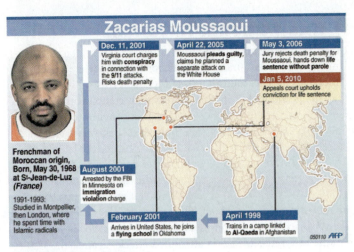

FIGURE 16–2 Zacarias Moussaoui.
Source: ea/js AFP/Newscom.

operations in the United States were grounded briefly on two occasions in September 2001. On December 11, 2001, the U.S. District Court for the Eastern District of Virginia indicted Moussaoui on six counts of conspiracy for his role in the events of September 11, 2001.

Recent Terrorist Threats

With the 2011 killing of Osama bin Laden by U.S. Navy Seals, the complexion of global terrorism changed. Although the full ramifications of his death are not yet known, the U.S. government continues to monitor how his death impacts al-Qaeda's organization and operations. Because of bin Laden's stature and his personal connections with leaders of al-Qaeda affiliates and allies, his death also may change the way terrorist groups relate to one another.[25]

The years following 9/11 have demonstrated that despite the counterterrorism efforts against al-Qaeda, its intent to target the United States remains constant. Numerous examples exist. In one case, an al-Qaeda homeland plot involved three operatives—Najibullah Zazi, Zarein Ahmedzay, and Adis Medunjanin—who were arrested by U.S. government agents in the fall of 2009. These individuals received terrorist training in Pakistan from al-Qaeda and then returned to the United States, where they planned to use homemade improvised explosive devices (IEDs) to attack the New York City subway system.

The 2009 scheme also demonstrated al-Qaeda's continuation of targeting trends that developed over the previous years, such as its interest in recruiting American citizens for an attack on U.S. soil, its preferred weapon (the crudely made IED), and its desire to target America's transit systems. Although these aspects of al-Qaeda's *modus operandi* (MO) have remained consistent, al-Qaeda has expanded its strategy in hopes of perpetrating more attacks. For example, while al-Qaeda remains committed to large-scale attacks, it also may pursue smaller, less sophisticated ones that require less planning and fewer resources and operational steps. Instead of plots reminiscent of 9/11 that involve more than a dozen operatives, future attacks may employ only a few.

▶ International Terrorism

In 2014, approximately 13 years after the 9/11 attacks, the United States faces a more divers terrorism threat than in 2001. Americans have learned all too clearly that terrorism is a threat that spans the globe. In this increasingly complex and ever-changing environment, not

LEARNING OUTCOMES 5 Explain the problem of international terrorism.

only does Pakistan-based al-Qaeda possess the ability to project itself across the globe to stage attacks against the West, but so do groups based in Yemen, Somalia, and Iraq. Thus, in many ways, al-Qaeda in the Arabian Peninsula poses as serious a threat to the nation as core al-Qaeda, with two attempted attacks against the U.S. homeland between 2009 and 2011.[26]

In this ever-changing threat environment, America continues to evolve to keep pace with this tenacious and creative enemy. In recent years, the United States has made significant progress in combating terrorism, most importantly with the May 2, 2011, death of al-Qaeda leader Osama bin Laden. Moreover, many lives have been saved by U.S. counterterrorism efforts, for example, the arrest of a homegrown violent extremist (HVE) who attempted to attack a Christmas tree-lighting ceremony in Portland and the arrest of three al-Qaeda-trained operatives in the United States before they could attack the New York City transit system.[27] These represent important domestic terrorism victories. Researcher Mantri concludes that the most alarming things about these attempted attacks have been both the apparent ineffectiveness of the Homeland Security apparatus put in place post-9/11 and the rise in what is commonly termed "homegrown terrorism": attacks conceived and launched by U.S. citizens on U.S. citizens.[28]

Islamic Terrorism

Islamic terrorism has its roots in **Islamism** (Islam + ism; Arabic: al-'islamiyya), a set of ideologies holding that Islam is not only a religion but also a political system and that modern Muslims must return to the roots of their religion and unite politically.

Islamism is a controversial term, and definitions of it sometimes vary. Leading Islamist thinkers emphasize the enforcement of sharia (Islamic law); of pan-Islamic political unity; and of the elimination of non-Muslim, particularly Western, military, economic, political, social, and cultural influences in the Muslim world, which they believe to be incompatible with Islam.[29]

Some observers suggest that Islamism's tenets are less strict and can be defined as a form of identity politics or "support for [Muslim] identity, authenticity, broader regionalism, revivalism, [and] revitalization of the community."[30] Still others define *Islamism* as "an Islamic militant, anti-democratic movement, bearing a holistic vision of Islam whose final aim is the restoration of the caliphate."[31]

Many of those described as "Islamists" oppose the use of the term, maintaining that they are simply Muslims and that their political beliefs and goals are an expression of Islamic religious belief.[32] Similarly, some scholars instead favor the term *activist Islam* or *political Islam*.[33]

It is important to distinguish between Islamists and Islamist terrorists:

> While ignoring the overwhelming majority of Islamists who have little or nothing to do with terror and making them virtually irrelevant and stigmatized in Western political discourse. . . . To ignore the complexity of political Islam and tar all Islamists with the same brush of terrorism guarantees bin Laden's success.[34]

The International Crisis Group warns that the tendency of "policy-makers. . . to lump all forms of Islamism together, brand them as radical and treat them as hostile. . . is fundamentally misconceived."[35] Furthermore, the International Crisis Group states,

> . . .the issues and grievances which have been grist to the mill of Sunni jihadism across the Muslim world have not been resolved or even appreciably attenuated since 2001, but, on the contrary, aggravated and intensified. The failure to address the Palestinian question and, above all, the decision to make war on Iraq and the even more extraordinary mishandling of the postwar situation there have unquestionably motivated and encouraged jihadi activism across the Muslim world. Unsophisticated Western understanding and rhetoric that tends to discredit all forms of political Islamism, coupled with the lumping together of the internal, irredentist and global jihadis. . . .[36]

Post–bin Laden Terrorism

While bin Laden's death in 2011 was an important "moral victory" for U.S. counterterrorism efforts, it does not necessarily mean that the threat of terrorism is over for the United States. As researcher Phillip Jenkins notes, "Terrorism is a tactic not a movement."[37] For example, after 2011 there was an increased threat from al-Qaeda affiliates like al-Qaeda in the Arabian Peninsula (AQAP) and Tehrik-e Taliban Pakistan (TTP).[38] These organizations have changed dramatically and probably point to the most significant difference in the terrorist threat

Think About It...

A Different Perspective The way people think is sometimes different depending on an individual's culture—what "makes sense" to us as Americans might make "no sense" to others, and vice-versa. This reality is important for police personnel who must consider actions and motivations beyond what they are used to dealing with. Why might cooperation between law enforcement and intelligence officials be so important when addressing international terrorism?

Asianet-Pakistan/Shutterstock.com

Osama Bin Laden Supporters.

Current List of Designated Foreign Terrorist Organizations

1. Abu Nidal Organization (ANO)
2. Abu Sayyaf Group (ASG)
3. Aum Shinrikyo (AUM)
4. Basque Fatherland and Liberty (ETA)
5. Gama'a al-Islamiyya (Islamic Group)
6. HAMAS
7. Harakat ul-Mujahidin (HUM)
8. Hizballah (Party of God)
9. Kahane Chai (KACH)
10. Kurdistan Workers' Party (Kongra-Gel, PKK)
11. Liberation Tigers of Tamil Eelam (LTTE)
12. National Liberation Army (ELN)
13. Palestine Liberation Front (PLF)
14. Palestinian Islamic Jihad (PIJ)
15. Popular Front for the Liberation of Palestine (PFLP)
16. PFLP-General Command (PFLP-GC)
17. Revolutionary Armed Forces of Colombia (FARC)
18. Revolutionary Organization 17 November (17N)
19. Revolutionary People's Liberation Party/Front (DHKP/C)
20. Shining Path (SL)
21. Al-Qa'ida (AQ)
22. Islamic Movement of Uzbekistan (IMU)
23. Real Irish Republican Army (RIRA)
24. United Self-Defense Forces of Colombia (AUC)
25. Jaish-e-Mohammed (JEM)
26. Lashkar-e Tayyiba (LeT)
27. Al-Aqsa Martyrs Brigade (AAMB)
28. Asbat al-Ansar (AAA)
29. Al-Qaida in the Islamic Maghreb (AQIM)
30. Communist Party of the Philippines/New People's Army (CPP/NPA)
31. Jemaah Islamiya (JI)
32. Lashkar-e-Jhangvi (LJ)
33. Ansar al-Islam (AAI)
34. Continuity Irish Republican Army (CIRA)
35. Libyan Islamic Fighting Group (LIFG)
36. Al-Qa'ida in Iraq (AQI)
37. Islamic Jihad Group (IJU)
38. Harakat ul-Jihad-i-Islami/Bangladesh (HUJI-B)
39. Tehrik-e Taliban Pakistan (TTP)
40. Jundallah
41. Army of Islam (AOI)
42. Indian Mujahidin (IM)
43. Jemaah Anshorut Tawhid (JAT)
44. Abdallah Azzam Brigades (AAB)
45. Haqqani Network (HQN)
46. Ansar al-Dine (AAD)
47. Boko Haram
48. Ansaru
49. al-Mulathamun Battalion
50. Ansar al-Shari'a in Benghazi
51. Ansar al-Shari'a in Darnah
52. Ansar al-Shari'a in Tunisia

Source: National Counterterrorism Center. (2014, January 14). Retrieved from http://www.state.gov/j/ct/rls/crt/2012/209989.htm.

environment since 9/11. The AQAP, which has attempted two U.S.-based attacks between 2009 and 2011, now poses as serious a threat to the homeland as the original al-Qaeda. Since 9/11, and especially since the death of bin Laden, the AQAP has proven itself an innovative and sophisticated enemy capable of striking beyond the Arabian Peninsula. While the tactics the original al-Qaeda developed and refined continue to threaten the United States, the inventive tactics created by the AQAP pose an additional threat.

With the 2009 Christmas Day attempt by Nigerian national Umar Farouk Abdulmutallab to detonate an IED onboard Northwest Flight 253, the AQAP became the first al-Qaeda affiliate to attempt an attack on the United States. With this attack, the AQAP broke from al-Qaeda's typical *modus operandi* in several ways. For example, Abdulmutallab was a single operative traveling alone. Rather than constructing his device in the target country, he carried an IED on his person all the way from the flight he first boarded in Africa to the airspace over Detroit, and he evaded detection systems in various airports. Abdulmutallab was not based in the United States, providing fewer chances for terrorist investigators to look for clues of possible terrorist associations.

After this attempted attack, the AQAP revealed its capacity to adapt and innovate by following with the October 2010 package-bomb plot. In this plot, the AQAP circumvented the need for a human operative by sending sophisticated IEDs concealed in printer cartridges inside packages aboard airfreight airlines. This tactic eliminated the potential for human error in the operation or detonation of the device. The AQAP claims the total operation cost was only $4,200, a vastly smaller figure than the estimated $400,000 to $500,000 spent by al-Qaeda to plan 9/11. In this approach, the AQAP moved the West to spend many times more than that to re-examine and strengthen its security procedures. From the AQAP's perspective, this failed attempt was a success—not in producing mass casualties, but in achieving a high economic cost.

In addition to conducting its own attacks, the AQAP also has sought to radicalize and inspire others to conduct attacks. In July 2010, the AQAP published the first edition of its English-language online magazine, *Inspire*, a glossy, sophisticated publication geared to a Western audience. As of the writing of this book, in the five published editions of *Inspire* the AQAP has provided religious justification and technical guidance, including information on manufacturing explosives and training with an AK-47, to encourage U.S. homegrown terrorists to stage independent attacks.

In all facets of its operations, the AQAP benefits from the expertise and insights provided by its American members to target an English-speaking audience. Anwar al-Aulaqi—a former U.S.-based imam—briefly became the leader of the AQAP until he was killed on September 30, 2011. In the years before his death, Aulaqi played an increasingly operational role in the AQAP. He recruited individuals to join the group, facilitated training at camps in Yemen, and prepared Abdulmutallab for his attempted bombing of Northwest Flight 253.

The AQAP is not the only al-Qaeda affiliate to pose an increased threat to the United States. Tehrik-e Taliban (TTP)—a Pakistani militant group that has also voiced its desire since 2008 to strike the United States—demonstrated for the first time its ability to stage attacks against America with Faisal Shahzad's failed vehicle-borne IED (VBIED) attack on Times Square in May 2010. Shahzad, a naturalized U.S. citizen of Pakistani origin, traveled to Pakistan to acquire terrorist training from the TTP and then used those skills to construct a VBIED when he returned to the United States.

Other al-Qaeda allies and affiliates also have expanded their focus. In July 2010, Somalia-based terrorist group al-Shabaab staged its first attack outside of Somalia with an attack in Uganda that killed dozens. Al-Shabaab also has attracted Western recruits, including Americans; at least two dozen have traveled to Somalia to train or fight over the past few years. Some of these Americans even have assumed leadership positions, raising the possibility that they could help expand al-Shabaab's global reach.

As these examples show, the rise of al-Qaeda affiliates presents an increasing and complicated terrorism threat. U.S. authorities no longer can prioritize al-Qaeda threats over those emanating from affiliate groups; they now must cover them all.

▶ *Threats of Mass Destruction*

Identify current threats of mass destruction.

In 2011, the U.S. Department of State identified four categories of weapons of mass destruction (WMD) that terrorists may seek to acquire

Four Categories of Weapons of Mass Destruction

Chemical   Biological   Radiological   Nuclear

and use in a WMD terrorist attack. These are chemical, biological, radiological, and nuclear.

Chemical

Chemical weapons are a potentially dangerous tool in the hands of terrorists. If they are dispersed in sufficient dosages, they could cause mass casualties, as was demonstrated by the use of chemical weapons during World War I and the Iran–Iraq War (1980–1988). Today's chemical terrorism threat includes the potential acquiring and use of chemical warfare agents and military-style delivery systems. Included are the use of toxic industrial chemicals, such as the industrial chlorine containers included in IED attacks in Iraq, and improvised dissemination systems, such as those used in the 1995 attack conducted by Aum Shinrikyo in the Tokyo subway system. Perpetrators of that attack used sharpened umbrellas to puncture plastic bags filled with the nerve agent sarin, causing the sarin to spill out and evaporate, killing 12 and injuring thousands.

Terrorists also have attempted to acquire commercially available materials such as poisons and toxic industrial chemicals. The growth of the worldwide chemical industry, including the development of complex synthetic and dual-use materials, may make the task of investigating this threat more difficult.

Biological

Bioterrorism, another deadly threat, is the deliberate dispersal of pathogens through food, air, water, or living organisms to cause disease. The 2009 Commission on the Prevention of WMD Proliferation and Terrorism concluded that it is more likely that terrorists would be able to acquire and use biological agents than nuclear weapons due to the difficulty in controlling the proliferation of biotechnologies and biological agent information.[39] If properly produced and released, biological agents can kill on a massive scale, and if terrorists use a pathogen that can be transmitted from person to person, the disease could quickly spread through commercial air travel across oceans and continents before authorities realize their nations have been attacked.

Even the use of a badly designed weapon that resulted in only a limited health impact could cause significant disruption. For example, a small-scale bioterrorism attack such as the 2001 anthrax attacks in the United States, which resulted in 5 Americans killed and an additional 17 individuals infected, had a substantial economic impact with the costs of decontamination, medical treatment for those exposed, decreased commercial activity, social distress, and lost productivity. The terrorists can often meet their objective of creating disruption and fear without causing large numbers of casualties.[40]

Radiological

Some terrorists seek to acquire radioactive materials for use in a radiological dispersal device (RDD) or **dirty bomb**. Radioactive materials are widely used in industrial, medical, and research applications and include devices used for power supply in remote locations, cancer therapy, food and blood irradiation, and radiography. Their widespread use in nearly every country makes these materials much more accessible than the materials required for nuclear weapons.

Most radioactive materials lack sufficient strength to present a significant public health risk once dispersed, whereas the materials posing the greatest hazard would require terrorists to have the expertise to handle them without exposure to incapacitating doses of radiation or detection during transit across international borders.[41] It is possible that the public panic and economic disruption caused by setting off an explosive radiological dispersal device could be substantial even if a weak radioactive source is used.

Nuclear

Some terrorist organizations, such as al-Qaeda, have openly stated their wish for acquiring nuclear weapons. The availability of scientific and technical information regarding the assembly of nuclear weapons, some of which is now available on the Internet, has increased the risk that a terrorist organization in possession of sufficient **fissile material** could develop its own crude nuclear weapon.[42] The complete production of a nuclear weapon strongly depends on the terrorist group's access to special nuclear materials as well as engineering and scientific expertise. Furthermore, with countries, such as North Korea, that have access to nuclear capabilities, the number of potential sources of unsecured nuclear weapons makes it difficult to investigate and monitor such materials.

▶ *Domestic Terrorism*

The term *domestic terrorism* was used commonly throughout the 1960s and 1970s. In a broad, general sense, acts of domestic

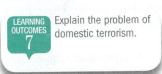

LEARNING OUTCOMES 7 — Explain the problem of domestic terrorism.

terrorism in the United States are considered to be rare, but this has not always been the case. For example, according to the FBI, between 1980 and 2000, 250 of the 335 incidents confirmed as or suspected to be terrorist acts in the United States were carried out by American citizens.[43]

The statutory definition of *domestic terrorism* in the United States has changed many times over the years; also, it can be

argued that acts of domestic terrorism have been occurring since long before any legal definition was set forth.

According to a memo produced by the FBI's Terrorist Research and Analytical Center in 1994, domestic terrorism was defined as "the unlawful use of force or violence, committed by a group(s) of two or more individuals, against persons or property to intimidate or coerce a government, the civilian population, or any segment thereof, in furtherance of political or social objectives."[44] Under current U.S. law, set forth in the USA PATRIOT Act, acts of domestic terrorism are those that

1. "Involve acts dangerous to human life that are a violation of the criminal laws of the United States or of any State;

2. Appear to be intended—(a) to intimidate or coerce a civilian population; (b) to influence the policy of a government by intimidation or coercion; or (c) to affect the conduct of a government by mass destruction, assassination, or kidnapping; and

3. Occur primarily within the territorial jurisdiction of the United States."[45]

Examples abound of domestic terrorism. One of the most memorable is the 1995 bombing of the Murrah Federal Building in Oklahoma City. In that case, a powerful truck bomb exploded outside the federal building in downtown Oklahoma City. As a result, 168 people died and hundreds more were wounded. The perpetrator, 29-year-old Timothy McVeigh, was found guilty

Domestic Terrorist Organizations in the United States

☑ *The Ku Klux Klan (KKK).* From Reconstruction at the end of the Civil War to the end of the civil rights movement, the KKK used threats, violence, arson, and murder to further its white supremacist, anti-Semitic, anti-Catholic agenda.

☑ *The Weathermen.* The Weathermen was a U.S. radical left organization active from 1969 to 1975. Its members referred to it as a "revolutionary organization of communist women and men." Their goal was the revolutionary overthrow of the U.S. government. Toward this end, and to change U.S. policy in Vietnam, they bombed a number of police and military targets. The group collapsed shortly after the U.S. withdrawal from Vietnam in 1975.

☑ *The Jewish Defense League (JDL).* The JDL was founded in 1969 by Rabbi Meir Kahane in New York City, with its declared purpose the protection of Jews from harassment and antisemitism.[I] FBI statistics show that from 1980 to 1985, 15 terrorist attacks were attempted in the United States by members of the JDL.[II] The FBI's Mary Doran described the JDL in 2004 Congressional testimony as "a proscribed terrorist group."[III] The National Consortium for the Study of Terror and Responses to Terrorism states that during the JDL's first two decades of activity, it was an "active terrorist organization."[IV] Kahane later founded the far-right Israeli political party Kach. The group's present-day website condemns all forms of terrorism.[V]

☑ *The Symbionese Liberation Army (SLA).* The SLA was an American self-styled, radical-left "urban guerrilla warfare group" that considered itself a revolutionary vanguard army. The group committed bank robberies, two murders, and other acts of violence between 1973 and 1975. Among the SLA's most notorious acts was the kidnapping and brainwashing of newspaper heiress Patty Hearst.

☑ *Army of God (AOG).* The AOG is a loose network of individuals and groups connected by ideological affinity and the determination to use violence to end the legal practice of abortion in the United States. Its affiliates consist of right-wing Christian militants who have committed violent acts against abortion providers. Acts of anti-abortion violence increased in the mid-1990s, culminating in a series of bombings by Eric Rudolph, whose targets included two abortion clinics, a gay and lesbian nightclub, and the 1996 Olympics in Atlanta. Letters Rudolph sent to newspapers claiming responsibility in the name of the AOG focused attention on the issue of right-wing extremism.

☑ *Animal Liberation Front (ALF).* The ALF is a name used internationally by animal liberation activists who engage in direct action tactics on behalf of animals. This includes removing animals from laboratories and fur farms and sabotaging facilities involved in animal testing and other animal-based industries. According to ALF statements, any act that furthers the cause of animal liberation, in which all reasonable precautions are taken not to endanger life, may be claimed as an ALF action. The group is listed by the U.S. Department of Homeland Security as a domestic terrorist organization.

☑ *Earth Liberation Front (ELF).* The ELF is a group associated with environmental extremism and advocates direct action against alleged high polluters. Several fire bombings of SUV dealerships have been attributed to the ELF.

☑ *Black Liberation Army (BLA).* A splinter group made up of the more radical members of the Black Panther Party, the BLA sought to overthrow the U.S. government in the name of racial separatism and Marxist ideals. The Fraternal Order of Police blames the BLA for the murders of 13 police officers. According to a Justice Department report on BLA activity, the BLA was suspected of involvement in more than 60 incidents of violence between 1970 and 1981.

[I] Anti-Defamation League. (2009). *Backgrounder: The Jewish Defense League*. Retrieved from http://www.adl.org/extremism/jdl_chron.asp.
[II] Bohn, M. K. (2004). *The Achille Lauro hijacking: Lessons in the politics and prejudice of terrorism.* Brassey: 67.
[III] Federal Bureau of Investigation. *Congressional testimony: Special Agent Mary Deborah (Debbie) Doran before the 9/11/2001 Commission,* June 16, 2004.
[IV] National Consortium for the Study of Terror and Responses to Terrorism. (2007). *Terrorist Organization profile: Jewish Defense League (JDL).*
[V] Council on Foreign Relations. *Militant extremists in the United States.*
Retrieved from http://www.cfr.org/terrorist-organizations/militant-extremists-united-states/p9236.

of 11 criminal counts, ranging from conspiracy to first-degree murder. He was sentenced to death and was executed by lethal injection at the U.S. penitentiary in Terre Haute, Indiana in 2001.

One year after the Oklahoma City bombing, 38-year-old Eric Robert Rudolph detonated a makeshift bomb during the 1996 Olympics, resulting in the death of 1 person and the injury of 111 others. This explosion, known as the Atlanta's Centennial Park bombing, resulted from Rudolph's antiabortion and antigay visions of America's future. After eluding police for years, Rudolph was captured, prosecuted, and sentenced to life imprisonment without the possibility of parole. These acts of domestic terrorism, termed "lone-wolf terrorism," continue to be a national security concern.[46]

Today, the domestic terrorism movement continues to remain active, and several recent domestic terrorism incidents demonstrate the scope of the threat. For example,

- In March 2010, nine members of the Michigan-based Hutaree Militia were indicted for their alleged involvement in a plot to kill law enforcement officers.

- In January 2011, a pipe bomb was discovered at a Martin Luther King Day parade in Spokane, Washington, and a subject was arrested by the FBI's Joint Terrorism Task Force (JTTF).
- In February 2011, three subjects were arrested on weapons and firearms charges in relation to alleged domestic terrorist activity in Fairbanks, Alaska.[47]

▶ Self-Radicalization: The Homegrown Terrorist

On September 24, 2009, 19-year-old Jordanian national Hosam Maher Hussein Smadi parked what he believed to be a large VBIED in the underground garage of Fountain Place—a beautiful, conspicuous skyscraper in the heart of the Dallas, Texas, business district. He armed and powered up the elaborate timing device, exited the building during the busy weekday lunch rush, and was picked up by an associate who he believed was a low-level soldier in al-Qaeda cell he had located after a long search.[48]

With the associate, Smadi drove to the top of a nearby parking garage, where he used his mobile phone to dial the number that he believed would detonate the VBIED—he had insisted on personally command-detonating the bomb—and destroy the building, killing thousands of innocent civilians in and around Fountain Place. The call, however, did not activate a VBIED; instead, it signaled the North Texas Joint Terrorism Task Force to arrest Smadi while he attempted to commit mass murder in the name of al-Qaeda.

Smadi had spent months planning the attack, modifying his plans as to which target he would focus on and what type of explosive device he would use. He believed he was fortunate to have found in the United States an al-Qaeda sleeper cell planning the next large-scale attack and that he could convince the cell to let him commit an enormous act of terrorism as an al-Qaeda soldier. In fact, Smadi had not found an al-Qaeda sleeper cell but an FBI undercover operation.[49] The Smadi investigation highlights the ongoing threat of lone offenders who operate without any ties to terrorist groups or states, can become radicalized by propaganda easily found on the Internet, and increasingly exist in America's rural areas.

Modern Islamist extremism emerged in the middle of the last century, but initially was limited to the Middle East. That dramatically changed in the aftermath of the assault on 9/11 when the threat Islamist terrorism posed to countries in the Western world became apparent. Although it was not the first time Islamist extremists targeted a Western country, the scale of the attack—which included killing almost 3,000 people and destroying the iconic Twin Towers—demonstrated that the threat from such organizations and individuals had shifted. Today, Western societies increasingly deal with an increase in so-called homegrown Islamist terrorism.

Homegrown terrorism or **self-radicalization** is not a new phenomenon, as nationals of the respective country conduct the vast majority of typical nationalistic or politically motivated terrorist activity. The terms **homegrown terrorism** and *homegrown violent extremism* typically describe self-radicalized Western citizens or local residents. They adopt an extremist religious or political ideology hostile to Western societies and values and turn to terrorism. The word *radicalization* has many definitions in intelligence and law enforcement communities. According to the FBI, homegrown terrorism is "the process by which individuals come to believe their engagement in or facilitation of non-state violence to achieve social and political change is necessary and justified."[50]

Who and How

The task of counterterrorism is more art than science. Radicalization, especially of Islamist extremists, has only recently become a serious topic of research by law enforcement organizations, intelligence agencies, and academia. Yet, data still are not extensive and have resulted mainly from shared analysis of terrorist attacks that have been either already executed or prevented. Baseline data for comparison have proven difficult to collect because of legal restrictions and other issues. Collection of data also presents challenges because as a rule, Islamist terrorism is not static, but highly flexible, including its recent manifestation into homegrown terrorism. To counter this threat, various government studies from Western European countries and comparable research in the United States have considered two key points of homegrown violent extremism: *who* becomes radicalized and *how* the radicalization process works.[51]

Research shows that in both Europe and the United States violent Islamist extremists represent a broad range of the population. In Western countries, most of these individuals have been nationals or have had legal status in the country. They are ethnically diverse, although in some European countries, the majority of identified Islamist terrorists comprise part of the largest immigrant Muslim community.

What is known is that most terrorists are male, but women also play a significant role. The majority of extremists are between 20 and 30 years old, but older men—and sometimes women—should also be considered. Although numerous individuals are single, many also have steady relationships and children.[52] Their educational backgrounds span the entire spectrum, from no formal qualifications to postgraduate degrees (although most work in relatively low-grade jobs). Some analysis indicated that many radicalized Islamists in Western Europe tend to seek a group-oriented life, and group dynamics also have proven a common factor in promoting terrorist activities in the United States.[53]

A disproportionately high number of Islamist extremists in the West converted to Islam, but this neither insinuates a general tendency toward radicalization among converts nor does it deny the fact that the majority of Islamist extremists were born into the Muslim faith.[54] Most of these terrorists' prior criminal involvement was minor or nonexistent. Homegrown Islamist extremists are so socially and demographically diverse that no universally accepted profile can be compiled using socio-demographic characteristics.

The Self-Radicalization Process

On the surface, the pathways to terrorism seem as varied as the actors themselves. Extremists have many varied starting points and follow very different paths that lead to their ultimate involvement in terrorist activities. The existence of a common end point has led many individuals and organizations with an interest in radicalization to characterize these pathways as variations of *the* radicalization process, and much effort has focused on identifying common aspects to understand and—in the end—counter this progression. In the course of this research, several analyses of the radicalization of identified Islamist terrorists have been conducted, mainly based on data from law enforcement agencies and intelligence services.

Although these explanations are not completely consistent, they suggest a prevailing radicalization model composed of three main components: (1) grievance, (2) ideology, and (3) mobilization.[55] Obviously, not all individuals who begin this process complete it. Many stop or even abandon this development at various points and for different reasons; some reenter later and begin again. Others do not follow the implied sequential development, but move from one radicalization stage to the next. Yet other individuals do not seem to make well-considered decisions within this process, but follow it like a slippery slope. The radicalization process can take several years for some persons, but develop very quickly for others.[56]

Grievance

Discontent appears to serve as the prerequisite of the radicalization process. Issues driving this attitude toward individuals in the West may include (1) perceived persecution of Muslims throughout the world; (2) a sense of uprootedness, alienation, or lack of acceptance; feelings of discrimination, especially among second- or third-generation immigrants; or (3) a general search for identity.

This discontent may be based on individuals' actual experiences or those of other people within their community, or it may result from the normal process of identity formation among young people. These latter feelings of uncertainty of oneself during adolescence and early adulthood are common and well known in developmental psychology, but after an individual feels rejected by society, these emotions can lead to a deep identity crisis and cause one to search for a new purpose of life. Some Muslim-born individuals may link experiences of disadvantage or non-belonging to their faith and judge them to be an expression of cultural and religious discrimination.

Ideology

Ideological framing adopts this rambling feeling of discontent and leads it in a defined direction. The idea of "us"—the *ummah* (community) or *ummat al-mu'minin* (the community of the believers)—defending against "them"—the nonbelievers conducting an alleged war against Islam—secures a strong bond among the followers while alienating them from Western citizens.[57]

This narrative typically finds its ideological footing in a form of Salafism, adherence to which is viewed as the ultimate distinguishing feature between right and wrong. Interpretations of Salafism range from a purely personal religious conviction with an emphasis on purifying the believer's way of life to a jihadi orientation that demands its followers to take on the fight against Western governments and "apostate" Muslim (especially Middle Eastern) regimes held responsible for the suffering of all Muslims. This jihadi Salafism emphasizes God's undisputed and sole sovereignty (*hakimiyyat Allah*) and views the Qur'an and the Sunnah of Muhammad as the only acceptable sources to define right and wrong. In consequence, this ideology bans the idea of democracy and man-made law in general as un-Islamic; Western societies are considered sinful and a danger to the right order of mankind.

Some well-read scholars justify these claims with in-depth theological arguments in favor of violent *jihad,* "the use of violence against persons and governments deemed to be enemies of fundamentalist Islam, especially the West." However, Islamism and Salafism, when presented as an ideology or narrative to promote radicalization rather than as a religion, tend to be kept simple and without theological depth.

The primary significance of the ideological component is significant because it is the way in which followers (true believers) are instilled with an idea of their "true purpose" and sense of belonging to a transnational community. By accepting this highly polarized worldview and its narrow set of rules, the uncertain individual searching for meaning receives simple answers, as well as a comprehensive framework of social and moral norms and values. Terrorist movements or ideologues then can build on this ideology by strengthening the perception of global Muslim suppression; the picture of Islam under threat, triggering the belief that the Muslim community and the radicalized individual exist in a state of permanent self-defense; and the view of violence as a legitimate response.

Mobilization

In the majority of cases, extremists become radicalized to a great extent through intensifying social interaction with other people with similar beliefs. This relationship results in a mutual push toward violence. Sometimes, a spiritual leader will prod individuals to take such actions. That said, the "lone wolf/lone offender" has served as the unusual exception.

From an investigative standpoint, mobilization is the only radicalization component involving specific actions possibly subject to criminal prosecution. Potential operatives are recruited by an extremist group or individual, small groups are prompted to form a terrorist cell of their own, and extremists begin preparing direct attacks or supporting others planning to attack. In the United States, mobilization also is the transition phase from ideology—protected under the First Amendment—to action, which becomes criminal activity. Logically, law enforcement and intelligence resources will focus on mobilization because activities conducted in this latter stage of radicalization present the opportunity to make arrests.

Role of the Internet

Online radicalization presents a primary concern. Extremists use a variety of tools that range from dedicated password-protected jihadist websites, forums, blogs, social networking resources, and video-hosting services to professionally produced online English-language propaganda magazines, such as *Inspire* magazine, established by the AQAP. These online assets, serving as a sort of "virtual *jihad* university," can play a role in all three radicalization components.

- *Grievance.* The Internet allows rapid and widespread dissemination of information about events that may fuel grievances. Often, such propaganda is intensified by highly emotional images combined with an amplifying comment or soundtrack. Because anyone can post content online, individuals have a forum to present the material in a way that supports their point of view, no matter how extreme.

- *Ideology.* Similarly, the Internet allows the extremist narrative to spread globally. Anwar al-Aulaqi, a Yemen-based American citizen and member of the AQAP, is perhaps the best example for English-speaking audiences. His lectures and contributions to *Inspire* magazine are widely available online. It no longer is necessary to have an ideologue at a local mosque or gathering place to inspire future extremists.

- *Mobilization.* How online interaction impacts mobilization poses pressing questions inside the United States and Europe. Because extremists interact online with other like-minded individuals despite geographical differences, can they develop the group dynamics that lead to violence? How effective are social networking sites as a venue for terrorists to spot and assess would-be extremists? In a recent case in Germany, a 21-year-old extremist accused of fatally shooting two U.S. soldiers and wounding two others at the Frankfurt airport on March 2, 2011, claimed to be radicalized through the Internet and motivated to take action after seeing propaganda videos.

Homegrown individuals engaging in Islamist extremism are both demographically and socioeconomically diverse, preventing the development of a reliable profile. Yet, all these persons develop a new mind-set as they undergo radicalization. Although no typical pathway exists for this radicalization process, as noted, three main components include deeply ingrained grievances as the basis for an identity crisis, an elementary Islamist/Salafist ideology providing a sense for one's existence and sense of belonging to a chosen community, and the individual's mobilization to join the terrorist movement.

Assassination as a Terrorist Tactic

Assassination is a tactic used by nearly all terrorist groups, although far less frequently than other types of armed attacks. Assassination, when used as a terrorist tactic, is the targeted killing of a country's public officials or individuals who represent the political, economic, military, security, social, religious, media, or cultural establishments. The killings can be motivated by ideology, religion, politics, or nationalism. Most terrorist groups conduct assassinations to eliminate enemies, intimidate the population, discourage cooperation, influence public opinion, decrease government effectiveness, gain media attention, or simply to exact revenge.

Simple terrorism-related assassinations can be carried out with a minimum of personnel, training, or equipment, and they are usually successful when aimed at public figures who are protected least. An example of such an attack was the 2004 killing of filmmaker Theo Van Gogh by a Dutch-Moroccan extremist in the Netherlands. By contrast, assassination operations directed against highly protected individuals, such as heads of state, are difficult and costly. Although impressive when successful—such as the 2007 killing of former Pakistan prime minister and party leader Benazir Bhutto—these operations are rare and prone to failure. Similar to attacks on other hard targets, they require extensive planning, financing, personnel, training, and equipment.

There have been 26 incidents of terrorism-related assassination attempts in the United States over the past 100 years.[58] The last events of this type were in 1990, when Jewish Defense League founder Meir Kahane and Qur'anic scholar and teacher Rashid Khalifi were killed by extremists linked to foreign terrorism. Only eight of these attacks may be directly or indirectly attributed to foreign groups or state sponsors of terrorism.

The majority of U.S. assassination attempts have been conducted by homegrown violent extremists with little or no connection to foreign organizations and most often directed against public figures having minimal security, if any. Terrorism-related attempted assassinations of highly protected public figures are an extremely rare occurrence in the United States, with the 1950 attempt on President Truman by Puerto Rican nationalists the only one that truly qualifies as such. Robert F. Kennedy, whose killer claimed an international nexus due to Kennedy's support for Israel, is on the chart but cannot be considered a highly protected official. He had minimal personal security when he was killed, and it was this assassination that generated future Secret Service protection for presidential candidates.

Tactics to Destabilize Terrorist Organizations

The most visible and immediately effective tactic of U.S. terrorist financing strategy has been designating and blocking the accounts of terrorists and those associated with financing terrorist activity. Publicly designating terrorists, terrorist supporters, and facilitators and blocking their ability to receive and move funds through the world's financial system has  been and is a crucial component in the fight against terrorism. On September 24, 2001, President Bush issued Executive Order 13244, Blocking Property and Prohibiting Transactions with Persons Who Commit, Threaten to Commit, or Support Terrorism.[59]

The Department of the Treasury's Office of Enforcement, in conjunction with the Treasury's Office of International Affairs and the Office of Foreign Assets Control, has helped lead U.S. efforts to identify and block the assets of terrorist-related individuals and entities within the United States and worldwide. Currently, 250 individuals and entities are publicly designated as terrorists or terrorist supporters by the United States, and

LEARNING OUTCOMES 8 — Describe the tactics used to destabilize terrorist organizations.

since September 11, 2001, more than $113 million in assets of terrorists has been frozen around the world.[60]

Currently, more than 165 countries and jurisdictions have blocking orders in force. Alternative financial mechanisms to combat terrorist financing conducted through these mechanisms include the following measures:

- *Protecting charities from terrorist abuse.* Under the authority of Executive Order 13224, the United States has designated 12 charitable organizations as having ties to al-Qaeda or other terrorist groups. The Financial Action Task Force (FATF) Special Recommendation VIII on Terrorist Financing commits all member nations to ensure that nonprofit organizations cannot be misused by financiers of terrorism.

- *Regulating hawalas.* Terrorists have also used hawalas and other informal value-transfer systems as a means of terrorist financing. The word **hawala** (meaning "trust") refers to a fast and cost-effective method for the worldwide remittance of money or value, particularly for persons who may be outside the reach of the traditional financial sector. In some nations, hawalas are illegal; in others, they are active but unregulated. It is therefore difficult to accurately measure the total volume of financial activity associated with the system; however, it is estimated that, at a minimum, tens of billions of dollars flow through hawalas and other informal value-transfer systems on an annual basis.

- *Controlling bulk cash smuggling.* Bulk cash smuggling has proven to be yet another means of financing adopted by terrorists and their financiers. Customs has executed 650 bulk cash seizures totaling $21 million, including $12.9 million with Middle East connections. Pursuing bulk cash smuggling from a domestic perspective, however, is not enough; disruption of this tactic requires a global approach.

- *Investigating trade-based terrorist financing.* With respect to trade-based financial systems, authorized enforcement agencies continue to investigate the use of licit and illicit international trade commodities (for example, diamonds, gold, honey, and cigarettes, as well as narcotics) to fund terrorism. The U.S. Customs Service has developed a state-of-the-art database system to identify anomalous trade patterns for imports and exports to and from the

Beyond simply freezing assets, these U.S. and international actions to publicly identify terrorists and their supporters advance global interests in terrorist financing and combating terrorism by

- shutting down the pipeline by which designated parties move money and operate financially in the mainstream financial sectors.

- informing third parties who may be unwittingly financing terrorist activity of their association with supporters of terrorism.

- providing leverage over those parties not designated who might otherwise be willing to finance terrorist activity.

- exposing terrorist financing "money trails" that may generate leads to previously unknown terrorist cells and financiers.

- forcing terrorists to use alternative and potentially more costly informal means of financing their activities.

- supporting diplomatic effort to strengthen other countries' capacities to combat terrorist financing through the adoption and implementation of legislation that allows states to comply with their obligations under U.N. Security Council Resolutions 1390 and 1373.

United States. In the past, customs has demonstrated this system to other nations, including Colombia, with excellent results.

- *Investigating terrorist cyberfundraising activities.* Terrorist groups now exploit the Internet to recruit supporters and raise terrorist funds. Developing a strategy to counter such **cyberfundraising** activities is a responsibility that the Treasury Department assumed in its 2002 National Money Laundering Strategy.

The field of criminal investigation faces many challenges in the twenty-first century. Although there have been operational and technical advancements in methods to detect and capture lawbreakers, those same lawbreakers are finding ways to avoid detection. As technology develops, it is crucial for criminal investigators across the nation to continue to use professional venues, such as conferences and professional magazines, and other ways to share investigative "best practices." Doing so will continue to professionalize the field of criminal investigation and further efforts to capture those who continue to victimize society.

The Reality of Criminal Investigations Dealing with Domestic Terror Threats

There are some who primarily consider domestic terrorism an issue for military personnel to deal with. The reality is that law enforcement personnel are at the heart of dealing with domestic terrorism, based on the fact that they are first responders when incidents happen within society. A case as recent as June 2011 demonstrates the importance of law enforcement taking seriously the problem of domestic terrorism.

In this case, several men were arrested in a plot to attack a military facility that dealt with recruits in Seattle, Washington. Their plot included the use of guns and grenades to kill recruits, but they were caught after attempting to purchase these weapons via a police informant. Those arrested were Abu Khalid Abdul-Latif (aka Joseph Anthony Davis) and Walli Mujahidh (aka Frederick Domingue Jr.). Their hope, allegedly, was that such an attack would inspire radical Muslims in the United States to take action. As part of the police investigation, the police informant had lunch with the suspects to discuss the plot. What the suspects did not realize was that the informant, a person the suspects approached for assistance believing he shared their values, did not in fact agree with their intentions and went immediately to the police to share the plot.

Sources: Riley, K. J., & Hoffman, B. (1995). *Domestic terrorism: A national assessment of state and local preparedness.* Santa Monica, CA: Rand Corporation; Davis, L. M. (2004). *When terrorism hits home: How prepared are state and local law enforcement?* Santa Monica, CA: Rand Corporation; Carter, M. (2011, June 23). Two men arrested in plot to attack Seattle military processing facility. *The Seattle Times.* Retrieved from http://seattletimes .nwsource.com/html/localnews/2015404971_terrorplot24m.html.

Terrorism represents one of the greatest challenges and responsibilities for criminal investigation:

1. **Pretend you are the lead investigator in this case. Based on the relevant material in the chapter, what is important about the police department's role in staying prepared to address domestic terror?**

Define *terrorism*.

LEARNING OUTCOMES 1

Terrorism is pervasive throughout the world and remains one of the most complex and difficult issues facing law enforcement in the twenty-first century. There is no single, universally accepted definition of the word *terrorism*. It is defined in a number of ways by a number of organizations.

1. What are the four primary elements of terrorism outlined in the federal Foreign Relations Authorization Act?

2. Why is it difficult to provide a precise, universal definition of terrorism?

3. What types of geo-political organizations have practiced terrorism over the years?

4. What form does terrorism take when practiced by ruling governments?

5. Why is it difficult to create a terrorist profile?

6. Other than where the act is committed, how do domestic terrorism and international terrorism differ?

terrorism Typical definitions of terrorism refer only to those violent acts that are intended to create fear (terror); are perpetrated for a religious, political, or ideological goal; and deliberately target or disregard the safety of non-combatants.

Describe who terrorists are.

LEARNING OUTCOMES 2

Persons who carry out acts of terror vary in age, race, and cultural background. Today's terrorists have a deep-seated belief in the justice of their causes. They have little regard for their lives or the lives of others. Terrorists can be a part of a large organization or can act with only a few persons who share similar beliefs.

1. What types of specific tasks are involved in planning terrorist acts?

2. What key criteria are used to describe terrorists and terrorist organizations?

3. Why is the media an important player in terrorist attacks?

4. How do terrorists gain access to the weapons used to carry out their acts of terror?

5. How is the structure of terrorist groups similar to the structure of organized crime groups?

Describe the various forms of terrorism.

LEARNING OUTCOMES 3

Terrorism has been classified in five distinct forms. Based on intentions, goals, and methods used to carry out terrorist acts, some forms of terror merit more attention than others from law enforcement.

1. How is terrorism categorized?

2. How do ideological and revolutionary terrorism differ?

3. What countries are considered strong supporters of state-sponsored terrorism?

4. What are the goals of state-sponsored terrorism?

5. What are the consequences (positive and negative) of state-sponsored terrorism?

6. What are key tactics used by revolutionary terrorists?

7. What is the ultimate goal of revolutionary terrorism?

Identify notable terrorist incidents.

LEARNING OUTCOMES 4

Notable terrorist incidents include the 1983 truck bombings of U.S. and French military barracks in Beirut, Lebanon; the September 11, 2001, attacks on the Pentagon and World Trade Center; the bombing of the *U.S.S. Cole* in October 2000; and the bombings of two U.S. embassies in eastern Africa in August 1998.

1. Beyond the number of people killed, what were the implications of the 9/11 terrorist attacks on the United States?

2. What terrorist group is considered the most dangerous threat to U.S. national security? Why?

3. What federal agencies are responsible for investigating and stopping terrorist threats against the United States?

4. What are the most notable recent terrorist threats against the United States and/or U.S. interests?

Explain the problem of international terrorism.

Experts in international terrorism point out that *jihadism*, or the Islamic Holy War movement, survives independent of any one organization and appears to be gaining strength around the world. Jihadist principles continue to serve as the organizing rationale for extremist groups in much of the Muslim world.

1. What makes the use of the term *Islamism* problematic?

2. Why has the war in Iraq aggravated and intensified the anti-Western sentiment of some people in the Middle East?

3. Why is it important to distinguish between Islamists and Islamist terrorists?

4. What techniques are used by al-Qaeda to carry out its terror attacks?

5. Until 2011, who was the leader of al-Qaeda?

6. What is the most effective tactic to destabilize terrorist organizations?

Islamism A set of ideologies holding that Islam is not only a religion but also a political system and that modern Muslims must return to the roots of their religion and unite politically.

Identify current threats of mass destruction.

The U.S. Department of State identifies four categories of weapons of mass destruction (WMD) that terrorists may seek to acquire and use in a WMD terrorist attack.

1. How does the U.S. State Department categorize weapons of mass destruction?

2. What factors make investigating terrorist acts via chemical weapons more difficult?

3. The 2001 anthrax attacks are an example of what form of terrorism?

4. Why is it more likely that a terrorist group can gain access to a radiological dispersal device than a nuclear weapon?

bioterrorism Terrorism involving the intentional release or dissemination of biological agents.

dirty bomb A speculative radiological weapon that combines radioactive material with conventional explosives.

fissile material Material capable of sustaining a nuclear fission chain reaction.

Explain the problem of domestic terrorism.

According to the FBI, between 1980 and 2000, 250 of the 335 incidents confirmed as or suspected to be terrorist acts in the United States were carried out by American citizens. Domestic terrorist groups include the Army of God, Animal Liberation Front, Earth Liberation Front, and the Jewish Defense League.

1. How does the Patriot Act define acts of domestic terrorism?

2. What organization may be deemed as the oldest and most recognizable terrorist organization in the United States?

3. What kinds of tactics has this terror organization used throughout its history?

4. Identify examples of "homegrown" terrorists.

5. What are some of the most recent examples of domestic terrorism?

6. How does the death of Osama bin Laden affect the direction of al-Qaeda?

self-radicalization A process by which an individual comes to adopt increasingly extreme political, social, or religious ideals and aspirations that reject or undermine the status quo.

homegrown terrorism Acts of terrorism on American soil that are normally considered domestic terrorism.

hawala An informal transfer system used primarily by money brokers in the Middle East, North Africa and the Horn of Africa.

cyberfundraising Fundraising initiatives by terrorist organizations utilizing the Internet or social media.

Describe the tactics used to destabilize terrorist organizations.

The most visible and immediately effective tactic of U.S. terrorist financing strategy has been designating and blocking the bank accounts of terrorists and those associated with financing terrorist activity. Publicly designating terrorists, terrorist supporters, and facilitators and blocking their ability to receive and move funds through the world's financial system has been and is a crucial component in the fight against terrorism.

1. Explain how the assets of terrorists can be identified.

2. Identify the U.S. government organizations that identify and block the assets of terrorist-related individuals.

3. Describe the alternative financial mechanisms to combat terrorist financing.

4. In what ways can hawalas and other informal value-transfer systems of terrorist financing be identified and stopped?

Additional Links

www.justice.gov
This is the official site of the Department of Justice. Visitors can read the USA PATRIOT Act in its entirety here; a PDF version of the bill is also available. In addition, visitors can view the Protect America Act, which also deals with the intelligence community and terrorism.

www.state.gov
This is the official site of the U.S. Department of State. The website menu includes policy issues, economics and energy, and arms control and security, to name a few. The site features a search engine, news and features, a media center, and careers links.

www.csis.org
This is the site of the Center for Strategic and International Studies. The website includes multimedia publications, a press menu, and a defense and security link under the topics menu. The link leads to information on terrorism, weapons, homeland security, and international security.

Glossary

abduction The process of proposing a likely explanation for an event that must then be tested.

absolute judgment When eyewitnesses compare each photograph or person in a lineup only with their memories of what the offender looked like.

acute maltreatment When a child's death is directly related to injuries suffered as a result of a specific incident of abuse or act of negligence.

admission A self-incriminating statement made by a suspect that falls short of an acknowledgment of guilt.

aggravated assault A personal crime associated with a high probability of death; serious, permanent disfigurement; permanent or protracted loss or impairment of the function of any body member or organ; or other severe bodily harm.

alligatoring The pattern of crevices formed by the burning of a wooden structure.

Amber Alert A system that quickly posts information about child abductions.

Amido black protein An amino acid-staining diazo dye used in biochemical research to stain for total protein on transferred membrane blots.

analysis A scientific examination.

anthropometry The measurement of the human individual used for identification, for the purposes of understanding human physical variation.

arrest The act of a police officer taking a person into custody after making a determination that he or she has violated a law.

associative evidence Evidence that links a suspect with a crime.

authentication A principal requirement to admit a photograph into evidence.

bank robbery The unlawful taking of money or other assets from a bank through the use of face-to-face contact between suspect and victims.

baseline technique Crime-scene measuring technique in which a line is drawn between two known points.

battered child syndrome A clinical term referring to the collection of injuries sustained by a child as a result of repeated mistreatment or beating.

Bertillon system An early criminal identification or classification system based on the idea that certain aspects of the human body, such as skeletal size, ear shape, and eye color, remained the same after a person had reached full physical maturity. This system used a combination of photographs and standardized physical measurements.

binding material Material used to incapacitate a victim during the course of a robbery.

bioterrorism The intentional release or dissemination of biological agents such as bacteria, viruses, and toxins.

Bobbies The name of London Metropolitan Police Department officers; They were named this after Home Secretary Sir Robert Peel.

Bow Street Runners A group of English crime fighters formed by Henry Fielding during the eighteenth century.

burglary A covert crime in which the criminal works during the nighttime, outside the presence of witnesses.

buy-bust When an undercover agent makes a purchase of illicit narcotics and the suspect is immediately arrested.

buy-walk When an undercover agent makes a purchase of illicit narcotics and the suspect is allowed to leave for the purposes of continuing the investigation.

chain of custody Documentation of all who handle evidence in a criminal case.

check kiting Drawing cash on accounts made up of uncollected funds.

child abuse The physical, sexual, or emotional abuse of children.

child pornography Pornography involving a child, either simulated or produced with the direct involvement of a child.

chronic maltreatment Occurs when a child's death is directly related to injuries caused by maltreatment or neglect occurring over an extended period.

closed files Intelligence files that are maintained apart from criminal investigation files to prevent unauthorized inspection of data.

Code Adam An internationally recognized "missing child" safety program in the United States (and Canada) originally created by Walmart retail stores in 1994.

coercion The use or threat of illegal physical means to induce a suspect to make an admission or confession.

collation The process of comparing texts carefully to clarify or give meaning to information.

Combined DNA Index System (CODIS) The generic term used to describe the FBI's program of support for criminal justice DNA databases as well as the software used to run these databases.

commercial robbery Robbery of stores and businesses located close to major thoroughfares such as main streets, highways, and interstates.

composite A freehand drawing of a suspected criminal.

confession Direct acknowledgment by the suspect of his or her guilt in the commission of a specific crime or as an integral part of a specific crime.

consent search When police gain permission to search without a warrant.

contamination log Documents any evidence that has been compromised or for which the chain of custody has not been observed.

contamination of evidence The act of adversely affecting evidence by allowing it to be tampered with or by not protecting the chain of custody.

coordinate method Measuring an object from two fixed points of reference.

***corpus delicti* evidence** Evidence that establishes that a crime has been committed.

cover story A fictitious story contrived by an undercover investigator to explain his or her presence as a drug buyer to criminal suspects.

covert information collection A clandestine process of data collection on criminal acts that have not yet occurred but for which the investigator must prepare.

credibility One's ability to be believed.

crime scene The location where the crime took place.

criminal investigative analysis Identifying psychological and social characteristics surrounding the crime as well as the manner in which it was committed.

cross-projection method Used in indoor crime scenes, it is basically a top-down view of the crime scene where the walls of the room have been "folded" down to reveal locations of bullet holes, blood-spatter evidence, and so on.

custodial interrogation A process of questioning a suspect when his or her liberty has been restricted to a degree that is associated with arrest.

cybercrime Any crime that involves a computer and the Internet.

cyber-extortion The use of email or another electronic medium as an offensive force.

cyberfundraising Exploitation of the Internet to recruit supporters and raise terrorist funds.

CYMBL A rule that helps officers remember to include the necessary information for a suspect vehicle description: Color, Year, Make and model, Body style, License number.

dactylography The study of fingerprints.

deadly force Actions of police officers that result in the killing of a person.

deductive reasoning The process of reasoning from one or more general statements or premises to reach a logical conclusion.

deep cover Working undercover for extended periods of time.

detention Something less than an arrest but more than a consensual encounter.

dirty bomb A radiological weapon that combines radioactive material with conventional explosives.

dissemination The phase of the intelligence process whereby information is shared with other law enforcement agencies.

DNA technology The science of identifying the genetic facsimile, or "blueprint," of any particular organism in every cell within each human body.

Drug Enforcement Administration (DEA) A United States federal law enforcement agency tasked with investigating drug offenses such as trafficking, manufacture, and abuse of illicit drugs.

duress The imposition of restrictions on physical behavior such as prolonged interrogation and deprivation of water, food, or sleep.

embezzlement A low-profile crime involving employees who steal large amounts of money over long periods of time.

entrapment When an undercover officer convinces a criminal suspect to commit a crime he or she was not predisposed to commit.

exclusionary rule The legal rule that excludes evidence that has been determined to have been obtained illegally.

exemplars Samples, as of a suspect's handwriting.

exigent circumstances Circumstances whereby a search may be legally conducted without a warrant.

family abduction An abduction related to a domestic or custody dispute.

fence A person who buys and sells stolen property with criminal intent.

field interview cards A method for documenting information on the street through the use of cards.

field notes An investigator's most personal and readily available record of the crime-scene search.

finished sketches A completed crime-scene sketch drawn to scale.

fire triangle What a fire needs to burn: heat, fuel, and oxygen.

fissile material Material capable of sustaining a nuclear fission chain reaction.

flash description An emergency radio broadcast, generally made by the first officer to reach a crime scene to other officers in the area, in which descriptions of the suspect and his or her vehicle are communicated.

fleeing-felon rule A legal doctrine, no longer in effect, allowing police officers to shoot suspected felons.

flowcharting An informational tracking system that demonstrates a chain of events or activities over a period of time.

forensic pathology A subspecialty of pathology that focuses on determining the cause of death by examining a corpse.

forward-looking infrared (FLID) A surveillance technology that measures radiant energy in the radiant heat portion and displays readings as thermographs.

fungible goods Items such as tools, liquor, and clothing that are indistinguishable from others like them.

global positioning system (GPS) A space-based global navigation satellite system (GNSS) that provides location and time information in all types of weather, anywhere on or near the earth where there is an unobstructed line of sight to four or more GPS satellites.

grid-search method A crime-scene search method whereby an area is sectioned off in square areas. Each square, averaging about 6 square feet, represents a specific search area that is a manageable size for each investigator.

hacker Someone who seeks and exploits weaknesses in a computer system or network.

hawala A word meaning "trust" that refers to a fast and cost-effective method for the worldwide remittance of money or value, particularly for persons who may be outside the reach of the traditional financial sector.

hearsay evidence Second-party statements offered to the court by a person who did not originate the statement.

homegrown terrorism Western citizens who adopt an extremist religious or political ideology hostile to Western societies and values and turn to terrorism.

homicide The unlawful killing of one human being by another.

Identi-Kit A computer-generated composite of a suspected criminal.

identity theft A type of larceny that involves obtaining credit, merchandise, or services by fraudulent personal representation.

inductive reasoning Reasoning in which the premises seek to supply strong evidence for (not absolute proof of) the truth of the conclusion.

informant Anyone who provides information of an investigative nature to law enforcement authorities.

inside team A surveillance team responsible for briefing officers concerning their actions if a crime occurs.

Integrated Automated Fingerprint Identification System (IAFIS) A national fingerprint and criminal history database maintained by the FBI's CJIS Division.

intelligence gathering The covert process of gathering information on criminal activity.

interrogation The systematic questioning of a person suspected of involvement in a crime for the purpose of obtaining a confession.

interview A relatively formal conversation conducted for the purpose of obtaining information.

Islamism A set of ideologies holding that Islam is not only a religion but also a political system and that modern Muslims must return to the roots of their religion and unite politically.

Jessica's law The informal name given to a 2005 Florida law, as well as laws modeled after the Florida law in several other states, designed to punish sex offenders and reduce their ability to reoffend.

labeling Classifying a missing child case.

latent fingerprints Fingerprints that are not visible unless developed through a fingerprint-lifting process.

lineup The police practice of allowing witnesses or victims to view several suspects for identification purposes.

link analysis A charting technique designed to show relationships between individuals and organizations using a graphic visual design.

lividity A bloodstain on the body of a deceased person.

Locard's exchange principle A scientific principle which holds that the perpetrator of a crime will bring something into the crime scene and leave with something from it, and that both can be used as scientific evidence in a criminal investigation.

manslaughter The deliberate killing of another person, characterized by either voluntary or involuntary classifications.

markers Items placed in crime-scene photos that call attention to specific objects or enable the viewer of the photo to get a sense of the size of the object or the distance between objects.

medical examiner A public official who makes official determinations of the cause and time of death in wrongful death cases.

Megan's law An informal name for laws in the United States requiring law enforcement authorities to make information available to the public regarding registered sex offenders, which was created in response to the 1994 murder of Megan Kanka.

method of operation (MO) The behavior of the criminal during the commission of the crime.

Mitochondrial DNA Population Database One of several DNA databases in the world.

mobile surveillance Observing a criminal suspect from a moving vehicle.

motivations Reasons why someone does something.

Mulberry Street Morning Parade An event instituted in 1966 by Thomas Byrnes that showcased all criminals arrested in the previous 24 hours.

Munchhausen syndrome by proxy A clinical term referring to when a parent or caretaker attempts to bring medical attention to him- or herself by inducing illness in his or her children.

murder The purposeful, premeditated, and unlawful taking of human life by another person.

National Academy A lengthy management training course sponsored by the FBI.

National Crime Information Center (NCIC) Criminal data maintained by the FBI on wanted persons and property stolen from all 50 states.

National Incidence Studies of Missing, Abducted, Runaway and Thrown Away Children (NISMART) project A research project supported by the U.S. Department of Justice to address the 1984 Missing Children's Assistance Act.

neighborhood canvass A door-to-door search of the area of a crime to identify witnesses.

noncustodial parent A parent who does not have legal custody of his or her child.

nonfamily abduction When a child is removed from his or her family through force or trickery.

olfactory Pertaining to smell. A distinguishable odor may indicate a specific type of crime.

open files Criminal information developed for the purpose of eventually making an arrest and gaining a conviction in a court of law.

outside team The arrest team in a surveillance.

overt information collection A method of collecting information involving personal interaction with individuals, many of whom are witnesses to crimes, victims of crimes, or the suspects themselves.

paper trail Evidence in an arson case that shows motive. This includes financial records, inflated insurance coverage, little or no inventory, and excessive debts.

parens patriae A Latin term for "parent of the nation."

plain-view doctrine A legal doctrine whereby police officers have the opportunity to confiscate evidence, without a warrant, based on what they find in plain view and open to public inspection.

plants Preparations used to set an arson fire.

plastic fingerprints A fingerprint impression left when a person presses against a plastic material, such as putty, wax, or tar.

point of origin The location on an arson scene where the fire originated.

polygraph A mechanical device designed to aid investigators in obtaining information.

preliminary investigation A term referring to the early stages of crime-scene processing, usually conducted by the first officer on the crime scene.

preventive response Prevention through deterrence that is sometimes achieved by arresting the criminal and by aggressive prosecution.

primary physical aggressor If the police have sufficient reason to believe that a person, within the preceding four hours, committed an active domestic violence or spousal battery, the officer is required to arrest a person. This person is known as the primary physical aggressor.

proactive response An investigative approach to crime solving in which criminal activity is investigated before it occurs.

probable cause The minimum amount of information necessary to cause a reasonable person to believe that a crime has been or is being committed by a particular person.

property crime A type of crime whereby the criminal is more concerned with financial gain and less prepared for a violent altercation with the victim.

protection order A legal document that orders one person to stay away from another.

protective search A search conducted for officer safety that includes a quick search of the premises for additional suspects/persons or any weapons that could be acquired by such persons.

rape Unlawful sexual intercourse, achieved through force and without consent.

reactive response An approach to crime solving that addresses crimes that have already occurred, such as murder, robbery, and burglary.

reasonable force The amount of force that is considered reasonable to capture or subdue a criminal suspect.

relative judgment When eyewitnesses compare lineup photographs or members with each other rather than with their memories of the offender.

residential robbery Robbery when an armed intruder breaks into a home and holds the residents at gun- or knifepoint.

resistance Physical or psychological unwillingness to comply.

rigor mortis The process of the stiffening or contraction of the muscles of a deceased person after the vital functions cease.

rogues' gallery A compilation of descriptions, methods of operation, hiding places, and the names of associates of known criminals in the 1850s.

rough sketch The initial crime-scene sketch drawn by officers on the crime scene.

runaway or lost child A category of missing children that is the most commonly encountered by law enforcement.

scene-conscious When the crime-scene investigator becomes aware of the crime-scene situation and is prepared to take certain immediate actions.

school robberies Instances of petty extortion or "shake-downs" of students and teachers in public schools.

scope of the search An officer's authority to search incident to an arrest.

Scotland Yard One of the first criminal investigative bodies originally formed in England in the mid-nineteenth century.

search warrant A legal document enabling a police officer to search.

seed money Money required to initiate an undercover drug transaction.

self-radicalization Western citizens who adopt an extremist religious or political ideology hostile to Western societies and values and turn to terrorism.

sequential lineup A police lineup method whereby people or photographs are presented to a witness one at a time.

serology The scientific analysis of blood.

shaken baby syndrome (SBS) A medical term for murder of infants who are violently shaken.

shoplifting A common form of theft involving the taking of goods from retail stores.

simple assault Threats by one person to cause bodily harm or death to another or purposely inflicting bodily harm on another.

simultaneous lineup A lineup procedure whereby the eye-witness views all the people or photos at the same time.

smash-and-grab robbery A type of robbery in which the robbers approach a car, break the window, and hold up the driver at gunpoint.

snitches Amateur pilferers who are usually respectable persons who do not perceive themselves as thieves, yet are systematic shoplifters who steal merchandise for their own use rather than for resale.

solvability factors Factors that logically guide the investigation and are likely to result in case solution.

span of the fire Physical characteristics of an arson fire such as smoke, direction, flames, and distance of travel.

stakeout Another term for stationary or fixed surveillance.

stationary surveillance Another term for fixed surveillance or stakeout.

stop and frisk When an officer stops and searches a person for weapons.

strategic intelligence Information that provides the investigator with intelligence as to the capabilities and intentions of target subjects.

street robbery Robbery committed on public streets and alleyways.

sudden infant death syndrome (SIDS) A diagnosis made when there is no other medical explanation for the abrupt death of an apparently healthy infant.

suggestiveness An identification technique that unduly narrows down the victim's/witnesses' options so a particular suspect is chosen.

surveillance Surreptitious observation.

tactical intelligence Information that supports police operations on a tactical level—such as raid planning—and that furnishes the police agency with specifics about weapons, dangerous individuals, and different types of criminal activity.

terrorism Violent acts that are intended to create fear (terror); are perpetrated for a religious, political, or ideological goal; and deliberately target or disregard the safety of non-combatants.

***Terry* stop** An investigative detention.

thief catchers People recruited from the riffraff of the streets to aid law enforcement officials in locating criminals.

trace evidence A minute or even a microscopic fragment of matter such as a hair or fiber that is not immediately detectable by the naked eye.

trailers Materials used in spreading an arson fire.

triangulation method A bird's-eye view of the crime scene using fixed objects from which to measure.

triggering condition An anticipated future event giving rise to a probable cause to search.

vehicle identification number (VIN) A 17-digit number assigned to each vehicle by the manufacturer at the time of production designed to distinguish each vehicle from all others.

visible fingerprints A type of fingerprint left at a crime scene that results from being adulterated with some foreign matter, such as blood, flour, or oil.

zone-search method A searching technique; also known as the quadrant method.

References

Chapter 1, Foundations of Criminal Investigation

1 Richardson, J. F. (1970). *The New York Police*. New York: Oxford, p. 37.

2 Mathias, W. J., & Anderson, S. (1973). *Horse to helicopter*. Atlanta: Community Life Publications, Georgia State University, p. 22.

3 Thorwald, J. (1965). *The marks of Cain*. London: Thames and Hudson, p. 129.

4 Wilson, O. W. (1953). August Vollmer. *Journal of Criminal Law and Criminology*, 44(I), Article 10.

5 Ibid.

6 Block, P., & Weidman, D. (1975). *Managing criminal investigations: Perspective package*. Washington, DC: U.S. Government Printing Office; Greenberg, B., Ellion, C. V., Kraft, L. P., & Proctor, H. S. (1977). *Felony decision model: An analysis of investigative elements of information*. Washington, DC: U.S. Government Printing Office.

7 Eck, J. (1983). *Solving crimes: The investigation of burglary and robbery*. Washington, DC: Police Executive Research Forum.

8 Nordby, J. J. (2002). *Dead reckoning: The art of forensic detection*. Boca Raton, FL: CRC Press.

9 Weisberg, M. W. (2001, March/April). Recent directions in crime scene investigations. *The Law Enforcement Trainer*, 44–48.

10 Goldstein, H. (1977). *Policing a free society*. Cambridge, MA: Ballinger, p. 1.

11 More, H. (1988). *Critical issues in law enforcement* (4th ed.). Cincinnati, OH: Anderson.

Chapter 2, The Crime Scene: Field Notes, Documenting, and Reporting

1 Gillium, J., & Eisler, P. (2011, January 10). *Suspect Jared Loughner known for bizarre behavior*. USA Today. Retrieved from http://www.usatoday.com/news/washington/2011-01-10-suspect10_ST_N.htm

2 Tyler, P. B. (1995). The Kelly-Frye "general acceptance" standard remains the rule for admissibility of novel scientific evidence: *People* v. *Leahy*.

3 Scientific Working Group Imaging Technology (SWGIT). (1999, June 8). *Definitions and guidelines for the use of imaging technologies in the criminal justice system*. Washington, DC: Federal Bureau of Investigation; International Association of Identification. (1997). *1997 Resolution and legislative committee, Resolution 97–9*.

4 Fox, R. H., & Cunningham, C. L. (1989). *Crime scene search and physical evidence handbook*. Washington, DC: U.S. Department of Justice.

Chapter 3, Processing the Crime Scene

1 Thornton, J. I. (1997). The general assumptions and rationale of forensic identification. In D. L. Faigman, D. H. Kaye, M. J. Saks, & J. Sanders (Eds.), *Modern scientific evidence: The law and science of expert testimony* (Vol. 2). Cincinnati: West Publishing Co.

2 The purpose of the entry by the officers affects the courts' views as to whether or not the entry was lawful. Courts have typically upheld an entry and protective sweep if the officers had any substantial reason to believe that there were victims within the premises who might be in need of help. In contrast, courts are much more likely to hold a warrantless entry unlawful when the entry was made primarily or solely for the purpose of apprehending a perpetrator thought to be inside.

3 In emergencies, entry to protect victims may have to take priority over communication with superiors. Even in emergency circumstances, however—whenever possible—communication should be simultaneous with emergency entries or the taking of other emergency measures, or if sufficient personnel are on the scene, one officer should communicate while other officers are performing emergency functions.

4 Note that police frequencies are often monitored by persons other than law enforcement officers and agencies. News media, curious citizens, and even the perpetrators themselves may be listening. This may require the use of discretion as to what is said on the radio. However, even when transmissions are subject to such monitoring, sufficient information must be provided by the responding officers to enable superiors to take appropriate action. The codes used must not be so cryptic that they fail to convey the information necessary to ensure an appropriate response from headquarters or other officers.

5 Persons who are or may be witnesses or have relevant information should not be allowed to leave the scene completely. They should, however, be moved out of areas in which their presence may result in loss or destruction of evidence. If the persons present at the scene include relatives of a victim or other persons who have a legal right to be on the premises, the clearing of the area must be accomplished with tact and, in some cases, may be subject to considerations of the welfare of the persons involved.

6 Local officials may, for various reasons not directly connected with the investigation of the crime, come to the scene of a major crime. Dealing with such persons requires tact. The officer in charge or some other experienced person should be designated to handle such situations.

7 The entry of any nonessential person into the crime-scene area threatens the integrity of the case. In any subsequent legal proceeding, the criminal defense may claim that the entry of such persons into the area compromised the scene and casts doubt upon the validity of the prosecution's case.

Chapter 4, Identifying Criminal Suspects: Field and Laboratory Processes

1 U.S. Department of Justice Drug Enforcement Administration. (1987). *Intelligence collection and analytical methods. Training manual.* Washington, DC: U.S. Government Printing Office.

2 Retrieved from http://www.fbi.gov/about-us/lab/biometric-analysis/codis/ndis-statistics.

3 Ibid.

4 Saferstein, R. (1990). *Criminalistics: An introduction to forensic science.* Upper Saddle River, NJ: Prentice Hall.

5 Davies, G. M., & Valentine, T. (2006). Facial composites: Forensic utility and psychological research. In R. C. L Lindsay, D. F. Ross, J. D. Read, & M. P. Toglia (Eds.), *Handbook of eyewitness psychology* (Vol. 2, pp. 59–96). Mahwah, NJ: Erlbaum.

6 Brace, N., Pike, G., & Kemp, R. (2000). Investigating E-FIT using famous faces. In A. Czerederecka, T. Jaskiewicz-Obydzinska, & J. Wojcikiewicz (Eds.), *Forensic psychology and law* (pp. 272–276). Krakow, Poland: Krakow Institute of Forensic Research Publishers.

7 Bruce, V., Hanna, H., Hancock, P. J. B., Newman, C., & Rarirty, J. (2002). Four heads are better than one: Combining face composites yields improvements in face likeness. *Journal of Applied Psychology, 87,* 894–902.

8 Ibid.

9 Strentz, T. (1988, April). A terrorist psychological profile: Past and present. *FBI Law Enforcement Bulletin,* 13–19.

10 Innocence Project website. (2009). Retrieved from www.innocenceproject.org/understand/Eyewitness-Misidentification.php.

11 Ibid.

12 Ibid.

13 *United States* v. *Wade,* 388 U.S. 218, 229 (1967).

14 *Neil* v. *Biggers,* 409 U.S. 188 (1972). See also *Manson* v. *Brathwaite,* 432 U.S. 98 (1977) (*Biggers* test applied to photo identifications).

15 Wells, G. L., Memon, A., & Penrod, S. D. (2006). Eyewitness evidence: Improving its probative value. *Psychological Science in the Public Interest, 7*(2), 45–75.

16 Wells, G. L., & Olson, E. (2003). Eyewitness testimony. *Annual Review of Psychology, 54,* 277–295.

17 Wells, Memon, A., & Penrod, S. D. (2006). Eyewitness evidence: Improving its probative value. *Psychological Science in the Public Interest, 7*(2), 45–75.

18 Gary L. Wells's comments on the Mecklenburg Report (see note 8). Retrieved from www.psychology.iastate.edu/faculty/gwells/Illinois_Project_Wells_comments.pdf.

19 Mecklenburgh, S. H. (2006, March 17). *Report to the Legislature of the State of Illinois: The Illinois Pilot Program on Sequential Double-Blind Identification Procedures.* Retrieved from www.chicagopolice.org/IL%20Pilot%20on%20Eyewitness%20ID.pdf

20 Schuster, B. (2008). Police lineups: Making eyewitness identification more reliable. *NIJ Journal.*

21 Steblay, N. M. (1997). Social influence in eyewitness recall: A meta-analytic review of lineup instruction effects. *Law and Human Behavior, 21,* 283–297.

22 Wells, G. L., Small, M., Penrod, S., Malpass, R., Fulero, S. M., & Brimacombe, C. A. E. (1998). Eyewitness identification procedures: Recommendations for lineups and photospreads. *Law and Human Behavior, Vol. II, 22*(6).

23 Wells, G. L., & Olson, E. (2003). Eyewitness testimony. *Annual Review of Psychology, 54,* 277–295.

24 Ibid.

25 Ibid.

26 Wells, G. L. & Seelau, E. (1995). Eyewitness identification: Psychological research and legal policy on lineups. *Psychology, Public Policy and Law, 1,* 765–791.

27 Mecklenburgh, S. H. (2006, March 17). *Report to the Legislature of the State of Illinois: The Illinois Pilot Program on Sequential Double-Blind Identification Procedures.* Retrieved from http://www.chicagopolice.org/IL%20Pilot%20on%20Eyewitness%20ID.pdf.

28 Ibid.

29 Located at Innocence Project website. (2009). Retrieved from http://www.innocenceproject.org/understand/Eyewitness-Misidentification.php.

30 *Simmons* v. *United States,* 390 U.S. 377 (1968).

31 After a witness has identified a photo, subsequent identifications may be influenced. The contention is that the witness thereafter is really only recognizing the previously seen photograph, not the actual criminal. For this reason, the practice of showing a witness a photograph of the defendant just before trial to "refresh the witness's memory" should be avoided.

32 Although it may surprise many officers to hear it, the average citizen still sees the police officer as a benevolent "father figure" (or perhaps, in the case of a female officer, a "mother figure"), with the result that the lineup witness is often extremely anxious to please the officer by making an identification—even though the citizen is not at all certain that the person chosen is the guilty party.

33 Even a photo array should be avoided. This is especially true if the suspect is the only person in the photo array who is also in the lineup.

34 See *Gilbert* v. *California,* 388 U.S. 263 (1967).

35 See *Foster* v. *California,* 394 U.S. 440 (1969).

36 See *Stovall* v. *Denno,* 388 U.S. 293 (1967).

37 *United States* v. *Wade,* 388 U.S. 218 (1967) and *Gilbert* v. *California,* 388 U.S. 263 (1967).

38 *Kirby* v. *Illinois,* 406 U.S. 682, 688–89 (1972).

39 *U.S.* v. *Ask,* 413 U.S. 300 (1973). At least one state supreme court has held that when simulated lineups are filmed or videotaped for later exhibition, there is no right to have counsel present when the film or videotape is subsequently shown to witnesses, *People* v. *Lawrence,* 481 P.2d 212 (1971). Showing witnesses a film or tape of a previously recorded simulated lineup has become known as a "Lawrence lineup."

Chapter 5, Legal Issues in Criminal Investigation

1 *Terry* v. *Ohio*, 392 U.S. 1 (1968).

2 Ibid.

3 State courts' decisions and statutes may place restrictions on officers not imposed by the Supreme Court of the United States.

4 See, for example *United States* v. *Mendenhall*, 446 U.S. 544 (1980); *Michigan* v. *Chesternut*, 486 U.S. 567 (1988).

5 *Illinois* v. *Wardlow* 528 U.S. 119 (2000); *Florida* v. *Royer* (460 U.S. 491 (1983).

6 *United States* v. *Brignoni-Ponce*, 422 U.S. 873 (1975).

7 It should be noted that the term "pat-down" does not necessarily describe the proper technique for searching a suspect for weapons. It is a legal term, not a descriptive one. It refers to the fact that the search must be confined to contact with the suspect's outer clothing unless and until the presence of a weapon is detected.

8 Del Carmen, R. V., & Walker, J. T. (2000). *Briefs of leading cases.* Cincinnati, OH: Anderson.

9 *U.S.* v. *Puerta*, 982 F.2d 1297, 1300 (9th Cir. 1992).

10 Adams, T. (1990). *Police field operations* (2nd ed.). Upper Saddle River, NJ: Prentice Hall.

11 *Stansbury* v. *California*, 114 S. Ct. 1526, 1529 128 L.Ed2d 293 (1994); *Yarborough* v. *Alvarado*, U.S. Supreme Court No. 02-1684 (decided June 1, 2004).

12 Peak, K. J. (1993). *Policing America: Methods, issues and challenges.* Upper Saddle River, NJ: Prentice Hall.

Chapter 6, Interviews and Interrogations

1 Inbau, F., Reid, J., Buckley, J., & Jayne, B. (2001). *Criminal interrogation and confessions*, 4th ed. Gaithersburg, MD: Aspen Publishing.

2 John E. Reid & Associates. (2012, April). Interviewing vs. interrogation. Retrieved from http://policetraining.net/blog/2012/04/18/interviewing-interrogation.

3 Memon, A., Bull, R. (1991). The cognitive interview: Its origins, empirical support, evaluation and practical implications. *Journal of Community and Applied Psychology, 1,* 1–18.

4 Loftus, E. F., & Guyer, M. J. (2002). Who abused Jane Doe? The hazards of the single case history. *Skeptical Inquirer.* Retrieved from http://www.csicop.org/si/2002-05/jane-doe.html.

5 Fisher, R. P., Geiselman, R. E., Raymond, D. S., Jurkevich, L. M., & Warhaftig, M. L. (1987). Enhancing enhanced eyewitness memory: Refining the cognitive interview. *Journal of Police Science and Administration, 15,* 291–297.

6 Fisher, R. P., Geiselman, R. E., & Amador, M. (1989). Field test of the cognitive interview: Enhancing the recollection of actual victims and witnesses of crime. *Journal of Applied Psychology, 74*(5), 722–727.

7 Willis, G. B. (1994). Cognitive interviewing: A "how to" guide. Retrieved from http://fog.its.uiowa.edu/~c07b209/interview.

8 Ibid.

9 Tousignant, D. D. (1991, March). Why suspects confess. *FBI Law Enforcement Bulletin,* 14–18.

10 Navarro, J., & Schafer, J. (2001, July). Detecting deception. *FBI Law Enforcement Bulletin.*

11 Ibid.

12 U.S. Department of Justice, Drug Enforcement Administration. (1988). *Drug enforcement handbook.* Washington, DC: U.S. Government Printing Office.

13 Ibid.

14 Evans, D. D. (1990, August). 10 ways to sharpen your interviewing skills. *Law and Order,* 90–95.

15 Coleman, R. (1984, April). Interrogation: The process. *FBI Law Enforcement Bulletin,* 27.

16 Innocence Project. (2009). False confessions. Retrieved from http://www.innocenceproject.org/understand/False-Confessions.php.

17 Forsyth, B., & Lessler, J. T. (1991). Cognitive laboratory methods: A taxonomy. In P. Biemer, R. Groves, L. Lyberg, N. Mathiowetz, & S. Sudman (Eds.), *Measurement errors in surveys.* New York: Wiley.

18 Ericsson, K. A., & Simon, H. A. (1980). Verbal reports as data. *Psychological Review*, 87, 215–251.

19 Willis, G. B. (1999). *Cognitive interviewing: A "how to" guide.* Short course presented at the 1999 Meeting of the American Statistical Association: Research Triangle.

20 Ibid.

21 Ibid.

22 Ibid.

23 Geller, W. A. (1983, March). Videotaping interrogations and confessions. *National Institute of Justice, Research in Brief.* Washington, DC: Department of Justice.

24 Kassin, S. A. (1997). The psychology of confession evidence. *American Psychologist, 52*(3), 221–233.

25 Lassiter, G. D., & Irvine, A. A. (1986). Videotaped confessions: The impact of camera point-of-view on judgments of coercion. *Journal of Applied Social Psychology, 16,* 268–276; Lassiter, G. D., Slaw, R. D., Briggs, M. A., & Scanlan, C. R. (1992). The potential for bias in videotaped confessions. *Journal of Applied Social Psychology, 22,* 1838–1851.

Chapter 7, Criminal Intelligence and Surveillance Operations

1 Federal Bureau of Investigation. (2001, February 20). Robert Philip Hanssen espionage case. Retrieved from http://www.fbi.gov/about-us/history/famous-cases/robert-hanssen.

2 Botsch, R. B. (2008). Developing street sources: Tips for patrol officers. *FBI Law Enforcement Bulletin, 77*(9).

3 See also Interview with Brian Michael Jenkins. (1994). *Omni, 17*(2), 77.

4 Suro, R. (1998, April 24). U.S. lacking in terrorism defenses: Study cites a need to share intelligence. *The Washington Post,* A-18.

5 IACP National Law Enforcement Policy Center. (1998). *Criminal intelligence* (Rev. ed.). Retrieved from http://www.ojp.usdoj.gov/BJA/topics/CI_Paper_0703.pdf.

6 U.S. Department of Justice. (1988). *Intelligence collection and analytical methods training manual.* Washington, DC: Drug Enforcement Administration.

7 Federal Bureau of Investigation. Counterintelligence. Retrieved from http://www.fbi.gov/hq/ci/cointell.htm.

8 Nason, J. (2004, May). Conducting surveillance operations: How to get the most out of them. *FBI Law Enforcement Bulletin.*

9 *Olmstead* v. *U.S.*, 277 U.S. 438 (1928).

10 *On Lee* v. *U.S.*, 343 U.S. 747 (1952); *Lopez* v. *U.S.*, 373 U.S. 427 (1963).

11 *Berger* v. *New York*, 388 U.S. 41 (1967).

12 *Lee* v. *Florida*, 392 U.S. 378 (1968).

13 *U.S.* v. *White*, 401 U.S. 745 (1971).

14 *U.S.* v. *Karo*, 468 U.S. 705 (1984).

15 Roland, N. (2007, March 20). Mueller orders audit of 56 FBI offices for secrete subpoenas. *Bloomberg News.* Retrieved from http://ww.bloomberg.com/apps/news?pid=newsarchive&sid=aBd9Zzld22w0&refer=home.

16 Pillar, C., & Lichtblau, E. (2009, July 29). FBI plans to fight terror with high tech arsenal. *LA Times.* Retrieved from http://articles.latimes.com/2002/jul/29/nation/na-technology29.

17 Odell, M. (2005, August 1). Use of mobile helped police keep tabs on suspect. *Financial Times.* Retrieved from http://www.ft.com/home/us.

18 Miller, J. R. (2009). Cell phone tracking can locate terrorists—but only where it is legal. *Fox News.* Retrieved from htttp://www.foxnews.com/story/0,2933,509211,00.html.

19 Zetter, K. (2009). Feds "Pinged" Sprint GPS Data 8 Million Times over a Year. *Wired Magazine.* Retrieved from http://www.wired.com/threatlevel/2009/12/gps-data.

20 Havenstein, H. (2008, September 12). One in five employers uses social networks in hiring process. *Computer World.* Retrieved from http://www.computerworld.com/s/article/9114560/One_in_five_employers_uses_social_networks_in_hiring_process.

21 Nakashima, E. (2007). FBI prepares vast database of biometrics. *Washington Post* (December 22). Retrieved from http://www.washingtonpost.com/wp-dyn/content/article/2007/12/21/AR2007122102544.html.

22 Ibid.

23 *People* v. *Deutsch*, 96 C.D.O.S. 2827 (1996).

24 *Kyllo* v. *U.S.*, 533 U.S. 27 (2001).

Chapter 8, Informant Management and Undercover Operations

1 Police upset by cancellation of *America's Most Wanted.* (1996, May 16). *USA Today.*

2 Puente, M. (1997, July 29). A no longer most wanted list. *USA Today*, 3A.

3 Ibid.

4 Gray, P. (1997, August 23). A heart in her hand. *Time*, 43.

5 U.S. Department of Justice, Drug Enforcement Administration. (1988). *Drug enforcement handbook.* Washington, DC: U.S. Government Printing Office.

6 Drug Enforcement Administration. (2009). Hundreds of alleged Sinaloa Cartel members and associates arrested in nationwide takedown of Mexican drug traffickers. Retrieved from http://www.usdoj.gov/dea/pubs/states/newsrel/2009/la022509.html.

7 Adams, T. (2001). *Police field operations* (5th ed.). Upper Saddle River, NJ: Prentice Hall.

8 Langworthy, R. (1989). Do stings control crime? An evaluation of a police fencing operation. *Justice Quarterly*, 6, 28–45.

9 Schoeman, F. (1986). Undercover operations: Some moral questions. *Criminal Justice Ethics*, 5(2), 16–22.

10 Black, D. (1971). The social organization of arrest. *Stanford Law Review*, 23, 1087–1111; Lafave, W. (1965). *The decision to take a suspect into custody.* Boston, MA: Little, Brown and Company; Smith, D. A., & C. Visher (1981). Street-level justice: Situational determinants of police arrest decisions. *Social Problems, 29*, 167–178.

11 Lyman, M. D. (2007). *Practical drug enforcement* (3rd ed.). Boca Raton, FL: CRC Press.

12 Motto, C. J., & June, D. L. (2000). *Undercover* (2nd ed.). Boca Raton, FL: CRC Press.

13 Girodo, M. (1991). Symptomatic reactions to undercover work. *The Journal of Nervous and Mental Disease*, 179(10), 626–630.

14 Marx, G. (1988). *Undercover: Police surveillance in America.* Berkeley: University of California Press.

15 Ibid.

16 Brown, J. (1990). Sources of occupational stress in the police. *Work & Stress*, 4(4), 305–318. Retrieved from http://www.informaworld.com/smpp/content~content=a782548838~db=all.

17 Marx, G. (1988). *Undercover: Police surveillance in America.* Berkeley: University of California Press.

18 Ibid.

19 Ibid.

20 Girodo, M. (1991). Drug corruptions in undercover agents: Measuring the risks. *Behavioural Science and the Law, 9*, 361–370.

21 Marx, G. (1988). *Undercover: Police surveillance in America.* Berkeley: University of California Press.

22 Ibid.

23 Girodo, M. (1991). Personality, job stress, and mental health in undercover agents. *Journal of Social Behaviour and Personality*, 6(7), 375–390.

24 Marx, G. (1988). *Undercover: Police surveillance in America.* Berkeley: University of California Press.

Chapter 9, Death Investigations

1 Federal Bureau of Investigation/Bureau of Justice Statistics. (2013). *Crime in United States, 2012.* Washington, DC: Federal Bureau of Investigation.

2 Ibid.

3 Ibid.

4 Ibid.

5 Ibid.

6 Keel, T. G. (2008, February 8). Homicide investigations: Identifying best practices. *FBI Law Enforcement Bulletin, 77*(2), pp. 1–2.

7 Ibid.

8 Ibid.

9 Ibid.

10 Ibid.

11 Ibid.

12 Ibid.

13 Ibid.

14 Ibid.

15 Ibid.

16 Adams, S., & Harpster, T. (2008, June 8). 911 homicide calls and statement analysis. *FBI Law Enforcement Bulletin*, 23.

17 Ibid.

18 Geberth, V. (1990). *Practical homicide investigation* (2nd ed.). New York: Elsevier.

19 Statheropoulos, M., Agapiou, A., et al. (2007). Environmental aspects of VOCs evolved in the early stages of human decomposition. *Science of the Total Environment, 385*(1–3), 221–227.

20 Eberhardt T. L., & Elliot, D. A. (2008). A preliminary investigation of insect colonisation and succession on remains in New Zealand. *Forensic Science International, 176*(2–3), 217–223

21 Ibid.

22 Smith, K. G. V. (1987). *A manual of forensic entomology.* Ithaca, NY: Cornell University Press, p. 464.

23 Ibid.

24 Ibid.

25 Buckberry, J. (2000). Missing, presumed buried? Bone diagenesis and the under-representation of Anglo-Saxon children. Retrieved from http:?/www.assemblage.group.shef .ac.uk/5/buckberr.html.

26 Smith, K. G. V. (1987). *A manual of forensic entomology.* Ithaca, NY: Cornell University Press, p. 464; Kulshrestha, P., & Satpathy, D. K. (2001). Use of beetles in forensic entomology. *Forensic Science International, 120*(1–2), 15–17.

27 Schmitt, A., Cunha, E., & Pinheiro, J. (2006). *Forensic anthropology and medicine: Complementary sciences from recovery to cause of death.* New York: Humana Press, p. 464; Haglund, W. D., & Sorg, M. H. (1996). *Forensic taphonomy: The postmortem fate of human remains.* Boca Raton, FL: CRC Press, p. 636.

28 Ibid.

29 Geberth, V. (1990). *Practical homicide investigation* (2nd ed.). New York: Elsevier.

30 Ibid.

31 Di Maio, V. J. M. (1985). *Gunshot wounds: Practical aspects of firearms, ballistics, and forensic techniques.* New York: Elsevier.

32 See also Mahoney, P. F., Ryan, J., Brooks, A. J., & Schwab, C. W. (2004) *Ballistic trauma— practical guide* (2nd ed.). New York: Springer.

33 Krug, E. E. (Ed.). (2002). *World report on violence and health.* Geneva: World Health Organization.

34 Note that some small-caliber bullets, such as .22s, may have the primer crimped into the rim of the bullet instead of in a center cylinder, and the hammer can strike the bullet anywhere on the rim to fire the slug. This is known as "rimfire."

35 Centers for Disease Control and Prevention, Agency for Toxic Substances and Disease Registry. (2007). *Toxicological profile for barium and barium compounds. Retrieved from http://www.atsdr.cdc.gov/toxprofiles/tp24.pdf.*

36 Magnetic susceptibility of the elements and inorganic compounds. In *Handbook of chemistry and physics* (81st ed.). Boca Raton, FL: CRC Press; United States Geological Survey. (2009). *Antimony statistics and information.* Retrieved from http://minerals.usgs.gov/minerals/pubs/commodity/ antimony/.

37 Brown, G. I. (1998). *The big bang: A history of explosives.* Sutton Publishing: UK.

38 Gunshot residue test results. Firearms ID.com. Retrieved from http://www.firearmsid.com/A_distanceResults.htm.

39 Ibid.

40 Bykowicz, J. (2005, March 27). Convictions tied to controversial gun-residue test: Prosecutor's office counts several cases over 5 years; defenders seek further review. *Baltimore Sun.*

41 Guzman, D. (2007, October 29). Judge rules out gunshot residue evidence in murder trial. *Houston News.* Retrieved from http://www.click2houston.com/news/14452905/detail .html.

Chapter 10, Robbery

1 Federal Bureau of Investigation. (2013). *Crime in America, 2012. Uniform crime reports.* Washington, DC: U.S. Government Printing Office.

2 Ibid.

3 Found at Lawyers.com. See: http://criminal.lawyers.com/ criminal-law-basics/the-crime-of-robbery.html (accessed May 20, 2014).

4 McClintocki, F. H., & Gibsson, E. (1961). *Robbery in London.* London: Macmillan, p. 15.

5 Ibid.

6 Ibid.

7 National Institute of Justice. (1990). *Computer crime: The new crime scene.* Washington, DC: U.S. Department of Justice.

8 National Institute of Justice. (1983). *Robbery in the United States: An analysis of recent trends and patterns.* Washington, DC: U.S. Government Printing Office.

Chapter 11, Assault and Related Offenses

[1] Federal Bureau of Investigation. (2013). *Crime in America, 2012. Uniform crime reports*. Washington, DC: U.S. Government Printing Office.

[2] Ibid

[3] Ibid

[4] Heise, L., & Roberts, J. (1990). Reflections on a movement: The U.S. battle against women abuse. In M. Schuler (Ed.), *Freedom from violence: Women's strategies round the world* (pp. 5–12). Line Village, NV: Copperhouse Publishing.

[5] Violence Against Women Grants Office. (1998). *Stalking and domestic violence: The third annual report to Congress under the Violence Against Women Act*. Washington, DC: U.S. Department of Justice (NCJ-172204).

[6] Tjaden, P., & Thoennes, N. (2000). *Full report of the prevalence, incidence, and consequences of violence against women: Findings from the National Violence Against Women Survey*. Washington, DC: National Institute of Justice.

[7] Federal Bureau of Investigation. (2013). *Crime in America, 2012. Uniform crime reports*. Washington, DC: U.S. Government Printing Office.

[8] Ibid.

[9] Brownmiller, S. (1975). *Against our will: Men, women, and rape*. New York: Simon & Schuster.

[10] See, for example, The American Prosecutors Research Institute. (1999). *The prosecution of Rohypnol and GHB related sexual assaults*. Alexandria, VA: Author.

[11] *People v. McCann*, 76 Ill. App. 3rd 184, 186, 394 N.E.2d 1055, 1056 (2d Dist. 1979).

[12] Griffiths, G. L. (1985, April). The overlooked evidence in rape investigations. *FBI Law Enforcement Bulletin*, 8–15.

Chapter 12, Missing and Abducted Persons

[1] Flores, J. R. (2002, October). *National incidence studies of missing, abducted, runaway and thrownaway children (NISMART)*. Washington, DC: U.S. Department of Justice.

[2] National Center for Missing and Exploited Children. (2009, May 18). Press release. Retrieved from http://www.missingkids.com/missingkids/servlet/NewsEventServlet?LanguageCountry=en_US&PageId=4046.

[3] Douglas, A. (2011, August). Child abductions: Known relationships are greater danger. *FBI Law Enforcement Bulletin*.

[4] Ibid.

[5] National Center for Missing and Exploited Children. (2009, May 18). Press release. Retrieved from http://www.missingkids.com/missingkids/servlet/NewsEventServlet?LanguageCountry=en_US&PageId=4046.

[6] Flores, J. R. (1999). *Non-family abducted children: National estimates and characteristics*. Washington, DC: Administrator of Office of Juvenile Justice and Delinquency Prevention.

[7] Flores, J. R. (2002, October). *National incidence studies of missing, abducted, runaway and thrownaway children (NISMART)*. Washington, DC: U.S. Department of Justice. This study commissioned by the U.S. Department of Justice,

Office of Juvenile Justice and Delinquency Prevention found that there were only approximately 115 stereotypical stranger abductions in 1999.

[8] Ibid.

[9] Ibid.

[10] Croft, R. (2006). Folklore, families and fear: Understanding consumption decisions through the oral tradition. *Journal of Marketing Management, 22*(9/10), 1053–1076.

[11] Ibid.

[12] The NCMEC can be contacted as a source for both model policies and excellent training, which it provides at no cost to a wide variety of agencies working with children.

[13] Allender, D. (2007). Child abductions: Nightmares in progress. *FBI Law Enforcement Bulletin 76*(7).

[14] National Center for Missing and Exploited Children. (1994). *Missing and abducted children*. Retrieved from http://www.missingkids.com.

[15] McKenna, R., Brown, K., Keppel, R., Weis, J., Skeen, M., & U.S. Department of Justice, Office of Juvenile Justice and Delinquency Prevention. (2006). *Investigative case management for missing children homicide investigation*. Retrieved from http://www.missingkids.com/en_US/archive/documents/homicide_missing.pdf.

[16] Douglas, A. (2011, August). Child abductions: Known relationships are greater danger. *FBI Law Enforcement Bulletin*.

[17] Ibid. For further information about the FBI's CARD team, visit http://www.fbi.gov/about-us/investigate/vc_majorthefts/cac/card. For further information about the FBI's Crimes Against Children Unit, visit http://www.fbi.gov/about-us/investigate/vc_majorthefts/cac.

[18] For further information about the FBI's Crimes Against Children Unit, visit http://www.fbi.gov/about-us/investigate/vc_majorthefts/cac.

[19] Flores, J. R. (2002, October). *National incidence studies of missing, abducted, runaway and thrown away children (NISMART)*. Washington, DC: U.S. Department of Justice.

Chapter 13, Crimes against Children: Child Abuse and Child Fatalities

[1] Walsh, B. (2005). *Investigating child fatalities*. Washington, DC: United States Department of Justice, Office of Justice Programs, Office of Juvenile Justice and Delinquency Prevention.

[2] Bonner, B. L., Crow, S. M., & Louge, M. B. (2002). Fatal child neglect. In H. Dubowitz (Ed.), *Neglected children* (pp. 156–173). Thousand Oaks, CA: Sage Publications.

[3] Ibid.

[4] Briere, J., Berliner, L., Bulkley, J. A., et al. (Eds.). (1998). *The APSAC handbook on child maltreatment* (2nd ed.). Thousand Oaks, CA: Sage Publications.

[5] Walsh, B. (2005). *Investigating child fatalities*. Washington, DC: United States Department of Justice, Office of Justice Programs, Office of Juvenile Justice and Delinquency Prevention.

[6] Pence, D., & Wilson, C. (1994). *Team investigation of child sexual abuse*. Thousand Oaks, CA: Sage Publications.

7 Walsh, B. (2005). *Investigating child fatalities*. Washington, DC: United States Department of Justice, Office of Justice Programs, Office of Juvenile Justice and Delinquency Prevention.

8 Pence, D., & Wilson, C. (1994). *Team investigation of child sexual abuse*. Thousand Oaks, CA: Sage Publications.

9 Reece, R. M. (Ed.). (1994). *Child abuse: Medical diagnosis and management*. Malvern, PA: Lea and Febiger.

10 Ibid.

11 Kelley, G. (2010, March). Child fatality boards. *FBI Law Enforcement Bulletin*.

12 Ibid.

13 Office of Juvenile Justice and Delinquency Prevention.

14 National Criminal Justice Reference Service.

15 Office of Juvenile Justice and Delinquency Prevention.

16 National Center for Injury Prevention and Control. (2006). *Child maltreatment: Fact sheet*. Centers for Disease Control and Prevention (CDC). Retrieved from http://www.cdc.gov/ncipc/factsheets/cmfacts.htm.

17 American Academy of Pediatrics: Committee on Child Abuse and Neglect. (2001). Shaken baby syndrome: Rotational cranial injuries. Technical report. *Pediatrics*, *108*(1), 206–210. Retrieved from http://pediatrics.aappublications.org/cgi/content/full/108/1/206.

18 Office of Juvenile Justice and Delinquency Prevention.

19 Geissinger, S. (1993, October 15). Boy Scouts dismissed 1,800 suspected molesters from 1971–1991. *Boston Globe*, p. 3.

20 Russell, D. (1983). The incidence and prevalence of intrafamilial and extrafamilial sexual abuse of female children. *Child Abuse and Neglect*, *7*, 133–146.

21 Wolfner, G., & Gelles, R. (1993). A profile of violence toward children: A national study. *Child Abuse and Neglect*, *17*, 144–146.

22 Lawson, L., & Chiffen, M. (1992). False negatives in sexual abuse disclosure interviews. *Journal of Interpersonal Violence*, *7*, 532–542.

23 Sorenson, E., Bottoms, B. L., & Perona, A. (1997). *Handbook on intake and forensic interviewing in the children's advocacy center setting*. Washington, DC: Office of Juvenile Justice and Delinquency Prevention.

24 Saywitz, K. J., & Goodman, G. S. (1998). Interviewing children in and out of court. In J. Briere, L. Berliner, J. A. Bulkley, et al. (Eds.), *The APSAC handbook on child maltreatment* (2nd ed., pp. 297–317). Thousand Oaks, CA: Sage Publications.

25 Ibid.

26 Sorenson, E., Bottoms, B. L., & Perona, A. (1997). *Handbook on intake and forensic interviewing in the children's advocacy center setting*. Washington, DC: Office of Juvenile Justice and Delinquency Prevention.

27 Saywitz, K. J., & Goodman, G. S. (1998). Interviewing children in and out of court. In J. Briere, L. Berliner, J. A. Bulkley, et al. (Eds.), *The APSAC Handbook on child maltreatment* (2nd ed., pp. 297–317). Thousand Oaks, CA: Sage Publications.

28 Flick, J., & Caye, J. (2001). *Introduction to child sexual abuse (curriculum)*. Chapel Hill, NC: UNC-CH School of Social Work.

29 Cordisco Steele, L., & Carnes, C. N. (2002). *Child centered forensic interviewing*. International Society for Prevention of Child Abuse and Neglect. Retrieved from http://www.ispcan.org/Tcbyauthor.htm.

30 Goldstein, H. (1977). *Policing a free society*. Cambridge, MA: Ballinger.

31 Ibid.

32 The National Center for Missing and Exploited Children. (2014). retrieved from http://www.missingkids.com/Exploitation/FAQ.

33 The National Center for Missing and Exploited Children. (2014). Retrieved from http://www.missingkids.com/en_US/documents/CCSE_Fact_Sheet.pdf.

Chapter 14, Theft-Related Offenses

1 Federal Bureau of Investigation. (2013). *Crime in America, 2012*. Washington, DC: U.S. Government Printing Office.

2 Ibid.

3 Ibid.

4 Ibid.

5 Federal Bureau of Investigation. (2011, October). *Crime in the United States, 2010*. Washington, DC: U.S. Government Printing Office.

6 American Bankers' Association. (2007). Banker's Association Deposit Account Fraud Survey Report. Retrieved from http://www.aba.com/Press+Room/112707Deposit+FraudSurvey.htm.

7 Cameron, M. O. (1983). The scourge of shoplifting. *Criminal Justice Ethics* (Winter–Spring), 3–15.

8 Hartmann, D., Gelfand, D., Page, B., & Walker, P. (1972). Rates of bystander observation and reporting of contrived shoplifting incidents. *Criminology*, *10*, 248.

9 Blankenburg, E. (1976). The selectivity of legal sanctions: An empirical investigation of shoplifting. *Law and Society Review*, *11*, 109–129.

10 Federal Bureau of Investigation. (2008). *Crime in the United States, 2007*. Washington, DC: U.S. Government Printing Office.

11 Woodard, T. (n.d.). Prosecutor to review MySpace suicide. *Fox2News, St. Louis*. Retrieved from http://www.myfoxstl.com/myfox/.

12 Pokin, S. (2007, November 11). "MySpace" hoax ends with suicide of Dardenne Prairie teen. *St. Louis Post-Dispatch*.

13 Parents say fake online "friend" led to girl's suicide. (2007, November 17). *CNN*. Retrieved from http://www.cnn.com/2007/US/11/17/internet.suicide.ap/index.html.

14 Collins, Lauren. (2008, January 21). Annals of crime: The friend game. *The New Yorker*, 34.

15 Taylor, B. (2007, December 5). Lawyer: Mother unaware of cruel messages. *Associated Press*.

16 Perry, R. (1986). *Computer crime*. New York: Franklin Watts.

17 Rosnoff, S. M., et al. (1998). *Profit without honor*. Upper Saddle River, NJ: Prentice Hall.

18 Hacker's ransom. (2000, January). *USA Today*, 11:3A.

19 National Institute of Justice. (1989, June). *Research in brief*. Washington, DC: U.S. Department of Justice, National Institute of Justice.

20 Clark, F., & Diliberto, K. (1996). *Investigating computer crime*. Boca Raton, FL: CRC Press.

21 State of Florida Attorney General. (2006, August 14). Retrieved from http://www.myfloridalegal.com.

22 Federal Bureau of Investigation. (2013). *Crime in America, 2012*. Washington, DC: U.S. Government Printing Office.

23 National Insurance Crime Bureau. (2014). Retrieved from https://www.nicb.org/home.

24 Ibid.

Chapter 15, Arson and Bombings

1 National Fire Protection Association. (1998). *Fire loss in the United States, 1987–1996* (11th ed.). Boston: National Fire Protection Association.

2 Ibid.

3 Federal Bureau of Investigation. (2013). *Crime in America, 2012*. Washington, DC: U.S. Government Printing Office.

4 Ibid

5 Ibid

6 Woodfork, W. G. (1990, December 28). Not just a fire department problem. *Police Chief*.

7 O'Conner, J. J. (1987). *Practical fire and arson investigation*. New York: Elsevier.

8 Saferstein, R. (1998). *Criminalistics. An introduction to forensic science*. Upper Saddle River, NJ: Prentice Hall, 265.

9 White, P. (Ed.). (1998). *Crime scene to court. The essentials of forensic science*. Glasgow, UK: The Royal Society of Chemistry, 133–138.

10 Moenssens, A. A., Starrs, J. E., Henderson, C. E., & Inbau, F. E. (1995). *Scientific evidence in civil and criminal cases*. Westbury, NY: The Foundation Press, 416–417.

11 Ibid.

12 O'Conner, J. J. (1987). *Practical fire and arson investigation*. New York: Elsevier.

13 Ibid.

14 Rider, A. O. (1980). The firesetter: A psychological profile. *FBI Law Enforcement Bulletin* (June–August), 9.

15 James, J. (1965, March 24). Psychological motives for arson. *Popular Government*.

16 Hart, F. (1990). *The arson equation [plus] circumstantial evidence*. National Emergency Training Center.

Chapter 16, Terrorism and National Security Crimes

1 Terrorism. (1989). *Oxford English Dictionary* (2nd ed.). Def. 2: "A policy intended to strike with terror those against whom it is adopted; the employment of methods of intimidation; the fact of terrorizing or condition of being terrorized."

2 Foreign Relations Authorization Act, U.S. Code, Title 22, Section 2656 f (d)(2).

3 Angus, M. (2002, February 12). *The right of self-defense under international law—the response to the terrorist attacks of 11 September*. Australian Law and Bills Digest Group, Parliament of Australia; Thalif D. (2005, July 25). *Politics: U.N. member states struggle to define terrorism*. Inter Press Service.

4 Hoffman, B. (2006). *Inside terrorism*. New York: Columbia University Press, 32. See review in the *New York Times*.

5 Record, J. (2003). *Bounding the global war on terrorism*. Retrieved from http://www.carlisle.army.mil/.

6 Abrahms, M. (2008). What terrorists really want: Terrorist motives and counterterrorism strategy. *International Security, 32*(4), 86–89. Retrieved from http://maxabrahms.com/pdfs/DC_250-1846.pdf.

7 Terrorism. Encyclopædia Britannica. Retrieved from http://www.britannica.com/eb/article-9071797.

8 Sageman, M. (2004). *Social networks and the jihad*. Philadelphia: University of Pennsylvania Press, 166–167.

9 Williams, P. (2008). Violent non-state actors and national and international security. Retrieved from http://se2.isn.ch/serviceengine/FileContent?serviceID=ISFPub&fileid=8EEBA9FE-478E-EA2C-AA15-32FC9A59434A&lng=en.

10 Library of Congress. (1999). *The sociology and psychology of terrorism*. Washington, DC: Library of Congress Federal Research Division.

11 Definition of terrorism retrieved from http://www.fbi.gov.

12 Friedlander, R. A. (1989). Terrorism: Documents of international and local control. New York: Oceana Pub.

13 Georges-Abeyie, D. E. (1983). Women as terrorists. In L. Freedman & Y. Alexander (Eds.), *Perspectives on terrorism* (pp. 71–84). Wilmington, DE: Scholarly Resources, Inc.

14 White, J. (2005). *Terrorism and homeland security*. Belmont, CA: Wadsworth Publishing.

15 Center for Strategic and International Studies. (2014). Retrieved from http://csis.org/expert/walter-z-laqueur.

16 Juergensmeyer, M. (2000). *Terror in the mind of God*. University of California Press, 125–135.

17 Ibid.

18 Bockstette, C. (2008). *Jihadist terrorist use of strategic communication management techniques*. George C. Marshall Center Occasional Paper Series. Retrieved from http://www.marshallcenter.org/mcpublicweb/MCDocs/files/College/F_Publications/occPapers/occpaper_20-en.pdf.

19 Juergensmeyer, M. (2000). *Terror in the mind of God*. University of California Press, 127–128.

20 Bockstette, C. (2008). *Jihadist terrorist use of strategic communication management techniques*. George C. Marshall Center Occasional Paper Series. Retrieved from http://www.marshallcenter.org/mcpublicweb/MCDocs/files/College/F_Publications/occPapers/occpaper_20-en.pdf.

21 Federal Bureau of Investigation. (2000). *Terrorism in the United States 1999*. Washington, DC: U.S. Government Printing Office. Retrieved from www2.fbi.gov/publications/terror/terror99.pdf.

22 United Nations. (2005, March 21). *UN reform.* Retrieved from http://web.archive.org/web/20070427012107/http://www.un.org/unifeed/script.asp?scriptId=73. The second part of the report, titled "Freedom from fear backs the definition of terrorism—an issue so divisive agreement on it has long eluded the world community" defines *terrorism* as any action "intended to cause death or serious bodily harm to civilians or non-combatants with the purpose of intimidating a population or compelling a government or an international organization to do or abstain from doing any act."

23 White, J. (2005). *Terrorism and homeland security.* Belmont, CA: Wadsworth Publishing.

24 Ibid.

25 O'Brien, L. (2011). The evolution of terrorism since 9/11. *FBI Law Enforcement Bulletin, 80*(9).

26 Ibid.

27 Ibid.

28 Mantri, G. (2011). Homegrown terrorism: Is there an Islamic wave? *Harvard International Review* (Spring).

29 Eikmeier D. C. (2007). Qutbism: An ideology of Islamic-fascism. *Parameters* (Spring), 85–98.

30 Fuller, G. E. (2003). *The future of political Islam.* New York: Palgrave MacMillan, 21.

31 Footnotes of *9/11 commission report Mehdi Mozaffari bin Laden and Islamist terrorism. Militant Tidsskrift.* (2002, March). Washington, DC: U.S. Government Printing Office, 131:1.

32 Kramer, M. (2003). Coming to terms, fundamentalists or Islamists? *Middle East Quarterly* (Spring), 65–77.

33 International Crisis Group. (2005). *Understanding Islamism.* Retrieved from http://merln.ndu.edu/archive/icg/Islamism2Mar05.pdf; Stanley, T. (2005). *Definition: Islamism, Islamist, Islamiste, Islamicist, perspectives on world history and current events.* Retrieved from http://www.pwhce.org/islamism.html.

34 Fuller, G. E. (2003). *The future of political Islam.* New York: Palgrave MacMillan, 21.

35 International Crisis Group. (2005, March 2).*Understanding Islamism Middle East/North Africa.* Report No. 37. Retrieved from http://www.crisisgroup.org/en/regions/middle-east-north-africa/north-africa/037-understanding-islamism.aspx.

36 Ibid.

37 Jenkins, P. (2011). After Al Qaeda: Hijacking and suicide bombings didn't start and won't end with Islamists. *American Conservative, 10*(Issue 9), 26–29.

38 O'Brien, L. (2011). The evolution of terrorism since 9/11. *FBI Law Enforcement Bulletin, 80*(9).

39 U.S. Department of State. (2011). *Country reports on Terrorism 2009.* Washington, DC: U.S. Government Printing Office. Retrieved from http://www.state.gov/s/ct/rls/crt/2009/.

40 Ibid.

41 Ibid.

42 Ibid.

43 Council on Foreign Relations. (2011, February 7). *Militant extremists in the United States.* Retrieved from http://www.cfr.org/terrorist-organizations/militant-extremists-united-states/p9236.

44 Presley, S. M. (1996). *Rise of domestic terrorism and its relation to United States Armed Forces.* Retrieved from http://www.fas.org/irp/eprint/presley.htm.

45 Retrieved from http://frwebgate.access.gpo.gov/cgibin/getdoc.cgi?dbname=107_cong_public_laws&docid=f:publ056.107.pdf.

46 Moskalenko, S., & McCauley, C. (2011). The psychology of "lone wolf terrorism." *Counseling Psychology Quarterly, 24*(2), 115–126.

47 Federal Bureau of Investigation. (2011). Comments from Mark Giuliano, Assistant Director Counter Terrorism Division, April 14, 2011. Retrieved from http://www.fbi.gov/news/speeches/the-post-9-11-fbi-the-bureaus-response-to-evolving-threats.

48 Petrowski, T. D., Howell, M., Marshall, D. W., & Zaidi, S. (2011, September). The Hosam Smadi case an example of success. *FBI Law Enforcement Bulletin.*

49 Ibid.

50 Hunter, R., & Heinke, D. (2011, September). Radicalization of Islamist terrorists in the Western world. *FBI Law Enforcement Bulletin.*

51 Ibid.

52 O'Brien, L. (2011). The evolution of terrorism since 9/11. *FBI Law Enforcement Bulletin, 80*(9).

53 Ibid.

54 U.S. Department of Justice, Federal Bureau of Investigation, Domestic Terrorism Operations Unit and Domestic Terrorism Analysis Unit. (2010). *Sovereign citizen danger to law enforcement.* Washington, DC: U.S. Government Printing Office.

55 Ibid.

56 U.S. Department of Justice, Federal Bureau of Investigation, Domestic Terrorism Analysis Unit. (2011). *Sovereign citizen extremist movement.* Washington, DC: U.S. Government Printing Office.

57 Ibid.

58 National Counterterrorism Center. (2014). 2014 calendar. Retrieved from http://www.nctc.gov/site/index.html.

59 International Monetary Fund. (2003). *Enhancing contributions to combating money laundering: Policy paper.* Retrieved from http://www.imf.org/external/np/ml/2001/eng/042601.htm.

60 U.S. Treasury Department. (2003). *High intensity money laundering and related financial crimes areas (HIFCAs) designations.* Retrieved from http://www.ustreas.gov/fincen/hifcadesignations.html.

Name Index

Subject Index

plants, **272**

plastic fingerprint, **66**

point of origin, **271**

Police: The Law Enforcement Magazine, 164

police-citizen encounter, 93, 95–96

police infiltration, 158. *See also* informant management and undercover operations

police interrogation room, 115, *115*

police lineup, 76–79

police report. *See* investigative report

police specialist, 14–15

polygraph, **117**–119, *119*

polymerase chain reaction (PCR) technique, 64

possession of burglary tools, 263

post-bin Laden terrorism, 288–290

postmortem lividity, 174

powder method (fingerprints), 68

power thesis (sexual assault), 202

prejudicial image, 35

preliminary investigation
    burglary, 249–250
    death investigation, 169–170
    defined, **45**
    elements of, 46
    motor vehicle theft, 261
    objectives, 18
    robbery, 188–189

President's Task Force on Combating Terrorism (PTFCT), 284

pretexting, 255

preventive response, **15**

prima facie evidence, 47

primary physical aggressor, **199**

primary solvability factors, 17

proactive response, **15**

probable cause, **88**, 98, 99

probable cause requirement, 87–88

probing technique, 113

processing the crime scene, 44–62
    chain of custody, 52
    collecting evidence, 54–57
    crime-scene evidence, 46–47
    crime-scene report, 57–58
    first responder, responsibilities of, 47–50

follow-up investigation, 57–58
    medical examiner, contacting the, 57
    neighborhood canvass, 57
    preliminary investigation, 45–46
    searches, 53–54
    securing and protecting the scene, 50–53
    walk-through, 52

Professional Criminals in America (Byrnes), 5

professional fence, 250

professional robber, 187

professional shoplifters, 255

profiling technique, 74–75

Progressive Era, 6

progressive or leapfrog method, 137

property crime, **248**

Protect America Act, 300

protection orders, **200**

protective search, **48**

pry marks, *250*

"Psychological Motives for Arson" (James), 274

psychological profiling, 75

pubic and head hair evidence collection kits, *206*

public safety exception to *Miranda*, 114

puncture wounds, 56

purging files, 135–136

purse snatching, 183

putrefaction stage of decomposition, 171

pyromaniac, 274

Q

quadrant or zone search, *53*

questioned document examination, 10

questioned documents unit, 64

R

radioactive materials (terrorism), 291

radiological dispersal device (RDD), 291

RAND study, 10–11

rape, **202**. *See also* sexual assault

rape evidence checklist, 203

RDD. *See* radiological dispersal device (RDD)

reactive response, **15**

Real ID Act, 285

reasonable deadly force, 104

reasonable expectation of privacy, 97

reasonable force, **102**

reasonable officer standard, 101, 102

reasonable suspicion, 99

receipt of stolen property, 249–250

recorded statement, 121

reformed informant, 152

relative judgment, **77**

relevant photograph, 35

report writing, 29
    crime-scene report, 57–58
    investigative report, 29–32

requested exemplars, 72–73

residential robbery, **185,** 188

resistance, **202**

responding officer. *See* responsibilities of first officer

responsibilities of first officer, 47–50
    actions while en route, 48
    arrest of perpetrator, 48–49
    assistance to victims, 48
    briefing investigators and superiors, 49
    flash description, 49–50
    follow-up communications, 49
    identification of witnesses and vehicles, 49
    initial actions upon arrival, 48
    overview (flowchart), 50
    protection of witnesses and bystanders, 48
    protective search, 48

restriction fragment length polymorphism (RFLP) technique, 64

revengeful informant, 152

revolutionary terrorism, 286

RFLP technique. *See* restriction fragment length polymorphism (RFLP) technique

Ridge ending, *66*

rifle, 175

right to counsel
    eyewitness identification, 80–81
    interviews and interrogations, 113

motor vehicle fraud, 262–263
motor vehicle insurance fraud, 263
motor vehicle theft, 259–262
motorcycle theft and fraud, 262
possession of burglary tools, 263
robbery, 182–195
sexual assault, 201–207
shoplifting, 254–256
stalking, 200–201
triangulation method, **38**, *38*
Trifurcation, *66*
triggering conditions, **92**
TTP. *See* Tehrik-e Taliban (TTP)
TV, impact of, on crime-scene processing, 59
twinned loop, *67*
two-car surveillance, 138
two-officer surveillance, 136
two-pronged *Aguilar* test, 154
type lines, *67*

U

ummah, 294
ummat al-mu'minim, 294
Unabomber, 278
Unabomber case, 74
undercover operations, 155–159
cover story, 157–158
FBI review committee, 156
infiltration, 158–159
job stress, 159
overview (flowchart), 156
protecting the officer's "cover," 158–159
risks, 158, 159
types of undercover operations, 157
undercover working environment, 157
Uniform Crime Reporting Handbook, 210
United States Secret Service, 5
United States v. Dunn, 97
United States v. Grubbs, 92
United States v. Irizarry, 96
United States v. Leon, 89

United States v. Wade, 75
University of Tennessee Anthropological Research Facility (Body Farm), 172, 181
urine, saliva, and feces, 56
U.S. v. Karo, 139
U.S. v. Lewis, 78
U.S. v. White, 139
US Antiterrorism and Effective Death Penalty Act (AEDPA), 285
U.S. Department of State, 300
U.S. Fire Administration, 280
U.S. Supreme Court (website), 105
USA Patriot Act, 285, 291, 300
use of force, 101–103, 104, *104*
use-of-force continuum, *103*
U.S.S. Cole, 287

V

vehicle identification number (VIN), **259**, 261, *261*
vehicle inventory search, 96–97
vehicle robbery, 186
vehicle search, 54, 96–97
vehicle surveillance, 137–138, *138*
vehicle theft, 259–261
ventilation period (interview of rape victim), 207
verbal-probing techniques, 113
Verint, 142
Verizon, 141
video-taped confession, 121
VIN. *See* vehicle identification number (VIN)
virtual *jihad* university, 295
visible fingerprint, **66**
voice stress analyzer (VSA), 119
voluntary manslaughter, *167*, 169
voluntary statement form, 121, *122*
VSA. *See* voice stress analyzer (VSA)

W

waiver of rights form, *114*
walk-through, 52

warrantless searches, 92–97
automobile search, 96–97
emergency search, 93–94
investigative detention, 93, 95–96, 97
open-field search, 97
plain-view search, 96
search by consent, 92–93
stop-and-frisk search, 94–95
weak induction, 12
weapons of mass destruction (WMD), 290–291
Weathermen, 292
Weeks v. United States, 88
whorl, *67*
wife battering, 198–200
William J. Burns Detective Agency, 4
wiretaps, 139–143
witness
arson, 272
eyewitness identification, 75–80
interview of, 19–20
robbery, 191
WMD. *See* weapons of mass destruction (WMD)
Wong Sun v. United States, 89
World Trade Center bombing (1993), 286
writing medium, 73
written statement, 120–121
www.findlaw.com, 43
www.Supremecourt.gov, 105
Wyoming v. Houghton, 96

Y

"you don't understand" tactic, 117

Z

Zodiac Killer, 74
zone search method, 53, *53*